'A fascinating account of the Mughal conquest of India that, to this layman at least, already feels like a classic. Like Stephen Runciman's books about Byzantium it is exciting in addition to being well-researched'   Giles Foden, *Tatler*

'The story of Mughal India is intensely colourful and dramatic, and Eraly's lively text does justice to its subject . . . *The Mughal Throne* makes exciting reading'   Philip Ziegler, *Daily Telegraph*

'In an environment where every fact is malleable and every interpretation politicised, the need for clear, unbiased accounts of history is all the greater, and it is hard to imagine anyone succeeding more gracefully in producing a balanced overview than Abraham Eraly . . . Eraly gives a richly readable account of one of the most crucial and misrepresented periods of Indian history. He writes well . . . with a lovely eye for detail and colour'   William Dalrymple, *Sunday Times*

'Eraly certainly succeeds in bringing the Mughal emperors to life . . . An engaging and accessible book'   Francis Robinson, *TLS*

'Majestic study of rulers of India for three centuries and who transformed the country and laid the foundations on which the British built'   *Sunday Herald*

'The author has given readers a very colourful and detailed history that in part reads like one of the great epics he has used in its preparation'   *Contemporary Review*

'Consistently readable . . . Eraly's writing is vigorous, supple and undogmatic'   *Indian Review of Books*

'The book marks the return of the narrative in historical writing. Eraly weaves together accounts of the people and politics of the empire and explodes myths about controversial emperors like Babur and Aurangzeb'   *Outlook*

Abraham Eraly, who was born in Kerala, has taught Indian history in Madras and the United States. He is the author of *Gem in the Lotus: The Seeding of Indian Civilization*. He lives in Madras.

THE MUGHAL THRONE

The Saga of India's Great Emperors

Abraham Eraly

PHOENIX

A PHOENIX PAPERBACK

First published in Great Britain in 2003
by Weidenfeld & Nicolson
This paperback edition published in 2004
by Phoenix,
an imprint of Orion Books Ltd,
Orion House, 5 Upper St Martin's Lane,
London WC2H 9EA

Originally published by Penguin Books India in 1997
and revised edition in 2000 under the title
Emperors of the Peacock Throne: The Saga of the Great Mughals

A CIP catalogue record for this book
is available from the British Library.

ISBN 0 75381 758 6

Printed and bound in Great Britain by
Butler & Tanner Ltd, Frome and London

For SATISH
who in the summer of
a year of crisis
asked, "What's it again? Can't begin
anything new at your age?
Why not?"
and got me going.

Akbar: *Tell me, if you please, what is the greatest
consolation that man has in this world?*
Birbal: *Ah, sire! it is when a father finds himself
embraced by his son.*

In this history I have held firmly to it that the truth should be reached in every matter, and that every act should be recorded precisely as it occurred . . . I have set down of good and bad whatever is known . . .
—Emperor Babur in *Babur-nama*

**

I give the story as I received it; to contradict it is not in my power.
—Francois Bernier in his report on Mughal India.

Contents

Acknowledgements

The gods have been kind to this unbeliever. At every moment of pressing need, as I plodded on interminably with the work on this book, I have received the needed support, often from unexpected sources and in unexpected ways, even without my asking for it, as a gift from the gods.

Several friends read portions of the manuscript at different stages and gave help and encouragement. Of them I have to make a special mention of two, Sita Srikanth and Nancy Gandhi, whose contributions have been direct and crucial, and have mattered to me far more than I have ever had the grace to show.

Sita, a colleague of mine when I was living disguised as the editor of a fortnightly magazine, was the first person with whom I discussed this project. She then scoured the libraries and pressed books on me, and did much to harden my tenuous idea into a firm project. Later, she read through the entire first draft of the book, making valuable suggestions and hectoring me to work harder, challenging me to be better than I am, often flinging at me the very precepts on which I used to hold forth at editorial meetings. Her support has been invaluable in sustaining this project.

Equally invaluable has been the contribution of Nancy, who came in when I was completing the second draft and was desperately looking for someone to read it before I went in for the final revision. Nancy, patient and thorough, punctilious in observing grammar conventions and puritanical in her aversion to ornamentation, has been the ideal editor for me, better than I could have dreamed of. She gave me the second wind needed to complete this work.

I should also record my gratitude to S. Krishnan, who read the early chapters of the book and buoyed me up with his enthusiasm; to Dr. C. T. Kurian, whose critical comments enabled me to firm up the chapter on Mughal economy; to David Davidar, Editor and Publisher of Penguin India, whose prompt and positive response to the book saved me all the soul-numbing publishing hassles; and to Ravi Singh, my editor at Penguin, who expertly put the book through its final paces.

Preface

I have in my study, on the old, worm-hole pitted teak desk at which I work, an antique stone head of Buddha, less than a foot high, which I had picked up many years ago in Madras from a pavement junkwallah. It is a fine piece, its chiselled features perfect, head slightly bent sideways, as if trying to anchor a memory or a dream, eyes half-closed meditatively. A thick patina of grime tinges the handsome, serene face with a peculiar sadness, the anguish of a compassionate outsider, concerned with the human predicament, but not involved with it.

Over the years, as I laboured on this book, the dispassionate compassion of Buddha had seemed to me the perfect ideal for students of history, though of course we would all fail disgracefully to live up to it, as the passions of our lives and the furies of our age knead and rework us continually on the slow wheel of time.

As time reworks us, we rework history. "All works of history are interim reports," says American historian John Noble Wilford. "What people did in the past is not preserved in amber . . . immutable through the ages. Each generation looks back and, drawing from its own experience, presumes to find patterns that illuminate both past and present."

Nothing ever quite dies. The past is nearly as alive as the present, and it changes as the present changes, the historical past as much as our personal past. The bare facts of history do not of course change, except for occasional emendations, but the way facts interlock and change colour to make patterns is unique to each generation, indeed to each historian. No particular representation of the past has therefore any absolute validity, and the value of any historical work depends largely on the felicitous catalysis of the personal vision into a universal vision. It is essentially a triumph of art.

The mutability of human perceptions apart, there are other obstacles to a definitive understanding of the historical processes. Man cannot, as Albert Camus says in *The Rebel*, grasp the totality of history "since he lives in the midst of this totality. History, as an entirety, could exist only in the eyes of an observer outside it and outside the world." It is in fact impossible for man to know the final truth even about any particular event in history, however trivial it might be, for he, himself swirling in time, does not have the perspective to see all its relevant connections and discern where it would ultimately lead, as its consequences, intersecting with the consequences of myriad other events, proliferate endlessly into the future. "Historical reason will never be fulfilled and will never have its full meaning or value until the end of history," argues Camus. "The purely historical absolute is not even conceivable."

When we consider these all too evident limitations of writing history, it seems amazing that academic historians in modern times have generally laid claim to scientific precision for their methodology, and objective validity for their theories. Historical investigation has of course become more sophisticated lately, especially in the evaluation of archaeological and philological data. But this has come about mainly because of advances in science and technology, and not because of any radical change in the methodology of history. The character of history has not changed.

But the garb of historians has changed, for they have suited up for their new role as social scientists. Unfortunately, many historians, in their excitement at being recognized as social scientists, overlooked the fact that while scientific discoveries are sequential and mark a linear progress—with new discoveries displacing or modifying old theories— new interpretations of history seldom displace old interpretations, for they are only tenets, at best philosophies, not discoveries. The unpredictability of human affairs makes historical analysis, for all its vaunted scientific methodology, essentially an act of faith. What we find depends a lot on what we are.

There were other complications too. Observes Harvard professor Simon Schama: "As historians institutionalized themselves into an academic profession," they turned away from "historical realities" to "historiographical obsessions". Their focus then shifted from persons and events, the flesh and blood of history, to abstract structures of their own construction. This pursuit trapped historians in a maze of sophistry, the sterile, self-abusive game of thought, involving over-elaborations and supersubtleties which made little sense.

Now at last historians are beginning to grope their way out of the maze. And gradually, renouncing the conceits of the recent past, they are returning to their primary function, to resuscitate the past and release it into the present. That is what history is all about. Herodotus, the fifth century BC Greek father of history, has said it all in the opening sentence of his book: "This is a publication of the researches of Herodotus Halicarnassus, in order that the actions of men may not be effaced by time . . ." The historian's profession, as the nineteenth-century French scholar Jules Michelet stated, is to bring "things back to life". Says Schama: "I have tried to bring a world to life rather than entomb it in erudite discourse."

In this role, the historian does not merely log and interpret data; he portrays life and tells a story. Meticulous research is essential, and so is vivid writing, to enable readers to vicariously experience life in other times, other places. When history is yoked to theories and formulas, its sap dries up. Then it neither enlightens nor sensitizes.

The sloughing off of the ill-fitting vestments of science by historians does not make history worthless, but it does change the nature of its worth. Sensitizing the present to the past is not a value neutral process. Every retelling of history, if it is anything more than just a banal catalogue of events, involves ideation, if only because, even at the primary level, a process of selection and evaluation of data, a pattern-making, is involved. The historian might not be overtly judgemental, but judgement is implicit in the very telling of the story. Facts speak for themselves, and when vividly presented, speak loud and clear.

The historian is not a moral eunuch. In fact, it is his moral voice that gives his work its unique timbre—not to raise the moral voice is to treat history like paleobotany, with bland detachment. So, even while the historian acknowledges the provisional nature of all historical perceptions, he, like the nineteenth-century Danish philosopher Kierkegaard, affirms his subjective certainty in the world of objective uncertainties. He might not have any cosmic conclusions to offer, but he does take positions that are appropriate and necessary to his time and place.

The essential corollaries of this relativistic attitude are moderation and tolerance. The historian affirms his views, but humbly, conscious that there are no absolutes. As the saying goes, the white heron in the snow has a different colour. All perceptions, all truth, are relative. As Vedantists would say, all are maya, mental constructs. The eye looks, the mind sees.

To acknowledge the subjective and provisional nature of historical perceptions is not to abandon the process of fair and unbiased collection and evaluation of data. To adapt Tom Wolfe's dictum, the historian sees with an impersonal eye, but speaks with a personal voice. The ideal of historical objectivity has been set down by several Mughal writers. "It is the duty of an historian to be faithful, to have no hope of profit, no fear of injury, to show no partiality on one side, or animosity on the other, to know no difference between friend and stranger, and to write nothing but with sincerity," says Khafi Khan, courtier historian of Emperor Aurangzeb. "In this history I have held firmly to it that the truth should be reached in every matter, and that every act should be recorded precisely as it occurred," writes Emperor Babur in his memoirs. Uncompromising exploration, clear, unbiased perception, candid presentation—these were Babur's ideals. There are no better precepts for historians.

Candour is a major charm of Babur's autobiography, and so is its richness of detail. Fine detail—nuance—is the life-blood of history, as of literature. Says Francois Bernier, a seventeenth-century French traveller in his report on Mughal India: "I agree with Plutarch that trifling incidents ought not be concealed, and that they often enable us to form more accurate opinions of the manners and genius of a people than events of great importance." Major events shape the contours of history, but it is the particulars that breathe life into it.

To give completeness to history and to establish the total context of life, it is as essential to examine the details of everyday life, as of political, economic and socio-cultural developments. In this, the historian of Mughal India is fortunate, for his sources are numerous and varied, and are rich in detail about every facet of life. And I have quoted extensively from them, somewhat in the manner of a reporter quoting eyewitnesses, to give immediacy and authenticity to the narrative, and to let the reader see Mughal life through the eyes of those who saw it directly.

The basic concern of the historian is, I believe, similar to that of any serious artist or creative writer—to share experience and to elucidate the human condition. The historian too uses imagination and insight, to visualize what happened in history and present a coherent picture, though he, unlike the creative writer, has to work strictly within the boundaries of known facts, and is not free to invent even the minutest detail. What Richard Feynman said of physicists applies to historians too: "Our imagination is stretched to the utmost, not, as in fiction, to imagine things which are not really there, but just to comprehend those things which are there." Imagination, says American historian Barbara Tuchman, enables the historian "to understand the evidence he has accumulated. Imagination stretches the available facts . . . the artist's eye: It leads you to the right thing." Methodical research builds the ship, imagination sails it.

This volume on late medieval Indian history, from 1526 to 1707, is part of a four-volume study titled India Retold, that would, when completed, cover the history of India from the beginning up to 1858; chronologically, this is the third volume in the proposed series, though the first to be ready.

My focus in this volume is on the Mughal empire; I have dealt with regional histories only in their links with Mughal history. Regional histories—indeed, even studies of sub-regions and towns—are valuable, but impractical for the general historian. I have therefore stayed close to the dominant theme of the period, and have tried to deal with it exhaustively, bearing in mind Thomas Mann's dictum that "only the exhaustive is truly interesting". But the exhaustiveness I have attempted is in presenting life in its fullness, not in cataloguing events. I have not, for instance, listed many of the battles, but have, on the other hand, described a couple of battles in great detail, to show how the Mughals fought. I have also dealt with everyday life—of the people as well as of the rulers—at great length, as my objective is to portray life rather than merely to chronicle history.

If history is the mirror in which we recognize ourselves as a people, then modern Indians can hardly recognize themselves in the mirror that is conventionally held up to them. Or, alternately, they imagine themselves to be something they are not, as distortions in the mirror distort their self-perceptions. This is a modern predicament, a consequence of the psychic morphing of India, induced initially by British imperial prejudice, then by European romanticism, and finally by Indian nationalism.

These distortions prevail even today, though times have changed. During the British rule, Indians, as a subject people, needed the comfort and strength of a presumed golden past to mould the nationalist sentiment and energize the freedom struggle. But now, half a century after independence, India cannot still subsist on the mindset of adolescent nationalism, chewing the cud of romantic fancy. To move on, it is imperative today to lift the veils of bias, romance and myth that obscure India's image, and look truth in the eye. The alternative is to remain snared in self-delusions, fighting quixotic battles with the spectres of the past—the unforgiven colonial rule, or (for some) the even more unforgiven Muslim invasion of India one thousand years ago.

Tradition, however glorious, is what a people have to grow out of. The future is not a replica of the past, but its fulfilment. In every other major civilization, the past has died so the future could be born, but

India seems to be killing the future so the past can live on. India's lofty boast is that its is the oldest living civilization, but is that anything to be proud of? That India has not evolved? There is something very wrong with a people who consider that the greatest that would ever be has already been, and that the best they can do is to duplicate the past.

There is of course much in the Indian heritage to be proud of, but there is also much to be ashamed of, and both have to be examined with candour. Not to do so would be irresponsible. It is possible that such candour would be controversial in a socio-political environment in which expedient myths tyrannize reality. As a Chinese saying has it, when the finger points to the moon, the idiot would look at the finger. That cannot be helped. The historian is not concerned with political correctness.

Abraham Eraly

Madras
December 1995

Mughal India

- Fergana
- Samarkand
- Herat
- Kabul
- Peshawar
AFGHANISTAN
- Kandahar
KASHMIR
Indus
Jhelum
Chenab
Ravi
- Lahore
- Multan
Satluj
BALUCHISTAN *Indus*
PUNJAB
Yamuna
- Panipat
Brahmaputra
- Delhi
Ganga
SIND
RAJASTHAN
Fatehpur Sikri • Agra
Chambal
- Chitor
- Gwalior
- Allahabad
- Patna
- Chausa
Ganga
Son
BIHAR
Brahmaputra
GUJARAT
Dharmat
MALWA
Narmada
- Calcutta
BENGAL
- Surat
- Burhanpur
Mahanadi
- Aurangabad
- Bombay
- Ahmednagar
- Pune
Godavari
ORISSA
D E C C A N
- Satara
- Bidar
- Bijapur
- Golconda
Krishna
- Goa
Arabian Sea
Bay of Bengal
- Madras
CARNATIC
- Pondicherry
Kaveri
- Thanjavur

Family of Itimad-ud-daula
(Its links with the Mughal dynasty)

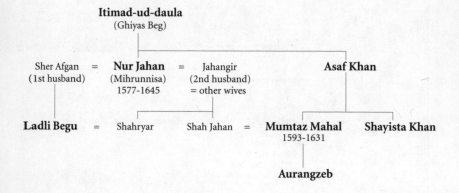

Itimad-ud-daula
(Ghiyas Beg)

| Sher Afgan
(1st husband) | = | **Nur Jahan**
(Mihrunnisa)
1577-1645 | = | Jahangir
(2nd husband)
= other wives | | **Asaf Khan** |

| **Ladli Begu** | = | Shahryar | | Shah Jahan | = | **Mumtaz Mahal**
1593-1631 | **Shayista Khan** |

Aurangzeb

The Great Mughals
(Years of rule are given in brackets)

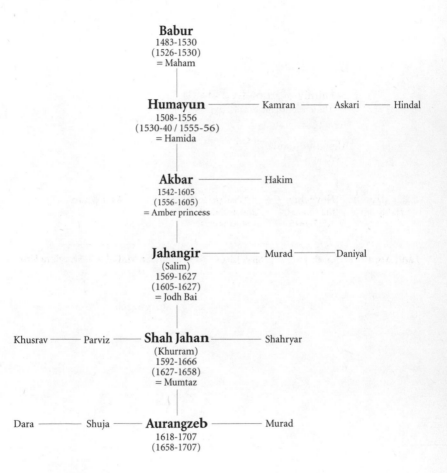

Babur
1483-1530
(1526-1530)
= Maham

Humayun ———— Kamran ———— Askari ———— Hindal
1508-1556
(1530-40 / 1555-56)
= Hamida

Akbar ———— Hakim
1542-1605
(1556-1605)
= Amber princess

Jahangir ———— Murad ———— Daniyal
(Salim)
1569-1627
(1605-1627)
= Jodh Bai

Khusrav ———— Parviz ———— **Shah Jahan** ———— Shahryar
(Khurram)
1592-1666
(1627-1658)
= Mumtaz

Dara ———— Shuja ———— **Aurangzeb** ———— Murad
1618-1707
(1658-1707)

(The mothers of the emperors are given. But except for Aurangzeb, the brothers of the emperors had different mothers.)

THE MUGHAL THRONE

Chapter One

THE MUGHAL ADVENT

Like a King on a Chessboard

"IN THE MONTH of Ramadan of the year 899, and in the twelfth year of my age, I became ruler in the country of Fergana." So begin the memoirs of Babur. The day was Tuesday, 9th June 1494. Babur's father, Umar Sheikh Mirza, king and pigeon fancier, had died in a freak accident the previous day at Akhsi, a northern fort of Fergana, when his dovecot, built on the edge of a ravine in a corner of the castle, tumbled into the river below in a landslide, bearing him down with it. "Umar Sheikh Mirza flew, with his pigeons and their house, and became a falcon," writes Babur.

Babur was born on 14th February 1483. He was named Zahiruddin Muhammad—Defender of the Faith, Muhammad—but that was a tongue-twister of an Arabic name for the rustics of Fergana, so they nicknamed the child Babur. The name meant tiger, and proved fitting.

Babur's lineage was awesome. On the paternal side, he was the grandson of Sultan Abu Said Mirza of Herat, a great-grandson of Timur, the legendary Tartar hero. On his mother's side, his grandfather was Yunus Khan of Tashkent, the Great Khan of the Mongols, the thirteenth in the direct line of descent from Chingiz Khan. Babur was thus a Turko-Mongol, as were most of the ruling class in the racial cauldron of Central Asia; he was in fact more a Mongol than a Turk, for his paternal ancestor, Timur, though a Turk by language and culture, was also of Mongol descent. Babur, however, preferred to call himself a Turk—he considered Mongols to be uncouth barbarians and despised them, saying, "Were the Mongols a race of angels, it would still be a vile nation."

Nothing much is known about Babur's mother, except her name, Qutluq Nigar Khanum, and her Mongol lineage. Babur himself has little to say about her. But there is a lively, candid profile of his father in his memoirs. Umar, as Babur describes him, was a short, stout, powerfully built man—"not a man but fell to his blow," he writes—slovenly in dress, gross in habits, but amorous, and addicted to alcohol, opium and the game of draughts. He was also, Babur wryly notes, a vapid poet.

WHEN THE NEWS of his father's death reached Babur, he was encamped, it being summer, in a garden outside Andizhan, the capital of Fergana. His immediate and characteristically Timurid concern, though he was but a child, was to secure his throne. As the eldest prince, the throne was his by right, but that right could be enforced, in the volatile political environment of Central Asia, only by the sword. He therefore hastily returned to Andizhan, escorted by his amirs. And there, after some uncertainty about whether he would be received as king or taken captive, he ascended the throne.

It was a shaky throne. At the time of Babur's accession, Fergana was under attack by two of his uncles, neighbouring monarchs who had been provoked into hostility by Umar, and who now, on Umar's death, considered the boy-king fair prey. And within Fergana itself a cabal of nobles were plotting to raise Babur's younger brother Jahangir to the throne. For the moment, however, Babur's stars were in the ascendant, and he triumphed over all his adversaries, partly by luck, but mainly because his affairs were taken in hand by his maternal grandmother, Aisan-daulat Begum. A nomadic Mongol of the wild steppes, she was a worldly-wise and formidable dowager, of whom Babur says, "Few amongst women will have been my grandmother's equals for judgement and counsel; she was very wise and farsighted and most affairs of mine were carried through under her advice."

Babur loved Fergana. It was a beautiful, river-laced land of hills and dales, celebrated for its orchards, gardens and abundant game. But Fergana was too small to sate Babur's ambition or contain his energy. The boy was a dreamer, awake with visions of empire and glory. Moreover, fratricidal wars were a Timurid rite of passage, a royal obligation. Babur could fulfil himself—indeed, even survive—only by the sword.

The entire mountainous country from the Aral Sea to the Hindu Kush, broken into half-a-dozen principalities, was ruled by the close relatives of Babur, turbulent descendants of Timur or Chingiz Khan, who were forever grappling with each other in ceaseless wars. There was scope enough there for Babur to fulfil himself.

Immediately to the west of Fergana was the kingdom of Samarkand, ruled by Baisanghar, a paternal cousin of Babur. Samarkand, Timur's fabled capital, was no longer the grand imperial city it had been once, but for Babur the throne of Timur was still the ultimate symbol of temporal power, and its possession now became his magnificent obsession. It was a possible dream, for Samarkand was in chaos at this time, with rival princes clashing over the throne. In mid-1496 Babur joined the fray, and though his initial campaign was a failure, and he was obliged at the onset of winter to retreat over the mountains to Fergana, he was able to seize the city the following year after a tenacious siege of seven months.

Babur was then just fifteen years old. But his career, as he saw it, had already peaked. To sit on the throne of Timur was the highest of highs for him, not eclipsed even by his later conquest of India, and till the end of his life he loved to roll in his mind the bitter-sweet memory of winning and losing Samarkand.

His moment of triumph was all too brief. For a hundred days he held Samarkand, despite desertions in his army. Then his run of luck ended—he fell seriously ill in Samarkand, meanwhile lost Fergana to rebels favouring his brother Jahangir, and when he marched out to quell the rebellion, lost Samarkand also, to Sultan Ali Mirza of Bokhara, a cousin. The fledgeling that had dared to soar had crashed ignominiously. "It came very hard on me," writes Babur. "I could not help crying a good deal."

Babur did eventually recover Fergana, and Samarkand too, but only to lose them both all over again, this time to the formidable Uzbeg chief Shaibani Khan, a descendant of Chingiz Khan, who had made it the mission of his life to extirpate the Timurids from Central Asia.

THE TEN YEARS from the time he ascended the throne of Fergana as a boy-king, till, as a young adult, he established himself as the ruler of Kabul, were years of unremitting adversity for Babur, punctuated by a few all too brief triumphs. For many years, says Mughal chronicler Ferishta, "Babur was like a king on a chess-board, moved from place to place, and buffeted about like pebbles on a seashore." Time and again he was a king without a kingdom, sometimes even without a home. Lamented Babur:

> Is there one cruel turn of Fortune's wheel
> unseen by me?
> Is there a pang, a grief my wounded heart has
> missed?

Homeless, for a while he wandered about in the mountains of Central Asia with a small band of ragged comrades, often sheltering with wild hill tribes. Finally, wretched and destitute, he took refuge with his maternal uncle, the Mongol chieftain, in Tashkent. There was no solace for him there either. "During my stay in Tashkent," he writes, "I endured much poverty and humiliation. No country, or hope of one!"

7

At one time, in despair and shame, he even thought of slinking off to China.

Then suddenly, in a dramatic turn of events, fate plucked Babur out of his misery and set him on the throne of Kabul. Kabul, like all the other kingdoms in the region, was ruled by a relative of Babur, Ulugh Beg Mirza, a paternal uncle. When Ulugh Beg died, leaving only an infant son as heir, the principality collapsed into turmoil as rebels and invaders swept the land. This was opportunity for Babur. His eyes had been on Kabul for some time, and now, desperate for a safe haven, he swooped down on the hapless city and claimed it for himself.

This was in 1504. Babur once again had a power base.

And a future.

Babur was only twenty-two years old when he took Kabul. A whole life lay ahead of him. Never again would he have to be anxious for a throne to sit on. He had suffered enough.

But suffering had not calloused him. Or dulled his verve for life. There were times when he wept and bemoaned his fate, but never for long. As he put it,

> All ill, all good in the count,
> Is gain if looked at aright.

Adversity made him wise, not cynical; it taught him what he needed to learn to merit what he had to achieve. There was a natural candour about Babur, a warmth and openness that endeared him to his men, with whom he shared all dangers and all hardships, always leading them from the front. "This prince was adorned with various virtues," writes his cousin Mirza Haidar, "above all of which bravery and humanity had the ascendant." Intelligence, compassion, energy, ambition, steadfastness, and, equally, the sheer joy of life—these are the traits we see in Babur in Kabul.

We do not know what Babur looked like. There are no descriptions. In a portrait in *Babur-nama* painted during the reign of Akbar, presumably with the guidance of those who had known Babur, we see him as a man of medium build, with a light beard—he was so lightly bearded that it was only in his twenty-third year that he first needed to shave—heavy eyelids, a sharp nose and a broad forehead. The setting in the painting is pastoral, the mood serene. But Babur, the nomadic blood of his ancestors surging in his veins, was a restless person. Always on the move, he had never since his eleventh year "kept the Ramadan feast for two successive years in the same place," he notes with pride in his journal.

Babur loved to call himself a dervish. His generosity was legendary. Possessions did not mean much to him. But self-fulfilment did. And self-fulfilment meant fulfilment as a monarch and empire-builder. For that, Kabul opened up unprecedented opportunities.

IN KABUL, BABUR'S eyes turned eastward, lured by the memory of Timur's Indian invasion, and impelled by his own compelling need to foray, to supplement the meagre revenue of his mountain kingdom. From the time Kabul was taken, "my desire for Hindustan had been constant," writes Babur. In 1505, the very year after he took Kabul, Babur led his first expedition towards India. "It was in the month of Shaban, the Sun being in Aquarius, that we rode out of Kabul for Hindustan," he records. That campaign however was little more than a border raid across the Khyber Pass. His first serious expedition into India would come only a full twenty years later, in 1524. For the time being, he was still preoccupied with Central Asian affairs, mainly with his indomitable adversary Shaibani Khan, who was always there just beyond the horizon, a constant menace.

Between Shaibani and the Timurids it was not just a power rivalry, but a blood feud. There could never be any peace between them, and as long as Shaibani was around, no Mughal would be safe on his throne. So when Sultan Husain Mirza of Herat, the grand patriarch of the clan, summoned Timurid princes to combine against Shaibani in a fight to the finish, Babur at once set out with his troops for Herat. Unfortunately, the aged sultan died before the campaign could be launched, and his two sons, both exquisitely over-cultured sybarites, who now became the joint rulers of Herat, could not bear to soil their hands in war. They did march out of Herat to encamp on the banks of the Murgab, and they talked incessantly about setting out to wage war, but that was about as far as they would go. "The Mirzas were good enough as company and in social matters, in conversation and parties, but were strangers to war, strategy, bold fight and encounter . . . . Dreamers, they moved through a dream!" writes Babur.

The Mirzas entertained their up-country cousin royally, introducing him to the refinements of high culture. "The social cups were filled," writes Babur of a party he attended, "the guests drank down the mere wine as if it were the water of life; when it mounted to their heads, the party waxed warm." Babur himself would not yet violate the Islamic injunction against alcohol, though he was tempted, but he did greatly enjoy the company of the Mirzas, and when they pressed him to go with them to Herat, he did not demur.

9

Babur's sojourn in Herat, which was then the cultural capital of the eastern Muslim world, had a great effect on him. He was both fascinated and repelled by the cloying decadence of the city, a honeyed world of luxury, culture, learning, and wanton sensuality. Enigmatists, men who made up riddles, were the pride of Herat. Almost all the luminaries of Herat wrote poetry, even wrestlers. Or they composed music, took to calligraphy or painting, or some such refinement. Chess was an obsession in the city, and chess parties were as common as wine parties. A city of dandies, Herat set the fashion for cultured Muslims everywhere. Naturally, Herat was also a merry den of vice; as Babur notes with gentle reprobation, in Sultan Husain Mirza, "in his sons, and in his tribes and hordes, vice and debauchery were extremely prevalent." Herat was hopelessly decadent. But it had flair.

Though enjoying himself, Babur was uneasy in Herat. The Uzbeg hurricane, he knew, was gathering across the Murgab. The Mirzas were living in a fool's paradise. Babur, though young in years, was a battle-toughened veteran; his instincts warned him to flee.

So, though it was the dead of winter, and the mountains impassable, after twenty days of merrymaking in Herat Babur tore himself away and trekked back to Kabul. Soon, as he feared, Herat fell to Shaibani. The Mirzas fled for their lives.

The fall of Herat left Babur as the only reigning prince of the house of Timur. Timurid princes and amirs from all over Central Asia, the debris of the Uzbeg flash-flood, now drifted to Kabul, the only high ground left for their refuge. To signify his new status as the chief of the Timurids, Babur, who like all Timurid rulers was till then known as a Mirza, prince, now styled himself as Padshah, emperor. This august title denoted Babur's ambition, presaged his destiny, but his position was as yet insignificant and precarious—not only was there no hope of his recovering his ancestral lands from Shaibani, but even his tiny principality of Kabul was in peril. In this predicament, Babur desperately needed to distance himself from his relentless adversary, and it was thus that he seriously began to look on India as a possible refuge.

Then unexpectedly the scene changed. Shaibani Khan, overreaching himself, made the mistake of clashing with Shah Ismail, the founder of the Safavid dynasty of Persia, who, even wilier than Shaibani, outmanoeuvred and decimated the Uzbegs in battle. Shaibani was killed, his body dismembered, and his skull, set in gold, made into a drinking cup for the Shah.

The news electrified the Timurids. From their diverse places of refuge they now hastened back to recover their lost lands. Babur himself sprang to action and, putting his brother Nasir Mirza in charge of Kabul, rode north towards Transoxiana, dreaming of Samarkand again. But Samarkand was not his destiny. Though he did, with the help of a Persian expeditionary force, occupy the city, now for the third time, he could hold it only briefly, that too virtually as a Persian vassal, before being driven out by the Uzbegs again.

He lingered on in Badakshan for a while, unable to reconcile himself to the loss of Samarkand, but in 1514, after an absence of three years, he finally returned to Kabul and resumed the throne from his brother. He would never again turn to the west. His destiny lay in the east, in India.

BACK IN KABUL, Babur's life settled into a routine, insofar as the life of a medieval prince could be routine. He was still involved with frequent military campaigns—punitive expeditions against refractory Afghan tribes, pillaging forays across the eastern mountains, coercive actions against rebellious nobles and ambitious relatives. But the eleven years that Babur spent in Kabul after his return from Badakshan till his final Indian expedition were, relatively speaking, a time of peace and tranquillity for him.

The season now turned to spring for Babur. He now had the leisure to indulge in his passion for literature and the arts, and to enjoy the pleasures of life. He delighted in good companionship, held numerous wine and opium parties, which often began at the crack of dawn and pleasured on late into the night.

These were new amusements for Babur. "I had had no inclination for wine in my childhood; I knew nothing of its cheer and pleasure," he writes. "If, as sometimes, my father pressed wine on me, I excused myself . . . Later on when, with the young man's lusts and the prompting of sensual passion, desire for wine arose, there was no one to press it on me, no one indeed aware of my leaning towards it; so that, inclined for it though my heart was, it was difficult of myself to do such a thing, one thitherto not done." In Herat his cousins had offered him wine, but he had decorously declined it, hoping that they would ask again. They had not.

So it was only in his thirties that Babur first tasted wine, but he briskly made up for lost time. Somewhere along the way he also started taking confections of opium, and possibly marijuana. But these habits did not debase Babur—in him intoxication was a refinement, a keenness of senses, not a vice. He loathed raucous revelry, and often broke up parties when they turned unruly. "There was much disgusting uproar," he writes about one such incident, "the party became intolerable and was broken up."

11

Babur loved the pleasures of the table too; fruits especially were a passion with him. He does not however seem to have been keen on the fourth component of Omar Khayyam's paradise, women. He was a good provider and a caring householder, affectionate and deferential towards his women, especially towards his elder relatives, but he was not, unlike his roly-poly father, a ladies' man. Babur preferred the macho bonhomie of his friends to the pleasures of the harem.

Babur's first wife was Aisha, a cousin, to whom he was betrothed at the age of five. Eleven years later, she joined him in Fergana. She found him a bashful lover. As Babur tells it, "Though I was not ill-disposed towards her, yet, this being my first marriage, out of modesty and bashfulness, I used to see her once in ten, fifteen, twenty days. Later on, when even my first inclination did not last, my bashfulness increased. Then my mother Khanum used to send me, once a month or every forty days, with driving and driving, dunnings and worryings." Babur had his first child, a daughter, by Aisha three years after she joined him, but the baby died in infancy, and Aisha herself deserted him during his days of homeless wandering. By and by Babur acquired other wives and several concubines, as behoved a prince, and he fathered a number of children, as duty required of him, to ensure the continuity of his line. But there was no ardour in him for women.

There was only one romantic infatuation in Babur's life, his unabashed love for a bazaar boy in Andizhan. Babur was sixteen then, and Aisha had just joined him. "In those leisurely days," he confesses, "I discovered in myself a strange inclination . . . for a boy in the camp-bazaar, his very name, Baburi, fitting in. Up till then I had had no inclination for anyone, indeed of love and desire, either by hearsay or experience, I had not heard, I had not talked . . . From time to time Baburi used to come to my presence, but out of modesty and bashfulness I could never look straight at him; how then could I make conversation and recital? . . . In that frothing-up of desire and passion, and under that stress of youthful folly, I used to wander, bare-head, bare-foot, through street and lane, orchard and vineyard. I showed civility neither to friend nor stranger, took no care for myself or others . . ."

Babur does not tell how the affair ended. But he got over it soon enough. Baburi was just an adolescent fancy, not unusual in an environment in which, among Central Asian aristocrats, bisexuality was common, and pederasty high fashion. In Babur's case, however, the affair appears to have been virginally romantic and without carnal expression. Later, in Kabul, when he once again had time to enjoy himself, he preferred the gentler seductions of literature, art, music and gardening to carnal pleasures.

Babur gave all of himself to every one of his many cultural pursuits, and his achievements in some of them were substantial. Still, they were only avocations for him, and not for one moment would he let himself forget that he was a king by profession, and that his ultimate ecstasy would be in the perilous thrill of the battlefield.

IN KABUL, THOUGH he did not yet know what fate had in store for him, Babur began to organize himself for the battles ahead, whipping his men into a superb fighting force. "I had been at great pains to train and exercise them to the utmost point," he writes. "Never, perhaps, were my troops in such perfect discipline." He also took care to modernize his army, introducing muskets and cannons (till then used mostly in siege operations) into field battle, a tactic he adopted from the Ottoman Turks. That innovation would give him a crucial advantage in India.

Meanwhile, the political jigsaw in India had rearranged itself, to open a passage for Babur. And Babur needed that exit, to get away from the ever menacing Uzbegs. "The foe mightily strong, I very weak, with no means of making terms, no strength to oppose," he laments. "In the presence of such power and potency, we had to think of some place for ourselves and, at this crisis and in the crack of time there was, put a wider space between us and the strong foeman. That choice lay between Badakshan and Hindustan and that decision must now be made."

The choice fell on India.

Babur states that from 1519 on he led five expeditions into India, but long before that, in fact from the time he took Kabul, he had been active along India's north-western marches. Those early campaigns were however only pillaging raids, and he probably did not cross the Indus till 1519, when he advanced as far as the Jhelum. Even then, till 1524 he had no ambition beyond Punjab, which he claimed as his Timurid legacy, by virtue of it having been a part of Timur's empire a century earlier. Then, fortuitously, a greater opportunity came knocking. The messengers of destiny were Dilawar Khan (son of Daulat Khan, the rebel Afghan governor of Punjab) and Alam Khan (an uncle of Ibrahim Lodi, the Sultan of Delhi), who arrived in Kabul to solicit Babur's help in ousting Ibrahim. Babur then took an omen, found it favourable, and agreed to their proposal, intending not so much to help them as to help himself.

The campaign of 1524 was abortive. The allies, after occupying Punjab, fell out over the division of the province. Daulat Khan wanted

13

all of Punjab for himself, while Babur had other ideas. Babur therefore prudently withdrew to Kabul, leaving a garrison in Lahore. It would have been dangerous for him to advance further into India, with a truculent Daulat Khan behind him in Punjab threatening his line of retreat.

Babur set out from Kabul on his final invasion of India in mid-November 1525, before the snows closed the mountain passes. He moved leisurely, holding frequent wine parties along the way. By mid-December he crossed the Indus, never to recross it. His immediate adversary was Daulat Khan, who had entered the field against him with two swords girded to his waist to display his victory-or-death resolve. That, it turned out, was just bluster, for as soon as Babur approached, the Khan's army scattered and the old man himself tamely surrendered. He was brought before Babur with his two swords hanging from his neck. Babur upbraided him: "I called thee Father. I showed thee more honour and respect than thou couldst have asked . . . What ill sayest thou I have done thee, that thus thou shouldst hang a sword on thy either side, lead an army out, fall on lands of ours, and stir strife and trouble?" The Khan had no answer.

But Daulat Khan was irrelevant. The real challenge lay ahead, at Panipat, where Ibrahim Lodi waited with his army. "I put my foot in the stirrup of resolution," writes Babur, "set my hand on the rein of trust in God, and moved forward against Sultan Ibrahim."

"If Fame Be Mine . . ."

BABUR DID NOT tarry in Punjab. Even then it took him a while to settle his affairs there, so that by the time he crossed the Satluj and advanced to the Yamuna, it was April, and the dreaded Indian summer was upon him. On reaching the Yamuna, at a point east of Kurukshetra, the epic battleground of the Mahabharata, Babur encamped.

Meanwhile Ibrahim Lodi, haughtily disregarding the dire warnings of his astrologers, had advanced with his troops to Panipat, eighty kilometres north of Delhi, to challenge the intruder. The opposing forces thus lay two marches away from each other, the Afghans immediately to the south of Panipat and the Mughals some way to the north of it.

The going had been easy for Babur in India till then, as he had met only desultory resistance from the Afghan provincial forces in Punjab. Now he had to face the imperial Afghan army. His own army was small by Indian standards. Four months earlier, when he was crossing the Indus, his army, Babur reports, numbered 12,000 men, "great and small, good and bad, retainer and non-retainer." He was later joined by the contingents he had left behind in India during his previous campaign, as well as by a few renegade Afghan officers and soldiers. With these accretions, by the time Babur reached Panipat his army had probably swelled to about 20,000 men.

The actual strength of the Afghan army is not known. Babur estimated it to be roughly 100,000 strong, with some 1000 elephants. Whatever the true count, the Afghan army was certainly much larger than the Mughal army. This Afghan advantage was somewhat offset by Babur's superior weaponry: a train of artillery (estimates vary from just two to a few hundred pieces) and a contingent of musketeers (again of unknown number, but probably about 4000) which would be used in India in a field battle for the first time at Panipat. Still, the balance of power favoured Ibrahim. Babur could win only by clever tactics.

MOST OF BABUR'S battles till then had been close combats in the hill country, in constricted battlefields where large forces could not be deployed, and it was not the size of the army but its spirit, the tactical use of the terrain and the element of surprise that decided the outcome of battles. Babur was now in flat, open country. Here numbers would matter. There was little scope for a surprise attack, no tactical advantage in the terrain. And valour, rapidity of response and manoeuvrability, though they all could make a difference, would not be decisive.

To defeat Ibrahim Lodi, Babur had to neutralize the awesome Afghan superiority in numbers and enable his own strengths in cavalry and gunnery to prevail. The critical requirement for him was to create· a narrow battlefront, to prevent the Afghans from sweeping around the flanks of his small army and encircling it. But that in itself was not enough, for however narrow the front, Babur would not have enough depth of array to withstand the Afghan onslaught which could, by its sheer mass and velocity, smash through the Mughal ranks like a giant tidal wave. Babur had to devise a means to steel his frontline, to hold the Afghans in check long enough for his slow-firing guns to break the Afghan formation. If he could do that, then the Mughal cavalry could charge into their midst and scythe them down.

What had Babur to do to gain that tactical advantage? In his quandary, he summoned his veterans to a war council. Together, reaching back to the lore of their turbulent land and the memory of Babur's own thirty-two years of incessant wars, they conceived a revolutionary new strategy that dexterously modified the traditional Mughal battle formation to accommodate the Ottoman wall-of-fire gunnery tactics and the wheeling cavalry charge of the Uzbegs—to halt the Afghan juggernaut in its tracks and annihilate it.

Having decided on the strategy, Babur sent out scouts to survey the prospective battlefield at Panipat. The stretch of open land on the eastern flank of Haryana along the Yamuna was the traditional passage into the Gangetic Plain, a corridor between the mountains on the north and the desert on the south, at the end of which lay Delhi. This was the arena of India's destiny where other decisive battles had been fought in the past, as they would be in the future. The ground at Panipat was ideal for a conventional field battle. It suited Ibrahim Lodi.

But it did not suit Babur. There was nothing at all in the terrain that he could take advantage of—it was just a vast, open, flat field, its monotony relieved only by a few trees and thorn bushes. Babur had somehow to modify the battleground to serve his particular strategic needs.

In two rapid marches southward along the Yamuna, Babur reached Panipat and deployed his army to the east of the town, between the town and the river, which in the sixteenth century flowed close by. His right wing abutted the buildings of the town, secure against being outflanked; to protect his left wing, he dug ditches and laid an obstacle of felled trees between the river and his position, thus effectively narrowing the width of the field to ensure that the battle would be fought precisely along the front on which he deployed his army. The enemy would have no chance to sweep around him, either on the left or on the right.

To protect his frontline and to impede the Afghan cavalry onset, Babur set up along his entire front a barrier of gun-carriages and other carts, some 700 of them, placed about four metres apart and with ropes of rawhide stretched between them. In between the carts, Babur placed his musketeers, six or seven in each gap, protected by breastworks. And to give an offensive potential to this essentially defensive deployment, he left several gaps, each about a bow-shot wide, between groups of carts through which a couple of hundred horsemen could charge abreast. By 12th April Babur was ready for the enemy, his preparations complete.

His was a perfect defensive-offensive arrangement, which could hold the enemy at bay until he was ready to attack. The only disadvantage, and this was a crucial factor, was that its success depended on the Afghans attacking his entrenched position; if they did not attack, all his elaborate preparations would be worth nothing. Babur confidently expected the Afghans to attack, for after all the Mughals had intruded into the Lodi domain and it was for Ibrahim Lodi to expel them.

Ibrahim Lodi viewed the situation differently.

He was close by, straddling the route to Delhi in a good blocking position. As Babur set about preparing his defences, the sultan made no move to interfere. Clearly, he was not planning to attack. He had no need to, as his objective was only to deny Babur passage to Delhi. Defence, in this case, was the best form of offence. By staying fast in his position, the sultan could force Babur to leave his entrenchments and attack him. Time was on Ibrahim Lodi's side. He could afford to wait.

But Babur could not. As an aggressor in an alien land, and facing a superior army, he needed quick results to keep his men in the high heat of martial zeal. For seven days, with increasing restlessness, he waited for the Afghan attack. Meanwhile, the morale of his army began to crumble. "Many of the troops," he notes, "were in great tremor and alarm."

Babur tried to calm them by ridiculing Ibrahim Lodi as "an unproved brave" from whom they had nothing to fear. At the same time he sought to incite the Afghans into action by sending provocative sallies into their camp, hurling insults and shooting arrows. These were

17

ignored by the Afghans. "Still he made no move; nor did his troops sally out," grumbles Babur. The unproved brave was proving to have a firm and sound strategy of his own.

In the end, it was Babur who was obliged to change his battle plan and launch, on 19th April, a night attack on the Afghans, hoping to take them by surprise. The main body of Babur's left wing, a contingent of some four or five thousand men, nearly a fourth of his army, was sent into the attack, while Babur himself stood at arms with the rest of his men, ready to press the advantage should the attackers make headway, or to cover their retreat should they fail.

The foray was a fiasco. Instead of surprising the Afghans, the Mughals were in for a surprise themselves—they found the Afghans alert and ready for them, so that, in peril of being decimated, they retreated abruptly, without engaging.

But such was Babur's luck that it was this apparent rout that got him what he wanted—an Afghan attack on his position.

APRIL 20TH, THE day after the failed night attack, was a quiet day in the Mughal camp, as Babur waited for the Afghan countermove. He waited in vain, though late that night the Mughal camp was thrown into panic by a false alarm about a surprise Afghan attack—"For twenty minutes there was uproar and call to arms," says Babur. The Mughals were edgy.

Then, as dawn broke over the plain on Saturday, 21st April, Mughal pickets reported that the Afghans were on the move. Apparently, the easy rout of the Mughal night-raiders had emboldened the Afghans. They scented an easy victory, and moved in for the kill.

This was a fatal error. The Afghans were walking into the trap cunningly laid by Babur.

Babur waited, his cavalry, his barricade of carts and breastworks, his cannoneers and musketeers, all in position. Behind the gun line, the Mughal army, with soldiers as well as horses clad in mail, was drawn up in the classic Timurid formation—the advance guard up front at the centre, with the main contingent directly behind it, flanked by the right and left wings, and flying squadrons at the far right and the far left. At the rear of it all, Babur kept a large reserve force ready for any contingency.

The Afghans came on at a fast gallop, as if they meant simply to overrun the Mughals.

But they were in trouble even before they engaged the Mughal army. Squeezed between the walls of Panipat on their left and Babur's ditches and hurdles on their right, the Afghans found themselves in a bottleneck when they closed in on the Mughals. As they sidled to squeeze though the constriction, their left wing angled ahead of the frontline, so it was in an odd, lopsided formation that the Afghans slammed, like a brittle wedge, into the right wing of the Mughal army.

Babur, who had positioned himself near the centre of the Mughal deployment in an overseeing position, noticed the Afghans bearing down on his right, and rushed a part of his reserve troops to reinforce that wing. But there was no need for anxiety. When the Afghans came up against the Mughal defences, and the Mughal guns opened up (an unexpected terror) their forward divisions faltered, and as they tried to rein in, the ranks behind, unable to break their momentum, slammed into them, throwing the entire Afghan army, already under a lateral squeeze because of the constriction in the wings, into disarray. It was precisely as Babur had planned. An army no more but a dense, seething horde, the Afghans were unable to fight effectively, or even to retreat.

Babur seized the moment and swung his flying squadrons into action, to wheel around the enemy and attack them from the rear. Simultaneously, he ordered his left and right wings to advance. His strategy was clear. He meant to roll up the Afghan wings and slam them into the Afghan centre, turning the Afghan army into compacted fodder for his cannons and muskets.

The Afghans fought on valiantly, repeatedly charging the Mughal position, but their plight was hopeless. It was not a battle any more, but carnage. "The sun had mounted a spear-high when the onset of battle began, and the combat lasted till mid-day, when the enemy was completely broken and routed, and my friends victorious and exulting," writes Babur. "By the grace and mercy of Almighty God, this arduous undertaking was rendered easy for me, and this mighty army, in the space of half a day, laid in the dust."

The slaughter was dreadful. The Afghan dead were set down by Babur as 15,000 or 16,000 men, a likely figure. Ibrahim Lodi himself lay dead amidst a pile of corpses, the only Muslim ruler of Delhi (Turk, Afghan or Mughal) ever to fall in battle. When the Mughals found the slain sultan's body, they, as was customary among them, severed his head and took it as a memento to Babur. Babur treated the grisly trophy with grave respect. "Honour to your bravery!" he exclaimed, lifting up the head solemnly. Before the battle he had spoken scornfully of Ibrahim Lodi, but now that the day was won, he would salute the brave dead. He called for a bolt of brocade to shroud the body, and commanded two of his top amirs, Dilawar Khan and Amir Khalifa, to bathe Ibrahim Lodi and to bury him with full honours at the spot where he had fallen.

AN EMPIRE HAD been won in a mere five-hour battle. "That very day," writes Babur, "I directed Humayun Mirza . . . to set out without baggage or encumbrances, and proceed with all possible expedition to occupy Agra (the Lodi capital), and take possession of the treasuries." Another contingent was rushed to occupy Delhi.

Babur himself rode on to seize the Afghan camp, then pitched his tents on the banks of a nearby stream for the night. The next day, a Sunday, he set out for Agra. On the way he stopped over in Delhi for a few days, securing treasuries and visiting palaces, gardens and shrines. He also arranged for the khutbah (a formal sermon, incorporating a prayer for the reigning monarch) to be read in his name at the main mosque in the city during the Friday noon congregational prayers, to legalize his rule. He reached Agra on 4th May, having covered the 280 kilometres from Panipat in two weeks at the height of summer. For a week he camped in an open field on the outskirts of the city. On Thursday, 10th May, he ceremonially entered Agra, and rode into the citadel of Ibrahim Lodi to take up residence there as the Emperor of Hindustan.

Babur was now forty-three years old. Three decades earlier, as a boy-king on the rickety throne of an obscure, war-torn principality, he had dared to dream grand dreams, and now at last, after endless struggles and many misfortunes, he had won a domain to match his vision. Fergana, his ancestral kingdom lost to the Uzbegs, was now a distant memory; Samarkand, the legendary Timurid capital which he had once ardently coveted, a forsaken passion; and Kabul, his capital for twenty-five years, just a provincial outpost. India was now home for Babur.

Babur's decision to settle in India was an unpleasant surprise to his men. They had expected him to return home to Kabul, laden with booty, as he had done on previous occasions. When Babur first launched his Indian campaigns, the annexation of Punjab as a province of his Kabul kingdom was the limit of his ambition. That still had seemed to be his goal as he set out on his last Indian invasion, for he had just before that entered into an agreement with Alam Khan, the Lodi pretender, by which, in return for help in ousting Ibrahim Lodi, Babur was to get Lahore and all the Lodi lands west of it. Babur's officers had therefore assumed that the expedition into the Indo-Gangetic Plain was just another pillaging sweep. India was opulent, but inhospitable. A good hunting ground, but no place to live in.

Such were the views of the Mughal amirs, and they resented Babur's decision to remain in India. His very generosity compounded his problems. "The treasures of five kings fell into his hands," writes Gulbadan Begum, his daughter; "he gave everything away." All his men—nobles and soldiers, even traders and scribes—received generous bounties from Babur, and so did his relations and friends back home, as well as holy men in Samarkand and Khurasan. "Every soul in the country of Kabul and the valley-side of Varsak, man and woman, bond and free, of age and non-age," was given a silver coin, records Babur. He kept nothing for himself.

His men were sated. Now all they wanted was to get back to the cool mountains of Afghanistan and enjoy their good fortune. As Khwaja Kalan, one of Babur's intimates, would write while leaving India for Kabul,

> If safe and sound I cross the Sind,
> Blacken my face ere I wish for Hind.

Babur knew how his men felt. He himself found India a dreary land. "Hindustan is a country of few charms," he frets. "Its people have no good looks; of social intercourse, paying and receiving visits, there is none; of genius and capacity none; of manners none; in handicraft and work there is no form or symmetry, method or quality; there are no good horses, no good dogs, no grapes, musk-melons or first-rate fruits, no ice or cold water, no good bread or cooked food in bazaars, no hot-baths, no colleges, no candles, torches or candlesticks."

More than anything else, the climate of India oppressed the Mughals. The summer of 1526 was savage in Agra, one of the worst in living memory. "Violent, pestilential winds struck people down in heaps together," writes Babur. And this was not all. Powerful adversaries—Afghans in the east, Rajputs in the south—were marshalling their forces and advancing against Babur. The Mughals, it was clear, would have to fight and win many more battles before they could claim Hindustan as their own.

There was no support for the Mughals anywhere in India. The people of the land were sullenly hostile, harassing the Mughals at every turn. "On our first coming to Agra, there was remarkable dislike and hostility between its people and mine," writes Babur. "All the inhabitants had run away in terror. Neither grain for ourselves nor corn for our horses was to be had. The villagers, out of hostility and hatred to us, had taken to thieving and highway robbery; roads became impassable." Towns and villages fortified themselves and would not submit without a fight. India, it seemed, would have to be conquered inch by inch.

WAS THE CONQUEST of India worth such a formidable effort? Babur thought so. India, he says, was "a large country . . . [that had] masses of gold and silver," and "workmen of every profession and trade . . . [were] innumerable, and without end." These were major attractions. There was, in addition—and perhaps, for Babur, ever so much more seductive than any material reward—the prospect of glory that would be his, his place in history as the founder of a great empire. As one of Babur's favourite sayings had it,

Give me but fame, and if I die I am contented.
If fame be mine, let Death claim my body.

In deciding to remain in India, Babur was looking at a time beyond his own time. The ambitions of his men, however, were yoked to their immediate appetites, and they clamoured to be sent back to Kabul. But Babur remained adamant. "By the labours of several years, by encountering hardship, by long travel, by flinging myself and the army into battle, and by deadly slaughter, we, through God's grace, beat these masses of enemies in order that we might take their broad lands," he reminded his men. "Now what force compels us, what necessity has arisen that we should, without cause, abandon countries taken at such a risk of life? Was it for us to remain in Kabul, the sport of harsh poverty? Henceforth, let no well-wisher of mine speak of such things!"

This exhortation chastened most, but not all. Some, including a couple of his most trusted old comrades in arms, such as Khwaja Kalan, pleaded with Babur to let them return to Kabul. Reluctantly, he let them go. But he missed them.

He missed Kabul too. "Boundless and infinite is my desire to go to those parts," he wrote in a letter to Khwaja Kalan in Kabul. Broiling in the summer heat of India, he longed for the mountains. Once, when a Kabul melon was brought to him and its aroma filled the air, he was awash with nostalgia—"I felt myself affected with a strong feeling of loneliness, and a sense of my exile from my native country, and I could not help shedding tears while eating it." He dreamed of returning to Kabul some day.

But not yet. He had a mission to accomplish in India.

Panipat had given Babur his place in history, but it was only a provisional place. If he abandoned India after Panipat, or if his successors failed to preserve his conquest (as nearly happened), Babur would be relegated to the nether regions of history crowded with petty potentates. Babur could not afford to rest on his laurels. He had, as he enigmatically noted in his memoirs, "seen his task whole".

There was, however, a lull in action after Panipat, as Babur's adversaries, the Rajputs and the Afghans, waited to see what his moves would be. Meanwhile, Babur's decision to make India his home brought him several Indian allies, including a few Afghan nobles, who sought to hitch their fortunes to the rising Mughal star. Also, the hostile public mood in India, which had troubled Babur initially, now began to dissipate, because, as Ahmad Yadgar puts it, "during the first two months of His Majesty's reign, he behaved to every one with such kindness and generosity that dread and terror were banished from the hearts of all men." Babur's position further improved around this time with the arrival of a number of Mughals from Central Asia to join him on his invitation. "The Most High has given us sovereignty in Hindustan," he had written to them; "let them come that we may see prosperity together."

Babur needed all the strength he could marshal, for his position in India was still perilous. By Central Asian reckoning, the domain that Babur acquired by his victory over Ibrahim Lodi was immense, but it was nevertheless only a strip of land staked out along the Lahore-Delhi-Agra belt. The Mughals were by no means the dominant power in India. The Afghans, defeated but not crushed, remained in power in Bihar and Bengal. Immediately to the south of the Mughal lands lay a powerful Rajput confederacy under Rana Sanga of Mewar, who dreamed of raising a Hindu empire from the ashes of the Delhi Sultanate. Further south was the prosperous Afghan kingdom of Gujarat, a rallying ground for ambitious Afghans. Still further south, beyond the Vindhya Mountains, were other powerful kingdoms, the Deccan sultanates and the Vijayanagar empire.

Babur's immediate concern was with the Afghan chieftains who had regrouped in eastern India and had menacingly advanced to Kanauj, some 200 kilometres east of Agra. But the Afghan challenge turned out to be a weak bluff. As the Mughals advanced, they scattered.

The Rajputs were quite another matter. Babur however remained curiously complacent about them, underestimating their power. "Rana Sanga," he notes in his memoirs, "is thought not to be the equal of the [Afghan] rebels." This was a serious miscalculation. Fortunately for Babur, the Rajputs were still a long way off. And the monsoon, during which no major military operation was possible in India, had broken over the land. Babur would have a few months rest.

He used this interlude of peace to lay out gardens and palaces in Agra, to make the city congenial to his lifestyle. Soon after arriving in Agra he had scouted around on the left bank of the Yamuna, in the crook of the river opposite the fort, for a place to build a garden complex, but had, he says, found "those grounds . . . so bad and unattractive that we traversed them with a hundred disgusts and repulsions." Still, he ingeniously transformed that cheerless landscape into a pleasant retreat, constructing tanks, water courses, bath-houses and other buildings, and laying out gardens with "order and symmetry, with suitable borders and flower-beds in every corner, and in every border rose and narcissus in perfect arrangement," as he puts it. The Mughal amirs followed Babur across the river, and soon the garden complex grew into a flourishing and lovely suburb. The local people, says Babur, "had never seen grounds planned so symmetrically and thus laid out," and they in their prosaic simplicity called the settlement Kabul.

THEN THE RAINS ceased, and it was time again for Babur to return to the battlefield. Rana Sanga of Mewar, heading a formidable Rajput confederacy, and joined by several Afghan chieftains, including Mahmud Lodi, the brother of Ibrahim Lodi, was rapidly advancing on Agra. Babur and the Rana had been in friendly contact with each other before the battle of Panipat, but now they had bitter grievances against each other—Babur accused the Rana of not keeping his word to make a diversionary attack on Ibrahim Lodi on the eve of Panipat, and the Rana resented Babur occupying lands to which he had a claim. These recriminations were, however, mere pretexts. The real issue was who should have sway over Hindustan.

Rana Sanga was a dangerous adversary. According to James Tod, an early-nineteenth-century chronicler of Rajput history, the Rana was so intrepid and ferocious a warrior that at the close of his life "he exhibited . . . but the fragments of a warrior. One eye was lost in a broil with his brother, an arm in an action with the Lodi king of Delhi, while he was cripple owing to a limb having been broken by a cannon ball. From the sword or lance he counted eighty wounds on various parts of his body."

As the Rana approached, Babur, who had been earlier sanguine about the Rajputs, recognized the gravity of the threat. "Rana Sanga the pagan . . . Satan-like he threw back his head and collected an army of accursed heretics," writes Babur. "Ten powerful chiefs, each the leader of a pagan host, uprose in rebellion, as smoke rises, and linked themselves, as though enchained, to that perverse one." Babur calculated the potential strength of the Rajputs as 200,000, an army much larger than that which Ibrahim Lodi had deployed at Panipat.

This alarmed the Mughals. The problem, however, was not just of numbers. There was also the Rajput valour to be reckoned with. As the advancing Rajputs decimated every probing contingent that Babur sent against them, "the fierceness and valour of the pagan army" made the Mughal troops "anxious and afraid," admits Babur. Some of Babur's Indian allies, especially the Afghans who had joined him after Panipat, now began to desert him. Even his own men were sullen, reluctant to fight a dangerous and uncertain battle, risking all their gains in India, their rich booty, merely to defend a land they hated and did not want to hold. They again pleaded with Babur to return to Kabul. "No manly word or brave counsel was heard from any one soever," laments Babur.

There were problems elsewhere too. "Trouble and disturbance rose on every side . . . Every day some unpleasant news reached us from one place or another," writes Babur. His stars, it seemed, were once again turning malevolent. To make matters worse, Muhammad Sharif, a reputed astrologer who had just then arrived from Kabul, predicted that, because of the adverse aspect of Mars, Babur would be defeated by Rana Sanga. This prophecy shattered the fragile morale of the Mughal army, though Babur himself, no stranger to adversity, was not perturbed: "We gave no ear to his wild words, made no change in our operations, but got ready in earnest for the fight."

On 11th February 1527, having marshalled his forces by calling in his outlying garrisons, Babur marched out of Agra to confront the Rajputs. He advanced with great caution, taking care at every halt to protect his camp with ditches, wooden tripods on wheels (which served as portable breastworks, a new innovation) and carts joined together with chains and ropes of rawhide. These precautions helped to ease the anxiety of his men. But this was not enough. Battles are not won by troops cowering behind defences. To win, Babur would have to ignite the blood of his warriors.

Mulling over the problem one day while out riding, Babur came up with a perfect solution. For over fourteen years he had been a heavy drinker, a grave though common infraction among the Mughals. Now, in his hour of crisis, he decided to "return to obedience"—to win divine favour, and, more importantly, to gain the moral authority to declare the war against Rana Sanga (his first war against a Hindu monarch) as a jihad, holy war, and thus to unleash the martial fury of his men.

25

What followed was high drama, as Babur turned the private renunciatory vow into a stirring sacramental rite. As his men stood in formation, glum and uncertain about what to expect, he faced them, and raising his arms to invoke the blessings of Allah, ceremonially took his pledge to renounce wine. Then, with splendid theatricality, he called for his abundant stock of wine to be brought, poured all the radiant ruby-red liquor on the ground in front of his aghast troops, smashed his flagons, his gold and silver goblets, and gave away the fragments to dervishes and the poor. A well was ordered to be dug where the wine was poured, and an alms-house built beside it. For good measure, Babur also swore not to trim his beard thereafter.

He then turned to address his men. "Noblemen and soldiers! Whoever sits down to the feast of life must, before it is over, drink of the cup of death . . . How much better, then, it is to die with honour, than to live with infamy," he declaimed. "The most High God has been propitious to us. He has now placed us in such a crisis that if we fall in the field, we die the death of martyrs; if we survive, we rise victorious, the avengers of his sacred cause. Let us, therefore, with one accord swear on God's Holy Word that none of us will for a moment think of turning his face from this warfare; or shrink from the battle and slaughter that ensue, till his soul is separated from his body."

The impact of these words on his men was electric. "All those present, officer and retainer, great and small, took the Holy Book joyfully into their hands and made vow and compact to this purport," Babur notes with gratification. "The plan was perfect. It worked admirably." The mood of the Mughal army then swung dramatically from dread to daredevilry. "From the effect of these soul-inflaming words, a fire fell into each heart," says Mughal chronicler Nizamuddin Ahmad.

AT DAWN ON 16th March, Babur reached Khanua, a small village about forty kilometres west of Agra. There, as his army was pitching its camp at a carefully chosen and prepared site near a low hill, he was informed by scouts that the Rajputs were approaching.

It was, as at Panipat, a Saturday, and it would be as lucky for Babur. The battle of Khanua was a virtual replay of the battle of Panipat, except that it lasted nearly double the time and was far more fiercely contested, resulting in heavy casualties on both sides. The battle commenced at about nine in the morning and raged on till late evening. The decisive factor at Khanua, as at Panipat, was the firepower of the Mughals, aimed at the enemy compacted into "one mass" by

Babur turning the Rajput flanks. Mustafa, the Ottoman Turk in charge of the Mughal artillery, "had the carts brought forward and broke the ranks of pagans with matchlock and cannon," reports Babur. And the Mughal soldiers, inflamed by Babur's oration, "fought with such delight and pleasure that it was more like a time of mirth than one of war," notes Nizamuddin Ahmad.

In the end the Rajputs fled, leaving so many dead in the battlefield that, according to Babur, the Mughal contingents chasing them "found no foot-space without the prostrate foe." Rana Sanga himself fled, with Babur in hot pursuit. But after a chase of about three kilometres beyond the enemy camp, Babur peeled away, leaving it to others to follow on, which enabled the Rana to escape. "There was a little slackness; I ought to have gone myself," writes Babur. Apparently he did not want to force his luck. Nor did he, as he would normally have done, follow up the victory with an invasion of Mewar, because of "little water and much heat on the road."

Returning to the battlefield, Babur ordered a pillar of severed enemy heads to be erected on the hill beside which the battle was fought. This was a Mughal military rite performed after almost every battle, to strike terror in potential adversaries and thus to cripple their spirit and defeat them even before the battle was fought on the ground.

By nightfall Babur returned to his camp, and there assumed the title of Ghazi, Holy Warrior. He then turned to Muhammad Sharif, the astrologer who had predicted a Mughal rout, but was now waiting to congratulate Babur on his victory. Babur tore into him: "I poured forth upon him a torrent of abuse." But eventually his generosity prevailed. "When I had relieved my heart by it, although he was a self-conceited fellow . . . and an intolerable evil-speaker, yet, as he was my old servant, I gave him a lakh in a present, and dismissed him, commanding him to depart from my dominions."

Black Fell the Day

THE BATTLE OF Khanua marked the end of the travails of Babur. There were still battles to fight—there would always be battles to fight—but Babur was now indisputably the Emperor of Hindustan. He was content. The pace of his life now eased, and he gradually reverted to the relaxed lifestyle of his balmy days in Kabul.

Everything interested Babur and most things delighted him. His curiosity was boundless, and there was in him, even after all he had had to endure in life, a charming, childlike faculty to find joy in the most humdrum things of everyday life. It thrilled him, for instance, to burn the leafy branches of holm-oak which crackled as they burned; "It is good fun to burn it!" he writes. For him, the shining moon, the flowering bush, the rushing stream, were all celebratory miracles. "Tonight I elected to take opium," he writes, "because of . . . the shining of the moon." Again: "On Thursday at sunrise . . . confection was eaten. While under its influence wonderful fields of flowers were enjoyed . . . There were flowers on all sides of the mound, yellow here, red there, as if arranged regularly to form a sextuple." It was with the same joyous wonder that he had first seen India, in 1505: "In Ningnahar another world came to view—other grasses, other trees, other animals, other birds, and other manners and customs of clan and horde. We were amazed, and truly there was ground for amazement."

In India, after Khanua, there was only one thing that sullied Babur's happiness—his vow to abstain from wine. "In truth the longing and craving for wine-party has been infinite and endless for two years past, so much so that sometimes the craving for wine brought me to the verge of tears," he wrote to Khwaja Kalan in Kabul, and lamented:

> While others repent and make vow to abstain,
> I have vowed to abstain, and repentant am I.

He would break his vow and revert to wine towards the end of his life, but in the meantime he consoled himself with the pleasures of good companionship. "In the company of friends, death is a feast," he used to say, quoting a Persian proverb. He enjoyed people and delighted in convivial parties. "There was much joking and laughter," he says, recalling with pleasure a party at the house of an amir. He revelled in clever repartee, but despised "vapid and empty" small-talk.

ONE OF THE enduring passions of Babur, in good times and bad, was his love of literature. He now had the leisure to luxuriate in it. His library was one of his most valued possessions, which he always carried around with him, and books were one of the treasures he hunted for in a conquered land. In his memoirs, when he listed the sovereigns and high nobles of a land, he also listed poets, musicians and intellectuals. They too mattered to him.

He was a fastidious connoisseur of literature, and he considered it a terrible depravity to write bad poetry. "His verse is flat and insipid," says he about his paternal uncle Sultan Mahmud Mirza of Badakshan, and adds: "Not to compose is better than to compose verse such as his." It greatly distressed him that his son Humayun was a negligent writer. "Though taking trouble . . . [your letter] can be read, it is very puzzling, and whoever saw an enigma in prose?" he once upbraided Humayun, and advised: "Thy remissness in writing seems to be due to the thing which makes thee obscure, that is to say, to elaboration. In future write unaffectedly, clearly, with plain words, which saves trouble to both writer and reader."

Babur himself was an acclaimed writer. He wrote in Turki as well as in Persian, but with greater felicity in Turki, in which he was a poet "second only to Amir Ali Shir", according to Mirza Haidar. Babur had several books to his credit, prose and poetry, even a treatise on jurisprudence and another on Turki prosody. But his best known work is his autobiography, a classic in its genre.

Babur wrote a good deal after Khanua. He found it a fair consolation for the loss of the pleasures of wine. Further, he had a curious notion that literature had healing powers—writing irreverent poetry, he believed, caused illness, while writing ennobling poetry cured it! He was, he says, once a careless versifier, stringing into verse whatever came to his head, "good or bad, grave or jest . . . however empty and harsh the verse might be," but became more discriminating while writing *Mubayyin*, his poetic magnum opus. At that time, says Babur, "this thought pierced through my dull wits and made way into my troubled heart, 'A pity it will be if the tongue which has the treasure of utterances so lofty as these, is wasted again on low words . . .' Since that time I have refrained from satirical and jesting verse."

Not quite. Babur did still occasionally relapse into frivolous

29

limericks—and suffered for it! A few days after one such trivial composition, notes Babur, "I had fever and discharge, followed by cough, and I began to spit blood each time I coughed. I knew whence my reproof came; I knew what act of mine had brought this affliction on me."

Unfortunately, very little of Babur's poetry has survived, so his literary reputation today rests solely on his autobiography, and even from this large portions are missing. Babur used to carry his journal with him all the time, even on military campaigns, working on it whenever he had a little time. This habit of his once led to a near disaster. He was at that time encamped at a riverside, sitting up late in the night, writing. Suddenly, a great storm burst over the camp. "Such a storm burst, in the inside of a moment, from the up-piled clouds of the rainy season, and such a stiff gale rose, that few tents were left standing," Babur records. "I was in the audience tent, about to write; before I could collect papers and sections, the tent came down, with its porch, right on my head . . . Sections and book were drenched under water and were gathered together with much difficulty. We laid them in folds of the woollen throne-carpet, put this on the throne and on it piled blankets . . . We, without sleep, were busy till shoot of day drying folios and sections." It was probably in some such mishap that the missing sections of his memoirs were lost.

The great charm of Babur's memoirs is its directness and simplicity, its total lack of affectation. Babur was a candid chronicler. "In this history I have held firmly to it that the truth should be reached in every matter, and that every act should be recorded precisely as it occurred," he writes. "From this it follows of necessity that I have set down of good and bad whatever is known, concerning father and elder brother, kinsman and stranger; of them all I have set down carefully the known virtues and defects."

This was his precept. His practice did not always quite match the high ideal. Babur was writing about himself, with his eyes on posterity, and he would not have been human if he did not intensify the drama of his life. Babur's descriptions of events do sometimes vary in detail from other contemporary sources, and it cannot be assumed that his version was always right. The discrepancies are, however, minor, and could be due to differences in perception or quirks of memory.

Apart from the books he wrote, Babur had to his credit several other cultural accomplishments, such as musical compositions, and the creation of a new and distinctive style of calligraphy, called Baburi. But his greatest passion outside literature was gardening. He would even pause in the midst of critical military campaigns to lay out gardens, as he did on the river-bank near Sirhind in Punjab on the way to Panipat. In Agra, one of his first projects was to build a garden complex. Later, he laid out another garden at the lake in Daulpur, where he had a six by six metre tank hewed out of a single mass of rock, saying, "When it is finished, I will fill it with wine." At Sikri, on his way back from Khanua, he ordered an octagonal platform to be built in the middle of the lake there, for him to repose and enjoy opium; he also loved boating in the lake, says Gulbadan.

Babur was a keen horticulturist. "I had plantains brought and planted there (in Kabul); they did very well," he writes. "The year before I had sugar-cane planted there; it also did well." In India, he was ecstatic when the grapes and melons which he had introduced into the Garden of Eight Paradises in Agra began to bear fruit. "To have grapes and melons grown in this way in Hindustan filled my measure of content," he writes.

THIS CAPACITY OF Babur to find joy in so many different things was what sustained him during his years of adversity, for some facet or other of the many facets of his personality always caught the light of the sun, whichever way the wheel of fate turned. Babur was a blessed dilettante, not a driven, obsessed genius. Whatever he did was a vigorous and cheerful expression of his own vigorous and cheerful self, open and spontaneous. Babur delighted in being Babur.

All things fresh and new gladdened him, and he travelled around his Indian empire with the feisty enthusiasm of a tourist. "They are wonderful buildings," he writes about the Gwalior fort complex, though he found the rooms dark and airless, and the palace itself "heavy and unsymmetrical". In the valley beneath the fort, he visited the Jain shrines alongside the lake, where, he notes, "the idols are shewn quite naked without covering the privities . . . Not a bad place . . . the idols are its defect. I, for my part, ordered them destroyed." He also visited the nearby Hindu temples, but says nothing about destroying the idols there—it seems that it was his aesthetic sensibilities that were offended by the Jain idols, not his religious sentiments.

The tours of Babur had a political purpose too: he was familiarizing himself with his empire, its land, its people. Whatever else his interests and activities, Babur always had one eye cocked vigilantly on state security. On that he would never relax. "No bondage equals that of sovereignty," he would write sternly to Humayun when that easygoing prince wanted to "retire" from government. "Retirement matches not with rule."

Curiously, despite all the attention he gave to matters of the state, and despite his scholarship in jurisprudence, Babur did not set up even a rudimentary administrative system in India. This failure cannot be explained away by the fact that he ruled India only for less than five years or that during that time he was continually engaged in wars, for under virtually the same circumstances, Sher Shah (the Afghan chief who later expelled Babur's successor from India) set up a complex, efficient and enduring administrative system.

But then, Sher Shah was of the land; he knew its ways, and had only to overhaul and energize the prevailing system. Babur was an alien in India, and he did not have the time to familiarize himself with local traditions. Besides, his administrative attitudes were conditioned by his experience in turbulent Afghanistan, which could be ruled only by *saifi* (sword), not *qalami* (pen), as Babur puts it.

All that Babur did in India by way of administrative action was to parcel out his domain among his amirs, for them to govern their fiefs as they pleased. He did not even have a regular system of revenue collection. Once, in October 1528, when he needed funds—he was short of funds in India, as he had given away virtually all the plunder he had gathered—he even had to requisition contributions from his amirs, ordering "that each stipendiary should drop into the royal treasury thirty in every hundred of his allowance, to be used for war *matériel* and appliances, for equipment, for powder, and for the pay of gunners and matchlockmen."

This was an unusual procedure, presumably adopted to meet some emergency. The primary source of revenue for Babur in India was pillage. As he candidly states in his memoirs, raids were often made specifically to seize plunder—for instance, he notes that he once decided, choosing from different alternatives, to march westward from Agra because that was where there was "treasure helpful for the army". The Mughals lived by war. Not to wage war was not to live, or at least not to have the means of livelihood.

It certainly was a failure of Babur that he did not make the transition from the ways of nomadic monarchy to those of a settled empire. As Sher Shah observed, the Mughals "have no order or discipline, and . . . their kings . . . do not personally superintend the government, but leave all the affairs of the State to their nobles and ministers . . . These grandees act on corrupt motive in every case."

BACK IN AGRA after the battle of Khanua, Babur rewarded his men suitably, distributed fiefs among his nobles, and, as he had promised he would, granted leave to those who wanted to return to Kabul. Humayun was dispatched to govern Badakshan, which had fallen to Babur in 1520. Then, as the monsoon was imminent, he sent the remaining officers to their fiefs, to get some well-earned rest and to re-equip their contingents. Babur himself remained in Agra, in the Garden of Eight Paradises, till Ramadan, and then moved to Sikri, because, he says, he did not want to break his custom of not holding the Ramadan feast in the same place for two successive years.

When the monsoon ended Babur set out on his campaigns again, this time against Medini Rai of Chanderi in north-eastern Malwa. Here for the first time he came across the macabre Rajput rite of jauhar, in which, faced with certain defeat, women and children immolated themselves or were slaughtered by their men, who then slew each other or rushed out naked to fight and die—to preserve their honour. The Rajputs kept their honour; Babur took the fort.

Meanwhile the Afghans were on the move again east of Agra, and though they initially scattered without fighting when Babur turned on them menacingly, they regrouped again soon after, this time under the command of Sultan Mahmud Lodi, the brother of Ibrahim Lodi, who had set himself up as the king of Bihar. Babur then launched a second eastern campaign, and in a battle fought at the confluence of the Ganga and the Ghaghara, near Patna. on 6th May 1529, he decisively routed the Afghans.

The battle of Patna was Babur's last major military campaign. By then, his attention had once again turned to developments beyond the Hindu Kush; in fact, even while he was marching against the Afghans, his eyes were on Central Asia, as he had received reports of Uzbeg-Persian clashes in Khurasan. An old gleam now returned to Babur's eyes—maybe the Timurid lands could yet be recovered, he thought, and ordered Humayun in Badakshan to join the fray. "Thank God! now is your time to risk life and slash swords," he wrote. "Neglect not the work chance has brought . . . He grips the world who hastens." Babur then made plans for himself to return to Kabul, to be close to the scene of action. "Matters are coming to some settlement in Hindustan; there is hope . . . that the work here will soon be arranged," he wrote to Khwaja Kalan. "This work brought to order, God willing, my start will be made at once."

Nothing came of those plans. In Central Asia, the Uzbegs recovered their initiative, the Persians retreated, and Humayun aborted his campaign. Babur was not destined to see Kabul again. However, towards the close of 1529, he did proceed as far as Lahore, and spent a couple of months there. Surprisingly, he did not make the short hop from there to Kabul, which he so passionately yearned to visit again. Instead, he returned to Agra. His memoirs do not tell why—they end abruptly in mid-sentence on 7th September 1529. Even the entries for the previous several months are sketchy. Something was amiss.

BABUR HAD NOT been in good health for quite some time. Despite his phenomenal physical vitality, he had always been prone to illness, and at least once, in 1498, when he was fifteen, was so critically ill that his life was despaired of. His memoirs are dotted with accounts of his numerous ailments. "It was a strange sort of illness," writes Babur about a bout of fever, "for whenever with much trouble I had been awakened, my eyes closed again in sleep. In four or five days I got quite well." On his final Indian expedition, as soon he crossed the mountains he fell ill. "That evening I had fever and discharge which led on to cough, and every time I coughed, I spat blood," he notes. In India, because of the oppressive climate and the rigours of incessant wars, he was ill quite often, especially in the last couple of years of his life—he suffered from recurrent fever, boils, diarrhoea, sciatica, discharges of the ears and spitting of blood.

Amazingly, despite his ill health, even late in his life Babur could perform physical feats from which a much younger man would have flinched. At forty-six we find him exuberantly swimming across the Ganga. "I swam the Ganga river, counting every stroke," he writes. "I crossed with thirty-three, then, without resting, swam back. I had swum the other rivers, Ganga had remained to do." Still, age had begun to tell on him. He suffered from ennui as much as from ill health. For all his vigorous enjoyment of life, Babur had a renunciatory streak in him, a predilection for mysticism. "I am a king but yet the slave of dervishes," he used to say. He had led a full life, had seen everything, done everything, and now he was tired. Sometimes he went into a deep depression and talked of becoming a hermit. "My heart is bowed down by ruling and reigning," he said. "I will make over the kingdom to Humayun."

His iron will began to falter. He returned to wine. And, though he had not till then shown any great fondness for the company of women, he now became attached to two Caucasian slave girls, Gul-nar and Nar-gul, whom he had received as a gift from Shah Tahmasp of Persia a couple of years earlier. The death of an infant son, Alwar, at this time upset him greatly. He missed his children, and kept asking to see Hindal, his youngest son, who was away in Kabul. There were signs of senility. His mind often wandered. He took little interest in government.

"He passed his time in . . . company with Mughal companions and friends, in pleasure and enjoyment and carousing, in the presence of enchanting dancing girls with rosy cheeks, who sang tunes and displayed their accomplishments," Yadgar reports. "Mir Khalifa . . . possessing the chief authority, managed the government, and his decrees were like those of the Sultan himself."

In that perplexing situation, Humayun abruptly returned to India from Badakshan without royal permission, a serious breach of propriety. It is likely that he had come to know of his father's condition. It could also be that he had heard the rumour that Mir Khalifa was plotting a succession coup—though none of Humayun's contemporaries mentions such a conspiracy, the writers of the next generation do; but if indeed there was such a plot, it fizzled out on the arrival of Humayun in Agra.

Babur upbraided Humayun for leaving Badakshan without permission, but soon forgave him. Humayun, though somewhat eccentric, and not as ambitious or energetic as Babur would have liked him to be, was nevertheless a lovable and highly cultivated prince, whose company Babur enjoyed hugely. Says Abul Fazl, "The Emperor many times declared that Humayun was an incomparable companion."

After spending a few days with his father in Agra, Humayun left for Sambhal, his fief near Delhi, and Babur himself with his wives moved to his gardens at Daulpur. There he presently received an urgent message from Humayun's camp: "Humayun Mirza is ill and in an extraordinary state. Her highness the Begum should come at once to Delhi, for the Mirza is much prostrated." Babur, says Gulbadan, was desolated by the news. When Humayun's mother, Maham Begum, consoled him, saying, "Do not be troubled about my son. You are a king: what griefs have you? You have other sons. I sorrow because I have only this one," Babur said, "Maham, although I have other sons, I love none as I love your Humayun. I crave that this cherished child may have his heart's desire and live long, and I desire the kingdom for him and not for others, because he has not his equal in distinction." Babur immediately returned to Agra and ordered Humayun to be brought by boat from Delhi to Agra for treatment, but by the time the prince reached Agra, he was delirious and critically ill.

Only god could save Humayun, it seemed. And god, an amir suggested, could be induced to save the prince if one of Humayun's valued possessions was offered as a propitiatory oblation. Babur seized the thought, but rejected the suggestion to offer a great diamond belonging to Humayun. Instead, he decided to offer his own life, characteristically placing sentiment above treasure and contending that it was the father's life that a son valued most. As Mughal chroniclers

35

tell the story, Babur then circumambulated the sick-bed and prayed fervently that his own life be taken in exchange for his son's life. Writes Abul Fazl: "When the prayer had been heard by God . . . he (Babur) felt a strange effect on himself and cried out, 'We have borne it away! We have borne it away!' Immediately a strange heat of fever surged upon his Majesty and there was a sudden diminution of it in the person of his Highness."

"That very day he (Babur) fell ill, and Humayun poured water on his head, and came out and gave audience," says Gulbadan, telescoping time in remembered pain. "Because of his illness, they carried my royal father within, and he kept to his bed for two or three months." Says Abul Fazl: "In a short time he (Humayun) entirely recovered, while Babur gradually grew worse and marks of dissolution and death became apparent."

As Babur's condition worsened, Humayun, who had returned to his fief, was called back to Agra. He was shocked at the sight of his father. "I left him well, what has happened to him all at once?" he asked the amirs. "They said this and that in reply," writes Gulbadan. Babur was suffering from an acute disorder of the bowels, and was in great pain. "Day by day he lost strength and became more and more emaciated," recalls Gulbadan. "Every day the disorder increased and his blessed countenance changed." Probably delirious, he kept asking for Hindal, and wanted to know how tall he had grown, even though he had seen the boy just a few months earlier. "Alas! a thousand times alas! that I do not see Hindal!" he lamented over and over. Babur was losing his mind.

But he still had lucid intervals when he could make clear decisions. The day after Humayun arrived, Babur, lying on a couch at the foot of the throne, called his amirs to him to give them his dying instructions. Then, taking Humayun's hand in his, he asked the prince to sit on the throne, and asked his nobles to acknowledge him as king. "For years it has been in my heart to make over the throne to Humayun and to retire to the Zer Afshan (Gold Scattering) Garden," said Babur. "By divine grace I have obtained in health of body everything but the fulfilment of this wish . . . Now when illness has laid me low, I charge you all to acknowledge Humayun in my stead." Babur then turned to Humayun. "Do nothing against your brothers even though they may deserve it," he counselled. "At these words," notes Gulbadan, "hearers and onlookers wept and lamented. His own blessed eyes also filled with tears."

On Monday, 26th December 1530, Babur passed away. "Black fell the day for children and kinsfolk and all," grieves Gulbadan.

Babur was laid to rest in the Garden of Eight Paradises in Agra, now renamed Aram Bagh, Garden of Rest, opposite which the Taj would rise four generations later. Some years afterwards, probably around 1543, during the reign of Sher Shah, the mortal remains of Babur were transferred to Kabul and buried, as Babur had desired, in his favourite garden on the Shah-i-Kabul hill overlooking a stream and a vast meadow, with the snows of the Paghman in the far horizon, in a simple grave open to the sky. The man of the mountains was back home.

Chapter Two

THE STRUGGLE FOR SURVIVAL

The Dreamer Cometh

FOUR DAYS AFTER Babur's death, on 30th December 1530, a day chosen by astrologers, Humayun, twenty-three, ascended the throne in Agra. For Humayun, whose name meant fortunate, life as a prince had been a lark. As king, he would never again know any real repose.

"Dreamers, they moved through a dream," Babur had once said of his hedonistic cousins in Herat. He could have said the same about Humayun, who was more awake in his dreams than when awake. Though personable, cultured and amiable, Humayun was, says Ferishta, "for the most part . . . disposed to spend his time in social intercourse and pleasure." He lacked the grit to match the turbulence of the world he lived in. Predictably, his reign, which began as a dream, darkened into an awful nightmare.

"I have seen few persons possessed of so much natural talent and excellence as he . . .," writes Mirza Haidar. "In battle he was steady and brave; in conversation, ingenious and lively; and at the social board, full of wit. He was kind-hearted and generous. He was a dignified and magnificent prince, and observed much state. But in consequence of his having dissolute and sensual men in his service, and of his intercourse with them . . . he contracted some bad habits, as for instance the excessive use of opium. All the evil that has been set down to the Emperor, and has become the common talk of the people, is attributable to this vice."

Humayun was a skilled mathematician, and was "unequalled in the sciences of astronomy and astrology and all abstruse sciences," says Akbar's courtier Badauni. But these talents had little to do with the stern business of government. Even in his esoteric pursuits, Humayun had no particular achievement to his credit—he was compulsively inventive, but in a bemused, eccentric way, and he lacked the tenacity of purpose to forge his airy whimsies into solid achievements. He loved playing at being an intellectual and an aesthete, just as he loved playing at being a king.

Even virtues turned into vices in Humayun. "The mildness and benevolence of Humayun's character were excessive," says Ferishta. "His conversation," writes Mushtaqui, "was so nice that he never addressed any person as *tu*, but as *shuma*." The harshest pejorative he is ever said to have used was, "You stupid!" Says Badauni: "He never opened his lips in a smile, nor did he ever cast an angry glance at anyone."

Humayun was a misfit in his time and place, an ease-loving prince among a warlike people, in charge of a nascent kingdom in a perilous setting. Though Babur had in three major encounters routed those who opposed his entry into Hindustan, the adversaries were still around, lurking in the shadows. Their challenges had to be met. Humayun could not even be certain of the loyalty of his own men, a motley crowd drawn from different Central Asian martial races. The prospect of plunder was their only unifying motive, and heroic leadership the only means of harnessing their energy. Humayun also had to contend with the ambitions of his own kin, brothers and cousins, all sons or grandsons of kings, all eager to be kings themselves. These hazards could be overcome only with a well-sharpened sword, for as Kamran, Humayun's younger brother, put it,

> Who'd to his bosom clasp dominion's bride
> Must kiss the glèaming sabre's lip.

Humayun, though personally courageous, had no particular enthusiasm for kissing the sabre's lip.

NASIRUDDIN MUHAMMAD Humayun was born in Kabul on 6th March 1508, "the sun being in Pisces", notes Babur. At twelve, he was sent off to Badakshan as governor. It is not known how he fared there—probably not too well, for Babur's very first comment on Humayun in his memoirs complains about his tardiness. Babur, then setting out from Kabul on his final Indian campaign, had ordered the prince to join him on the way, but Humayun was long in coming. "I wrote harsh letters to Humayun," says Babur, "lecturing him severely because of his long delay beyond the time fixed for him to join me."

Humayun did well in India, though. He was blooded in battle near Ambala in Punjab, where he routed an Afghan auxiliary force and returned with a clutch of severed enemy heads. Babur considered that auspicious. "At this same station and this same day the razor or scissors were first applied to Humayun's beard," records Babur. The boy had become a man. Later, at Panipat as well as at Khanua, Humayun commanded the right wing of the Mughal army.

After Khanua, Babur sent Humayun back to Badakshan as governor.

He was then nineteen years old, an age at which Mughal princes were normally battle-hardened veterans in the thick of the struggle for survival and domination. But there was in Humayun a disturbing lack of earnestness, an unbecoming capriciousness. This troubled Babur. And it infuriated him when Humayun raided, perhaps as a prank, the treasury of Delhi on his way to Badakshan from Agra. "I never looked for such a thing from him," writes Babur. "It grieved me very much. I wrote and sent off to him very severe reproaches." Humayun was not serious about governing Badakshan either, but kept pestering Babur to allow him to "retire" from there, so that Babur had to chide him again: "As for the retirement—'retirement' spoken of in thy letters—retirement is a fault for sovereignty . . . Retirement makes not rule."

Still, Humayun was Babur's chosen heir. There was no dispute about his succession. But troubles began immediately thereafter. The first to challenge Humayun was his brother Kamran. On Babur's death, his throne and the overlordship of the empire, along with the Mughal lands in Hindustan, went to Humayun; Kamran got Kabul and Kandahar; Askari and Hindal, the other two surviving sons of Babur, received subordinate fiefs; Badakshan was given to Sulaiman Mirza, a second cousin of Humayun. The division of the empire between Humayun and Kamran was more or less according to the 6:5 ratio that Babur had specified. But Kamran, an inordinately spirited youth, was not content with his share, and seeking to measure out his domain with a drawn sword in the Timurid tradition, he crossed the Indus and laid claim to the entire territory west of the Satluj.

This could have meant war. But Kamran had taken care to cloak his aggression behind a pretence of subservience by sending emissaries to Humayun to profess fealty and seek indulgence. Humayun on his part, out of his natural softness of heart as well as out of regard for the advice of his dying father to be indulgent towards his brothers, treated Kamran with forbearance and acceded to his demands. In fact, he gave Kamran more land than he asked for. Kamran in turn, matching sentiment with sentiment, wrote to Humayun:

> May every mist which rises on thy way,
> Be the dimming of the light of my own eyes.

The sons of Babur were a curious lot. They were violent adversaries in their fight for land and power, but otherwise entirely loving and brotherly. They showed genuine mutual affection even in the midst of their most savage clashes, and often wept over each other's fates—fates which they inflicted on each other!

43

AROUND THE TIME that Kamran invaded Punjab, Humayun also had to face a rebellion by his cousins (who held important fiefs near Agra) as well as resurgent Afghan belligerence in Bihar under Mahmud Lodi. Humayun dealt with these threats with an uncharacteristic show of spirit, first subduing the Afghans, then turning to chase off his cousins. His cousins would continue to be a nuisance for a while longer, but they would never again directly threaten his power, and as for Mahmud Lodi, he now finally gave up his struggle to regain the imperial sceptre.

The field of action then shifted to Gujarat. A small kingdom grown rich on the trade of its port emporiums, Gujarat was at this time ruled by Bahadur Shah, an ambitious and energetic monarch who stood forth as the standard-bearer of the Afghans after the defeat of Mahmud Lodi. To Gujarat flocked defiant Afghans from all over Hindustan, as well as a few Mughal rebels. Even Alam Khan, the tireless Lodi pretender, who had initially brought Babur into India, was there. The presence of these volatile elements in Gujarat ignited Bahadur Shah's own ambitions, and presently he began to move aggressively in several directions. He sent his armies south to threaten the Deccan sultanates, north towards Rajasthan and Punjab, and east towards Malwa and beyond, as if he meant to gobble up the Mughal lands in one gargantuan bite.

There was, however, a fatal flaw in Bahadur Shah's strategy. He mistook territory for power, and in ranging out in too many directions, spread his power thin, instead of concentrating it against the one man—Humayun—whom he had to defeat to realize his ambitions. For all his apparent aggressiveness there was a certain timidity in Bahadur Shah's bearing towards the Mughals—he was reluctant to confront Humayun directly, and in battle he seemed more anxious not to lose than to win!

Inevitably, he lost. Though initially Bahadur Shah and his allies did make some gains against the Mughals, and one army under Tartar Khan, Alam Khan's able son, even penetrated the environs of Agra, soon they were in full retreat everywhere, and Bahadur Shah himself fled without engaging when Humayun confronted him in Mewar. Darting from place to place, pursued by Humayun, Bahadur Shah finally escaped into the island of Diu, a safe refuge from the land-bound Mughals.

Humayun chased Bahadur Shah as far as Cambay, where he paused briefly to have a look at the sea (which no Timurid had ever seen before) and then doubled back to besiege Champanir, a strong fort in deep forest where the fabled royal treasures of Gujarat were reputed to be hidden. The siege dragged on for four months, but in the end Humayun—whose spirit had not yet been liquefied by opium and dissipation—stormed the fort in a daring night action, personally leading some 300 Mughal braves to scale the fort on spikes driven into rock and stonework in a remote and unguarded part of the citadel built over a precipitous hillside. It was Humayun's finest hour.

Treasures beyond imagination fell to the Mughals at Champanir, even though Bahadur Shah had removed the crown jewels and part of the hoard to Diu. "Humayun gave his officers and soldiers as much gold, silver, and jewels as could be heaped on their respective shields, proportioning the value to their rank and merit," says Ferishta. The emperor and his men then fell to revelry. Humayun diverted himself, says Abul Fazl, by "holding magnificent banquets and constantly arranging royal entertainments on the banks of the Du Ruya tank." He had no thought of consolidating his conquest.

DISCIPLINE IN THE Mughal army was so lax at this time and such was the general quixotry that one day, records Abul Fazl, a band of inebriated subordinate staff, "book-bearers, armour-bearers, ink-horn-bearers and the like", while listening to the exploits of Timur being read out at the camp fire, took it into their heads to desert the army and set out—to conquer the Deccan, no less!

The revellers were overtaken and brought back. To their misfortune the day was a Tuesday, when Humayun, according to his astrologically determined fancy, "wore the red vesture of Mars and sat on the throne of wrath and vengeance." The culprits were therefore handed out, in a weird application of poetic justice, punishments "fitting their destiny"—those who had acted in a headstrong manner had their heads chopped off, those without discretion ("not distinguishing between their feet and their hands," as Abul Fazl puts it) had their feet and hands severed, and so on. Not only that, an imam, whose prayers that day were thought to have implied a criticism of Humayun's eccentric punishments, was ordered to be trampled to death under the foot of an elephant—though when Humayun realized that the poor imam did not mean any criticism all, he "spent the whole night in sorrow and weeping," says Abul Fazl.

Inflicting such savage and arbitrary punishments was a medieval royal privilege, a demonstration of the king's absolute power. Humayun's peculiar fault was not arbitrariness but capriciousness. There was in him a certain quirkiness of character that often made him look silly. Especially so were his astrology-linked pranks, such as the "carpet of mirth" that he invented. It had circles marked out on it in different colours to represent the planets, on which the courtiers

45

positioned themselves according to the planet that was appropriate to them, and played a curious game, in which they either stood, sat or reclined according to the fall of the dice—this, according to Abul Fazl, "was a means of increasing mirth". The courtiers, we should assume, dared not but enjoy.

Not all of Humayun's innovations were frivolous. The prefabricated, portable bridge he designed was an excellent device, and his floating palace, with its bazaar and garden, an elegant creation. Unfortunately, Humayun often turned even good ideas ludicrous by over-elaborating them. For instance, the drum of justice which he set up near the durbar hall in Agra, to enable people to appeal to him directly, was in itself a thoughtful arrangement, but when he went on to specify different number of beats for different complaints—one beat for a matter of dispute; two for the non-receipt of wages and dues; three in case of oppression—it trivialized the idea.

The stars ruled Humayun's life in a manner which even professional astrologers would have found bizarre. He allowed astrology to carry him so far out that it virtually took him out of this world altogether. What he did on each day was determined not by the exigencies of government, nor by any rational mode of time management, but by the attribute of the planet of the day—Sunday and Tuesday, for example, were given to government affairs because, as Abul Fazl (himself an astrologer) explains, "Sunday pertains to the sun whose rays regulate . . . sovereignty, while Tuesday is Mars's day and Mars is the patron of soldiers." For similar reasons, Saturday and Thursday were assigned to matters of religion and learning, while Monday and Wednesday were "days of joy", and Friday was a day open to all matters and all classes of men. On each day Humayun wore clothes of the colour appropriate to the planet of the day—on Sundays he wore yellow, on Mondays green, and so on.

To match the three functional divisions of the week, Humayun grouped his courtiers into three functional classes, administrators, men of religion and culture, and a third group called "people of pleasure", which, according to Khvand Amir, was made up of "those who possessed beauty and elegance, those who were young and most lovely, also clever musicians and sweet singers". Within each of these three classes, Humayun created twelve grades, and then divided each of the grades into three ranks!

This did not exhaust the fancy of Humayun. He went on to organize government departments on the basis of the four elements: fire (armed forces), air (wardrobe, kitchen and stable), water (canals and wine cellar) and earth (agriculture, land and buildings), each under a minister who had to wear clothes of the colour suited to his department. The minister in charge of the army, for instance, had to wear red. Humayun thus constructed a marvellously intricate yet neat and elegant bureaucratic structure. Its only flaw was that it served no useful purpose.

Categorization and systematization were a mania with Humayun, and he busied himself with arranging and rearranging his courtiers and officers, not looking at the functional value of the arrangements, but only at their abstract harmony and perfection. There was certainly a method in his madness, an internal consistency in all that he did. But what he did was not consistent with the ways of the world. Nor with the grim business of government.

WHILE THE MUGHALS were revelling in Champanir, Bahadur Shah emerged from Diu and tried to recover his kingdom, but was again driven off by Humayun, who then went on to occupy Ahmadabad, the capital of Gujarat, thereby completing the conquest of the kingdom. At that point, Humayun's counsellors, according to Humayun's personal attendant Jauhar, suggested that since he had "obtained the objects for which he had commenced this war"—to defeat Bahadur Shah and to obtain treasure—"it would now be advisable to advance one or two years' pay to the army, to keep the remaining treasure in deposit for future emergencies, and then appoint Bahadur Shah as his deputy to rule the province of Gujarat." Such graciousness, they maintained, "would redound much to his fame, and would afford him leisure to look after his other dominions."

Humayun rejected the advice; he would not negotiate away what he had won by the sword. This decision was a blunder. Had he accepted the plan, he could have retained suzerainty over Gujarat and secured an annual tribute from there, instead of losing the state altogether, and losing Malwa too, as it happened.

After capturing Ahmadabad, Humayun left his brother Askari in charge of Gujarat and moved to Mandu in Malwa, a town for which he had taken a fancy. There he once again sank into a life of soothing dissipation. As soon as Humayun left Gujarat, Bahadur Shah re-emerged from his sanctuary in Diu and, gathering the support of local chiefs, advanced on Ahmadabad. Askari offered him little resistance. Instead, prodded on by some disgruntled amirs, he abandoned Gujarat and marched to Agra, his intention ambiguous, but probably to usurp the throne.

By then Humayun himself was at last on the way to Agra, to deal with renewed rebel activity in the north. The two armies converged in Mewar. There was a risk of a clash then, but Humayun characteristically overlooked Askari's incipient disaffection, and together the brothers marched to Agra as one army, there to receive the happy news that Hindal, their younger brother, who had been left in charge of the capital, had already subdued the rebels.

Meanwhile Malwa was lost to the Afghans, and in Gujarat, as Askari retreated, Bahadur Shah reoccupied the entire state. Humayun had spent twenty months, from November 1534 to August 1536, in his Malwa-Gujarat campaigns, but had no territorial gains to show for it. The action now shifted to Hindustan.

"The Feast Is Over . . ."

FOR A YEAR after his return to Agra, Humayun remained inert, diverting himself with opium and the pleasures of the harem, and busy with his abstruse studies and fanciful inventions. There was some talk of launching a fresh campaign against Bahadur Shah, but nothing came of it.

Meanwhile there was an unexpected and alarming resurgence of Afghan power in Bihar, under the wily leadership of Sher Khan, a local chieftain. During his 1531 campaign against Mahmud Lodi, Humayun had clashed briefly with Sher Khan, and had reduced him to submission. Sher Khan had thereafter remained, outwardly at any rate, a Mughal vassal. But that was only a pretence. The Khan was biding his time.

It was not Sher Khan's nature to act rashly. He had begun his career as a lowly officer in the Afghan kingdom of Bihar, then built up his power brick by brick and tier by tier, hastening slowly, to establish himself, after many years of patient and circumspect endeavour, as the virtual ruler of Bihar, a king in all but name. That was a very substantial achievement. But Bihar was only a halfway house for Sher Khan, the middle rung on his ladder of ambition. His eyes were on the Mughal throne. He had in his early youth spoken of his ambition to overthrow the Mughals, but no one had taken him seriously. Since then he had taken care not to reveal, by word or deed, what his inner eye was focused on.

Sher Khan was so discreet in action that Humayun had no inkling of what he was up to till it was too late. After consolidating his power in Bihar, the Khan began to push into Bengal. This move, though in a direction away from Mughal territory and carefully timed to coincide with Humayun's absence in Malwa and Gujarat, brought Sher Khan into conflict with Humayun for the second time.

Humayun was initially inclined to regard Sher Khan merely as a troublesome vassal who did not merit his personal attention, but when the Khan extended his rule into Bengal he became virtually a rival monarch and a threat to Mughal suzerainty. Sher Khan, it seemed, was turning east against Bengal only to gather strength to turn west later against the Mughals. This realization at last roused Humayun from his torpor. In mid-July 1537, having marshalled his forces from the provinces, and placing his lands in the secure charge of trusted nobles, he set out from Agra with a grand army against Sher Khan, sending part of the army and most of the heavy equipment down the Yamuna in a flotilla of barges. It was a portentous beginning.

But it ended, predictably, in disaster. Humayun was a negligent and lethargic campaigner, and in Sher Khan he was up against a relentless and exceptionally crafty adversary, a Machiavellian tactician who had no compunction in resorting to deceit and trickery to gain his goals. Compared to Sher Khan, Humayun was a babe in the woods.

THE FIRST TACTICAL error of Humayun was that, instead of promptly hunting down Sher Khan in Bengal, he paused on the way to besiege Chunar, an Afghan fort on the Ganga near Varanasi (Benares), wasting time and energy on a peripheral target. The delay enabled Sher Khan to complete his conquest of Bengal.

Humayun arrived at Chunar after a five-month leisurely trip from Agra, and spent the next three months besieging the fort. He gained little by taking it. Chunar was important to Sher Khan, but not vital. He had for a while, during his Bengal campaign, left his harem and treasure in Chunar, but had since then moved them to safety in Rohtas, a newly captured hill fort on the upper reaches of the Son River, in a rugged hill country impenetrable to the cumbersome Mughal army.

The Rohtas action was typical of Sher Khan. He desperately needed the fort as a sanctuary from the advancing Mughal forces, but he did not have the time, nor probably the means, to take it by force; in any case, it was his policy to avoid the use of force where stratagem would do. He therefore pleaded with Raja Hari Kishen, the chieftain of Rohtas, to allow him to leave his harem—and his treasure—in the fort, saying that he would rather see his treasure go to the raja than have it fall to the Mughals. For good measure, he also bribed a minister of the raja to plead his case. When the raja, lured by the prospect of seizing the treasure, acceded to the request, Sher Khan (according to Mughal sources, but denied by Abbas Khan, an Afghan chronicler) smuggled into the fort a band of his soldiers in covered litters supposedly carrying the begums, and they seized the fort in a flash. The poor, duped raja fled for his life through a back gate.

His family and treasure safe in Rohtas, Sher Khan returned to Bengal, while Humayun continued his futile siege of Chunar. By the time the emperor resumed his eastward march, joined on the way by Mahmud Shah, the fugitive king of Bengal, Sher Khan was on his way back to Bihar, having virtually completed the subjugation of Bengal.

Around this time Humayun made an effort to cajole Sher Khan into submission. He offered to return Chunar to Sher Khan and, in addition, to give him Jaunpur or any other place of his choice, if he would give up Bengal, hand over to Humayun the treasure he had taken there, including the *chhattar* (royal umbrella) and throne, and agree to rule under Mughal overlordship. Sher Khan was not tempted. He received the Mughal envoy courteously, but told him (according to Jauhar) that since it had "cost him five or six years' toil to subdue Bengal, with the loss of a great number of his soldiers, it was impossible he could resign that conquest." Instead, he made a counter-proposal—he offered to relinquish the regalia of Bengal, surrender Bihar, and pay an annual tribute of one million rupees to Humayun, provided he was allowed to retain Bengal.

Humayun was initially inclined to accept Sher Khan's proposal, but decided against it when he learned that Sher Khan's hold on Bengal was tenuous and that he could easily be dislodged from there. Moreover, Sher Khan himself had returned to Bihar by that time, leaving only a part of his army in Bengal under the command of his son Jalal Khan. Humayun believed that these circumstances favoured him, so he rejected Sher Khan's offer and continued to advance on Bengal, certain of victory.

This decision was the turning point in Humayun's career. It was also a turning point in Sher Khan's career, for he too now decided on a fight to the finish. He had gone to the limit of what he could concede to Humayun to avoid a clash. He would yield no more. So he hurried back to Bengal, where, at Gaur, the capital of Bengal, he assumed the title Sher Shah. He was no longer a mere khan (chieftain), but a shah (king), though he did not yet presume to ascend the throne. From that point on it would be all or nothing for Sher Shah. To survive, he had to eliminate Humayun. The two could not coexist in the same land.

HUMAYUN TOO HASTENED towards Gaur, though by then the monsoon had broken, making the campaign arduous. Sher Shah made no move to stop him. It suited him to have Humayun advance, for his plan was to bottle up the Mughals in Bengal. Sher Shah's only problem was that he had taken so much treasure in Gaur that he had difficulty in finding enough porters to carry it to Rohtas. To gain time, he sent Jalal Khan to block the narrow Teliyagarhi pass north-west of Rajmahal, through which the Mughal army had to pass to enter Bengal, and hold them off for a while. Jalal did more than just hold off the Mughals.

Though Sher Shah, ever cautious, had ordered him to take a strictly defensive position, Jalal found the Mughal advance forces so carelessly deployed at the pass that he attacked and scattered them. This was Sher Shah's first victory over Humayun, and a portent.

Jalal Khan's triumph enabled Sher Shah to get away safely to Rohtas with the Bengal treasure. It was not however his intention to hole up in Rohtas, but to use it as a base from where to stretch out his arms and garrotte Humayun in Bengal, by squeezing tight the Mughal lines of communication and supply.

Humayun innocently walked into the trap.

When Jalal Khan withdrew from the pass he was guarding, Humayun proceeded triumphantly to Gaur. He found it a desolate city, ravaged by a long drawn out war, its streets choked with the dead, the living barely alive. Humayun, perhaps ironically, renamed the city Jannatabad (Paradise), but his men found it a hell. Indeed, they found Bengal itself a hell, and loathed it so intensely that when Humayun offered the governorship of the province to one of his amirs, he deserted, protesting that the posting amounted to a death sentence.

But Humayun himself took to Bengal. "When His Majesty reached Gaur, he found everywhere a paradise full of fairy-faced girls and handsome maids, along with exhilarating gardens and soothing tanks," says Mushtaqui. He liked the climate of Bengal, and its lush fecundity. Moreover, Sher Shah, according to Niamatullah, had furnished the palace at Gaur "with an exquisite variety of ornaments and embellishments" in the hope "that Humayun, charmed with it, would be induced to prolong his stay there."

The charm worked. Besides, Humayun had, as he viewed it, accomplished the task he had set out to achieve, to drive Sher Shah out of Bengal. So he now parcelled out the province among his amirs and retreated into the harem, taking no further interest in the affairs of the state. Humayun, says Jauhar, "very unaccountably shut himself up for a considerable time in his harem, and abandoned himself to every kind of indulgence and luxury." For three months he admitted no one to an audience with him. Says Abul Fazl, "His Majesty . . . found the climate of Bengal agreeable and sat down to enjoy himself." It is not clear how long Humayun was in Bengal; a good conjecture is that in all he spent about nine months in the province, including at least three months in Gaur itself.

While Humayun idled, Sher Shah got busy and took the offensive in Bihar. Virtually the entire province soon fell to him, including the city of Varanasi. Jaunpur and Chunar were invested. As a precaution, he seized the families of the principal zemindars of the region and held them in Rohtas as hostages, to eliminate any residual local support for the Mughals. When Humayun heard of these activities, he was incredulous, says Jauhar, and he asked in wonder, "How could Sher Khan dare so much?"

But Sher Shah had more surprises in store. He now blocked the passes between Bihar and Bengal, so that supplies, and even communication, no longer reached Humayun. At that critical juncture, Humayun's brothers, fearing that he would perish in Bengal, began to desert him, and Hindal, who was holding a back-up position to secure the lines of communication and supply, abandoned his station and proceeded to Agra to claim the throne for himself.

The noose was tightening around Humayun. He had to get out of Bengal. But by the time he got moving, the monsoon had once again burst over Bengal, turning the land into a quagmire. The imperial troops, especially the cavalry, suffered great hardship and losses trudging through the deep, viscous slush—it was as if the very soil of Bengal were clutching at Humayun's feet and dragging him down to bury him. The Mughals were utterly dispirited and exhausted by the time they lurched back into Bihar to challenge Sher Shah.

When Sher Shah heard of Humayun's retreat from Bengal, he lifted the siege of Jaunpur, in which he was then engaged, crossed to the right bank of the Ganga and withdrew to south Bihar, intending to play hide-and-seek with Humayun, to exhaust and frustrate him. Sher Shah was still reluctant to fight an open battle against Humayun—he had from his humble beginnings built up a great career, acquired immense wealth and power through tireless effort, and he did not want to chance it all on the luck of a battle. His plan was therefore to retreat to Bengal in case Humayun attacked him, or to hang around the Mughal army and harass it in case Humayun proceeded to Agra.

Sher Shah's retreat from Jaunpur forced Humayun, who was then marching on that city, also to cross to the right bank of the Ganga—it would have seemed unmanly for him to remain on the left bank when the rebel (as Humayun still thought of Sher Shah) was on the right bank. Humayun however made no effort to seek out Sher Shah, but proceeded towards Agra. Moving along the right bank of the Ganga now, passing Patna, crossing the Son, the Mughal army reached Chausa, where the river Karmanasa (Destroyer of Karma) joined the Ganga. All along the way, the Mughals were trailed by Afghan scouts, watching their every move and engaging in occasional skirmishes, but avoiding any major battle.

Then, suddenly, the scene shifted. When Sher Shah came to know of the disarray and low morale of the Mughal army, and sensed the zeal of his own men to fight the Mughals, he changed his strategy and decided to seek battle with Humayun. "Now that I have overthrown his armies which were in Bihar and Jaunpur, and taken those countries, the way to peace is closed," he told a conclave of his commanders. "If you agree with me, I will try my fortune." They were even more eager for battle than he was.

The die was thus cast. Sher Shah then emerged from south Bihar and advanced to confront Humayun. Closing in, he skirted the Mughal army, crossed the Karmanasa, and presently, to the utter surprise of the Mughals, appeared in front of them when they thought he was behind them.

The two armies reached Chausa at about the same time, on opposite banks of the Karmanasa, with Sher Shah blocking the passage to Agra. Humayun's councillors were divided in their advice on how to deal with the situation, says Jauhar. One group recommended immediate attack, arguing that Sher Shah had come by forced marches and his army was tired and vulnerable; the other group advised Humayun to adopt the time-tested Mughal tactic of fighting from an entrenched position, saying that "there was no necessity for hurry or perturbation."

Humayun chose the latter option, crossed the Karmanasa and encamped. For two months the foes lay facing each other across a narrow but steep-banked rivulet called Toram Nathi, Small Stream, engaging in occasional skirmishes but avoiding general action. The military advantage at that point seemed to be with Humayun. Skirmishes invariably favoured the Mughals. Moreover, with each passing day the Mughal army swelled in size, as stragglers from Bengal caught up with the main body of the army. But the morale of the Mughal army was low, and it was battle weary after the exhausting Bengal campaign. And Humayun himself was vacillating, vexed as much about what his brothers were up to as about Sher Shah's threat.

The wild card in this game was the possible line of action of Kamran and Hindal. Both were susceptible to the temptations that Humayun's vulnerability offered them. Hindal, nineteen years old and impressionable, one moment eager for the throne, and the next shamed into fraternal duty by his mother, Dildar Begum, was finally prodded by a few perfidious amirs into declaring himself king. Dildar Begum was so upset by Hindal's imprudent act that she put on mourning clothes when he ascended the throne. When he asked her why she was so dressed on such a joyous occasion, she answered, "I am mourning for you... You have girded your loins for your own destruction." But such admonitions had no effect on Hindal, whose attitude was, as Abul Fazl says,

Advice of man is wind in mine ear,
But 'tis a wind that fans my fire.

From Agra, Hindal advanced north to take possession of Delhi, but was rebuffed there by Humayun's loyal officers, who called in Kamran from Kabul to subdue the rebel. When Kamran arrived in Delhi at the head of a large cavalry force, Hindal retreated to Agra, and when Kamran pursued him, he submitted. The erstwhile rebel and his chastiser then joined together, crossed the Yamuna, and advanced to relieve Humayun.

Sher Shah was now in danger of being trapped between two Mughal armies. Fortunately for him, Kamran and Hindal, after advancing for a few days, inexplicably turned back and returned to Agra. Kamran's own ambitions might have had something to do with it—when he realized how hopeless Humayun's plight was, "there arose in him," says Gulbadan, "a desire for sovereignty." Clearly, there was a crisis of leadership among the Mughals. Humayun had little confidence in himself, and therefore could inspire none in others. His brothers could see no future in remaining with him.

Meanwhile the summer was almost over, and the rains broke over the land with great fury, creating an unforeseen problem for Sher Shah. He had not chosen his ground carefully, so his camp was inundated with rain water, and he was forced to move his army to a position some eight kilometres away, leaving only his artillery and a covering force in the original entrenchments. That unplanned manoeuvre put Sher Shah in great jeopardy. But Humayun failed to seize the moment— this was his greatest failing, his lack of energy in responding to shifting strategic situations.

SO THE AWFUL waiting continued. Humayun soon realized that he could expect no aid from his brothers; on the contrary, he feared that they could be scheming to usurp the throne themselves, and had thus become a greater threat to his power than Sher Shah. For the moment, then, getting to Agra became for him more important than suppressing Sher Shah's rebellion. It was essential for him to secure an uncontested but honourable passage to Agra.

In this predicament Humayun sent an emissary, Mullah Muhammad Barghiz, to Sher Shah to negotiate peace. When the mullah reached the Afghan camp, he found—as Erskine, Humayun's nineteenth-century biographer, describes the scene—Sher Shah "busy with his spade, in the heat of the day, among his soldiers who were employed in digging a trench. On seeing the ambassador, the king washed his hands, a temporary awning was spread, and he sat down under it on the ground, without ceremony, and received the envoy." Sher Shah's reply to the mullah when he broached the subject of peace was as casual. He said: "Go, tell your Emperor this from me: he is desirous of war, his troops are not; I do not wish for war, my troops do."

Negotiations, however, continued. Sher Shah, ever cautious and crafty, and, according to Abbas, "wavering in his decision as to peace or war", then wrote a conciliatory letter to Humayun, stating "that if the Emperor would give him the kingdom of Bengal and be satisfied that the khutbah be read and money struck in the Emperor's name, he would be the Emperor's vassal." Humayun, anxious for peace, readily agreed to these terms, but with the face-saving provision that Sher Shah should first—before Humayun formally condoned his rebellion and granted him Bengal—retreat for a couple of marches and let Humayun chase him in a mock pursuit.

It is not clear what was finally agreed, but some sort of an armistice seems to have been reached. Perhaps even a formal treaty was concluded. But while Humayun was trusting, Sher Shah intended to deceive. "I [have] lost all hope in his goodness . . . He is but playing with me, and will eventually not abide by this peace," said Sher Shah, conveniently shifting the onus of perfidy to Humayun.

Whether a treaty was formalized or not, both armies behaved as if it were as good as signed, and they got busy with preparations to break camp. There were convivial visits between the Mughals and the Afghans. Sher Shah even acted out a charade for a couple of days by arraying his army and sending it out some twelve kilometres, as if to chastise a local chieftain, and then bringing it back, so that (he later explained) he "might put the Emperor off his guard". The Mughals meanwhile were busy constructing a bridge of boats over the Ganga for their return to Agra by the traditional route through the Doab.

All along, while Humayun relaxed in the assurance of peace, Sher Shah was awake and alert, scheming, prowling. When he was satisfied that the prey was entirely limp and unwary, he pounced. On 25th June 1539, just before midnight, he summoned his chiefs, told them of his decision to attack the Mughals, and ordered his army to be arrayed immediately. At about three in the morning they set out, but in a direction away from the Mughals, Sher Shah still keeping up the pretence that his target was the rebel chieftain, so as not to rouse Mughal suspicions. After the army had gone some distance, he wheeled it around—"Now is the time to regain the Empire of Hindustan," he told his men—and swooped down on the barely awake Mughal army.

"In the twinkling of an eye they routed the Mughal forces," says Abbas.

The Mughals were thrown into utter chaos, with camp-followers and women screaming and fleeing helter-skelter. Humayun, roused from his sleep by the startling hubbub, immediately mounted and, fighting valiantly, tried to rally his forces. But the battle had already been lost. In imminent danger of being cut down—"His Majesty's blessed hand was wounded," says Gulbadan—he was saved by one of his captains, who seized the reins of his horse and turned him away, saying, "This is not the time for dallying. The feast is over, why linger near the food?" They galloped towards the Ganga and plunged in, swimming their horses across the river. In mid-stream Humayun fell off his mount and nearly drowned, but was rescued by a water carrier named Nizam, who gave him an inflated water bag and helped him to swim across.

On reaching the opposite bank, Humayun, with characteristic impulsiveness, promised Nizam: "Thou shall sit on my throne." So when Humayun got to Agra, and Nizam, perhaps not hoping for much, presented himself at the public durbar, Humayun, true to his word, gravely invited the water-carrier to sit on "the throne of the world", says Jauhar. Nizam played emperor for a couple of hours, but no harm was done, for he prudently confined himself to issuing orders to enrich his family. The farce, however, further damaged Humayun's reputation, and Kamran, says Abul Fazl, "displayed the wrinkle of cavil on the forehead of criticism."

For the Mughals, Chausa was an awful disaster. Thousands were slaughtered by the Afghans, many more drowned in the Ganga, attempting to flee. There was, however, no random violence or rapine by the Afghans, no severed heads on spikes, no tower of heads. Sher Shah, unlike the Mughals, was a magnanimous victor, seeking no revenge beyond victory itself. Triumphant, he rode into the Mughal royal enclosure, dismounted at the durbar tent and prostrated himself in thanksgiving prayer. He then ordered the protection of the families of the Mughal officers and men, especially of Humayun's harem; they were shown every courtesy, taken to the safety of Rohtas and later sent to Humayun with a special escort.

SHER SHAH DID not pursue Humayun to Agra, not wanting to force his luck. Instead, he returned to Bengal, expelled Jahangir Kuli, the Mughal governor, and spent several months there organizing his government. He would consolidate his gains before turning on Humayun again. And it would be as an equal that Sher Shah would face Humayun next, a king against a king, not a rebel against his liege. After his victory at Chausa, when he was at the Mughal camp, Sher Shah, seeking to validate his expedient action as a divine dispensation, had spoken of a strange dream he had the previous night, of god taking the crown from Humayun and placing it on his (Sher Shah's) head, and advising him to rule justly. This felicitous dream was fulfilled soon after at Gaur, when Sher Shah, then in his early fifties, was formally enthroned as king in a grand ceremony, legitimizing the royal title he had assumed the previous year.

The suggestion that he should ascend the throne was made, perhaps on a hint from Sher Shah, by a distinguished Afghan amir at an assembly of officers, and was received with general acclamation. Sher Shah, as courtesy required, demurred before agreeing. "The kingly office is a very exalted thing, and is not devoid of trouble," he said, "but since the noble minds of my friends have decided to make me king, I agree."

On a chosen day, at an auspicious hour designated by astrologers, Sher Shah ascended the throne, and the royal umbrella was unfurled over his head. Sher Shah then assumed a new title, signifying the theme of his reign—Sultan-ul-Adil, The Just Ruler. "For seven days drums were beaten in token of rejoicing," Abbas reports. "Afghan youths came in troops from every tribe, and danced according to the custom of the Afghans. Gifts were made to these musicians, and the servants of Sher Shah sprinkled saffron and musk, mixed with rose-water and ambergris of various colours, upon the heads of the dancing youth." All were treated to grand feasts.

The gloom that had settled on the Afghans after the battle of Panipat had at last lifted. When the coronation festivities were over, Sher Shah turned westward again, retook Jaunpur, and established himself as the undisputed master of Bihar and Bengal. It would soon be the turn of Agra.

"What Is to Be Done?
Where Am I to Go?"

ON REACHING AGRA from Chausa, Humayun went straight to the Zer Afshan Garden, where Kamran lay encamped. The brothers embraced tearfully, and were seen sitting together for a long time on the porch of the pavilion there, talking. Kamran appealed to Humayun to pardon Hindal's rebellion, so when Hindal pleaded that, being young and inexperienced, he was misled by others, Humayun said, "Well, at Kamran Mirza's entreaty, I do forgive thee." It was not the time for recriminations. "What is past is past. We must now all join manfully to repel the common enemy," Humayun urged.

Join manfully! That seldom was the way of royal siblings. "Seven months were wasted in weary indecision," writes Mirza Haidar, who was then in Agra with Kamran, "until the opportunity was lost and Sher Khan was on the Ganga ready for war." Kamran offered to take on his brother's burden and lead his Kabul cavalry against Sher Shah. That probably was the most viable line of action, but Humayun would not agree to it. He could not. "No," he said to Kamran, "Sher Khan defeated me, and I will have my revenge of him." Humayun could not afford to let the credit of humbling Sher Shah go to Kamran—given his own feeble reputation and the growing rivalry between himself and Kamran, that would have been nearly as damaging to him as another defeat at Sher Shah's hands.

Humayun tried to get Kamran to play a subordinate role, but Kamran was averse to that. Instead, he desired to return to Kabul, on the ground that the climate of Agra did not suit him. "However much he [Humayun] scoured the rust of contrariety with the burnisher of advice, the brightness of concord could not by any means be developed in the mirror of his [Kamran's] fortune," says Abul Fazl. Humayun was reluctant to let Kamran go, but when he fell seriously ill around that time—there was a suspicion, probably unfounded, that he was poisoned—Humayun could hold him no more, and Kamran returned to Lahore with most of his men.

"The retreat of Kamran," says Haidar, "was the efficient cause of the rise of Sher Khan, and of the fall of the Chaghatai dynasty." This is not quite true. Humayun's position did not become hopeless in direct consequence of Kamran's departure. Collecting a fresh army was not a problem, as the Mughal amirs, realizing that if Humayun fell they would fall too, flocked to him with troops from their fiefs. Humayun was also able to persuade a few of Kamran's amirs, including Mirza Haidar, to join him with their retainers.

Meanwhile Sher Shah, having consolidated his power in Bihar and Bengal, had crossed the Ganga into the Doab, the very heartland of the Mughal empire. In a daring show of force, he then sent an Afghan army across the Yamuna towards Malwa, traversing the Mughal domain. But that army, under Qutb Khan, Sher Shah's youngest son, was defeated at Kalpi by a Mughal force under Yadgar Nasir Mirza, a cousin and brother-in-law of Humayun. Qutb Khan was slain, and his head, along with a bunch of other severed Afghan heads, was sent to Agra to rouse the flagging spirit of the Mughals.

The tide was at last turning, thought Humayun. So in the summer of 1540, he issued out of the Agra fort and pitched his tents in the Zer Afshan Garden in the outskirts of the city to marshal his forces against Sher Shah. In a short time a vast concourse of men gathered under his standard, but it was more a rabble than an army, lacking in training and discipline. Nor was it well led. A good number of Mughal veterans had perished in Bengal and at Chausa, and most of the remaining amirs, says Haidar, were "amirs only in name . . . [and] had not a tincture of prudence or knowledge, or energy or emulation or dignity of mind or generosity, qualities from which nobility draws its name." Humayun himself was hardly a heroic leader, who could whip the mob into a sinewy fighting force. There was "a general languor and disaffection" in the Mughal camp, writes Erskine. "The officers showed little zeal, the troops little ardour; all was disorganized."

Still, the Mughals had one great advantage—they had, according to Haidar, 700 swivel guns and twenty-one heavy cannons, and a battalion of some 5000 musketeers. This was, for that age, formidable fire power. The awareness of this power, coupled with the characteristic caution of Sher Shah, made the Afghans retreat across the Ganga when Humayun, advancing from Agra, closed in on them near Kanauj. The two armies then encamped, Sher Shah on the left bank of the river and Humayun on the right bank. There they lay for about a month.

THE WAITING DID no good to the Mughals. The morale of the Mughal army, fragile to begin with, crumbled during the interlude. Then the desertions began. A trickle at first, they soon became a flood, and even some of Humayun's highest nobles deserted. "Everybody began to desert," says Haidar. "An excited feeling ran through the army and the cry was, `Let us go and rest in our homes.'" Humayun's entire army was in danger of vanishing, leaving it to Sher Shah to stroll over and occupy the imperial throne.

To stanch the haemorrhage and to force the battle, Humayun then crossed over to the left bank of the Ganga. The crossing was also prompted by a message from Sher Shah daring Humayun to cross the river and fight, and offering to move the Afghan army away from the riverside to facilitate the crossing.

Sher Shah would keep his word. He wanted an honourable battle for once. When his generals suggested a surprise attack while the Mughals crossed the river, he said, "I have never before had any advantages, and have been compelled to use stratagems in warfare. Now by the favour of the All-Powerful, my force is not inferior to the Emperor's. I will not now, notwithstanding my advantages, break my promise . . . With my army arrayed in the open field, I will give battle without fraud or stratagem."

Humayun thus crossed the river unopposed. Yet, for quite a while the armies did not engage, but lay entrenched close to each other. "Every day skirmishes occurred between the adventurous, swaggering spirits of both sides," says Haidar, but there was no general action. Then the fates intervened to end the impasse by sending unseasonal May showers to flood the ground occupied by the Mughals, compelling them to shift camp, thus offering Sher Shah an opportunity similar to the one that Humayun had missed at Chausa. "To move was indispensable," notes Haidar. And when the Mughal army was manoeuvring to shift its camp, at noon on 17th May 1540, Sher Shah attacked.

The Mughal army, even after all the desertions, was a considerable force, some 40,000 strong. "All mounted on tipchak horses, and clad in iron armour, they surged like the waves of the sea," recounts Haidar. Sher Shah's army, in contrast, was much smaller, less than 15,000 strong. Still, the advantage was with the Afghans, for their spirit was high. The Mughals, in contrast, were cringing. On the day of the battle, notes Haidar contemptuously, many of the Mughal amirs were so timid that they hid their yak-tail standards, "lest the enemy might see and bear down upon them". The Mughal army was more ready for flight than for fight. So the battle was lost even before it began. "It was not a fight, but a rout, for not a man, friend or foe, was even wounded . . . Not a cannon was fired—not a gun," writes Haidar, who commanded a division of the Mughal army in the battle.

Haidar exaggerates. The Mughal rout was not precipitate. Nor was the Afghan victory certain. In the initial stages of the encounter, the battle in fact favoured the Mughals, as the Mughal left under Yadgar Nasir Mirza pushed back the Afghan right, and at the centre, the Mughal advance forces under Hindal prevailed. But everything was lost when the Mughal right under Askari, the least of the sons of Babur, collapsed without resistance when attacked by the Afghans under their great general Khavass Khan. "A cry of `defeat' was heard, and that instant a panic seized the men; and before an arrow was shot from a bow, they fled," recalls Haidar.

After scattering the Mughal right, Khavass Khan wheeled around the Mughal army and got to the rear of the Mughal camp, where lay huddled a vast mob of camp-followers, probably as many as 200,000 men and women, for normally camp-followers were about five times the size of the fighting force. Khavass Khan charged the camp and drove the rabble stampeding into the midst of the Mughal army, spreading panic. That decided the battle.

"By the pressure of the masses of these men, the troops were quite unable to keep their ranks," writes Haidar. "The camp-followers, crowding behind, bore them so down that they were thrown into disorder; and the crowd, continuing still to press on, some on one side, some on another, pushed the soldiers upon the chains of the carriages. Even then the camp-followers, who were behind, went on urging those before, till in many instances the chains burst, and every person . . . stationed at the chain so broken [was] driven out beyond it, while the order, even such as kept within, was totally broken and destroyed, and, from the pressure and confusion, not a man could act . . . When, to this confusion, the rush of the terrified men flying from the right was added, the defeat was sure, and the day irretrievable."

Meanwhile, Sher Shah, moving in from the reserve, charged to halt the advance of the Mughal left, and drove that wing too into the Mughal centre, making the mêlée there utterly chaotic. In that dreadful turmoil the Mughal artillery, on which Humayun had placed much reliance, could not be brought to bear upon the enemy, for there was no enemy in front of the guns, only Mughal fugitives from the right and the left.

The battle was fought some six kilometres east of the Ganga, and to the river the Mughal fugitives now fled. Hotly chased by the Afghans, they plunged headlong into the river, without even pausing to take off their armour. Thousands drowned. Humayun himself crossed the river on one of Babur's old elephants, and had to be literally dragged up the steep bank of the river on the other side by some of his men—they "tied their turbans together and threw an end of the cloth to him, and he with some difficulty climbed up. They then brought him a horse on which he mounted and proceeded towards Agra," says Jauhar. "When we emerged from the river on the other bank, a monarch, who at noon had a retinue of seventeen thousand men, was mounted upon a wretched, spavined horse, with both his head and feet bare," notes Haidar. Sher Shah was disappointed that Humayun had managed to escape. "I had intended that he should perish," he said, "but he has escaped."

HUMAYUN RODE STRAIGHT on to Agra. He was so vulnerable at this time—an army in flight was anybody's game—that on the way he even had to suffer the humiliation of being set on by a band of villagers! In Agra, Humayun stopped at the suburban house of Sayyid Rafia-e-din, an eminent Sufi. The sage consoled him, speaking of the fickleness of temporal fortunes; he then served him a meal of bread and melons, and advised him not to attempt to defend Agra but to go on to Lahore and join up with Kamran.

Humayun heeded the advice, gathered his family and treasure from Agra, and hastened northward. It was a pell-mell flight. On one occasion, between Agra and Delhi, when an alarm was raised that the Afghans were close behind, Humayun in panic at once mounted his horse and rode off, leaving his men to fend for themselves. Jauhar, who attended on Humayun during the flight, writes of the scene: "No one attempted to assist another; the son paid no attention to his father, nor the father to the son, but each person endeavoured to conceal whatever valuables he had, and to make his escape; and, to add to their distress, a very heavy rain fell. In short, God preserve us from seeing such another day." Calm was eventually restored, and the Mughals reached Delhi in reasonable order. Humayun rested there for a couple of days, then left for Punjab.

He reached Lahore in early July, and was received by Kamran. Askari and Hindal, who had gone to their fiefs to collect their possessions, also joined them there. The brothers were all together again. The fate of the Mughal empire depended on their accord. "Several times they gathered together . . . and deliberated and made vows and promises of unity and concord," writes Abul Fazl. "At length one day, all the mirzas, nobles and grandees having been assembled, wrote out a deed of concord and unanimity, and to this auspicious record all the officers gave their signatures."

What they agreed formally and what they decided in their own hearts were, however, quite different. This was unavoidable. The interests of the princes were divergent. Kamran especially was worried that Humayun would dispossess him of Kabul and Punjab to compensate for the loss of Hindustan. Indeed, there was a suggestion at this time that Humayun should eliminate Kamran and take his lands, but Humayun rejected the plan out of hand, saying, "No, never for the vanities of this perishable world will I imbrue my hands in the blood of a brother!"

Predictably the brothers could not, despite their formal accord, agree on a concerted plan of action—Kamran wanted to take the royal family to safety in Kabul and then return with reinforcements; Hindal and Yadgar wanted to conquer Gujarat and from there re-enter Hindustan; Haidar suggested the conquest of Kashmir. Humayun himself spun between these alternatives, unable to decide what to do. "They conferred and took counsel and asked advice, but they did not settle on any single thing," says Gulbadan.

As the Mughals were bickering, the Afghans entered Punjab. At that point Kamran opened negotiations with Sher Shah. "All his endeavour was that every one should be ruined, and he counted it a gain that he himself might go to Kabul and secure a corner for his own enjoyment," charges Abul Fazl. This is an unfair indictment, for Humayun himself was at that time seeking accommodation with Sher Shah. "I have left you the whole of Hindustan. Leave Lahore alone, and let Sirhind . . . be a boundary between you and me," he appealed to Sher Shah through an emissary. Sher Shah gruffly turned down the plea. "I have left you Kabul. You should go there," he warned.

Sher Shah had the means to enforce his will. So when the Afghans crossed the Beas and advanced on Lahore, the Mughal princes scattered in panic. "It was like the day of resurrection," writes Gulbadan. "People left their decorated palaces and furniture just as they were, but took with them whatever money they had." Some 200,000 people were in flight. It was the Mughal exodus from India.

Kamran and Askari set out westward to Kabul. Hindal and Yadgar went south towards Gujarat. Haidar proceeded to Kashmir, which he would conquer and rule for many years with distinction. Humayun, as usual, could not make up his mind; he became totally distracted, accepting one suggestion at one moment, quite the opposite one the next. At one time he thought of going to Badakshan, but Kamran would not hear of that, as the route to Badakshan passed through Kabul. Humayun finally decided to join Hindal and Yadgar, and they, passing through the land of the fierce Baluchis and continually harassed by them, crossed the Indus and reached Sind.

HUMAYUN WAS NOT welcome in Sind, which was at that time ruled by Shah Husain Mirza, a relative of Humayun, who, though nominally subordinate to the Mughal emperor, was in fact an independent sovereign. The arrival of Humayun in Sind distressed Husain, though Humayun assured him that he meant no threat but was only seeking help to conquer Gujarat. This assurance by a fugitive king on the hunt for a throne to occupy carried little conviction with Husain, especially as it was in similar circumstances that Babur had seized Kabul from Husain's family. Husain therefore sought to ensure that Humayun did not become a burden on him or a challenge to his power—he strung Humayun along, holding out promises of help but really doing nothing and in fact thwarting every move of Humayun without seriously provoking him.

It took Humayun six frustrating months to realize that he was never going to get any help in Sind, either by his own force or by the favour of Husain. Yet, in a way, Humayun's sojourn in Sind was fortunate for him, for it was there that he met and married Hamida, and begot by her a son, Akbar, who would become one of the greatest rulers of India. As Jauhar tells the story, Humayun first saw Hamida at Pat in western Sind during an entertainment given by Dildar Begum, Hindal's mother. A Persian and a Shiah, Hamida was a descendant of Ahmad Jani, a celebrated Muslim sage popularly known as His Reverence the Terrible Elephant, and her father was one of Hindal's preceptors. "The king was much pleased with her, and inquired if she was betrothed," writes Jauhar. "He was informed that she had been asked, but that the ceremony had not taken place. The king then said, I will marry her.'"

A king's desire, even a fallen king's desire, in such matters could not be denied in that age, but both Hindal and Hamida bitterly opposed the marriage proposal, possibly because they were involved with each other. Hindal in fact became furious and made a scene when Humayun spoke of his desire for Hamida. "I thought you came here to do me honour, not to look out for a young bride," he stormed at Humayun. "If you commit this (ridiculous) act, I will leave you." Hamida too firmly rejected the proposal. Humayun, offended, left the feast in a huff.

It was Dildar Begum's tact and considerable persuasive powers which eventually won Hamida for Humayun. She pacified Hindal, and wrote to Humayun holding out hope of obtaining Hamida's consent. Hamida, however, remained adamant. She was then fourteen, and he thirty-three; but more than the difference in age, Humayun, ravaged by dissipation and hounded by calamities, was hardly an ideal match for the romantic and spirited maiden. Once, when Humayun sent for her, she refused to go, saying, "If it is to pay my respects, I was exalted by paying my respects the other day. Why should I come again?" Another time Humayun sent a messenger to ask Hindal to send her, but the prince told him, "Whatever I may say, she will not go. Go yourself and tell her." And when the messenger approached Hamida, she said, "To see kings once is lawful; a second time is forbidden. I shall not come."

Still Dildar persevered. "For forty days the begum (Hamida) resisted and discussed and disagreed," recalls Gulbadan. "At last her highness my mother, Dildar Begum, advised her, saying: `After all you will marry someone. Better than a king, who is there?' The begum said: `Oh yes, I shall marry someone; but he shall be a man whose collar my hand can touch, and not one whose skirt it does not reach.' Then my mother again gave her much advice." In the end Hamida relented.

When Humayun was informed about Hamida's consent, he, says Gulbadan, "took the astrolabe into his own blessed hand and, having chosen a propitious hour," fixed the time for marriage, and gave "two lakhs of ready money for the dower". Little Hamida thus became Hazret Maryam-makani, Hamida Banu Begum, the queen. A few days later, the odd couple boarded the royal barge and proceeded to Humayun's camp in Charbagh, a pleasant garden on the outskirts of the town of Lohri.

Whatever idyll the couple enjoyed was brief. Humayun's position was utterly hopeless, and his men could see no future in remaining with him. Many deserted. Hindal, as expected, left Humayun soon after the Hamida affair, and proceeded to Afghanistan, where he lived for a while as a dervish. Yadgar Mirza, seduced by Shah Husain with grand promises, was vacillating in his loyalty. Even such loyal veterans as Munim Beg and Tardi Beg were inclined to flee. On one occasion, Humayun, warned of their possible flight, stayed awake through the night to keep an eye on them, so that they would not sneak away; even then, in the morning, when Humayun went to have a bath, the two made a run for their horses—Humayun "ran after them and with great difficulty prevailed on them to return," says Jauhar. That was what the Mughal emperor was reduced to, running after his servants to plead with them to stay.

How long could he go on like that? Humayun seemed to be at the end of his tether. "What is to be done? Where am I to go?" he kept asking. There were no answers.

YET SOMEHOW HUMAYUN plodded on, maybe drawing solace from

astrology, blaming the stars for his misfortunes and finding hope in their shifting configurations. "The bucket of success," an amir would later tell Humayun, "must at one time come up full from the waters of hope and at another, it must by a revolution of the wheel, go down empty." Humayun must have found comfort, and hope, in such thoughts. Or perhaps, more practically, he heeded the harsh but sensible advice of Mirza Haidar on what the future portended for him. "It involves great hardships," said Haidar, "but it is you who have made hard what was once easy. And moreover, if you do not bear patiently your present troubles, they will become yet more onerous."

Humayun was living off the land at this time, taking by force whatever he could find, like a common marauder. Often there was nothing at all for him to take, for people fled at the approach of the Mughals. For days on end they had to live on wild berries, and once when they caught a wild animal for food, it was like a celebratory feast.

Humayun's tribulations only got worse when he moved into the desert of Rajasthan on the invitation of Maldev of Marwar. "It was extremely hot," writes Gulbadan. "Horses and [other] quadrupeds kept sinking to the knees in the sand . . . On they went, thirsty and hungry." For several days they found no water, and men fought, sometimes killed, for water. Several perished of thirst, both men and animals. Sometimes, when they found water, they drank too much and some animals died of that too. Desertions continued.

And, at the end of the awful desert trek, the Marwar refuge turned out to be a mirage. Maldev—"that ravening demon," as Abul Fazl describes him—was proffering help only to entice Humayun and betray him to Sher Shah, it appeared. But where could Humayun go? The only prospect was Umarkot, a forlorn little town on the edge of the desert on the Sind border, whose Rajput chief, Rana Prasad, had offered help.

This was the nadir of Humayun's life. He and his family had to endure great hardship as they toiled through the desert towards Umarkot, with hostile Rajputs hovering around, harassing them and filling up the wells on the route. Humayun's personal reputation was so low at this time that even his closest amirs showed him scant regard, and Tardi Beg churlishly—"throwing the dust of meanness on his own head," as Nizamuddin Ahmad puts it—even turned down Humayun's request to give one of his horses for the heavily pregnant Hamida to ride on. Humayun did not amount to much in the eyes of anyone.

His retinue had at this time dwindled to a mere handful. When he entered Umarkot there were but seven horsemen in immediate attendance on him. So badly equipped was he that he did not even have a change of clothing with him, so when he gave what he wore for washing, he had only his bathing gown to wear. Nor did Humayun have the means to give the customary presents to the Rana (though he had with him, hidden safely, some valuable jewels), so he had to, by a ruse, take possession of the hidden valuables of his amirs. He also had to borrow money from Tardi Beg. "The treasury was empty," writes Gulbadan. "Tardi Beg Khan had a great deal of money, and the emperor having asked him for a considerable loan, he lent 80,000 ashrafis at the rate of two in ten (twenty per cent). His Majesty portioned out this money to the army. He bestowed sword-belts and cap-a-pie dresses on the rana and his sons. Many people bought fresh horses here."

In the eyes of the weary refugees, dreary Umarkot was "a beautiful place with many tanks . . . Many things were very cheap indeed; four goats could be had for one rupee," says Gulbadan. Humayun rested there for about seven weeks. He also persuaded the rana to vacate the fort for the use of his family, and lodged Hamida there, under the care of her brother Khwaja Muazzam. He and the Rajputs then set out for Sind and an uncertain future.

Four days out, when Humayun was encamped by a lake some forty kilometres from Umarkot, he received the happy news that Hamida had given birth to a son—as Abul Fazl would have it, "the nursling of Divine light had emerged from the womb of concealment into the world of manifestation." Humayun "was highly delighted" with the news, says Gulbadan, and by way of rewarding Tardi Beg, the bearer of the news, pardoned all his past offences. He then broke a pod of musk in a china bowl and divided the pieces among his men, enveloping the desert camp with fragrance and good cheer. "This is all the present I can afford to make you on the birth of my son, whose fame will I trust be one day expanded all over the world, as the perfume of the musk now fills this apartment," said Humayun. Drums were beaten, and trumpets proclaimed the birth of the prince. Humayun gave the child a name he had heard in a dream: Jalaluddin Muhammad Akbar.

HUMAYUN BROKE CAMP that same evening and continued on to Sind, eventually reaching the fertile district of Jun to the north-west of the Rann of Kachchh (Kutch), where, in a garden around which trenches were dug, he camped for the next several months. He was joined there by Hamida and the infant Akbar.

There, for a short while, Humayun's position improved as a number of local chiefs joined him, and his army swelled to some 15,000 horse.

Then, in quick succession, the usual misfortunes began to pile up on the hapless fugitive. The Rajputs, always touchy about their honour, rode off in a huff over some petty squabble—"Any attempt to assist the Mughals is a loss of labour and time," they grumbled. Munim Khan, a distinguished veteran, quarrelled with Tardi Beg, and he too departed in pique. Others followed. The fates were giving Humayun another turn over the grill.

In that bleak hour, Humayun was joined by Biram Khan, one of his distinguished generals, who had fallen into Afghan hands after the battle of Kanauj, but had managed to escape. The arrival of Biram Khan turned the face of the day. The emperor, Jauhar recalls, "was much rejoiced by the arrival of so celebrated a character".

With Biram Khan joining Humayun, there was at last a plan of action. It was clear that there was no point in Humayun lingering on in India. His position in Sind, closely invested as he was by Shah Husain, was untenable. Negotiations were therefore opened with Husain, who readily agreed to let Humayun leave Sind with honour; he even built a bridge of boats across the Indus to speed Humayun on his way.

On 11th July 1543, Humayun crossed the Indus and began his trek out of India.

In the thirteen years since his accession, Humayun had conquered Malwa and Gujarat, only to lose them soon after; he then conquered Bengal, but lost that too; and in the end lost his throne as well. He was now a destitute fugitive. It was the end of the Mughal empire, it seemed.

Chapter Three

THE AFGHAN
INTERLUDE

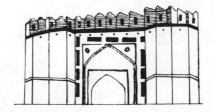

Man of Destiny

DURING HUMAYUN'S FORLORN wanderings in Sind and Rajasthan, the Afghans were nowhere in sight. Sher Shah had pursued Humayun up to the Chenab, then turned away, leaving the chase to his generals, directing them "not to engage the Emperor, but to drive him beyond the borders of the kingdom", says Abbas Khan. Sher Shah had more pressing matters to attend to than hunting down a crippled and hapless fugitive.

Sher Shah was in his mid-fifties when he took Agra, an old man. He had come a long, long way from his troubled childhood and meagre patrimony in the grubby little town of Sasaram in southern Bihar. Fortune had favoured him, but at every stage he had worked hard and acted with care and caution to take advantage of the opportunities that fate offered him. He was at last the master of Hindustan, a vast empire. But much work still remained to be done. Frontiers had to be firmed up, potential enemies combated, potential rebels neutralized. Administration had to be organized. For all that Sher Shah needed time.

And time was running out for him. "Alas!" he lamented, looking in the mirror, "I have attained the empire only when I have reached old age, and when the time for evening prayer has arrived. Had it been otherwise, the world would have seen what I would have accomplished."

EVERYTHING THAT HAPPENED in Sher Shah's life, both good and bad, had prepared him, in a steady cumulation of experience, to play the role that destiny had allotted to him. His family originally came from Roh, the highlands of the Sulaiman Range in southern Afghanistan close to the Indus. His grandfather Ibrahim, a lowly Afghan of the Sur tribe, a horse trader by profession, migrated to India during the reign of Buhlul Lodi and took to soldiering, hoping to improve his fortune. Later chroniclers would assign to Ibrahim a royal pedigree to match the status won by Sher Shah, but the truth seems to be that he was only a trader, and that too, as Abul Fazl slightingly notes, one without "any distinction among the crowd of tradesmen".

The family first settled in Punjab, then moved on to Narnaul, near Delhi, where Ibrahim was able to secure a jagir as a commander of forty. On Ibrahim's death, his son Hasan Khan inherited the jagir. Somewhere along the way, in a year that is not recorded, but probably around 1486, a son was born to Hasan, his first-born, the future Sher Shah. They named him Farid.

Hasan eventually sired eight sons by his four wives. His career too prospered, and he shifted to Bihar, where, under Lodi governor Jamal Khan, he rose to become a commander of 500, and held the parganas of Sasaram and Khavaspur Tanda in southern Bihar, close to the Rohtas hills. It was not a soft assignment. Hasan's jagir was mostly rugged hill country, only partly under cultivation, and the wilderness was infested with robbers and turbulent chieftains. But it was a good place for young Farid to hone his survival skills.

Farid's was not a happy childhood. Hasan had wearied of the faded charms of Farid's mother, and, as Abbas Khan puts it, he "did not care for or love [her] . . . but was very fond of his slave girls, and was especially attached to . . . a Hindu slave girl, and she gained such influence over Hasan Khan, that she entirely ruled him." Farid suffered with his mother, and was bitter towards his father. "Angry words often passed between Hasan and Farid," says Abbas. It is possible that Farid fell in with a bandit gang at this time. The story, attributed to Sher Shah himself and told in detail by Mughal chroniclers Mushtaqui and Abdullah, is quite credible, given the wild nature of young Farid and the bandit-infested milieu in which he lived. In medieval India, the distinction between the brigand and the chieftain or king was hazy: a brigand could grow and consolidate his power and become recognized as a king, a king could lose his power and descend to brigandage. In any case, according to the story, a close brush with death in a forest encounter chastened Farid, and he returned home.

He did not, however, remain at home, but moved on to Jaunpur, the capital of Bihar. Jaunpur broadened his horizon, roused his ambition. The city was a centre of Islamic learning in those days, and Farid immersed himself in studies, concentrating on "books of history and the lives of ancient kings", according to Abbas. It is not known how many years Farid spent in Jaunpur, nor what he did apart from studying, but he was there long enough to acquire a reputation for learning and ability, and was probably employed in some executive capacity in the provincial government.

A reconciliation was meanwhile effected between Farid and his father through the intervention of their kinsmen, and Hasan handed over the administration of his jagir to the precocious youngster. Many years later, as king, Farid would take Sultan-ul-Adil, The Just Ruler, as his title, but he had, if we are to believe contemporary chroniclers, set justice as the hallmark of his rule right from the time he assumed charge of Sasaram. "Justice alone is the mainstay of government and the source of prosperity to the governed," he is reported to have declared on that occasion. "Injustice is the most pernicious of things; it saps the foundation of the government and brings ruin upon the realm."

EVEN AT THAT young age, Farid's actions were marked by clarity of purpose and resoluteness. "I have set my heart on improving the prosperity of the district . . . and by this means I hope to establish my reputation," he told a gathering of village headmen and officers soon after taking over the administration of Sasaram. He was especially concerned with the lot of the peasants. "I shall always watch over their condition so that no man may oppress or injure them," he vowed, "for if a ruler cannot protect the humble peasantry from the lawless, it is tyranny to exact revenue from them." And he assured the cultivators: "I won't allow anyone to tyrannize over you. Be engaged heart and soul in sowing and reaping."

He then turned to tax collectors and village headmen. "I know the oppressions and exactions of which you have been guilty towards cultivators," he told them. That had to stop, he warned, for "cultivation depends on the humble peasants; if they be ill off they will produce nothing, but if prosperous they will produce much." Turning finally to soldiers, he warned them that while he would ignore their past misdeeds, he would brook no further indiscipline. "If it reaches my ears that any one has taken even a blade of grass forcibly from the ryots, I shall inflict such punishment upon him that others should take a lesson from it. I shall not allow any one to transgress my orders." At the same time, he offered to share the gains of prosperity with his soldiers. "My wish is that, as the effect of my administration, all persons, both high and low, may prosper, and no trace of oppression or violence may remain," he told them.

Would the young man be taken seriously? Words did not rule, only arms did.' To prove himself, Farid had to demonstrate that he had the will and the power to compel obedience. And he did that with ruthless efficiency, terrorizing most villages into submission, and sacking those that resisted him. "Pay me my rights; if not, I will sell your wives and children, and will not suffer you to settle anywhere again," Farid threatened the headmen. "Wherever you may go, thither will I pursue you; and to whatever village you may go, I will command the headmen to seize you and make you over to me, or else I will attack them also." The terror tactic worked, and in a short time Farid was able to establish his absolute and unquestioned sway over virtually the entire jagir.

Only the forest chiefs, mostly Cheros, an unruly Dravidian tribe whose main occupation was dacoity, remained defiant. Farid considered these tribal chieftains to be dangerous outlaws who had to be extirpated, not just forced into submission. He therefore rejected their offers to surrender, and set on their hamlets with deliberate brutality, butchering the men and enslaving the women and children. That was not, as Farid saw it, an act of mindless savagery, but a cool, judicious application of terror, essential for the security of his jagir.

After that convincing demonstration of his coercive power, Farid turned his attention to revenue and judicial matters. "If any soldier or peasant had a complaint," Abbas writes, "Farid would examine it in person, and carefully investigate the cause, nor did he ever give way to carelessness or sloth." For some seven years he thus laboured in Sasaram, in ceaseless and resolute endeavour. The results were impressive. As Abbas puts it, "In a very short time both the Parganas became prosperous and the soldiery and peasantry were alike contented . . . He gained a reputation among men and pleased all his friends and others, except a few enemies . . ."

Except a few enemies . . . There was trouble ahead for Farid. In the seventeen or eighteen years since he first left home, his father's young wife, the "Hindu slave girl", had borne her own sons, Sulaiman and Ahmad, and was understandably anxious to secure their interests. Farid's success thwarted the chances of her own children. They could rise only if he fell. And she, according to Abbas, nagged Hasan day and night, denied him her bed, even threatened to commit suicide, to gain favours for her sons. Finally Hasan, "entangled in the noose of her love", yielded to her entreaties and took away the management of the jagir from Farid and entrusted it to Sulaiman. "I know it is not right to grieve Farid, but what can I do?" Hasan confessed to those who protested against the action. "Sulaiman and his mother have driven me into this strait, nor do they give me a moment's peace."

Once again, Farid had to leave home.

THIS TIME HE went to Agra, to plead with Sultan Ibrahim Lodi to transfer his father's jagir to him. Ibrahim rejected the request outright, saying, "He is a bad man who complains against and accuses his own father." Later, however, when Hasan died, Farid was able to secure a royal firman conferring Sasaram on him. In 1520, he returned to Sasaram, a jagirdar in his own right.

That brought Farid once again into confrontation with his stepmother, who manoeuvred to secure at least a part of the jagir for her sons. The issue became further complicated when the firman of Ibrahim Lodi, under which Farid claimed Sasaram, lost its validity on the death of the sultan at Panipat. Farid therefore sought the patronage of Bihar Khan (formerly the governor, but now, after Panipat, the ruler of Bihar) for protection against the machinations of his stepmother, and to seek new avenues for his advancement in the rapidly changing political scene in Hindustan.

Entering the king's service, Farid, says Abbas, "employed himself day and night in his (the king's) business, nor did he rest one moment from it, and from this good service he gained Bihar Khan's favour, so that he had access to him in public and private and became one of his intimate friends. In consequence of his excellent arrangements he became celebrated throughout the country of Bihar." In a short time, Farid rose to become the Vakil (royal deputy) of Bihar Khan, as well as the guardian of Jalal Khan, the heir-apparent. He also received the title Sher (Tiger) Khan from the king, for his feat of killing a tiger singlehanded.

These were, however, "days of confusion" in Hindustan, following the overthrow of the Lodi dynasty, and "no man put entire confidence in another", says Abbas. Presently, misunderstandings arose between the ambitious Vakil and his insecure king, and in consequence Farid (from now on known as Sher Khan) once again lost Sasaram. And once again he set out for Agra, this time to seek succour from the Mughals. In Agra, he found a patron in Junaid Barlas, one of Babur's top amirs, and was able to recover Sasaram with Mughal help, probably during Babur's eastern campaign.

In Hindustan, it was a time of opportunity for the ambitious. The three-century-old power structure of the Delhi Sultanate had collapsed. Everything was in flux. Anything was possible. And Sher Khan was alive to every possibility.

After recovering Sasaram, Sher Khan returned to the Mughal camp. There, observing the careless ways of the Mughals, the seed of an idea took root in his fertile mind, that the Mughals could yet be driven out of India and the Afghan imperial power restored. "If luck and fortune favour me," he told the Afghan officers in the Mughal camp, "I will very shortly expel the Mughals from Hind, for the Mughals are not superior to the Afghans in battle or in single combat; but the Afghans have let the empire of Hind slip from their hands on account of their internal dissensions . . . If fortune extends a hand to me . . . I shall bring the Afghans under my control and never permit them again to become divided." But he was alone in this dream. No one took him seriously. "Come," Afghan officers used to tell their friends, "come to Sher Khan's quarters and hear his impossible boastings, which all men are laughing at." Sher Khan had become something of a camp joke.

The only person who saw Sher Khan in a different light was Babur. "Keep an eye on Sher Khan," Babur cautioned Mir Khalifa, his minister. "He is a clever man, and the marks of royalty are visible on his forehead . . . As soon as I saw this man, it entered into my mind that he ought to be arrested, for I find in him the qualities of greatness and marks of mightiness." Mir Khalifa advised Babur against arresting Sher Khan, saying that it would scare away the Afghans who were just beginning to flock to the Mughals, and that in any case Sher Khan did not have the power to do any mischief. So the matter was dropped. But Sher Khan sensed that he had come under the adverse notice of Babur. "The emperor today looked much at me, and said something to the minister, and cast evil glances towards me," he said to his men when he got back to his quarters, and that very day fled from the Mughal camp to return to Sasaram. When Babur was told of Sher Khan's flight, he reproached Mir Khalifa, "If you had not hindered me, I would have arrested him at once; he is about to do something, God only knows what!"

IN BIHAR, SHER KHAN rejoined the service of the sultan, who graciously restored him to his favoured position as Vakil. The timing of his return was fortuitous. A short while later, Bihar Khan died, to be succeeded by his young son, Jalal Khan, with Dudu, the king's widow, as the regent. When Dudu too died soon after, Sher Khan became the de facto ruler of Bihar.

Around that time, Sher Khan strengthened his position through two strategic marriages, both with rich and childless widows. By one marriage he acquired the strong fort of Chunar, and by the other great wealth. These resources enabled him to create for himself what was in effect a state within the state. "Sher Khan during a space of four years elevated himself to a state of complete independence," writes Niamatullah, "and gained the attachment of the greater part of the army by the bounties and honours lavished upon them; so much so that within the frontiers of Bihar no one dared disobey his orders."

Sher Khan's career suffered a major setback, however, when Mahmud Lodi, the brother of Ibrahim Lodi, as the rightful heir to the

Lodi throne, took over Bihar by chasing away Jalal Khan. Sher Khan then reverted to his old position as a mere jagirdar. And when Mahmud summoned the local Afghan chieftains to join him against the Mughals, Sher Khan had no alternative but to obey. But he did so reluctantly. He had no faith in Mahmud, and so tried to protect his interests against the expected certain defeat of Mahmud by parleying with Humayun and offering to withdraw his forces without engaging when the Afghan and Mughal armies met.

Sher Khan kept his promise, but demurred when Humayun demanded that he surrender Chunar as well. For four months he withstood the Mughal siege of the fort, but finally offered to submit. And Humayun, his attention meanwhile diverted by developments in Malwa and Gujarat, hastily accepted the offer and pulled out.

Sher Khan then returned to the service of Jalal Khan (who had been restored to his throne by the Mughals as their vassal) and once again became the virtual ruler of Bihar. His main concern at this time was to rebuild the self-confidence of Afghans, many of whom, on account of their misfortunes, had taken to the life of mendicants. Sher Khan brought them back to soldiering, using coercion when necessary, even putting a few to death and declaring that "he would kill every Afghan who refused to be a soldier".

The old but dormant dream of Sher Khan, of driving out the Mughals and restoring Afghan imperial power, now became an obsession with him. Portents, by which medieval man set much store, favoured him. Niamatullah reports that one night, while Sher Khan was, as was his habit, secretly depositing cash and clothes beside sleeping mendicants in the bazaar in Jaunpur, a dervish suddenly raised his head and exclaimed, "God be praised! The Emperor of Delhi has come." Sher Khan took it as a prophecy.

But he was in no hurry. His immediate objective was to preserve his power and position in Bihar against the intrigues of envious amirs, mainly Lohani Afghans, who were rivals of the Sur tribe to which Sher Khan belonged. Besides, he had to neutralize Jalal Khan, who, now old enough to want to govern and not just reign, sought to subvert the Khan's authority by secretly supporting the Lohanis. There was also a threat of invasion from Bengal.

But nothing daunted Sher Khan. He converted every one of the problems to his advantage by boldly seizing the initiative from his adversaries—he repulsed the invading Bengal forces, took to the offensive himself and annexed a large tract of Bengal, and then went on to use the leverage of his enhanced power and prestige to discomfit the Lohanis. Pushed to a corner, his adversaries plotted to assassinate him with the connivance of Jalal Khan. The plot failed. And that made Jalal Khan's position in Bihar untenable, so he, a master in terror of his servant, fled to Bengal for refuge, along with several Lohani nobles. Their flight suited Sher Khan perfectly. His authority in Bihar was now untrammeled, except for his nominal subordination to the Mughal emperor, in whose name he continued to read the khutbah and mint coins.

After the flight of Jalal Khan, Sher Khan could have proclaimed himself king and ended the ambiguity of his position. But to do so would have been to formally renounce the Mughal overlordship and openly challenge Humayun. Sher Khan was not yet ready to do that. The throne of Bihar was left vacant.

Sher Khan kept up the pretence of subservience to the emperor for some more years, till he had annexed all of Bengal in a series of major battles. Paradoxically, even Humayun's victories against Afghans— against Mahmud Lodi in Bihar and Bahadur Shah in Gujarat—helped Sher Khan's rise. The old Afghan aristocracy had previously mocked him as an upstart, calling him derisively The New Man, but now, after the fall of Gujarat to the Mughals, they began to flock to him. "Several powerful chiefs, who had at first scorned to enter Sher Khan's service, when they saw his power day by day increasing, put their pride aside and volunteered to serve under him," says Abbas. The New Man had become the new hero.

MEANWHILE HUMAYUN, BACK. in Agra from Gujarat, realized that Sher Khan, though nominally still his vassal, had, by his victories in Bengal, grown far too powerful to remain under the Mughal wing. Yet Humayun was slow to act. He first called for a report on Sher Khan from Hindu Beg, the Mughal governor at Jaunpur. And Hindu Beg sanguinely wrote: "Sher Khan is a loyal servant of your Majesty and strikes coins and reads the khutbah in your name, and has not transgressed the boundaries of your Majesty's territory or done anything since your departure which could be any cause of annoyance to you."

That was indeed the factual position. There was no outward act to indict Sher Khan. Even in the Bengal districts that he had annexed, he was reading the khutbah in the name of Humayun. But Hindu Beg, whom Sher Khan had won over with lavish presents, failed to probe beneath appearances to assess Sher Khan's true potential. Humayun was told the facts, but not the truth. Thus misled, he deemed that no immediate action was required against Sher Khan, and this decision gave the Khan a free hand in Bengal. By the time Humayun finally decided to act, it was too late, and his strategy all wrong.

The tussle between Humayun and Sher Khan was unusually long drawn out—if Humayun was sluggish, Sher Khan was cautious and shifty, so that the conflict that began in July 1537, when Humayun set out from Agra against Sher Khan, ended only three years later, in May 1540, with the rout of Humayun at Kanauj.

Peaceable Kingdom

FROM KANAUJ IT was a headlong flight out of India for the Mughals, with Sher Shah in hot pursuit. After chasing off Humayun from Lahore, Sher Shah remained for a while in Punjab, securing the vulnerable north-west frontier.

Meanwhile, there was trouble in Bengal. For the rulers of India, Bengal had always been a problem province, and its capital Gaur, formerly called Lakhnauti, had long been known by the sinister sobriquet Bulghakpur, the City of Strife. Sher Shah had left Khizr Khan, a trusted veteran, as the governor of Bengal, when he set out westward in pursuit of Humayun. But with Sher Shah far away in Punjab, it was not long before the peculiar chemistry of Bengal began to work on Khizr Khan. He married the daughter of Sultan Mahmud, the former king of Bengal, took to sitting on the *toki* (upper palace) after the manner of the rulers of Bengal, and, though he did not dare to assume the royal title, generally began to act as if he were king.

The news infuriated Sher Shah. He immediately set out for Bengal, and by forced marches suddenly appeared in Gaur, to surprise and confront Khizr Khan. Khizr Khan tried to mollify Sher Shah by submitting humbly and arranging a regal reception for him, but Sher Shah remained unrelenting. "Why did you without my order take in marriage the daughter of Sultan Mahmud, and seat yourself on the *toki*?" he rebuked, and ordered him to be put in chains and punished severely, as a warning to potential rebels. "It becomes not a noble of the State to do a single act without the King's permission," warned Sher Shah.

Exemplary punishment of rebels was necessary to discourage rebellion, but that in itself was not be enough, for the basic problem was the structural weakness of the state. Provincial insubordination had been a perennial problem in the Delhi Sultanate, and Sher Shah, who knew his history well, realized that the key solution to the problem was to set up a strong administrative grid to integrate the empire.

During the long journey from Punjab to Bengal, Sher Shah had apparently thought over the problem thoroughly, for by the time he got to Gaur, he had a solution ready. To curtail the power of the governor and to increase primary imperial control, he split Bengal into a number of districts (Sarkars) and made the district chiefs directly responsible to the emperor. Simultaneously, he replaced the provincial governor with a provincial coordinator. The coordinator had no military power, no authority over the officers of the districts, and therefore no sinews to challenge imperial authority; he was merely the emperor's eyes and ears.

In the districts themselves Sher Shah effected a separation of powers, to prevent the dangerous concentration of power in any one officer—he entrusted the maintenance of law and order to the chief military administrator, while revenue and civil administration, including civil justice, was assigned to the Chief Munsif. A Kazi looked after religious affairs. Elaborating the pattern further, Sher Shah divided the districts into sub-districts (Parganas), each with an administrative structure similar to that of the district. Major towns were treated as separate administrative units, with the Kotwal (town prefect) as the officer responsible for general administration and the maintenance of law and order. To prevent anyone from developing a vested interest in his territory, Sher Shah rotated provincial officers every two years.

He did not disturb the traditional village organization, except to rationalize its revenue administration, but he strictly required the village headman to bear personal responsibility for the crimes committed in his village—if the criminal was not caught, the headman had to suffer the punishment, on the premise (says Abbas) that "headmen and cultivators were alike thieves", and nothing happened in a village without the knowledge of the headman. The system did not necessarily yield justice, but it deterred crime by ensuring that someone or other got punished for every crime. "In the days of Sher Shah and of Islam Shah," notes Abbas, "the headmen used to protect the limits of their own villages, lest any thief or robber . . . might injure a traveller, and so be the means of their destruction and death."

Such general awe of government was unusual in medieval India, for the sweep of royal authority normally went no farther than the immediate reach of the king's arms. Sher Shah overcame this limitation by setting up several military outposts (Thanas) in the provinces, thereby greatly increasing his military control. On the whole, Sher Shah's was an excellent system of checks and balances, to avert rebellion and to ensure effective government.

Sher Shah was a superb practitioner of realpolitik, but not a radical innovator. He was not interested in abstract ideas, but only in doing what was necessary to make his government effective. He, says Abbas, "made certain laws, both from his own ideas, and by extracting them from the works of the learned." He revived several proven but defunct institutions of the Delhi Sultanate and adapted them to his needs. Practicality was his byword. He did not impose a uniform system throughout his empire, but kept everything flexible to meet specific circumstances. The administrative restructuring that he affected in Bengal, for example, was only for Bengal. In provinces like Ajmer, Malwa and Punjab, Sher Shah retained the prevailing system of military governorship.

PREVENTION OF FRAUD was a mania with Sher Shah. He trusted no one. From the highest to the lowest, all officers were susceptible to corruption, he knew, so he set up an elaborate network of confidential agents to keep an eye on royal officers and to report to him on what was happening in the empire, for, as he put it, "the courtiers and ministers, for purposes of their own, do not report to the king the whole state of the kingdom."

Eradication of corruption was, for him, not an issue of morality, but of efficiency. "A king should not have corrupt Vakils or Viziers," he maintained, "for a receiver of bribes is dependent on the giver of bribes, and one who is dependent is unfit for the office of Vizier, for he is an interested personage, and to an interested person loyalty and truth in the administration of the kingdom are lost." As he candidly admitted, "The corruption of ministers of contemporary princes was the means of my acquiring the worldly kingdom I possess." He would not let the same fate befall his own kingdom.

As a disciplinarian he was uncompromising, but he was also fair in his dealings with his men. "The stipend and the maintenance which I may agree to give you, I will pay you in full, and not diminish them by a single falus (copper coin), but you shall not oppress or quarrel with anyone," he exhorted those who entered his service. "If you do, I shall visit you with such punishment as shall be an example to others." To ensure that the common soldier got a fair deal, and the government was well served, the salary of each soldier was fixed by Sher Shah personally, and was paid directly by the government. "He himself fixed the monthly salary by looking at the men, and in his presence he had the descriptive rolls taken down and the horse branded," notes Abbas. This combination of fairness and firmness enabled Sher Shah to sustain high morale and efficiency among his officers and men.

He maintained a large and well-equipped standing army directly under his command; in addition, army divisions were stationed at different strategic points of the empire, which again were supplemented by feudal levies in times of need. To prevent malpractices in the army, Sher Shah revived two old regulations of Alauddin Khilji—horses were required to be branded to ensure that they were not lent out from contingent to contingent at the time of roll call; similarly, descriptive rolls of soldiers were maintained to prevent substitutions. Sher Shah, says Mushtaqui, would not pay salary or allowance to anyone even in his harem without having their horses branded. Even sweepers had to have their descriptive rolls recorded.

Parallel to these administrative reforms, Sher Shah also built the infrastructure he needed to govern efficiently. He constructed a number of new forts and planned to build several more. "If my life lasts long enough, I will build a fort in every Sarkar, on a suitable spot, which may in times of trouble become a refuge of the oppressed and a check to the contumacious," he stated. "And I am rebuilding all the earthen-work caravanserais in brick, that they also may serve for the protection and safety of the highway." He repaired old highways and laid out several new roads. "He constructed a road from Gaur to the river Indus," says Mushtaqui, but it is more likely that Sher Shah only repaired and realigned the road, for there had been a highway along that grid from ancient times. Feeder roads linked Lahore with Multan, Agra with Rajasthan and Malwa. The major highways were lined on both sides with shade and fruit trees, and had, at every six kilometres or so, a caravanserai, about 1700 of them in all. These serais, while providing security and convenience to travellers, also served as intelligence gathering and relaying centres (*dak chauki*), where post horses to carry government mail were stabled.

Sher Shah could effectively control what happened in the empire, for he knew much of what was brewing. He paid thorough and unblinking attention to all aspects of government so that, though his reign over Hindustan lasted a mere five years, he earned an enduring reputation as one of the most efficient rulers in the long history of India.

If Abbas is to be believed, north India under Sher Shah was probably the safest place in the world for the traveller. "Travellers and wayfarers, during the time of Sher Shah's reign, were relieved from the trouble of keeping watch; nor did they fear to halt even in the midst of a desert," writes Abbas. "They encamped at night at every place, desert or inhabited, without fear: they placed their goods and property on the plain, and turned out their mules to graze, and themselves slept with minds at ease and free from care, as if in their own house; and the zemindars, for fear that any mischief should occur to the travellers, and that they should suffer or be arrested on account of it, kept watch over them. And in the time of Sher Shah's rule, a decrepit old woman might place a basket full of gold ornaments on her head and go on a journey, and no thief or robber would come near her, for fear of the punishments which Sher Shah inflicted." Much of this is no doubt hyperbole, but there is certainly a core of truth in it, for nostalgia for the benevolent rigour of Sher Shah's peaceable reign persisted for many generations.

WITH PEACE AND security came prosperity. From his early days in Sasaram, Sher Shah had given high priority to caring for the peasant. Where the peasant is ruined, the king is ruined, he believed. He therefore took great care to ensure that the protectors of peasants—the army and the revenue officials—did not, as often happened, become their oppressors.

Sher Shah was especially careful to ensure that the movements of the army did not damage crops. "When he marched, he personally examined into the state of the cultivation, and stationed horsemen round it to prevent people from trespassing on any one's field," Abbas reports. "If he saw any man injuring a field, he would cut off his ears with his own hand, and hanging the corn (which the man had plucked off) round his neck, would have him to be paraded through the camp. And if from the narrowness of the road any cultivation was unavoidably destroyed, he would send amirs, with a surveyor, to measure the cultivation so destroyed, and give compensation in money to the cultivators. If unavoidably the tents of his soldiery were pitched near cultivation, the soldiers themselves watched it, lest any one else should injure it, and they should be blamed and be punished by Sher Shah, who showed no favour or partiality in the dispensation of justice. If he entered an enemy's country, he did not enslave or plunder the peasantry of that country, nor destroy their cultivation. `For,' said he, `the cultivators are blameless, they submit to those in power; and if I oppress them they will abandon their villages, and the country will be ruined and deserted, and it will be a long time before it again becomes prosperous.'"

This regard for the welfare of the peasant was also reflected in the flexible revenue system of Sher Shah, which accommodated the diverse customs and cropping patterns in different parts of the empire—in some places, land was surveyed and revenue settled according to the fertility of the soil; in other places, as in Multan, for example, there was no survey, and the state merely collected a portion of the gross produce. The jagirdari and zemindari systems were allowed to continue in some areas. Sher Shah's revenue system was a hybrid, but it worked well, and would be the base on which the Mughals, and later the British, would build their revenue administration.

Records are not clear about Sher Shah's revenue demands—they probably varied from place to place, and ranged from one-fourth to one-third of the produce. The dues could be paid in cash or kind, cash being preferred by the government. Revenue officers were instructed to be lenient at the time of assessment but strict during collection, making adjustments only for damage to crops due to natural and other calamities, for Sher Shah's objective was to leave the peasant with sufficient surplus to encourage him to sustain and expand cultivation, and at the same time to ensure that the peasant did not cheat the king of his dues, nor hinder his authority.

The same concerns ruled Sher Shah's dealings with traders. "He directed his governors and Amins (revenue officers) to compel the people to treat merchants and travellers well in every way, and not to injure them at all, and if a merchant should die by the way, not to stretch out the hand of oppression and violence on his goods as if they were unowned," writes Abbas. To encourage trade, Sher Shah simplified trade imposts, collecting taxes only at the point of entry and the point of sale, and abolishing all irregular levies. "No one dared to levy other customs, either on the road or at the ferries, in town or village," writes Abbas. "Sher Shah, moreover, forbade his officials to purchase anything in the bazaars except at the usual bazaar rates and prices." Trade also benefited from the general prosperity of rural India at this time, and from the security and convenience of the roads and caravanserais that Sher Shah built. His currency reforms, by which he standardized the metal content of gold, silver and copper coins, also facilitated trade. So good were the currency standards he set that they endured through the entire Mughal period, and became the basis of the coinage under the British.

Sher Shah, true to his title, set high value on even-handed administration of justice, and there are many tales about his fairness and rigour. One such story is about the punishment he is said to have meted out to his son, Adil Khan. The prince, while riding an elephant through Agra, happened to look over a crumbled compound wall and see the wife of a shopkeeper undressed and bathing. Smitten by her beauty, he "fixed his eyes upon her" and threw a paan at her. When the woman, fearing that her honour was compromised, tried to kill herself, her husband complained to Sher Shah. The sultan then decreed that the prince's wife should suffer the same indignity at the hand of the merchant, saying that, in the administration of justice, the prince and the peasant were the same in his eyes. The sentence however was not carried out, as the merchant prudently withdrew his complaint.

The judgment that Sher Shah passed against his son was not arbitrary or unconventional, but strictly in conformity with the Islamic judicial principle of retaliation, by which the offender is made to suffer exactly the same injury he inflicted on the victim. Sher Shah worked entirely within Islamic judicial tradition; what was exceptional about him was his thoroughness and impartiality in enforcing the law, so it was said of him:

> Sher Shah, he in dread of whom,
> The lion and the goat drank at the same source.

It was equally remarkable that Sher Shah was able to keep the proud and turbulent Afghans totally pliable to his will. "Sher Shah's authority, whether he was absent or present, was completely established over the race of Afghans," says Abbas. "There was not a creature who dared to act in opposition to his regulations . . . During his time, all quarrelling, disputing, fighting, and turmoiling, which is the nature of the Afghans, was altogether quieted."

IN RELIGION SHER SHAH was an orthodox and devout Sunni—Abbas claims that he never ate breakfast except in the company of the ulema and pious men. In the treatment of Hindus, he followed the usual policy of the Delhi Sultanate—they were treated as a subject people, but were not unduly oppressed. He retained a fair number of Hindu officers in his service; his infantry was almost exclusively Hindu, and his musketeers predominantly so. There is no record of any communal disturbance during his reign.

As was incumbent on kings, he practised charity on a large scale. His kitchen, Abbas reports, "was very extensive, for several thousand horsemen and private followers . . . fed there, and there was a general order that if any soldier or religious personage or any cultivator should be in need of food, he should feed at the king's kitchen, and should not be allowed to famish. Places for the dispensing of food to the poor and destitute, and to all necessitous persons, were established . . . The daily cost of these meals . . . was 500 gold pieces (ashrafis)."

Further, he gave stipends from the treasury to "destitute people, who were unable to provide for their own subsistence, like the blind, the old, the weak in body, widows and the sick," says Abbas. And "to every pious Afghan who came into his presence from Afghanistan, Sher Shah used to give money to an amount exceeding his expectations, and he would say, `This is your share of the kingdom of Hind, which has fallen into my hands; this is assigned to you, come every year to receive it.' And to his own tribe and family of Sur, who dwelt in the land of Roh, he sent an annual stipend in money, in proportion to the numbers of his family and retainers; and during the period of his dominion no Afghan, whether in Hind or Roh, was in want, but all became men of substance."

Sher Shah looked on his charities as an investment to earn divine favour. "It is incumbent upon kings to give grants to imams," he used to say, "for the prosperity and populousness of the cities of Hind are dependent on the imams and holy men . . . Whoever wishes that God Almighty should make him great, should cherish the ulema and pious persons, that he may obtain honour in the world and felicity in the next."

In his short reign Sher Shah did not have much time to indulge in the royal pastime of building new cities and palaces. He did however begin (but could not complete) the construction of a new walled city in Delhi, close to the Yamuna in the place of Humayun's fort, which later came to be known as Purana Qila (Old Fort), where the mosque he built is of some architectural interest. For some inexplicable reason, he also demolished the ancient city of Kanauj, and built a new fort there, which was, according to Abbas, a "very unpopular act". And he built his own mausoleum in Sasaram. In architecture, he generally followed the prevailing style, and his original contribution was negligible.

THE RANGE OF Sher Shah's achievements during his all too brief reign was phenomenal. He was extremely hardworking. His day began "when two-thirds of the night were passed", probably at around 3 a.m., when he had a bath and spent some time in prayers and devotions. At dawn he held his first meeting with his officers, and was thereafter continually engaged in work until bedtime, the work interrupted only for meals and obligatory prayers, and a short nap in the afternoon. He managed his time well, dividing, as Abbas puts it, "both day and night into portions for each separate business, and suffered no sloth or idleness to find its way to him."

As he drove himself hard, so did he drive everyone else, in the spirit that, as one of his officers put it, "Ease is for women, it is shameful to honourable men." But in all that he demanded of his officers and men, he himself set the best example, paying minute attention to every detail of government, often working shoulder to shoulder with his men, even in digging trenches. His attitude, as he himself put it, was: "It behoves the great to be always active."

The Fiery End

THE CARE AND thoroughness that Sher Shah displayed in his administration were also evident in the manner in which he set about expanding and consolidating his empire. His means, if judged by chivalric code, were not always honourable, but the question of honour seldom troubled medieval rulers, as long as they could vindicate themselves by being victorious. Sher Shah's adversaries often charged that "deceit and cunning are his ways", but their real grievance was that he outsmarted them.

Sher Shah generally preferred to attain his goals by persuasion and guile, without bloodshed, but if forced to fight he used stratagems to ensure victory and minimize casualties in his army. His well trained soldiers were his chief asset, and he was reluctant to squander them. "Sher Shah would not give the head of one of his soldiers for a kingdom," says Badauni.

Persuasion worked well for Sher Shah in Gwalior, Malwa and Ranthambhor, where his "smooth-tongued ambassadors" were able to pressurize local chieftains into submitting without a fight. But that did not work with Puran Mal, the raja of Raisen, who refused to surrender. Sher Shah then decided, according to Abbas, to "take the fort by the exercise of his skill and prudence." The ensuing siege lasted several months, but in the end heavy Afghan bombardment forced Puran Mal to seek accommodation, and on Sher Shah giving him a solemn assurance that he "shall suffer no injury in property or person", the raja came out of Raisen with his family and retinue.

Sher Shah did not mean to keep his word. With treachery in mind he allotted to the Rajputs a camp-site in the midst of his army, and had them watched carefully, to prevent them from fleeing. Then, late one night a few days later, he ordered his troops to assemble secretly and at sunrise encircle the Rajputs. As Abbas describes the scene, when the Afghans surrounded his camp, Puran Mal went "into the tent of his beloved wife, Ratnavali, who sang Hindi melodies very sweetly, cut off her head," and ordered his captains also to slay their women and children. "While the Hindus were employed in putting their women and families to death, the Afghans on all sides commenced the slaughter of the Hindus. Puran Mal and his companions . . . failed not to exhibit valour and gallantry, but in the twinkling of an eye all were slain." Only a few women and children among the Rajputs survived. A daughter of Puran Mal who fell to the Afghans was given to itinerant minstrels to be brought up as a dancing girl; three of his young nephews were castrated.

For his inexcusable treachery, Sher Shah had of course an excuse. He was, he claimed, obliged to slaughter the Rajputs for their heinous crime of enslaving Muslim women and turning them into dancing girls and concubines; moreover he had, he said, once taken a vow, when seriously ill, to extirpate the Rajputs of Raisen. As for breaking his pledged word, his conscience was clear, for the ulema had assured him that no faith need be kept with infidels.

After Raisen, Sher Shah, rejecting the counsel of his amirs to invade the Deccan, turned against Maldev of Marwar, "that accursed infidel", as Sher Shah described him. Maldev was the most dangerous of Sher Shah's enemies, a powerful neighbour. He had greatly extended his territories during the Mughal-Afghan tussle, and now his frontier lay a bare fifty kilometres from Delhi. Wedged as they were so close together, a clash between Sher Shah and Maldev was inevitable, especially as fractious Rajput chiefs envious of Maldev's growth at their expense were enticing Sher Shah into Rajasthan.

Sher Shah prepared very carefully for the Marwar campaign, assembling the largest army he had ever deployed, an army so large that, says Abbas, "its whole length and breadth were never visible together." Despite such overwhelming power, Sher Shah proceeded with customary caution, entrenching himself at each halt. "One of the maxims of Sher Shah, from which he never departed, was to throw up an entrenched position round his army, no matter how few the enemy might be," writes Badauni. About midway between Ajmer and Jodhpur, Sher Shah's advance was blocked by Maldev. The two armies remained facing each other for about a month, without engaging. But soon Sher Shah found himself in a bind—he was running out of provisions and could not afford to lie entrenched for long; on the other hand, he was reluctant to risk a battle. As Badauni puts it with partisan fervour, Sher Shah did not want "to involve his army in a calamity with the ignorant, boar-natured and currish Hindus."

Sher Shah therefore decided to use a ruse to ensure victory—he forged some letters, purportedly from Maldev's commanders to Sher Shah, offering to betray Maldev, and had the letters dropped in the Rajput camp. When the letters fell into Maldev's hands, as was intended, he suspected the worst. And, despite protestations of innocence by his chiefs, he cancelled the planned attack on the Afghans, and that very night withdrew from the field with the bulk of his army.

This left a stain on the honour of the Rajput chiefs, which could be washed off only with their own blood. At dawn the next day, the chiefs and some 12,000 of their men, all bent on heroic death, charged into the Afghan army, and by sheer impetuosity smashed through the enemy frontline and threatened the very person of Sher Shah, before they could be halted and cut down. "I had nearly given the kingdom of Delhi for a millet seed," Sher Shah would later comment ruefully, recalling the great risk he had taken to conquer the barren lands of Marwar.

FROM MARWAR, SHER SHAH advanced into Mewar—where Rana Udai Singh surrendered Chitor without a fight—and then, turning sharply eastward, proceeded to Kalinjar in Bundelkhand, where a grim fate awaited him.

According to Abbas, it was a siren that enticed Sher Shah to Kalinjar, a Patar dancing girl of Raja Kirat Singh of whom Sher Shah "had heard exceeding praise", though he no doubt had other good reasons too for attacking the fort. Kalinjar, a strong fort, was a prize in itself. And, after the easy fall of the renowned fort of Chitor, Sher Shah had probably expected the prompt capitulation of Kalinjar. But the fort proved to be impregnable, the raja resolute. The siege dragged on for nearly a year.

Finally, trenches were run to the ramparts, and close to the fort an observation tower built, which overtopped the fort walls, so the Afghans could pick off the people in the fort with arrows and muskets. On Friday, 22nd May 1545, Sher Shah as usual had breakfast with Muslim divines, and then ascended the observation tower and amused himself for a while shooting arrows into the fort. He then came down to supervise the firing of huqqa (rocket grenades) into the fort. As ill fate would have it, one of the rockets hit the fort wall, "and recoiling with great force, exploded . . . [and] its fragments fell among the other grenades, which exploded, burning Sher Shah severely from head to foot," reports Badauni.

Physicians rushed to attend on him, but there was nothing that they could do to save his life. His body was on fire. In the tent where Sher Shah lay, "the air was terribly hot," says Badauni, "and although they sprinkled his body constantly with sandal [paste] and rose water, it was utterly useless to relieve the scorching heat whose intensity increased hour by hour."

Sher Shah remained fitfully conscious. "Whenever he recovered his consciousness a little, he shouted to his men encouraging them to seize the fort," says Badauni, "and if any one came to see him he signed to him to go and fight, so that in his absence the amirs in command worked harder than if he had been present and behaved with utmost gallantry." Sher Shah would not die defeated.

A few hours later, by the afternoon prayer, the fort fell. "At the very moment of hearing the good tidings of victory, he yielded up his life," says Badauni. "Praise be to God! This was my very desire," Sher Shah breathed. These were his last words.

SHER SHAH'S BODY was temporarily interred at Kalinjar, but was later borne to Sasaram, his childhood home, to be buried in a mausoleum he had built there, close to the grave of his father, whose love-hate for him was the friction that had initially fired Sher Shah's ambitions.

Who would succeed the sultan? Sher Shah had two surviving sons, Adil Khan and Jalal Khan, but he had not nominated either as his successor. It therefore fell to the Afghan amirs to choose the king, and they, meeting in an emergency conclave, chose Jalal Khan, the younger son. It was the natural choice. Jalal had proved himself time and again in battle—in fact, it was he who had won the first battle for Sher Shah against the Mughals, at the Teliyagarhi pass—while Adil Khan was inclined to indolence and sensuality. Moreover, Jalal was close by at Rewa, while Adil was far away at Ranthambhor, and that too weighed in favour of Jalal, for the throne could not be left vacant for long without setting off disorder in the state. Jalal was therefore quickly brought to Kalinjar, and four days after the death of Sher Shah, on 26th May 1545, he was enthroned as king. Jalal assumed the title Islam Shah, which was corrupted in common usage as Salim Shah.

The enthronement itself, however, meant little. For the throne to be truly his, Islam Shah had to win it all over again on his own. As a Persian poet puts it,

> None, by inheritance,
>   can kingdom grasp,
> Till he, with both his hands,
>   the sword doth smite.

Islam Shah, very much his father's son, would prove himself equal to the challenge, but initially there were problems and uncertainties. Would not the amirs who had put Islam Shah on the throne exact a price for their support? And if the price were not paid, play king-makers again? What would Adil Khan do? He had acquiesced in his younger brother's accession, but would he not be the nucleus around which disgruntled or ambitious nobles would coalesce? Would the great Afghan amirs—many of whom, like Khavass Khan, had toiled shoulder to shoulder with Sher Shah to build the Sur empire—give Islam Shah the same respect and allegiance they had given his father?

The first imperative of Islam Shah was to eliminate the potential threat from his brother, and he set about this task with a deviousness that Sher Shah would have admired. Soon after his accession, he wrote to Adil Khan in Ranthambhor offering to vacate the throne in his favour. "As you were at a distance, and I was near, I have, in order to put down all disturbances, attended to the protection of the army up to the time of your arrival," wrote Islam Shah. "I have no other alternative but to serve and obey you." Adil Khan was surprised by the offer, but not fooled—he demanded that his safety should be guaranteed by four great nobles before he came to visit Islam Shah.

The guarantee given, the two brothers met near Sikri and together they set out for Agra. In Agra, Islam Shah cajoled Adil to ascend the throne, and himself stood aside, flawlessly playing the role of a deferential brother and faithful subject. But this was just theatre, as even the easygoing Adil surely knew. In any case, kingship was a burden that Adil was reluctant to shoulder, so he rose from the throne, made Islam Shah sit on it, made obeisance, and withdrew to Bayana, his chosen jagir.

This, however, did not settle the issue between the brothers. As long as Adil was around, Islam Shah could not be secure on the throne. He tried to solve the problem quietly, by sending a confidential officer to Bayana with "golden fetters" to imprison Adil. But the prince evaded capture and, gaining the support of a few powerful amirs, advanced on Agra against his brother. In the ensuing battle he was routed, and he "fled alone and unaccompanied towards the hills of Bhata, and no one knew what had become of him," says Abdullah.

In the fratricidal war, some of the nobles, including Khavass Khan, had sided with Adil Khan, and that soured the temper of Islam Shah, who was in any case, as Abdullah says, "a monarch of vindictive disposition". He suspected widespread disaffection and conspiracy among his amirs, a reasonable conjecture given the Afghan predilections. An attempt on his life at this time further embittered him, and he resolved:

> I am so vexed with my friends,
> I will never take one
> even to save myself from ruin.

ISLAM SHAH THEN embarked on a cold-blooded and systematic purge of the great nobles of the state, spreading such terror and consternation that in a short time no one dared to challenge his authority. But the mowing down of the veterans deprived the state of talent. Islam Shah had inherited his father's relentlessness, but not his tact; he, unlike Sher Shah, had to coerce his amirs into obedience instead of winning their loyalty.

But in his own way Islam Shah was quite a remarkable monarch, and even in the shadow of his great father, he stands out as a ruler of substantial achievements. He further improved on the administrative machinery that Sher Shah had built, and sent, according to Badauni, "written orders to all the Sarkars, containing comprehensive instructions on all important points of religion, and all political and civil questions, entering into the minutest essential detail, and dealing with all regulations which might ' be of service to the soldiery and civil population, to the merchants and other various classes." The main thrust of his policies was to secure the absolute subordination of nobles to royal authority. With this objective, he abolished the jagir system altogether and paid amirs in cash from the treasury, deprived them of the privilege of keeping war elephants, overhauled the organization of the army, garrisoned royal troops at strategic centres throughout the empire, and augmented the intelligence network by building additional caravanserais between those built by Sher Shah.

Knowing the potency of symbols, he reserved certain paraphernalia, such as the purple tent, exclusively for royal use, introduced new court customs that set the king on a plane far above the nobles, and ordered durbars to be held in districts on all Fridays, when officers were required to make their obeisance to the shoes and quiver of the sultan as symbols of royal authority. The amirs resented these innovations "as acts tending to dishonour them", and that probably was in part Islam Shah's purpose. There was a certain brashness about him, a callous disregard for the feelings of others. Still, his reforms were by and large the logical extensions of the centralization policies of his father.

Islam Shah did not have any major conquest to his credit, but this was more due to lack of opportunity than due to lack of ambition or skill. He was in fact high-spirited and impetuous in battle. Thus when he heard that Humayun, having recovered Kabul, had crossed the Indus and intruded into Hindustan, his response was instantaneous. "Islam Shah just at the very moment when this tidings arrived, had applied a leech to his throat," writes Badauni, "but instantly took it off, dashed some water upon his head, and binding up his throat with linen rags, ordered his army to proceed." He would not even wait for bullocks to be collected to pull the cannons, but ordered soldiers to pull them instead, though "some of the large mortars were of such a size that it took one or two thousand men, more or less, to drag each one." The advance, however, did not lead to battle, because by the time Islam Shah got to Lahore, Humayun had retreated to Kabul.

For all the violence in his life, Islam Shah died in bed, but painfully. In November 1554, when he was in Gwalior, his favourite residence, he was suddenly taken ill "by a painful retention of urine, and a disease of the bladder", reports Abdullah. Further, he was "afflicted by an impostume in his privy parts", which he cauterized himself, with fatal consequences.

On his death-bed Islam Shah regretted nothing, but acknowledged his human condition, and lamented to one of his amirs, "O Taj Khan, I had great confidence in my own strength, and I have subdued all men. But this thing is stronger than I am, and I find myself weaker and more helpless than an ant. I now know myself!" He passed away on 22nd November, after a reign of nine years and six months. Abul Fazl pays the ultimate accolade to Islam Shah and Sher Shah by stating that if they had been in the Mughal service, it would have been an invaluable advantage. "Both father and son behaved properly in the management of affairs," he writes.

ISLAM SHAH SEEMS to have had a presentiment of what would happen after his death. He suspected—Badauni says that this was based on his knowledge of physiognomy—that his cousin Mubariz Khan (son of Sher Shah's younger brother Nizam) was conspiring to usurp the throne. "If you value your child, keep clear of your brother," he had warned his wife, Bibi Bai, sister of Mubariz. But she had said, "My brother spends all his time in amusing himself, and the robe of royalty is in no way suitable to his standard of ambition."

Bibi Bai did not know her brother.

On the death of Islam Shah, his twelve-year-old son, Firuz Khan, was raised to the throne in Gwalior. Soon after, Mubariz Khan came visiting and, on the pretext of offering homage to his nephew, barged into the royal chambers. Bibi Bai at once sensed what was in store, and fell at her brother's feet to implore: "Ah my brother, spare the life of this poor harmless boy, and let me take my own away and bear him away to some place where no one will have a trace of him, and where he will have nothing to do with sovereignty, nay, will not even mention the name of kingship." But Mubariz, who had earlier feigned madness to escape being liquidated by Islam Shah, tore the boy away from his mother, and before her very eyes cut off his head.

A few days later Mubariz ascended the throne as Adil Shah, and salved the easily assuaged conscience of amirs with extravagant presents and grand titles. He was equally extravagant in his eccentricities—Muhammad bin Tughluq, the infamous fourteenth-century sultan of Delhi, was his hero—and for a while amused himself by shooting gold-tipped arrows at random from the palace into the city, and giving rich presents to the households where the arrows fell. "This fitful habit, however, quickly came to an end after a few days," says Badauni.

Adil Shah's accession was marked by a devastating famine in the Delhi-Agra region, but this did not trouble the sultan. The throne gave him certain privileges, but he accepted none of the responsibilities that went with it. "Inasmuch as Adil had originally been accustomed to the profession of music and dancing, and was fond of a life of ease and luxury, and was indolent in his habits, he was by no means fitted for the conduct of military affairs, or the duties of civil administration," writes Badauni. His amirs then, having little to do at the court, retired to their fiefs and assumed virtual independence. There were several rebellions. Two of Adil Shah's cousins set themselves up openly as independent sovereigns—Sikandar in Punjab, Ibrahim in Delhi and Agra—and so did Muhammad Shah in Bengal, so that Adil Shah's authority was virtually confined to Bihar, with Chunar as his capital.

Even in Bihar, Adil Shah gradually relinquished the management of the state to Hemu, a low born Hindu of high ability, who quietly, almost imperceptibly, gathered into his own hands the reins of power that fell from Adil Shah's limp hands. In a way, it was good policy on the part of Adil Shah to put Hemu in charge. An Afghan noble in that position would have been a potential usurper; Hemu, however great his ambitions, could not threaten the throne.

Meanwhile, Humayun was back in the Indian theatre. The history of the Afghans in India then once again merged with that of the Mughals. It was quite a melee in Hindustan for a while, with the three Sur monarchs fighting among themselves as well as with Humayun, and Hemu determinedly carving out a niche for himself.

As his kingdom crumbled around him, Adil Shah fiddled away—literally. But he fiddled exquisitely. This depraved and sanguinary monarch was one of the greatest musical virtuosi of his age. "Adil was so highly skilled in singing and dancing that Miyan Tansen, the well-known kalawant, who is a past master in this art, used to own to being his pupil, and Baz Bahadur . . . who was also one of the most gifted men of his age and had no equal in this life-wasting accomplishment, acquired the art (of music) from Adil," says Badauni.

In 1557, after an inglorious reign of three years, Adil Shah was defeated and killed by the sultan of Bengal. Of the other two Sur monarchs, Ibrahim, expelled from Delhi by Sikandar, took refuge in Orissa and died there in obscurity; Sikandar himself was driven out by the Mughals and died in Bengal. The dynasty of Sher Shah thus became extinct in just two decades. Adil Shah's music was the dirge of the Sur dynasty.

Chapter Four

THE MUGHAL
RESTORATION

Humayun in Exile

FOR FIFTEEN YEARS, from the time he was driven out of Hindustan by Sher Shah till his triumphant return to reclaim the Indian empire, Humayun led a perilous life on a crumbling ledge of fortune. Yet, in a sense, the worst was over for him when, after his desolate wanderings in Rajasthan and Sind, he finally crossed the Indus in the autumn of 1543 and ascended the mountains into Afghanistan. There were yet the undertows of the old calamities for him to contend with, and there were new sorrows and new pitfalls ahead, but the climb was now mostly upward.

For a while though, the going was still extremely arduous for Humayun, as he and Hamida, with their infant son Akbar and an entourage of some forty men and two women, made their way through the frigid, bandit-infested badlands of southern Afghanistan. The climate was extreme in those mountain wastelands. Jauhar notes: "In the hot season the semum blows with such violence, that the very limbs of a man are melted, and he dies, but in the winter the cold is so severe, that if a person takes his broth out of the pot, and pours it into a plate, it becomes instantly a piece of ice." Provisions were scarce. Once they killed a horse for meat, but "there was no cooking-pot, so they boiled some flesh in a helmet, and some they roasted," says Gulbadan, ". . . and with his own blessed hand the Emperor roasted some meat which he ate. He used to say: `My very head was frozen by the intense cold.'"

Humayun's initial plan was to go to Kandahar, but this was folly, for there was no place more dangerous for him than the domains of his brothers. As he crossed the Bolan Pass and proceeded towards Afghanistan, Askari, on the instruction of Kamran, issued out of Kandahar—to wait on Humayun, as he coyly described his mission. This could have been the end of the road for the fugitive. Luckily, Humayun, warned in the nick of time, managed to flee into the wilderness just as his brother rode into his camp.

But he had to leave Akbar behind in the care of a few trusted servants, out of fear that the infant might not be able to endure the rigours of the flight through the mountains in the dead of winter.

Leaving him behind was the lesser risk. Askari in fact took to the winsome baby right away, cradling him in his arms and fondling him with great affection, says Jauhar. Taken to Kandahar, Akbar was entrusted to Askari's wife, Sultanum Begum, who brought him up with loving care, as if he were her own son.

Humayun's course was now set—he would flee to Persia and, if well received, seek assistance there to recover his kingdom; if not, he would go on to Mecca on pilgrimage. With this plan in mind he sent a letter to the Shah of Persia, explaining his predicament and seeking help. Then, in January 1544, without waiting for the Shah's reply, Humayun, anxious to get out of the reach of Kamran, crossed the Helmand River into Persia and safety.

It had taken Humayun over three years after his rout at Kanauj to leave India, and now, by fleeing into Persia, he had taken himself out of the Mughal political arena altogether, leaving the field to Kamran, who then proclaimed himself king in Kabul. Humayun was out of the reckoning, a refugee in a foreign land.

Happily, the Shah regarded Humayun as an honoured guest, not as a refugee, and he had the kettle-drum beaten for three successive days at the royal residence in Kazvin to announce the joyous event of Humayun's arrival in Persia. "This is excellent that . . . the king hath exalted this country by his distinguished advent," wrote the Shah to his provincial governors.

The moment Humayun entered Persia, his life changed. In India and Afghanistan, local rulers had treated the fugitive emperor with antagonism, as a threat to their own power and position. The Shah had no such anxiety. By giving shelter to the Mughal emperor, the Shah added lustre to his own prestige, and by the magnificence of the reception given, he emphasized the prestige of the refugee, and consequently his own grandeur as the refuge.

FOR PERSIANS, COURTLY hospitality was the hallmark of culture, and they spared no effort to exalt and entertain Humayun as he travelled to the royal court. Shah Tahmasp, who was then in his late twenties, was a demon for detail, and he sent precise and minute instructions to his provincial governors for the reception of Humayun along the way. Typical was his firman to the governor of Herat. Describing Humayun (without a touch of irony) as the "pearl of success and sovereignty's ocean, goodly tree ornamenting the garden of government and world sway, world-illuminating light of the portico of sovereignty and glory . . . king of land and sea, world-warming sun of felicity's heaven, exalted full moon of the zenith of the khilafat and world rule", and so on—there were twenty-nine such attributes lauding Humayun in the letter—the Shah ordered the governor to send 500 "prudent and experienced men" to bear royal gifts to Humayun at the Persian border and welcome him.

To receive Humayun at the second stage of his journey through Persia, the governor was directed to send his son and grandson with 1000 cavaliers—"Let the uniforms of the one thousand be coloured and smart," the Shah advised. At the third stage, the governor himself with 30,000 soldiers ("which number must be exact") was commanded to meet and escort Humayun to Herat. Four days were specified for the eighty-kilometre third leg of the journey to Herat, during which the governor was required to "continually keep him (Humayun) pleased by conversation of a reassuring character." On no account should "unfriendly glances" be cast on Humayun's entourage by the Persian escort, the Shah cautioned, and commanded his men to serve Humayun "in the manner that one would serve one's own king."

"Let arrangements be made day by day for sweet and pleasant drinks, with white loaves kneaded with milk and butter and seasoned with fennel seeds and poppy seeds," the Shah ordered. "Be it also arranged that at the places where his Majesty will halt, there be arranged and pitched, on the previous day, cleansed, pleasant, white, embroidered tents and awnings of silk and velvet, and also pantries and kitchens and all their necessary out-offices, so that every requisite apparatus be in readiness. When he, in his glory and fortune, shall direct a halt, let rose water sherbet and wholesome lemon juice be prepared and poured out, after having been cooled with snow and ice. After the sherbet, let conserves of . . . apples . . . watermelons, grapes, etc., with white loaves, made as already directed, be tendered; and let care be taken that all the beverages be examined by the protector of sovereignty, and that rose-water and gray ambergris be added to them. Each day let five hundred dishes of varied food be presented, together with the beverages . . . After food has been partaken of, let sweetmeats and faluda, prepared from candy and refined sugar, and various conserves, and *rishta-i-khatai*, which shall have been perfumed with rose-water, musk and gray ambergris, be brought in . . ." The Shah specified that "the total of the food, sweetmeats and liquids be not less than 1500 dishes", and that the food should be served on "*langari* dishes known as Muhammad Khani, and also on other plates of porcelain, gold and silver, placing covers of gold and silver over them . . ."

The Shah ordered his eldest son, Sultan Muhammad Mirza, a

young lad who was the nominal ruler of the province, to receive Humayun ceremonially at Herat, and he gave the governor, the prince's guardian, specific directions about the attire and comportment of the prince. "Put on him the dress which we sent him last year on New Year's day . . . When the son shall come out of the city, strive that all the troops mount in the prescribed order and that they proceed towards the welcoming," the Shah advised. "When near that king . . ., viz, when the space intervening be an arrow's flight, let . . . [the guardian] advance and beg the king not to dismount. If he agrees, let him return immediately and dismount the happy son, and let the last go quickly and kiss the thigh and stirrup of that king . . . and show all the points of service and respect and honour which are possible. Should the fortunate Nawab not agree, and should he dismount, let the son dismount before him and do homage and, his Majesty having first mounted, let our son kiss the king's hand and mount, proceeding on thus, ride according to etiquette to the camp and the fixed quarters. And let . . . [the guardian] be in attendance on the king, and close to the son, so that, if the king should put any questions to the son, and the son, out of bashfulness, be unable to reply, the . . . [guardian] may make a proper reply . . . Our son will proceed alongside of his Majesty, but so that the head and neck of the latter's horse be in front. You . . . will follow close behind . . ."

On the eve of Humayun's entry into Herat, heralds were "to proclaim that all the men and women of the city shall assemble on the morning . . . in the Avenue, and that in every shop and bazaar, where carpets and cloths shall be spread in order, the women and maidens will be seated, and, as is the rule in that city, the women will engage in pleasant sayings and doings with the comers and goers. And from every ward and lane let the masters of melody come forth, so that the like of it will not be seen in any other city of the world. And bid all the people come forth to offer welcome," the Shah instructed.

Elaborate security arrangements were prescribed for Humayun's safety along the way. The governor was also asked to arrange for "a good writer, who is a man of experience, to write a full diary . . . and let all the stories and remarks, good or bad, which pass in the assemblage, be reduced to writing and be sent by the hands of trusted persons, so that we be fully informed of all that occurs." And the Shah warned: "Having acted, paragraph by paragraph, and day by day, in accordance with the procedure set forth in this edict, let there be no remissness concerning the paramount instructions." The firman, as reproduced in Abul Fazl's *Akbar-nama*, cover fourteen printed pages in English translation! Shah Tahmasp was a very thorough man.

HERAT WAS ONE of the great cities of the medieval Muslim world, renowned for its urban sophistication and luxury, an ambience very pleasing to Humayun, and he relaxed there for about a month, staying at a royal palace. He had endured much hardship in the previous four years, and now he desired to take life easy for a while. Even when he finally set out for Kazvin, the Persian capital, he proceeded by slow stages, sightseeing, hunting and hawking along the way, lingering in some places for as many as forty days, so that by the time he got to Kazvin, some seven months after his entry into Persia, the Shah had moved to his summer retreat in the mountains. It was there that the two monarchs met. "When his Majesty entered the paradise-like court of the monarch of Persia," writes Jauhar, "the latter advanced to the edge of the carpet, where the two kings embraced; after which the Persian monarch placed Humayun to his right, and they sat down on the same cushion."

It was not however all cordiality between the two monarchs. There was a moment of tension even at their very first meeting. Humayun had on that occasion put on the robe of honour sent to him by the Shah, but he, being a Sunni, omitted to wear the cap sent along with the dress, a jewelled, high conical cap of crimson silk worked in gold, called the *taj*, which was worn by Persian monarchs and was a symbol of the Shiah faith. The Shah noted the omission, and demanded, "You must put on the Persian cap." And Humayun, in no position to object, amiably replied, "A *taj* is an emblem of greatness; I will with pleasure wear it." The Shah then with his own hands placed the cap on Humayun's head. Thereupon the royal band struck up, trumpets blared, and Persian nobles prostrated themselves in thankful prayer, as if the Shah had converted Humayun to Shiism.

Then the two monarchs dined together. Afterwards, Humayun retired to the palace of Prince Bahram, the Shah's brother, who had been appointed as the prince in attendance on the Mughal monarch. There Humayun tonsured his head in the Persian style, had a hot water bath, put on the dress of honour presented to him, and, as Jauhar puts it, "passed the night in feasting and carousing." It was like the good old times when he was emperor in India. Even better, for he did not now have the chore of governing.

The only annoyance in Humayun's life of ease and felicity in Persia was the Shah's insistence that Humayun and his men should become Shiahs. To change sect was probably a matter of no great moment for the easy-going Mughal, but the Shah's vehemence distressed him, and he resisted the pressure. Still the Shah persisted, cajoling and threatening alternately, and in the end he prevailed, at least temporarily, with

107

Humayun yielding in the spirit of doing in Persia as the Persians do.

The blow-hot, blow-cold relationship between the two monarchs ended on a celebratory note, with the Shah organizing a grand ring hunt and a farewell party in Humayun's honour. The party, held at the ancient city of Persepolis, lasted three full days, and was rounded off by a night-long drinking party. The Shah then formally undertook to provide Humayun with an army of 12,000 cavalry, along with 300 veterans from the Shah's personal bodyguard, as well as all the requirements of the camp, including tents, horses, camels, carpets and whatever else Humayun needed, so that he might recover his lost domains. Said the Shah: "O Humayun, if I have been deficient in anything, I trust your generosity to excuse it." In return for the military aid, Humayun agreed to hand over to the Persians the city of Kandahar, after taking it from Kamran.

Before Humayun departed he gave a farewell banquet to the Shah, who had expressed a desire for Indian entertainment and cuisine. The Shah, Jauhar says, especially liked the "dish of rice with peas (dal khuske)" among all the Indian dishes served. Humayun then rode with the Shah to the Persian camp, and, as it was raining heavily by then, spent the night there.

The next morning the Shah bade farewell to Humayun: "Now, Humayun, you may go, and the blessing of God be with you!" As a parting gift he gave Humayun two apples and a knife, and presented him with a ring taken off his finger. Prince Bahram accompanied Humayun to the Mughal camp, where, on parting, Humayun said to him, "I would willingly remain with you all my life, but my reputation is at stake, and obliges me to leave you."

But Humayun was in no great hurry to redeem his reputation. Instead of hastening back to Kabul and certain victory, he went sightseeing in Persia, to Tabriz and places along the Caspian Sea, so that when Shah Tahmasp returned to Kazvin, he was amazed to find Humayun still encamped nearby, and had to send word that the Mughals should march out immediately.

AND SO, AFTER a leisurely stay of over a year in Persia, Humayun reluctantly set out homeward. When he reached Sistan, the Persian province bordering Afghanistan, he found the promised Persian troops waiting for him under the nominal command of the Shah's third son, a child about three years old. In the summer of 1545 Humayun led the army into Afghanistan.

Humayun's immediate objective was to seize Kandahar, which he took from his brother Askari after a siege of four months, and handed over to the Persian commander, in fulfilment of his agreement with the Shah. He gave it away too soon. Strategically it was imperative for Humayun to retain Kandahar, as a base from which to mount the attack on Kabul; moreover, with winter approaching, he required the fort to shelter his troops. So when the Shah's infant son died in Kandahar, Humayun reoccupied the fort, expelling its Persian commander on the specious charge of dereliction of duty. Luckily for Humayun, the Shah did not retaliate, probably because Humayun kept up the pretense that he was holding the fort on behalf of the Shah. But Kandahar would thereafter remain a bone of contention between the Mughals and the Persians, changing hands several times over a span of a hundred years, till the Persians finally wrested it from the Mughals in 1649, during the reign of Shah Jahan.

Humayun now, for a change, looked like a winner. The Persian contingent remained with him, despite the Kandahar tangle. His brother Hindal, his cousin Yadgar, and several amirs deserted Kamran at this time and joined Humayun, and when he advanced on Kabul in mid-November 1545, the city surrendered to him virtually without resistance. Kamran fled to Sind with his family.

In Kabul, to crown Humayun's happiness, his son Akbar, now a robust young lad of three, was restored to him. Akbar, who had been shifted from Kandahar to Kabul when Humayun advanced into Afghanistan, was then in the loving care of his grand-aunt, Babur's elder sister Khanzada Begum. "She was very fond of him," says Gulbadan, "and used to kiss his hands and feet and say: `They are the very hands and feet of my brother, the Emperor Babur, and he is like him altogether.'"

Celebrations marked Humayun's return to Kabul. "There were many festive gatherings, and people sat from evening to dawn, and players and singers made continuous music," says Gulbadan. "Many amusing games, full of fun, were played." In the spring Hamida arrived in Kabul from Kandahar, and soon after that Akbar's circumcision ceremony was performed. The next few months were a time of happy domesticity for Humayun.

But Kabul was not Humayun's to hold in peace. The lethal game between Humayun and Kamran, with the throne and their own lives as stakes, was yet to be played out. In the ten years following Humayun's return to Afghanistan, Kabul would change hands between the two as many as five times, and there were occasions when Humayun lost everything in the struggle, and once, very nearly his life.

As the struggle between Humayun and Kamran intensified, so did its viciousness. On one occasion, when Humayun was investing Kabul, Kamran, defending the fort, turned murderously on the women and children of the besiegers trapped in the fort, killing several and flinging their bodies over the ramparts, and suspending others from the fort walls, to make the attackers desist. He even exposed Akbar, a child he was otherwise fond of, to the cannonade. "Bring him and put him in front," he ordered, according to Gulbadan. When the child was noticed on the ramparts, Humayun immediately ordered the firing to stop—or, as Abul Fazl would have it, even before Humayun noticed Akbar, god intervened to protect his own, so that "the hands of the marksmen trembled, the arrows flew crooked, and the linstocks congealed."

Humayun, when he finally took the fort, matched the brutality of Kamran, executing many of the defenders and allowing his soldiers to plunder the city. He was however magnanimous to his brothers, though he initially made a show of sternness. When Kamran, who had escaped from the fort, but was pursued and caught, was brought in, Humayun sat in full durbar to receive his surrender—it was a formal function of the state, the surrender of a rebel to his sovereign, not fighting brothers meeting in reconciliation. As Kamran approached, he took a whip from one of the courtiers and put it around his own neck, and presented himself as a common criminal. Touched, Humayun exclaimed, "Alas! alas! there is no need for this! Throw it away!" Humayun then rose to embrace Kamran, and, says Abul Fazl, "wept so violently that all those present were touched to the heart." Kamran was also in tears and sobbing. "Sit close to me," Humayun told Kamran. A cup of sherbet was then brought, of which Humayun drank half and passed the cup to Kamran, who drank the other half. The adversaries were brothers again.

The four brothers (Askari too had been restored to favour) then dined together, sitting on the same carpet. A two-day long festivity marked the reconciliation. Humayun then assigned different fiefs to his brothers, and they departed.

The arrangement did not last. Between Mughal royal siblings there could be only the peace of the grave. Of Babur's four sons, fortune would favour only one to live and reign. The others would perish. And it so happened that it was luckless Humayun who turned out to be lucky in the end. Askari was taken prisoner by Humayun and ordered to go on pilgrimage to Mecca, a customary form of kindly exile; he died there in 1558. Hindal died in a night skirmish with Kamran. Kamran too, after a futile attempt to seek help from Islam Shah—"in the expectation," says Badauni, "that the water which had flowed away would return to its source"—was caught. Humayun's counsellors now insisted that Kamran should be executed. "Brotherly custom has nothing to do with ruling and reigning," they warned him. "If you wish to act as a brother, abandon the throne. If you wish to be king, put aside brotherly sentiment . . . This is no brother! This is your Majesty's foe!"

Humayun, remembering the words of his dying father, did not have the heart to take Kamran's life, but he agreed to have him blinded. Kamran would have preferred death. "Kill me at once," he told those who went to blind him, but stoically bore the lancing of his eyes. When the brothers met again, predictably it was Humayun who broke down and wept, overcome with remorse. Kamran remained calm. "Whatever has happened to me, has proceeded from my own misconduct and fault," he said consolingly. "If it be known that his Majesty has shown favour to me, let it also be known how little I have deserved it." The prince then asked permission to go on pilgrimage to Mecca, which was granted. He died in Mecca four years later, in October 1557.

With Kamran and Askari gone, and Hindal dead, only Humayun now remained in the Mughal royal arena. After a decade-long struggle, he was the unchallenged lord of Afghanistan.

He could now resume his interrupted imperial career.

IN NOVEMBER 1554 Humayun set out from Kabul for India. He left his family behind, with his younger son Muhammad Hakim as the nominal governor of Kabul, and the veteran general Munim Khan as his guardian. But he took Akbar with him. On reaching Jalalabad, Humayun floated down the Kabul River on a raft to Peshawar. It was smooth sailing for him. And so it would be all the way to Delhi.

Humayun's invasion of India turned out to be an absurdly easy undertaking. He had only a tiny army with him when he set out from Kabul, a mere 3,000 cavalrymen, and though this force was later augmented in Punjab by the Kandahar contingents brought by Biram Khan, the total strength of the Mughal army amounted to not very much more than 5,000, a ludicrously small invading force. But it was enough, for the Sur empire had fragmented and there was no dominant power in Hindustan to oppose him. The Afghan forces in Punjab simply scattered on the approach of the Mughals, like chaff in the wind, so that Humayun was able to occupy the province, even the great city of Lahore, without any opposition, and then move on to retake the whole of his former Indian empire without a single serious reverse.

Mughal valour was a major factor in this easy conquest, and so was

111

the Afghan disarray, but Humayun was also lucky. When he entered Punjab, its monarch, Sikandar Shah, was away in Delhi with his army, battling his cousin Ibrahim. Sikandar hastily sent reinforcements into Punjab, an army of some 30,000 men, but they were routed by Biram Khan in a twilight action on the banks of the Satluj. Even the much larger main Afghan army, led by Sikandar himself, did not fare any better when it engaged the Mughals at Sirhind. Worsted, Sikandar fled to the foothills of the Himalayas, leaving Delhi defenceless. On 23rd July 1555, fifteen years after he was chased out of the city by Sher Shah, Humayun reoccupied Delhi, unopposed.

Agra fell soon after, again without resistance. Then one by one the old Mughal provinces fell to Humayun's generals. Only in Punjab was there was some residual resistance, as Sikandar re-emerged from the hills to menace the Mughal lifeline to Kabul, but even that proved to be only a fleeting problem. Biram Khan, accompanied by Akbar as his ward, presently stormed into Punjab and once again drove Sikandar into the hills. Soon all was quiet in the empire.

In Delhi, Humayun relaxed, his life-work done. "The remainder of this year was spent in ease and enjoyment," writes Nizamuddin Ahmad. Humayun refurbished the Sher Mahal, one of Sher Shah's mansions in Delhi, to accommodate his library and to set up an observatory there to pursue his astronomical studies. He also busied himself with dreaming up a novel administrative organization, by which he planned to divide the empire into several virtually autonomous provinces, with himself as the overlord who would constantly tour the provinces with a praetorian guard of 12,000 horse, to ensure discipline and good government and to exact tribute.

It was not a bad scheme, but Humayun did not have the chance to implement it. In January 1556 we find him preparing to shift his residence to Agra; he even sent ahead his *peshkhana*, the advance tents, in preparation for the journey. But before he moved, he wanted to make some important appointments, for which he considered Friday, 24th January as auspicious. The rise of Venus that night, he believed, had a special astrological significance for him. So, as the night fell, he summoned his astronomers to the roof of the Sher Mahal, to sit in the small open pavilion there to watch Venus rise.

If Venus indeed had a message for him, Humayun misread it. After watching the skies for a while, Humayun, staff in hand, entered the staircase to return to his quarters. As he was descending the steep, narrow steps, the call of the muezzin was heard, so Humayun paused, as was expected of a pious Muslim, to repeat the creed of Islam, and then proceeded to sit down on the steps "till the crier had done", says

Ferishta. Unfortunately, at the moment of sitting down, says Abul Fazl, "his blessed foot caught in the skirt of his robe . . . and his good staff slipped. He lost his feet and fell upon his head, his right temple receiving a severe blow, so that some drops of blood issued from his right ear." When attendants rushed to him, he was unconscious.

For a couple of days Humayun lingered, occasionally regaining consciousness, but died on the evening of 26th January. He was forty-eight. His last words: "I accept the divine summons."

Humayun seems to have had a premonition of death. After his return to Delhi he often spoke of death, and liked to tell of a dream he had in which a supernatural voice recited these verses:

> O Lord! of thine infinite goodness
>   make me thine own;
> Make me a partaker of the knowledge
>   of thy attributes;
> I am broken-hearted from the cares
>   and sorrows of life;
> O call to thee thy poor madman!
>   O grant me release!

WHAT A LIFE Humayun had had! No other Mughal monarch, except Babur, had to endure as much suffering and privation, as many twists and turns of fate, as this hapless prince. And what a contrast he makes to Babur! While Babur took on adversity with cheerful, exuberant energy, Humayun submitted to it with an equanimity that was almost repellent in its passivity. He sleepwalked through life in exquisite romantic languor, more often than not induced by opium, which he took with rose-water. Humayun's life was eventful, but undramatic. In the colourful phrase of Lane-Poole, "Humayun stumbled out of life as he had stumbled through it."

The Reluctant Boy King

AT THE TIME of Humayun's fatal accident, Akbar and Biram Khan were in Punjab, encamped on the banks of the Ravi. Akbar, says Abul Fazl, broke down when he was told of his father's death, "weeping and lamenting as befitted the condition of affection and love." Akbar wept, we should assume, as much for himself as for his lovable though eccentric father. The burden of the empire was on him suddenly, and he was not yet done with childhood.

Meanwhile, as the arrangements for Akbar's enthronement were being made, Humayun's death was kept secret in Delhi, to prevent unrest, and for a couple of weeks one Mullah Bekasi was made up to resemble the emperor and present himself to the public every morning from the riverside balcony of the fort, as Humayun used to do. It was only on 11th February that Humayun's death was made public, and Akbar proclaimed as emperor.

AKBAR WAS FOURTEEN years old when he became king. At that age his grandfather Babur was already a veteran in war and politics and was on his way to Samarkand, dreaming of empire. Akbar showed no such precocity—we look in vain in the child for the father of the man that Akbar would become. Yet, this was no ordinary child, and this is evident even through the thick fog of hyperbole and fanciful tales with which Abul Fazl mythologizes Akbar's childhood.

According to Abul Fazl, the first intimation of Akbar's future greatness appeared as "a strange light perceptible from the bright brows" of Hamida when she was pregnant with Akbar. That portent was confirmed by the splendid star configuration in Akbar's horoscope, though the impetuous infant very nearly missed his rendezvous with the stars by being born too early. "In a short time a glorious moment will arrive, such as does not happen once in a thousand years," fretted the royal astrologer when Hamida was in labour. "What an advantage if the birth could be delayed." Luckily, fate intervened in the form of a "country midwife" to delay the birth, a woman so repulsive in appearance that at the very sight of her Hamida's labour pains ceased!

This enabled Akbar to be born at an astrologically ideal time, at about 2 a.m. on Sunday, 15th October 1542, a night of the waxing moon. And Akbar, if Abul Fazl is to be believed, was born with a smile to match the radiance of the night. "Contrary to the way of other infants," says Abul Fazl, "his majesty, the king of kings, at his birth and the first opening of his eyes on the visible world, rejoiced the hearts of the wise by a sweet smile."

The baby was first put to the breast of his mother, and then handed over to wet nurses. Hamida herself, as was the royal custom, would never again give milk to the child. Ten wet nurses were provided for the lusty infant, and there was quite a competition among them to suckle Akbar, for foster-motherhood established an advantageous link with the heir-apparent, by which they could later promote the careers of their husbands and sons, especially of sons, who, as foster-brothers of the king, were linked with him, as Akbar would later remark, by "a river of milk".

The infant grew up in what must have been to him a bewildering world of ever-changing environment, people and climate. He was always in the thick of danger, whether in India with his fugitive father, or in Afghanistan caught in the fight between his father and uncles. The one constant in Akbar's world in the midst of all these upheavals was Maham Anaga, the superintendent of Akbar's foster-mothers. Although she most probably did not herself suckle Akbar, she was the dominant early influence on him, being his surrogate mother when Hamida was away with Humayun in Persia. A woman of great ability, with ambitions to match, Maham Anaga would later play a major role in court politics in the early years of Akbar's reign, when he was, in Abul Fazl's phrase, "behind the veil".

Akbar was a burly child, tough and strong, able to wrestle down older, bigger boys; he had a robust appetite, and ate voraciously. He was also hyperactive and intractable, and, to the great disappointment of his erudite father, could not be made to sit down and study. From the very first day, Akbar's education went awry. Humayun had chosen an astrologically suitable time to begin his instruction, but when the auspicious moment arrived, the boy was nowhere to be found, for he had run away to play.

Later, four tutors in succession tried their hand at teaching Akbar. All failed. Humayun in despair then chose a tutor by lot, but this did not work either. Nor did it work when, after Akbar's accession to the throne, Biram Khan tried to educate him. Akbar imbibed a love for Sufi poetry from his new tutor Abdul Latif, but he still refused to learn to read and write.

Akbar's interests in his childhood and early youth were almost entirely physical. Playing truant, the restless child forever romped about the hills, hunting with dogs, racing camels and horses, flying pigeons, but more than anything else applying himself to the martial arts. Akbar excelled in horsemanship, archery and fencing, and was a superb marksman with the musket.

These skills, along with an intuitive understanding of human nature and the ability to control and manipulate men, were far more relevant to Akbar's profession as king than all the book learning he could have had. Book learning had done little good to Humayun. Abul Fazl is not therefore entirely ludicrous when he claims that through sport Akbar "practised wisdom under the veil of concealment". Akbar's wisdom, says Abul Fazl, "was not learnt or acquired, but was the gift of God."

ACCESSION TO THE throne made little immediate difference in Akbar's life. He paid hardly any attention to affairs of state, and left governance almost entirely to Biram Khan. In a way it was fortunate that Akbar did not attempt to govern for the time being, for the situation of the Mughal empire on Humayun's death was far too complex and precarious for the callow boy-king to handle. Biram Khan's exceptional skills in the management of men and affairs were essential to consolidate the empire. He made India safe for Akbar. Akbar himself had little to do with it.

And it is to Biram Khan's credit that he never allowed his personal ambition to override the interests of the dynasty he served, despite all the opportunities for self-aggrandizement he had during the four years when he enjoyed absolute power in the empire as Akbar's regent. Akbar's throne was safe in the care of Biram Khan.

Biram Khan, a Turk, was originally in the service of the Shah of Persia, and had served as a captain in the Persian expeditionary force that assisted Babur in his last Samarkand campaign. Babur took to him and induced him to join the Mughal service. Nothing much is known about Biram Khan's career under Babur, but under Humayun he rose rapidly; he played a prominent role in Humayun's Gujarat campaign, and was elevated to the high office of the keeper of the royal seal. Later, he helped Humayun to extricate himself from Sind and escape into Persia, where his suave diplomacy helped to soothe the tension between Humayun and the Shah. When Humayun conquered Afghanistan, Biram Khan was appointed the governor of Kandahar, from where he joined Humayun in Punjab for the Indian invasion, and was appointed Akbar's guardian.

On the death of Humayun, Biram Khan swiftly assumed control of the government. His first task was to ensure that the kingdom had a king. For over two weeks, from the day of Humayun's death to the reading of the khutbah in Akbar's name in Delhi, there was no Mughal emperor. Biram Khan had to wait for news of the formal announcement of Humayun's death before he could arrange for Akbar's enthronement. This took a few days. But as soon as the news was received, Akbar's accession was formalized, without any elaborate ceremony. At Kalanaur, a small town on the Ravi to the west of Gurdaspur in Punjab—where Babur had once camped briefly during his invasion of India—in a garden which Monserrate describes as "very large and beautiful", on a hastily built brick throne resting on a masonry platform, Akbar was crowned emperor at midday on Friday, 14th February 1556, "when Orion was on the ascendant".

Akbar's inheritance, notwithstanding Orion's ascendancy, was precarious, his kingdom as rough and temporary a construct as the throne on which he was crowned. The Mughal power in India was at this time largely confined to garrison camps and had no administrative grid bracing it. Even from a purely military point of view, the Mughal position was hazardous. There were still a couple of Sur monarchs around—Sikandar Shah in Punjab, Adil Shah in Bihar—and they had to be eliminated before Akbar could be safe. And, as yet unknown to the Mughals, the mysterious power of Hemu was rising, like a spectre out of the debris of the collapsed Sur empire, to menace Akbar. Not even Kabul, the Mughal power base, was secure, as Akbar's covetous relatives hovered around the city. But the most pressing and troublesome problem of all was that the very power configuration at the Mughal court was unsettled. Would Akbar's authority—Biram Khan's authority—be respected and obeyed by the great Mughal amirs? If they turned defiant, chaos was inevitable.

Biram Khan could not expect automatic subservience from the amirs—he was, after all, only the first among equals. Already Shah Abul Maali, a brilliant but erratic general and a favourite of Humayun, who used to sit on the same carpet as Humayun and eat from the same plate, had turned truculent in Punjab when Akbar, presumably on the advice of Biram Khan, would not grant him the same honour. Biram Khan had nipped this problem in the bud by throwing Maali into prison—he would have preferred to execute him, but Akbar would not consent—but there were bound to be others to challenge the Khan.

The immediate decision that Biram Khan had to make was whether to remain in Punjab or to move on to Agra, the Mughal capital. Agra was over 600 kilometres from Kalanaur, a great distance by medieval reckoning, and normally it would not have been advisable for a newly crowned monarch to stay so far away from the capital city. Nevertheless, Biram Khan decided to remain in Punjab.

It was a prudent decision. Punjab, where Sikandar Shah still lurked, had to be secured before Akbar could be moved safely to Agra. Kabul too needed watching; it had to be safeguarded as a base to which the Mughals could return for refuge if driven out of India. Kabul was then under the governorship of Akbar's younger brother and potential rival, Muhammad Hakim, a risky arrangement in itself, but made worse by the fact that Hakim's guardian was Munim Khan, a rival of Biram Khan. Further, the city was then being menaced by Sulaiman Mirza, who had received the kingdom of Badakshan as a gift from Humayun but had since outgrown his gratitude. Such being the situation in Punjab and Kabul, it was imperative from a strategic point of view for Biram Khan to remain in Punjab.

There were other considerations too. At the time of Akbar's accession, the Delhi-Agra region was in the grip of a severe famine because of a combination of drought, anarchy and incessant wars, so it was not a good time to move the court there. Besides, the royal begums, along with the families of Mughal amirs, were on their way from Kabul to India at this time—they were, says Abul Fazl, being brought to India "so that men might become settled and be restrained in some measure from departing to a country to which they were accustomed"—and Biram Khan had to wait in Punjab to escort them to Agra. It is also likely that he was apprehensive that Tardi Beg and other Mughal veterans in Delhi would inhibit his freedom of action or even challenge his authority. Biram Khan needed time to consolidate his position.

MEANWHILE HEMU WAS on the move, his power swelling like a tidal wave as he advanced, threatening to engulf and destroy the rickety Mughal state.

Hemu's climb to power is a fascinating, almost incredible saga. Outwardly, everything was against him. He had, as Abul Fazl brutally states, "neither rank nor race nor beauty of form nor noble qualities." A Hindu in a Muslim state, his religion was against him. Even among Hindus, his caste was against him, he being, as Abul Fazl says, a Baniya of "the Dhusar tribe, which is the lowest class of hucksters in India." In an age in which heroic persona and martial skills determined political fortunes, Hemu was puny and gnomish—he never wore a sword and could not even ride a horse. But he was an incomparable manipulator of men, and he overcame all his disabilities by sheer craftiness, fortitude and tenacity, driven by the grand vision of an empire of his own. "That evil-looking one of puny form . . . [had] lofty designs," says Abul Fazl.

We first come across Hemu in the small town of Alwar near Delhi, where he was known as Hemachandra, a hawker of saltpetre (according to Abul Fazl) or vegetables (according to Badauni). He gradually rose to become a "government huckster", in which capacity he somehow caught the attention of Islam Shah, who raised Hemu to the post of superintendent of the Delhi market. From there Hemu steadily slithered his way up, and by "masterpieces of feline trickery" (as Abul Fazl puts it) became the head of Islam Shah's intelligence department, and gained the king's complete trust.

When Adil Shah usurped the throne from Islam Shah's young son, but could not be bothered about government chores, Hemu filled the power vacuum and, as Abul Fazl records it, "annexed the whole of the administration and rose to lofty offices . . . Hemu undertook all appointments and dismissals, and the distribution of justice." While Adil Shah sang and danced, Hemu ran the government.

He ran it efficiently, with skill and discretion. He served his master well. But he also served himself well in the process. "Outwardly he was behaving loyally towards his master, in reality he was seeking his own ends," writes Abul Fazl. As the power behind the throne, Hemu accumulated immense wealth, which he spent prodigiously to acquire more power—wealth and power were like two legs to him, one enabling the other to step up, as he climbed the ladder of success. Hemu was so bounteous that, says Abul Fazl, his "debtors worshipped him and did his behests."

All along, Hemu maintained extreme humility, not to rouse envy among the amirs or suspicion in his master. He in fact used his disadvantages to great advantage, as his puny form and shrinking demeanour made his adversaries underestimate him. On one occasion, when Hemu led an army against a rebel amir in Gwalior, the amir contemptuously sent his stable keeper to engage Hemu in battle while he himself went hunting—and lived to regret it. Though no warrior himself, Hemu was a brilliant strategist and a great general, and he won as many as twenty-two battles for Adil Shah.

When Humayun returned to India, Hemu hung around at the Mughal frontier, looking for an opening. "The proud Hemu, who joined extreme daring to craft, was ever following feline stratagems," says Abul Fazl with grudging admiration. "On none of those former occasions was there a ruler of India possessed of such courage, enterprise and plan . . . He was ever meditating the conquest of distant climes and kept hidden in his heart the designs of great expeditions. And . . . fortune had favoured Hemu in a way which the rulers of India had not attained in those former days."

Hemu's opportunity came when Humayun suddenly died. But when he suggested to Adil Shah an immediate invasion of the Mughal kingdom, the court astrologer opposed it, stating that Akbar's stars were invincible. Hemu nevertheless persuaded the king to let him lead the Afghan army against the Mughals, arguing that Akbar was but a boy and that the Mughals were not yet firmly established in India. "It is easy to root up a small plant," he said.

He very nearly did that. First, he took Gwalior, expelling Ali Quli Khan, the Mughal governor, and then advanced on Agra, which was taken without a battle, as Iskandar Khan Uzbeg, the Mughal commander, thought it prudent to retreat to Delhi and there join up with the army of Tardi Beg. There was no resoluteness in Delhi either, as Tardi Beg wanted to retreat to Punjab, or even to Kabul. Tardi Beg's plan was, however, opposed by other Mughal amirs, who wanted to stay and fight. But with divided counsels and in two minds, their defeat at the hands of Hemu was certain, especially as Tardi Beg with his contingents stood aloof in the ensuing battle. Tardi Beg and Iskandar Khan then fled to Punjab ("with the speed of the wind," as Abdullah puts it) where they were joined by Ali Quli Khan. It was a precipitate flight of the Mughals from the Indo-Gangetic Plain.

Hemu, once he came into possession of the imperial capitals of Delhi and Agra, won entirely by his own enterprise and valour, assumed a royal title, Raja Vikramaditya, and "raised the imperial canopy over him, and ordered coin to be struck in his name," reports Yadgar. But he did it all tactfully, with the concurrence of Afghan amirs, and by continuing to humour Adil Shah with professions of fealty. Hemu's bountiful generosity also helped him to win over potential opponents—when he took Delhi, for instance, he distributed all the spoils, keeping only the elephants for himself. Nothing speaks so well of Hemu's genius as that he was able to carry the proud and turbulent Afghans with him all the way and get them to accept him, a low caste Hindu, as their sultan. They called him Hemu Shah. Abul Fazl, however, saw it all in a different light: "Hemu entered Delhi and increased his arrogance so that his intoxication became madness," he writes.

Meanwhile in Punjab, Tardi Beg was in trouble. He had failed in his duty to his sovereign by his hasty flight from Delhi, and he compounded that misdeed by clamouring for a retreat to Kabul, thus undermining Mughal morale, on which their future in India depended.

To restore authority and unity of purpose, it became thus essential to punish Tardi Beg in an exemplary manner.

Dereliction of duty was not, however, the only reason for punishing Tardi Beg. Probably it was not even the primary reason. If it were so, Iskandar Khan and Ali Quli Khan were equally guilty, but they, instead of being punished, were given important commands. Tardi Beg was singled out because he was subverting Biram Khan's authority by insisting on retreating to Kabul, while unity of leadership was critical for the survival of the Mughals in India. Tardi Beg, who had first come into India with Babur, and was even then a noted commander, was not just a rival noble, but a rival centre of power.

There were also other and more personal factors involved in the action against Tardi Beg. Though Biram Khan usually addressed Tardi Beg as 'tugan', elder brother, he, according to Abul Fazl, "recognized Tardi Beg Khan as his rival and was always apprehensive of him. Tardi Beg too regarded himself as a leader of the army and was lying in wait for an opportunity to overthrow Biram Khan." Further, they belonged to different sects—Biram Khan was a Shiah, Tardi Beg a Sunni—and that provided them "additional reasons for watching for opportunities to ruin one another".

Cultural and personality differences aggravated these problems. Biram Khan was a suave aristocrat connected to the old Persian royal family, a consummate diplomat and leader of men, while Tardi Beg was a rugged, coarse and eccentric soldier with no finesse or sophistication, a dervish whom Babur had raised to the status of an amir. Tardi Beg feared Biram Khan and resented his success, flavouring his envy with a trooper's contempt for the courtier. Biram Khan in turn looked on Tardi Beg as a rogue elephant who could ruin his carefully laid plan to stabilize Mughal power.

Tardi Beg had to go. Personal rivalry as well as the interest of the state converged to seal his fate. There was, however, a court-martial, as Badauni explicitly states, and Akbar's acquiescence was most likely obtained in executing Tardi Beg, though at the time of the execution Akbar was (conveniently) out hawking on the plains of Sirhind.

The execution of Tardi Beg had the intended salutary effect on the Mughal army. It ended dissidence and unequivocally established the authority of Biram Khan. There was no more talk of the Mughals fleeing to Kabul. Biram Khan then boldly decided to wrest the initiative, and, despite the inferiority of his forces and the low spirit of his soldiers, he advanced towards Delhi to confront Hemu.

HEMU TOO GOT ready, for what he knew would be the decisive

121

battle of his career. Panipat was once again the battlefield of India's destiny. For the Mughals, the campaign opened auspiciously, when a division under Ali Quli Khan defeated Hemu's advance force and captured his artillery. Still, Mughal morale remained brittle, for Hemu's army was much larger than the Mughal army and was moreover a victorious, spirited army. When Hemu approached, "perturbation found its way into the hearts of imperial servants, through the instrumentality of empty-headed babblers, from whom no army is ever free," says Abul Fazl.

Hemu had problems of a different kind. Ill omens—morale depressants—beset him. On the way to Panipat he had a nightmare, in which he saw the elephant he was riding being swept away in a flood, and a Mughal soldier putting a chain around his neck and pulling him out as he was about to drown. The dream was analyzed by the "interpreters of dreams" as signifying the defeat and death of Hemu in battle. But Hemu was not disheartened. "The very reverse of this dream will happen," he asserted. When, however, heavy rain fell the next day and Hemu's best war elephant was killed by lightning, it seemed to confirm the warning of Hemu's nightmare.

On the Mughal side, the omens were favourable, for Ahmad Beg, "the madman, who was unequalled throughout the world in foretelling the future by what he saw in the blade-bone of a sheep", feasted on mutton and predicted certain victory for the Mughals, says Yadgar.

It was however Mughal defeat that seemed certain when the battle was joined on 5th November 1566. As Yadgar reports, "Hemu advanced, fought, and routed the Moguls, whose heads lay in heaps, and whose blood flowed in streams." Hemu's wings worsted the Mughal wings, and his victory seemed assured when he, mounted on his great elephant Hawai, led his elephant corps against the Mughal centre.

A lucky accident saved the Mughals. At the point of Hemu's victory, exults Abul Fazl, "suddenly . . . an arrow from the bended bow of divine wrath reached Hemu's eye, and piercing the socket, came out at the back of his head." When Hemu fell, his army, says Abul Fazl, became "handless and footless, and no more girded up the loins of courage." They scattered at once.

Hemu's mahout tried to lead his elephant away from the battle to save his master, but was captured. Meanwhile Akbar—whom Biram Khan had till then kept at a safe distance from the battle, on an elevated position, with 3000 horse to guard him,—arrived at the battlefield, and Hemu, half dead, was taken to him. "This is your first war," Biram Khan said to Akbar. "Prove your sword on this infidel, for it will be a meritorious deed." Akbar refused, saying, "He is now no better than a dead man, how can I strike him? If he had sense and strength, I would try my sword." Then, as Badauni describes the scene, Biram Khan, "as a warrior of the faith", himself slew Hemu. His head was sent to Kabul as a trophy and his torso to Delhi to be placed on a gibbet.

Soon after the battle, Iskandar Khan, chasing the fleeing enemy, occupied Delhi. Two days later, Akbar himself made his triumphant entry into the city, where he stayed for a month. Then he and Biram Khan returned to Punjab, to deal with Sikandar Shah, who had become active again. Sikandar eluded the Mughals for a while, but eventually surrendered, and was treated generously; he was assigned a fief in Bihar, but fled from there to Bengal and faded into obscurity.

In Punjab, Akbar was joined by Hamida Banu Begum and the other members of the royal family, who had arrived from Kabul. After resting in Punjab for some four months, they set out for Delhi. On the way, at Jalandhar, Akbar, not yet fifteen, took his first wife, Ruqaiya, Hindal's only daughter. And Biram Khan, who was then in his fifties, married another young cousin of Akbar, the richly talented Salima Begum, daughter of Humayun's sister Gulrukh.

The Mughals were at last ready to settle down in India.

Behind the Veil

IN OCTOBER 1558, two and a half years after his accession, Akbar and the royal court finally moved to Agra, travelling from Delhi down the Yamuna in barges. With that began the imperial phase of Mughal history. Babur and Humayun, however fascinating their careers, were transient rulers in India; without Akbar's achievement, their reigns would have been mere passing episodes in the long history of India.

Akbar's reign began on a deceptively low key. Initially he took little direct interest in government, and was content to let Biram Khan rule in his name. Outwardly, the arrangement worked well, for there seemed to be perfect trust and harmony between Akbar and Biram Khan. But beneath the surface there were undercurrents of tension. Evidently, as Abul Fazl states, Akbar, even while he remained "behind the veil", was carefully observing what was going on and taking stock, growing and changing in ways concealed from the eyes of others.

Akbar was a wilful youth, and had already twice defied his guardian openly, by refusing permission to execute Maali and by declining to slay Hemu. The incipient friction between the two gradually developed into a full-blown clash of personalities soon after the arrival of the royal household in Punjab, as the presence of Akbar's mother Hamida Banu Begum and foster mother Maham Anaga in the royal camp ended Akbar's exclusive dependence on Biram Khan, and provided him with opportunities for alternate alignments.

The basic cause of friction between Akbar and Biram Khan was that Akbar was no longer a child, and did not like being treated as a child. Biram Khan was taking his guardianship a trifle too earnestly, tightly controlling even Akbar's household expenses, which was galling, especially as Biram Khan was lavish in his own household expenses and in conferring largess on his favourites. Significantly, it was a family matter, and not an issue of government, that led to the first major clash of wills between them. Soon after the begums arrived in Punjab, Akbar had taken his first wife, but when he wanted to take a second wife soon after, Biram Khan strenuously objected, on the ground that it was not a politically desirable alliance, as the intended bride was a niece of Kamran's wife. But Akbar remained adamant and finally had his way, though only after other amirs intervened to persuade Biram Khan to relent.

The harmony between Akbar and Biram Khan was thus broken. Soon irritations began to pile one on another, and inconsequential incidents came to be blown out of proportion into intolerable affronts. Typical was an incident in Punjab in which, during an elephant fight, two of Akbar's elephants came close to Biram Khan's tent, causing disturbance and some panic. It was clearly an accident, but in the prevailing environment of intrigue and suspicion, Biram Khan concluded that it was deliberately engineered. He suspected that Maham Anaga or Atga Khan (a foster-father of Akbar) was behind it, and he berated Atga Khan: "As His Majesty occasionally treats me with disfavour, I believe this must come from your contrivances and calumnies."

It is of course possible that Maham Anaga, a canny schemer, was at this time plotting Biram Khan's fall, but the elephant incident could not have been a part of the plot. In any case the rupture between Biram Khan and Akbar did not require any outside instigator, but was inherent in the nature of their evolving relationship. The clique of foster relations who surrounded the young emperor, backed by Akbar's masterful mother, no doubt played a key role in the ouster of Biram Khan, and were responsible for its specific orchestration, but the ouster itself was not dependent on them, and probably was not even initiated by them.

BIRAM KHAN THOUGHT of himself, not without justification, as the co-founder of the Mughal empire, and considered himself indispensable to Akbar in governing the empire. He took his power for granted. He took Akbar for granted. And, though he meticulously observed all the formalities of obeisance due to his sovereign, he virtually ignored Akbar in the routine administration of the empire.

As the scene changed and Akbar began to slip out of his control, Biram Khan naturally grew anxious about his position, and that affected his judgement. Once a cool, suave, prudent leader, he now became irritable, brusque and overweening. He saw conspiracies where none existed, insults where none were intended. More and more, he turned to sycophants for reassurance, and they further distorted his perception of reality. Uncharacteristically, he now became indiscreet in his words and deeds, which, in a court where nothing was a secret, inevitably reached the ears of Akbar, further exacerbating their relationship. Biram Khan, says Badauni, was "somewhat touchy on the subject of precedence."

The irritants between Akbar and Biram Khan were numerous, but most of them are remarkable only for their pettiness, and seem unbecoming of the exalted personages involved. Biram Khan, says Abul Fazl, was guilty of several "unseemly actions", but the wrongs he lists are all trivial, though they were good enough as levers to pry the Khan out of his office. Abul Fazl also speaks of "some sinister designs" of Biram Khan, but gives no details. A major offence of Biram Khan in the eyes of the predominantly Sunni amirs of the Mughal court was that he, a Shiah, unduly favoured the members of his sect for appointment in government. The nomination of Sheikh Gadai to the high office of the minister for religious affairs was especially resented— the Mughal nobles, says Badauni, "flew into rage at the advancement, honour and unreasonable exaltation of Sheikh Gadai."

Yet another issue that agitated the anti-Biram Khan cabal was the Khan's abrupt dismissal of Pir Muhammad, a harem favourite, from service. Pir Muhammad was once a protege of Biram Khan and had served as his office manager. In this capacity, he "was the person to whom the nobles and officers had to make their applications, and of the many, high and low, who attended at his door, he admitted hardly any one," writes Nizamuddin. "His temper now became arrogant and perverted." His worst infraction, however, in the eyes of Biram Khan, was that he wormed his way into the favour of the harem clique and betrayed the Khan's trust, and was impudent even towards the Khan. Matters came to a head one day when a page barred the Khan's way when he went to visit the ailing Pir Muhammad, and though Pir Muhammad apologized for the incident, saying, "Forgive me, for my porter did not know you," the Khan retorted: "Nor did you."

Three days later Biram Khan cut the presumptuous subordinate down to size, writing to him: "You were wearing the dress of a poor scholar when you came to Kandahar. As you appeared simple and honest, and did good service, you were raised to high office by me, and from being a mullah you became a leader of armies. As your capacity was small, you easily became intoxicated and got out of hand after one cup. We fear that some great mischief may be committed by you which it will be difficult to remedy. It is better that for some time you should draw in your feet under the blanket of disappointment, and sit down in a corner. You will now make over your standard, drum and other insignia of distinction and of your exaltation, and betake yourself to the mending of your disposition, for this is good both for yourself and for the world."

Biram Khan reinforced this lesson in humility by confining Pir Muhammad for a while in Bayana, and then sending him on forced pilgrimage to Mecca. Pir Muhammad proceeded as far as Gujarat, but halted there, biding his time and waiting for the turn of events. He did not have to wait for long.

BY EARLY 1560, after riding on Biram Khan's shoulders for four years, Akbar, eighteen, was impatient to stand on his own feet. In March that year he made his move.

The decision to break with Biram Khan could not have been easy for Akbar. The Khan, whom he used to affectionately call Khan Baba, was like a father to him. He owed his very throne to Biram Khan. And Biram Khan, with his immense power and prestige, was not a person to be trifled with. But these very factors, which made Biram Khan so very powerful, also made it imperative for Akbar to remove him from the scene before he could take charge of the government—Akbar had to step out of Biram Khan's broad shadow to find his own place in the sun.

In his manoeuvre to break with Biram Khan, Akbar found an eager ally in Maham Anaga, who was, in the words of Abul Fazl, "a marvel of sense, resource and loyalty." When Akbar confided his intention to her, she immediately took charge of the operation, and it was she who choreographed all the moves.

Her first step was to remove Akbar from the immediate physical control of Biram Khan, without rousing suspicion. On the morning of 28th March, Akbar came out of Agra with a small retinue, as if to go hunting. After travelling some distance, he proceeded on to Delhi on the pretext of wanting to visit his ailing mother, Hamida. An unsuspecting Abul Kasim, Kamran's son, was taken along, so as not to leave behind a pretender to whom Biram Khan could latch on, should he choose to rebel. Meanwhile Maham Anaga, who had been secretly recruiting partisans, advised Shihabuddin Ahmad Khan, the governor of Delhi and a member of the harem clique, to strengthen the defences of the Delhi fort and get ready to receive Akbar.

The operation was meticulously planned. Soon after Akbar reached Delhi, he dispatched letters to the veteran amirs of the empire, informing them that he had broken with Biram Khan—because the Khan "had deviated from the straight path", wrote Akbar—and ordering some of them to join him in Delhi, and giving others detailed instructions on what they were to do. As the harem clique had shrewdly calculated, most of the nobles, crass opportunists that they were, turned away from Biram Khan the moment they realized that he was out of royal favour.

When Biram Khan received the first reports of Akbar's moves, he dismissed them as wild rumours. He could not believe that Akbar would defy him. "Biram Khan," writes Abul Fazl, "in spite of all his wisdom and discernment, was unaware that the throw of the dice had been the reverse of his wish and the scheme of the world had taken another form, and was unconcernedly beating the drum of power." But when he finally realized what was happening, his response was dignified and correct in every respect—he decided to submit to the will of his sovereign and proceeded to Delhi to surrender.

Biram Khan's advance towards Delhi threw the harem clique into confusion—they did not know what to make of it, and feared the worst. Their anxiety was such that some even suggested that Akbar should retreat to Lahore, and then to Kabul, if Biram Khan advanced on Lahore. Akbar rejected the timid course. If it came to war, he would stand and fight. To force the issue, Akbar ordered Biram Khan to return to Agra.

Would Biram Khan obey? Some of his followers suggested that he should not submit, but fight, arguing that it was Maham Anaga and her clique who were causing all the trouble, not Akbar himself, and that Biram Khan had the obligation to rescue Akbar from the faction that had ensnared him. Biram Khan rejected the advice. He would not fight his sovereign—whoever was behind Akbar, the man up front was Akbar himself. Yet there was some ambivalence in Biram Khan's stance, and though he often spoke of taking to asceticism, he simply could not, in the words of Abul Fazl, "admit the idea that the administration of India could go on without him."

Akbar then issued a firman to Biram Khan, detailing the charges against him and ordering him to go on pilgrimage to Mecca. At the same time Akbar assured the Khan that no punitive action would be taken against him. "You are still dear to us . . . and we wish your welfare," wrote Akbar.

Akbar further softened the harshness of the dismissal order by following it up with a conciliatory oral message. "Your services and your fidelity to this great family are known to mankind," said the message. "As owing to our tender age, we gave our attention to promenading and hunting, we did not cast our glance on political and financial affairs, and all the business of sovereignty was entrusted by us to your excellent capacity and knowledge. Now that we have applied our own mind to the affairs of government, and the administration of justice, it is right that this sage well-wisher, who ever boasted of his sincerity and devotion, should . . . offer up endless thanks for it. He should for a time gather up his skirts from business and turn his attention to the bliss of pilgrimage of which he was always desirous, and with regard to which he was constantly, in public and private, expressing his great longing . . . We shall grant him whatever place and whatever extent of land he may wish for in India, so that his servants may remit him the proceeds, harvest by harvest and year by year."

The order to go to Mecca was banishment, but Biram Khan decided to comply with it. Fortune, he knew, was an ass: "when it goes forwards, it does go forward, when it goes back, it does go back," says Badauni. At Nagaur in Rajasthan, he asked all the amirs with him to leave him, and kept with him only his close relatives, and, as Nizamuddin records, he "divested himself of his standard and kettle drum, and all the paraphernalia of his rank as amir, and sent them . . . to the sublime threshold." Said Biram Khan, "My heart has grown cold to the world and the burden thereof." Akbar had, it seemed, won the gamble.

THEN, SUDDENLY AND unexpectedly, Biram Khan spun around to confront his adversaries. He was driven into rebellion by a dreadful tactical blunder of Maham Anaga, who pushed him to make him lick the dust even as he knelt down to submit. In a totally unnecessary and vindictive act, she sent Pir Muhammad (Biram Khan's reprobate servant, who had returned to the court the moment he heard of the Khan's fall) to Rajasthan to speed his former master out of the empire—"to pack him off as quickly as possible to Mecca," as Badauni puts it. This, as Nizamuddin records, made Biram Khan "terribly despondent and grieved in heart", and made it impossible for him to exit with dignity. He had no alternative but to turn and fight.

Biram Khan rightly suspected the hand of Maham Anaga in the attempt to humiliate him. "A faction had spoken words for the purpose of perverting the noble mind of Akbar," Biram Khan wrote to Mughal amirs, justifying his action and soliciting their support. "Especially Maham Anaga . . . had wrought this, and was making it her business to ruin him." Biram Khan pledged to resume his pilgrimage after setting things right at the court.

Akbar quickly countered Biram Khan's move by issuing to him a fresh firman, accusing him of nepotism and cronyism. "To his own menial servants . . . he gave the titles of Sultan and Khan, and presented them with flags, kettledrums, rich fields and productive territories, while he with total want of consideration made the Khans, the princes, the officers, and the trusted servants [of Humayun] . . . to be in want of even dry bread," wrote Akbar. "Nay, he aimed at the life and honour of all of them . . . He committed various immoderate and disproportioned acts." Akbar charged that while Biram Khan allowed his own servants to get away with murder, the slightest faults of others were severely dealt with. The letter, probably drafted by Maham Anaga, went on to accuse Biram Khan of planning to separate from Akbar those close to him, "reducing him to solitude".

Akbar assured Biram Khan that he "had no design against his life, property or honour", but insisted that he should relinquish his powers, arrest the trouble-makers and send them to the court. "As we, during these five years, have respected his wishes and have not shown any recusancy, and have not gone beyond his good pleasure in anything that he proposed, whether it was acceptable to us, or unacceptable, he likewise should at once submit to this our order, and not be vexed therewith," wrote Akbar. "Whenever he acts according to this order, we shall clear our heart with regard to him and entirely forgive his crimes and offences. And whenever he is inclined to serve, and there is occasion for it, we shall summon him to our service, so that the evil over him may be removed. And as his services are still appreciated and approved by us, though he has received a thousand favours equal to them, we desire that his name, which has for years been celebrated in all countries and cities for sincerity, devotion, obedience and reliability, may not become notorious for rebellion, contumacy and sedition." If however Biram Khan did not submit, Akbar threatened to "abolish him from the earth," and quoted an expository couplet:

> Who puffs a God-lighted lamp,
> Sets fire to his own beard.

But it was too late for Biram Khan to back out. The die had been cast. The issue could now be settled only in the battlefield. Biram Khan, who had been proceeding through Rajasthan towards Gujarat to take ship to Mecca, now turned course at Bikaner, advanced into Punjab and, lodging his family in the fort of Bathinda, moved up to Jalandhar, intending to take Lahore.

At Jalandhar, the Khan's path was blocked by the imperial army. It was by no means certain how the battle would go. Akbar disdained to lead the army personally against the rebel, and Atga Khan, whom Akbar appointed to command the royal army, was hardly confident of himself, or sure of his men. Biram Khan had only a few soldiers with him, but, as Abul Fazl notes, "they were of good quality. He also placed much reliance on the royal army, as many from an evil disposition and double-tonguedness were sending him letters." Indeed, the battle favoured Biram Khan in its early stages, and he would probably have won the day if his elephants had not got bogged down in a paddy field in the course of the battle. That forced him to retreat. Fleeing north, Biram Khan took refuge in the fortress of Tilwara in the Shiwalik Hills, but offered to submit when he was besieged there by imperial forces.

Akbar treated his fallen guardian with grace, honour and magnanimity. "When the Khan-i-khanan approached the royal camp, all the amirs and khans went out, by the emperor's order, to meet him, and conducted him to the emperor with every mark of honour," writes Nizamuddin. Akbar, Abul Fazl reports, "with his sacred hand raised Biram Khan's head from the ground of humiliation and embraced him. He took the cloth from his neck and wiped from his face the tears of penitence and the dust of shame. With his gracious lips he inquired about his health and bade him sit on his right hand, as had been the rule when Biram Khan was prime minister."

The wrong that had been done to Biram Khan was thus set right— he would be allowed to retire with self-respect. Akbar offered Biram Khan three options: of staying on at the court as an emeritus prime minister and Akbar's confidential advisor, of retiring to any fief of his choice in India, or of going on pilgrimage to Mecca. There was however really only one choice for Biram Khan. He could not possibly stay on in the Mughal empire in any capacity whatever, after having been its de facto ruler for over four years. He had to leave for Mecca. But there would now be no disgrace in going. It would not be exile. The decision to go would be his.

Two days after his meeting with Akbar, Biram Khan took the road to Gujarat. Reaching Patan he encamped, to rest there for a few days before taking ship. There, while on a lakeside excursion, he was tragically ambushed and stabbed to death by an Afghan gang on a personal vendetta. There was no one even to bury his body, and it lay unattended "in the dust and in his blood . . . till some fakirs and poor men lifted up his bloody corpse and committed it to earth," says Abul Fazl.

It was a sad end for a truly great man. Says Abul Fazl, "Biram Khan was in reality a good man, and of excellent qualities" and "he relied upon his rectitude and probity, and did his work without a wrinkle on the brow of his heart, or a knot in the eyebrow of his soul." Says Badauni, "In wisdom, generosity, sincerity, goodness of disposition, submissiveness, and humility he surpassed all . . . The second conquest of Hindustan and the building up of the empire were due to his strenuous efforts, his valour and his wide policy."

Biram Khan's camp was ransacked by his assassins, but his family was rescued. Akbar had them brought to the court; he married Biram Khan's widow, Salima Begum, and took on himself the responsibility of bringing up the Khan's four-year-old son, Abdur-Rahim, who would later rise to become the highest noble of the empire, the Khan-i-khanan, the very position once held by his father.

WHEN BIRAM KHAN fell a new power configuration emerged in Agra to run the government, as Akbar still preferred to remain "behind the veil". He would wait another eighteen months before taking charge. In the intervening period it was Maham Anaga who managed the affairs of the state. Writes Abul Fazl: "In those days, though Bahadur Khan had the name of Vakil, yet in reality the business was transacted by Maham Anaga . . . . to whose knowledge and perspicacity the bridle for opening and closing all affairs, political and financial, was . . . entrusted at this time."

Maham Anaga was in many ways like her former adversary, Biram Khan, a sagacious and resourceful leader of men, masterful in action, always in perfect self-control. Though she assiduously promoted herself and her own, she was totally loyal to Akbar and never betrayed his interests or subverted his will. And when at last the time came for her to depart from the scene, her submission was total and unquestioning. But the source of her power was entirely different from that of Biram Khan's, who had earned his position by his services to the state. Biram Khan had a power base independent of the emperor. Maham Anaga's position, on the other hand, was wholly dependent on her personal equation with Akbar. But theirs was a felicitous alliance, and it would probably have endured much longer than it did, but for the provocative actions of her unruly son, Adham Khan. Maham Anaga herself was careful not to give any offence to Akbar in speech or deed, but Adham Khan was presumptuous, perhaps even disloyal. Her fall was his doing.

Early in 1561 Akbar, in his first major expansionist move, had sent Adham Khan (with Pir Muhammad as his second in command) to invade Malwa. Malwa was at this time ruled by Baz Bahadur, a Sur Pathan who was exceptionally talented in music and dance, but had only a peripheral interest in ruling. "Music and melody, which the wise and farsighted have employed at times of lassitude and depression . . . as a means of lightening the mind and of cheerfulness, were regarded by this scoundrel as a serious business, and he spent upon them all his precious hours," writes Abul Fazl censoriously. "Baz

Bahadur was the most accomplished man of his day in the science of music and in Hindi song," says Nizamuddin. Nearly as celebrated as Baz Bahadur himself was his muse, Rupmati, a Hindu enchantress, who was, as even Abul Fazl concedes, "renowned throughout the world for her beauty and charm. Baz Bahadur was deeply attached to her and used to pour out his heart in Hindi poems descriptive of his love." It was an infatuation that would pass into bardic lore and make the lovers immortal.

The Mughals had no difficulty in defeating Baz Bahadur and occupying Sarangpur, his capital. Baz Bahadur saved himself by flight, but his harem, along with his other treasures, fell to the Mughals. Rupmati herself, though wounded by her bodyguards (presumably on her entreaty to take her life) was seized by Adham Khan. But she preferred death to Adham Khan's embrace. "From love for Baz Bahadur," writes Abul Fazl, "she bravely quaffed the cup of deadly poison and carried her honour to the hidden chambers of annihilation." Baz Bahadur, after taking refuge in various courts, including Chitor, and once even briefly recovering his kingdom, eventually submitted to Akbar, who, himself a keen patron of music, treated him well. Inducted into the imperial service, he ended his days as a commander of 2,000, and was reputedly buried, along with the remains of Rupmati, in Ujjain, in a tomb built in the middle of a lake.

The invasion of Malwa was accompanied by general slaughter. "On the day of the victory, the two captains remained on the spot, and had the captives brought before them, and troop after troop of them put to death, so that their blood flowed river upon river," reports Badauni, who was aghast that even Sayyids and Sheikhs with the Koran in their hands were slain. It was a savage act, but a common Mughal practice— Babur and Humayun were guilty of such acts, and so would Akbar be. Pir Muhammad offered an additional defence: "In one night all these captives have been taken, what can be done with them?" And when he was told that it was not lawful to put to death women and children, Pir Muhammad replied, "If we keep them for the night what will happen to them?"

There is no indication that Akbar disapproved of the butchery. What roused his wrath was another aspect of the Malwa action. Adham Khan, instead of sending to the emperor the choicest of the spoils, sent only a few elephants as a token offering, and kept for his own enjoyment most of the treasure, including the beautiful women who fell into his hands. In doing that, he violated the Mughal custom of surrendering all the spoils to the emperor and receiving his reward as the emperor's gift. Adham Khan was not taking Akbar seriously.

That infuriated Akbar, and he set out post-haste from Agra, disregarding the brutal summer heat, and was upon Adham Khan even before the fast messenger sent by Maham Anaga to warn her son could reach him.

Adham Khan was taken aback by Akbar's sudden appearance at Sarangpur and hastened to make his obeisance, but was treated coldly. Akbar would not even accept the change of dress offered by Adham Khan. Soon however Maham Anaga herself arrived in Malwa, to make her hot-headed son give up the spoils and thus prevent any clash with Akbar. Even then Adham Khan managed to appropriate for himself, in the bustle of Akbar's return march, "two special beauties" who had already been shown to Akbar. When Akbar found the girls missing, he halted the march and ordered a search, but Maham Anaga had the girls quietly murdered, to prevent Adham Khan being found guilty. Akbar tactfully ignored the crime, but the Malwa episode fractured the relationship between Akbar and his foster-mother. Soon, another incident would sunder it.

FIVE MONTHS AFTER his return from Malwa, Akbar made his next move. In November 1561 he removed Munim Khan, a confidant of Maham Anaga, from the office of Vakil and appointed Atga Khan to the post. This curtailed Maham Anaga's power and set the stage for the next act in the drama. Maham Anaga herself was inclined to bend with the wind, but Adham Khan, who had been recalled from Malwa, wanted to force the issue.

Adham Khan considered Atga Khan the villain of the piece, and turned on him in fury. And one sweltering mid-May afternoon in 1562, when Akbar was resting in the harem and the chief officers of the state were in an adjoining hall transacting business, Adham Khan swaggered in with a few cronies and strode up threateningly to Atga Khan, his hand on his dagger. As Atga Khan, not expecting any outrage in the royal palace, rose to greet Adham Khan, he was wordlessly stabbed in the chest by one of Adham Khan's men. The amir tried to save himself by running out, but was chased and struck down, and he fell dead in the courtyard, on a heap of lime which had been collected there for building purposes.

Astonishingly, no one present, neither amir nor guard, drew his sword against the felons. Nor did any one move to stop Adham Khan when he, sword in hand, climbed the steps from the hall to the outer balcony that girded the harem. But as Adham Khan tried to push into the harem through one of the doors, he met with the first check—the eunuch on guard there shut and bolted the door.

Meanwhile Akbar, who was asleep, but whose fortune, as Abul Fazl puts it, was awake, started up on hearing the hubbub. When he inquired what the matter was, Rafiq, an old servant of the family, told him what had happened and showed him the mangled corpse in the courtyard. At the sight of his murdered foster-father, Akbar's blood rose. He immediately emerged from the harem, wrapping a cloth around himself. As he passed through the door, a servant handed him one of his special scimitars, and sword in hand Akbar hurried down the terrace.

As he turned a corner he saw Adham Khan standing at a door clamouring to be let in, and strode up to him. "You son-of-a-bitch (*batcha-i-lada*), why have you killed our Atga?" he bellowed, his usually loud voice even louder now in anger. His hand was on his sword. Adham Khan mumbled an answer and grasped Akbar's hand to restrain him, but Akbar wrenched his hand free and smashed it into Adham Khan's face with such force that he, as Mutamid Khan puts it, "tuned like pigeon" and fell unconscious. The blow left a mark like that of a mace-wound on Adham Khan's face.

Akbar ordered Adham Khan to be bound and thrown down from the harem terrace. But that did not kill him, perhaps because the height of the terrace was only about eight feet—"height of a man and a half," says Abul Fazl—or because the servants were timid. So he was hauled up and flung down again, this time headlong, "so that his neck was broken, and his brains destroyed."

The news of the fray soon reached Maham Anaga, who was lying ill in her house, but apparently she was told only that Adham Khan had been imprisoned, not that he had been executed. She immediately rushed to the palace, perhaps hoping to secure her son's release. Akbar told her: "Adham Khan killed our Atga; we have inflicted retaliation upon him." She said quietly, "You did well."

It probably did not then register in her mind that Adham Khan had been killed. But even when she learned the truth soon after, she "did not complain or lament, but she became inwardly wounded by a thousand fatal blows," says Abul Fazl. "The colour left her face." She wanted to see the body, but Akbar forbade that, as he did not consider it fit that she should see her son in that condition. Maham Anaga never recovered from the shock and sorrow of the incident, and forty days later she too died.

THUS ENDED ONE phase of Akbar's life, and another now began. In a sense, the new phase had already begun. Four months before the

Adham Khan episode, Akbar had gone on a pilgrimage to Ajmer, and on the way had received the homage of Raja Bhara Mal of Amber, a prominent Rajput chieftain, and accepted the raja's offer of his eldest daughter's hand. The marriage was performed at Sambhar on Akbar's way back from Ajmer.

There was nothing unusual in the raja's offer, nor in Akbar's acceptance. The custom of Hindu rulers offering their daughters in marriage to Muslim rulers, though not common, has been known in India for several centuries. Yet Akbar's marriage with the princess of Amber is significant, as an early indication of his evolving policy of religious eclecticism. Contrary to the usual practice of the sultans, he allowed the princess to remain a Hindu and to maintain a Hindu shrine in the royal palace, and he himself occasionally participated in the puja she performed.

Akbar was now twenty. He had swept away his past. He was ready for the future.

Chapter Five

THE EMPIRE
TAKES HOLD

Earth Hunger

"A MONARCH SHOULD be ever intent on conquest," Akbar maintained, "otherwise his enemies rise in arms against him. The army should be exercised in warfare, lest from want of training they become self-indulgent." Peace, Akbar believed, could be secured only by war. At other times he justified his conquests on humanitarian grounds, as he did in a letter to Abdullah Khan Uzbeg, a Central Asian monarch. "[My conquests] did not proceed from self-will and self-indulgence," he wrote. "We had no object except to be kind to mortals, and to obliterate the oppressors."

These were pretexts rather than reasons for aggression. Akbar, for all his intellectual refinements, was very much a ruthless medieval warlord, driven by earth hunger and blood thirst. Kings fed on land, it was their sustenance. A great monarch necessarily had also to be a great warrior, for unless he was successful in the battlefield, he could not be successful on the throne. Akbar therefore spent a good part of his life on military campaigns. Besides, he enjoyed war, as he enjoyed hunting, a perilous sport, and often personally led the charge against the enemy, as no other Mughal ruler, not even Babur, had done in India. Policy dictated wars, but war was also a pleasure in itself.

Explosive energy characterized Akbar's reign. From the time he took over the reins of government until his death, for over forty years, he was ever on the move, engaged in incessant wars, directed internally against rebels or externally against his neighbours along the ever-widening frontiers of his empire.

Territorial expansion under Akbar began during the regency of Biram Khan itself, when Ajmer, Gwalior and Jaunpur were annexed, thereby extending Mughal power over nearly all the territories that Babur had once ruled—a broad band of land across the sweep of the Indo-Gangetic plain, from Afghanistan to the eastern border of modern Uttar Pradesh. The empire was still relatively small, only about a third of what it would be at the end of Akbar's reign, though it was already the largest and the most powerful state in the subcontinent, as India was at this time fragmented into over twenty kingdoms.

In 1561, soon after the fall of Biram Khan, Akbar annexed Malwa.

This was followed in 1564 by the invasion of the adjacent Gond kingdom ruled (as regent) by Rani Durgavati, a legendary warrior queen. Akbar did not personally lead these campaigns, but he swung into action when a powerful clan of Uzbeg provincial chiefs broke out in rebellion. In two decisive campaigns, in Malwa and Bihar, he crushed the rebellion, but pardoned its leaders, hoping to conciliate them. But they mistook his magnanimity for weakness, so he had to quell their uprising a second time. Again he pardoned them. But the Uzbegs were incorrigible and they revolted a third time, now committing the ultimate treasonable act of proclaiming Muhammad Hakim, Akbar's step-brother, as their king. Simultaneously the Mirzas, a group of Akbar's distant cousins who held important fiefs near Agra, also rose in rebellion. That exhausted Akbar's patience. In the ensuing battle the Uzbeg chieftains were slain and several of the rebel leaders trampled to death under elephants. The Mirzas were driven out of the empire.

Meanwhile Akbar also had to deal with his brother. Hakim, who governed the province of Kabul as a virtually independent ruler, was susceptible to the enticement of the rebels because of the vexing contrast between his tiny domain and the vast empire of Akbar. In November 1566 he crossed the Indus into Punjab, dreaming of usurping the Mughal throne, or at least seizing Punjab. But it was the prick of envy rather than drive of ambition that spurred Hakim. He was no match for Akbar, and he tamely slunk back to Kabul when the emperor advanced against him into Punjab.

AKBAR RETURNED TO Agra from these campaigns in mid-July 1567, but was on the march again within a few weeks, this time against Mewar in Rajasthan, ruled by Rana Udai Singh, son of Rana Sanga. Mewar was strategically important to Akbar, as it lay on the route from Agra to Gujarat and the Deccan. Besides, though most other Rajput kingdoms had tamely accepted Akbar's suzerainty, the Rana stood aloof proudly, insisting on special privileges. And this hampered the consummation of Akbar's evolving Rajput policy, by which he sought to bind the rajas to him as his loyal vassals.

Udai Singh's claim for prerogatives was based on the unique status the Ranas of Mewar enjoyed among the Rajputs. The Rana, says Jahangir, "was the greatest of the . . . rajas of Hindustan. All the rajas and rais of the country have acknowledged him and his ancestors to be their chief and head." The Ranas prided themselves as the embodiment of Rajput valour, though this claim was based, as such claims usually are, on a mound of myth and a pinch of truth. The Ranas were not a class apart. Internecine feuds were as common in Mewar as in any other Rajput kingdom, and the princes of Mewar had no compunction in colluding with neighbouring rulers (Muslim or Hindu) against their rivals. On occasion, Mewar too had meekly surrendered to Muslim invaders, the last time to Sher Shah.

Indeed, Mewar was willing to submit to Akbar too, as evidenced by the fact that Sakat Singh, son of Udai Singh, was in attendance on Akbar at Daulpur just before the commencement of the emperor's Mewar campaign. What Mewar demanded of Akbar was preferential treatment, not independence—the Rana wanted to be exempted from personal attendance on the emperor (though he was willing to send his sons to the court) and he stipulated that he would not give a Mewar princess in marriage to the Mughal.

Initially Akbar was inclined to humour the Rana in these matters. Securing a Mewar bride was of little interest to him. Such marriages were political in nature, a way of sealing alliances; what was important was the alliance itself and not the manner in which it was sealed. The refusal of the Rana to attend on the emperor in person was a more serious matter, but Akbar might have overlooked that too. According to Abul Fazl, what led to war was a misunderstanding. Akbar had, it seems, one day in jest (but perhaps only half in jest) remarked to Sakat Singh that though other Rajput chiefs had paid their respects to him in person, the Rana had not, and that "therefore he proposed to march against him and punish him". The prince took the threat seriously and fled to warn his father. The departure of the prince without permission, says Abul Fazl, stirred up Akbar's wrath, "and jest became earnest".

The Rana had no strength to oppose Akbar. So when the Mughal army advanced into Mewar, Udai Singh prudently left Chitor under the command of his generals, Jai Mal and Patta, and took refuge in the Aravalli Range, where he built a new capital, Udaipur. Akbar then settled down to besiege Chitor.

Perched atop an isolated, rocky hill rising sheer from the plains, Chitor was a difficult fort to storm. But it was not impregnable, and had fallen to Alauddin Khilji early in the fourteenth century, and more recently to Bahadur Shah of Gujarat. The problem at Chitor was to get to the fort walls without being mowed down by enemy fire. Akbar, like Bahadur Shah before him, overcame the difficulty by building a couple of massive covered approach corridors called *sabats*, which rose from the middle of the hill at a musket shot distance from the fort walls, and snaked their way up like mammoth reptiles, finally to bite into the fort wall. The *sabats*, with brick walls and roofs of planks covered with rawhide, were massive constructions, one of them broad enough for ten

141

horsemen to ride abreast, and high enough for a "a man on an elephant with spear in hand" to pass under its cover, according to Badauni.

Some 5000 men were engaged in building the *sabats*, but work was slow and hazardous. More than a hundred workers were killed every day by enemy fire, though they were protected by bull-hide screens. Sometimes there were dreadful accidents, such as when two mines that were set to go off simultaneously near each other under the fort walls exploded one after the other, because the fuses were not properly adjusted. Some 500 "specially selected soldiers" who had rushed into the breach opened by the first explosion were killed in the second explosion, which, says Maulana Ahmad, "blew friend and foe together into the air, scattering their limbs in all directions . . . The vast quantities of dust and smoke prevented all movement in the imperial army for a time; stones, corpses, and limbs fell from the air, and the eyes of the soldiers were injured."

What finally ended the Rajput resistance was a lucky shot by Akbar. On the night of Tuesday, 23rd February 1568, Akbar, who was a crack shot, happened to notice, in the light "of the flashing of the fire of the cannon and guns", a Rajput of commanding presence at a breach in the fort, supervising the repairs. Akbar did not know who the man was, but he lifted his favourite gun, Sangram—guns had names in those days—and shot him down. The man was Jai Mal, the Rajput general.

Presently Rajput soldiers began to withdraw from the ramparts, and smoke could be seen billowing up from the fort—it was, Raja Bhagwan Das explained to Akbar, jauhar, "the last awful sacrifice which Rajput despair offers to honour and the gods." Jauhar meant that the Rajputs were conceding defeat, but it did not mean that they were giving up the fight. As the Mughals stormed into the fort, the battle raged on, street by street and house by house, each Rajput fighting till he fell, taking with him as many of the enemy as he could, seeking honourable death. Among the defenders, only the mercenary musketeers from Kalpi, about a thousand of them, managed to escape from the fort, by binding their wives and children and driving them before them as if they were captives, so as to pass off as Mughal soldiers.

Akbar, furious at the bitter resistance he faced, and affronted by the trick played on him by the Kalpi marksmen, ordered a general massacre in the fort, "which ceased only for lack of victims." Some 30,000 people, mostly peasants who had taken refuge in the fort, were slaughtered, according to Abul Fazl, but this is probably a vastly inflated figure. Badauni simply states that "eight thousand valorous Rajputs were slain", without mentioning the peasants killed. According to the fanciful account of James Tod, Akbar had the sacred threads of the slain collected and weighed, to estimate the number killed—it weighed over 200 kilograms! The slaughter was not merely vengeance. There was also a policy behind it—the greater the resistance, the greater the retaliation, was the Mughal rule, to strike terror in potential adversaries and cripple their will to fight.

Akbar remained in Chitor for three days, then returned to Agra, where, to commemorate the victory, he set up, at the gates of his fort, statues of Jai Mal and Patta mounted on elephants. What it signified is not clear. If it was meant to honour their valour, it was an odd compliment, to represent the Rajput heroes as imperial gatekeepers. Chitor itself fell into decay. The Mughals forbade the repair of its fortifications, and in the course of time the fort turned into a dense jungle, home to tigers and other wild animals, and a refuge for hermits.

Udai Singh never again ventured out of his mountain refuge. Akbar let him be. But hostilities broke out again soon after the death of the Rana in 1572. Udai Singh's son and successor, Pratap Singh, was initially inclined to be submissive to Akbar, and had, soon after his accession, sent his son Amar Singh to the Mughal court, though he himself, like his predecessors, refused to serve in person. Akbar insisted that the Rana should submit personally. There were other irritants too. Akbar, an obsessive collector of elephants, had heard much about a great elephant named Ramprasad in the Rana's possession, and was keen to acquire it, but the Rana, contrary to normal courtesy, declined to present it. Further, when Raja Man Singh, imperial commander and a close friend of Akbar, visited Udaipur, the Rana slighted him by refusing to receive him in person or to eat with him. The Rana was also reported to be strengthening his forts, a hostile act.

Evidently, Pratap Singh meant to abandon his father's passive policy and resume war, desiring, as Rajput bards sang, "to make his mother's milk resplendent". That brought the Mughal forces back into Mewar, though Akbar did not himself lead the army. In the ensuing war the Mughals won nearly all the engagements, often inflicting terrible slaughter on the Mewaris; even Udaipur was taken, and Pratap Singh had to flee for safety ever deeper into the jungle, beyond the reach of the Mughals. But he never gave up. And the Mughals, despite all the battles they won, could not crush him. The Rajputs simply scattered into the jungle when defeated, to strike again at their convenience. Trying to subdue the Mewaris was like trying to tether the wind. So the desultory war dragged on interminably, and would end only in 1615, when Amar Singh, Pratap Singh's successor, surrendered to Jahangir, Akbar's successor, half a century after Akbar first invaded Mewar.

Pratap Singh's war against Akbar is often regarded as a fight for Rajput honour, or even for Hindu honour. It was hardly that. The Rana's army was not all Rajput or even all Hindu in composition—there were several Afghan chiefs in his army, and one of them, Hakim Sur, distinguished himself in the greatest battle of the war, the engagement at Haldighat, in June 1576. And on the Mughal side was arrayed the cream of Rajput nobility, the princes of Amber, Bikaner and Bundi; even the Rana's own brother Sagaraj was with the Mughals. The Mughal-Mewar conflict was primarily a fight for power, as between any two kings. Honour was certainly involved, but it was the personal honour of Pratap Singh, not Rajput or Hindu honour.

WITHIN MONTHS AFTER the fall of Chitor, Akbar was back in Rajasthan, besieging the great fort of Ranthambhor, held by a vassal of the Rana of Mewar. The fort was reputed to be one of the strongest in India, but its defenders offered only a token resistance, not wanting to suffer the fate of Chitor. And Akbar, who had by then come to respect Rajput valour, offered them honourable terms.

Terror, as at Chitor, was very much a part of Akbar's policy, but so was magnanimity. The two were complementary means to achieve the same goal, of integrating the Rajputs into the Mughal empire. Akbar recognized that while the Rajputs could be troublesome as antagonists, as Pratap Singh was, they could be invaluable as allies, strong wheels for the Mughal empire to roll on. Furthermore, it was important for Akbar to win Rajput allegiance and broaden the military and political base of his power, as a counterpoise to the growing antagonism of orthodox Muslims towards him.

In broad terms, Akbar's Hindu policy was not unprecedented. Several Muslim rulers before Akbar had associated Hindu chieftains with their government, and the practice of Hindu rajas offering their daughters in marriage to sultans to cement political alliances was known even under the Delhi Sultanate. In the Deccan, Deo Raj of Vijayanagar had married a daughter to Firuz Shah Bahmini, and Mukund Rao Maratha, the Raja of Idar, had given his sister in marriage to Yusuf Adil Shah, the first Sultan of Bijapur. Similarly, Maldev of Marwar had married a daughter to Sultan Mahmud of Gujarat, and another to Islam Shah.

Akbar took several Rajput princesses in marriage, and so did his sons. The initiative for such alliances invariably came from the rajas themselves, for they, as vassal kings, had much to gain from links with the imperial family. And political expediency made such marriages respectable for the Rajputs, especially as Akbar had Hindu proclivities and allowed his Hindu wives to perform their customary rites in the royal palace. Though racial and religious considerations were important in the Middle Ages, they were never as important as political considerations. Religion subserved politics. Significantly, as Mughal power declined, such alliances ceased, Aurangzeb's great-grandson Farrukh-siyar's marriage with the daughter of Raja Ajit Singh of Marwar being the last.

The special vibrancy of Akbar's Rajput policy was derived from the bond of rapport and mutual admiration between him and the Rajputs. The Rajputs were a proud people, touchy about honour. Akbar understood this and heaped honours on them, so that as imperial officers they came to enjoy even greater prestige than as independent chieftains. He treated the rajas as trusted comrades in arms and as esteemed members of the ruling elite, and conferred on them prerogatives enjoyed only by the highest amirs of the empire—they were permitted to go up to the outer gate of the citadel beating kettledrums and ride armed to the public durbar hall, and were assigned to mount guard at the imperial palace, all signal honours.

The Rajputs benefited greatly, and lost little, by submitting to Akbar, for though their domains were annexed to the empire, they were normally given back to them as *watan* (hereditary) jagirs, which they could bequeath to their successors. The rajas were not however autonomous rulers. Their successors had to be approved by the emperor and invested in office by him by presenting them with a ceremonial dress and putting the *tika*, the vermilion mark, on their foreheads. Further, Mughal administrative regulations applied to the domains of the rajas as to any other part of the empire, and the revenue from their lands was adjusted against their salaries. The rajas, for all their privileges, were not kings, but only imperial officers.

The rajas did not mind losing independence, for in the process they gained freedom from the constricting clan politics of Rajasthan. Their power was no longer dependent on the support of their feuding clan chiefs, the Thakurs, and their thrones, protected by imperial authority, were safe from the machinations of their rivals within or enemies without. On the whole, being a Mughal amir raised rather than lowered the stature of the rajas, and this was reflected in the pomp and solemnity they now assumed. While the traditional Rajput durbar was an informal, casual assembly of near equals, it now, in imitation of the Mughal practice, became a formal affair, regulated by elaborate court

145

etiquette. The people of Rajasthan too benefited, as the Mughals brought peace to their land and introduced a relatively stable administration.

Perhaps the greatest benefit for the rajas was that, by joining the imperial service, they were able to break out of the confines of their desert homeland and range over the length and breadth of India, even to cross the Indus westward, which they had not done since the fall of the Hindushahi kingdom 600 years earlier. Instead of being petty chieftains, they now became commanders of a grand imperial enterprise, and their political role expanded exponentially. Further, they now enjoyed incomes several times greater than what they had ever got from their arid ancestral lands, for they were assigned, in addition to their *watan* jagirs, lands in other provinces to make up their salaries.

The rajas of Amber especially benefited from their close association with the Mughals, and acquired immense wealth and power. Of the twenty-seven Rajputs in Abul Fazl's list of mansabdars, thirteen were of the Amber clan, and some of them rose to positions nearly as high as those of the imperial princes. Raja Bhagwan Das, for instance, became a commander of 5000 and bore the proud title Amir-ul-Umara (Chief Noble), and his adopted son, Raja Man Singh, rose even higher, to became a commander of 7000.

The dual policy of Akbar towards the Rajputs—of high reward for those who submitted and relentless pressure on those who opposed—paid rich dividends, and soon all of Rajasthan came under his control, except for the hills where Pratap Singh lurked. Around the time Ranthambhor submitted, Kalinjar, where Sher Shah had met his nemesis, surrendered to the Mughals; within three months, Jodhpur, Bikaner and Jaisalmer also submitted, with the royal families of Jodhpur and Jaisalmer offering princesses to the Mughal harem.

AFTER THE MEWAR campaign, Akbar was militarily inactive for a couple of years, while he was busy with the construction of his new capital at Sikri. Then he was on the move again. His first target was Gujarat, a kingdom lying in the crook of the Mughal provinces of Rajasthan and Malwa, and alluringly rich from its flourishing overseas trade. Akbar could claim Gujarat as his patrimony, for it was once, for a short while, a province of Humayun's empire. The possession of Gujarat was of some importance to the Mughals, as it was the sea gate for pilgrims from the empire going to Mecca. But the immediate and compelling reason for Akbar's action was that the rebel Mirzas, who had previously been driven out of Hindustan, were now operating out of a base in southern Gujarat. Moreover, factional squabbles had broken out in Gujarat at this time, and Akbar had received an invitation from a clique in Gujarat to take over and restore order in the state.

Akbar set out from Sikri in the first week of July 1572, hunting along the way as usual. "He moved on," says Abul Fazl, "hunting and administering justice as he went." It was a leisurely expedition, almost an excursion, which took nearly five months to reach Gujarat. Akbar met with hardly any resistance in the kingdom. Muzaffar Shah, the king, took to his heels in terror as the Mughals approached Ahmadabad, but was caught hiding in a corn field; he was pensioned off by Akbar with a small allowance.

From Ahmadabad, Akbar moved south to deal with the Mirzas. On the way, he halted for a while at Cambay, where he, like Humayun before him, set eyes on the sea for the first time, and even went on a pleasure cruise. "His Majesty boarded a fast-moving boat and ordered that an assembly of pleasure and enjoyment be arranged . . . and he gave himself up to a drinking bout there," reports Muhammad Arif Qandahari. After a week-long sojourn at Cambay, Akbar pushed on against the Mirzas. It was during this phase of the campaign that he demonstrated for the first time his awesome intrepidity, when he, with a contingent of just about one hundred men, charged into a thousand-strong force of the enemy and scattered them by the sheer ferocity of the assault. Then, driving the Mirzas before him, Akbar advanced into Surat, the commercial capital of Gujarat, where he received Portuguese envoys and, in the words of Abul Fazl, showed "kindness to that crew of savages".

Akbar then left his favourite foster-brother Aziz Koka as the governor of Gujarat and returned to Sikri early in June 1573. To commemorate his victories, he renamed Sikri as Fatehpur (City of Victory) and constructed there the monumental Buland Darwaza, the majestic gateway of the Jama Masjid. But he was celebrating too soon. The trouble in Gujarat was not yet over. Soon after he had left the province, the Mirzas sallied forth again, threatening even Ahmadabad. So, after barely three months in Fatehpur Sikri, Akbar set out again for Gujarat.

This time he did not tarry on the way, but sped to Gujarat with a small force of 3000 cavalry, and, covering the 800-kilometre distance in just eleven days, surprised and routed the Mirzas in a sharp engagement, slew their leader, erected a tower of severed enemy heads in the battlefield, and was back in Fatehpur Sikri early in October 1573, after being away for just forty-three days. He then sent Raja Todar Mal to Gujarat to organize its revenue administration, and the raja made such an excellent job of it that soon the province was yielding more than five million rupees annually to Akbar's treasury, after expenses.

After Gujarat, Akbar turned to Bengal. In 1564, on the collapse of the Sur power, an Afghan noble named Sulaiman Kararani had established an independent kingdom in Bengal, but he was politic enough to read the khutbah in the name of Akbar and to maintain good relations with him. The scene changed in 1572, when Sulaiman died, and his younger son Daud, described by Nizamuddin as "a dissolute scamp", usurped the throne by murdering his brother. Daud read the khutbah in his own name, denying Akbar even the courtesy of a nominal subordination.

Akbar then ordered Munim Khan, the governor of Bihar, to chastise Daud, but later, noticing slackness in the aged governor, himself set out against the rebel. He travelled down the Yamuna in a couple of royal barges, followed by an entourage of amirs in their own barges, and a flotilla carrying all the royal equipment. Akbar took his infant sons with him on this trip, and also, as usual, a few select members of the royal zenana, for whose pleasure a floating garden was provided. Two giant war elephants, Bal Sundar and Saman, each solicitously accompanied by two female elephants, also travelled in barges.

The army marched along the river and kept within sight of the royal fleet. The river cruise did not prevent Akbar from indulging in his insatiable passion for blood sport. "Every day," says Nizamuddin, "he (Akbar) left the boat and went hunting on shore." On reaching Patna, where Daud was holed up, Akbar with characteristic daredevilry offered to fight him in single combat to settle their dispute. Daud refused to accept the challenge and fled by night from the city.

Disgusted, Akbar returned to Fatehpur Sikri, leaving it to his generals to complete the campaign. Daud evaded capture for a while, but was eventually seized, and, after some hesitation—"for he was a very handsome man," says Badauni—beheaded. His head, stuffed with straw and anointed with perfumes, was sent to Akbar, and the headless trunk gibbeted at Tanda, the capital of Bengal. Bengal was then annexed to the Mughal empire, but it took a long while to pacify the province effectively, the Mughal authority there being largely confined to the urban centres, while Afghan and Hindu chieftains had free run of the countryside. Bengal would ever live up to its reputation as the land of rebels, and it would be in Bengal that the rebellion most threatening to Akbar would break out.

Invincible Emperor

SUCCESS CAME EASILY to Akbar, and never once in his long reign did he have to suffer the humiliation of defeat in the battlefield. Yet curiously, there were more rebellions during Akbar's reign than that of any other Mughal—the *Akbar-nama* mentions as many as 144 such incidents. "His people are continually in revolt against him," says Monserrate, a Jesuit priest in Akbar's court. The rebellions, however, do not signify any weakness in Akbar, but are, paradoxically, an indication of the magnitude of his endeavour and the radical nature of much of what he did. The harder the bow is drawn, the more the wood complains.

The most serious uprising against Akbar broke out midway through his reign. Predictably, the trouble began in Bengal, with a clamour by the Mughal officers there against the growing rigour of Akbar's administration. The crisis came to a head when the newly appointed governor of the province, Muzaffar Khan Turbati, tried tactlessly to bulldoze the Bengal amirs into discipline—he was, says Nizamuddin, "harsh in his measures; he offended men with his words and he deprived many amirs of their jagirs." When Muzaffar Khan in a brusque show of authority revoked unauthorized alienations of land, enforced the branding of horses, cut the extra field allowances of troops and even demanded the repayment of the excess already paid, he was asking for trouble.

And trouble was what he got. Not only were his measures harsh, but his timing was deplorable, for storm clouds were already darkening the Mughal skies at this time, rising from the resentment among Muslim amirs over Akbar's religious aberrations and the growing role of Hindus in government. "To them (Hindus) belong half the army and half the land," charges Badauni. "Neither the Hindustanis (Indian Muslims) nor the Mughals can point to such grand lords as the Hindus have among themselves." Akbar was even accused of apostasy, the most heinous crime in a Muslim state, which not even the most autocratic monarch could commit without serious consequences.

Orthodox Muslim outrage against Akbar was stoked by the mullahs, who had their own grudge against him, for he, apart from deviating from the norms of Islam, had slashed the power of the Sadrs, the influential coterie of officers who administered the religious department of the government and controlled charitable grants. Their charity often began at home, and nepotism and corruption were rampant among them. Akbar's awareness of their venality, along with his growing disenchantment with Islam, inclined him to restrict their powers and order the resumption of the lands they had arbitrarily given away. His action was not altogether unprecedented. Sher Shah, for instance, had taken similar action against the Sadrs, but in his case it was seen as a purely administrative measure, while Akbar's religious deviancy made it seem as if the action were against Islam itself, not just against the dishonest officers.

That set the mullahs on the warpath. And into that explosive, darkening environment stepped Muhammad Yazdi, a mullah frenzied with an all-consuming hatred for Akbar. Yazdi was, not surprisingly, a former confidant of Akbar, one of only four persons ever hauled up the wall of the royal residence at Fatehpur Sikri at night for confidential discussions with Akbar on religion. Apparently Akbar found Yazdi tiresome and packed him off as the Kazi of Jaunpur. The banishment from court made Yazdi turn on Akbar with fury, bitterly denouncing him as an infidel and issuing a fatwa calling on all Muslims to rise in revolt against him. This sparked the blaze.

In January 1580 mutinies broke out almost simultaneously in Bihar and Bengal, and soon entire eastern India was in revolt. In April the rebels overran the royal forces at Tanda, and Muzaffar Khan was brutally tortured to death. They then proclaimed Muhammad Hakim, Akbar's besotted younger brother, as emperor, and read the khutbah in his name. Todar Mal, who was sent by Akbar to suppress the rebellion, was himself besieged and pinned down at Munger.

Akbar then raised the level of military pressure on the rebels by sending his foster-brother Aziz Koka to Bengal at the head of a large army. Even with all that concentration of military might, it was hard going for the loyalists for quite a while, and it took them about four years to gain control of the situation in Bihar and Bengal, and yet another couple of years for order to be fully restored. The troublesome mullahs were quietly got rid of through contrived accidents.

AKBAR DID NOT personally march against the mutineers, because he judged that the real threat to his throne came not from the provincial rebels in the east, but from the pretender in the west. In December 1580, Hakim invaded Punjab, as he had done fourteen years earlier, in eager response to the revolt in Bihar and Bengal. He had been given to believe that there would be a general uprising of Muslims in India in his favour. Perhaps if Hakim had looked like a winner, and if the rebels in the east had been more strikingly successful, many Muslims would have risen in his favour. As it was, none did, not even the mullahs of Lahore.

On 8th February 1581, Akbar set out from Fatehpur Sikri to deal with his brother. As before, when Akbar advanced, Hakim retreated to Afghanistan. Comments Badauni:

> He that cannot seize the skirt of fortune
>   by might,
> His bootless effort is like dyeing the
>   the eyebrows of the blind.

Though Hakim withdrew from Punjab, Akbar pressed on, determined to end the threat from his brother once and for all. He had made unprecedented preparations for the campaign, and led an army of 50,000 cavalry, 500 elephants, a camel corps, matching infantry, and the usual legion of camp followers who probably numbered four or five times the size of the army. Akbar looked into every detail of the campaign with meticulous care, for, as Nizamuddin writes, "although he had full trust and hope in heavenly assistance, he neglected no material means of success." So thorough were the arrangements that, despite the immensity of the operation, there was no confusion at all during the long march. The commissariat arrangements were such that there was no shortage of supply at any time, and prices in the camp remained low and steady, as Monserrate, who went with Akbar, noted. The soldiers too were content, having received eight months pay in advance.

The only snag in the operation was a general reluctance in the army to proceed to Kabul. In contrast to the problem that Babur once had to get his amirs to stay on in India, the problem now was to get them to leave India, even for a short military campaign. They were, says Abul Fazl, "afraid of the cold of Afghanistan." The Hindu officers were additionally inhibited by their traditional taboo against crossing the Indus. But Akbar spurred them on.

On the way to Kabul, Akbar made a nostalgic detour to visit Kalanaur, where, as a reluctant teenager, he had been enthroned king a quarter century before. In August 1581 Akbar entered Kabul virtually unopposed (Hakim having fled into the mountains) and took up residence in Babur's old citadel, which was for him redolent with the memories of his childhood. He stayed there for about three weeks, then, in the absence of his timid brother, who had written offering submission but dared not appear before him in person, handed over the province to his sister Bakhtunnisa Begum, and returned to India. It did not matter to Akbar any more whether Hakim returned to Kabul or not. He had made the point: he was the big brother.

The Kabul campaign went off without a flaw, except for one unfortunate incident—the patently unjust execution of Shah Mansur, Akbar's revenue minister, who was suspected of treason and was executed at Shahabad near Ambala on the way to Kabul. The incident, though trivial in itself, is significant in what it reveals about the Mughal ethos.

Mansur was probably the most unpopular Mughal officer of his time. He was, says Abul Fazl, "an adept at the mysteries of accounts", but his skill in unraveling the complex weave of corruption among government officers hardly endeared him to the amirs. It did not help matters that Mansur was also acerbic and tactless, without courtly graces. He had many enemies in high places.

Mansur's methods were inquisitorial. "From his practice in accounts, and seeking after profit (for the government), he looked narrowly into the transactions of the army, and giving his attention to one side only of a minister's duties, he pressed forward the rules of demand," says Abul Fazl. "The Khwaja went out of his proper course and set himself to increase the revenue. Nor did he consider the disturbances of the time and the crisis of the age, but demanded payment of arrears . . . From love of office and cupidity he was always laying hold of trifles in financial matters, and displaying harshness." Even so eminent an officer as Todar Mal had to complain to Akbar about receiving from Mansur "sharp letters . . . claiming a good deal of money."

As the discontent with Mansur spread, Akbar suspended him from office for a while, hoping to placate the amirs, but had to reinstate him soon after, as his services were found indispensable. This upset the amirs, for an honest officer in a corrupt system, like a dog in a house full of cats, was a menace to everything and everybody. "Many of the amirs and officers of State were on bad terms with the Khwaja, and these exerted their influence to secure his death," says Nizamuddin.

Mansur first came under suspicion towards the end of 1580, when letters purportedly written by Muhammad Hakim to Mansur, indicating collusion, were seized by Raja Man Singh in Punjab and forwarded to Akbar. Then, when Akbar was at Sonipat just north of Delhi on his way to Kabul, letters from one of Mansur's officers, again hinting at intrigue, were discovered. Around this time Hakim's revenue minister defected and approached Akbar through Mansur for employment, which was also construed as evidence that Mansur was in contact with Hakim's court. Akbar then summoned Mansur and showed him the incriminating letters. During the inquiry, Mansur, though he swore his innocence, offended Akbar by uttering, according to Abul Fazl, "injudicious words". That sealed his fate.

Abul Fazl then, on the order of Akbar, charged Mansur with ingratitude and treason despite all the favours that had been shown to him. Akbar, says Monserrate, commanded Abul Fazl "to urge the criminal to undergo his punishment with a stout heart, accepting it as only his due. He was further instructed to convince those present that the King had planned no injustice against Shah Mansur, and to warn them to abide by their duty." The arraignment was only a formality. Akbar had already passed judgment.

After his trial, Mansur was taken out and unceremoniously strung up on a tree. No one protested. The execution of Mansur was in fact one of the few popular acts of Akbar in that difficult year. "Throughout the whole camp, the punishment of the wicked man was approved with rejoicing," writes Monserrate.

In all probability Mansur was the victim of a frame-up, as Akbar seems to have discovered when he made inquiries about him in Kabul. According to Badauni, Akbar was told that some of the amirs in Kabul "had concocted all this forgery and deception, and that the last letter also, which had been the cause of his being put to death, was a forgery of the amirs."

Mansur was an unlikely conspirator. He was not a politician; he knew accounts and he knew the rules, but he did not know men. In any case, Mansur and the rebels were in opposite camps, and the amirs were revolting as much against his revenue measures as against Akbar's religious policy.

Did Akbar make a scapegoat of Mansur? Possibly. Akbar was in a vulnerable position at this time, faced with a rebellion in the east and an invasion in the west. It was essential for him to retain the loyalty of the officers still with him, for which it may have seemed necessary to sacrifice Mansur. It was safer for Akbar to execute Mansur than not to execute him. But he would later regret the action—for administrative reasons, not for the miscarriage of justice. "From that day," Akbar would lament, referring to the execution of Mansur, "the market of accounts was flat and the thread of accounting dropped from the hand."

BY THE FIRST week of December 1581 Akbar was back in Fatehpur

Sikri—the entire Kabul campaign had taken just ten months! Four years later, when Muhammad Hakim, thirty-one, died of palsy, Kabul lost its special status and became just another province of the Mughal empire.

Soon after his return to Fatehpur Sikri, Akbar was faced with an uprising in Gujarat. Long years in exile had hardened Muzaffar Shah, the once ineffectual king of Gujarat, into a tough adversary, and in September 1583, taking advantage of the general discontent among imperial officers over Akbar's policies, he expelled the Mughals from Ahmadabad and occupied the city. Though the Mughals promptly retook the city under the command of Abdur-Rahim, Biram Khan's son, Muzaffar fought on tenaciously in the wilderness of Kachchh (Kutch) and Kathiawar, and it was only ten years later, in 1593, that he was finally captured. Two days after he was caught, Muzaffar committed suicide by slitting his throat.

Long before that, Akbar's attention had once again turned to the west, where a new spectre had arisen. The Uzbegs, hereditary adversaries of the Mughals, had, under Abdullah Khan Uzbeg, extended their power from Transoxiana into Badakshan—and that put Kabul, and possibly even Hindustan, in jeopardy. The western frontier of the empire therefore needed careful watching. Of additional concern to Akbar at this time were the activities of the turbulent Afghan tribes around the Khyber Pass, who were menacing the Mughal lifeline from India to Kabul. So in mid-1585 Akbar, who was at that time busy building a fort in Allahabad, to protect the road to Bengal and to serve as a jump-off point for the invasion of the Deccan, changed his plans and set out again for Punjab.

He would stay in Punjab for the next fourteen years, till 1598, securing his western frontier and seizing new lands. For about a decade after the annexation of Bengal, there had been no major expansion of the Mughal empire, but now that the rebellions and mutinies that beset him for several years were behind him, Akbar was ready to move again.

Over a period of thirty years, Akbar, by waging ceaseless war, had built up his kingdom into one of the most powerful empires on earth, arguably the most powerful empire of the age, as the Mings in China and the Safavids in Persia were on the decline at this time, and the rise of European powers was still in the future. But Akbar was not sated. While he was in Punjab his eyes fell on the unconquered territories in that region—Kashmir, Baluchistan and Sind. He would annex them all one by one before he returned to Agra. But Akbar, forty-three now, was slowing down. Both his father and his grandfather had died in their forties. He was almost sedentary in Punjab, leaving it to his generals to wage the battles.

The most difficult of these campaigns turned out to be the one against the Afghan tribes, who were in a peculiar turmoil at this time, under the influence of Bayazid, a self-proclaimed prophet. Bayazid had synthesized out of Hinduism and Islam a weird pantheistic faith, which held that since god was immanent in everything in the universe, all acts were divine acts, and there was therefore no distinction between right and wrong, good and bad. Bayazid further assured his followers— known as Raushanais (Illuminati)—that they, as the chosen people of god, were destined to inherit the earth, and that they could, in anticipation of the fulfilment of divine promise, seize what they could of the land and possessions of unbelievers. This made pillage a religious duty for his followers, which perfectly suited the temperament of the turbulent hill tribes among whom Bayazid preached, and galvanized them into action.

When Bayazid died, his youngest son, Jalaluddin, a charismatic lad of sixteen, took over as the head of the movement. Soon the entire region was plunged into turmoil, and the route from Kabul to Punjab became so unsafe that sometimes even foreign ambassadors with military escort on the way to the Mughal court were not able to get through.

Akbar then fitted out an expedition under Zain Khan to chastise the Afghan tribes. Raja Birbal, a celebrated litterateur and close friend of Akbar, and Hakim Abul-Fath, a renowned physician, were also given military commands in this campaign on their entreaty with Akbar to give them a chance to win glory in the battlefield. Abul Fazl had also vied for the honour, so Akbar had had to draw lots to choose between Abul Fazl and Birbal, which Birbal to his misfortune won. The expedition was a disaster, and on its retreat from the mountains, was ambushed by the Afghans at the Malandarai Pass in February 1586. Birbal, who sensibly tried to save himself by running away, was taken and presumably killed. His body was never found.

Some 8000 men perished in the retreat, but what grieved Akbar most was the loss of Birbal. "For two days and nights he did not take his daily food and drink," reports Abul Fazl. Birbal, a weary looking man with prominent cheekbones and deep-set eyes, had been Akbar's constant companion for many years. Born Mahesh Das, he was a poor brahmin from Kalpi, and was originally in the service of Raja Bhagwan Das, who brought him to Akbar's court. He was fourteen years older than Akbar, but the emperor took to him instantly, and soon he achieved renown as a poet, musician, wit and raconteur, and was given the title Kavi Rai, King of Poets. Later he received the title Raja Birbal, and enjoyed the rank and pay of a commander of 2000 cavalry. His poetic works have not survived, though snatches attributed to him are common, and his witty exchanges with Akbar are part of Indian folklore.

AKBAR AVENGED BIRBAL'S death by sending Todar Mal to hunt down the Afghans; Man Singh, the newly appointed governor of Kabul, also engaged them. Yet it took the Mughals a few years to force the tribes into even a semblance of submission.

Meanwhile Akbar turned to Kashmir. Some years earlier the sultan of Kashmir had sent Akbar a princess as bride, but Akbar had refused to accept her or to receive the presents she had brought. The rebuff had nothing to do with the person of the princess. She was rejected because what was involved was not merely a marriage but an alliance—by rejecting the princess, Akbar was rejecting the proposed alliance, for the sultan, though deferential towards Akbar, did not consider himself a Mughal vassal as Akbar desired. Later, however, when another Kashmiri princess was sent for Prince Salim, she was accepted, for by then Mughal-Kashmir relations had improved, and the khutbah was being read and coins struck in Akbar's name in Kashmir.

Still, problems persisted between the emperor and the rulers of Kashmir. This eventually led to war, and in 1586 Akbar annexed the kingdom. Kashmir then became the private garden of the Mughal emperors, their favourite summer retreat. Akbar vacationed there thrice, first in the summer of 1589, when he spent a couple of months there, again in August 1592, when he spent a week, and for a third time in the summer of 1597, when he spent six months. During the second visit, which followed the suppression of an uprising in Kashmir against Akbar's strict revenue policy, the entire state was converted into crown lands.

After Kashmir came the turns of Sind and Baluchistan, annexed in 1591 and 1595. At about the same time, Raja Man Singh invaded Orissa and brought it under Mughal rule. Akbar's attention then turned to Kandahar. When Humayun broke his word to the Shah and kept Kandahar for himself, the Shah had let it be, biding his time, but in 1558, two years after Akbar's accession, he seized the city by force. For the next thirty-six years Kandahar remained in Persian hands. Its recovery was not a priority for Akbar, but after the Mughal conquest of Sind and Baluchistan, a push against neighbouring Kandahar seemed desirable.

Circumstances favoured the Mughals. Kandahar was at this time under threat from the Uzbegs, but the Shah of Persia, himself beleaguered by the Turks and the Uzbegs, was unable to send any reinforcements. So the governor of Kandahar, who was in any case in an adversary relationship with the Shah, surrendered the city to the Mughals in April 1595.

The Kandahar development did not overtly disturb the Mughal-Persian relationship. Akbar and the Shah continued to exchange ambassadors and presents. In the beginning, the Persian monarch was inclined to be patronizing towards the Mughal emperor, because of the help he had given Humayun to recover his kingdom. Even after the power equation between the two changed in favour of the Mughals—when Akbar built a large and secure empire for himself, and in contrast Persian power declined—Persians continued to consider themselves as superiors, as Mughal culture was patterned on Persian culture. The Mughals and Persians were however far too refined to offend each other by flaunting either superior power or superior culture.

As with Persians, Akbar was careful in his dealings with the Uzbegs. He wanted his western frontier to be quiet. He had no great Central Asian ambitions. The Mughals, now in their third generation in India, had severed the umbilical cord. India was home; Badakshan and Transoxiana were foreign lands. The cool highlands to which Babur's amirs had looked back with desperate longing were now frigid, forbidding lands in the eyes of Akbar's amirs. As for Akbar, enough territories yet remained to be conquered in India itself to sate his earth hunger. He therefore consistently rejected invitations to meddle in the affairs of Badakshan. He certainly did not want to tangle with Abdullah Khan, the Uzbeg chief, even though Abdullah had annexed Badakshan and sent Sulaiman Mirza, the Mughal protege there, scurrying into India for refuge.

As for his northern neighbour, China, the Himalayas secured the frontier, and Akbar did not even know what was going on beyond the mountains. He was curious about China, and once thought of sending an ambassador there, "as for a long time there had been no news of that country, nor was it known who ruled it," writes Abul Fazl. "His Majesty also wished to know with whom he was at war, and what degree of enlightenment and sense of justice he possessed, what kind of knowledge was current, who among the ascetics had a lamp of guidance, who was supreme for science." Nothing came of the proposal.

The only trans-Indian power against whom Akbar assumed an antagonistic posture was Turkey. Soon after Akbar's accession, Biram Khan had sent to Sulaiman the Magnificent, the ruler of Turkey and the "Caliph on earth sent by God", a letter in the name of Akbar, offering friendship. Sulaiman ignored the letter. This indifference galled the Mughals. Further, as Turkish power declined, and Mughal power grew,

Akbar seemed to resent that in Mecca the khutbah was still recited in the name of the Sultan of Turkey, though Akbar was the most powerful Muslim ruler in the world at that time. Akbar's assumption of the titles of Imam and Khalifa in 1579 may have had something to do with his latent rivalry with the Sultan of Turkey. At one time Akbar approached the Shah of Persia and the Uzbegs, and even the Portuguese, for an alliance against Turkey. But this was all just a fancy. Turkey was too far away to have any practical effect on Mughal affairs.

A MAJOR DEVELOPMENT in Akbar's time was the growing presence of Europeans in India, though it would take another couple of centuries for their potential to be manifest. The Portuguese had landed in India over a quarter century before Babur took Delhi, and they had over the decades occupied a few tiny pockets of land along the coast of the peninsula, but as yet their political role in India, even after a century of operations, was insignificant. They, of course, dominated the Indian seas, but that did not concern the Mughals.

Akbar first came into contact with the Portuguese during his 1572-73 Gujarat campaign, and they aroused his ravenous curiosity by opening up an altogether new world for him to explore. A flurry of contacts with the Portuguese followed—a couple of years after returning to Fatehpur Sikri from Gujarat, Akbar sent to Goa an officer with several skilled artisans to procure European products and to learn European crafts; in 1578 a Portuguese ambassador arrived at Fatehpur Sikri; the following year Akbar sent an envoy to Goa to invite Christian priests to the court; in early 1580 a Jesuit mission arrived in Fatehpur Sikri. Akbar was engrossed in religious explorations at this time, and his primary interest in the Portuguese was to learn about their religion. He also desired to secure from the Portuguese safe passage for Indian pilgrims going to Mecca by sea. Later, when he launched his Deccan campaigns, the Portuguese, who had close contacts with the Deccani powers, became a factor, though a minor one, in the Mughal military calculations.

Akbar did not consider the Portuguese as adversaries, and he took no action against them, though he did once speak of a plan to suppress them. "I have kept before my mind the idea that when I . . . [am free of other] tasks, I should, under the guidance of God's favour, undertake the destruction of the Feringi infidels who have come to the islands of the ocean, and have lifted up the head of turbulence, and stretched the hand of oppression upon the pilgrims to the holy places," wrote Akbar to Abdullah Khan Uzbeg. "They have become a great number and are stumbling-blocks to the pilgrims and traders. We thought of going in person and cleansing that road from thorns and weeds." It is doubtful whether Akbar meant it seriously. He did not act on the plan. In any case, he could have cleared the "thorns and weeds" only on the land, not on the sea. The Portuguese were amphibians—challenged on land, they could always retreat to the security of the sea, beyond the reach of the Mughals.

As for the British, though their first ambassador would arrive at the Mughal court only during the reign of Jahangir, a few English merchants did visit Akbar's court. In 1585 a deputation of three English traders, representing the 'Merchants of the Levant' and headed by John Newbery, arrived at Fatehpur Sikri, bearing a letter from Queen Elizabeth of England, in which she, addressing Akbar as "the most invincible and most mightie prince, lord Zelabdim Echebar, king of Cambaya", requested that favours be shown to the merchants bearing the letter. Akbar was just then setting out for Punjab, and it is doubtful whether he received the delegation. There is no record of it.

In 1603, another Englishman, John Mildenhall, representing the newly formed East India Company, arrived at the court, travelling through the Mediterranean to Syria, and then overland to Agra through Persia and Kandahar. He brought yet another letter from Elizabeth to Akbar. Mildenhall claimed to be the British ambassador (which he was not) and was therefore admitted to the Mughal court, the first Englishman to have that privilege. He presented the emperor with twenty-one horses and some jewels, hoping to win favour, but could make little headway despite his long stay in Agra, for the Jesuits at the court, who doubled as the political agents of Portugal, obstructed him in every way and spread the word that the English were a nation of thieves and that Mildenhall was a spy. The good fathers bribed Akbar's councillors, lied in their teeth, and even tried to silence the Englishman by spiriting away his interpreter; they were not, it was rumoured, even above using poison to gain their objectives.

But then, Mildenhall himself was not above chicanery; he was, as one English historian puts it bluntly, "a dishonest scoundrel". Neither bluster nor deception could, however, get him any concessions from Akbar. It was only later, during the reign of Jahangir, that he managed to get some sort of a firman, and even that proved to be of no practical value.

IN FEBRUARY 1598 Abdullah Khan Uzbeg died, and with him passed the threat of an Uzbeg invasion of India. Relieved, Akbar returned to Agra, and soon after launched his long deferred Deccan campaign.

"The rulers of the Dakhin, every one of them severally, had been accustomed to send their envoys every year with tribute and presents to the Imperial court," claims Nizamuddin Ahmad. But they were independent rulers, not Mughal vassals, and Akbar could not countenance that. The objective of Akbar's Deccan policy, according to Abul Fazl, "was to clear the territory of Ahmadnagar of the weeds and rubbish of rebellion, and then to prevail over Bijapur, Golconda and Bidar, so that the rulers of these places should make binding treaties of obedience."

The first foray of the Mughals into the Deccan was in 1561, when Pir Muhammad entered Khandesh in hot pursuit of Baz Bahadur, the ruler of Malwa. Three years later, in 1564, when Akbar was in Malwa chastising rebels, he demanded the submission of Khandesh. Khandesh yielded and sent him a princess as bride. After that Akbar virtually ignored the Deccan for the next twenty-seven years, till 1591, when he sent envoys to the courts of the Deccan sultanates to demand that they acknowledge his suzerainty. Bijapur and Golconda received Akbar's envoys courteously, and sent through them valuable gifts, but they balked at acknowledging Mughal overlordship. Khandesh, already a Mughal tributary, once again sent a princess, this time for Salim. But Ahmadnagar, a frontline state, grew agitated over Akbar's claim of overlordship and its Nizam Shahi sultan gruffly dismissed the Mughal envoy. Akbar noted the affront and bided his time.

Four years later, in 1595, a chaotic succession struggle in Ahmadnagar (with four claimants to the throne, each a puppet of a feudal faction) opened a passage for the Mughals to enter the Deccan. When one of the factions sought Mughal help, Akbar ordered Prince Murad, who was then governor of Gujarat, to move in. But Murad was an alcoholic and a poseur—he preened as "a ripe grape, when he was not even an unripe grape," says the acerbic Badauni—and he and his second in command, Abdur-Rahim, the Khan-i-khanan, could not pull together. This hampered the Deccan campaign, and though the Mughals penetrated deep into the state and laid siege to its capital, Ahmadnagar city, the capture of the city seemed a remote possibility.

The dominant faction in the kingdom of Ahmadnagar at this time was the one led by Chand Bibi (Lady Moon), a Nizam Shahi princess who, though she was the dowager queen of Bijapur, ruled Ahmadnagar as the regent of her grand-nephew, Bahadur, an infant. Faced with Mughal invasion, Chand Bibi adopted a two-pronged strategy to protect her power—on the one hand, she persuaded Bijapur and Golconda to mobilize in her aid, by impressing on them the common danger they faced from the Mughals, and at the same time she tried to placate the Mughals by ceding to them Berar, an Ahmadnagar protectorate. Murad, running short of provisions, and aware of the troop movements of Bijapur and Golconda, accepted Chand Bibi's offer and withdrew from Ahmadnagar.

But factional chaos persisted in the state, and hostilities with the Mughals broke out again within a year. In the ensuing battle the Mughals worsted the combined forces of Ahmadnagar, Bijapur and Golconda, but were not able to press home their advantage, mainly because of the friction between Murad and Abdur-Rahim. Two years later, in May 1599, Murad, twenty-nine, died of delirium tremens, and Prince Daniyal, twenty-seven, took his place as the commander of the Mughal forces in the Deccan. But Daniyal too was an alcoholic, and his appointment hardly improved matters. Morale was low in the Mughal camp at this time. There was a shortage of funds, and the pay of soldiers was long in arrears; moreover, the Mughal amirs abhorred serving in the Deccan, and there were several desertions. It was clear that if the situation were to be retrieved, Akbar himself would have to move into the Deccan.

In the last week of September 1599 Akbar, fifty-seven now, set out from Agra with an army of 80,000 horse, and ordered Daniyal to push on against Ahmadnagar. In the face of such a mammoth invasion, Chand Bibi was inclined to sue for peace, but that prudent advice was not heeded by her amirs, who charged her with collusion with the Mughals. They incited the city rabble to storm her palace and kill her, and girded themselves to oppose the invader. And, fighting tenaciously, they succeeded in preserving Ahmadnagar as a fragmentary state for several decades, though the Mughals annexed a good part of the kingdom, including Ahmadnagar city.

From Ahmadnagar the Mughals turned to Khandesh. Khandesh had been the first Deccani state to submit to Akbar, but now, thirty-six years later, its young ruler, Bahadur Faruqi, taking his cue from the defiance of Ahmadnagar and relying on the strength of Asirgarh, one of the strongest hill forts in the world, threw off his allegiance to the emperor. This led to war, and in January 1601 Akbar seized Asirgarh, allegedly by stratagem, and annexed Khandesh.

The Khandesh campaign marked the end of Akbar's career of conquest. The Mughal empire now covered the whole of India north of the Godavari River, except the tribal belt south of Bihar. In the north the empire extended into Kashmir, in the west to the Helmand River in Afghanistan, and in the east to the valley of the Brahmaputra River. It was one of the largest empires in Indian history, with a population of over a hundred million people. Akbar would probably have stayed on in the Deccan a while longer, extending his frontiers further, but he was obliged to return to the north to deal with Prince Salim, his eldest son, who had risen in rebellion. The eagle would soar no more.

Person and Persona

AKBAR IS ONE of the only two monarchs in the entire span of Indian history to be called 'great', the other being Asoka, who lived eighteen centuries before Akbar. Akbar's name meant 'great', and he would live up to its promise.

The passage of time has been kind to Asoka, gently washing away the common sludge of life and enveloping him in the misty, golden glow of myth, but Akbar lived too close to our own time for us not to know the person behind the persona, the deeply troubled man who, despite all his great triumphs, was unhappy with himself and unsure of the world. There was no halo around Akbar's head. Yet, in his own way, Akbar, like Asoka, was a compassionate king, especially in his later years. But his compassion was not of character, which was violent, but of intelligence.

They were both great visionaries, Asoka and Akbar, who dared to pursue the ideal of perfection beyond the ordinary limits of the possible. Akbar's ambition was to gather the diverse peoples of the subcontinent under his benevolent wings, to enable them, through religious and cultural syncretism, to live in peace and amity. In this vision, and in his intellectual openness and rationalism, this sanguinary medieval autocrat was a thoroughly modern man, ahead of his time, and in some ways ahead even of our time.

Akbar, unlike Asoka, was not a gentle person, but a driven, possessed man. What distinguished him most was energy, physical and intellectual, a sparking, supercharged electric potency. He was invincible in the battlefield, a great empire builder. "Every enterprise that the sublime genius of the Shahinshah engaged in was accomplished with the greatest ease, however difficult it might appear to ordinary eyes," says Abul Fazl. And Du Jarric writes, "Echebar was one of the most fortunate monarchs of his time. Everything came to him that he wished for."

Gradually Akbar came to be regarded as a man of superhuman powers. And the legend of his omnipotence, by the none too mysterious process of the extrusion of myth into reality—of the man growing to fill the contours of the myth—made Akbar in fact invincible, as his adversaries, with terror in their hearts and flight in their thoughts, could never take a firm stand against him. Omens, an important determinant of fortune in medieval times, always favoured Akbar, even when they were ill omens. Once when Akbar was going by boat on a campaign, a large fish leapt out of the water and fell before Akbar, and "soothsayers knew that this was a sign of success, and gave thanks to God," says Abul Fazl. Similarly, when there was a sudden change in the wind direction when he was setting out, it was not seen as portending a change of fortune, but as foretelling victory. On another occasion, when the nose-piece of his helmet fell off when he was on a campaign, it too was read as a sign of victory, and not of misfortune. "It is a good omen," said Akbar, "for our front has been made clear."

Akbar seemed to ride on a beam of the energy of time itself. In most cases there was no rational explanation for why he succeeded in impossible situations. A divine providence was therefore assumed. Akbar himself attributed his success to celestial favour: "In all my enterprises . . . all my reliance is on divine aid," he said. Explains Abul Fazl: "Verily, these doings are of Grace and not manufactured. They are Fortune and not contrivance." But there was contrivance too. Akbar had full trust in his good fortune, but he also made careful preparations for all his major campaigns. "He has an acute insight, and shows much wise foresight both in avoiding dangers and in seizing favourable opportunities for carrying out his designs," says Monserrate.

AKBAR'S CONTEMPORARIES, ALL under his spell, even Jesuit missionaries, speak of his majestic bearing. Monserrate writes: "The Prince is of a stature and of a type of countenance well-fitted for his royal dignity, so that one could easily recognize, even at first glance, that he is the King . . . His expression is tranquil, serene and open, full also of dignity, and when he is angry of awful majesty."

Akbar, according to his son Jahangir, "was of middling stature, but with a tendency to be tall, of wheat-complexion, rather inclining to dark than fair, black eyes and eye-brows, stout body, open forehead and chest, long arms and hands. There was a fleshy wart, about the size of a small pea, on the left side of his nose, which appeared exceedingly beautiful and which was considered very auspicious by physiognomists, who said that it was the sign of immense riches and increasing prosperity. He had a very loud voice, and a very elegant and pleasant speech. His manners and habits were quite different from those of other persons, and his visage full of godly dignity." There was a touch of melancholy in the face, in the way his head drooped sideways. Laughter, Monserrate says, did not become Akbar: "When he laughs, his face becomes almost distorted."

He was slightly bow-legged, from much horse riding in his childhood, and limped on his left leg, "though indeed he has never received any injury there," says Monserrate. "His body is exceedingly well built and is neither too thin nor too short. He is sturdy, hearty and robust." His shoulders were broad and muscular, his face square, with a cleft jaw. He sported no beard, but wore long sideburns, reaching beneath his earlobes. His mouth, framed by a drooping, trimmed moustache, was small and resolute, the lips thin. There was a suggestion of impatience there. "His nose is straight and small, though not insignificant," says Monserrate. "His nostrils are widely opened, as though in derision," and hinted an explosive temper held in check by the force of will; his widely set, heavy-lidded eyes beneath sparse, thin eyebrows were "so bright and flashing that they seem like a sea shimmering in moonlight. His eyelashes are very long."

Akbar's dress was rich but not gaudy. A simple turban of tightly rolled cloth covered his head and a good part of his broad, open forehead; the turban was usually adorned with pearls and gems, yet appeared simple and unostentatious, more apparel than imperial diadem. He wore hardly any jewels, except often a string of pearls around his neck. "The king is apparelled in a white *cabie* (muslin tunic) made like a shirt and tied with strings on the one side, and little cloth on his head coloured oftentimes with red or yellow," says Ralph Fitch. Akbar wore his hair long, not close-cropped as was usual among his people, probably as "a concession to Indian usages, and to please his Indian subjects," says Monserrate. "He generally sits, with crossed legs upon a couch covered with scarlet rugs."

If Jesuit missionaries are to be believed, Akbar occasionally wore European dress in private, in the presence of Europeans. Wearing the European dress was not, however, a mere fancy for Akbar. "That he did in order to please his guests," says Monserrate. The Jesuit priest Acquaviva once found Akbar clad in a silk dhoti. Whatever dress he wore, it was heavily perfumed. "His Majesty is very fond of perfumes," writes Abul Fazl. "The court hall is continually scented with ambergris, aloeswood, and compositions according to ancient recipes, or mixtures invented by His Majesty; and incense is daily burnt in gold and silver censers of various shapes; whilst sweet-smelling flowers are used in large quantities. Oils are also extracted from flowers, and used for the skin and hair."

COMPLEX AND MULTI-FACETED, Akbar was an enigma to his

contemporaries. He never revealed himself fully to anyone. Says Bartoli, a late-seventeenth-century Jesuit historian: "And in all business this was the characteristic manner of King Akbar—a man apparently free from mystery and guile, as honest and candid as could be imagined, but in reality so close and self-contained, with twists of words and deeds so divergent one from the other, and most times so contradictory that even by much seeking one could not find the clue to his thoughts. Thus it often happened that a person, comparing him today with what he was yesterday, could find no resemblance; and even an attentive observer, after long and familiar intercourse with him, knew no more of him on the last day than he had known on the first."

No one had the measure of Akbar, for he lived tightly rolled into himself. As emperor, he was always in the public eye. Even his private life was public. The courtiers knew where he was at all times, and heard rumours about what he said and did, wherever he was, even in his apartment in the harem. There was no private place anywhere to which Akbar could retreat, except into himself. So he kept concealed within himself a good part of what he thought and felt.

That hidden, interior space was what gave Akbar's character its depth and resonance, and also its mystery. He was perceived by different people in different ways, so that, though there are voluminous contemporary writings about Akbar, his personality remains elusive. Often his motives were misunderstood, but he was philosophical about it, as he once wrote to Abdullah Khan Uzbeg:

> Of God people have said that He had a son;
> Of the Prophet some have said that he
>   was a sorcerer;
> Neither God nor the Prophet has escaped
>   the slander of men,
> Then how could I?

Akbar radiated awesome power. His effect on people was mesmeric. A ruler is primarily a ruler of men, and Akbar was supremely masterful in that role. "Indeed he was a great King," says Du Jarric, "for he knew that the good ruler is he who can command, simultaneously, the obedience, the respect, the love, and the fear of his subjects."

Usually Akbar was pleasant mannered, in perfect self-control, and therefore in cool control of others. Sometimes though, a shadow of melancholia fell over him, and he did strange things. And he did have a temper, which was a fearsome thing when it flared up. But these were aberrations. Akbar was generally lenient towards offenders, and kept in service even those who betrayed him. "The noblest quality of princes is the forgiveness of faults," he maintained. He was strong enough to bear and forbear the faults of others.

"The world of existence is amenable only to kindness," Akbar professed. "No living creature deserves rejection." Notes Father Jerome Xavier, a Jesuit missionary in Akbar's court: "He was great with the great, and lowly with lowly." Bartoli elaborates: "With small and common people, he was so sympathetic and indulgent, that he always found time gladly to hear their cases, and to respond graciously to their requests. Their little offerings, too, he used to accept with such a pleased look, handling them and putting them in his bosom, as he did not do with the most lavish gifts of the nobles, which, with discreet pretence, he often seemed not even to glance at." Though generally considered tightfisted, Akbar used to keep a heap of gold and silver coins beside him, to give away as presents. Once he emptied the pool in the courtyard of the Fatehpur Sikri palace and filled it with gold, silver and copper coins and gave it all away as alms.

Despite all the controversies surrounding him, Akbar was a popular monarch. "He was a prince beloved of all," says Du Jarric, "firm with the great, kind to those of low estate, and just to all men, high and low, neighbour or stranger, Christian, Saracen, or Gentile; so that every man believed that the king was on his side." As Abul Fazl would have it, Akbar was

Sagacious, liberal and gentle
An angel in the form of man.

Not quite. Akbar was no angel. But he did work very hard to be a good ruler. His day was long, and began early. About three hours before daybreak, musicians struck up to awaken the emperor and the court. After ablutions, Akbar spent some time in prayers and meditation—or, as Abul Fazl puts it, "His Majesty retires to his private apartments, brings his external appearance in harmony with the simplicity of his heart, and launches forth into the ocean of contemplation." Then for the rest of the day, except for a nap at midday, Akbar was busy with work till late at night. He slept little. "He passed his nights in wakefulness, and slept little in the day," says Jahangir; "the length of his sleep in a whole night and day was not more than a watch and half (four and a half hours)." Said Akbar: "Although sleep brings health of body, yet as life is the greatest gift of God, it were better that it should be spent in wakefulness."

Akbar was essentially a man of action. Though there was in him a strong predilection for mysticism and philosophy, he had no patience with abstract, pointless speculation and metaphysical hair-splitting. Everything in some way had to have a practical relevance and had to energize action, for, as he said, "Although knowledge in itself is regarded as the summit of perfection, yet unless displayed in action, it bears not the impress of worth; indeed, it may be considered worse than ignorance."

In battle, Akbar delighted in plunging in where the fight was thickest and the danger greatest—so impetuous was he that sometimes his officers deliberately had to frustrate his battle plans to save him from himself. He did not know what fear was. When the need was pressing, he could move at lightning speed, often travelling from midnight to midday, to confound his adversaries. But he would not crawl up on the enemy treacherously in the night for a surprise attack, for he held, as Abul Fazl puts it, that "a night attack is the trade of cowards."

Akbar's energy was prodigious, and few could match his stamina. Once when he walked from a hunting ground near Mathura to Agra, a distance of nearly sixty kilometres, only three of his companions were able keep up with him and stay the course. Yet, for a man who used up so much energy, his diet was frugal. In his youth he was gluttonous, but his habits changed and became spartan as he grew older. "In the course of twenty-four hours, His Majesty eats but once, and leaves off before he is fully satisfied," says Abul Fazl; "neither is there any fixed time for this meal, but the servants have always things so far ready, that in the space of an hour, after the order has been given, a hundred dishes are served up."

Akbar was indifferent to food. "'What dinner has been prepared today?' never passes over his tongue," says Abul Fazl. Towards the end of his life he virtually gave up eating meat; vegetables and fruits, especially fruits, then constituted his main diet. "During three months of the year he ate meat, and for the remaining nine contented himself with Sufi food, and was no way pleased with the slaughter of animals," notes Jahangir. "His Majesty cares very little for meat . . . If his Majesty had not the burden of the world on his shoulder, he would at once totally abstain from meat; and now it is his intention to quit it by degree," reports Abul Fazl. "It is not right that a man should make his stomach the grave of animals," Akbar maintained. "My father the late king was exceedingly fond of fruit, especially melons, pomegranates and grapes," says Jahangir. Akbar had fruits served to him even when he took opium or wine. Adds Abul Fazl: "His Majesty looks upon fruits as one of the greatest gifts of the Creator, and pays much attention to them . . . Ever since the conquest of Kabul, Kandahar, and Kashmir, loads of fruit are imported."

Though indifferent to food, Akbar was particular about water. He preferred water from the Ganga—"the water of immortality", he called it—and arranged to procure it even when he travelled to far-off places. When Akbar was in Punjab, Ganga water was brought from Haridwar. "Some trustworthy persons are stationed on the banks of that river, who dispatch the water in sealed jars . . . ," notes Abul Fazl. "On journeys and hunting parties, his Majesty, from his predilection for good water, appoints experienced men as water-tasters." The water was cooled with ice, if available, otherwise with saltpetre. For cooking, rain water or water from the Yamuna or the Chenab was used, "mixed with a little Ganga water".

Unlike his father or his sons, Akbar was not a heavy drinker, nor was he an opium addict, though he had a fondness for arrack, the common spirituous liquor of India, and for pousta, a drink of opium cut with various spices. "He rarely drinks wine, but quenches his thirst with pousta or water," says Monserrate. Sometimes, while listening to the discourses of the Jesuits, he fell asleep from the effect of opium or alcohol, or perhaps out of boredom. Tobacco was introduced into the Mughal court towards the close of Akbar's reign, but he did not take to it.

AS AKBAR GREW older, he grew in stature. Not only that, his very character underwent a mutation, as he evolved from a youth of ravenous appetites—for food, for sex, for adventure, for conquest—into an austere, somewhat saddened man in middle age. Only his appetite for conquest remained unabated till the end.

As a young man, Akbar was a sexual predator. He married early and often. Abul Fazl lists seven wives of Akbar, three in excess of the liberal four permitted by Islam, and these were just his legal wives, married by the formal *nikah* ceremony. In addition, he had several wives by informal *mutah* marriages, which involved no ceremony and had little legitimacy. He also had numerous concubines. In all, Akbar probably had in his harem, as wives and concubines, some 300 women, from many races and different religions. But contrary to the prevailing custom of bisexuality, he was strictly heterosexual.

In his youth Akbar had not, as he himself once admitted, regarded the question of the number of permitted wives and had married whatever number of women he pleased. But later, when he had put on the mantle of an arbiter in religion, his early marital excesses became an embarrassment, and he sought the help of the ulema to somehow legitimize his illegitimate marriages. And sure enough, they obliged, compliantly interpreting that four could also mean nine or even eighteen. They further drew a distinction between *nikah* wives and *mutah* wives, and concluded that a man may take as many *mutah* wives as he desired.

In his twenties, Akbar's sexual appetite had seemed insatiable. In 1564, when he was twenty-two and already a much married man, we find him casting about for fresh mates, sending panders and eunuchs into the harems of nobles to select women for him. His eyes fell even on married women, and, as Badauni reports, in one case at least he forced an amir to divorce his "wonderfully beautiful and altogether a charming wife without peer" and send her to the imperial harem. The amir, Sheikh Abdul Wasi, had no option but to consent, for it was the Mughal custom that "if the emperor cast his eye with desire on any woman", the husband should divorce her and give her over to the emperor.

Akbar's raids into the households of amirs caused considerable resentment, says Badauni, "and a great terror fell upon the city", which may have had something to do with an assassination attempt on Akbar around this time, in which a slave named Fulad shot an arrow at Akbar from the balcony of a seminary in Delhi, when he was passing by after visiting the tomb of Sheikh Nizamuddin Auliya. Abul Fazl describes the scene: "It (the arrow) struck His Majesty's right shoulder and penetrated about the length of a span. A cry rose from heaven and earth, and devoted followers fell upon that wretch. They wished to examine him and not to kill him at once, but His Majesty indicated that he should be speedily put to death lest a number of loyalists should fall under suspicion. In an instant they cut him to pieces."

Still, Akbar's eyes continued to rove. Seven years later, in 1571, when he was living in the hermitage of Sheikh Salim Chishti at Sikri during the construction of his new capital, not even his veneration for the sage inhibited him. Chishti had allowed Akbar entry into his private apartments, and Akbar roamed a bit even there, so that the sheikh's sons and nephews complained, "Our wives are becoming estranged from us." But the worldly-wise sage advised them, "There is no dearth of women in the world. Since I have made you amirs, seek other wives, what does it matter!" Badauni rationalizes:

> Either make no friendship with an
> elephant driver,
> Or make a house fit for an elephant.

Akbar's sexuality was intense but short-lived, and by early middle age he was sated. Gradually he became continent. "Had I been wise earlier, I would have taken no woman from my own kingdom into my seraglio," he penitently confessed, "for my subjects are to me in the place of children." He even recommended monogamy, saying, "To seek more than one wife is to work one's own undoing. In case she were barren or bore no son, it might then be expedient."

Monogamy was not however practical for a medieval ruler; infant mortality being what it was in those days, a number of wives, and as many children as possible, were the only insurance against the line dying out. Politics too played a role in determining the size of the royal family—Akbar simply had to keep marrying princesses to bind his alliances with the vassals and tributary rulers of his expanding empire.

He took his first wife, Ruqaiya Begum, a cousin, when he was about fifteen years old; she outlived him by many years and died at 84. Childless herself, she tended Akbar's grandson Khurram who eventually ascended the throne as Shah Jahan. His other noteworthy spouses were Salima Begum (Biram Khan's widow) and Raja Bhara Mal's daughter, the mother of Salim.

Before Salim's birth, "the emperor had had several children in succession born to him, but they had all passed away at a tender age," notes Badauni. His first child was a daughter, Fatima Banu Begum, but she died in infancy, and so did the first sons born to him, twins named Hasan and Husain, born in 1564; they lived only a month. In 1562 Akbar began his annual pilgrimages to the tomb of Sheikh Muinuddin Chishti in Ajmer, sometimes travelling part of the way on foot, in the hope of winning divine favour for an heir, and continued to do so till 1579, though by then he had three sons, and he himself had become disenchanted with Islam.

It was the lack of an heir that made Akbar seek the blessings of Sheikh Salim Chishti, a devotee of the saint of Ajmer and himself a revered holy man, who lived in a hermitage amidst the rocky hills of Sikri. The sheikh assured Akbar that his prayers would be answered, and he would be blessed with three sons. So when his Rajput wife was with child, Akbar sent her to the hermitage at Sikri for her confinement, for the childbirth to be made auspicious by the spiritual potency of the place. The child, a son, born in August 1569 when Akbar was twenty-seven, was named Salim, after the sage. Akbar celebrated the birth of his heir with a seven-day festival, during which prisoners were released, so that the child might be blessed by their gratitude. A few months later, in January following, Akbar set out on a thanksgiving pilgrimage to Ajmer, walking the entire 360 kilometres on foot, covering it in sixteen stages, averaging twenty-three kilometres a day.

Three months after the birth of Salim a daughter was born to Akbar, and then Murad, born to Salima Begum in June 1570. Two years later, in September 1572, was born Akbar's last son, Daniyal, and finally two more daughters. Akbar was particularly fond of his last daughter, Aram Banu Begum, a hot-tempered and saucy girl.

Illiterate Savant

AKBAR WAS JUST thirty when his third son was born. His line was now secure. He had achieved most of his political ambitions too, and was the absolute ruler of a vast empire. Gradually then, he began to turn away from the quest for temporal and carnal gratifications to cultural and spiritual pursuits, though the expansion and consolidation of his empire would ever remain his primary goal. And whatever he did, whether leading a cavalry charge, debating religious issues, or even playing a game, he applied himself to it with resolute intensity. "At one time he would be deeply immersed in state affairs, or giving audience to his subjects," says Du Jarric, "and the next moment he would be seen shearing camels, hewing stones, cutting wood, or hammering iron, and doing all with as much diligence as though engaged in his own particular vocation."

A lifelong passion of Akbar was music, and he gathered in his court the finest musical talent from all over his far-flung empire, including Tansen, the most renowned Indian musician-composer of the age. The emperor himself was a skilled drummer, and had learned singing from Lal Kalawant, who taught him, in the words of Jahangir, "every breathing and sound that appertains to the Hindi language". A discerning lover of poetry, Akbar also occasionally composed verses. "The inspired nature of his Majesty is strongly drawn to the composing of Hindi and Persian poetry and is critical and hair-splitting in the niceties of poetic diction," writes Abul Fazl, and goes on to quote one of Akbar's compositions:

> It is not the chain of insanity on the neck
> of the afflicted Majnun;
> Love hath laid a loving hand on his neck.

Akbar had a special affinity for the soaring, mystical works of Sufi poets, but mere jugglery of words repelled him. "A rope-dancer performs with feet and hands, a poet with his tongue," said Akbar about commonplace, banal versifiers. And again: "Since the poet builds on fiction, his creation cannot be seriously accepted." There was much truth in this reproach, for most medieval Indian poets, especially the panegyrists in the court, were hollow pedants and verbal jugglers. Though some of the great devotional poets of the age, including Tulsi Das, the greatest Hindi epic poet of all time, were Akbar's contemporaries, he does not seem to have been familiar with their works.

In his time Akbar enjoyed a considerable reputation as a savant. But he was illiterate, barely able to sign his own name—the only sample we have of his handwriting is a signature on the margin of a manuscript book, written laboriously, like a child. "He is illiterate," states Monserrate. "Although illiterate... [he had acquired so much knowledge] that no one knew him to be illiterate," says Jahangir. Being unlettered was not, however, a disability in the Mughal emperor—there was no functional need for him to be literate, for he could always hire people to read and write for him.

And this was what he did. He had an insatiable thirst for knowledge, and had books read out to him regularly, so that in the course of time, because of his keen interest and retentive memory, he became quite a learned man. He possessed a vast personal library, which, according to an inventory said to have been taken of his treasures after his death, contained 24,000 volumes, valued at 6.5 million rupees. He also maintained an extensive translation department at the court, which could handle many languages, including Greek, and translated from Sanskrit into Persian such works as the Hindu epics *Mahabharata* and *Ramayana*, and *Leelavati*, a poetic treatise on arithmetic. Some of Akbar's amirs themselves were distinguished scholars. Abdur-Rahim, the Khan-i-khanan, for instance, was a great linguist, fluent in Persian, Arabic, Turki, Sanskrit and Hindi; it was he who translated Babur's memoirs from Turki into Persian. The memoirs of Gulbadan Begum and Jauhar were also written at Akbar's request: "There was an order issued—write down whatever you know of the doings of Babur and Humayun," notes Gulbadan.

For all his passion for knowledge, Akbar did not care for printed works, and gave away the books presented to him by the Jesuits. He collected only manuscripts, valued equally for their calligraphy and illustrations as for their contents. All were exquisitely bound. The books were works of art. This was important to Akbar, for he was an ardent and discerning patron of art. "His Majesty, from his earliest youth, has shown a great predilection for this art (drawing)," says Abul Fazl. As a boy he had eagerly taken to drawing, and when he became emperor he gathered in his court several noted artists, and commissioned from them major illustrated works.

Abul Fazl mentions the names of eighteen eminent artists in Akbar's court, thirteen of whom were Hindus, indicating the prevalence of a lively indigenous art tradition. But Persian influence dominated Mughal art, and towards the end of Akbar's life, European influences also began to be felt. Once, when Akbar saw a painting of the Madonna in the Jesuit chapel, he personally carried the picture into the royal harem to show it to his wives. His own drawing master, Khwaja Abdus Samad, was a well-known artist; a disciple of Bihzad, the celebrated artist of Herat, he was brought to India from Persia by Humayun. Akbar appointed him as the head of the imperial mints, and it was presumably he who designed the admirable coins of Akbar that are regarded as the finest coins minted anywhere in the world at the time.

The most renowned artist in Akbar's court was Daswanth, son of a poor palanquin-bearer, who used to wander about the streets of Fatehpur as a child, drawing on walls. Akbar noticed him, and took him to the court to be coached by Abdus Samad. Soon Daswanth outshone his master. But tragically, after ten years in the imperial atelier, he committed suicide. "All at once," says Abul Fazl, "melancholy took possession of him, and he wounded himself with a dagger."

As in arts, Akbar was also keenly interested in crafts and machinery. He loved pottering about in workshops, especially in the gunsmithy, and was an inventor of sorts himself. Abul Fazl mentions that Akbar fabricated a wheel contraption turned by a cow, by which sixteen gun barrels could be cleaned simultaneously; he is also said to have made a number of modifications in the designs of weapons.

THE WARRIOR KING that he was, Akbar was an avid sportsman, though it is probable that, as Abul Fazl claims, he was seeking other gains than mere pleasure in sports. "Inasmuch as the wise make use of sport to test men when they are at ease... His Majesty was studying all the groups [of amirs playing various games] with the norms of knowledge," says Abul Fazl, echoing Ovid's maxim that "In our play we reveal what kind of people we are."

What Akbar enjoyed most in sports was hunting, which was a substitute—and sometimes a warm-up—for battle. As Laurence Binyon, a modern biographer of Akbar, puts it, the Mughal was "possessed with the fever of the hunt, whether of beasts or of men." Here again, Abul Fazl attributes occult motives to Akbar: "Superficial, worldly observers see in killing an animal a sort of pleasure... But deep inquirers see in hunting a means of acquisition of knowledge, and the temple of their worship derives from it a peculiar lustre."

Akbar invariably opened his military campaigns with a hunt, and has to his dubious credit some of the most massive hunts ever organized anywhere. Early in 1567 he arranged a *battue* hunt near Lahore, in which 50,000 beaters laboured for a month to drive all the game in the area into a slaughter arena of sixteen kilometres circumference. For five days Akbar hunted there, using every conceivable weapon—sword, lance, musket, arrows, even the lasso—slaughtering a prodigious number of animals. Hunting with trained cheetahs was a special joy for Akbar, and he had at one time as many as a 1000 cheetahs in his various stables, of which 50 were kept at the court. His favourite cheetah, Madan Kali, had the honour of having a drum beaten before it in procession. Akbar was a daring hunter. Once, on the way from Malwa to Agra, when he came across a tigress with cubs, he, just nineteen years old then, fearlessly approached it on foot, despite the ferocity of the beast protecting its young, and slew it with his sword—a feat which, along with other similar exploits, went into the making of the legend of his superhuman powers.

Akbar prided himself on having special powers over birds and animals. Wild deer, it is said, used to eat out of his hand, and when his courtiers marvelled at this, Akbar remarked that "it was not extraordinary that such things occurred, if one did not ill-treat animals and spoke kindly to those dumb creatures." He was a keen pigeon flier from his childhood, and as emperor maintained some 20,000 carefully bred pigeons, divided into ten groups; he loved watching their antics, which he called *ishkbazi*, love-play. He also had 12,000 deer, of which 101 were kept in the citadel.

To the horror of orthodox Muslims, Akbar also maintained a kennel of dogs. Badauni charges that Akbar, "in contempt of Islam ceasing to consider swine and dogs as unclean, kept them in the harem and under the fort, and regarded the going to look at them every morning as a religious service." Akbar justified his fondness for dogs by claiming that they had ten virtues and that "if a man had but one of them he would be a saint." His favourite dog was named Mahuwa, charmer.

But the animal that Akbar favoured most was the elephant, with which he is said to have had a special rapport. When the Sultan of Bijapur once asked Asad Beg, historian and bureaucrat, what Akbar had "the greatest taste for", Asad had a ready answer: "Rare jewels and choice elephants." Akbar was utterly fearless in handling elephants, and could ride unruly elephants that others feared to mount, climbing on them by stepping on their tusks, even when they were in the rutting season. In his youth he sometimes used to leap onto the backs of rampaging elephants from a wall or a tree, and make them fight other elephants, often endangering his life.

Why did he take such risks? Explained Akbar: "Our knowingly and intentionally mounting on murderous elephants in musth, when they have a moment previous brought their drivers under their feet and killed them, and when they have slain many a man, has this for its cause and motive: that, if I have knowingly taken a step which is displeasing to God or have knowingly made an aspiration which was not according to His pleasure, may that elephant finish us, for we cannot support the burden of life under God's displeasure." He was testing his fate, he claimed. Fortunately, his luck held, whatever the reason for his daredevilry.

Wrestling was another favourite sport of Akbar, and so was *chaugan* (polo), which he played with great verve, often hitting the ball in mid-air. He took polo so seriously that courtiers were required to play it regularly, and any one who did not exert himself well was liable to be sent out of the court—or even banished from the empire. To induce the amirs to play, betting on the game was allowed, and Akbar had "knobs of gold and silver... fixed to the tops of the *chaugan* sticks," says Abul Fazl. "If one of them breaks, any player that gets hold of the pieces may keep them." To play the game at night, Akbar introduced a luminous ball of *palas* wood, which smouldered when ignited.

Akbar also played a variety of indoor games, and is credited with inventing a dice game called Chandal Mandal. In a scene described by Abul Fazl, we see Akbar and his amirs at play at the lakeside in Fatehpur Sikri: "Some were playing at draughts, some at chess, and many were occupied with cards." Akbar played all games in a deadly competitive spirit, as if they were battles, and at least one death was recorded while he was playing polo.

If sport was battle for Akbar, sometimes battle was sport. Once, when he was encamped at Kurukshetra, a centre of Hindu pilgrimage some 140 kilometres north of Delhi, two rival groups of sadhus, Kurs and Puris, sought the emperor's permission to settle in a fight a dispute between them over the place to sit to receive alms. Akbar, amused, agreed, and even let some of his own soldiers smear their bodies with ash and join the Puris, the weaker side, so that it would be an even fight. The battle of the sadhus left several dead, but "the holy heart [of the emperor]... was highly delighted with this sport," notes Abul Fazl, and goes on to comment, "The asceticism of most of these men arises from the world's having turned its back on them, and not from their having become cold-hearted to the world. Consequently, they are continually distressed and overcome of lust and wrath and covetousness."

AKBAR DID NOT have quite the same passion for gardens as Babur and Jahangir, but he did lay out gardens at Fatehpur and Sikandra, and built a floating palace with gardens in Kashmir. "As in this country there were more than 30,000 boats but none fit for the world's lord, able artificers soon prepared river-palaces, and made flower gardens on the surface of the water," reports Abul Fazl. "Men of note, and near relatives, also prepared boats so that more than a thousand were ready, and there was a city upon the waters."

More than gardening, architecture was the true creative medium of Akbar, and it was in it this he made a unique cultural contribution. Though Babur was fascinated by Indian architecture and was alive to its possibilities, the Indian phase of his career was too short for him to plan any major building complexes. Nor did Humayun, compulsively inventive but too harassed in life, build anything enduring. Akbar had the interest, the time and the resources. His first buildings were a couple of palaces in Agra, built around 1562, the year he finally emerged 'from behind the veil'. Two years later he built a garden palace complex called Nagarchain (Abode of Peace) in Kakrali village, some eleven kilometres south of Agra. He used it as a country retreat, where he "amused himself with carousing, pigeon-flying and polo", though occasionally formal state functions, like receiving ambassadors, too were held there. The palace was abandoned after a short while, and by the end of Akbar's reign it had disappeared almost without a trace.

In 1565, Akbar began extensive renovations in Agra, replacing the dilapidated old brick fort there—built by Sikandar Lodi fifty years earlier—with a new fort of hewn stone, and erecting, according to Abul Fazl, "five hundred buildings of masonry after the beautiful designs of Bengal and Gujarat." Three or four thousand workers laboured for some five (according to Badauni), eight (according to Abul Fazl) or fifteen (according to Jahangir) years to complete the construction, which cost three and a half million rupees, and was financed by a special tax.

But Agra was not lucky for Akbar, and he abandoned it for Sikri. Monserrate offers a credible medieval explanation: "When the king went to reside in his new fortress and palace, he found . . . the place overrun with ghosts, who rushed to and fro, tore everything to pieces, terrified the women and children, threw stones, and finally began to hurt everyone there." All the children born to Akbar in Agra died in infancy.

In contrast, Sikri, about forty kilometres west of Agra, was considered lucky for Akbar. It was there that his first surviving son, Salim, was born, and the idea of building a city there was born with him. Some work on the city probably began in 1569 itself, the year of

Salim's birth, but it was only two years later, in 1571, when Akbar took up residence at Sikri, that the construction began in earnest. There were already some Mughal structures there, pavilions that Babur had built. The area was mostly a jungle, swarming with wild beasts. But with Akbar moving in, "in a short time there was a great city, and there were charming palaces," says Abul Fazl. "Beautiful gardens were made in the vicinity. A place of great concourse was brought together such as might move the envy of the world." Akbar personally supervised the construction, sometimes himself quarrying the locally available red sandstone of which the city was built.

Sikri, whatever its auspciousness, was not a good choice for a great city. "The site," says Monserrate, "was rocky and not very beautiful." Situated on an outcrop of the Aravalli Range, its climate was scorching in summer and freezing in winter. An even more serious problem was that Sikri, being not on a river bank, did not have adequate water supply. British traveller William Finch says that the water in the town was "brackish and fretting." "Fatehpur," says Jahangir, "has little water, and what there is, is bad." Its only source of good water was the lake, which Akbar strengthened by shoring up its embankments and laying out parks and an amphitheatre (for elephant fights and polo) on its banks. But the lake was a vulnerable source of water. In 1582, when Akbar along with a number of princes and nobles was at the lakeside on a picnic, the embankment burst suddenly, and though the royal party was lucky to escape the disaster, many people lost their lives and much of the city was flooded. The breach was repaired, but the city was doomed.

Akbar stayed on at Fatehpur Sikri for only three more years after the dam-burst. In the autumn of 1585, a mere fifteen years after it was founded, he abandoned the city. He would return to it only once, on a fleeting visit in 1601, on his way back to Agra from the Deccan. Soon the jungle repossessed the city, and so rapidly, that William Finch, who passed through Fatehpur just four or five years after the death of Akbar, found it already a ghost town. "It is all ruinate," writes Finch, "lying like a waste desart." Only the palace complex remained inviolate, conserved by the descendants of Sheikh Salim.

The royal mansions remain today, frozen in time, a fitting memorial to Akbar. Fatehpur Sikri is Akbar himself congealed into stone, strong, sharp and vital. Daringly original. Open, eclectic, soaring, yet earthy. And full of surprises.

Chapter Six

AN EXPERIMENT
IN SYNTHESIS

"My Mind Is Not at Ease . . ."

"THE WORLD IS A bridge: pass over it, but build no house upon it," cautions the inscription on the facade of Buland Darwaza, the towering portal that Akbar built at the Friday Mosque in Fatehpur Sikri to celebrate his conquest of Gujarat. "The world endures but an hour: spend it in prayer . . ."

The incongruity of this renunciatory advice on a monumental structure celebrating a worldly achievement reflects the dichotomy in Akbar's own life. Outwardly, he had every reason to be contented and happy. Almost till the very end, everything in his life had gone exactly as he had wished; every ambition fulfilled, every desire consummated. Yet he was unhappy. "Although I am the master of so vast a kingdom, and the appliances of government are to my hand, yet . . . my mind is not at ease . . . and my heart is oppressed by this outward pomp and circumstance," he lamented. "How I wish for the coming of some pious man, who will resolve the distractions of my heart . . . If I could but find any one capable of governing the kingdom, I would at once place this burden upon his shoulders and withdraw therefrom."

This renunciatory refrain would be heard periodically throughout Akbar's adult life, but to abdicate power would be, Akbar felt, irresponsible. "The difficulty," he said, "is to live in the world and to refrain from evil, for the life of a recluse is one of bodily ease."

WHAT TORMENTED AKBAR? We do not know, but even in his teens, when physical pursuits had seemed all that interested him—the thrills of the chase and battle, the pleasures of the table, the rapture of sex— there was something dark and mysterious stirring in him, beneath the surface.

The first intimation of psychic disturbance in Akbar was in 1557, during the siege of Mankot, when he, barely fifteen then and on the throne for just one year, was one day possessed by a strange mood, and rode out into the desert all by himself to get away, as Abul Fazl states, from "the presence of short-sighted men" who distressed him. Five years later, just after he assumed full sovereign power, there was another crisis. "On the completion of my twentieth year," says Akbar, "I experienced an internal bitterness, and from the lack of spiritual provision for my last journey my soul was seized with exceeding sorrow." All of twenty and already grieving about mortality!

There seems to have been a streak of melancholia in Akbar. Abul Fazl repeatedly mentions it as the reason for his occasional abnormal behaviour. Akbar himself brought this out once, while visiting the retreat of Sheikh Jalal, a Muslim hermit. "You have spent a long life, and have enjoyed the society of the good—can you tell of a cure for melancholy?" he asked the sage. "And have you obtained a remedy for a heart distracted by opposing desires?"

It is probable that Akbar suffered from some disorder of the nervous system. Possibly he, like his son Murad, was epileptic; Du Jarric, a contemporary French Jesuit historian, explicitly states, on the evidence of Christian missionaries, that Akbar was an epileptic. It is also possible that there was a genetic predisposition in Akbar towards psychic disturbance—there was a strain of eccentricity, even a touch of madness, in his mother's family; his maternal uncle, Khwaja Muazzam, was subject to violent mood swings, and died insane. Some of Akbar's own actions were suicidal, such as riding musth elephants into fight with other elephants, sometimes when he was himself drunk. His claim that he was in perfect self-control on such occasions and was merely testing divine favour, is too neat an explanation to be convincing.

The most bizarre of these incidents took place in 1573, when Akbar was thirty-one, and was encamped at Surat. Abul Fazl tells the story: "One night there was a select drinking party. Discourse fell upon the bravery of the heroes of Hindustan, and it was stated that they paid no regard to their lives. For instance, some Rajputs would hold a double-headed spear and two men, who were equally matched, would run from opposite sides against the points, so the spear transfixed them and came out at their backs. The divine wrestler of the world, for the sake of screening his glory, or for testing men, or from melancholy engendered by his being in the outer world, fastened the hilt of his special sword to a wall, and placing the point near his sacred breast declared that . . . he would rush against this sword. Awe fell upon those who were standing at the feast, and none had the power to utter a word, not even to offer any opposition. Just then Man Singh ran with the foot of fidelity and gave such a blow with his hand that the sword fell down and cut His Majesty's hand between the thumb and index finger. Those present removed the sword, and His Majesty angrily flung Man Singh on the ground and squeezed him. Saiyid Mozaffar . . . by twisting Akbar's] wounded finger released Man Singh."

The incident cannot be dismissed as a freak drunken act, though drunkenness was a part of it. There was something strange and preternatural about Akbar, which probably also accounts for his obsessive preoccupation with religion.

In his later years, Akbar was inclined to be coolly rational, maintaining that nothing whatever could be accepted without proof, but mystical and ecstatic forms of religion had a strong appeal to him in his youth. "My father was very submissive to dervishes," says Jahangir. Often, when religious works were read out to him, especially the poems of Jalaluddin Rumi, the great Persian mystic of the thirteenth century, tears could be seen rolling down his eyes. Even Badauni, hardly sympathetic to Akbar in matters of religion, notes that Akbar used to spend whole nights in praise of god and "would sit many a morning alone in prayer and meditation on a large flat stone of an old building which lay near the palace in a lonely spot, with his head bent over his chest, gathering the bliss of the early hours of dawn." As usual with men of ecstatic faith, Akbar too was subject to mystical dreams and hallucinations, and used to speak of strange visions that appeared to him in sleep to comfort his spirit weary of the burden of life.

Akbar had an early affinity for Sufism, a mystical Muslim sect to which he was introduced by Abdul Latif, his tutor. Sufism was by its very nature open and tolerant and permeated with the sensibilities of other sects and faiths, and Akbar would later adopt its precept of universal toleration (*sulh-i-kull*) as his own guiding principle. The unorthodox and questing nature of Sufism was particularly appropriate to the closing years of the sixteenth century, when, as the end of the first millennium of Islam approached, devout Muslims confidently expected the Mahdi, the last prophet, to come forth and propound new teachings. That belief gave a special energy to religious disputations, even a certain legitimacy to heterodoxy.

Akbar was one with this spirit of the times. His family tradition too inclined him towards cultural openness and religious syncretism— Chingiz Khan is said to have participated in Nestorian, Christian, Muslim, and Buddhist religious observances; Timur was inclined towards Sufism; Babur and Humayun had no qualms about subordinating their faith to their temporal interests. In Akbar's own time, one of his elder relatives, Sulaiman Mirza of Badakshan, was a renowned mystic.

In such an environment, and with such a family background as his, and having the kind of intellectual and spiritual susceptibilities which he had, it was natural that Akbar should go foraging far afield in religion. In doing so, he was pushing along a path that was already open, though he went farther than most.

INTELLECTUAL AND SPIRITUAL explorations were not mere cultural indulgences for Akbar, as they were to his father and grandfather, but intensely earnest pursuits, to slay the dragon of whatever it was that tormented his spirit. Yet he was also very much a creature of his age, and some of his ideas and experiments were, like Humayun's, rather odd. He had, for instance, the curious notion that there was an innate, natural human language, or maybe even an innate religious faith, which he thought he could discover by insulating infants from society for a few years from their birth. To verify the idea, he bought twenty new-born babies from their parents and had them brought up in a secluded place where they would not hear any human speech. Even their nurses were not allowed to speak in their presence. The children were brought out after three or four years, but as Abul Fazl sadly notes, "nothing came out of them except the noise of the dumb."

Normally Akbar was not so credulous, but showed a healthy scepticism in his investigations. Once, when a 'miracle man' was brought before him—one who claimed that he had the power of psychokinesis, and could go from one place to another instantly— Akbar told the man, "We are fond of investigating this sort of thing. If you can show us this miracle, all the wealth and dominions that we possess are yours, and we will become your property." The man remained silent. So Akbar said, "Very well then, we will bind you hand and foot, and cast you [into the river] from the top of the castle. If you come out of the water safe and sound, well and good, if not, you will have gone to hell." Thus cornered, the poor man pointed to his stomach and said: "I have done all this merely for the sake of filling this hell of my own."

Akbar himself was commonly believed to have miraculous powers, but he looked upon the idea with benign scepticism. "The vulgar believe in miracles," he said, "but the wise man accepts nothing without adequate proof." Not that he doubted the possibility of miracles, but he knew that the potency of miracles was not in the shrine or in the saint, but in the faith of the supplicant himself. "Miracles occur in the temples of every creed," said Akbar. "This is the product of mental enthusiasm."

Despite such discernment, Akbar would not deny himself to those who sought his blessings, for he recognized that people needed an external stimulus to activate their own miraculous powers. Thus when people requested from him water on which he had breathed, which was believed to be the panacea for all ailments, he always obliged. "Not a day passes but people bring cups of water to him, beseeching him to breathe upon it," says Abul Fazl. Jerome Xavier gives the story a Christian twist: "He works miracles through healing of the sick by means of the water in which he washes his feet. Women make vows to him for the restoration of health to their children, or for the blessing of bearing sons, and if it happens that they regain health, they bring their offerings to him, which he receives with much pleasure, and in public, however small they may be." Says Coryat, "Ecbar Shaugh had learned all kinds of sorcery."

Occasionally Akbar also resorted to harmless subterfuge to promote the myth of his miraculous powers. "His Majesty even learned alchemy," says Badauni naively, "and showed in public some of the gold made by him." Once, during a thunderstorm, "the wonder-worker emitted his glorious breathings on a mirror and then put it into a fire," says Abul Fazl. "From the wondrous effect of the breath of him whom the spheres obey, the celestial turbulence ceased." If Akbar could stop rain, he could bring rain too. "One of the occurrences was the fall of rain at the wish of His Majesty," writes Abul Fazl. Another time, when one of Akbar's special pigeons was attacked by a hawk, Akbar cried, "Strike and seize," and "suddenly a troop of crows gathered from the plain and surrounded the hawk, and he withdrew his claws from the pigeon and fell into consternation," claims Abul Fazl. And, of course, the emperor was omniscient; he knew everything, even the events in the womb of time, according to Abul Fazl. "And thus after a time the titles, The Only One, The Absolute, The Perfect Man, became commonly applied to the just, majestic and magnanimous Emperor," says Badauni.

AKBAR'S PRIMARY INTELLECTUAL interest was in metaphysics. "Discourses on philosophy have such a charm for me that they distract me from all else," he once confessed, "and I forcibly restrain myself from listening to them, lest the necessary duties of the hour should be neglected." States Badauni: "From childhood to manhood, and from manhood to his declining years, the Emperor had combined in himself various facets from various religions and opposite sectarian beliefs, and by a peculiar acquisitiveness and a talent for selection, by no means common, had made his own all that can be seen and read in books."

In 1575, when he was thirty-three, Akbar set up at Fatehpur Sikri a centre for inquiry into religion and philosophy, called the Ibadat Khana, the House of Worship. The vacant hermitage of a Chishti disciple in the gardens of the palace complex was rebuilt with spacious halls on all four sides to accommodate the Ibadat Khana, into which, according to Nizamuddin Ahmad, none were allowed to enter except

187

"Sayyids of high rank, ulema and sheikhs". In setting up the centre Akbar was possibly influenced by the Bengal ruler Sulaiman Kararani's practice of holding night-long discussions on religion, but the immediate reason seems to have been the expected arrival in India of Sulaiman Mirza, the fugitive king of Badakshan, with whom Akbar apparently hoped to spend long hours in discussion.

The structure that housed the Ibadat Khana has not been satisfactorily identified among the extant buildings in Fatehpur Sikri. Possibly, different buildings were at different times designated as the Ibadat Khana—for instance, when the discussions there were thrown open to non-Muslims, the venue would necessarily have been shifted from its original facility built around a Muslim hermitage. It could be also that the original Ibadat Khana, hastily built for the arrival of Sulaiman Mirza, was pulled down later, or was destroyed in some natural calamity, like the flooding of the town when the embankment of the lake at Fatehpur Sikri breached.

It is tempting to fancy that the building commonly identified as the Diwan-i-khas was really the Ibadat Khana. This is a curious edifice, about thirteen metres square, with a single lofty chamber, from the dead centre of which rises an ornate stone column which flares into an immense circular capital ten feet in diameter, like a lotus open on its stem—to seat the emperor? Narrow stone catwalks with low lattice-work parapets stretch diagonally from the capital to the four corners of the hall to connect with the galleries along the walls. On the outside, balconies on ornate brackets run on all sides. In all this, the building appears to be the very crystallization into stone of Akbar's quest to draw wisdom from all quarters—or, for himself to radiate wisdom to all quarters. The cruciform plan of the hall also fits the known four-sided disposition of debaters in the Ibadat Khana. There is, however, no hard proof that this building was indeed the Ibadat Khana.

The architectural plan of the Ibadat Khana is not precisely described in any contemporary chronicle, but Nizamuddin Ahmad says that it had four wings and that the participants in the discussions there (a small number of special invitees) were segregated into four groups: on the eastern side were the great amirs; Sayyids, the descendants of Prophet Muhammad, occupied the western wing; the ulema were in the south, and "sheikhs and men of ecstasy" were in the north. The groups had to be thus separated, for discussions at the Ibadat Khana often generated considerable heat, and initially there were even disputes about seating and precedence.

"Questions of Sufism, scientific discussions, inquiries into philosophy and law, were the order of the day," says Badauni about the deliberations in the Ibadat Khana. The subjects discussed, according to Nizamuddin Ahmad, were "science . . . ancient and modern history of religions and people and sects, and . . . all matters of worldly interest . . ." Invariably, Akbar personally presided over the assembly and took active part in its debates. Says Abul Fazl: "The world's lord would, with open brow, a cheerful countenance, a capacious heart and an understanding soul, pour the limpid waters of graciousness on those thirsty-lipped ones of expectation's desert, and act as a refiner. Lofty points and subtle words passed from the holy lips . . ."

The deliberations in the Ibadat Khana began on Thursday night (Friday, according to the Muslim calendar, which reckons the day as beginning at sunset) and often went on till noon on Friday. "The Friday nights he passed without sleep in purity in that house, and the whole night was spent in charitable and devotional gifts and offerings," says Badauni. Initially the forum was open only to Muslims, and Akbar's objective was limited to an attempt to resolve the differences among the various warring Islamic sects. "My sole object, oh wise mullahs," said Akbar to the assembly, "is to ascertain truth, to find out and disclose the principles of genuine religion, and trace it to its divine origin."

That objective, to ascertain religious truth through debate, was clearly unattainable. Akbar could not pit creed against creed and expect reason and good sense to prevail. Soon he got tired of the raucous, hairsplitting squabbles of the mullahs. "The vein of the neck of the Ulema of the age swelled up, and a horrid noise and confusion ensued," grumbles even the orthodox Badauni. The discussions, instead of strengthening Akbar's faith in Islam, in fact shattered it. "Doubt was heaped upon doubt," writes Badauni, "so that after five or six years not a trace of Islam was left in him . . . . The differences among the ulema, of whom one would pronounce a thing as unlawful, and another by some process of argument would pronounce the very same thing lawful, became to His Majesty another cause of unbelief."

Like an explorer bored with a familiar landscape, Akbar longed to break free from the confines of orthodox Islam and set out to probe new continents of thought and experience. But contrary to what Badauni imagined, Akbar did not at this time renounce Islam—in fact, he would never do so formally. For the time being, he remained, in appearance at any rate, a devout and orthodox Muslim, and did whatever was expected of him in the patronage of the religion. In 1575 he sent his wife Salima, his aunt Gulbadan and several other distinguished Mughal ladies on a haj pilgrimage. He himself expressed a strong desire to go to Mecca, and when dissuaded by his advisors on the ground that he could not leave India without imperilling the empire, he is said to have donned the pilgrim's garb and walked some distance with those going to Mecca. But while Akbar thus outwardly remained an orthodox Muslim, the internal springs of his faith were beginning to dry up.

"Reason, Not Tradition . . ."

THE YEAR 1578 was a watershed year for Akbar. He was then thirty-six. In May that year something strange and traumatic happened to him, which would hasten his transformation from an orthodox Muslim monarch to a radical reformer. The precise nature of what happened is not known. None of the contemporary chroniclers describe the incident plainly, but refer to it in veiled hints, deepening its mystery. Whatever it was that happened, the event was in some way pivotal to the changes in Akbar's lifestyle and beliefs that took place around this time.

Akbar was then at Bhera, on the banks of the Jhelum in Punjab, on a *battue* hunt. For some ten days beaters in a tightening circle had driven animals from an eighty kilometre circumference of forest into a compact arena, for Akbar to begin the purgatorial slaughter and slake the fire in his blood. When everything was ready, and Akbar had taken his position under a fruit tree to begin the hunt, "suddenly, all at once, a strange state and strong frenzy came upon the Emperor," writes Badauni, "and an extraordinary change manifested in his manner, to such an extent as cannot be accounted for." The hunt was abruptly abandoned, and Akbar ordered that "no one should touch the feather of a finch and they should allow all animals to depart according to their habits," records Abul Fazl.

Akbar was in some dire crisis at this juncture, perhaps even on the point of death. "He was nearly abandoning this state of struggle, and entirely gathering up the skirt of his genius from earthly pomp," says Abul Fazl enigmatically. "A sublime joy took possession of his bodily frame. The . . . cognition of God cast its ray." Says Qandahari: "A mysterious divine call had descended on the emperor, which tranced him completely." It seems likely that Akbar had fallen into a trance or delirium. Or maybe he had a severe epileptic seizure. The crisis, whether physical or mental, was critical enough for Hamida Banu Begum to rush from Fatehpur Sikri to Bhera to care for her son.

Meanwhile, as news of the emperor's mysterious disorder spread, "strange rumours and wonderful lies became current in the mouths of common people," reports Badauni, "and some insurrections took place among the peasants." Fortunately, notes Abul Fazl, "in a short time he (Akbar) by god-given strength turned his face to the outer world and attended to indispensable matters." The insurrections were quelled. The crisis passed.

The incident at Bhera however had a lasting effect on Akbar. He himself considered it as a turning point in his life. When he recovered, he tonsured his head as an expiatory act, distributed alms to fakirs and the poor, and to mark the spot where the eerie change had come over him, laid out a garden there and erected a memorial building. And when he returned to Fatehpur Sikri, he filled the Anup Talao (Peerless Pool) in the courtyard of his palace with "red and white and black coins (gold, silver and copper coins), the whole of which he gave away to the amirs, the poor, the holy, and the learned," says Nizamuddin. "The total of this money amounted to twenty crores of tankas (ten million rupees), and the distribution of it lasted for three years."

SHORTLY AFTER THE hunting incident, Akbar threw open the discussions in the Ibadat Khana to all faiths. Apart from various Muslim sects, Hindus, Jains, Jews, Zoroastrians and Christians were now invited to the assembly; even an obscure Semitic sect called Sabians were there, as were Charvakas, an ancient and nearly extinct school of Indian materialists. Akbar "associated with the good of every race and creed and persuasion, and was gracious to all in accordance with their condition and understanding," says Jahangir. "We associate at convenient seasons with learned men of all religions and thus derive profit from their exquisite discourses and exalted aspirations," stated Akbar in a letter addressed to Philip II of Spain.

It was an unprecedented free-for-all in the Ibadat Khana for a while. Any one could propound any wild theory, and many often did. "Persons of novel and whimsical opinions" flaunted their "pernicious ideas and vain doubts" in the Ibadat Khana, says Badauni. Akbar was an active participant in these deliberations, and, being the emperor, had the prerogative of being always right, for, as Badauni points out, none could argue effectively against a man who had the power of life and death. Abul Fazl saw Akbar's role differently. "The difficulties of sect upon sect of mankind are made easy by the flashings of his sacred soul," he writes, emphasizing Akbar's wisdom rather than his power. "Continually, in those day-like nights, glorious subtleties and profound words dropped from his pearl-filled mouth."

Abul Fazl, for all his hyperbole, could well be right, for Akbar probably was the only person wholly without religious prejudice in that assemblage of zealots. Said Akbar: "He is a man who makes justice the guide of the path of inquiry, and takes from every sect what is consonant to reason. Perhaps in this way the lock, whose key has been lost, may be opened."

Religious exclusiveness was abhorrent to Akbar, and he held that "the contempt of any religion was the contempt of God," according to Thomas Coryat, a British traveller in the early sixteenth century India. Akbar put it this way: "Most persons . . . think that outward semblance, and the letter of Mohammadanism, profit without internal convictions. Hence we by fear and force compelled many believers in the Brahman religion to adopt the faith of our ancestors. Now that the light of truth has taken possession of our soul, it has become clear that in this distressful place of contrarieties (the world) . . . not a single step can be taken without the torch of proof, and that that creed is profitable which is adopted with the approval of wisdom. To repeat the creed, to remove a piece of skin and place the end of one's bones on the ground (to prostrate) from dread of the Sultan, is not seeking after God."

Seeking after god was, for Akbar, seeking after truth. Predictably, no orthodox religion could satisfy him. He was especially disappointed with Islam, for Islam was his own religion and he could forgive it the least for failing him. Akbar, says Badauni, denounced many of the Muslim religious practices as vain superstitions, and "acknowledged man's reason, not tradition, as the only basis of religion."

COINCIDING WITH THESE changes in the religious attitudes of Akbar, certain changes took place in his lifestyle too. His habits grew austere and he became a near-vegetarian. Akbar had always, even in his teens, shown an affinity for Indian customs, to which he was introduced by Khwaja Ambar Nazi, an old servant from Kabul in his service. "The manners and customs of India, and . . . their ways thus became pleasing to him," says Abul Fazl. Later, when he married Hindu princesses, through his association with them, or out of his natural predilection, or probably as a policy to reconcile his Hindu subjects to his rule, he over the years adopted some Hindu practices. He permitted the Hindu inmates of his harem to perform their rituals in the palace, and even participated in them. "From early youth, in compliment to his wives, the daughters of the Rajahs of Hind, he had within the female apartments continued to offer *hom*," says Badauni. Akbar even allowed one of his sons, Daniyal, to be brought up by Bhara Mal's wife in Amber, as a gesture of honour to the raja's family.

When Raja Birbal became a major influence on Akbar, he, as

Badauni bitterly complains, persuaded the emperor to worship the sun and the fire, and venerate "water, stones, and trees, and all natural objects, even down to cows and their dung; that he should adopt the sectarian mark, and Brahmanical thread . . . He began also, at midnight and early dawn, to mutter the spells which Hindus taught him." Further, he ordered that "the sun should be worshipped four times a day, in the morning and evening, and at noon and midnight," alleges Badauni. "His Majesty had also one thousand and one Sanskrit names for the sun collected and recited them daily at noon, devoutly turning towards the sun; he then used to get hold of both ears, and turning himself quickly round about, used to strike the lower ends of his ears with his fists. He also adopted several other practices connected with sun worship. He used to wear the Hindu mark on his forehead . . . Mosques and prayer-rooms were changed into store-rooms and into Hindu guard-rooms . . . The cemetery within the walls was allowed to run to waste."

Akbar generally tended to favour Hindu customs and festivals over Muslim customs and festivals. "The Diwali festival was celebrated," writes Abul Fazl, "and by order the boats, the river banks and the roofs were adorned with lamps." Adds Badauni: "On the festival of the eighth day after the Sun's entering Virgo in this year he came forth to the public audience chamber with his forehead marked like a Hindu, and he had jewelled strings tied to his wrist by Brahmans, by way of blessing. The chiefs and nobles adopted the same practice in imitation of him . . . It became the current custom also to wear the rakhi (a Hindu protection charm) on the wrist . . . Every precept which was enjoined by the doctors of other religions he treated as manifest and decisive, in contradistinction to this religion of ours, all the doctrines of which he set down to be senseless, and of modern origin, and the founders of it as nothing but poor Arabs, a set of scoundrels and highway-robbers."

Badauni exaggerates. Akbar did turn away from Islam, but he did not turn against Islam. Nor did he turn to any other religion, for though he found something good in all religions, none satisfied him entirely. Writes Badauni: "A faith of a materialistic character became painted on the mirror of his mind and the storehouse of his imagination . . . that there are wise men to be found and ready at hand in all religions, and men of asceticism, and recipients of revelation and workers of miracles among all nations, and that the Truth is an inhabitant of every place: and that consequently how could it be right to consider it as confined to one religion or creed . . . [especially to] one which had only recently made its appearance and had not as yet endured a thousand years! And why assert one thing and deny another, and claim pre-eminence for that which is not essentially pre-eminent?"

The proposition that all religions were equally true would have seemed abominable to most of the participants in the discussions in the Ibadat Khana. The objectives of Akbar and those of the disputants were totally divergent. He wanted new perceptions of religious truth; they only wanted to entrench known positions. He hoped for a reconciliation of warring religions, perhaps even a synthesis; they were only interested in proving themselves right and every one else wrong. He wanted to conciliate and heal; they only wanted to fight and subdue. Neither Akbar nor the theologians were getting anywhere. The more vehemently the sectarians argued, the less convinced Akbar became. They sought to win him over with the passion of faith and the authority of tradition, but he wanted to test everything against reason. Eventually Akbar lost all interest in the discussions, and moved towards a religious formulation of his own. The Ibadat Khana then lost its focus, and though the assembly continued to meet till 1582, its spirit had died long before that.

AKBAR THEN TURNED from public debates to private discussions to continue his philosophic explorations, and in this exercise favoured Indian sages. Writes Badauni, "Samanas (Buddhist or Jain ascetics) and Brahmans, as far as the matter of private interviews is concerned, gained the advantage over every one in attaining the honour of interviews with His Majesty, and in associating with him . . . [A brahmin named Debi used to be] pulled up the wall of the castle sitting on a *charpai* (rope cot) till he arrived near a balcony, which the Emperor had made his bed chamber. Whilst thus suspended he instructed His Majesty in the secrets and legends of Hinduism, in the manner of worshipping idols, the fire, the sun and stars, and revering the chief gods of these unbelievers . . . He became especially firmly convinced of the doctrine of the transmigration of souls."

In addition to the orthodox preceptors of Hinduism, Akbar sought out and visited Hindu mystics, like Chid Rup, a Vaihsnava anchorite who lived in a tiny cave near Ujjain. Akbar also summoned yogis to him, says Badauni, "and gave them at night private interviews, and inquired into abstract truths; their articles of faith; their occupation; the influence on pensiveness; their several practices and usages; the power of being absent from the body; or into alchemy, physiognomy, and the power of omnipresence of the soul." Around this time Akbar ordered Hindu religious texts like the Vedas and the epics to be translated into

Persian—the translation of the *Mahabharata* was entrusted to Badauni, to his utter disgust.

Akbar had overtly got so close to Hinduism at this time that bards even extolled him as an incarnation of Rama or Krishna, says Badauni. But Akbar was not about to become a Hindu. Or to be converted to any other religion. In fact, though he became estranged from orthodox Islam, he remained attached to Sufism, and Sheik Tajuddin, a Sufi sage, continued to exert a dominant influence on him.

Tajuddin, notes Badauni with envy and sectarian venom, used to be "drawn up the wall of the castle in a blanket, and His Majesty listened the whole night to his Sufi obscenities and follies . . . arguments concerning the Unity of Existence . . . Thus he became a chief cause of the weakening of the Emperor's faith in the commands of Islam." Indeed, the mystic perceptions of Sufism, reinforced by the monistic views of high Hindu metaphysics, became the basic religious creed of Akbar, though he did also adopt from various other religions bits and pieces of beliefs and rituals to garnish his faith. "Each person according to his condition gives the Supreme Being a name," Akbar maintained, "but in reality to name the Unknowable is vain."

Perhaps next only to Tajuddin, the favourite guru of Akbar was Dastur Mahyarji Rana, a Parsee whom he had met in Gujarat in 1573. Mahyarji arrived in Fatehpur Sikri in 1578 on Akbar's invitation, and under his influence Akbar set up a sacred fire in the imperial palace, and began the custom of prostrating himself in public before the fire as well as before the sun. Birbal also had a role in persuading Akbar to revere the sun. Says Badauni, "The accursed Birbal tried to persuade the Emperor that since the sun gives light to all, and ripens all grain, fruits and products of the earth, and supports the life of mankind, therefore that luminary should be the object of worship and veneration." Akbar put Abul Fazl in charge of keeping the sacred fire burning all the time. At the court, all were required to rise when lamps were lit in the evening. Akbar probably also took to wearing the sacred shirt (*sadra*) and girdle (*kusti*), which all Parsees are required to wear.

IT WAS IN MARCH 1580 that Akbar adopted, openly and in public, the Parsee rites of fire worship. At that time there were at the court three Jesuit missionaries from Goa—they had arrived a month before—but they seemed to have taken no notice of the event at all. The Jesuits had come with the fixed notion that Islam was their enemy in the Mughal empire, and that it was from that religion that they had to wean away the emperor and the people. So fixed was their belief, and so blind were they to the obvious and growing disenchantment of Akbar with Islam, that in December that year, after having been at the court for ten months, they could still write to their Rector in Goa: "Our ears hear nothing but the hideous and heinous name of Mahomet . . . In a word, Mahomet is everything here. Antichrist reigns."

Seeing only what they wished to see, and reporting only what their superiors wanted to hear, the Jesuit missionaries greatly exaggerated their own role in the Mughal court, and paid little attention to the influence of other religions on Akbar. Three Jesuit missions in succession visited Akbar, and they were at the Mughal court for a total of about twenty-six years, overlapping into the reign of Jahangir. Yet they had the least influence on Akbar, and there is no indication that he adopted any Christian rites or subscribed to any Christian beliefs.

Akbar's first recorded contact with Christians was in 1572, when Portuguese traders and officers met him during his Gujarat campaign. This roused his curiosity, and a few years later, soon after he set up the Ibadat Khana, he summoned to the court Father Julian Pereira, the Vicar-General in Bengal, to question him about Christianity. But Pereira was a preacher, not a theologian; he could not satisfy Akbar's curiosity.

A more systematic contact was established in 1578, when the Portuguese viceroy at Goa, Dom Diego de Menezes, sent to the imperial court an emissary, Antonio Cabral. This revived Akbar's interest in Europe and in Christianity, and prompted him to send one of his amirs to Goa with a letter to the head of the Jesuit mission there. "Send . . . to me . . . two of your learned men, who should bring the books of the law, and above all the Gospels, because I truly and earnestly desire to understand their perfection," wrote Akbar. "With great urgency I again demand that they should come with my ambassador . . . and bring their books. For from their coming I shall obtain the utmost consolation; they will be dear to me, and I shall receive them with every possible honour. As soon as I shall have become well instructed in the law, and shall have comprehended its perfection, they will be able, if willing, to return at their pleasure, and I shall send them back with great honours and appropriate rewards."

The viceroy received the Mughal envoy with the highest honour and ceremony. The Jesuits were, of course, exultant. For them, Akbar's letter was god's answer to their fervent prayers to open a passage to the Mughal court. So it was with great care that they chose the missionaries to be sent to Akbar, balancing pedigree with ability. Rodolfo Acquaviva, thirty, scion of a Neapolitan noble family, though timid and ineffectual, was chosen to lead the mission, as befitted his lineage, which, it was hoped, would enable him to establish a rapport

197

with the emperor. But the effective leader of the mission was Antonio Monserrate, an astute and enterprising Catalan Spaniard, who was also the chronicler of the mission. Francesco Enriquez, a Muslim convert to Christianity, was the third member of the mission, and its interpreter.

The Jesuits arrived at Fatehpur Sikri in February 1580, and roused considerable curiosity among the public by their quaint appearance. "They became the cynosure of all eyes on account of their strange attire," writes Monserrate. "Everyone stopped and stared in great surprise and perplexity, wondering who these strange-looking, unarmed men might be, with their long black robes, their curious caps, their shaven face, and their tonsured heads."

Akbar had been waiting impatiently for the Jesuits, and called them to him the very day they arrived in the city, and kept them talking till two in the morning. The discussion continued on subsequent days. Lodging was provided for the Jesuits in the palace complex itself, and Akbar sent them food from the royal table. The Jesuits presented Akbar with a richly bound copy of the Bible, which he received with great reverence, kissing it and, removing his turban, placing it on his head. Later, Prince Murad, ten, and some children of the amirs were handed over to the Jesuits for Christian instruction. "The young prince was an ideal pupil as regards to natural ability, good conduct and intellectual capacity," notes Monserrate. "In all these respects it would have been hard to find any Christian youth, let alone a prince, surpassing him. He was obedient to his teachers, and so submissive that he sometimes did not even dare to raise his eyes to his teacher's face when he was reproving him."

The favours that Akbar showed to the Jesuits reinforced their optimism about their mission—they believed that they could convert Akbar to Christianity and thus turn India into a land of faith. In this they would be bitterly disappointed. Though Badauni says that "His Majesty firmly believed in the truth of the Christian religion, and wishing to spread the doctrines of Jesus, ordered Prince Murad to take a few lessons in Christianity", the fact was that Akbar, though intensely curious, was not convinced about the merit of Christianity. He refused to acknowledge the divinity of Christ, ascribing his miracles to his skill as a physician, and he was puzzled by the concepts of virgin birth and the Trinity. The Jesuit insistence on monogamy baffled him; he considered monogamy impractical, at least for the monarch.

Akbar insisted on proof for everything, and, perhaps with a touch of mischievousness, pressed the Jesuits to show him a miracle, which obviously they could not. He, however, continued to favour the Jesuits, and seemed to have taken a liking for the painfully shy Acquaviva. "Several times he paced up and down with his arm round Rodolfo's shoulders," says Monserrate. And when Monserrate fell ill, the emperor solicitously visited him, greeting him in the Portuguese style, which he had learned specially for the occasion, to humour and cheer up the sick alien.

Akbar told the Jesuits that they were free to propagate their religion in his realm, and that his own sons were free to adopt any religion of their choice. As for Akbar himself, he took the exhortations and chidings of the missionaries—"the Fathers frequently and freely admonished the King," says Monserrate—in good spirit, though he often got bored with the long-winded discourses of the Jesuits, and changed the subject in mid-exposition. In the Ibadat Khana, Akbar assigned Abul Fazl to expound Christianity, and the quick-witted sophist did it so brilliantly that the Fathers themselves, writes Monserrate, "were greatly astonished as they listened to him". Akbar even allowed the Jesuits to set up a chapel in the palace complex, and himself visited it, removing his turban reverentially as he entered. And when a Portuguese at the court died, the priests were permitted to take out a procession through the city with crucifixes and lighted candles.

THAT HOWEVER WAS as far as Akbar was willing to go. And gradually it dawned on the Jesuits that their mission was a failure. In 1582 Monserrate left for Goa, but Akbar would not let Acquaviva go. Explained Abul Fazl to the puzzled Jesuit: "The king, having a desire for all kinds of knowledge, and liking to show his greatness, delighted to have in his court people of all nations." So it was another year before Acquaviva could leave Fatehpur Sikri.

Akbar, who had by then enunciated his own creed, soon lost interest in Christianity. But when a priest of the Greek church visited him in Lahore in 1590, his interest perked up again, and he made over to the Greek "some quick-witted and intellectual persons to be instructed by him in order that the translation of Greek books might be carried out," records Abul Fazl. When the Greek left, Akbar sent through him a letter to Goa, "summoning the most learned and virtuous of the Fathers, by whom I would be taught many things concerning the faith of the Christians and of the royal highway whereon they travel to God's presence."

Once again, though this time with some reluctance, the Jesuits sent a couple of missionaries to Akbar. They arrived in Lahore in 1591, but found that Akbar was interested only in the secular knowledge that they could impart. He had them set up a school in Lahore to teach Portuguese to the royal children. That was not, however, the mission that the Jesuits had in mind, so after a few months at the court, they returned to Goa, frustrated.

In 1595 the third and final Jesuit mission arrived at the Mughal court, headed by Jerome Xavier, a grand-nephew of Francis Xavier, the legendary early-sixteenth-century Spanish missionary. The Jesuits were, as usual, graciously received by Akbar, and were allowed to preach and convert as they pleased. One day Akbar even attended the litany service in the Jesuit chapel, "on bended knees and with clasped hands, like a Christian prince." But it was curiosity, not faith that moved Akbar.

The missionaries however had a great opportunity to win souls for the church when a famine devastated Punjab and Kashmir soon after their arrival in Lahore. The good Fathers religiously went about baptizing abandoned and dying infants wholesale, imagining that they were thus ensuring a heavenly passage for the dying, and earning for themselves the merit of good deeds. But with Akbar himself, or with his successor, they could make no headway, though Jerome Xavier stayed on at the Mughal court for twenty-three years, well into the reign of Jahangir.

Akbar tantalized the Jesuits, but would not satisfy them. The Jesuit labour at the Mughal court was not however entirely wasted. They, serving as political agents in addition to being missionaries, were for many years able to use their entrenched position at the court to block the penetration of other European powers into Mughal India and frustrate their trade moves. Though they failed in god's work, the Jesuits succeeded in serving Caesar and Mammon well.

WHERE THE JESUITS failed, the Jains fared better. In 1582 a three-member Jain delegation, summoned by Akbar from Gujarat, arrived at the court, headed by Hiravijaya Suri, who had walked all the way to Fatehpur Sikri, as his creed prohibited him from using any conveyance. Suri was received with imperial pageantry and was honoured with the title Jagat-guru (Teacher of the World), but he politely refused the presents that Akbar heaped on him. He wanted nothing from the emperor. Akbar nevertheless was able to persuade him to remain at the court for a couple of years. The gentle and pacific Jains made a profound impression on the fiery and combative emperor; he now began to lead an austere life, curtailed his food and drink, especially meat; he gave up hunting, imposed restrictions on animal slaughter, even on fishing; prisoners and caged birds were released. Reported Jerome Xavier: Akbar "adores God, and the Sun, and is a Hindu (Gentile); he follows the sect of the Jains."

What changed in Akbar under Jain influence was his lifestyle, not his faith. What his true faith was, no one knew. He gave the exponents of each religion the impression that he favoured them, but all were in the end equally disillusioned. It might not be that he deliberately and hypocritically intended to mislead them. As Abul Fazl notes, it was Akbar's nature not to reveal his true thoughts to anyone, but speak "with every group, nay with every individual, suitably to the latter's comprehension. Accordingly, the acute of every group conjecture, or rather are certain, that the prince of the world has no other understanding or knowledge except what he shows to them!"

Bartoli, a seventeenth-century Jesuit historian, viewed Akbar from a slightly different perspective: "He (Akbar) never gave anybody a chance to understand rightly his inmost sentiments or to know what faith or religion he held by; but, in whatever way could best serve his own interests, he used to feed one party or other with the hope of gaining him to itself, humouring each side with fair words, and protesting that he had no other object with his doubts than to seek and find out by the guidance of their wise answers the simple truth till then hidden from him. The answers given, however, never sufficed to satisfy him; the disputes, and with them the hopes and vexation of the disputants, never came to an end, because each day they began again at the beginning." Monserrate made this cool assessment: "It may be suspected that Jalal-ud-din (Akbar) was moved to summon the Christian priests, not by any divine inspiration, but by a certain curiosity, and excessive eagerness to hear some new thing . . ." Akbar, writes Du Jarric, did know "what heaven to make for."

It is difficult to determine who exerted what influence on Akbar. His psychic circuitry was complex, and often responded to pulses of influence unpredictably, sometimes ludicrously. For instance, Badauni mentions that when Akbar heard that the Lamas in Tibet lived up to 200 years, he, "in imitation of the usages of these Lamas, limited the time he spent in the harem, curtailed his food and drink, but especially abstained from meat. He also shaved the hair of the crown of his head, and let the hair at the sides grow, because he believed that the soul of perfect beings, at the time of death, passes out of the crown (which is the tenth opening of the human body) with a noise resembling thunder, which the dying man may look upon as a proof of his happiness and salvation from sin, and as a sign that his soul by metempsychosis will pass into the body of some grand and mighty king."

Reason, by which Akbar swore, often failed him.

Allahu Akbar!

WHAT DID NOT fail Akbar was his vision.

Even while he was diligently exploring other religions and trying out exotic rites and modes of life, he was quietly formulating a syncretic, regi-centric creed of his own, Din Ilahi, Divine Faith.

The enunciation of Din Ilahi would be the most controversial act of Akbar, and the most misunderstood. Akbar's objective in launching Din Ilahi was not to challenge or displace the existing creeds, but to establish a central point of convergence and concord in their midst, to which all could subscribe even while remaining true to their own faiths. It was nevertheless a risky undertaking, in that age of bigotry, to step between warring religions. So it was with deliberation and caution that Akbar proceeded with his religious reform, taking one wary step at a time, first establishing his authority over Islam, then stepping outside it (but not renouncing it) to offer himself as the nucleus of a religious synthesis.

Akbar made his first move in the summer of 1579. On 26th June that year, a Friday, which also happened to be the birth anniversary of Prophet Muhammad, Akbar took the unusual step of mounting the pulpit of the Jama Masjid in Fatehpur Sikri during the noon congregational devotions to read the khutbah, the Friday sermon, which was usually delivered by the imam. He made no significant deviation from the normal format of the khutbah, but merely recited a short verse composed for the occasion by Faizi, the poet brother of Abul Fazl:

> The Lord who gave us sovereignty,
> Who gave us a wise heart and a strong arm,
> Who guided us in equity and justice,
> And drove from our thoughts all save equity,
> His description is higher than the range of thought,
> Exalted is His majesty—Allahu akbar!

After delivering these lines, Akbar 'read' a passage from the Koran and recited the *fatiha*, the opening passage of the Koran constituting the

Lord's Prayer of Islam, then came down from the pulpit and joined the congregation in prayers.

There was nothing radical or objectionable in what Akbar recited, even from the orthodox point of view, nor was it unheard of for a Muslim ruler to read the khutbah himself, though it was not common. The Caliph of Turkey, as the secular and spiritual head of the community, routinely read the khutbah; among the Timurids, the founder of the clan, Timur, had himself read the khutbah. Abul Fazl places Akbar's action in its historical context: "As at this time it came to his hearing that the guiding imams and legitimate caliphs did not leave worship to others, but took this weighty matter on their own shoulders, he resolved to imitate them in this, and to reap the reward thereof."

The incident nevertheless created quite a commotion. The controversy centred on the closing words of Akbar's discourse: *Allahu akbar*! That was a common enough invocation in Muslim prayers and meant, in Arabic, that god (Allah) is great (*akbar*). But it could be also taken to mean, if one chose to see it that way, that Akbar was god. To orthodox Muslims, already agitated over Akbar's unorthodox spiritual explorations, the reading of the khutbah by him sounded like a clap of thunder warning them of the storm about to burst over them.

They were not mistaken about that portent. But was Akbar really claiming godhead? That seems unlikely. According to Abul Fazl, when Akbar heard of the rumpus about the khutbah, he exclaimed, *Ya Allah!*—Oh God! He could not believe that he was being accused of claiming divinity.

Akbar's surprise is not credible. He could not have been unaware of the double meaning of the phrase he used, or of the possibility of his opponents reading only one meaning into it. Badauni says that while reading the khutbah Akbar "stammered and trembled, and though assisted by others, he could scarcely read three verses of the poem." This could have been stage fright. It could also have been his guilty conscience.

THE CONTROVERSY DID not make Akbar retreat. He was cautious but resolute. On 2nd September 1579, two months after reading the khutbah, Akbar took the next step. Following up on a suggestion originally made by Sheikh Mubarak (the father of Abul Fazl) six years earlier, Akbar obtained from the principal ulema of the empire a declaration (often called the Infallibility Decree) certifying that Akbar, as a just ruler (*sultan-i-adil*), could act as the final arbiter in matters of religion.

The document, drafted by Sheikh Mubarak, read: "Whereas Hindustan has now become the centre of security and peace, and the land of justice and beneficence . . . we, the principal Ulema . . . have duly considered the deep meaning, first, of the verse in the Koran, `Obey God, and obey the Prophet, and those who have authority among you,' and, secondly, of the genuine Tradition: Surely the man who is dearest to God on the day of judgement is the Imam-i-adil; whosoever obeys the Amir, obeys Thee, and whosoever rebels against him, rebels against Thee,' and thirdly, of several other proofs based on reasoning or testimony; and we have agreed that the rank of Sultan-i-adil is higher in the eyes of God than the rank of Mujtahid (interpreter of law). Further, we declare that the king of Islam, Amir of the Faithful, shadow of God in the world, Abul-Fath Jalaluddin Akbar Padshah Ghazi (whose kingdom God perpetuate!) is a most just, most wise, and most God-fearing king.

"Should therefore in future a religious question come up, regarding which the opinions of the Mujtahids are at variance, and His Majesty in his penetrating understanding and clear wisdom be inclined to adopt, for the benefit of the nation, and as a political expedient, any of the conflicting opinions which exist on that point, and issue a decree to that effect, we do hereby agree that such a decree shall be binding on us and the whole nation.

"Further, we declare that should His Majesty think fit to issue a new order, we and the nation shall likewise be bound by it; provided always, that such order be not only in accordance with some verse of the Koran, but also of real benefit to the nation; and further, that any opposition on the part of his subjects to such an order passed by His Majesty shall involve damnation in the world to come and loss of property and religious privileges in this.

"This document has been written with honest intentions, for the glory of God and the propagation of Islam . . ."

The declaration of the ulema became an imperial decree when it was endorsed by Akbar. There was nothing at all exceptionable in the declaration, either from the point of view of Islam or of good government, and it certainly did not confer infallibility on Akbar. In matters of religion Akbar could not give any decision of his own, but had to choose from among the rulings of the Mujtahids, and in matters of government his decrees were required to be in conformity with the Koran and for the good of the people.

That was what the declaration said. What it meant in practice was quite another thing. The stipulations in the declaration, it was evident, could all be easily manipulated by an absolute monarch to make his will prevail. Akbar no doubt knew it. And so did his critics. "There was brisk market of inappreciation," says Abul Fazl. "Especially this was so with paper-worshipping scholiasts, sunk in the mire of routine, and recognizing no knowledge except the garnering of old materials and market-worn beads of small value and writings in black and white on ancient folios which had been fabricated by servile decorators . . . On every side there arose the dust of commotion and the black smoke of darkness. Assemblages of wickedness congregated together . . . Some of the heated fanatics of the desert of destruction said that the Prince of the Age wished to claim to be the prophet of the incomparable Deity."

The problem here, apart from the religious antagonism that Akbar's actions roused, was that the Muslim religious elite, many of whom held positions of power and prestige at the interface of religion and politics in the theocratic state, feared that Akbar's syncretic predilections, and now his intrusion into religious authority, threatened their privileges. There was a danger of Akbar dismantling the theocratic state, they feared. Many would then lose their religious sinecures. Orthodox Muslims therefore had good reason to grieve over Akbar's reforms.

And they hit back at Akbar where he was most vulnerable, charging him with apostasy, with having become a Hindu. "The ground for this improper notion," says Abul Fazl, "was that the prince out of his wide tolerance had received Hindu sages into his intimacy, and had increased the rank of Hindus for administrative reasons, and had for the good of the country showed them kindness."

The charge of apostasy against Akbar was not, at that time, tenable. He was unorthodox, but still a Muslim. Nevertheless, to blunt the thrust of his adversaries, it became necessary for Akbar to demonstrate his faith, and he did so by a series of canny manoeuvres. First, soon after the promulgation of the 'infallibility decree', he went on a pilgrimage to the tomb of Khwaja Muinuddin Chishti in Ajmer (his last to the shrine), which, says Abul Fazl, was expressly undertaken "as a means of calming the public and enhancing submission of recalcitrants". Also, he now had a portable mosque built, and carried it with him on tours and campaigns to say his daily prayers. And when a stone supposedly bearing the footprint of Prophet Muhammad was brought to the court, he received it with ostentatious veneration. Finally, Akbar offered to fund haj pilgrimages, so that whoever wanted to go to Mecca could do so at state expense, and he designated an officer titled Mir Haji to conduct pilgrims from India to Arabia.

In all this Akbar was dissembling. He had no intention of retreating from the path he had chosen. Though he was still a Muslim, and would remain so nominally till the end, he was rapidly spinning away from the orbit of Islam, and gathering elements from different religions to mould a faith of his own. He was encouraged in this endeavour by Sheikh Tajuddin, the Sufi sage. It was Tajuddin who, according to Badauni, told Akbar about "the faith of Pharaoh". This struck a responsive chord in Akbar. Like Pharaoh Ikhnaton of ancient Egypt, Akbar too would look into himself to invent a creed for his age and his people.

THIS WAS A perilous enterprise in a Muslim society. But Akbar, secure now as the absolute and omnipotent monarch of a vast empire, could dare what no other Muslim ruler anywhere had ever dared before. He could play the Pharaoh. So in 1582, two years after the issue of the 'infallibility decree', Akbar promulgated Din Ilahi.

Alauddin Khilji, an early-fourteenth-century sultan of Delhi, had also thought of founding a new faith, but he, unlike Akbar, did not proceed with the plan. Moreover, Alauddin's motivations and methods were entirely different from those of Akbar—Alauddin had no serious interest in religion, but only wanted to gain renown as the founder of a new sect, which he believed he could propagate by the power of his arms. In Akbar too there might have been a desire for personal glory, but Din Ilahi was also the culmination of his long and earnest study of religions, and there was in it a broad and commendable political objective, to end communal discord in the empire and to enable his subjects to live in harmony. Alauddin's project was megalomaniacal, Akbar's was a vision of a new India.

Characteristically, Akbar convened a council at Fatehpur Sikri to discuss his ideas. "For an empire ruled by one head, it is a bad thing to have the members divided among themselves and at variance one with the other," Akbar is reported to have said, addressing the assemblage. "We ought, therefore, to bring them all into one, but in such fashion that they should be both one and all; with the great advantage of not losing what is good in any one religion while gaining whatever is better in another. In that way, honour would be rendered to God, peace would be given to the people, and security to the empire."

Akbar then asked the assembled amirs to speak up freely on his proposal. Many spoke, but not freely. Writes Bartoli: "The men of note, especially the commandants, who had no God other than the king, and no law other than his will, all with one voice replied, Yes, inasmuch as he who was nearer to heaven, both by reason of his office and by reason of his lofty intellect, should prescribe for the whole empire gods, ceremonies, sacrifices, rules, solemnities, and whatever else was required to constitute one perfect and universal religion."

There was only one dissenting voice at the meeting. Raja Bhagwan Das of Amber, according to Badauni, protested: "I would willingly believe that Hindus and Musalmans have each a bad religion, but only tell us what the new sect is and what opinion they hold, so that I may believe." Akbar had no ready answer to that. He had no revelation to proclaim. What he was proposing was not a religion in the conventional sense.

Five years later Raja Man Singh, the adopted son of Raja Bhagwan Das, raised the same objection when Akbar prodded him to embrace Din Ilahi. "If Discipleship means willingness to sacrifice one's life, I have already carried my life in my hand—what need is there for further proof?" asked Man Singh. "If, however, the term has another meaning and refers to faith, I certainly am a Hindu. If you order me to do so, I will become a Musalman, but I know not of the existence of any other religion than these two."

Outside the court, the reactions of orthodox Muslims were not so polite—there was dismay and fury; worse, the mullahs found Akbar ridiculous. One satirical poet wrote,

> The king this year had laid claim to be
>   a prophet,
> After the lapse of a year, please God,
>   he will become God!

THIS CHARGE WAS unfair. Not even his fawning courtiers ascribed godhead or prophethood to Akbar, though Abul Fazl came fairly close to it. Akbar himself certainly did not make any such claim. What he claimed was that kings were touched with divinity, not that they were divine persons; the divinity of the king was of the office, not of the man.

As for Din Ilahi, its appeal was to reason, not to faith or ardour. And that was its main weakness—it could not give people the crutch of faith they needed to hobble through life.

Din Ilahi was, in fact, not even really a religion, and was never intended to be one; it was more like a fraternity, and its primary concerns were socio-political rather than religious. Akbar himself was the nucleus of the creed. Indeed, he was the reason for its very existence. And this, in Akbar's view, was as it had to be, because, as he put it, "The very sight of kings has been held to be a part of divine worship. They have been styled conventionally as the Shadow of God; and, indeed, to behold them is a means of calling to mind the Creator, and suggests the protection of the Almighty."

If the veneration of the emperor was the core of Din Ilahi, then what would the emperor himself venerate? Akbar had a ready answer to this. "Divine worship in monarchs consists in their justice and good administration," he maintained. "The justice of one hour is better than the saying of prayers all night, and of fasting all days for sixty years." And what would be the emperor's reward for being a just and good king? Akbar believed that being a monarch was a reward in itself. "Sovereignty is a supreme blessing," he held, "for its advantages extend to multitudes."

Akbar certainly had a good idea in Din Ilahi. He did not, however, seem to have thought it through with thoroughness, but improvised the concept as he went along. While some of the beliefs and practices of Din Ilahi—like the four degrees of devotion to the emperor—were already there as part of the emperor veneration that had been growing even before the enunciation of the new creed, others were added on haphazardly, so that it ended up being something of a mishmash. And in combining his socio-political vision with a creed akin to religion, Akbar straddled two boats moving in opposite directions, one surging into the future and the other drifting into the past. This accounts for many of Din Ilahi's ambiguities.

On one thing Akbar was clear. Din Ilahi was not for the masses. Abul Fazl repeatedly speaks of Akbar's reluctance to initiate indiscriminately all who wanted to join the fraternity. "The words of kings resemble pearls," Akbar maintained; "they are not fit pendant to every ear." The fraternity was frankly elitist. Akbar was especially careful to see that Din Ilahi did not become a means of advancement for opportunistic careerists. "To make a disciple is to instruct him in the service of God, not to make him a personal attendant," said Akbar. "The real object of those who became disciples was to get into office," writes Badauni, "and . . . His Majesty did everything to get this out of their heads."

Badauni charges that Akbar favoured Hindus for admission into Din Ilahi. "Of Hindus . . . he could not get enough," he says. "But if other than Hindus came, and wished to become disciples at any sacrifice, His Majesty reproved or punished them. For their honour and zeal he did not care, nor did he notice whether they fell in with his view or not." Badauni's complaint seems baseless. There is no evidence that Akbar favoured Hindus—or that, if he did indeed favour Hindus, they favoured Din Ilahi—for in the list of eighteen prominent members of the fraternity compiled by Blochmann from the names mentioned by Abul Fazl and Badauni, there is only one Hindu: Raja Birbal.

Apart from these eighteen leading members, there were no doubt scores of lesser adherents of Din Ilahi. But their number could never have been very large, for each member had to be individually initiated by the emperor himself. The initiation—which was a secret rite, not many details of which are known—seems usually to have been performed on Sundays, because of the Zoroastrian and Hindu reverence for the sun. The novice approached Akbar with his turban in his hand and prostrated at his feet; Akbar then raised him up and replaced the turban on his head. This, according to Abul Fazl, symbolized that the neophyte had "from seeming existence . . . now entered into real life". Continues Abul Fazl: "His Majesty then gives the novice the *shast*, upon which is engraved `the Great Name', and His Majesty's symbolical motto *Allahu Akbar.*"

Jahangir says that the novice was "given the *shast-o-shabah* (token and likeness) . . . At the time of initiation some words of advice were given to the disciple: he must not . . . [indulge in] sectarian quarrels, but must follow the rule of universal peace with regard to religions; he must not kill any living creature with his own hand and must not flay anything. The only exceptions are in battle and the chase . . . Honour the luminaries (the Sun, Moon etc.) which are manifesters of God's light, according to the degree of each, and recognize the power and existence of Almighty God at all times and seasons. Be careful indeed that whether in private or in public you never for a moment, forget Him."

It does not seem to have been necessary for the initiate to renounce his old faith—he could remain a Hindu or a Muslim and yet be a member of Din Ilahi—but many, according to Badauni, on their own submitted statements renouncing their religion, writing, "I, who am so and so, son of so and so, do voluntarily, and with sincere predilection, utterly and entirely renounce and repudiate the religion of Islam . . . of my fathers, and do embrace Din Ilahi of Akbar Shah, and do accept the four grades of entire devotion, viz, sacrifice of Property, Life, Honour and Religion." Members of the cult wore on their turbans a medallion with Akbar's likeness, and greeted each other with the salutation *Allahu Akbar*, to which the response was *Jalla Jalaluhu* (Glorious is His Glory), the greeting as well as its response playing on Akbar's names. The emperor himself was saluted by his disciples with the *sijda*, the prostration used for worship in the mosque.

It is not clear whether Din Ilahi addressed itself to any metaphysical questions, though Akbar personally believed in transmigration. It had no gods, no prayers, no rites. There were, however, numerous minor regulations, some of them droll, issued by Akbar over a period of several years, specifying the social, family and personal obligations of cult members. They were to show concern for animal welfare, accept the remarriage of widows, reject child marriage and marriage of close relations, reject forced sati. They were encouraged to practice monogamy and chastity, and to become vegetarians. Further, members were required to give a party and distribute alms on their birthdays; during their birth month they were not to eat meat or even go near meat; they were not to use the vessels used by butchers, fishers and bird-catchers; they were not to cohabit with pregnant, old, barren or underage women. And so on. There were also precise regulations for the burial or burning of the dead, as also directions for sleeping—the cult members were required to sleep with their heads to the east.

AKBAR'S TENTATIVENESS with Din Ilahi, evident in its conceptualization, was also evident in his manner of propagating it. Though, according to Bartoli, he did send, soon after the council meeting at Fatehpur Sikri, "one of the sheikhs, a most distinguished old man, to proclaim in all quarters that in a short time the law to be professed throughout the Mughal empire would be sent from the Court", no formal, empire-wide promulgation of Din Ilahi seems actually to have been made. No organization was set up to propagate it, and there is no indication that the machinery of the state was in any way used to promote it.

There is little doubt that if Akbar had used the resources of the empire to propagate Din Ilahi, it would have won, at least temporarily, numerous adherents. Ordinary human susceptibilities would have ensured that. In fact, long before the enunciation of Din Ilahi, and without any initiative whatever from Akbar, a community of brahmins called Darshaniyas had become demonstrative devotees of Akbar—they would not touch food or water, or set about their work, without first venerating Akbar as he presented himself to the public at sunrise from a fort window.

As for courtiers, they would have swung whichever way Akbar swung. Thus when Akbar started wearing the *rakhi*, the nobles, says Jahangir, "carried this extravagance to [such an] excess" that Akbar had to ban the practice. Writes Badauni about the situation in 1579, three years before the founding of Din Ilahi: "In these days, when reproach began to spread upon the doctrines of Islam . . . base and low men of the higher and lower classes, having accepted the collar of spiritual obedience upon their necks, professed themselves his disciples. They became his disciples through the motives of hope and fear, and the word of truth could not proceed out of their mouths." And when Din Ilahi was introduced, says Abul Fazl, "many thousands, men of all classes . . . cast over their shoulders the mantle of belief, and look[ed] upon their conversion to the New Faith as the means of obtaining every blessing." Says Badauni, "Indeed, if His Majesty, in setting up his claims and making his innovations, had spent a little money, he would easily have got most of his courtiers and much more the vulgar into his devilish nets."

But that was not Akbar's style. "No man should be interfered with on account of his religion," said Akbar, "and any one should be allowed to go over to any religion he pleased." To use coercion or bait to gain converts would have been to violate the very ideals on which Din Ilahi was founded—that truth may be found in all religions, and that reason should be the sole basis for belief and action. "His Majesty was convinced that confidence in him as a leader was a matter of time and good counsel, and did not require the sword," says Badauni.

Akbar therefore made no great effort to propagate Din Ilahi. It is doubtful that any large number of people outside the court circle knew about Din Ilahi, and it is even more doubtful that, if they came to know about it, it would have appealed to them, except as a means to win royal favour. Din Ilahi, a faith without passion, a cult without a god, was not for the masses, for people needed their gods and goddesses, their prayers and rituals, penances and festivals, to anchor their lives. Akbar evidently meant to keep Din Ilahi exclusive to a small, closed fraternity of intimates and true adherents, a core group not divided by conflicting religious loyalties, but united in their devotion to the emperor.

Akbar was the very life of Din Ilahi. Din Ilahi existed because Akbar lived. Inevitably, when he died, the fraternity died too. Its prominent members had all died before Akbar himself; there were no apostles to continue his mission. Din Ilahi simply vanished, without a trace.

ONE TANTALIZING thought remains. Din Ilahi, by its secular orientation and faith in reason, had held in it the promise of modernization of India. The promise of renewal and growth. If Akbar had energetically applied himself to the propagation of Din Ilahi, would not its electric stimulus on the elite of the land have awakened India from her slumber and brought her out of the dungeon of medievalism, out into the open, into sunlight and fresh air?

The potential was there. Indeed, for a short while the society around the Mughal court did scintillate with intellectual and artistic effervescence. "Astronomy, philosophy, medicine, mathematics, poetry, history, and novels, were cultivated and thought necessary," says censorious Badauni. "Many families plunged into these discussions . . . At night, when there were social assemblies, His Majesty told forty courtiers to sit down as The Forty, and every one might say or ask what he liked. If any one brought up a question connected with law or religion, they said: `You had better ask the Mullahs about it, as we only settle things which appeal to man's reason.'" It seemed like the dawn of the age of reason in India. For a brief shining moment a new and brilliant star blazed over Fatehpur Sikri.

Then the moment passed. And the night closed in again.

Would the light have abided if Akbar had persevered with Din Ilahi? Possibly. On the other hand, it was equally possible that, if Akbar had used force to propagate Din Ilahi, his adversaries would have used countervailing force to resist it, creating chaos and wrecking everything that Akbar had built. Though Din Ilahi, being not itself a religion, did not require its adherents to abandon their faiths, its basic thrust was against religion itself, and this would have made orthodox Muslims, perhaps even Hindus, unite against Akbar. Even as it was, in the eyes of orthodox Muslims, Akbar was beyond the pale. His sins were many. To begin with, he was tolerant towards other religions, and that was intolerable. He then went on to meddle with Muslim laws and traditions, and that was criminal, for Prophet Mohammed had warned that "anything new which is introduced in my religion is condemnable". And in enunciating Din Ilahi, he had become an apostate.

This at any rate was how orthodox Muslims saw Akbar. Many of his views were certainly incompatible with Islam—his belief in transmigration, for instance, implied the rejection of the basic Islamic tenets of resurrection and the last judgement. It is not, however, clear whether Akbar actually renounced Islam. The evidence is confusing, and the witnesses suspect. The Jesuit missionaries, a major source of information on the subject, were rabidly anti-Muslim, and they exaggerated Akbar's disenchantment with Islam, while other pressures and prejudices warped the judgement of Mughal chroniclers.

From Akbar himself the evidence is contradictory. In 1583, the year after he enunciated Din Ilahi, he founded a citadel at the confluence of the Ganga and the Yamuna and named it Allahabad, City of Allah. And in his letter to the sharifs in Mecca a little before the proclamation of Din Ilahi, as well as in his letters to the Uzbeg chief Abdullah Khan a couple of years later, he declared himself unambiguously to be a Muslim. "Places which from the time of the rise of the sun of Islam till the present day had not been trod by the horse-hoofs of the world-conquering princes . . . have become the dwelling-places and homes of the faithful," Akbar wrote to Abdullah, describing what he had accomplished by his conquests. "The churches and temples of the infidels and heretics have become mosques and holy shrines."

This affirmation of faith by Akbar is not convincing—in those letters Akbar was probably dissembling diplomatically, for he was writing to orthodox Muslim leaders who expected, and needed, to hear that reassurance from him. At other times, Akbar's position was entirely different. "Formerly I persecuted men into conformity with my faith and deemed it Islam," he said. "As I grew in knowledge, I was overwhelmed with shame. Not being a Muslim myself, it was unmeet to force others to become such."

Badauni is forthright in denouncing Akbar as an apostate, and goes on to level a series of charges against him. While at one time Akbar used to encourage and even fund pilgrimages to Mecca, "he cannot now bear even the name of such a thing, and merely to ask leave to go on a pilgrimage is enough to make a man a malefactor worthy of death," complains Badauni. "The prayers of Islam, the fast, nay even the pilgrimage, were henceforth forbidden. Some bastards, such as the son of Mullah Mubarak, a worthy disciple of Sheikh Abul Fazl, wrote treatises, in order to revile and ridicule our religious practices, of course with proofs." Not even the Prophet and his family were spared, says Badauni.

Badauni charges Akbar with violating Muslim conventions by allowing "dice playing and usury . . . and other forbidden things in like manner. And gambling houses were set up at the Court, and the Emperor lent money to the players at interest from the treasury." Further, according to Badauni, Akbar issued an order "that all people should give up the Arabic sciences, and should study only the really useful ones, namely, astronomy, mathematics, medicine, and philosophy . . . Reading and learning Arabic was looked on as a crime." The Hegira era was abolished, and a new era beginning with Akbar's accession, called Tarikh-i-Ilahi, was introduced, along with Zoroastrian festivals and the Persian calendar. Brahmins, not kazis, were directed to adjudicate in disputes among Hindus. Of Muslim customs, Friday prayer alone was retained, says Badauni. There were rumours that in the harem the begums were chanting, "There is no god but Allah and Akbar is his prophet."

There were other charges too—that Akbar disapproved children

213

being named Muhammad, that he banned the construction of new mosques, prohibited cow slaughter as in a Hindu state, disfavoured the consumption of garlic and onions and the keeping of beards, and so on. It is not clear whether these regulations applied to the general public or only to the adherents of Din Ilahi. But there was certainly a strong anti-Muslim bias in Akbar in the last phase of his life.

Badauni charges, and the Jesuits gloat, that, apart from rejecting Islam personally and delinking the apparatus of the state from the religion, Akbar actively persecuted Muslims. The Jesuit Provincial in Goa reported in 1590 that "the name Muhammad was as hated at the Mogul's court as in Christendom", and that Akbar had turned some of the mosques in Lahore "into stables for elephants or horses, on the pretence of preparation for war". Ferishta says that "Akbar ordered the chief mosque at Asirgarh to be destroyed and replaced by an idol-temple."

There might be considerable exaggeration in these stories of persecution of Islam, for religious intolerance was against Akbar's tenets and was uncharacteristic of him. But there is no doubt that Akbar saw Islam as the main obstruction to his progressive ways, and that in the last ten or fifteen years of his life he had ceased to be a Muslim in the conventional sense. But he does not seem to have formally abjured Islam, and it is possible that till the end he considered himself a Muslim of sorts. Writes Sir Thomas Roe, the British ambassador at the court of Jahangir: "Ecbar-sha himself continued a Mahometan, yet hee began to make a breach into the law, considering that Mahomet was but a man, a King as hee was, and therefore reverenced, hee thought hee might prove as good a Prophet himselfe. This defection of the King spread not farre, a certain outward reverence detayned him, and hee dyed in the formall profession of his Sect."

So the mystery remains. "He died as he lived," writes Du Jarric, "for as no one knew what law he followed in his lifetime, so no one knew in which he died." Says Maclagan: "Among the people there are various opinions regarding the emperor; some holding him to be a Christian, others a heathen, others a Muhammadan. The more intelligent however consider him to be neither Christian nor heathen nor Muhammadan, and hold this to be the truest."

Tyranny is Unlawful

DIN ILAHI, FOR all the promise it held, was a mere historical curiosity. It had little practical consequence. Akbar's administrative reforms, on the other hand, were of enduring value. And, in contrast to the mystery surrounding his faith, there is a wealth of lucid information about his administration. This is found mainly in Abul Fazl's monumental work *Ain-i-Akbari*, an encyclopaedic manual of the Mughal empire, giving minute information about virtually everything anyone would ever want to know about the conditions in India under Akbar, including matters of everyday life—the state of society, religion and culture, the administrative structure of the empire, the law, the prevailing military technology, the state of the economy, the crops grown and the prices of produce, the manner of refining gold, the method of extracting silver from ash, estimates of house building, the weight of different kinds of wood, rules for estimating the loss in wood chips, recipes for common dishes, rules of card games, and so on.

In its general characteristics, the history of Akbar's administrative reforms is similar to that of his religious reforms, with Akbar pushing everything to the limit of its potential. Yet the story is also quite different—in matters of administration Akbar could not range as freely as he did in religion, but had to work within the limits of what was practicable in the given conditions of his empire. There could be no basic institutional changes in the mode of government, for the only known (and conceivable) form of government in those days was royal autocracy. Nor was there scope for any radical restructuring of the administrative organization. The uniqueness of Akbar's government was therefore not so much in its institutions, as in the modulation that Akbar gave to the institutions, in the spirit that he infused in them— what was distinctive about Akbar's government was what was distinctive about him, as a person.

The common orientation of the medieval state was to protect and enhance the power of the ruler without regard to the welfare of his subjects, and this dichotomy was further accentuated in the Muslim kingdoms of India because of the racial and religious differences between rulers and subjects. One of Akbar's major administrative thrusts was to mitigate the harshness of this dichotomy by treating all his subjects as equal—his government was as secular as any government could have been in that age.

Akbar took the first step towards the political integration of his empire in the very year that he assumed full control of the government, in 1562, when he prohibited the enslavement of prisoners of war. The conquered too were his subjects, he held, and they merited his protection as much as anyone else. The following year, while on a tiger hunt near the Hindu sacred city of Mathura, he abolished the pilgrim tax collected from Hindus, saying that it was an offence to tax people who were gathered to honour god, to whichever religion they might belong.

Within months after this, in early 1564, Akbar, then just twenty-two, abolished jizya—the poll tax which non-Muslims had to pay in a Muslim state—maintaining that he would not discriminate between his subjects on the basis of religion, as all were equal in his eyes, and in any case his treasury was full. Jizya was first imposed in India 852 years earlier by Muhammad bin Kasim, the Arab conqueror of Sind, and had been since then commonly imposed (though not systematically collected) by Muslim rulers. The exaction of jizya was a theocratic obligation of the Muslim state; its formal abolition by Akbar was therefore a radical departure from convention.

The decision to abolish jizya was Akbar's most acclaimed act, but he was not the first to take this audacious step in India—jizya had been abolished in Kashmir by Sultan Sikandar in the early fifteenth century, and in Golconda by Sultan Quli Qutb-ul-Mulk just before Akbar abolished it. Akbar's abolition of jizya was not in any case an anti-orthodoxy measure, but only a sagacious political act, for he himself was very much an orthodox Muslim at this time, and there is in fact some evidence to indicate that, under orthodox pressure, he reimposed jizya temporarily in 1576, before finally abolishing it in 1579.

The reimposition of jizya by Akbar, if true, indicates the constraints under which even an absolute monarch had to function. Seemingly, all the power in the state was concentrated in the hands of the emperor, but in reality his freedom of action was dependent on his ability to quell contingent rebellion. Akbar's radicalism in the latter part of his reign was successful only because he had by then established his absolute military sway.

Equally important was the strength he gained by setting up an efficient administrative system. Neither Babur nor Humayun had done anything much to systematize the government, but Akbar, blessed as he was with "a wise heart and a strong arm", was as masterly in administrative organization as he was indomitable in battle. He had no doubt the advantage of being able to build on the strong foundation of Sher Shah's excellent administrative system, but he also introduced several innovations and refinements of his own. His system as it finally crystallized endured through the entire Mughal period and later formed the basis of the British administration in India.

Akbar's administration was, for a medieval system, remarkably efficient, though of course its efficiency was in serving the interests of the emperor, not in providing good government. There was much misgovernment in Mughal India, especially in outlying provinces, as was common in most kingdoms of the age. But the problem was especially acute in the Mughal empire, as its vast size made it impossible for the emperor, given the limitations of the medieval transportation and communication systems, to monitor efficiently and control systematically the provincial officers.

The Mughals were not in any case keen on minute control, nor did they have the complex interlocking administrative organization necessary to effect such control. As long as the broad political, military and revenue requirements of the emperor were met, provincial governors could quietly ignore imperial directives, and function as virtually autonomous rulers. Akbar would issue firman after firman, and governors would receive them with utmost reverence and obedience—and then go on to do precisely as they pleased. "This order quickly disappeared like a reflection on the water," says Badauni about one of Akbar's regulations; "it never attained currency, although firmans went forth to this effect," he writes of another.

AKBAR, LIKE SHER SHAH before him, prided himself on being a just ruler. "Tyranny is unlawful in everyone, especially in a sovereign who is the guardian of the world," he maintained. And again: "If I were guilty of an unjust act, I would rise in judgment against myself. What shall I say, then, of my sons, my kindred and others?"

Such statements are not to be taken literally—in medieval society there was no question of all men being equal under law. Akbar did however take special care in administering justice. Says Monserrate: "As to the administration of justice, he is most zealous and watchful . . . In inflicting punishment, he is deliberate, and after he has made over the guilty person to the hands of the judge and court to suffer either the extreme penalty or the mutilation of some limb, he required that he should be three times reminded by messages before the sentence is carried out." Such precautions were necessary because the Mughal system of justice was rough-and-ready, often brutal. "We, during the time of our rule have tried not to hurt an ant," Akbar is reported to have said. But this presumably meant only that he had tried to be as just and humane as possible in a harsh world, not that he abjured extreme punishments, for he had himself handed out savage punishments for trivial offences. Stern, deterrent punishments were unavoidable in medieval society to maintain law and order. The defect of the Mughal system of justice was not so much that it was pitiless, but that, though it operated within the general ambit of Muslim law and tradition, its exercise was largely arbitrary, and depended on the temper of the person administering justice.

Similar problems also plagued the Mughal general administration, though Akbar's system was a great improvement on the ad hoc procedures of Babur and Humayun. He organized his officers in tiered ranks, and made an effort to improve efficiency and contain corruption by such measures as regulating jagir assignments, maintaining descriptive rolls of soldiers, and branding horses. However, these measures were only partially successful, for they were systematically subverted by the amirs, whose power and freedom they abridged.

Akbar was more successful in his revenue administration. Neither Babur nor Humayun had any systematic revenue policy, but Akbar streamlined the administration and introduced several radical reforms. And he claimed for himself all the credit for it. "It was the effect of the grace of God that I found no capable minister," he is said to have remarked, "otherwise people would have considered that my measures had been devised by him." This was not a fair comment. Akbar no doubt was himself the source of most of the innovative ideas of his administration—under royal autocracy all reform ideas necessarily had to come, or at least appear to come, from the emperor—but he certainly had a few ministers of exceptional talent, and a good part of the success of his government was due to them. In fact, an aspect of Akbar's greatness was that he was a great leader of men, who could command the respect and allegiance of talented officers, and get the best out of them.

THE MUGHAL RULER—all medieval rulers, for that matter, whatever their religious persuasion—had, in addition to his basic political and military functions, considerable religious duties to perform. Akbar took these responsibilities seriously and issued a large number of regulatory orders on socio-religious matters. The scope and effectiveness of these regulations are not known. Most of them were apparently meant only for the adherents of Din Ilahi, and in any case it is unlikely that they were systematically enforced outside the penumbra of the Mughal court, and probably were not even known outside the urban centres of the empire. In addition to these decrees, Akbar also issued many directives of an advisory nature, to his disciples as well as to the general public, on matters ranging from weighty religious and social issues to such arcane topics as whether it was better to bathe before or after sexual intercourse.

As part of the new morality that he sought to inculcate in his people, Akbar tried to regulate the sale and consumption of alcoholic beverages. Liquor might be drunk, he decreed, only if it was prescribed by physicians, and he laid down severe punishments for those who indulged in excessive drinking, carousal, or disorderly conduct. To implement his prohibition regulations, he even set up, much to the outrage of orthodox Muslims, a liquor shop near the royal palace, with fixed tariff. To get liquor, the buyer had to register, identifying himself by giving the names of his father and grandfather. The measures were not successful. "In spite of all precautions," writes Badauni, "confusion and wickedness raised its head, and however many persons were every day punished, no practical result was effected."

No more successful was Akbar's effort to control prostitution. "The prostitutes of the imperial dominions," records Badauni, "had gathered together in the capital (Fatehpur Sikri) in such swarms as to defy counting and numbering. These he made to live outside the city, and called the place Shaitanpurah (Devilsville). And he appointed a Keeper, a Deputy and a Secretary for this quarter, so that any one who wished to associate with these people, or take them to his house, could do so, provided he first had his name and condition written down . . . But if any one wished to have a virgin, if the petitioner was a well-known courtier, he sent a petition by the Deputy, and obtained permission from Court. Nevertheless, in spite of the rule, all libertines carried on these affairs under assumed names, and so drunkenness and debauchery led to many acts of bloodshed, and however many were brought to punishment, another troop [of rakes] would strut arrogantly past the Inspector of the department."

Akbar also issued a number of dietary regulations, seeking to restrict the consumption of beef—on the ground that physicians held "the flesh of cows to be productive of sundry kinds of sickness, and to be difficult of digestion," says Badauni—and to discourage the use of garlic and onions. However, he recommended that the flesh of the wild boar and the tiger might be eaten, as a means of acquiring their qualities of courage. Slaughter of animals on Sunday was strictly prohibited, as the day was sacred to the sun.

Several of Akbar's regulations were directed against orthodox Muslim practices. Thus he decreed that boys should not be circumcised before they were twelve years old, and that they could then decide for themselves whether to be circumcised or not. Similarly gold and silk were required to be worn during prayer, in direct violation of Islamic rules. Further, he abrogated the common Muslim law of death for blasphemy, and ordered that "if a Hindu, when a child or otherwise, had been made a Musalman against his will, he was to be allowed, if he wished, to go back to the religion of his fathers." In the same spirit, he ruled that "if any of the infidels chose to build a church, or a synagogue, or idol temple, or Parsee tower of silence, no one was to hinder him." Akbar even found a reason to disfavour beards. "Certain pandering pimps brought forward proofs in favour of shaving the beard," says Badauni. "They affirmed that the beard drew its nourishment from the testicles, and that since for this reason they never saw any eunuch with a beard, what could be the virtue and distinction of preserving it!"

Family and social health were major concerns of Akbar. He was against high dowries, and he disapproved of marriage between close relatives, on the ground that "in such cases the sexual appetite is but small". He further decreed that "boys were not to marry before the age of sixteen, nor girls before fourteen, because the offspring of early marriages is weakly." He was firmly against the Hindu custom of child marriage, holding: "The marriage of a young child is displeasing to the Almighty, for the object which is intended is still remote, and there is proximate harm. In a religion which forbids the remarriage of the widow, the hardship is grave." Akbar was also of the opinion that if a woman were older than her husband by twelve years, he should not lie with her.

To ensure compliance with these regulations, Akbar required marriages to be registered. "No son or daughter of the common people was to be married until they had gone to the office of the Chief of Police, and been seen by his agents, and the correct age of both parties had been investigated," reports Badauni, who goes on to note that the regulation led to a brisk trade in false certificates. There was also a marriage tax, imposed at rates fixed according to the wealth and status of the contracting families. As for sati, Akbar did not consider it prudent to ban it, but sought to regulate it by directing that no one should be forced to commit sati, and that "a Hindu woman of tender years, who could have got no enjoyment from her husband, should not be burnt". He also sought to restrict slavery.

In formulating these regulations, Akbar was guided by reason (to his own satisfaction at any rate) and he had reasoned explanations even for his seemingly whimsical prescriptions. For instance, he justified his recommendation that people should bathe before sexual intercourse, not after, on the ground that though people have to wash after excreting and urinating, there was no need to do that after "the emission of so tender a fluid". Similarly, he maintained that base people should be prohibited from learning the sciences, "because insurrection often arose from these people".

Akbar's objective in issuing these canons and edicts seems to have been mainly to give the public the benefit of his wisdom. He had no systematic plan to transform society, though it could be that he hoped that the ripple effect of his reformist ideas would in some way eventually transform society, and make reason instead of blind faith prevail.

This was an impossible goal. People, secure in the yoke of their familiar faiths, preferred their old delusions to new dreams, and shrank from venturing from their burrows into the terror of the light.

The Long Farewell

TOWARDS THE CLOSE of Akbar's reign, the Mughal empire was only nominally a Muslim state, but there was not even a whisper of protest from anyone any more, even from the die-hard mullahs, for Akbar had by then acquired the aura of a superhuman hero, and even the stiffest, toughest knees in the Mughal court turned to jelly in his presence. Akbar's only worry now was his son and heir apparent, Salim.

Salim had been waiting in the wings for a long time, with growing impatience, to move to centre stage. As the sixteenth century drew to a close, his impatience turned into despair. He found it an intolerable affront to be thirty-one years old and yet not be king. Akbar at fifty-eight was still in robust health; he had been king for forty-four years, and it looked as though he would reign for many more years, and might even outlive Salim. One of Salim's brothers, Murad, was already dead; his other brother, Daniyal, was an alcoholic wreck with one foot in the grave; and Salim himself, because of his excesses, was in poor health. Time, it seemed to Salim, was running out faster for him than for his father. He could not afford to wait for the natural course of events to make him king. He had to force the pace.

There had been tension between father and son for years. Even ten years earlier, in 1591, Akbar had an apprehension that Salim might be up to some mischief. That year Akbar had suffered from an inexplicable stomach complaint, which would not yield to treatment. Poisoning was suspected, and Akbar, according to Badauni, suspected Salim. "Baba Shaikhuji," Akbar is said to have mumbled in a semi-conscious state, mentioning Salim by his nickname, "since all this sultanate will devolve on thee, why hast thou made this attack on me?"

Akbar's suspicion did not mean that Salim was guilty, but it indicated the uneasy relationship between father and son. Around that time Akbar seemed to be shifting his favour to his second son, Murad, and when he died, to his youngest son Daniyal, who was even authorized to use a red tent, which was normally reserved for the emperor. The amirs, alert weathercocks that they were, then began to flock to the younger princes, which confirmed Salim's fears and heightened his anxiety. Salim, according Muhibb Ali (who completed

Akbar-nama after the death of Abul Fazl), was perturbed that "his father's neglect of him was increasing daily."

Matters came to a head when Akbar set out for the Deccan in September 1599. Before he left Agra, he had charged Salim to resume the long neglected offensive against Mewar, but the prince, reluctant to get bogged down in what he knew would be a long and frustrating campaign, dawdled in Ajmer in sullen discontent. In mid-1600, in open disobedience of his father, if not in rebellion, Salim left Ajmer and proceeded to Agra. There he made a halfhearted attempt to seize the treasury, and when that failed, swerved and headed for Allahabad, avoiding meeting his grandmother, the venerable Hamida Banu Begum, who was very fond of him and wanted to divert him from his reckless course. On reaching Allahabad, he seized the treasury there and set himself up as a virtually independent ruler, appointing his own officers and distributing fiefs among them. He also began to raise an army.

When the startling development was reported to Akbar, his reaction was low key; he was inclined to treat it as a family affair rather than as a matter of state, as the misconduct of a son rather than as a rebellion. So, instead of sending a punitive force against Salim, he sent one of his amirs—Khwaja Muhammad Sharif, a childhood friend of Salim—to Allahabad to guide the prince back to obedience. Nothing came of it, for Salim induced Sharif to join him as a minister. Still, Akbar forbore. And Salim vacillated. There was something tentative about the whole affair, in Salim's challenge as well as in Akbar's response.

Meanwhile, with Ahmadnagar and Asirgarh fallen, Akbar concluded his southern campaign and returned to Agra in August 1601. He then resumed the contact with Salim, to find out what was troubling him and how his anxieties could be assuaged. The parley went on for some eight or nine months. Then, unexpectedly, Salim took to the field, advancing towards Agra with a cavalry force of over 30,000. Ostensibly he was going to pay his respects to his father, but in the prevailing charged atmosphere anything could have happened. He got as far as Etawah, a mere 100 kilometres from Agra, but Akbar remained cool— he ordered the prince to disband his army and visit him only with a small escort, or to return to Allahabad if he did not feel safe without his army. Salim dared not disobey a direct command from Akbar. He returned to Allahabad.

AKBAR THEN ISSUED a firman appointing Salim as the viceroy of Bengal and Orissa, denoting that he did not consider the prince to be

223

a rebel. Salim, however, preferred to stay on in Allahabad, where he (if de Laet is to be believed) now struck coins in his own name, and even sent some of them to Akbar—perhaps for his father to appreciate their artistic quality, or perhaps to indicate that he now considered himself an independent sovereign, though he showed Akbar the doubtful courtesy of calling him the Great King.

Akbar was not amused. Salim was clearly moving towards open rebellion. He had to be stopped. To work out a plan for that, Akbar recalled Abul Fazl, his trusted advisor, from the Deccan for consultations. But this only deepened the crisis. Salim and Abul Fazl disliked and distrusted each other. "Since his feelings towards me were not honest," writes Salim about Abul Fazl, "he both publicly and privately spoke against me. At this period, when, through strife-mongering intriguers, the august feelings of my revered father were entirely embittered against me, it was certain that if he obtained the honour of waiting on him, it would be the cause of more confusion, and would preclude me from the favour of union with him." Abul Fazl, on his part, openly boasted that he would soon truss up 'the king of Allahabad' and bundle him off to the court.

Salim pre-empted that prospect by having Abul Fazl assassinated by Bir Singh, the roguish Bundela chief of Orchha, through whose territory Abul Fazl had to pass on his way to Agra. Abul Fazl had been warned of the danger lurking ahead, but scorned to take any precaution—"I cannot flee from this unwashed thief," he said. He was therefore easy prey for Bir Singh, who intercepted him in the hill country south of Gwalior, speared him down, and sent his severed head to Salim in Allahabad. The prince, it is said, had the head "thrown into an unworthy place". He was entirely unrepentant about the murder of Abul Fazl, which, in his view, was an act of imperative political exigency. "Although this event was a cause of anger in the mind of the late king," he writes in his memoirs, "in the end it enabled me to proceed without disturbance of mind to kiss the threshold of my father's palace, and by degrees the resentment of the king was cleared away."

Akbar was shattered by the outrage. When Abul Fazl's deputy sombrely presented himself before the emperor with a blue handkerchief around his wrist, Akbar immediately knew what it meant—it was the custom at the Mughal court not to mention death directly before the emperor, but to signify it with a blue cloth. Akbar, who was at that time relaxing with his tumbler pigeons, "uttered a cry and became insensible," says Muhibb Ali. "That day and night he neither shaved, as usual, nor took opium, but spent his time in weeping and lamenting," adds Asad Beg, a close associate of Abul Fazl. "If Salim wished to be emperor," Akbar lamented, "he might have killed me and spared Abul Fazl."

Akbar's close confidants were all gone now, one by one—Birbal in 1586, Raja Bhagwan Das and Todar Mal in 1589, and now Abul Fazl, all those who had always been there beside him as he adventured through life. Soon it would be his turn for the long farewell.

THOUGH AKBAR WAS deeply hurt by Salim's involvement in Abul Fazl's assassination, he still made no move to chastise him. It was as if Akbar had had enough of military campaigns, enough perhaps even of reigning. He was weary. In this predicament, the great ladies of the harem took the initiative to deal with Salim—not to castigate him, but to affect a reconciliation between father and son.

Salima Begum, Akbar's favourite wife, took the task on herself. "That chaste lady, in order to soothe the prince's apprehension, took from His Majesty an elephant named Fath Lashkar, a special horse, and a robe of honour and went off with them" to Allahabad, reports Muhibb Ali. In Allahabad, she berated Salim into submission, and brought him back with her to Agra.

One stage outside Agra, Hamida Banu Begum took over, and led Salim to her residence. There, contrite and distraught, Salim wanted to consult astrologers to determine the propitious time to throw himself on his father's mercy, but Akbar said that "all hours were equally auspicious for an interview of harmony and concord", and himself went to his mother's residence to see the prince. As Akbar approached, Hamida rose with Salim and flung the prince at the emperor's feet. Akbar lifted him up, and removing the turban from his own head placed it on Salim. The reconciliation was complete. Salim's three-year rebellion was over.

Or so it seemed. But when Akbar ordered Salim to proceed against Mewar, the conquest of which was an unfinished task in Akbar's calendar, the prince demurred. He marched out obediently, but halted at Fatehpur Sikri, and then, on the ground that the forces given to him were insufficient for the task, requested Akbar to permit him to return to Allahabad. Reluctantly, Akbar agreed. "On receiving this message, the Prince, joyful, drinking wine, and pleasuring himself, crossed the Yamuna at a ferry near Mathura and went off gaily," says Muhibb Ali. Once in Allahabad, Salim sank into a life of shocking depravity. He seemed bent on self-destruction.

This distressed Akbar, for the future of the Mughal empire depended on Salim. Akbar's other surviving son, Daniyal, was a helpless alcoholic, unfit to rule. Akbar had tried to wean Daniyal from drink, and had sternly entrusted the task to Abdur-Rahim, the Khan-i-khanan, whose daughter was married to the prince. But all efforts failed. The guards charged with preventing liquor from reaching Daniyal were easily corrupted, and the boon companions of the prince did him what they considered to be the great favour of smuggling liquor to him, in the entrails of cows concealed in their clothing, or even in the barrels of muskets. Towards the end, Daniyal was in great pain; he gave up eating altogether, and, according to Muhibb Ali, "no other word but wine passed from his lips. For forty days he lay in bed, and . . . he died while longing for wine." This was in April 1604, at Burhanpur.

Now Akbar had only Salim to turn to. It was clear from the reports from Allahabad that Salim too was heading for disaster. Akbar could not let this happen; Salim had to be saved from himself. So in the summer of 1604 Akbar set out for Allahabad to take charge of his son. But the Fates would not let him go. While previously they favoured his every enterprise, now they hampered him in every way. Accidents and problems dogged him at every step—the barge in which he set out struck a sandbank immediately after it was launched, the camp of the army he had assembled for the campaign got inundated in rain, and his ailing mother, anxious to prevent a clash between her son and grandson, kept entreating him not to leave Agra. Akbar proceeded nevertheless. But he had not gone far when he received reports that the condition of his mother had become critical. He then had no alternative but to abort the campaign and return to Agra.

By the time he got to Agra, Hamida had lost consciousness, and though he spoke to her several times, she could not answer. On 10th September 1604, the grand old dowager empress passed away, aged seventy-seven, having outlived her husband by forty-eight years. Akbar bore her bier for a short distance, which was then carried by relays of nobles to Delhi to be buried in the mausoleum of Humayun. The emperor, according to Muhibb Ali, "fell into uncontrollable lamentation" on the death of his mother; he tonsured his head, shaved off his moustache, even his eyebrows, "and cast off his turban and donned the garb of woe".

WHEN HIS MOTHER died, something died in Akbar too. Her death increased his sense of isolation and loneliness. He now had nobody to turn to. It had thus become imperative to get hold of Salim and bring him to his senses.

Two months after Hamida's death, early in November 1604, Salim was again persuaded to return to the court, on the promise of full pardon. This time, though, his submission was not a private affair but a state occasion—the emperor received the prince formally in public audience, yet with affection and honour. But as the court broke up, Akbar abruptly seized Salim and drew him into an inner apartment, where he slapped him repeatedly in fury, reproaching him bitterly for his irresponsible conduct, mocking him for not daring to fight though he had an army of 70,000. Salim was then kept in confinement in the palace, in the charge of Raja Salivahan, a physician, with the strict instruction to deny him opium and wine. Many of Salim's principal adherents were imprisoned.

The cold turkey treatment lasted ten days, after which Salim was released, raised to higher honours, and assigned a fitting residence, though he was still kept under surveillance. For one year Salim lived there quietly, in apparent harmony with his father, and in reasonable self-control. The cure had worked.

Salim's recovery was a good portent. But Akbar was still anxious about the future. Would Salim's reform hold? Would there be a war of succession, for which Salim and his (Salim's) eldest son Khusrav seemed to have squared off? Why did Murad and Daniyal drink themselves to death? And why had Salim too grimly set himself on that self-destructive path? How had Akbar failed his children, and in failing them, failed his dynasty?

Akbar in his last years was not the emperor the world had known. Time no longer waited on his pleasure. And the world began to close in on him, this king for whom the world had once expanded boundlessly to accommodate his immense talents and ambitions.

His will to win, perhaps his will to live, had snapped. A year after his mother's death, towards the end of September 1605, Akbar was "taken somewhat ill, and in a short time was very much broken down," says Asad Beg. In that weakened condition, on 2nd October 1605, he arranged for a fight between an elephant of Salim and one of Khusrav, probably hoping to find in it an omen about the vexing issue of succession. The fight, presaging the future accurately, ended in an unseemly squabble between the partisans of Salim and Khusrav. Khusrav, whose elephant was routed, then rushed to the aged emperor and made a scene. The incident, says Asad Beg, made Akbar "exceedingly angry, vexed and enraged, and this so much increased his illness".

Akbar was restless that night and slept fitfully. By morning he was ill with an acute attack of diarrhoea, which he thought was brought on by his mortification over Khusrav's behaviour. For eight days his chief physician, Hakim Ali Gilani, refrained from giving him any medicine, hoping that his body would mend itself. But when there was no improvement, and the emperor grew progressively weaker, astringents were given, which stopped the diarrhoea, but brought on fever. When the fever was treated, diarrhoea set in again. "Every medicine which he used to check the disease, assisted it," writes Muhibb Ali. On the nineteenth day of the illness the helpless physician "withdrew his hand from applying remedies". Akbar's time had come.

AS AKBAR LAY dying, succession manoeuvres at the court intensified, and a powerful cabal of amirs plotted to set aside Salim in favour of his son Khusrav. This group, headed by Khusrav's maternal uncle Raja Man Singh and father-in-law Aziz Koka (Khan Azam), was however opposed by the majority of the top amirs of the court, who at a meeting convened to discuss the succession issue, contended that it was "contrary to the laws and customs of the Chaghatai Tatars" to bypass the father in favour of the son. The view of the majority prevailed.

On 21st October Salim visited the sinking emperor. Akbar was conscious but unable to speak. As Salim bowed at his feet, "the Emperor once more opened his eyes, and signed to them (the amirs around the bed) to invest him (Salim) with the turban and robes which had been prepared for him, and to gird him with his own dagger," reports Asad Beg. This was Akbar's last deed.

In his youth Akbar had often played tag with death, taunting and defying the Grim Reaper. But now there was no fight in him. And as he lay beaten and inert, death crept up on him. On the night of 25th. October 1605, as the midnight hour turned, Akbar, sixty-three, passed away.

As dawn broke over Agra, a section of the wall of Akbar's palace was knocked down, as was the custom, and the emperor's body, bathed and placed in a bier, and borne by his son, grandsons and the great nobles, was brought out of the palace. Salim "took the foot of the bier of the deceased King upon his shoulder, and carried it as far as the door of the public reception room," writes Asad Beg; "from thence, the great nobles, each anxious for the honour, relieving one another in quick succession, carried His Majesty as far as the gate of the fort. Thence the nobles and ministers, and courtiers and imams, and all his servants and troops, followed the bier with head and feet uncovered" to the mausoleum at Sikandra, eight kilometres west of Agra.

The mausoleum, planned and begun by Akbar himself, but

completed only in 1613, is a unique structure, which, like the palace complex in Fatehpur Sikri, embodied the spirit of the king who had conceived it—complex and full of surprises, seeming curiously unfinished, its possibilities not exhausted, open to all winds, all lights.

"These are the Gardens of Eden: enter them to dwell therein eternally," invokes the inscription on Akbar's mausoleum. Unfortunately, Akbar would not be left in peace in his grave. Eighty-six years after his death, in 1691, when his great-grandson Aurangzeb was in the Deccan pushing the frontiers of the empire to the very limits of the subcontinent, a band of wild Jats, who had no true knowledge of the man who had been laid to rest there, and probably would not have cared even if they did, broke into Akbar's mausoleum, pillaging and desecrating. "Most of the graves and tombs erected there had also been razed to the ground," reports Ishwardas Nagar, Aurangzeb's courtier historian. "They began their pillage by breaking in the great gates of bronze which it had, robbing the valuable precious stones and plates of gold and silver and destroying what they were not able to carry away," elaborates Niccolao Manucci, an Italian traveller who was then in India. "Dragging out the bones of Akbar, they threw them angrily into the fire and burnt them."

A Hindu end for Akbar, after all.

Chapter Seven

THE MIDDLE EMPIRE

His Father's Son

A WEEK AFTER the death of Akbar, on Thursday, 3rd November 1605, shortly after sunrise, Salim, thirty-six, ascended the imperial throne in the Hall of Public Audience in the Agra Fort.

Salim crowned himself. "Having . . . seated myself on the throne of my expectations and wishes, I caused also the imperial crown, which my father had caused to be made after the manner of that which was worn by the great kings of Persia, to be brought to me," Salim writes in his memoirs, "and then, in the presence of the whole assembled amirs, having placed it on my brows, as an omen auspicious to the stability and happiness of my reign, kept it there for the space of a full astronomical hour."

There was hardly any other ceremony. For the Mughals—indeed, in Muslim polity in general—enthronement was not a high ritual. The Mughals especially ruled by their arms, not by the sanctity of rites. They had therefore no accession ceremonies, no anointing or crowning, no priestly involvement. There was not even any regalia for the emperor to assume. The crown that Salim mentions had no particular significance; it was just a royal ornament. The only Mughal accession requirements were that the new monarch should formally take his seat on the throne, have the khutbah read and coins struck in his name.

It was however common for the emperor to assume a title on his accession, to mark his transition from prince to king. Salim took the title Jahangir, Seizer of the World—because, says Salim, "the business of kings is controlling the world"—and it would be by this name that he would be known in history.

AT THIRTY-SIX, SALIM was well past his prime when he became the emperor, almost an old man by medieval reckoning. Though several members of the Mughal royal family, especially women, had lived to ripe old ages, the average life span of Mughal princes, given their hazardous lives and self-indulgent lifestyles, was short. Salim's two brothers, Murad and Daniyal, both younger than he, died when they were twenty-nine and thirty-three; Akbar's brother Muhammad Hakim died at thirty-one; Humayun died at forty-eight, Babur at forty-seven, and Babur's father at thirty-eight. When Babur's maternal grandfather, Yunus Khan, lived beyond forty years, it was considered as something of a wonder. "None of the Chaghatai Khans who preceded him had passed the age of forty," says Mirza Haidar; "nay, most of them never reached that age."

Salim's advancing years had caused him considerable distress as he awaited his turn to rule. He was an intelligent, able young man, well-educated, with broad cultural interests. He needed a chance to prove himself, but with Akbar in vigorous health even in his late fifties, he had feared that he might not get the chance, or get it too late, when he was too old to prove himself. As the shadows lengthened, Salim, who was "of a hot disposition", had begun to seethe, and in the end had broken out in rebellion.

It could not have been an easy decision for Salim to rise against Akbar, and he would never admit, even to himself, that he had in fact rebelled. Instead, he flatly denies it in his otherwise candid memoirs. "Short-sighted men in Allahabad had urged me . . . to rebel against my father," he writes. "Their words were extremely unacceptable and disapproved by me."

Salim protests too much. In his memoirs he speaks repeatedly of his reverence and affection for Akbar. "I went on foot to see the resplendent sepulchre of my father," he writes. "If I could, I would travel this distance upon my eye-lashes or my head." Once, when a tray of fruits was presented to him, Jahangir was moved by the memory of Akbar—"When I see and enjoy these luxuries, I regret that my father is not here to share them," he writes. There is no reason to doubt the sincerity of these statements. But filial sentiment was one thing, politics quite another. As Salim would remark in another context, "Sovereignty does not regard the relation of father and son." It was a natural, almost animal instinct in Mughal princes to test themselves against their fathers; Salim himself, as well as Shah Jahan and Aurangzeb after him, would face major rebellions by their sons.

VERY LITTLE IS known about Salim's childhood. He was born on 30th August 1569, at noon, in the hermitage of Sheikh Salim Chishti at Sikri. A child of many prayers, he had a pampered childhood. Akbar was fond of children and doted on Salim, always lovingly calling him by his nickname, Shaikhu Baba. The ladies of the harem smothered him with love; Salima Begum, his step-mother, and Hamida Banu Begum, his grandmother, were particularly fond of him—in their eyes he could do no wrong, and they always found excuses for his peccadilloes. His mother, the Amber princess, was not very much in the picture. There are altogether only a dozen references to her in Jahangir's memoirs, and when she died in the eighteenth year of his reign, it merits only a casual reference by him. "On this day news came from Agra that Her highness Maryam-zamani, by the decree of God, had died," he writes; "I trust that Almighty God will envelop her in the ocean of His mercy." He did not attend her funeral, though he was nearby, in the outskirts of Fatehpur Sikri.

At the age of four, Salim, along with his two brothers, was circumcised, an occasion for a grand celebration. The ceremony inspired Abul Fazl, royal panegyrist, to write:

> Was the petal of the red rose scattered
>   by the wind,
> Or did the rosebud draw the veil from
>   her face?
> Nay, nay; when the fruit of the tree
>   of desire formed,
> The expended blossom dropped from the branch.

When Salim was four years, four months and four days old, he was, in conformity to the custom of the Mughal royal family, ceremonially initiated into the alphabet. Maulana Mir Kalan Haravi, a venerable scholar, was appointed by Akbar as Salim's first tutor, and he accepted his charge by raising the prince on his shoulders amidst acclamations and a shower of gems. Salim was then made to recite the name of god and the Muslim creed, and taught the first letter of the alphabet.

Other tutors followed. Salim presumably also had various guardians, at least nominal guardians, for that was the Mughal custom, though Abul Fazl states that Akbar "kept his children under his own care and did not appoint any guardian to them, and was continually educating them in the most excellent manner of which there are few instances in ancient times." Salim was a diligent student. He also excelled in martial arts, and grew into a robust young man who delighted in sport, hunting and athletics. He was, like all the Mughals, totally fearless, ever ready to meet danger head on. Akbar was proud of this son of his.

Salim's first battle experience, according to the Rajput tradition recorded by Tod, came quite early, when at the age of seven he was given nominal charge of the Mewar campaign. Around this time his rank was raised to that of a commander of 10,000, with an income to match. When he was around twelve, he accompanied Akbar on the

Kabul campaign, and was given command of a large detachment. Soon after, to initiate him into the administrative processes of the empire, two important departments (justice and celebrations) were put in his charge, with Abdur-Rahim, the Khan-i-khanan, as his guide. In all, Salim seemed to be shaping up well.

Then inexplicably, for the next eighteen years, from the age of about thirteen till he broke out in rebellion in 1600 at the age of thirty-one, Salim virtually disappears from Mughal chronicles, with only a few stray references to him, most of them towards the very end of the period. Throughout his youth no important responsibilities are recorded to have been assigned to the heir apparent. In 1598, when there was a proposal to send a Mughal army into Badakshan, Salim was sought to be put in command, but nothing came of it—Akbar did not proceed with the campaign, and in any case Salim was reluctant to take charge. Nor was Salim eager when the command of the Deccan forces was offered to him the following year. It was apparently a case of too little too late.

SOMETHING HAD SOURED the relationship between Salim and Akbar. Though Akbar was affectionate towards his children, he was also usually short with them. "The King's nature was such that, though he loved his children very dearly, he used to give them orders rather roughly whenever he wanted anything done," says Monserrate; "and he sometimes punished them with blows as well as with harsh words." And when his sons grew into manhood, Akbar's affections shifted to his grandsons—"The affectionate sovereign loved grandsons more than sons," says Abul Fazl. It was almost as if Akbar considered his adult sons as his rivals. There was an evident reluctance on his part to assign major tasks to them. He gave the impression that they did not quite measure up to his expectations. In the eye of Akbar's disapproval, Daniyal and Murad resigned themselves to a life of debauchery and early death, but Salim, who was tougher, survived, though sparks often flew between father and son.

Akbar's ire against Salim frequently exploded over seemingly trivial matters, indicating an undercurrent of tension between the two. Once, when Salim was twenty and the imperial family was on its way to Kashmir, Akbar worked himself into a fury one day when Salim, because of inclement weather, delayed bringing the royal harem to Akbar's camp as he had been directed to do. So infuriated was Akbar that, despite rain and slippery ridges, he immediately set out to fetch the women himself, and could be persuaded to return to camp only with great difficulty. Salim naturally felt humiliated by what seemed to him to be his father's unreasonable rage, and, according to Abul Fazl, "the prince shut himself in his tent, and abstained from food and sleep."

There seems to have been an Oedipal conflict between Akbar and Salim. The Mughal court was rife with rumours about the tension between the two, because of Salim's escapades and Akbar's resentment over them. The most romantic and persistent of these stories linked Salim in secret liaison with Anarkali (Pomegranate Blossom), a beautiful and accomplished concubine of Akbar and possibly the mother of Daniyal—legend has it that a wrathful Akbar entombed Anarkali alive for the crime of exchanging a smiling glance with Salim. Another tale was about Salim's infatuation with Mihrunnisa (Nur Jahan), which Akbar is said to have thwarted. Whether these particular incidents were true or not, the very fact that such rumours persisted is significant, and indicates that probably there was some sex-related tension between Akbar and Salim.

There was also the curious incident of Salim being thrashed one evening, hit with sticks and clods, by the amazonian guards of the royal harem. The improbable story, as Abul Fazl tells it, is that a mad man had wandered into the harem because of the carelessness of the sentinels, and Salim caught him, but was himself mistaken for a stranger and set on, and that Akbar came upon the scene and was about to strike with his sword when he recognized Salim. It is incredible that a stranger, that too a lunatic, could enter the royal harem undetected, that Salim was not immediately recognized, and that he did not identify himself when attacked. The incident remains a mystery.

Whatever the cause of the tension between Akbar and Salim, Akbar's death burned out the canker of resentment in Salim against his father. Salim—from now on to be known as Jahangir—was equally forgiving towards those who opposed his accession. What was past was past; he would not look back in anger. He took no vindictive action. Instead, he won over several of Khusrav's supporters by raising their ranks, and was solicitous enough to take Abul Fazl's son under his wing and appoint him as a high-ranking officer. But the main beneficiaries of his accession were of course his own followers. Zamana Beg, a long-time associate of Jahangir and a captain of his praetorian guard, was conferred the title Mahabat Khan and given the rank of a commander of 1500; he would now begin the climb through the ranks that would in the end make him, though only for a few months, the military dictator of the empire. Also honoured was Bir Singh Bundela, who received the rank of 3000; "the cause of his elevation," admits

237

Jahangir with brazen candour, "was the murder of Abul Fazl."

Jahangir's ambition was to be known as a just ruler. "The first order which I issued [on accession] was for the setting up of a chain of justice," he notes in his memoirs, "so that if the officers of the courts of justice should fail in the investigation of the complaints of the oppressed and in granting them redress, the injured persons might come to this chain and shake it, and so give notice of their wrongs." The chain, which was probably inspired by the drum of justice that Humayun had once set up at the fort, was made of gold, with some sixty bells on it, and was stretched from the battlement of the Agra fort to a stone column on the bank of the Yamuna.

The chain was not a mere symbol. English merchants William Hawkins, Nicholas Withington and William Finch, who were at the Mughal court in the early years of Jahangir's reign, each testify that the chain of justice was in actual use. "They (supplicants) came to a certaine place where a long rope is fastened unto two pillars, neare unto the place where the King sitteth in justice," says Hawkins. "This rope is hanged full of bels, plated with gold, so the rope being shaken the bels are heard by the King; who sendeth to know the cause and doth his justice accordingly." Frivolous ringing of the bells was not tolerated. Says Finch: "Let them be sure their cause be good, lest they be punished for presumption to trouble the King."

On his accession, Jahangir also promulgated a set of twelve ordinances, prohibiting the collection of unauthorized taxes, providing for the security of roads, safeguarding property rights, ensuring compensation to farmers for loss during military operations, banning disfiguring punishments like cutting off the nose and ears, and so on. He further banned the sale of hemp drugs and sought to enforce prohibition, although, as he happily confesses, "I myself have been accustomed to take wine, and from my eighteenth year to the present, which is the thirty-eighth year of my age, have regularly partaken of it." Later, he also forbade smoking. "In consequence of the disturbance that tobacco brings about in most temperaments and constitutions, I had ordered that no one should smoke it," says Jahangir.

These regulations were meant "to rearrange the withered world", says courtier historian Asad Beg. Hardly. The regulations were mere gestures; they were of little practical consequence. Jahangir no doubt meant well, but he simply did not have the sustained interest, nor the administrative machinery, to implement the regulations systematically.

JAHANGIR'S REIGN FALLS in the exact middle of the 180-year span from Babur to Aurangzeb, and marks a plateau in Mughal history. In many respects, his reign was like an afterglow of Akbar's reign. Jahangir did not strike out on his own in any new direction, but merely continued his father's policies. And whatever he built, was built on foundations laid by Akbar. Still, Jahangir cannot be dismissed as just an interlude between Akbar and Shah Jahan. Though he was prone to ease and luxury, and his main interests were in science and culture, not in empire building and governance, his reign was on the whole marked by stability and peace. There were only three major revolts during his reign, and each of them he overcame with shrewdness and resolute energy.

Jahangir was not a failure, as he is often portrayed to be. He might be found wanting in stature when measured against Akbar, and his stature might shrink further when seen through the frowning glance of Victorian historians who disapproved of his libertine ways and despised him for being henpecked. But if we are to judge a ruler by the security and prosperity enjoyed by his subjects, then Jahangir's reign should be reckoned as the best of the Mughal times. Also, next only to Babur, Jahangir is the most endearing of the Mughals, who dared to show the human face behind the Pharaonic persona of the emperor.

In religion, Jahangir was eclectic and tolerant like Akbar. "All religions are tolerated," says Terry, an English clergyman in Jahangir's court. Jahangir, says Della Valle, a medieval Italian traveller, "makes no difference in his dominions between the one sort and the other, and both in his court and armies, and even amongst men of the highest degree, they are of equal account and consideration." He even restored some of the Hindu practices that Akbar had initially adopted but later abandoned—for instance, he resumed the *rakhi* ceremony that Akbar had given up and "ordered that the Brahman should bind strings (of cotton) and silk after the ancient manner." Out of regard for Hindu sentiments, he forbade cow slaughter "on pain of death, though buffaloes may be freely killed," says Pelsaert. He further banned the sale of meat on certain days, though people were free to prepare meat at home.

In all these, Jahangir followed Akbar's precepts and practices. But there were also significant differences between the two. Jahangir lacked Akbar's earnestness, and now and then he lapsed from the policy of religious tolerance, sometimes for political reasons but often due to some vagrant impulse. Occasionally he was guilty of temple destruction.

The worst of these incidents took place in 1620, when the hill fort of Kangra, with its ancient shrine of Jwalamukhi, was taken. "I gave orders that the Kazi, the Chief Justice, and others learned in the law of Islam, should accompany me, and perform the ceremonies required by our religion," writes Jahangir. "We mounted the fort, and by the grace of God, prayers were said, the khutbah was read, a cow was killed and other things were done such as never had been done before from the foundation of fort to the present time. All this was done in my presence and I bowed myself in thanks to the Almighty for this great conquest, which no previous monarch had been able to accomplish. I ordered a large mosque to be built in the fortress."

In another instance, at Pushkar near Ajmer, on seeing there an image of Varaha (an incarnation of Vishnu, with a man's body and a boar's head) he "ordered them to break that hideous form and throw it into the tank," writes Jahangir. In Gujarat he hounded out the Jains, demolished their temples, and had their idol thrown on the steps of a mosque for Muslims to tread on. Before that, early in his reign, Jahangir had executed Sikh Guru Arjun Singh, though the provocation for that was political, not religious, for the guru had aided prince Khusrav's rebellion. Jahangir also persecuted the Mahdis, a sect of Muslim fundamentalists, whose virulence disturbed social harmony. And in Kashmir, when he heard that Hindus lately converted to Islam there were taking and giving daughters in marriage alliances with Hindu families, his ruling-class pride was outraged. "Taking them is good, but giving them, God forbid!" he writes. "I gave an order that hereafter they should not do such things, and whoever was guilty of them, should be capitally punished."

These were however random acts. There was no systematic religious persecution by Jahangir. His faith was not ardent enough to make him a zealot. During the succession tussle he had undertaken to uphold orthodoxy in return for the support of Muslim amirs, and he did take a few measures to fulfil that promise, such as sanctioning daily allowances to new converts to Islam, but he did not adopt a sustained orthodox policy. And, though by and large he conformed to the external observances of Islam throughout his life, he seems to have done so more out of inertia than faith. Similarly, the numerous references to god in his memoirs—"I trust that my life will be spent in doing God's will, and that not a breath of it will pass without remembering Him," he says in one place—sound more like a literary mannerism than a confession of faith. Indeed, some contemporary observers doubted whether Jahangir had any faith at all.

"His religione is his owne invention," says Sir Thomas Roe, the British Ambassador at the court of Jahangir; "he envyes Mahomett, and wisely sees noe reason hee should not bee as great a prohet as hee." Elsewhere Roe flatly states that "Jhe-hangier-Shah . . . is an Atheist." Says Francois Bernier, a French physician in India during the closing years of Shah Jahan's reign: "Jahangir died, as he had lived, destitute of all religion." According to Niccolao Manucci, Aurangzeb refused to pray at the mausoleum of Jahangir, "saying that it was the burial place of an infidel".

It is unlikely that Jahangir was really an infidel or an atheist, but he certainly was ambivalent in religion, even rather playful. "Some time he will make profession of a Moor," says Roe; "but always observe the holidays and do all ceremonies with the Gentiles too." Like Akbar, Jahangir held public discussions on religion for a while—he spent "euerynight for one yeare . . . in hearing disputation" on religion, says Roe. He loved to egg on the Jesuits against the mullahs, "slapping his thighs with delight at their retorts to their opponents," says Maclagan. Fernao Guerreiro, a seventeenth century Jesuit historian, reports that Jahangir once asked a Hindu courtier whether he considered Muhammad a prophet, to which the courtier replied, "'Yes, Sire! He is a false prophet,' at which the king laughed exceedingly."

Jahangir was equally disdainful of the popular beliefs of Hinduism and Christianity. The idea that Christ was the son of god seemed absurd to him, as did the Hindu myths about incarnations. How could that which had no limitations limit itself through incarnations, he asked, and why should the supreme spirit that was immanent in everything, specially incarnate itself in particular beings? There could be no answers to such questions—faith could not satisfy reason any more than reason could undermine faith. Predictably, popular religions bored Jahangir. But Sufism fascinated him, and so did the mystical and intellectual sects of Hinduism. He considered Vedanta "the science of Sufism".

What Jahangir sought in religion was esoteric knowledge, not faith. Like Akbar, he was fond of the company of ascetics. Sir Thomas Roe once found him closeted with a Hindu ascetic. "I found him sitting on the Throne, and a Beggar at his feet, a poore silly old man all asht, ragd, and patchet, with a young roague attending on him," writes Roe. "With these kind of professed poore holy men, the Countrey abounds, and are held in great reverence . . . his Majestie talked with [him] about an houre, with such familiaritie and shew of kindnesse, that it must argue an humilitie not found easily among kings. The Beggar sate, which his sonne dares not doe: he gave the King a Present, a Cake, asht, burnt on coales, made by himself of course graine, which the King accepted most willingly, and brake one bit and ate it, which a daintie mouth could scarce have done. After he tooke the clout, and wrapt it up, and put in the poore mans bosome, and sent fore one hundred Rupias, and with his owne hands powred them into the poore mans lap, and what fell besides, gathered up for him; when his collation of banquetting and drinke came, whatsoever he took to eate, he brake and gave the Beggar halfe, and after many strange humiliations and charities, rising, the old Wretch not being so nimble, he took him up in his armes, which no cleanly body durst have touched, imbracing him, and three times laying his hand on his heart, calling him father, he left him . . ."

Jahangir's (as well as Akbar's) favourite Hindu sage was Chid Rup, a Hindu hermit who lived in a tiny cave in the hills near Ujjain. "On Saturday, for the second time, my desire for the company of Chid Rup increased," says Jahangir about one of his many meetings with the sage. "After performing the midday devotion, I embarked in a boat and hastened to meet him, and at the close of day I ran and enjoyed his society in the retirement of his cell. I heard many sublime words of religious duties and knowledge of divine things." Jahangir sought out Muslim ascetics too. "As it was reported to me that in Lahore one Miyan Sheikh Muhammad Mir by name, who was a dervish, a Sindhi by origin, very eloquent, virtuous, austere, of auspicious temperament, a lord of ecstasy . . . and was rich in his poverty and independent of the world, my truth-seeking mind was not at rest without meeting him, and desire to see him increased," writes Jahangir.

In contrast, Christianity did not make much impression on him, though, continuing Akbar's policy, he allowed the Jesuits to preach and convert freely in the empire, and gave them stipends from the treasury, initially fifty rupees a month, which was later raised to one hundred, with thirty given additionally for the maintenance of their church. He also handed over to them, in what was the high point of Jesuit missionary achievement at the Mughal court, three sons of his dead brother Daniyal to be baptized.

It was an abrupt and baffling decision, which probably had something to do with court or harem intrigues. The Jesuits were summoned to the court at midnight one day in July 1610 and the boys, the eldest of whom was ten, handed over. "The fathers (Xavier and Pinheiro) in their enthusiasm fell to their knees and kissed his feet, while he good-humouredly patted them on their shoulders," writes Maclagan. The princes were baptized a couple of months later, presumably after proper Christian indoctrination. It made quite a stir in Agra when they, riding elephants, went in procession to the church, wearing Portuguese costumes, with gold crosses around their necks. At baptism, the princes were given Portuguese names—Tahmuras became Don Felipe, Baisanghar became Don Carlos and Hoshang became Don Henrique.

It was a day of wild joy for the Jesuits, and as the princes approached the church, the sextons rang the church bell with such gusto that they broke it. This was a portent of what was to come. After four years at playing Christians, the princes, as the Jesuits bitterly reported, "rejected the light and returned to their vomit".

Jahangir's main interest in the Jesuits was to procure from them European paintings. "His desire for Christian pictures became almost embarrassing," says Maclagan. The Jesuits—"Going and coming, and throwing the hook into the water, hoping that the fish will bite," as Jerome Xavier puts it—believed that one day they would be able to convert the emperor to Christianity. According to Maclagan, Jahangir used to attend the church on Christmas day, and had a portrait of himself placed in the church, so the Fathers would not forget to remember him in their prayers. But there was never any question of his becoming a Christian. According to Roe, Jahangir told the Jesuits: "If yee will cast the Crucifix and Picture of Christ into a fire before me, if it burne not, I will become a Christian." The Jesuits did not take up the challenge. Nor could they have been pleased when, while visiting their church in Lahore, Jahangir found the ambience there so very agreeable that he wanted to feast and drink in the church!

Scientist Emperor

THE DESIRE TO carouse in the church was typical of Jahangir. The Herat tradition of hedonism and passionate dilettantism, which had once surfaced in Humayun, surfaced now again in Jahangir. A keen naturalist and a connoisseur of painting, he was an equally ardent epicure, and though he was Mughal enough to harden himself for grim action when provoked, he believed that there was more to life than tearing around on horseback.

There was quite a bit of the child in Jahangir, as in Humayun. Manucci tells a charming story about Jahangir which he had heard late in the reign of Shah Jahan: "One day he (Jahangir) was passing through Lahore city when he saw a number of little children playing in the street. He descended from his elephant, sat himself down on the ground in their midst, and distributed sweets, flowers, clothes, gold and silver coins. After embracing and kissing them he said tearfully: 'Better were it for me to die or to be a little one like you, not to be as I am today, with my conscience entangled in the affairs of this weary world.' At these words he took his departure with a salutation, tears streaming from his eyes."

The story might be apocryphal, but it tells a truth about Jahangir. Highly emotional, his thrills and miseries were like those of a child, sudden and fleeting. There was no mystery about him. Unlike Akbar, who was impenetrable behind many veils, there was a charming simplicity and transparency about Jahangir, as in Babur. And, as with Babur, a great deal is known about Jahangir's private life, from his candid memoirs—which he wrote in his own hand for seventeen years from his accession—as well as from several contemporary works by Mughal chroniclers and European travellers. There are also a number of revealing portrait paintings of Jahangir.

WHAT IS IMMEDIATELY striking as we look at the portraits of Jahangir and compare his face with that of his father is the contrast between the two. Akbar appears self-contained; there is about him the inner orientation of a man who has to prove himself to no one but himself. In contrast, Jahangir's is a face in the mirror of the world, a man who has to see his worth in the eyes of other people. He appears a little unsure of himself, but bravely posturing. His expression—the arch look he favours, the fake firmness of his weak mouth—seems contrived. The very physiological mould of Jahangir is different from that of Akbar. There is a certain angularity in Jahangir's features, a hewn rather than moulded look; it is more Indian, with Rajput characteristics cutting another race into the smooth, rounded, Mongoloid face of his ancestors.

His complexion was typically Indian. "Hee is of a complexion neither white nor blacke, but of a middle betwixt them," says Coryat; "I know not how to expresse it with a more expressive and significant epitheton than olive; an olive colour his face presenteth." Jahangir, in the fashion of Akbar, sported no beard, but wore a neat moustache that dropped sharply at the edges and curled outward. The curve of the moustache was repeated in the long, narrow sideburns descending to curl at his earlobes. In most paintings a halo enveloped his head. One allegorical painting shows him as a plump and radiant monarch standing on a lion and protectively embracing a squat and shrinking Shah Abbas of Persia standing on a lamb and looking up humbly at the Mughal. Jahangir loved to swagger.

Unlike Akbar, he dressed opulently. In public, he was always heavily bejewelled, "clothed, or rather laden with Diamonds, Rubies, Pearles, and other precious vanities, so great, so glorious!" writes Sir Thomas Roe. "His head, necke, breast, armes, above the elbowes, at wrists, his fingers every one, with at least two or three rings, fettered with chaines, or dialled Diamonds; Rubies as great as Wall-nuts, some greater; and Pearles, such as mine eyes were amazed at." According to William Hawkins, who preceded Roe to the Mughal court, Jahangir wore a different set of jewels each day of the year.

A debonair man, Jahangir designed his own clothes, the fabric and style of which others were forbidden to use, except by royal permission. According to Bernier, Jahangir once had a fancy to clothe the whole court in European costume, and had arrayed himself in such a dress before his principal amirs, but their reaction "was so appalling that Jahan-Guyn abandoned the design and affected to pass the whole affair as a joke." The incident could well be true. Jahangir had a fascination for the exotic, and was an unabashed sybarite.

Appearances mattered to him, perhaps even more than substance. Gregarious and warm-hearted, he enjoyed good companionship. Once, when a descendant of the Lodi royal family visited him, Jahangir immediately took to him. "The Mir is of an exceedingly good disposition,

245

endowed with personal nobility and acquired excellencies, of good manners and approved ways, with a very pleasing face and open forehead," Jahangir writes. "I have never seen a man of this country of such a pleasing disposition as the Mir." And of a visitor from Transoxiana he writes: "He was an old man of very pleasing face, and full of talk and anecdote."

"He (Jahangir) is very affable," says Roe, "and of a cheerefull countenance. . . and not proud in nature, . . . full of gentle conversation . . . the wisdome and goodness of the King appeares aboue the malice of others . . ." Highly emotional, he wept easily, often uncontrollably and without reason. "Weeping came easily to Jahangir, for without any reason at all he would burst into tears. Anything and everything made him cry," says Manucci. Once, says Roe, "in extreme drunkennesse he fell to weeping, and to diverse passions, and so kept us till midnight."

This was one side of Jahangir. There was another. "This King's disposition seemes composed of extreames: very cruell, and otherwhiles very milde," says Edward Terry. Jahangir was susceptible to violent and unpredictable mood swings, perhaps because his early alcoholism and opium addiction had warped his temperament. Says Inayatullah: "The practice of indulgence in wine drinking, and of the excessive use of opium had affected the health of . . . Sultan Salim, and had made his temper so irritable and tyrannical, that the slightest offences were visited with the severest punishment, that pardon was never thought of, so that his adherents were struck dumb with terror."

Jahangir was often sadistic. "When he did wickedly, none could be worse," says Terry. "Hee delighteth to see men executed himself and torne in peeces with elephants," writes Hawkins. Once, according to Hawkins, when a favourite China dish of Jahangir's broke while being transported to camp, he had the amir in charge of his wardrobe mercilessly flogged and sent to prison—and when the poor man recovered from his wounds, he was given 5000 rupees and sent to China to procure another dish like the one broken, which had originally cost just seventy rupees!

Hunting was for Jahangir, as it was for Akbar, a way to cool the fever of his blood. But even here his attitudes were self-contradictory. He was a keen naturalist, who studied animals and birds with loving devotion. But he loved to kill them too. In 1617 he calculated that his hunting tally till then was 28,532 animals, of which he personally accounted for 17,168, including 86 tigers, 889 nilgais, 1,372 deer, 36 wild buffaloes, 90 wild boars, 23 hares; in addition, he had bagged 13,964 birds, including 10,348 pigeons, 3,276 crows, 156 waterfowl and 41 sparrows; he also accounted for 10 crocodiles. "I have such a liking for tiger shooting that whilst I can get it I do not go after other sport," he writes. He enjoyed fishing too, and there are many references to it in his memoirs; sometimes he amused himself by throwing the fish back into the water—after stringing pearls in their noses! On his tours, he always hunted along the way. "No day either of marching or halting, on land or water, passed without sport," says Jahangir about a trip from Lahore to Agra. The very last thing Jahangir did in his life, just a couple of days before he died, was to go on a rifle shoot.

JAHANGIR WAS REPUTED to have been a marksman in his youth, but by the time he became the emperor he could not have been much of a shot, for his health, as he admits it himself, was so broken by alcohol and drugs that his hands shook badly and he could hardly hold a wine cup to his mouth. "Up to my fourteenth year I had never drunk wine, except two or three times in childhood, when my mother or nurses had given me some as a remedy for some childhood ailment. Once also my father called for some arrack to the amount of a tola, and mixing it with rose-water, made me drink it as a remedy for cough," writes Jahangir. On his own, he drank wine for the first time during a hunt in Punjab. He had that day "met with many mishaps and was very tired," he writes, so when one of his attendants suggested that if he would drink a cup of wine it would relieve fatigue and weariness, he agreed. "I was young, and prone to indulgence . . ."

"From that time I took to wine drinking," continues Jahangir, "and from day to day took more and more, until wine of the grape had no effect upon me, and I resorted to spirit-drinking. In the course of nine years I got up to twenty cups of double-distilled spirit, fourteen of which I drank in the day, and the remaining six at night. The weight of this was six *seers* of Hindustan . . . My food in those days was one fowl and some bread. No one dared to expostulate with me, and matters reached such an extreme that when in liquor I could not hold my cup for shaking and trembling. I drank, but others held the cup for me."

At this point some residual instinct of self-preservation made Jahangir seek medical help. "At last I sent for the hakim Humam . . . and placed my case before him. With great kindness and interest, he spoke to me without concealment, and told me that if I went on drinking spirits in this way for six months longer, my state would be past remedy. His advice was good, and life is dear. I was greatly affected by his words, and from that day I began to diminish my potations, but I took to eating *faluha* (a marijuana concoction) and I

247

directed that my spirits should be mixed with wine of the grape, two parts wine and one spirit. Lessening my allowance daily, I reduced it in the course of seven years to six cups, each cup weighing eighteen *miskals* and a quarter. For fifteen years I have now kept to this quantity, taking neither more nor less. I take it at night, except on Thursday, that being the day of my accession to the throne, and on Friday, which is the most holy day of the week . . . On Thursday and on Sunday I eat no meat, that being the day of my accession, this my father's birthday. These days are held in great honour. After some time, instead of *faluha*, I took to opium . . . Now that my age is forty-six solar years and four months, I eat eight *surkhs* (small seeds used as a weight) of opium when five *gharis* (about two hours) of the day has passed, and six *surkhs* after one watch (three hours) of the night." According to Manucci, Jahangir took wine mixed with rose-water and "flavoured with costly spices and aromatic drugs".

In the evenings, when he met with his senior ministers in the Ghusl-khana, his cabinet room, Jahangir, says William Finch, drank "by number and measure, sometimes one and thirtie, and running over, mixing also among severe judicatures." Sometimes the conduct of business at the meeting was "prevented by a drowziness which possesseth His Majestie from the fumes of Backus," says Roe. Usually, after the official work was done, Jahangir would turn the meeting into a soiree, and occasionally, drowsy with opium and alcohol, he would stretch himself and go to asleep during the party. Attenders would then snuff out the candles, and the nobles quietly shuffle out. "After he hath slept two houres, they awake him and bring his supper to him," says Hawkins, "at which time he is not able to feed himself, but it is thrust into his mouth by others; and this is about one of the clocke, and then he sleepeth the rest of the night."

Despite his own weakness, Jahangir was particular not to admit into the Ghusl-khana any amir who smelt of alcohol, for it offended his sense of decorum. Hawkins, who had a weakness for drink, was once ordered out of the chamber for violating the regulation about alcohol and was never again allowed to take his usual place near the emperor "within the red rayles". Says Roe, "Though drunkennesse be a common and glorious vice . . . yet it is so strictly forbidden that no man can enter the Gusel-Chan, where the king sits, but porters smell the breath: and if hee have but tasted wine, is not suffered to come in." Jahangir, says Terry, was "often overcome with wine, but severely punishing that fault in others."

The prohibition applied to nobles only while attending the court on work. They could drink on the emperor's invitation. "On Thursday, the

25th, a wine-fest was held on the banks of Mahi, and some of my intimate servants who had admittance to such assemblies had their hearts delighted by brimming cups and ample favours," writes Jahangir about a party he held for nobles. And of a party to celebrate Aurangzeb's birthday, he says: "The day was passed in enjoyment . . . My private servants who have the entree into this kind of parties and assemblies were delighted with brimming cups." Jahangir seemed to consider wine drinking as a royal prerogative, even a royal duty. "My boy, you are the father of children, and kings and princes drink wine," he once told his son Khurram (Shah Jahan), but he went on to advise moderation: "To drink to excess and weaken the intellect is avoided by the wise."

Like Akbar, Jahangir too was fond of fruits, especially mangoes, and had fruits served as relish with his drinks. "Of all the fruits, I am very fond of mangoes," he says. "Notwithstanding the sweetness of the Kabul fruits, not one of them has, to my taste, the flavour of the mango." He even exempted the cultivation of fruits from tax, to encourage horticulture. "Thanks to Almighty God, no revenue on fruit trees has been taken during my reign; and I gave order that if any one were to plant a garden in cultivated land, he was not to pay any revenue," he states. In Kashmir he loved to pick cherries. "Everyday I plucked with my own hand sufficient to give a flavour to my cups. Although they sent them by runners from Kabul as well, yet to pick them oneself from one's home garden gives additional sweetness," he writes.

Jahangir was fastidious about food. He often cut open animals to find out what they had eaten, to make sure that their flesh would not be disagreeable to him. "As . . . the flesh of animals I have killed with my own hand is very much to my taste, in consequence of the suspicions and caution that I have in such matters, I order them to be cleaned in my presence, and myself inspect their stomachs to see what they have eaten and what the food of the animals is," writes Jahangir. "If by chance I see anything to which I have a dislike, I forbear from eating the flesh." When once he saw ducks eating "horrible worms" he gave up eating the bird.

In Gujarat, Jahangir developed a liking for the humble kichery of bajra (a mixture of split peas and millet boiled together) which then became his favourite dish. "It suited me well," he says. In milk, he favoured the camel—"It suited me admirably, and was to my taste." He was fond of fish too, but abhorred scaleless fish. "I eat no fish but those that have scales, but not because the professors of the Shiah faith look on those without scales as unlawful, but the cause of my aversion is that I have heard from old men, and it has become known to me by

249

experience as well, that fish without scales eat the flesh of dead animals and fish with scales do not eat it." His favourite fish was rohu, and he craved for it so much that once when a man in Gujarat presented him with a rohu, which he had not eaten for eleven months, he rewarded him with a horse.

FOR ALL HIS hedonism, there was also a serious side to Jahangir. His interest in art and nature studies, for instance, had a keenness and dedication that went far beyond idle dilettantism. Like his great-grandfather, he was alive to nature, and his memoirs are rich with graphic descriptions of the places he visited, their peculiarities, their flora and fauna, and their history. Sometimes he took care even to record the things not found in a particular region; there is, for example, a two-page list in his memoirs of the birds not seen in Kashmir.

Jahangir's zoological studies were as scientific as they could have been in his time, and he might be regarded as the first (and only) scientist emperor of India. At one time, for some five years, he carried around with him a pair of Saras cranes, wryly named Laila and Majnun—the Romeo and Juliet of the Islamic world—for him to observe, study and record their behaviour. His notes on the cranes, such as on their mating habits, would do any naturalist proud. "The female having straightened its legs went down a little: the male then lifted up one of its feet from the ground and placed it on her back, and afterwards the second foot, and immediately seating himself on her back, paired with her," records Jahangir. "He then came down and stretched out his neck, put his beak on the ground, and walked once around the female."

In due course the crane laid eggs. "On Monday . . . the Saras . . . gathered together some straw and rubbish in the little garden, and laid first of all one egg. On the third day (afterwards) it laid a second egg," notes Jahangir. "The female used to sit on the eggs the night alone, and the male stood near her on guard. It was so alert that it was impossible for any living thing to pass near her. Once a large weasel made its appearance, and he ran at it with the greatest impetuosity, and did not stop until the weasel got into a hole. When the sun illuminated the world with his rays, the male went to the female and pecked her back with his beak. The female then rose, and the male sat in her place . . ." When the eggs hatched, Jahangir continued his observation and noted their ways of feeding the young.

There are several such accounts in his memoirs. Even in examining phenomena that were merely curious, his approach was methodical. Thus when it was reported to him that a tiger and a goat lived together peaceably in a cage and "used even to couple and consort together", he decided to conduct an experiment in animal psychology. First he removed the goat from the cage, which made the tiger "disconsolate and uneasy". Then another goat of the same colour and size was put in the cage, but the tiger smelt it and broke its neck. A sheep was then put into the cage, but the tiger killed and ate it. "They then brought the old goat back again, when it was received with undiminished regard. The tiger lay on his back, and took the goat upon its breast, and licked its face," notes Mutamid Khan, Jahangir's surrogate diarist.

Jahangir took a child-like delight in these experiments, as when he cross-bred goats by pairing Markhur goats with Barbary goats, and a litter was born. "Of their liveliness and laughable ways and their manner of gamboling and leaping, what can be written? Some of their ways are such that the mind derived uncontrolled pleasure from looking at them. As it pleased me, I ordered them always to be kept near me, and I gave each of them an appropriate name," writes Jahangir, but spoils the effect of this charming scene by adding, "Perhaps their flesh would be very pleasant to taste." He dissected birds, reptiles and animals to study their physiology. Sometimes his investigations led to curious conclusions: seeking an explanation for the lion's courage, Jahangir inferred that the secret was in its gall bladder being enclosed in its liver.

He loved to verify tall claims. Thus when he was told in Kashmir about an "unfathomably deep" lake, he "ordered a stone to be tied to the end of a rope and thrown into it, and thus it was found that its depth did not exceed the height of a man and a half." Another time he experimented with bitumen from a mine in Persia to check its reputed effectiveness in mending broken bones—he found the claim untenable. Similarly, when it was claimed that "laughter arises from eating saffron, and that if it is taken in large quantities, there is fear of death supervening", he had a condemned criminal brought to him, and made him eat a *seer* (about half a kilogram) of saffron in his presence. As it produced no change, the next day double the quantity of saffron was given, "but it did not cause him even to smile, much less laugh!" says Mutamid Khan. And once when a yogi who had "a wonderful persistence" was brought to him, Jahangir had the yogi plied with vast quantities of arrack. "But not the least change took place," Jahangir notes. "At last his senses left him, and they carried him out like a corpse."

JAHANGIR PRIDED HIMSELF on being a poet. "As I have a poetical disposition," he says matter-of-factly, "I sometimes intentionally, sometimes involuntarily, compose couplets and quatrains." Sample:

> Turn not thy cheek, without thee
> I cannot live a moment
> For thee to break one heart
>   is equal to a hundred murders.

This is noteworthy only because of the stature of its author, but Jahangir had several distinguished literary men in his court—even his chief goldsmith was a poet—and among them was Talib Amuli, titled King of Poets, who wrote these classic lines of a typically Jahangiri sentiment:

> Two lips have I;
>   one for drinking,
> And one to apologize.

Writing poetry was an idle conceit in Jahangir, but his competence in art was genuine and substantial. A talented calligrapher himself, Jahangir was a great authority on art, and under him Mughal painting reached its acme. "My liking for painting and my practice in judging it have arrived at such a point that when any work is brought before me, either of deceased artists or of those of the present day, without the names being told to me, I say on the spur of the moment that it is the work of such and such a man," writes Jahangir. "And if there be a picture containing many portraits, and each face be the work of a different master, I can discover which face is the work of each of them. If any other person has put in the eye and eyebrow of a face, I can perceive whose work the original face is, and who has painted the eye and eyebrows."

Jahangir's taste in art was eclectic. He was particularly fond of European paintings, and endlessly pestered Europeans at his court—the Jesuits, the Dutch and English traders and diplomats—for paintings. The emperor, says van Ravesteyn, a Dutch trader in India, was "an amateur of all rarities and antiquities". Jahangir's was a collector's passion, not greed; he prized objects of value, not of high cost. "He affects not the value of anything but rarity in everything, insomuch that some pretty newfangled toys would give him high content, though their value were small, for he wants no worldly wealth or riches, possessing an inestimable treasury," noted the English in Surat in 1609. Among the presents given to him by Roe, what Jahangir prized most were paintings, and he had them copied and used as murals in palaces and tombs. And when Roe showed him a miniature painting of his fiancee, Jahangir had five copies of it made for presenting to his principal wives.

The Jesuits gave Jahangir religious paintings, and they too were copied as decorative murals. Notes Fernao Guerreiro: "On a wall of one of the halls he had painted figures of the Pope, the Emperor, King Philip, the Duke of Savoy, whose portraits he possessed, all on their knees adoring the holy cross." There was even a mural of the Virgin Mary on the wall of the throne balcony, says Guerreiro, which pleased the Jesuits, for they could tell their beads even as they bowed to the infidel emperor.

Court painters always accompanied Jahangir on his tours, and worked at the interface of his interest in art and nature studies—they painted precise pictures of birds and animals, apart from vivid portraits of people. Jahangir also commissioned a number of political paintings of an allegorical nature, like the one of himself with the Shah of Persia. When Inayat Khan, one of Jahangir's "intimate attendants" (who was addicted to alcohol and opium and had been reduced to skin and bones) was brought to the palace in a couch to take leave of the emperor, Jahangir, though touched by his appalling condition, was detached enough to order a drawing to be made of the dying man, because, as he put it, "though painters have strived much in drawing an emaciated face, yet I have never seen anything like this, nor even approaching to it." The portrait is a Mughal classic.

Little is known about Jahangir's interest in architecture, but he, unlike Akbar, seems to have disliked Hindu architecture. On visiting the Ranthambhor fort, he found the rooms there airless and cramped. "Built after the fashion of the Hindus . . . they did not please me, nor was I disposed to stay there," he writes. Elsewhere he writes, "The buildings Hindus construct after their fashion, however much they decorate them, are not pleasant."

Jahangir undertook no major building projects of his own, though he does mention in his memoirs that he once sent an architect to Lahore "to build a handsome palace for me". He did intervene in the construction of Akbar's mausoleum at Sikandra, but apparently only to restore Akbar's original design. In the first couple of years of his reign, Jahangir, because of his preoccupation with his son Khusrav's rebellion, could not pay much attention to the erection of the tomb, and when he visited the site in the third year he found, he says, that the builders "had altered the original design at their discretion." He therefore ordered "the objectionable parts" to be pulled down, and "by degrees a very large and magnificent building was raised, with a nice garden round it, entered by a lofty gate, consisting of minarets made of white stone."

Jahangir had Babur's passion for gardening, and wherever he camped for any length of time, he tried to enhance the charm of the place by laying out pleasances, and he has to his credit the best known of the Mughal gardens, the Shalimar Bagh in Kashmir, on the Dal Lake, against the backdrop of the great mountains, a perfect memorial for an incurable romantic.

Sons and Rebels

JAHANGIR HAD ON the whole an easy time of being the emperor. He "enjoyed a very peaceable reign . . . [and was] equally beloved by his subjects and his neighbours," says Jean-Baptiste Tavernier, a French jewel-merchant in India in the mid-seventeenth century. Confirms Mughal chronicler Muhammad Amin: "At the present time . . . the people of this country, whether rich or poor, high or low, are in the enjoyment of all the blessings of comfort and content, and slumbering secure from all danger." Facts generally corroborate these views. But the tranquillity that the Mughal empire enjoyed at this time was more a bequest of Akbar than an achievement of Jahangir. Akbar had so decisively established his authority, that his reputation of invincibility, like a force-field, continued to protect the Mughal emperors long after his death. Jahangir could rest on Akbar's laurels.

As we move from Akbar to Jahangir, the tempo of history changes from hyperactivity to languor. There was no noteworthy expansion of the empire under Jahangir, only a few minor conquests, though he had to his credit the final subjugation of defiant Mewar, the last pocket of Rajput resistance. His reign was also relatively free of major rebellions, except for one at the very beginning, and two towards the end. On the debit side, he lost Kandahar to Persia.

On his accession, Jahangir pardoned, as he had promised he would, the usurpation manoeuvres of his eldest son Khusrav, and restored him to favour, though, as a precaution, a careful watch was kept on him. Khusrav was then barely eighteen, and the sensible course of action for him would have been to win back Jahangir's trust and bide his time, for he had, as the eldest son, a fair chance of succeeding his father in the normal course.

But this was not Khusrav's destiny. He was a popular prince, handsome and charming—"He was a gentleman of a very lovely presence and fine carriage, so exceedingly beloved of the common people . . . the very love and delight of them," says Terry—but he had no strength of character, having inherited from his Rajput mother a tendency towards neurosis. "I invariably found Khusrav preoccupied and distracted," notes Jahangir. Khusrav had fantasized about being the emperor, and could not reconcile himself to waiting out his father's lifetime to ascend the throne. Furthermore, he had no respect for Jahangir and often slandered him openly. He fancied himself better suited to rule.

As Khusrav sulked in bitterness and frustration, he was egged on into rebellion by the usual band of sycophants and strife-mongers who buzzed around every prince. Khusrav, says Jahangir, came under the influence of "evil companions, [and] got some absurd notions into his head," because of "the petulance and pride which accompany youth" and from his "want of experience and prudence".

On 6th April 1606, just five months after Jahangir's accession, Khusrav broke out in rebellion. That evening, on the pretext of visiting Akbar's tomb, he secretly set out from Agra with a small cavalry contingent. The flight was discovered by a lamp-lighter who found Khusrav's mansion empty and reported the matter to officials. Jahangir, who had by then retired into the harem, was called out and informed. He ordered immediate pursuit. Simultaneously, messengers were rushed to Rajasthan to recall, for the defence of Agra, the army that had been sent against Mewar shortly before—Jahangir feared that there might be others behind his son's revolt and did not want to take any chances. The next morning Jahangir himself set out in hot pursuit of Khusrav, on the way sending back orders to Agra to imprison the sons of Muhammad Hakim, reasoning that "if my son could act in the way he had done, what might I expect from my uncle's sons?"

Khusrav, Jahangir feared, might flee to the Uzbegs or the Persians "and thus dishonour would fall upon my throne". Such was his perturbation that he even forgot to take "the allowance of opium" that morning, says Jahangir. "My distress arose from the thought that my son, without any cause or reason, had become my enemy." His bitterness hardened his heart. When the amir assigned to pursue Khusrav asked Jahangir how the prince should be dealt with, he was directed to treat him as an ordinary rebel. "Sovereignty does not regard the relation of father and son, and it is said, a king should deem no one his relation," said Jahangir.

Initially it was thought that Khusrav would head for Bengal, where his maternal uncle and former champion, Man Singh, was the governor. But it was westward that he fled, storming past Delhi towards Lahore. As Khusrav proceeded, his forces swelled, as turbulent elements in the countryside joined him, lured by the prospect of plunder. But the increase in numbers added nothing to Khusrav's strength; in fact it weakened him, for the rabble loosened military discipline and antagonized the populace. "Everyone whom they met on the road they plundered, and took from him horse and goods," writes Jahangir. "Merchants and travellers were pillaged, and wherever these insurgents went, there was no security for the women and children."

On his way through Punjab, Khusrav sought the help of Guru Arjun Singh, the patriarch of the Sikhs. The guru at first refused to help him, saying that whatever money he had was for the poor, not for princes, but when Khusrav pleaded that he was destitute, the guru gave him 5000 rupees. It was an act of charity—the guru was not supporting the prince's rebellion.

Arriving at Lahore, Khusrav proceeded to besiege the city with a rabble of some 12000 men, but when the imperial forces arrived in Punjab, he abandoned the siege and turned to confront them. Jahangir— then encamped at Sultanpur, about eighty kilometres south-east of Lahore—was just sitting down to a meal when the news was brought to him that the battle was joined. "Directly I heard it, although I had a very good appetite, I merely swallowed a mouthful for good luck, and then mounted," writes Jahangir. He called for his padded great coat, but did not wait for it, nor did he wait for his escort to form, but hastened to join the battle, armed only with a sword and a spear, and accompanied by some fifty cavalrymen. But before he reached the battleground, Khusrav had turned and fled.

A dragnet was immediately spread for the prince. "I was determined that . . . I would not return till I had got him into my hands," writes Jahangir. Khusrav and his comrades attempted to escape by fleeing across the Ravi at night, but the ferry-men refused to carry them, and when they tried to row themselves across the river, their boat drifted and ran aground. In the morning the hapless, marooned rebels surrendered, and they were taken in chains to Jahangir, who had by then arrived in Lahore. The rebellion had lasted just over three weeks.

Jahangir was overwhelmed by the news of Khusrav's capture and had to retire to his private tent to compose himself. He then convened a durbar to receive the formal surrender of the rebel. "Khusrav was brought into my presence . . . with his hands bound and a chain on his leg, and he was led up from the left side, according to the rule of Chingiz Khan." The prince was flanked by two amirs, his principal supporters, and he stood between them "trembling and weeping", writes Jahangir coldly.

When Khusrav tried to prostrate before Jahangir, he was curtly told to stand back. There would be no mercy for the rebels. The prince was forthwith ordered to be confined in prison, his legs chained. The two rebel amirs were stripped naked and sewn up tightly in the fresh skins of an ass and a cow, and paraded through the streets of Lahore seated on asses, with their faces towards the tail; one of them perished in the ordeal, as the animal skin dried in the sun and squeezed him to death, but the other somehow survived. Some 300 other partisans of Khusrav were impaled alive—the "most excruciating punishment", exults Jahangir—on a double row of stakes, and Khusrav was led between them on an elephant to review that grim guard of honour. The prince was so overcome with grief by the cruel turn of events that he "neither ate nor drank for the space of three days and three nights, which he consumed in tears and groans, hunger and thirst," says Jahangir.

It was not however the end of the Khusrav affair. From Lahore, Jahangir proceeded to Kabul, to parry an anticipated Persian move against Kandahar. In Kabul, Khusrav raised his hand against his father again, luring his jailer into an assassination plot. And once again Jahangir moved swiftly and ruthlessly to quell the revolt. The principal conspirators were summarily executed. He even considered executing Khusrav, but held his hand. "Although Khusrav had been repeatedly guilty of improper action, and was deserving a thousand punishments," writes Jahangir, "yet paternal affection did not allow me to take his life. To bear with such wicked proceedings was incompatible with the rules of government and policy, yet I overlooked his offences, and he was kept in great comfort and ease." Khusrav was however blinded, to incapacitate him from causing further trouble, though later, on the entreaty of his sisters, physicians were allowed to treat the prince, and his vision was partly restored. For a while he was even allowed to attend the court. "But he showed no signs of frankness of spirit," says Jahangir, "and always seemed sad and downcast, so I forbade his coming to see me."

Khusrav remained in confinement for about fourteen years. He was then released, and there was said to have been an effort to rehabilitate him by marrying him to Ladli Begum, daughter of Nur Jahan (Jahangir's all-powerful queen) by her first marriage. But the prince, bent on self-destruction, refused. In the end, he was put in the custody of Khurram (Shah Jahan), and he died in Burhanpur in 1622 under mysterious circumstances. Khurram reported that he had died of colic, but rumour had it that he was murdered on Khurram's order—which is not improbable, considering Khurram's later liquidation of his rivals to the throne. Another casualty of the Khusrav rebellion was Guru Arjun Singh—he was executed for aiding the prince. "Having confiscated his property, I commanded that he should be put to death," writes Jahangir.

KHUSRAV'S REVOLT FORCED Jahangir to shelve the grand plan of conquest he had conceived on his accession—to subdue Mewar, then to establish his suzerainty over the Deccan, and finally to conquer Tansoxiana—for, as he put it,

Though a king should seize the seven climes,
He still would labour to take others.

The Mughal empire was strong and secure enough for Jahangir to contemplate such grand imperial projects, but it is doubtful whether, even without the impediment of Khusrav's rebellion, he had the physical and mental stamina required for the endeavour. As it was, he had to content himself with a few minor conquests. Eastward the Mughal empire now expanded into Cooch Behar; further east, Kamrup was conquered, and even Assam penetrated. The hill fortress of Kangra in north-eastern Punjab, which had till then defied the Mughals, was reduced. There were also some minor gains in Orissa and Kachchh (Kutch).

The proudest achievement of Jahangir was the subjugation of the Rana of Mewar. Jahangir had a guilty conscience about Mewar, for the task of subduing the Rana had been twice entrusted to him by Akbar, and on both occasions he had shirked the responsibility. The issue between the emperor and the Rana was largely one of face, not of territory or power. The Mughals had already seized the plains of Mewar, and had driven the Rana deep into the mountains, so there was nothing more for them to take from him, except his pride. Yet the Rana, despite all his hardships and his near total isolation, would not submit.

Immediately after his accession Jahangir had sent an army into Mewar under his son Parviz, but the campaign had to be abandoned because of Khusrav's rebellion. The moment Jahangir was free of the enemy within, he turned to Mewar again, sending Mahabat Khan, Abdullah Khan and Prince Khurram in succession against Rana Amar Singh. The long war of attrition had already exhausted the Rana's scant resources, and now relentless military pressure broke his will to fight. In 1615, he at last submitted, ending the conflict that had begun forty-eight years earlier when Akbar first invaded Mewar. Even heroism had a price, and the Rana had paid for it far more than he could afford.

When Amar Singh sued for peace, Jahangir instructed Khurram to treat him chivalrously, for he was, says Jahangir, "always desirous, as far as possible, not to destroy the old families". The prince received the Rana with courtesy and honour when he arrived at the Mughal camp to surrender. "When the Rana clasped his (Khurram's) feet and asked forgiveness for his faults, he took his head and placed it on his breast, and consoled him in such a manner as to comfort him," notes Jahangir. The Rana and the prince then exchanged gifts.

The terms of the settlement were a clever formula that safeguarded the self-esteem of both the Rana and the emperor—the Rana submitted in person, and this saved the Mughal face; but the Rana was excused (because of his old age) from attending the emperor's court in person, which saved the Rana's face. Mewar, including Chitor, was restored to the Rana as his *watan* jagir, which was great gain for the Rana, but the Mughals secured their interests by laying down the condition that Chitor's fortifications should never be repaired.

After Amar Singh's formal surrender, Khurram and Karan Singh, the crown prince of Mewar, set out for Ajmer, where the emperor was then encamped. Jahangir appointed Karan Singh as a commander of 5000, a high rank. "As it was necessary to win the heart of Karan, who was of a wild nature and had never seen assemblies and lived among the hills, I every day showed him some fresh favour," says Jahangir. When he returned to Agra, Jahangir commemorated his victory over Mewar by installing full-size marble statues of Amar Singh and Karan Singh in the garden below the jharokha balcony of his citadel.

MEANTIME, EVEN WHILE the Mewar offensive was going on, Jahangir had resumed Akbar's interrupted Deccan campaign. Here Jahangir's chief adversary was Malik Ambar, an Abyssinian slave who had risen to a high position in the service of the sultans of Ahmadnagar. When Akbar annexed the capital city and a good part of the kingdom of Ahmadnagar, Malik Ambar retreated to Khirki, where he raised a scion of the royal family to the throne, and briskly set about to recover the lost territories, using the Marathas in guerrilla war with deadly effect. He also expertly revamped the state's revenue administration, to provide a strong economic base for its military operations. In diplomacy, his endless and complex manoeuvres bewildered even his most astute adversaries.

In 1608 Jahangir sent Abdur-Rahim, the Khan-i-khanan, to the Deccan to restore Mughal authority. Though Abdur-Rahim had grandly promised quick success, nothing came of his campaign, as his commanders could not act in concert. Soon Ahmadnagar city itself was lost. Jahangir then recalled Abdur-Rahim in disgrace, but the other generals he sent (with prince Parviz in overall command) could act with no greater unity, and were no more successful. In 1616 the southern command was therefore given to Khurram, who had just then triumphantly completed the Mewar campaign. Jahangir sanctioned

Khurram ten million rupees for campaign expenses, and when Khurram moved to Burhanpur, the Mughal command post in the Deccan, Jahangir himself moved to Mandu from Ajmer, to be close to the theatre of operations.

Khurram, combining military pressure with diplomacy, quickly brought the Deccan campaign to a successful conclusion, persuading Malik Amber and his ally, the Sultan of Bijapur, to restore the Mughal territories they had seized, including the city of Ahmadnagar, and to pay tribute.

Pleased, Jahangir conferred great honours on Khurram when he returned to the court. "After he had paid me his respects, I called him to the balcony where I was sitting," writes Jahangir, "and with the impulse of excessive paternal affection and love, I immediately rose up and took him in my arms. The more he expressed his reverence and respect for me, the more my tenderness increased towards him. I ordered him to sit by me." Jahangir poured trays of gems and gold coins over the prince's head, bestowed on him the title Shah Jahan (Lord of the World), and accorded him the unique privilege of being allowed to sit in the Diwan-i-am in the presence of the emperor, in a chair that was specially placed near the throne. Further, he was raised to the unprecedented rank of the commander of 30,000, and appointed as the governor of the rich province of Gujarat.

But there was not really all that much for Jahangir to celebrate. Not an inch of additional territory had been taken, only the status quo ante restored. Even that proved to be a fleeting gain. When Jahangir returned to the north, Malik Amber quickly advanced to besiege Ahmadnagar, and then, moving northward, threatened Burhanpur, even Mandu. So in 1620 Jahangir, who was then in Lahore, once again dispatched Shah Jahan to the Deccan, again with ten million rupees for campaign expenses.

This time Shah Jahan laid down terms for accepting the command. With Jahangir's health uncertain, succession manoeuvres had already begun at the court, and Shah Jahan was uneasy. He did not want to leave for the distant Deccan, separated from the court by over 1500 kilometres, without some insurance to protect his interests. He therefore demanded, and received, the custody of Khusrav before he set out from Lahore.

In the Deccan, Shah Jahan set about his task with his usual resolute enterprise. He quickly relieved Mandu, Burhanpur and Ahmadnagar, and forced Malik Amber to sue for peace. Under the peace terms, Ahmadnagar agreed to surrender all the territories it had seized from the Mughals and also cede a forty-five-kilometre-wide strip along the

Mughal frontier. In addition, Ahmadnagar, Bijapur and Golconda agreed to pay a tribute of five million rupees to the Mughals.

Before the monsoon set in in 1621, Shah Jahan was back in Burhanpur, celebrating victory. Jahangir was delighted. Malik Amber however remained a force to reckon with till he died in 1626, aged 80 lunar years, earning a rich tribute even from Mutamid Khan, the diarist of Jahangir: "This Ambar was a slave, but an able man. In warfare, in command, in sound judgment, and in administration he had no rival or equal. He well understood the predatory (*kazzaki*) warfare, which in the language of the Dakhin is called *bargi-giri*. He kept down the turbulent spirits of that country, and maintained his exalted position to the end of his life, and closed his career in honour. History records no other instance of an Abyssinian slave arriving at such eminence."

The capitulation of the Deccan sultanates in 1621 marked the zenith of Jahangir's career. Till then his reign had on the whole gone well, with even the triumphs that had eluded Akbar turning easy for him. But soon there would be one humiliation after another for him, loss of territory, rebellions, and finally the indignity of being made a prisoner by one of his own generals.

Another Son, Another Rebel

EVEN WHILE JAHANGIR was basking in the sunshine of his Deccan victories, storm-clouds were gathering in the north-west, over Kandahar. The town had changed hands four times between the Persians and the Mughals since Humayun first handed it over to the Persians in 1545. But the Mughal-Persian tussle over Kandahar had been all along a civilized affair, a sort of military minuet, and neither the Shah nor the emperor had allowed it to vitiate their otherwise cordial relationship.

Kandahar was not worth a war. At one time it had been of some economic importance, as it straddled the major overland trade route between India and the Middle East, but its importance was rapidly declining, with the seas becoming the favoured trade highways. Even the pilgrim traffic from India to Arabia had shifted to the sea route. Nor was Kandahar of any great strategic value to the Mughals, as there had never been a major invasion of India through the town. In fact, neither the Persians nor the Mughals were particularly energetic in defending (or attacking) the town, indicating its low priority in their scheme of things. The Shah spoke of Kandahar as a "petty country", and Jahangir called it "a petty village".

Yet Kandahar, though unimportant in itself, held in it the seeds of a major confrontation between the Persians and the Mughals. Persians certainly had a greater claim to it, by the terms of Humayun's agreement with the Shah, and they could not allow themselves to be cheated out of what was rightfully theirs. On the other hand, it was not in the nature of the Mughal to give away what he had seized. The Shah had made a tentative move against Kandahar early in Jahangir's reign, but did not press the siege, and explained it away as the unauthorized action of a provincial officer. He requested Jahangir to overlook the incident.

Despite the Shah's profession of innocence, Jahangir was wary of Persian intentions. This was why early in his reign, after quelling Khusrav's rebellion, he had gone on to Kabul, to watch over Kandahar. Now, at the close of his reign, he again had reason to suspect a Persian attack. He therefore placed Kandahar under a capable general and gave him adequate funds to provision the town. But inexplicably he did not increase the strength of its garrison, which had at this time dwindled to just a few hundred soldiers. Meanwhile, towards the end of 1620, yet another Persian ambassador, Zambil Beg, arrived at the Mughal court, and for the first time made an open claim to Kandahar. Then, without waiting for Jahangir's response, the Shah struck, and the city fell to the Persians without much of a fight.

Shah Abbas tried to soften the blow of the assault by sending a fresh conciliatory embassy to Jahangir, to explain his action and to proffer continued friendship. Addressing Jahangir as a "brother dear as life", the Shah wrote: "As Kandahar was held by the agents of your lofty family, I regarded you as myself and did not make any objection. From feelings of unity and brotherhood we waited, thinking that you would, after the manner of your ancestors who are in Paradise, voluntarily take the matter into your consideration. When you neglected to do this, I repeatedly, by writing and verbal messages, directly and indirectly, asked for the disposal of the question, thinking that perhaps that petty country was not regarded worthy of your notice."

The Shah then described the circumstances in which he seized Kandahar—he had, he said, gone hunting near the city, hoping that he would be received as an honoured guest by the Mughal commander there, but facing obstinacy, invested and took the fort. The incident, he hoped, would not disturb the friendly relationship between the two empires. "May the ever-vernal flower of union and cordiality remain in bloom, and every effort be made to strengthen the foundation of concord, and to cleanse the fountains of disagreement," wrote Abbas. "You will regard all our dominions as belonging to you, and will . . . proclaim that it (Kandahar) has been given up to him (Abbas) without any objection, and that such trifles are of no importance."

In his reply, Jahangir presumed to treat the Shah's letter as a "loving letter apologizing" for his action over Kandahar, but nevertheless went on to call the Shah a liar and a cheat, though by circumlocution. "Let it not be hidden from the world-adorning mind of my exalted and prosperous brother that until the arrival of the letter and messages brought by Zambil Beg no mention had been made by you in letters or verbal messages of your wish for Kandahar," said Jahangir in his sweetly venomous letter. "In the jewelled and pearl-dropping letter (sent through Zambil Beg) there was no mention of a wish for Kandahar. It was mentioned verbally by Zambil Beg. In reply, I said to him that I made no difficulty with regard to anything that my brother wished . . . "

So, wrote Jahangir, he was "entirely astonished" that the Shah took Kandahar by force. "What could there be in a petty village that he should set out to take it, and that he should shut his eyes to so much friendship and brotherly feeling? . . . Up to now the relationship of brotherhood stands firm . . . But it would have been right and brotherly that he should have waited till the arrival of the ambassador. Perhaps he would be successful in the object and claim for which he had come . . . May God preserve you at all times!"

Jahangir was furious. Kandahar did not matter. But his prestige did. He was honour bound to strike back. Further, there was a fear that a major Persian invasion of India through Sind might be in the offing. Jahangir therefore began to make extensive military preparations, not only to retake Kandahar, but to invade Khurasan and maybe even push on to the Persian capital itself, in alliance with the Uzbeg ruler of Samarkand, Imam Quli. Preparations were also set afoot to meet the supply and transport requirements of a vast army marching through sparsely populated, inhospitable regions. Shah Jahan, the victor of Mewar and the Deccan, was summoned to command the army.

ON RECEIVING JAHANGIR'S order, Shah Jahan obediently set out from Burhanpur. But as he proceeded he seemed to have second thoughts. At Mandu he halted. Something about the proposed campaign bothered him, and he tarried there, saying that he would advance further only after the rains. Also, he laid down several conditions for assuming the command of the Kandahar campaign—he wanted sole command of the army, the governorship of Punjab, and the great fort of Ranthambhor to be given to him for the safe residence of his family. Shah Jahan was clearly worried about what would happen if Jahangir—whose health was rapidly failing—died while he was away from India.

Jahangir was dismayed by Shah Jahan's apathy in the face of the Persian slur on the prestige of the Mughal dynasty. To him, it seemed like betrayal. Characteristically, his attitude towards Shah Jahan now swung from extreme favour to extreme disfavour. "His report was read," writes Jahangir. "I did not like the style of its purport nor the request he made, and, on the contrary, the traces of disloyalty were apparent . . . Fire had fallen into his mind, and (he had) let fall from his hand the reins of self-control."

Around this time, intelligence reports were received at the court that Shah Jahan had seized some jagirs of Shahryar (Jahangir's youngest son) and Nur Jahan, and that there was a clash between the officers of Shah Jahan and Shahryar over the disputed possession of Daulpur. Shah Jahan seemed to be heading towards open rebellion. Incensed, Jahangir ordered that Shah Jahan, whom he had regarded till then as his favourite son—"whom I considered in all things the first of all my sons"—should henceforth be called Bi-daulat, The Wretch. "I can safely assert that the kindness . . . which I have bestowed upon him no King has ever yet bestowed upon a son . . . I exalted his titles, made him lord of a standard and drum . . . The pen cannot describe all that I have done for him," he writes. And he cursed: "When, with a father like me, who . . . [has] raised him to the great dignity . . . and denied him nothing, he acts in this manner, I appeal to the justice of Allah that He may never again regard him with favour."

Jahangir grieved that "in pain and weakness in a warm climate that is extremely unsuited to my health, I must still ride and be active, and in this state must proceed against such an undutiful son." It distressed him that a number of his officers had joined Shah Jahan in rebellion. "Many servants cherished by me for long years and raised to the dignity of nobility, whom I ought to employ today in war against the Uzbeg and the Persian, I must punish for their vileness, and destroy them with my own hand," he writes. Jahangir was especially bitter that Abdur-Rahim, the Khan-i-khanan (who was his own guardian once, and had in fact joined him in his revolt against Akbar) should side with Shah Jahan. "In the seventieth year of his age [he] had blackened his face with ingratitude," writes Jahangir about Abdur-Rahim. "But he was by nature a rebel and a traitor. His father, at the close of his days, had acted in the same shameful way towards my revered father . . .

In the end a wolf's cub becomes wolf
Even though reared by man."

Events moved swiftly now. Jahangir ordered that if Shah Jahan was not willing to head the Kandahar campaign, he should immediately send to Lahore the officers and the army that were with him in the Deccan. He then appointed Shahryar as commander of the Kandahar forces, and transferred to him Shah Jahan's jagirs in the Ganga-Yamuna doab, even Hissar Firoza, the heir apparent's jagir.

Dismayed by the severity of the emperor's response to his tentative revolt, Shah Jahan apologized and sent his Diwan to the court to entreat with Jahangir. "But I took no notice of him, and showed him no favour," writes Jahangir. His heart had hardened against his favourite son.

WHY WAS JAHANGIR so implacable? Because of the influence of Nur Jahan, his domineering wife? He was very much under her sway at this time, and it is unlikely that he would have taken any major decision without consulting her. Yet it seems probable that even without her advice Jahangir would have acted in the manner he did, for his response was very much in character, and similar to his reaction to Khusrav's rebellion seventeen years earlier. A son who had rebelled was no longer a son but a foe, and had to be dealt with as such. That was Jahangir's view. Jahangir did not have Akbar's strength of character or broadness of mind to accommodate and manage human frailties.

The real mystery of the crisis is not why Jahangir was so harsh, but why Shah Jahan rebelled at all. He had everything going for him. His power and prestige and wealth were such as not enjoyed by any Mughal prince before him, and he had been designated as the heir-apparent. By rebelling, he was staking all that for what was virtually already his. It did not make sense.

Shah Jahan was at this time thirty years old, about the same age at which Jahangir broke out in rebellion against Akbar, so was he getting impatient to ascend the throne? This seems doubtful. Unlike Akbar, who was in vigorous health when Jahangir rebelled, Jahangir was in frail health, and in the natural course of events Shah Jahan would not have had to wait for very many more years to succeed him. It could not therefore have been impatience that drove him into rebellion. Shah Jahan in fact rebelled just when his succession seemed imminent. Did he then fear that he might not be the one to succeed? It seems likely that around the time he rebelled something new had come between him and the throne, so that he was no longer certain of succession, which made rebellion worth the risk.

Who, or what, stood between Shah Jahan and the throne? Nur Jahan? Likely. Nur Jahan and Shah Jahan had been allies for many years, and he was as much her favourite as Jahangir's. Yet Shah Jahan had good reason to resent her. He was the heir-apparent, but she, not he, was the second most powerful person in the empire. She was in fact the de facto emperor. Would she not try to retain that role even after Jahangir's death? If Shah Jahan succeeded Jahangir, she risked losing her privileged position. She needed a week successor. So, as Jahangir's health failed, the interests of Nur Jahan and Shah Jahan diverged. They both wanted power, but only one could have it. Did she then drive Shah Jahan into a corner to ruin him?

It is impossible to know what really happened. The Mughal court was a snake-pit in which countless rumours for ever hissed around, distorting facts, warping judgment. In such an environment it was easy for any small irritant to become a major issue. Further, astrologers invariably played a major role in any developing crisis in medieval

India, and we do not know what part they had in Shah Jahan's rebellion. Nor do we know the exact role of Shah Jahan's advisors. According to Jahangir, Shah Jahan's chief advisor at this time—"his guide to the desert of error"—was a brahmin officer named Sunder Rai, who bore the title Raja Bikramajit and administered Gujarat for Shah Jahan. "When the futile ideas entered his (Shah Jahan's) ungrateful mind, he sent for that dog of a Hindu, who was always shaking the chain of enmity and perversity," says Jahangir.

There were probably also harem factors involved—if Jahangir was under the influence of Nur Jahan, Shah Jahan was similarly under the influence of his wife, Mumtaz Mahal. Mumtaz was Nur Jahan's niece, but given the imperious character of the two begums and the susceptibility of close relatives among the Mughals to become adversaries, their relationship could not have been cordial.

A crucial development that drove Shah Jahan into rebellion seems to have been the betrothal in 1620 of Nur Jahan's daughter Ladli Begum to Shahryar, which indicated a change in the power equation at court. If Shahryar, a weak prince, almost an imbecile, became emperor, it would still be Nur Jahan who would be the power behind the throne. Was this why the betrothal was arranged? And was this what finally snapped the relationship between Nur Jahan and Shah Jahan?

Interestingly, the first indication of friction between Jahangir and Shah Jahan came around this time, when Shah Jahan, ordered to proceed to the Deccan, demanded that he be given the custody of his elder brother Khusrav. But was the betrothal of Ladli Begum to Shahryar the consequence or the cause of Shah Jahan's hostility? And if Shahryar was the rival claimant to the throne, why did Shah Jahan have to secure Khusrav's custody? We do not have the answers to these puzzles, but circumstantial evidence is strong that one way or another Nur Jahan was involved in the estrangement between Jahangir and Shah Jahan. Nur Jahan and Shah Jahan had become rivals. A collision between them was inevitable.

SHAH JAHAN'S REBELLION changed Jahangir's priorities. He had first to deal with the threat to his throne before he could deal with Persia. He therefore scuttled his Kandahar campaign plans, recalled his trusted general Mahabat Khan from Kabul and ordered him to suppress the rebellion. Commanded Jahangir: "Take him (Shah Jahan) alive, or drive him out of the imperial territory." Parviz, the emperor's second son, was given overall charge of the campaign. Jahangir, who was in Lahore when Shah Jahan broke out in rebellion, then proceeded towards

Agra, gathering a vast army as he advanced, so that, he says, "by the time I reached Delhi such an army had assembled, that the whole country was covered with men as far as the eye could reach."

Meanwhile Shah Jahan, with Abdur-Rahim at his side, stormed into Agra. He plundered the unwalled city—but could not take the fort and its treasure—and then swung north to meet the advancing imperial forces. Near Mathura he peeled off from his army and sent Sunder Rai to oppose Mahabat Khan. In the ensuing battle there was a moment of anxiety in the imperial camp when Abdullah Khan, who commanded the royal advance force, went over to the rebels with 10,000 soldiers, but still Mahabat Khan managed to rout the rebels. Sunder Rai was killed in the fight, and this was a major blow to Shah Jahan. "One might say that his good fortune and courage and understanding lay in that dog of a Hindu," says Jahangir.

Now Shah Jahan was on the run. He retreated to Mandu, and, as the imperial army closed in—Jahangir himself had moved to Ajmer to oversee the operations—he fled across the Narmada into the Deccan. Presently, as Shah Jahan's fortunes seemed to sink, officers and men began to desert him in hordes. Even Abdur-Rahim, who was sent to treat with Mahabat Khan, submitted to the imperialists. Gujarat, which was in the charge of Shah Jahan and from where he had expected much support, was lost. Malik Ambar refused him help. And the only help that the ruler of Golconda would give him was to allow him to flee through the kingdom into Orissa.

In Orissa, Shah Jahan had his first victory, as the Mughal governor surrendered the province without a fight. Shah Jahan's fortune now turned, and he advanced triumphantly to occupy Bihar and Bengal, where he captured rich booty and many elephants. Rohtas, Jaunpur, Varanasi (Benares) and Allahabad all fell to him. For a moment Shah Jahan looked like a winner.

But only for a moment. Presently Mahabat Khan, doubling back from Burhanpur, arrived in Bihar to hound Shah Jahan. He chased the prince relentlessly from pillar to post, and in the end forced him to flee from the Mughal realm altogether and take refuge in Berar. In his desperation Shah Jahan even sought the help of the Shah of Persia—the Shah advised him to be obedient and loyal to his father! To add to his misery, Shah Jahan fell seriously ill at this time. And Abdullah Khan, his chief lieutenant, became a fakir out of frustration. Shah Jahan had been on the run for three years, and now it was the end of the road for him. He decided to surrender. There was no other way out.

Shah Jahan's letter seeking forgiveness softened Jahangir, and he replied in his own hand that full pardon would be granted to him if he surrendered the forts of Asirgarh and Rohtas still held by his officers and sent his sons Dara and Aurangzeb to the court as hostages. These were very generous terms. Shah Jahan was being treated far more leniently than Khusrav had been in a similar situation. There were no chains for Shah Jahan, no imprisonment, no blinding. Instead, he was appointed governor of Balaghat, in central India. It was an insignificant assignment compared to the high position he had held earlier, but in his predicament it was far more than Shah Jahan could have dared to expect.

Shah Jahan accepted the surrender terms, and withdrew to Nashik and then to Junnar, to bide his time.

Light of the World

WITH SHAH JAHAN in virtual exile, Nur Jahan's influence, which had been growing steadily over the previous decade, peaked. "From the sixth year of the late emperor's reign, when she was united to him in the bond of matrimony, she gradually acquired such unbounded influence on His Majesty's mind that she seized the reins of government and arrogated to herself the supreme civil and financial administration of the realm, ruling with absolute authority till the conclusion of his reign," writes Inayat Khan, Shah Jahan's chronicler. "At last her authority reached such a pass that the King was such only in name," says Mutamid Khan, courtier of Jahangir. Muhammad Hadi confirms: "Nothing was wanting to make her an absolute monarch but the reading of the khutbah in her name."

Nur Jahan had come rather late into Jahangir's life, when he was forty-two, and she thirty-four. Jahangir mentions her for the first time in his memoirs in his ninth regnal year, two years after their marriage, when he writes of an illness which he kept a secret from everyone except Nur Jahan "than whom I did not think anyone was fonder of me," he says.

Before Nur Jahan became empress, she was Mihrunnisa, Sun Among Women, daughter of a destitute Persian migrant noble. Her grandfather, Muhammad Sharif, was a high officer in Persia, connected by marriage to the Safavids, but after his death the family fortunes sank, and his son, Ghiyas Beg, finding no scope for his talents in Persia, migrated to India. Mihrunnisa was born to him in Kandahar in 1577, on his way to India.

Persian officers were at this time highly valued in the Mughal empire, so Ghiyas Beg, who joined Akbar's service at Fatehpur Sikri, rose rapidly to become the superintendent of the royal household, a confidential and prestigious post. Ghiyas Beg was perfect for the Mughal court. He was erudite and suave, exceptionally able, immeasurably generous—and totally corrupt! As Muhammad Hadi puts it, "Mirza Ghiyas Beg was so charitably disposed that no one ever left his door dissatisfied; but in the taking of bribes he certainly was most uncompromising and fearless."

Ghiyas Beg was appointed as revenue minister by Jahangir on his accession, and was given the title Itimad-ud-daula, Pillar of the Government. Then for a short time he came under a cloud, when one of his sons was executed for being embroiled in a Khusrav conspiracy, and he himself was detained for a while. But this was only a tiny squiggle in the smooth and rising chart of Itimad-ud-daulah's career, which would eventually take him to the highest executive office of the empire, that of the Vizier. In every post he occupied, he acquitted himself creditably. "He was a wise and perfect Vizier, and a learned and affectionate companion," lauds Jahangir. "Though the weight of such a kingdom was on his shoulders, and it is not possible or within the power of a mortal to make everyone contented, yet no one ever went to Itimad-ud-daula with a petition or on business who turned from him in an injured frame of mind. He showed loyalty to the sovereign, and yet left pleased and hopeful him who was in need."

Meantime, while Itimad-ud-daula was energetically climbing the ladder of success in the Mughal hierarchy, his infant daughter had grown into a beautiful, vivacious and richly talented young woman. When Mihrunnisa was seventeen, she was married off to another Persian migrant noble, Ali Quli Beg Istajlu, a former table attendant of Shah Ismail of Persia. Popularly known as Sher Afgan (Tiger Grappler), a title given to him by Jahangir for subduing a tiger unarmed, Ali was a strapping young man, a great soldier, but hot-tempered and tactless, with a restless ambition that would not bide its time. Jahangir on his accession posted Sher Afgan to Barddhaman (Bardwan) in Bengal, but there he came under suspicion of colluding with local Afghan insurgents. When Qutbuddin Khan, the governor of Bengal, went to investigate the case, Sher Afgan preempted judgement by running his sword through the governor, but was himself slain by the governor's guards.

This was in 1607, when Jahangir was in Kabul. Later chroniclers would lay the blame for Sher Afgan's death on Jahangir, but no contemporary of Jahangir mentions it, not even the European travellers who thrived on exotic gossip and would certainly have noted so sensational an incident if there had been even a whisper about it. In any case, if Jahangir desired Nur Jahan, there was no need for him to murder Sher Afgan; he only had to ask for her, for it was the Timurid custom that if the emperor desired a woman, her husband should divorce her and give her to the emperor.

On Sher Afgan's death, Mihrunnisa returned to Agra and was appointed lady in waiting to Ruqaiya Begum, Jahangir's stepmother, in whose care Shah Jahan had also been brought up. There "she remained some time (four years, in fact) without notice," says Mutamid Khan.

"Since, however, Fate had decreed that she should be the queen of the world and the princess of the time, it happened that on the celebration of the New Year's day, in the sixth year of the Emperor's reign (1611), her appearance caught his far-seeing eye and so captivated him that he included her among the inmates of his select harem."

By the time Jahangir married Mihrunnisa, he was a much married man, with many wives and numerous concubines. He had, according to Terry, "four wives, and . . . concubines and women beside, . . . enough to make up their number a full thousand." Says Hawkins: Jahangir had "three hundred wives, whereof foure be chiefe as queenes." Modern scholars give the count as twenty wives and 300 concubines. Nur Jahan was his last wife. He had no children by her.

Jahangir took his first wife when he was fifteen. The bride, Man Bai, was a daughter of Raja Bhagwan Das of Amber. Abul Fazl says that Akbar selected her as the crown prince's bride on principles of eugenics, to ensure good offspring. But it was a bad choice, especially on principles of eugenics: both Man Bai and her father were mentally unstable—while Raja Bhagwan Das once attempted suicide and finally died under mysterious circumstances, Man Bai died by her own hand. Moreover, Man Bai was Jahangir's first cousin, his mother being the sister of Bhagwan Das. Khusrav was the unhappy progeny of this inbreeding.

Man Bai, titled Shah Begum, though described by Abul Fazl as "endowed with beauty and graces", was a neurotic woman, quick to take offence over imagined slights, for which there was plenty of scope for the Rajput princess in Jahangir's polygamous and predominantly Muslim household. "The lady was ever ambitious of an ascendancy over the other inmates of the harem, and grew violent at the slightest opposition to her will," says Inayatullah. "From time to time her mind wandered, and her father and brothers all agreed in telling me she was insane," writes Jahangir. In 1604, when Jahangir was thirty-five, she committed suicide by taking an overdose of opium.

What finally drove her to suicide, according to Jahangir, was her unhappiness over her son Khusrav's surliness towards him. "She had an excellent understanding and her affection for me was such that she would have given a thousand sons or brothers as ransom for one hair of mine," says Jahangir. But Muhibb Ali gives a different reason for her suicide: "As the Prince Royal always behaved improperly to her, her mind became jealous and she killed herself by taking opium." Whatever the circumstances of her death, Jahangir deeply mourned her. At least so he says. "How can I describe her excellences and good nature!" he writes. "Her death took such an effect upon me that I did not care to live, and had no pleasure in life. For four nights and days, that is for thirty-two watches, in the depth of distress and sorrow, I did not care to eat or drink." Jahangir had a great capacity for self-delusion.

MIHRUNNISA, MASTERFUL, calm and equable, was the exact opposite of Man Bai in character and temperament. Right from the beginning, Jahangir placed her on a plane different from that of all his other wives. At the time of their marriage, he gave her the title Nur Mahal, Light of the Palace; later, as her stature and role grew, she was given the title Nur Jahan, Light of the World, and on the death of Salima Begum she was designated as Padshah Begum, the first lady of the empire.

What was Nur Jahan's special hold on Jahangir, this king who had numerous wives and concubines? She was undoubtedly an imperiously beautiful woman. This is evident from her portraits. Though the paintings, many of them late copies, are stylized portraits in the prevalent mode, and none are authenticated, there is a consistency of features in them which indicates genuineness. The male artists who painted these portraits of course could not ever have set eyes on Nur Jahan, but it is probable that they had the works of women artists of the harem as models. Besides, they had Jahangir, an authority on painting, to advise them. We must therefore assume that Nur Jahan's portraits are fairly accurate. We see in them a vivacious woman, vital and energetic, her eyes large and lustrous, her forehead broad and open, her high-bridged nose sharp. She has a strong chin; her mouth is small but well formed, with the hint of a smile playing at its corners. It is a strong face, but not hard.

She was as talented as she was beautiful. A gifted artist, she designed new patterns for carpets, brocade and lace, and developed a distinctive style in interior decoration. And, though she herself dressed in simple elegance, usually in white or soft colours, the dresses and jewellery she designed remained in high fashion for well over a century. Similarly, the recipes attributed to her are considered to be the finest in Mughalai gourmet cuisine. In architecture, she broke new ground with the exquisite white marble mausoleum that she built for her father, a jewel of a building and a precursor of the Taj Mahal. She was also an accomplished poet, well versed in Persian literature and clever in repartee.

But more than everything else, Jahangir was pleased with Nur Jahan, for she made a conscious effort to please him. He loved feasts and displays, and she was inventive in the ways to stimulate his jaded spirit. Says Jahangir of a feast she held at Mandu, at her residence: "Summoning the amirs and courtiers to the feast which had been prepared by the begum, I ordered them to give the people cups of all kinds of intoxicating drinks according to the desire of each . . . All sorts of roast meats and fruits by way of relish were ordered to be placed before everyone. It was a wonderful assembly. In the beginning of the evening they lighted lanterns and lamps all round the tanks and buildings, and an illumination was laid out the like of which has perhaps never been arranged in any place. The lanterns and lamps cast their reflection on the water, and it appeared as if the whole surface of the tank was a plain of fire. A grand entertainment took place, and the drinkers of cups took more cups than they could carry."

Nur Jahan and Jahangir were good companions, who shared many interests. She was as enthusiastic about hunting as he was, and was an excellent shot, who once felled four tigers in six shots. "Until now such shooting was never seen, that from the top of an elephant and inside of a howdah six shots should be made and not one miss, so that four beasts found no opportunity to spring or move," exults Jahangir. For this feat Jahangir rewarded her with a pair of diamond bracelets worth 100,000 rupees, and also showered 1,000 ashrafis over her. And Nur Jahan could, like Jahangir, enjoy a drink—one portrait shows her with a dainty wine cup in hand.

They were a perfect pair, her strength firming up Jahangir and reassuring him of his self-worth. Thomas Roe offers a charming picture of Jahangir and Nur Jahan returning to the camp one night from a romantic bullock-cart ride all by themselves—Roe was in the royal courtyard, waiting for Jahangir, when "suddenly news came to put out all lights, the King was come, who entered on an open wagon, with Normahall, drawne by bullocks, himself carter, and no man neare."

Roe, a prim and proper Englishman, was not alive to the romantic resonances of that twilight scene. What fascinated him was the power that Nur Jahan wielded. She "governs him, and wynds him up at her pleasure," says Roe. "All justice or care of any thing or publique affayrs either sleepes or depends on her, who is more unaccesable than any goddesse or mystery of heathen impietye."

Should Nur Jahan be commended or condemned for her role? Gender prejudice, of her age as well as of later times, condemns her, but against the evidence of facts. Nur Jahan won her place in the empire by Jahangir's favour, but her place in history by her own exceptional political and administrative skills. Says Bernier: Her "transcendent abilities rendered her competent to govern the Empire without the interference of her husband." Jahangir did not abdicate power to Nur Jahan, he delegated it to her. And she merited the role he assigned to her, and played it with consummate skill, equal to every crisis she faced, exercising power with sagacity and grace. True, she tried to retain her role even after the scene had changed and she was no longer needed at centre stage, but it should be also said of her that when she finally lost power, she accepted that too with grace.

"It is impossible to describe the beauty and wisdom of the Queen," says Mutamid Khan. "In any matter that was presented to her, if a difficulty arose, she immediately solved it. Whoever threw himself upon her protection was preserved from tyranny and oppression." Her generosity, like that of her father, was legendary. "If ever she learnt that any orphan girl was destitute and friendless, she would bring about her marriage, and give her a wedding portion," continues Mutamid Khan. "It is probable that during her reign no less than 500 orphan girls were thus married and portioned." Often she interceded to moderate the harshness of Mughal justice. "In order to please and satisfy her, the pen of pardon was drawn through the record of his faults," writes Jahangir of a man whom he pardoned. Says Muhammad Hadi, "Nur Jahan won golden opinions from all people."

But there was one fatal flaw in her. She was a woman. An ambitious woman. And in the prejudice of the age, women had no public role, and ambition was the prerogative of men. Inevitably, there was a steady rumble of complaint against Nur Jahan at the court, and in one instance, Mahabat Khan, Jahangir's top general, even made bold to protest to the emperor about her. "The whole world is surprised that such a wise and sensible emperor as Jahangir should permit a woman to have so great an influence over him," said Mahabat Khan. History, he said, did not record "any king so subject to the will of his wife", and he advised Jahangir to think about how future generations would judge him.

MAHABAT KHAN PROTESTED in vain. As the anonymous author of *Intikhab-i Jahangir-Shahi* puts it, "The influence of Nur Jahan Begum had wrought so much upon his (Jahangir's) mind, that if 200 men like Mahabat Khan had advised him simultaneously to the same effect, their words would have made no permanent impression upon him." Nur Jahan's power only continued to grow.

"Day by day her influence and dignity increased," notes Mutamid Khan. "The Emperor granted Nur Jahan the right of sovereignty and government . . . Coin was struck in her name, with this superscription: 'By order of King Jahangir, gold has a hundred splendours added to it by receiving the impression of the name of Nur Jahan, the Queen Begum.' On all firmans also receiving the imperial signature, the name of 'Nur Jahan, the Queen Begum' was jointly attached. At last, her authority reached such a pass that the king was such only in name. Repeatedly he gave out that he had bestowed the sovereignty on Nur Jahan Begum and would say, 'I require nothing beyond a *seer* (about half a kilogram) of wine and half a *seer* of meat.'" Says Peter Mundy: "He became her prisoner by marrying her . . . (and she) in a manner ruled all in ruling him."

As her power grew, so did the resentment against her among the nobles. Part of the problem with the rise of Nur Jahan was that she did not rise alone. Her family rose with her. This was inevitable. Nur Jahan needed her family as the medium through which to exercise her power. She could not rule directly, by herself; she had to stay in purdah and could interact only with her family members. Though Mutamid Khan says that she did "sometimes . . . sit in the balcony of her palace, while the nobles would present themselves and listen to her dictates", she could not do it routinely. So the formation of a Nur-Jahana clique consisting of her family members was an administrative necessity.

The clique consisted of Nur Jahan herself, her father Itimad-ud-daula, her brother Asaf Khan, and, for a while, Shah Jahan, who had married Asaf Khan's daughter, the lady of the Taj. It was a foursome of formidable talent; Itimad-ud-daula and Asaf Khan were high officers of the empire, and Shah Jahan was the heir-apparent. When her father died and Shah Jahan dropped out by rebelling, the government was run by Nur Jahan and Asaf Khan. Jahangir "is king in name only," writes Pelsaert, "while she (Nur Jahan) and her brother Asaf Khan hold the kingdom firmly in their hands."

"The King does not trouble himself with public affairs, but behaves as if they were no concern of his," continues Pelsaert. "If anyone with a request to make at Court obtains an audience or is allowed to speak, the King hears him indeed, but will give no definite answer of Yes or No, referring him promptly to Asaf Khan, who in the same way will dispose of no important matter without communicating with his sister, the Queen, and who regulates his attitude in such a way that the authority of neither of them may be diminished."

There was much social intercourse between the royal family and the family of Itimad-ud-daula, with the emperor sometimes going out to dine with Itimad-ud-daula or Asaf Khan. Itimad-ud-daula had even the privilege of entering the royal harem without the ladies having to veil themselves. It was almost as if the two families had become one. The meteoric rise of Itimad-ud-daula and Asaf Khan brought up the bile of envy in many, especially as their advancement impeded the progress of many other amirs. Mahabat Khan, for instance, was left without a promotion for twelve years, which very likely was the reason why he pleaded with Jahangir to curb the power of Nur Jahan.

Jahangir saw no reason to do so. The arrangement was working perfectly, for himself as well as for the empire. Nor was such an arrangement unprecedented in Muslim polity, though usually the exercise of power by women from behind the throne was kept discreet. What was unusual in Nur Jahan's involvement in public affairs was that Jahangir, instead of keeping it quiet, flaunted it, as in his *seer*-of-wine-and-half-a-*seer*-of-meat remark.

This remark however is not to be taken literally—it was only Jahangir's way of paying a high compliment to Nur Jahan. Jahangir had not become effete or senile. Nur Jahan could not act against his will. Even at the peak of her power, Jahangir continued to attend to his daily work, maintaining the usual rigorous court routine, till his health broke down completely. "It has become my habit not to surrender . . . more than two or three sidereal hours of the coin of Time to the plunder of sleep . . . 'Be wakeful, for a wondrous sleep is ahead,' " writes Jahangir in his memoirs. Jahangir's routine, says Roe, was rigid and relentless, "as regular as clock that striks at sett howers."

An English Aristocrat in the Mughal Court

SIR THOMAS ROE was the first British ambassador accredited to the Mughal court. He presented his credentials to Jahangir at Ajmer in Rajasthan in January 1616, then travelled with the emperor to Mandu in Malwa, and finally to Ahmadabad in Gujarat. "I am yet following this wandering King over mountaynes and through woods, so strange and unused wayes," he wrote home, grumbling. Roe never got to Agra, the imperial capital.

During the three years he was at the Mughal court, Roe, according to his own perhaps self-serving report, became an intimate of Jahangir, and even joined him at his cups. But despite the long and supposedly close relationship between Jahangir and Roe, there is no mention of Roe in Jahangir's memoirs or in any other contemporary Mughal chronicle. His reports are therefore unverifiable. Roe spoke no Persian or Turki, lacked empathy for Mughal culture, and so was unable to evaluate human behaviour in its cultural context. Sometimes he embroidered his reports, to present himself in a favourable light to his masters. Nevertheless we should grant Roe's account fair credibility, for he was a quintessential English gentleman, punctilious, stiffly dignified, but also witty, meticulously mannered, and on the whole decent and fair.

Several British traders and adventurers had visited the Mughal court before Roe. The most prominent of them was William Hawkins, a representative of the newly formed East India Company, who arrived at Jahangir's court in 1609, bearing a letter of commendation from King James. Hawkins was an old hand of the Levant trade; he spoke Turki and Persian, was a *bon vivant*, and so was able to establish (according to his account) an easy rapport with Jahangir, who appointed him as a mansabdar of 400, and called him the English Khan. "Both night and day his delight was very much to talke with mee, both of the affairs of England and other countries," says Hawkins, no doubt vastly exaggerating his role, for there is no mention of Hawkins either in Jahangir's memoirs. Roe in fact considered Hawkins "a vayne foole".

In any case, Hawkins could not get the trade concessions he sought, for he was continually stymied by the Portuguese, who warned Jahangir that the British meant to capture the port cities of the Mughal empire, and cited, as proof of that, the riotous behaviour of the shipwrecked crew of a British ship near Surat. Jahangir dismissed the charge as preposterous. And that, says Hawkins, turned the Portuguese into "madde dogges, labouring to worke my passage out of the world". Whatever the truth of the Portuguese machinations—they were very likely true—Hawkins grew embittered, and he vented his spleen on "those prattling, juggling Jesuits", "the lying Jesuits", especially on Fr. Pinheiro, whom he considered "an arch Knave". "I being now in the highest of my favours," writes Hawkins, "Jesuits and Portugalls slept not, but by all meanes sought my overthrow."

Hawkins exaggerates. The Jesuits probably had some marginal effect on the articulation of Mughal policy, but the policy itself was dictated by hard realities. The emperor had no naval ambition, no interest in the sea tussle between European powers; his only concern was to protect the overseas pilgrim traffic from India, for which it was essential to maintain good relations with whoever dominated the Arabian Sea, which at that time happened to be the Portuguese. Moreover, Indian merchants in Surat were not in favour of a trade connection with the British, which they feared would not amount to much and would jeopardize their far greater trade with the Portuguese.

Hawkins thus had to leave Agra empty handed in 1611. He was succeeded by Paul Canning and William Edwards, but they made little impression at the court, with the Portuguese working to frustrate their every move—when Canning played a cornet at the court and Jahangir was pleased with it and tried to play it himself, the Portuguese produced a Neapolitan juggler to divert the emperor!

Gradually however the balance of power in the Arabian Sea began to shift in favour of the British. In September 1612, in a naval action off Surat, a couple of British ships under the command of Thomas Best prevailed over a strong Portuguese fleet sent from Goa, and three years later, in 1615, in yet another naval battle in the same area, the British again worsted the Portuguese fleet. "Most of their vessels were burnt by the English," notes Jahangir in his memoirs, in the first ever mention of the British in a Mughal chronicle.

The naval victories of the British raised their stature in the eyes of the emperor. Their relative position further improved when, around that time, the Portuguese inopportunely antagonized the Mughals by seizing at sea an Indian ship with rich cargo, despite the ship having a valid Portuguese pass. This attracted swift and severe Mughal reprisals, for Jahangir's step-mother, Salima Begum, happened to have a considerable commercial interest in the ship. Jahangir ordered his officers in Surat to exact compensation from the Portuguese. A Mughal contingent besieged Daman. Father Jerome Xavier was arrested. The favours conferred on the Jesuits were withdrawn, their activities banned. Thus pressured, the Portuguese treated for peace, and after prolonged haggling, agreed to pay compensation; they did not trouble the Mughals again during Jahangir's reign.

These developments made the timing of Roe's visit opportune. Moreover, Roe was far better equipped than his predecessors to negotiate with the Mughal emperor; unlike Hawkins, who was a mere trade representative, Roe was a royal ambassador. He was an aristocrat, a friend of the British royal family, and was well educated, at Oxford and the Middle Temple. He was already something of a celebrity in England, for having explored the Amazon in the wilds of Guiana, for which he was knighted. Roe was therefore a good choice to be the British ambassador to the Mughal court. At thirty-five he was, as the British court minutes of 7th September 1614 record, "in the prime of his life, of a pregnant understanding, well-spoken, learned, industrious, of a comely personage."

ROE AND HIS MEN set sail from England on 2nd February 1615 and landed at Surat on 18th September. Immediately on landing, right on the lading pier itself, Roe got into a dispute with Mughal officers, to fend off what he considered to be Mughal slights—he would not allow the customs officers to search his person, and he would not meet those who had come to receive him unless they stood up to greet him instead of sitting on their carpets. On both these issues he had his way. Roe was self-conscious of his status as an aristocrat and a representative of his king, and in India he would scrupulously guard his Englishness against the seduction of native ways.

From Surat, Roe set out for Ajmer, but on the way called on Prince Parviz at Burhanpur. There he refused to perform the Mughal obeisance of kornish, on the ground that he had, as he put it, "come in honour to meet the Prince, and was free from the custom of servants". Taken to the inner enclosure in front of the seat of the prince, Roe noticed that the great men of the town stood humbly before the prince, "with their hands before them like slaves". Roe decided that he would not degrade himself so. "I demanded the licence to come up and stand by him (the prince)," says Roe. "Hee answered, If the King of Persia or the Great Turke were there, it might not be admitted. I replyed that I must bee excused, for I doubted not hee would come downe and meete them at his gate."

It is difficult to believe that Roe actually said this; more likely it was a thought that passed through his mind—after all, he was a diplomat and had come to seek favours, so it seems unlikely that he would have been so impudent during his very first meeting with a Mughal prince as to give offence. But with Roe, we can never say. In any case, permission to move up to the prince was refused. Roe then asked for a chair so that he could sit and talk to the prince! This too was of course refused, but he was allowed to "ease my selfe against a pillar" of the prince's canopy, gloats Roe.

Roe was probably given considerable latitude in how he behaved, for in the eyes of the Mughals he was a feringhee unfamiliar with the courtly ways of Muslim civilization. Moreover, the Mughals, from the emperor down to petty local officials, were eager for the exotic presents they expected from Europeans, which ranged from worthless curios to paintings, riding coaches and bottles of liquor. Roe in fact sent Parviz a case of spirits, on which the prince feasted too well to keep his appointment with the ambassador for a private interview that evening.

From Burhanpur, Roe proceeded on to Ajmer, where Jahangir was camping. He arrived there just before Christmas, but the journey had worn him out and he fell ill on reaching Ajmer. Two weeks later, on 10th January 1616, he presented himself at the court during the afternoon durbar. To avoid the embarrassment of submitting to Mughal court etiquette, which he considered not befitting his dignity, Roe sought and obtained advance permission to salute the emperor in the English manner, perhaps with a bow and a flourish. The permission that was granted to Roe was not unusual, for foreign envoys were often allowed to greet the emperor according to their custom. Roe writes that he did three "reverences" on approaching the throne: on entering, at the inner railing, and in front of the emperor. He then presented a letter from King James to Jahangir, which addressed the emperor as, "To the high and mightie Monarch the Great Mogor, King of the Orientall Indies, of Chandahar, of Chismer and Corazon, &c. Greeting!"

Roe, tall and handsome, was quite a dandy—his lovingly groomed moustache was like the wings of a bird in flight, and his Vandyke beard like a silken bird's tail. He was an exotic presence in the Mughal court, and the begums often gathered behind the screens of the durbar hall to ogle him—"[their] curiositie made them breake little holes in a grate of Reed that hung before it, to gaze at mee," says Roe.

Soon, if Roe is to be believed (we have only his word for it), he established an easy, informal, joshing relationship with the emperor. They become friends, this starchy Englishman and the debauched Mughal. Jahangir wanted to know what Roe drank, how much, how often. The emperor, Roe says, wanted to know "what Beere was? how made? and whether I could make it heere?" When Jahangir made copies of a painting that Roe had brought, and Roe had difficulty in identifying the original from the copies, the emperor chaffed him, "with many passages of jests, mirth, and bragges concerning the arts of his country." Jahangir, says Roe, "was very merry and joyful, and cracked like a Northern man."

There were moments of embarrassment too. Roe was mortified when Jahangir once called him to explain a painting of Satyr. Another time Jahangir summoned Roe to the court at ten in the night, as he had just then been told that Roe had a painting that he had not shown Jahangir, and wanted to know why it was held back. "I replyed, that I esteemed it more then any thing I possessed, because it was the image of one that I loved dearely and could never recover," reports Roe. Roe nevertheless presented the miniature to the emperor, who graciously returned it to him after making copies of it to present to his queens.

Roe often attended Jahangir's drinking parties, and though no tippler himself—he found the liquor served too strong—he enjoyed the parties. "So drinking and commanding others, his Majestie, and all the Lords became the finest men I ever saw, of a thousand humours," Roe writes about a party he attended. "When he could not hold up his head, he lay downe to sleepe, and we all departed." Sometimes Jahangir shared with Roe the meat he personally hunted, especially boar, a forbidden meat for Muslims.

Despite such easy camaraderie with Jahangir, Roe felt frustrated at court, because even after some three years of negotiations, he was not able to make any headway with the trade treaty he had hoped to conclude, to regularize British trade with Mughal India. Jahangir would not commit himself to a treaty, for England was, in the eyes of the Mughals, an obscure and far off country, with which it would be beneath the emperor's prestige to enter into a treaty. Nor would he agree to Roe's plea to exclude the Portuguese from Gujarat. The most that Roe could secure was an edict from Shah Jahan (who was then the governor of Gujarat) towards the close of 1618, granting trade concessions, but forbidding the British from purchasing or constructing any buildings and from carrying arms. Roe had to be content with that.

Roe blamed his discomfiture on the manipulations of the Jesuits, and on the antagonism of Shah Jahan (who treated Roe with disdain) and Asaf Khan (who was believed to be in the interest of the Portuguese). "The Portugall pursues us heere with virulent hatred," bemoaned Roe. He was also handicapped by the fact that the presents he could offer to the emperor and the courtiers were commonplace—Jahangir rightly wanted to know why the presents were cheap if the King of England was a great monarch. Roe gamely dissembled: "My Master knew he (Jahangir) was Lord of the best part of Asia, the richest Prince of the East. That to send his Majestie rich Presents, were to cast Pearles into the Sea, the mother and store-house of them, that therefore his Majestie thought it unnecessary."

At Ahmadnagar, when Roe took leave of the emperor to return home, he was given a letter for King James: "Unto a King rightly descended from his Ancestors, bred in Military Affairs, and clothed with Honour and Justice,

"A Commander worthy of all command, strong and constant in Religion, which the great Prophet Christ did teach, King James, whose love hath bred such impression in my thoughts, as shall never be forgotten, but as the smell of Amber, or as a Garden of fragrant flowers whose beautie and Odour is still increasing, so be assured my love shall grow and increase with yours."

Roe sailed from Surat in February 1619.

SOON AFTER ROE left, Jahangir himself set out from Gujarat for Agra. He had been in Gujarat for about two years, having arrived there from Mandu in 1617. He had gone there to inspect the province, to hunt for elephants, and to view the sea. At Cambay, like his father and grandfather before him, Jahangir set eyes on the sea for the first time, and like Akbar, he too went on a sea cruise. "On Monday the 11th, I embarked on a boat, and sailed about one kos," he notes.

From Cambay Jahangir went on to Ahmadabad, but the city did not find favour with him. "I do not know what to call it—whether Samumistan (the home of hot winds), Bimaristan (abode of sickness), Zaqqum-zar (cactus land) or Jahannumabad (hell), for all these names are appropriate," he writes. To make matters worse, there was at this time a fever epidemic in Gujarat, and both Jahangir and Shah Jahan were infected. Yet they could not return to Agra, for a worse epidemic was raging in that city, bubonic plague, which had been sweeping through Hindustan in waves since 1616 and would continue till 1624, and was attributed by seers to the appearance of a comet at this time. The plague was still causing about a hundred deaths a day in Agra in the first quarter of 1619, when Jahangir was returning to the capital, so he had to break his journey for three months at Fatehpur Sikri, before proceeding on to Agra in April.

Jahangir did not stay in Agra for long. He abhorred Agra, and avoided staying there as much as possible. "The extreme heat of Agra was uncongenial to my constitution," he writes. At one time he thought of shifting his capital to a cooler place, on the foothills of the mountains, along the upper reaches of the Ganga, but could not find a suitable place. So, after a reluctant six-month stay in Agra, in October 1619 Jahangir left the city and set out for Kashmir, to seek refuge from the heat and dust, the ugliness and afflictions of the plains of Hindustan. It was his first visit to Kashmir as emperor—he had been there twice before, with Akbar—and he took a leisurely trip from Agra to Srinagar, taking five and a half months to cover the distance. He would stay in the valley for seven months, from March to October 1620. There was no hurry. Everything was quiet and peaceful in the empire.

Kashmir enthralled Jahangir. "If one were to praise Kashmir, whole books would have to be written," he says, hazarding a paean all the same. "Kashmir is a garden of eternal spring . . . a heart-expanding heritage . . . Its pleasant meads and enchanting cascades are beyond all description. There are running streams and fountains beyond count. Wherever the eye reaches, there are verdure and running water . . . In the soul-enchanting spring the hills and plains are filled with blossoms; the gates, the walls, the courts, the roofs, are lighted up by the torches of banquet-adorning tulips. What shall we say of these things of the wide meadows and the fragrant trefoil."

Jahangir, says Bernier, "became so enamoured of this little kingdom as to make it the place of his favourite abode, and he often declared that he would be rather deprived of every other province of his mighty empire than lose Kachemire." According to Pelsaert, "the reason of the King's special preference for this country (Kashmir) is that, when the heat in India increases, his body burns like a furnace, owing to the consumption of excessively strong drink and opium." In the cool, pleasant ambience of Kashmir, and under careful treatment by the most renowned physicians of the land, Jahangir's ravaged body recovered some of its old strength.

Unfortunately, in Kashmir Jahangir was afflicted with asthma. "On the day of the Dasehra, when I was in Kashmir, I was seized with a catching and shortness of breath," he writes. "In the air passages of my left side near the heart, an oppression and catching was felt. It gradually increased and became fixed." Medicines gave him some relief, but on returning to the plains, the bouts of asthma recurred, which his physicians could not relieve. "In despair of obtaining any relief from medicine, I gave up all doctoring, and threw myself upon the mercy of the Universal Physician . . . As I found relief in drinking, contrary to my habit, I resorted to it in the daytime, and by degrees I carried it to excess. When the weather became hot, the evil effects of this became apparent, and my weakness and suffering increased."

At this point Nur Jahan took over nursing Jahangir. "Nur Jahan Begum, whose skill and experience are greater than those of the physicians, especially as they are brought to bear through affection and sympathy, endeavoured to diminish the number of my cups and to carry out the remedies that appeared appropriate to the time, and soothing to the condition," writes Jahangir. "She, by degrees, lessened my wine, and kept me from things that did not suit me, and food that disagreed with me." When he recovered somewhat, she celebrated the happy occasion with the feast of his solar birthday, which cost her 200,000 rupees. At the customary ceremonial weighing of the emperor, it was found that his weight had come down from "three *maunds* and one or two *seers* more or less" to "only two *maunds* and 27 *seers*," notes Jahangir.

THE ELEVEN YEARS from his marriage to Nur Jahan in 1611 to the outbreak of Shah Jahan's rebellion in 1622 were the best years of Jahangir. They were years of peace and prosperity in the empire, contentment for the emperor.

This was largely the achievement of Nur Jahan. And of her clique. They worked closely together, and were dependent on each other—she was the power, they were the gears that transmitted the power to run the government. As long as the gears meshed well, everything ran smoothly. But in the early 1620s the Nur Jahana clique began to break up. The first to go was Asmat Begum, Nur Jahan's mother, who died in 1621. Heartbroken, Itimad-ud-daula followed her in January 1622. The deaths of her parents desolated Nur Jahan and disrupted the fine balance of her secure world—it was their good sense and loving authority that held the clique together, and now that they were gone, on whom was she to depend? What if Jahangir, whose health was failing rapidly, too died? There was little possibility of Shah Jahan giving Nur Jahan any political role if he succeeded to the throne. And whom would Asaf Khan support, his son-in-law or his sister? Suddenly Nur Jahan was faced with uncertainties.

It was in this clouded environment that Nur Jahan arranged the marriage of her daughter Ladli Begum to Shahryar. The marriage further altered the power equation in the empire. Shahryar, born of a concubine, was in his late teens then, and though he was "the most beautiful of all the princes", he was childish and frivolous, and was generally considered a nincompoop. The marriage was therefore seen as a manoeuvre by Nur Jahan to facilitate the continuation of her grip on power through the succession of the weak prince.

Shah Jahan seemed to have thought so, and this probably was the crucial factor that drove him into rebellion. Nur Jahan however handled the crisis well, even retaining the loyalty of Asaf Khan, who helped to crush his son-in-law's rebellion. But Nur Jahan did not gloat over her triumph. There was no ruthlessness in her pursuit of power. Nor was there any indication that she was bent on the ruination of Shah Jahan. The surrender terms offered to him were generous. She could have destroyed him. But she didn't.

The Coup

NO SOONER WAS Shah Jahan neutralized than Nur Jahan was up against another crisis, the rebellion of Mahabat Khan. A long time close associate of Jahangir, Mahabat Khan had always chafed under Nur Jahan's authority, and he hated and feared Asaf Khan, whom he considered an implacable enemy bent on ruining him. Equally, Nur Jahan and Asaf Khan were apprehensive about Mahabat Khan, for the Khan's crucial role in crushing Shah Jahan's rebellion had made him the most powerful amir in the empire, a rival power centre. Prince Parviz, Jahangir's eldest surviving son, was with him—and Parviz, thirty-six, though a weak and self-indulgent prince, was a likely successor to the throne, now that Khusrav was dead and Shah Jahan was in disgrace. If Parviz succeeded to the throne, would not Mahabat Khan be the power behind the throne? Where would that leave Asaf Khan? In fact, where would that leave Nur Jahan? Once again the interests of brother and sister converged. It was essential for them to separate Parviz from Mahabat Khan, and to reduce the Khan's stature.

As a first step towards this, Mahabat Khan was transferred to Bengal and Parviz to Gujarat, in opposite corners of the empire. Then, deliberately casting a slur on Mahabat Khan's integrity, he was asked to account for the booty that had fallen to him during the campaign against Shah Jahan, surrender the elephants that he had taken, and appear before the emperor to answer the charges against him. Mahabat Khan regarded those orders as a manoeuvre by Asaf Khan "to bring him to disgrace, and to deprive him of honour, property and life," says Mutamid Khan.

A grave act of impropriety committed by Mahabat Khan at this time, of arranging the marriage of his daughter with an imperial officer without first obtaining the customary royal permission, further vitiated the atmosphere. "The emperor made a great noise about this," says Mutamid Khan. "He sent for the young man, and having treated him with great insult and harshness, he gave orders for binding his hands to his neck, and for taking him bareheaded to prison." The presents that Mahabat Khan had given to his son-in-law were confiscated.

That was about as much as Mahabat Khan could take. It is not however certain that he had rebellion in mind when he set out for Lahore in response to the royal summons. He was accompanied by a contingent of four or five thousand Rajputs, but that in itself did not indicate sedition, for great amirs usually travelled with large retinues. In March 1626 Mahabat Khan arrived at the imperial camp on the east bank of the Jhelum, where Jahangir was encamped on the way to Kabul, but the emperor, to show his displeasure with the Khan, ordered him not to present himself at the court till summoned. Among the royalists there was no sense of any danger from Mahabat Khan. In fact, virtually the entire royal camp—the army, the officers and their families, even the domestics—crossed over to the western bank of the river after Mahabat Khan's arrival, leaving only the royal household on the eastern bank to cross the river the next morning. Nobody could even imagine that Mahabat Khan would dare to act against the person of the emperor.

WHAT ENSUED WAS the unimaginable. When Mahabat Khan realized that Jahangir was without protection, he impulsively decided the grab the chance. A contingent of some 2000 Rajputs was sent at the crack of dawn to secure the boat bridge over the Jhelum to prevent the imperial army from crossing back, and Mahabat Khan himself proceeded to the royal enclosure with a band of Rajputs.

Mutamid Khan, then an officer in the imperial household, had just finished his early morning prayers and was on his rounds when he heard the sudden cry, "Mahabat Khan is coming!" When he came out of his tent, his sword drawn, he saw Mahabat Khan approaching, leading his horse in the midst of about 100 Rajputs on foot, carrying spears and shields, all enveloped in a cloud of dust. Reports Mutamid Khan: "When he saw me, he addressed me by name, and asked for His Majesty," but without pausing for an answer, he hastened towards the state apartment and, still surrounded by the Rajputs, moved towards the Ghusl-khana, the antechamber where the emperor held confidential meetings. At this point Mutamid Khan spoke up. "This presumption and temerity is beyond all room. If you will wait a minute, I will go in and make a report." Mahabat Khan made no reply. Instead, his men began to tear down the boards of the antechamber.

Just then Jahangir, informed of the affront, came out of his tent and took his seat in a palanquin that was waiting to take him across the river. Seeing this, Mahabat Khan approached the emperor—not audaciously but deferentially—and pleaded, "I have assured myself that escape from the malice and implacable hatred of Asaf Khan is impossible, and that I shall be put to death in shame and ignominy. I have therefore boldly and presumptuously thrown myself upon Your Majesty's protection. If I deserved death or punishment, give the order that I may suffer it in your presence."

Jahangir twice laid his hand on his sword and, according to Mutamid Khan, "seemed intent on cutting off Mahabat Khan's head". But each time he was cautioned by an attendant, who said in Turkish (which Mahabat Khan could not understand): "This is a time for fortitude. Leave the punishment of this wicked, faithless fellow to a just God. A day of retribution will come." Jahangir checked himself.

Reprieved, Mahabat Khan requested Jahangir to ride out with him as if for hunting. "Let the necessary orders be given as usual, so that your slave may go out in attendance upon you, and it may appear that this bold step has been taken by Your Majesty's order." Mahabat Khan offered his own horse to Jahangir to ride, but Jahangir refused to mount it, and called for his own steed.

Thus the bizarre procession set out. When they had gone a few hundred metres, Mahabat Khan persuaded Jahangir to mount an elephant and sit in the howdah, so that people could see him better and gain the impression that nothing was amiss. Two personal attendants of the emperor, one of them his cup-bearer, were also allowed to mount, after a scuffle. But when the imperial elephant was brought up for Jahangir, the officers who brought it were cut down by the Rajputs, fearing a rescue attempt. The group then proceeded to Mahabat Khan's camp, where the emperor was placed under the guard of the Khan's sons.

In the excitement of the action, and because of the unplanned nature of the abduction, Mahabat Khan had overlooked to secure Nur Jahan, so he rode back to the royal camp with the emperor in search of her. But she, either because she was unaware of what had happened (as Mutamid Khan says), or because she was aware of it, as seems likely, had crossed over to the west bank of the river, to which the Rajputs guarding the bridge offered no objection, as their order was only to prevent the royal army from crossing back.

Mahabat Khan then thought of seizing Shahryar, and took Jahangir to the camp of the prince. "Apprehension and fear for his life so distracted the traitor that his deeds and words were not at all sensible," says Mutamid Khan. "He neither knew what he said nor what he did, nor what was to be done. Every minute some design or some anxiety entered his mind, and caused regret. His Majesty made no opposition to any of his proposals."

Across the river, Nur Jahan went straight to Asaf Khan's tents, to which she summoned all the chief amirs. "This has all happened through your neglect and stupid arrangements," she berated them. "What never entered into the imagination of any one has come to pass, and now you stand stricken with shame for your conduct before God and man. You must do your best to repair this evil, and advise what course to pursue." It was then decided that the army should be drawn out to recross the river the next morning and rescue the emperor. When Jahangir heard of the plan, he sent word to advise against it. "With what hope and what zeal could they fight, while . . . [the emperor] was on a different side of the river?" he asked. But the imperial officers, suspecting that the message was a ruse of Mahabat Khan, proceeded with their preparations.

The operation was a disaster. The ford selected for the army to cross the river—the bridge had been burnt by Mahabat Khan's men— "was one of the worst fords," says Mutamid Khan, and the crossing was disorderly and unsuccessful. "No one cared for or gave ear to another, no one showed any resolution." Nur Jahan herself, riding in a closed howdah on an elephant with Shahryar's infant daughter in her lap, had to turn back at mid-river, with her elephant badly wounded and the baby's nurse struck by an arrow. Though there were many instances of individual heroism, and a few braves even reached Shahryar's tent where Jahangir was lodged, the rescue attempt had to be abandoned. Some, including Mutamid Khan, then went over to Mahabat Khan's camp, on the pretext of wanting to be with the emperor. Many simply fled for their lives.

Among the first to flee was Asaf Khan, who, says Mutamid Khan, "was the cause of this disaster, and whose folly and rashness had brought matters to this pass." He had the most to fear from Mahabat Khan. A courtier, Asaf Khan was no soldier, nor much of a general, and had failed time and again in the battlefield, as in Mewar and the Deccan and now in Punjab. Not surprisingly, he abandoned his sister and the emperor to their fate, and fled to save his skin, taking refuge in the fort of Attock on the Indus.

Nur Jahan thus found herself in a helpless predicament. She therfore crossed the river to join Jahangir in captivity. There was nothing else that she could do. Outwardly, Mahabat Khan was still the humble servant of Jahangir, and did everything on his orders. But this was only a facade. The real power lay with Mahabat Khan, and he took command of the imperial army. Presently Asaf Khan himself, on being promised security of life, submitted to Mahabat Khan, and, as Mutamid Khan puts it, "bound himself by promise and oath to uphold Mahabat".

The imperial convoy then proceeded on to Kabul, which Jahangir entered in May 1626, riding an elephant and scattering gold and silver as usual. Throughout, Mahabat Khan was punctilious in his courtesy and deference towards the emperor. Jahangir and Nur Jahan on their part appeared reconciled to their figurehead status.

The new dispensation had come to stay, it seemed.

THIS WAS AN illusion. Mahabat Khan was way out of his depth in his role as the de facto ruler. He was a great soldier, a great general, bold and forthright, but court politics required a suavity and tortuous cunning that was not in him, and it was entirely beyond him to counter the subtle manoeuvres of Nur Jahan. Nor was Mahabat Khan skilled in manipulating the complex system of wires and levers that made the Mughal government work. Besides, the moment he seized power, whatever support he had among the great amirs of the empire began to crumble, as the acid of their envy corroded his links with them.

Mahabat Khan's first major mistake was in allowing Jahangir to proceed to Kabul. The general's main support was among the Rajputs, and it would have been desirable for him to keep the emperor in Hindustan, the home ground of the Rajputs. In Kabul the Rajputs, swaggering in their new role as king-makers, got into trouble with the Ahadis, the emperor's praetorian guards, as well as with the local population. When the Rajputs grazed their horses in the hunting ground reserved for the emperor, a riot broke out, in which several hundred Rajputs were killed, and many others captured and sold into slavery. To restore calm, Mahabat Khan dealt harshly with the instigators of the riot, and that further isolated him from the Mughal amirs.

Meanwhile Nur Jahan and Jahangir devised a plan to neutralize Mahabat Khan. On his part, Jahangir lulled the Khan's anxieties by acting as if he were reconciled, indeed happy, with the new power arrangement. The emperor, says Mutamid Khan, "set Mahabat's heart at rest, and removed that doubt and suspicion with which Mahabat had at first regarded him"; he disclosed to the Khan what he claimed Nur Jahan had told him in secret, and even warned him against her designs. While Jahangir was playing this role to the hilt, Nur Jahan quietly began to gather her support and organize her forces. "Nur Jahan Begum worked against him (Mahabat Khan) both in private and in public," says Mutamid Khan.

When everything was ready, Nur Jahan struck. On their return journey from Kabul in November 1626, at Rohtas on the Jhelum, Jahangir ordered Mahabat Khan to march one stage ahead, as he wished to review Nur Jahan's troops. Suddenly Mahabat Khan felt the ground crumbling under his feet. He marched ahead to obey the royal order, but instead of halting after one stage, barreled on in headlong flight, in which he took Asaf Khan and his son (the future Shayista Khan), and the sons of Daniyal as hostages.

Nur Jahan now pressed hard her advantage. She ordered Mahabat Khan to release the hostages, and threatened to send the imperial forces against him if he delayed. Mahabat Khan hedged. He released Daniyal's sons, but kept Asaf Khan and his son, saying that he would release them after he had put a safe distance between himself and the imperial army. But Nur Jahan would not relent; she again peremptorily ordered him to release Asaf Khan. At this point Mahabat Khan lost nerve; he released Asaf Khan, his son a few days later, and continued on his flight.

Shah Jahan meantime, on hearing of Mahabat Khan's coup, had marched northward with a small force—to rescue his father, he claimed. Though by the time he got to Sind his force had dwindled through desertions to a mere three or four hundred cavalry, and he himself was in poor health—at one time he had to be carried in a litter—Shah Jahan felt compelled to press on, to be near the scene of action, for fear of being denied his legitimate role in the power struggle. But he got bogged down in Sind. Before he could extricate himself from there, Nur Jahan had wrested back the reins of power from Mahabat Khan, and she ordered Shah Jahan to withdraw to the Deccan. Shah Jahan in frustration thought of fleeing to Persia, but the governor of Sind barred his way, so he had to retreat in humiliation to the Deccan. The only good news he had at this time was that his brother Parviz had died in an alcoholic coma in Burhanpur. This simplified the succession equation to two factors, Shahryar and Shah Jahan.

Meanwhile Nur Jahan, uncertain of Shah Jahan's intentions, ordered the fleeing Mahabat Khan to proceed to Sind to block the way of Shah Jahan, but the general swerved eastward hoping to seize the treasure coming from Bengal, and, failing in the attempt, took refuge in Mewar, from where he proceeded with some 2000 troops to join Shah Jahan at Junnar.

The Mahabat Khan escapade had lasted just eight months. It never had any real chance of success, and the only surprise about it was that it lasted as long as it did. The coup was unplanned; it began on an impulse and was sustained by inertia; it collapsed when a countervailing force was applied.

NUR JAHAN WAS now back in control. Her brother Asaf Khan stood by her. Appointed Vakil, the royal deputy, he now became the executive head of the imperial government. "The order was given for him to preside permanently over the administration of all affairs, revenue and political," notes Mutamid Khan.

Jahangir was by then very ill. So from Punjab he turned northward, to Kashmir, to rest from the trials that he had gone through, and to seek in the cool, crisp air of the valley relief from the asthma that had been racking him for eight years. But Kashmir gave him no relief; in fact he became so ill that he even lost the craving for opium. "His sufferings were great," says Mutamid Khan. "He lost all appetite for food, and rejected opium, which had been his companion for forty years. He took nothing but a few cups of wine of the grape." The royal family suffered another misfortune in Kashmir when Shahryar was stricken with an illness which, says Mutamid Khan, "robbed him of his honour", for all the hair on his head and body, even his eyelashes, fell off. Shahryar was advised by physicians to return to the plains, and he left.

Soon after, Jahangir himself set out for Lahore. On the way down he halted at Bairamkala, one of his favourite hunting grounds, and there, though quite ill, the urge came upon him to sport with the gun again. So he seated himself on the slope of a mountain, and as beaters drove in the animals, he raised his matchlock, and steadying it on a parapet specially built for the purpose, fired, wounding a deer, which bounded off to its herd and fell. But the joy of this good shot turned into horror for Jahangir a moment later, when a foot soldier, who leapt after the wounded deer, slipped and hurtled down the cliff before his very eyes. "The fate of the poor man greatly affected the Emperor," says Mutamid Khan. "It seemed as though he had thus seen the angel of death. From that time he had no rest or ease, and his state was entirely changed."

Jahangir continued his journey to the plains, but his condition turned critical a couple of days later, at Chingiz Hatli near Bhimbhar, and he was not even able to swallow a sip of the wine he had called for. The next day, 7th November 1627, soon after sunrise, he died. He was fifty-eight years old and had reigned twenty-two years.

Jahangir's death was long expected and it at once set off a flurry of activity plotted well ahead by the principal players in the succession drama. The immediate impact of the death of Jahangir was on Nur Jahan. The moment he died, her power too died—when she summoned a meeting of the amirs to determine what to do about the succession, the call was ignored, probably on the advice of Asaf Khan. As the premier noble of the empire, Asaf Khan now assumed charge and controlled the course of events. He held Nur Jahan incommunicado, and removed Shah Jahan's sons from her charge.

Surprisingly, Nur Jahan remained inert in the midst of all the frantic activity. Though Mutamid Khan says that "the Begum's wish was to raise Shahryar to the throne", and Abdul Hamid Lahori (one of Shah Jahan's chroniclers) repeats the charge, saying that "Nur Mahal . . . now clung to the vain idea of retaining the reins of government in her grasp, as she had held them during the reign of the late emperor", she did not take any resolute action. This was uncharacteristic. The fight seemed to have gone out of her.

But Asaf Khan worked energetically, though secretly, to ensure the succession of Shah Jahan, his son-in-law, who also had the support of most of the amirs. The main rival of Shah Jahan was Shahryar, the only other surviving son of Jahangir. Though considered an imbecile, he had the advantage of being close by, at Lahore, and of having the potentially powerful backing of Nur Jahan. Shah Jahan was far away in the Deccan, and it would be weeks before he could be informed of Jahangir's death and for the khutbah to be read in his name. The throne could not be left vacant for so long. It was therefore essential to have a stopgap emperor, "a sacrificial lamb", as Mutamid Khan puts it. Asaf Khan chose Dawar Bakhsh, a son of Khusrav, for the role. But when the throne was offered to him, Dawar was naturally suspicious. "He did not believe them," writes Mutamid Khan, "and placed no confidence in their proposals till they had bound themselves with stringent oaths." Then he agreed. And by that he signed his own death sentence.

THESE MANOEUVRES HAD taken place within hours of Jahangir's death. The next day the royal camp moved to Bhimbhar, on the edge of the plains, where the emperor's funeral rites were performed, and his body sent to Lahore to be interred in a garden which Nur Jahan had laid out at Shahdara, a suburb of the city. The khutbah was then read in the name of Dawar Bakhsh, and the royal camp proceeded to Lahore.

Meantime in Lahore, when the news of Jahangir's death reached the city, Shahryar—"urged on by his intriguing wife," according to Mutamid Khan—proclaimed himself emperor. He seized the treasury there and distributed some seven million rupees to win over the allegiance of the nobles. But Shahryar did not have it in him to make a fight for the throne. His hastily recruited army, commanded by Baisanghar (once Don Carlos), a son of Daniyal, was easily dispersed by Asaf Khan. Lahore was besieged and taken, and Shahryar, who had hid himself in the harem, was brought out by a eunuch and made to pay homage to Dawar Bakhsh. He was then thrown into prison and blinded.

All this was by-play. The real action was taking place behind the scenes. Immediately on the death of Jahangir, Asaf Khan had sent to Shah Jahan a fast runner, one Banarasi, with his signet ring for identification, bearing the news of Jahangir's death and requesting him to hurry north. It took Banarasi twenty days to reach Shah Jahan, who was then at Junnar, living in the beautiful mansion that Malik Ambar had built there. The prince, after a becoming delay of a few days to observe the rites of mourning (as well as to wait for the astrologically auspicious time), set out for Agra along with Mahabat Khan, taking a circuitous route through Gujarat, to avoid Khan Jahan Lodi at Burhanpur, who was suspected to be inimical to him.

On the way to Agra, Shah Jahan sent a firman to Asaf Khan, written in his own hand, to do away with all potential contenders to the throne—Shahryar, Dawar Bakhsh and his brother Gahrasp, and Daniyal's two sons. That was the best way to secure peace and avoid bloodshed, Shah Jahan believed. To exterminate them was "conducive to the common good" and therefore "entirely lawful", says Shah Jahan's chronicler Muhammad Salih Kambu. On the night of Wednesday, 2nd February 1628, soon after Shah Jahan was proclaimed emperor in Lahore, the princes "were all seized and put to death", reports Inayat Khan. This succession rite would be faithfully performed at the death of most Mughal emperors thereafter—a blood sacrifice to prevent bloodshed!

Meanwhile Shah Jahan continued on to Agra, which he entered "with great . . . splendour, mounted on an elephant", and was acclaimed by all as the sovereign. A few days later, Asaf Khan with the imperial entourage arrived from Lahore, and was received with honour. He was confirmed as the Vakil. The succession issue was closed. The new reign had begun.

Nur Jahan remained in Lahore, with Ladli Begum, her daughter. She received an ample annual allowance of 200,000 rupees from Shah Jahan, and she busied herself with the construction of her husband's mausoleum (which she built at her own expense) and with charitable work. There was no attempt on her part to interfere in politics. That phase of her life was over, and she made a smooth, intelligent and graceful transition from public to private life, as she had made other transitions in her life. After eighteen years of contented obscurity, on 18th November 1645, the great empress, aged sixty-eight, passed away. She was buried in a mausoleum she had built for herself beside that of her husband.

Chapter Eight

THE PARADISE
ON EARTH

The Man Behind the Mask

WITH SHAH JAHAN a Pharaonic mask slides into place. The person virtually disappears behind the persona, as Shah Jahan's official chroniclers scrub him clean of all the grime of life and present him as The Great Mughal, gilded, bejewelled and perfumed, larger than life but lifeless.

There are three meticulous chronicles of the reign of Shah Jahan, official histories by his courtiers, every chapter of which was approved by the emperor personally or by his authorized representative. They tell us little about the man. Probably no one even really knew Shah Jahan as a person, for there was a cold hauteur about him that did not permit intimacy. Shah Jahan did not write his memoirs. Nor were there any secret diarists in his reign, like Badauni in Akbar's court, to expose what official biographers papered over. Only the journals of European travellers provide the colour and spice, light and shade needed to make the image of this seemingly immaculate emperor credible.

SHAH JAHAN WAS born on the night of 15th January 1592 in Lahore to the Rajput princess Jagat Gossain, also called Jodh Bai, daughter of Uday Singh Rathor of Marwar, nicknamed Mota Raja (Fat Raja) by Akbar. On the sixth day of his birth, the child was named Khurram (Joyous) by Akbar, and was then handed over to Ruqaiya Begum, Akbar's childless wife, in whose care he grew up. When the prince was four years, four months and four days old, his *maktab* ceremony was held, as was the Mughal custom, to begin his formal education.

We know little else about the childhood of Khurram, but it seems to have been an uneventful, pampered life in the plush cocoon of the harem. When he was around seven, he was laid up with smallpox, but apparently recovered unmarked. We next find him with Akbar at the jharokha of the Agra palace at the end of Akbar's life, watching the combat between the elephants of Jahangir and Khusrav, and it was he who conveyed Akbar's admonition to his father and elder brother when they squabbled over the elephants. Khurram was Akbar's favourite grandson. Says Jahangir: "My father . . . frequently told me there was no comparison between him and my other children." The prince reciprocated his grandfather's love, and "remained in attendance on him day and night," says Jahangir. When Akbar lay dying, Khurram remained at his bedside, and not even his mother could persuade him to leave, though in the tense political situation then prevailing he was in some personal danger.

Khusrav's rebellion was the turning point in Khurram's career, and marked the beginning of his rise in Jahangir's favour—when Jahangir set out against his rebel son, it was Khurram whom he left behind in Agra as the nominal head of the regency council; later, when the prince joined his father in Kabul, it was he who first warned the emperor of Khusrav's assassination plot against him.

In the summer of 1607, when Khurram was sixteen, he was betrothed to Asaf Khan's daughter, Arjumand Banu Begum, the future Mumtaz Mahal. Khurram was thereafter treated as an adult, and was appointed as a commander of 8,000 and given an appropriate salary, instead of the daily allowance he was receiving till then. Soon after, he was formally designated as the heir-apparent, and allotted Hissar Firoza, the traditional fief of the crown prince. The seal of the emperor was then entrusted to him, with the authority to authenticate imperial decrees; he was also assigned a flag as his insignia, and granted the royal prerogatives of using a parasol and a red tent.

Khurram's engagement to Arjumand was unusually long—they were married only five years after their betrothal, on 10th May 1612, when he was twenty and she nineteen. In the intervening period, Khurram took his first wife, the daughter of a great-grandson of Shah Ismail of Persia. Later, five years after he married Arjumand, Khurram took a third wife, a grand-daughter of Abdur-Rahim, the Khan-i khanan. Somewhere along the way he seems also to have married a Rajput princess. Khurram's first child, a daughter, was born to him by his first wife; by his third wife, Khurram had a son, but the child died in infancy. Presumably some of his concubines also conceived, for Manucci reports that Khurram had several pregnancies of his women aborted. Apart from his first child, he would rear only the children of Arjumand. "Raise not issue on any other woman," Arjumand is said to have pleaded with him, "lest her children and mine should come to blows over succession."

Arjumand was a fecund woman, and she bore Khurram all the children he needed, fourteen in all, eight sons and six daughters, in the nineteen years of her life with him, averaging a child every sixteen months. She died young, only thirty-eight years old, giving birth to her fourteenth child. Half of her children survived, a good average for medieval times, four boys and three girls—Jahanara Begum, Dara

Shukoh, Shah Shuja, Raushanara Begum, Aurangzeb, Murad Bakhsh and Goharara Begum, her last child.

As the number of Khurram's children increased, so did his fortune. "Prince Sultan Coronne [is] his (Jahangir's) third son by birth but the first in favour," notes Roe. In 1615, to reward his victory over the Rana of Mewar, Jahangir raised Khurram to the rank of 15,000, which was raised again the following year to 20,000. Two years later, in 1617, after his successful campaign in the Deccan, the emperor conferred on Khurram the title Shah Jahan and accorded him the privilege of a seat in the durbar, honours which, says Inayat Khan, "no king during his own lifetime had ever bestowed on a son". Shah Jahan rode on that high wave of royal favour for about six years, till 1622, when he suddenly and unexpectedly turned rebel.

The rebellion was a mistake, but luckily not a fatal one. Shah Jahan was defeated, disarmed and packed off to a far corner of the empire, but he was still free. Jahangir did not imprison Shah Jahan, as he did Khusrav, presumably because Shah Jahan, bottled up in the Deccan, did not, as Khusrav did, pose any danger of joining up with the Persians or the Uzbegs, the peer rivals of the Mughals. Jahangir in any case could not afford to destroy Shah Jahan. His other two surviving sons were worthless, Parviz a frivolous alcoholic, Shahryar an imbecile. Shah Jahan was the only hope of the dynasty. Nor did Nur Jahan dare to destroy Shah Jahan, for it would have antagonized Asaf Khan, who was essential for her as the medium through which to exercise her power. So it was that this prince, who at the time of Jahangir's death had hardly any army with him, could boldly cut across the empire to enter Agra unopposed and claim the throne.

On 6th February 1628 Shah Jahan ascended the throne in Agra, the first monarch of the second century of the Mughal empire. The enthronement was a mere formality—he had already been proclaimed emperor in Lahore and the khutbah read in his name—but it was an essential formality, an occasion to confer honours and gifts on his supporters and other powerful amirs, and bind them to his throne. A great quantity of gold and silver was given away in charity during the accession celebrations. And to Arjumand, now titled Mumtaz Mahal, Paragon of the Palace, Shah Jahan presented 200,000 ashrafis and 600,000 rupees, and settled on her an annual allowance of one million rupees. It was a fitting inauguration for the reign of this most opulent of the Mughals.

SHAH JAHAN WAS the quintessential Great Mughal. "The King

appeared seated upon his throne, at the end of the great hall, in the most magnificent attire," reports Bernier, who saw Shah Jahan at the close of his reign. "His vest was of white and delicately flowered satin, with a silk and gold embroidery of the finest texture. The turban, of gold cloth, had an aigrette whose base was composed of diamonds of an extraordinary size and value, besides an Oriental topaz, which may be pronounced unparalleled, exhibiting a lustre like the sun. A necklace of immense pearls, suspended from his neck, reached to the stomach."

Shah Jahan had the poise to carry with authority the opulence of his dress and setting. He was of moderate stature, but powerfully built, broad-shouldered and barrel-chested, a wheat-complexioned handsome man with a sharp, chiselled nose and a tight mouth, large, heavy-lidded eyes, arched eyebrows, a broad sweep of forehead. As prince, he like his father and grandfather had sported only a moustache, but as emperor he wore a full beard, which added to the gravity of his countenance. Everything about Shah Jahan, from demeanour to dress and jewels and setting, was carefully designed to project imperial grandeur and magnificence. This was the role he had chosen for himself, to be The Great Mughal, and he worked hard at being magnificent.

Sometimes the effort showed. "I never saw so settled a countenance, nor any man keepe so constant a gravity, never smiling, or in face showing any respect or difference of men, but mingled with extreme pride and contempt of all," says Sir Thomas Roe, himself a high practitioner of starchy dignity. "Yet I found some inward trouble now and then assayle him, and a kind of brokenness and distraction in his thoughts." Roe is here writing about Shah Jahan as a young man of twenty-four, years before the failure of his rebellion and the early death of his beloved wife turned his beard gray and his mood saturnine. Whatever it was that oppressed him, Shah Jahan kept his woes to himself.

In a way, Shah Jahan was the culmination of the process of Mughal cultural mutation from Turko-Mongol rumbustiousness to Persian formalism and courtliness which began with Humayun's sojourn in Persia, in fact with the sojourn in Persia of Yunus Khan, Babur's maternal grandfather. The process quickened under the influence of the Persian wives of the emperors and the growing number of Persians in high offices in the Mughal court—Maham Begum (Humayun's mother) was Persian, and so were Hamida Banu Begum, Nur Jahan, Mumtaz Mahal and several others; and among the Persians (or men of Persian background) occupying the prime-ministerial office under the Mughals were Biram Khan, Abdur-Rahim, Itimad-ud-daula and Asaf Khan.

Persian was the language of culture of the Mughals, as well as their official language. It is significant that while Babur wrote in Turki, his mother tongue, Jahangir wrote in Persian and considered it an unusual accomplishment of his to be able to write at all in Turki. As for Shah Jahan, as a child he simply refused to learn Turki, which had come to be considered a vulgar language.

Persian courtly formalism suited Shah Jahan's temperament. He was not given to mood swings like his father, but was soft-spoken and unfailingly polite, always correct and formal in speech and manner. Self-control was everything to him. This was evident in his attitude towards wine. It was on his twenty-fourth birthday that he first tasted wine, when his father virtually forced him to have a drink. "It was only after a great deal of trouble that he could be persuaded to take a little wine," says Jahangir. Then for about six years Shah Jahan took wine occasionally, mostly red wine, but always in moderation.

"He did not drink of his own choice and inclination, but rather, at the Emperor's insistence," says Inayat Khan. "He had occasionally taken a few cups at gatherings during festivals and on cloudy days." In 1620, when he set out on his second Deccan campaign, he gave up drinking altogether, pouring his entire stock of wine into the Chambal river. There were presumably political and religious considerations involved in this act—he had just begun his succession manoeuvres—but he avoided drinking primarily because he did not want to do anything that would rupture the taut membrane of self-control encasing him.

Shah Jahan was an orthodox Muslim. But he was not an ascetic. He loved luxury nearly as much as Jahangir, and delighted in erotic pleasures, and in music and dance. Says Manucci: "Although warlike . . . he was at the same time fond of music and dancing to such a degree, more or less, as his father Jahangir. His usual diversion was to listen to various instruments, to verses and poetry; and he was very fond of musicians." Shah Jahan was himself a pleasing singer. If court historians are to be believed, his singing was so sweet that "many pure-souled Sufis and holy men with hearts withdrawn from the world . . . lost their senses in the ecstasy produced by his singing." He maintained a large troupe of singing and dancing girls called Kenchens (*kanchanas*: radiant ones) who, according to Bernier, were admitted into the seraglio during festivals, and sometimes for the whole night he "amused himself with their antics and follies", which, in Bernier's view, "transgressed the bonds of decency".

Kenchens were professional public entertainers, and the emperor consorting with them scandalized even the permissive Mughal court, especially when he took one of the girls into his harem as a concubine. But Shah Jahan, according to Manucci, justified himself saying, "Sweetmeats are good, whatever shop they come from." The emperor, says Bernier candidly, was "fond of sex". Says Manucci: "It would seem as if the only thing Shah Jahan cared for was the search for women to serve his pleasure." Not only was Shah Jahan's sexual appetite voracious, but it persisted well into his old age, and his death at the age of seventy-four was attributed by some to sexual excess. "The Great Mogoll, who seeking by artificiall meanes to stirre up lust, which was naturally decaying in him, beeing 73 years of age, wrought his owne death," says Peter Mundy, a seventeenth century European traveller in India.

SHAH JAHAN'S PROMISCUITY was a late development. As long as Mumtaz was alive he was totally devoted to her, neglecting even his other wives, who "enjoyed nothing more than the title of wifeship," according to Aminai Qazvini, one of Shah Jahan's official chroniclers. "The intimacy, deep affection, attention and favour which His Majesty had for the Lady, he did not have for any other. And always that Lady of the Age was his intimate companion, colleague, and close confidante in distress and comfort, joy and grief, on journeys or in residence." Says Inayat Khan: "He did not feel towards the others one-thousandth part of the affection that he did for Her late Majesty, and he never allowed . . . (her) to be separated from him whether at home or abroad." Confirms Peter Mundy: "The Kinge . . . thought in her life tyme to use noe other women."

Mumtaz was not just a beautiful woman with whom Shah Jahan was in love; she was his helpmate, the anchor on which he moored himself. He was as dependent on Mumtaz as Jahangir was on Nur Jahan. But unlike Jahangir, who did not care for convention and was not bothered about who knew of his dependence, Shah Jahan was careful about appearances. Still, it was widely known that he consulted her on all important state matters, and it was she who placed the royal seal on his firmans, which gave her a chance to examine the final drafts of documents. Unfortunately, she died within four years of his accession; had she lived longer, her influence and authority would undoubtedly have grown and would probably have been exercised more openly.

Mumtaz died at Burhanpur on 17th June 1631, a painful death, after a thirty-hour labour, giving birth to her fourteenth child, Goharara Begum. Shah Jahan was devastated by her death. "For a whole week after this distressing occurrence, His Majesty from excess of grief did not appear in public nor transact any affairs of state," writes Inayat Khan. "After this calamity, he refrained from the practice of listening to music, singing, and wearing fine linen. From constant weeping he was forced to use spectacles; and his august beard and moustache, which had only a few white hairs in them before, became in a few days from intense sorrow more than one-third white." He was even inclined to abdicate, but restrained himself because he considered kingship to be a sacred charge which could not be relinquished because of personal tragedies. "Empire has no sweetness, life itself has no relish left for me now," he lamented. There was no solace for him in the harem either. "Nobody's face can delight me now," he grieved.

Mumtaz was first buried in a garden on the banks of the river Tapi (Tapti) in Burhanpur. Six months later, her body, escorted by Prince Shuja, was taken to Agra, and on 8th January 1632 reburied on the banks of the Yamuna, where her great mausoleum, Taj Mahal, was raised. Shah Jahan named the tomb Rauza-i-munavvara, The Illumined Tomb, but it came to be commonly called Taj Mahal, a corruption of Mumtaz Mahal.

WHEN SHAH JAHAN came out of mourning, he loosened the bonds of self-control which had bound him to virtual monogamy till then. Though he did not marry again, nor apparently turn to his other wives, he now acquired several concubines, and entered into numerous illicit liaisons, even committing, according to bazaar gossip, adultery with married women, perhaps even incest.

The stories about Shah Jahan's dalliances mainly come from Manucci and Bernier. Their accounts cannot be taken entirely at face value—they both arrived at the Mughal court only at the very end of Shah Jahan's reign, and in any case they had no direct access to information on what went on in the palace, but had to depend on court and bazaar gossip. Nevertheless, their reports cannot be dismissed altogether, for they have been found otherwise generally credible. At the least they establish that there was gossip in court circles on these matters, smoke that indicates fire somewhere. The silence of the contemporary Mughal chroniclers, all royal officers, disproves nothing.

The Meena Bazaar, the week-long annual amusement fair held in the fort exclusively for women during the spring festival, in which the wives and daughters of amirs participated, was when Shah Jahan is said to have cast about for paramours. During the fair "no one was allowed to enter [the fort] except women," says Manucci. "In those eight days, the king visited the stalls twice every day, seated on a small throne carried by several Tartar women, surrounded by several matrons, who walked with their sticks of enamelled gold in their hands, and many eunuchs . . . there were also a set of women musicians."

"Shah Jahan moves past with his attention fixed, and seeing any seller that attracted his fancy, he goes up to the stall, and making a polite speech, selects some of the things, and orders whatever she asks for them to be paid to her," continues Manucci. "Then the king gives an agreed-on signal, and having passed on, the matrons, well-versed in these matters, take care that they get her; and in due time, she is produced in the royal presence. Many of them come out of the palace very rich and satisfied, while others continue to dwell there with the dignity of concubines."

Manucci as well as Bernier maintain that Shah Jahan had adulterous liaisons with married women, wives of amirs, and that the begums were often taunted by vagabonds in the bazaar, who would call out, "O breakfast of Shah Jahan! Remember us!" or "O luncheon of Shah Jahan! Succour us!" Bernier states that Jahanara, Shah Jahan's favourite daughter, connived with him in these affairs, procuring for him, according to Manucci, even the wife of her uncle, Shayista Khan. "The procuress in this affair was [Jahanara] . . . who, in compliance to her father, invited the said woman to a feast, at the end of which Shah Jahan violated her," says Manucci.

Whatever the truth of the particular stories, Shah Jahan's post-Mumtaz promiscuity seems to be a fact. But even in his amours Shah Jahan was careful not to compromise himself unduly, choosing his mistresses with care. Says Manucci: "Although Shah Jahan delighted in well-made women, he also required them to have good sense . . . The lasciviousness of Shah Jahan did not interfere with his care to govern his kingdom most perfectly."

BY FAR THE MOST outrageous scandal about Shah Jahan was his rumoured incestuous relationship with his prodigiously talented daughter Jahanara, which is mentioned by Bernier but denied by Manucci. On the death of Mumtaz Mahal, Jahanara, though only seventeen then, took over the responsibility of caring for her father. Shah Jahan bestowed on her half of Mumtaz's movable property worth ten million rupees, and only the remainder on her six other children. At the same time, Jahanara's annual stipend was raised from 600,000 rupees to one million. The royal seal, which used to in the custody of Mumtaz, was entrusted to her, and, says Inayat Khan, "all the duties appertaining to Her late Majesty were also now entrusted by His Majesty to Her Highness Jahanara Begum."

Jahanara was, says Bernier, "very handsome, of lively parts, and passionately beloved by her father . . . Chah-Jehan reposed unbounded confidence in this his favourite child; she watched over his safety, and was so cautiously observant, that no dish was permitted to appear upon the royal table which had not been prepared under her superintendence." Confirms Manucci: "Her father loved [her] to an extraordinary degree, as most lovely, discreet, loving, generous, open-minded, and charitable. She was loved by all, and lived in a state of magnificence."

Was there an incestuous relationship between Shah Jahan and Jahanara? We will never know. All deep affections, even between a parent and child, have a sensuous vein, and given Shah Jahan's ardour, and Jahanara's frustrations of maidenhood in the lascivious ambience of the seraglio, it was only natural that there should be titillating rumours about them. Bernier, generally a far more discerning reporter than Manucci, not only mentions incest but goes on to claim that some courtiers justified it, saying that "it would have been unjust to deny the King the privilege of gathering fruit from the tree he had himself planted."

Manucci, claiming insider information—"I was deep in the confidence of the principal ladies and eunuchs in her (Jahanara's) service," he says—dismisses Bernier's story as mere gossip. He however goes on to claim, as does Bernier, that Jahanara had lovers smuggled into her residence, and that she used to indulge in Bacchanalian orgies. "The lady's drinking was at night, when various delightful pranks, music, dancing, and acting were going on around her," says Manucci. "Things arrived at such a pass that sometimes she was unable to stand, and they had to carry her to bed." But whatever her secret vices, Jahanara was a beautiful, erudite, cultured woman of a benevolent disposition, inclined to Sufism, and was highly respected in Mughal society.

Shah Jahan very nearly lost her once in a fire accident in the palace. The mishap occurred on 4th April 1644, two days after Jahanara's thirty-first birthday. "After bidding His Majesty good night, that sum of modesty was proceeding to her own sleeping apartment when the border of her chaste garment brushed against a lamp left burning on the floor in the middle of the hall," reports Inayat Khan. "As the dresses worn by the ladies of the palace are made of the most delicate fabrics and perfumed with fragrant oils, her garment caught fire and was instantly enveloped in flames. Four of her private attendants were at hand, and they immediately tried to extinguish the fire; yet as it spread itself over their garments as well, their efforts proved unavailing. As it all happened so quickly, before the alarm could be given and water procured, the back and hands and both side of the body of that mine of excellence were dreadfully burned."

The tragedy, thirteen years after the untimely death of Mumtaz Mahal, shattered Shah Jahan. "As His Majesty's affection for Her Royal Highness exceeded all that he felt towards his other children, this lamentable accident cast a deep gloom over his spirits; so much so that contrary to his habitual practice, he did not stir out of the seraglio apartment all the next day," writes Inayat Khan. Shah Jahan summoned the best surgeons and physicians—Hindu, Muslim and European—to treat Jahanara. "From his earnest attachment to her, he took upon himself the task of administering her medicine and diet, and applying and removing her bandages with his own hand," continues Inayat Khan. "In short, owing to His Majesty being constantly occupied in tending the invalid, he repaired to public audiences and private conferences very late and quitted them early."

On the twentieth day of her injury, a physician just then arrived from Persia began to treat her, and her condition improved steadily for about four months. Then for the next few months there was no further progress. At this point, says Inayat Khan, "one of the royal pages, named Arif Chela, composed a dressing which after two months finally caused the wounds to close, and thereafter began to heal fairly quickly." To facilitate her recovery, a change of residence was recommended, so Jahanara moved to Dara's house, and Shah Jahan himself moved in there. Jahanara's recovery was celebrated with a week-long festivity.

Unfortunately, her wounds opened again after a while, when the court was on the way to Ajmer, but a mendicant called Hamun applied a plaster which healed her completely in three weeks. "In gratitude to the indigent Hamun, His Majesty ordered him to be weighed against gold—a man who had always been in want even of his evening meal— and bestowed on him a vast sum of money, with a robe of honor, a horse, and a female elephant," records Inayat Khan. "A grant in perpetuity of a village in his native place was also made to him." By March 1645, eleven months after the fire accident, Jahanara recovered fully.

SHAH JAHAN'S TENDER nursing of Jahanara and his earlier inconsolable grief over the death of Mumtaz Mahal, reveal a surprising sentimentality and emotional vulnerability in this seemingly frosty emperor. He would not, however, allow his frailties to get the better of him, but contained himself tightly through a rigorous self-discipline that froze blood into ice. Cold, hard perfection was Shah Jahan's ideal, and it is cold, hard perfection that we see in his cultural expressions, especially in the Taj. Only Shah Jahan could have built the Taj. The qualities of the Taj—opulent and startlingly beautiful, and yet also austere, perfect in symmetry and balance, meticulous and painstaking in craftsmanship—are all qualities which Shah Jahan cherished in his own life.

Shah Jahan had shown a talent for architectural design quite early in his life—at the age of fifteen he had elegantly remodelled the quarters allotted to him in Kabul, to the pleasant surprise of Jahangir, no mean aesthete himself. In time, Shah Jahan honed his talent to perfection, achieving great sophistication in architectural expression, so that, as his court historian Abdul Hamid Lahori claims, "for the majority of buildings he (the emperor) himself draws the plans." Shah Jahan had in his service many architects and designers, and several of them—including perhaps the Venetian jeweller Geronimo Verroneo, to whom Manrique preposterously attributes the design of the Taj—no doubt contributed ideas for the Taj, but the Taj matches the personality of Shah Jahan so perfectly that it is inconceivable that anyone other than the emperor himself could have been responsible for its design concept.

The site of the Taj was originally the residence of Raja Man Singh, and was acquired by Shah Jahan from his grandson, Raja Jai Singh. Construction began in 1632, and was completed in about sixteen years, though work around the complex went on for some more years. Cost was no consideration as Shah Jahan pursued perfection. Peter Mundy, who visited the site when the building was in its early stage, reports that "gold and silver [were] esteemed common metall, and Marble but as ordinary stone." An endowment of thirty hamlets yielding 200,000 rupees annually was established for the maintenance of the mausoleum and its garden.

It was at one time believed that Shah Jahan had planned for himself a replica of the Taj in black marble across the Yamuna, the two to be connected by a bridge; Tavernier specifically mentions that its construction was actually begun by Shah Jahan but had to be abandoned because of the civil war between his sons. The yin-yang harmony of the twin Taj concept is fascinating, but it is only a traveller's tale. There is no material evidence of any such construction, nor is there any reference to it in any other source. Shah Jahan would be buried beside his wife in the Taj.

The Taj Mahal overshadows everything else in Mughal architecture, but Shah Jahan had a number of other noble structures to his credit: the palace complex and the Jama Masjid in Delhi, the Pearl mosque in Agra, another mosque in Tatta in Sind, and the Shalimar Bagh gardens in Lahore. He also built extensively in Agra, and to a lesser extent in Lahore. Unfortunately, in these cities he pulled down many of Akbar's red sandstone buildings to make room for his white marble structures— and several of Shah Jahan's own buildings in Delhi were demolished by the British in the aftermath of the Sepoy Mutiny of 1857.

Next only to the Taj, Shah Jahan's most renowned building is the white marble palace complex he built in Delhi (Shahjahanabad), where, on the Diwan-i-Khas, the hall of private audience, is inscribed,

> *Agar firdaus bar ru-yi zamin ast*
> *Hamin ast, u hamin ast u hamin ast!*

> (*If there be a paradise on earth,*
> *It's this, it's this, it's this!*)

This was indeed what it was in the seventeenth-century world. It was to be expected that Shah Jahan would build a capital city of his own; it was common, indeed obligatory, for an emperor to found his own city, to perpetuate his memory. The site of the ruined city of Tughlaqabad, to the north of the then existing Delhi, was chosen for Shahjahanabad "after a long search", says Inayat Khan. The foundation of the new citadel was laid on 29th April 1639, "at the exact moment appointed by astrologers". Carts to transport materials for the construction were commandeered in such large numbers that trade was disrupted in the Delhi-Agra region for quite a while, and English factors there were not able to move their goods to ports. And "from throughout the imperial dominions, wherever artificers could be found, whether plain stone-cutters, ornamental sculptors, masons, or carpenters, by the mandate worthy of implicit obedience, they were all collected together," reports Inayat Khan, "and multitudes of common labourers were employed in the work." Still, despite all the massive endeavour, it took nine years and some months to complete the complex. The cost: 6.5 million rupees, including the cost of fortifications.

Shah Jahan held a grand, ten-day long celebration to inaugurate Shahjahanabad. An immense gold embroidered velvet canopy, sixty-four metres by forty-one metres, ordered from Gujarat at a cost of 100,000 rupees, was put up in the courtyard of the Diwan-i-am, the durbar hall, for the occasion. The canopy, according to Inayat Khan, could accommodate 10,000 men, and it took 3000 labourers one month to erect it, using "the most powerful tackle and machinery". From Agra, Shah Jahan travelled by the Yamuna in the royal barge to his new fort, and he entered it on 18th April 1648, to mount, at the time specified by astrologers as auspicious, the "Jewelled Throne in the Hall of Public Audience," says Inayat Khan.

The jewelled throne that Inayat Khan refers to is the fabulous Peacock Throne that Shah Jahan had commissioned on his accession, to display the vast collection of gems accumulated during preceding reigns. The Mughals were great connoisseurs of gems. Akbar was an avid collector, and the Mughal gem collection was largely accumulated by him. Jahangir, according to Terry, was an authority on gems, and in Shah Jahan we have the ultimate cognoscente, who, says Bernier, "understood better than any man the value of every kind of precious stone".

The Peacock Throne was a unique achievement of the jeweller's art. "It is the richest and most superb throne which has ever been seen in the world," says Tavernier. "It was . . . ordered that, in addition to the jewels in the imperial jewel-house, rubies, garnets, diamonds, rich pearls and emeralds, to the value of 200 lakhs (twenty million) of rupees should be brought for the inspection of the Emperor, and that they, with some exquisite jewels of great weight, exceeding 50,000 *mishals*, and worth eighty-six lakhs (8.6 million) of rupees, having been carefully selected, should be handed over to Be-badal Khan, the superintendent of the goldsmith's department," says Lahori. "There was also to be given to him one lakh (100,000) *tolas* of pure gold, equal to 250,000 *mishals* in weight and fourteen lakhs (1.4 million) of rupees in value."

"The throne," continues Lahori, "was to be three *gaz* (about 2.5 metres) in length, two and a half (about two metres) in breadth, and five (about four metres) in height, and was to be set with the above mentioned jewels. The outside of the canopy was to be of enamel work with occasional gems, the inside was to be thickly set with rubies, garnets, and other jewels, and it was to be supported by twelve emerald columns. On the top of each pillar there were to be two peacocks thick set with gems, and between each two peacocks a tree set with rubies and diamonds, emeralds and pearls. The ascent was to consist of three steps set with jewels of fine water. This throne was completed in the course of seven years at a cost of 100 lakhs (ten million) of rupees. Of the eleven jewelled recesses (*takhta*) formed around it for cushions, the middle one, intended for the seat of the Emperor, cost ten lakhs (one million) of rupees. Among the jewels set

311

in this recess was a ruby worth a lakh of rupees, which Shah Abbas, the king of Iran, had presented to the late Emperor Jahangir."

The ten million rupees that Lahori mentions as the cost of the Peacock Throne was only the cost of materials used in it. Bernier estimates the total cost of the Peacock Throne at thirty or forty million rupees; Tavernier, who examined it with a jeweller's eye and describes the gems used on it with precision, states, without committing himself, that he was told that the throne cost 107 million rupees. Shah Jahan sat on the Peacock Throne for the first time in 1634, the eighth year of his reign, during the celebration of the vernal equinox that year in Agra; later the throne was taken to Delhi, when the emperor shifted the capital to Shahjahanabad.

SHAH JAHAN WAS probably the wealthiest man in the world in his time. "In order to preserve with great security the immense wealth, which tributes and extortions augment every year, he (Shah Jahan) caused to be constructed, under his palace of Dely, two deep caves, supported by vast marble pillars," says Bernier. "Piles of gold were stored in one, and of silver in the other, and to render more difficult any attempt to carry away his treasure, he caused, of both metals, pieces to be made of so prodigious a size as to render them useless for the purposes of commerce."

Shah Jahan's annual revenue in 1647, according to the figures given by Lahori, was 220 million rupees, of which his privy purse (the income from crown lands) was thirty million rupees. According to Jadunath Sarkar, Shah Jahan had jewellery worth fifty million rupees; one of his rosaries, with five rubies and thirty pearls, was valued at 800,000 rupees, and the aigrette he wore on his turban on the anniversary of his coronation at 1.24 million rupees. Sarkar further reckons that Shah Jahan gave away ninety-five million rupees in gifts in the first twenty years of his reign.

There was of course a price to be paid for such extravagance. And that price was paid by the common people, whose poverty and wretchedness contrasts dismally with the opulence of the Mughal ruling class. There was a substantial increase in the revenue of the empire under Shah Jahan, but this was achieved by a tighter squeezing of the people than through economic progress. States courtier historian Rai Bhara Mal: "The pargana, the income of which was three lakhs (300,000) of rupees in the reign of Akbar . . . yielded, in this happy reign, a revenue of ten lakhs (one million)!" But this three-fold increase in revenue was nullified by a four-fold increase in expenditure. "The expenditure of former reigns, in comparison with that of the one in question, was not even in the proportion of one to four," says Bhara Mal.

Similar incongruities were evident in almost every facet of Mughal life. The high culture of the elite, for instance, contrasted sharply with the squalid, primitive life of the common people. Even the seeming military might of Shah Jahan was more flab than muscle, as his Balkh and Kandahar fiascoes revealed. Similarly, the general efficiency of Mughal administration slumped sharply under Shah Jahan, even as the bureaucracy proliferated monstrously.

The quality of justice too suffered. This is evident in what can be read between the lines of the panegyrics of the Mughal chroniclers. "Notwithstanding the great area of this country, plaints were so few that only one day in the week, Wednesday, was fixed upon for the administration of justice," writes Bhara Mal, "and it was rarely even then that twenty plaintiffs could be found to prefer suits." Unable to keep up the show of administering justice, Shah Jahan had to chide his officials that "although so many confidential persons had been appointed to invite plaintiffs . . . yet even the small number of twenty plaintiffs could be very seldom brought into Court."

Why were the plaintiffs so few? "Owing to the great solicitude evinced by the king towards the promotion of the national weal and the general tranquillity . . . the people were restrained from committing offences against one another and breaking the public peace," rationalizes Bhara Mal. Moreover, continues the panegyrist, the administration of justice at the lower levels was so efficient under Shah Jahan that few appeals needed to be preferred to the emperor. Bhara Mal's idyllic picture of a peaceable and contented people does not match the known facts of life in India under Shah Jahan. Corruption had always been rampant in the Mughal judicial system, and now the channel of appeal to the emperor was also blocked, as Shah Jahan haughtily distanced himself more and more from the people.

Shah Jahan's administrative difficulties were compounded by the drying up of the flow of migrant talent into India, especially from Persia, because of his wars with Persians and Uzbegs. At the same time, native talent, which had flowered under Akbar—stimulated by his policy of cultural and racial synthesis, and the opening up of vast opportunities for talent in his fast expanding and dynamic empire— now began to wither, because of Shah Jahan's gradual abandonment of Akbar's policies and the slackening of the pace of growth of the empire.

METHODICAL AND EARNEST by nature, Shah Jahan found comfort

313

and strength in the security that orthodoxy provided. His religious policy was entirely conventional. Muslim theocratic tradition required that though non-Muslims might be permitted to practice their religion in an Islamic state, they should not be allowed to build new temples or repair the old ones. Thus in January 1633 "His Majesty, the defender of the faith, gave orders that . . . throughout all his dominions in every place all temples that had been begun should be cast down . . . ," reports Lahori. "Seventy-six temples had been destroyed in the district of Benares." Similarly, Shah Jahan resumed the land and building given to the Jesuits for their church in Agra, and several churches in other parts of the empire were demolished.

Again, in conformity with Islamic convention, Shah Jahan prohibited Muslims from changing religion, but encouraged conversions to Islam by offering stipends and other favours to converts. The zemindar of Jogu and 5000 of his men were thus induced to become Muslims; in Kashmir, where Muslims and Hindus often intermarried, Shah Jahan decreed that if a Hindu had a Muslim wife, he could keep her only if he became a Muslim; otherwise he was to be fined and his wife separated. Captured enemies—Portuguese from Hugli (Hooghly), Rajputs from Bundelkhand—were often given the option of buying their life and liberty through conversion. In the same spirit, Shah Jahan directed that Hindus should keep to their own style of dress, tying their tunics on the left, unlike Muslims, who tied it on the right. Further, Hindus were asked to discontinue practices which were offensive to Islam, such as the sale of alcohol, the cremation of the dead or the performance of sati near a Muslim cemetery.

Shah Jahan himself was strict in conforming to an orthodox Muslim lifestyle. He grew a beard, abjured wine, forbade amirs from wearing miniature portraits of the emperor on their turbans—a custom which Akbar had introduced and had become widespread under Jahangir— and modified the manner of obeisance in the Mughal court to conform to Islamic customs. "The first order which was issued . . . at the court of this Defender of the Faith and King of Islam, was the prohibition of prostration (sijda) by those who approached the threshold of the Caliphate," writes Inayat Khan. In its place, after some experimentation, Shah Jahan ordered that "the usual mode of salutation by bowing and touching the head should be restored, with the difference that instead of doing so only once as before, the act should be performed three . . . times," says Bhara Mal. The Illahi Era of Akbar was replaced with the conventional calendar.

Shah Jahan mellowed somewhat in the final years of his reign, probably under the growing influence of Dara; he even presented a stone railing to the great temple built in Mathura by Bir Singh, the Bundela chief, during the reign of Jahangir. And, despite his great fondness for Persian cultural forms, Shah Jahan enjoyed Hindi music and poetry, and they flourished under his patronage. Hindu chieftains of course continued to serve the emperor in top positions, as indeed they would even under Aurangzeb.

But undeniably the elan of the Mughal empire, so striking under Akbar, was missing in the reign of Shah Jahan. In every respect, when the Mughal empire was apparently at its most brilliant, the light within was beginning to fade.

Pyrrhic Victories

AFTER THE RELATIVE peace of Jahangir's reign, the tempo of military action picked up again under Shah Jahan, with armies ranging over the length and breadth of the subcontinent, conquering new territories or suppressing rebellions. But Shah Jahan, unlike his predecessors, did not, as emperor, ever personally lead the army into battle, though he usually stayed close to the theatre of war and kept an eye on the action.

Shah Jahan's first major military action, soon after his accession, was against Jujhar Singh, the rebellious successor of Bir Singh Bundela, the assassin of Abul Fazl. The rebel was quickly brought to submission, but he remained truculent, so Shah Jahan had to send yet another army against him, this time under Prince Aurangzeb. The second Bundela campaign, in 1635, was in some ways a portent of the future. It was in this, his very first military assignment, that Aurangzeb, seventeen, revealed the grim resoluteness that would set him apart as a man of destiny. The campaign also marked the beginning of Shah Jahan's deliberate abandonment of Akbar's tolerant religious policy. At the conclusion of the offensive Shah Jahan joined Aurangzeb at Orchha, the Bundela capital on the banks of the Betwa River, and there demolished the great temple built by Bir Sigh and erected a mosque in its place. The captured members of Jujhar's family were taken to Agra, where the women were consigned to the harem and the young princes ordered to be brought up as Muslims. The adult members of the clan were offered the choice of death or conversion to Islam, but they, "from their innate vileness . . . spurned the offer and met their fate," says Inayat Khan. Jujhar, who had fled into the deep forest, was killed by wild Gond tribesmen.

Far more serious than the Bundela uprising was the rebellion of Khan Jahan Lodi, which, as it unfurled, engulfed the whole of the Deccan in war. Khan Jahan, the Mughal governor of Malwa and a descendent of the old Afghan dynasty of Delhi, was a favourite of Jahangir. Shah Jahan suspected him to be a Nur Jahan loyalist and was wary of him. His fears were confirmed when the Khan, on a plea of illness, did not go to Agra to pay his respects to the emperor on his accession, a serious discourtesy. Further, it was suspected that he, bribed by Ahmadnagar, had compromised Mughal interests in the Deccan.

Recalled to the court, Khan Jahan remained, says Lahori, "moody and discontented" in Agra for several months, but finally decided to stake his fortune on his sword rather than on royal whim, and one night in October 1629 took the road to the Deccan at the head of a 2000-strong Afghan contingent. Shah Jahan, who had been warned of the possible flight, immediately sent a royal force in pursuit, which intercepted the rebels at the Chambal River, about fifty-six kilometres south of Agra. But Khan Jahan and a few of his men managed to cut their way through, and, passing through Bundelkhand and Gondwana, eventually escaped into Ahmadnagar.

Ahmadnagar, which had been a victim of Mughal inroads since the time of Akbar, welcomed Khan Jahan as an ally. This conjunction turned the rebellion into an inter-state conflict. Shah Jahan then converted the problem into opportunity and launched a massive invasion of the Deccan, not just to subdue the rebel but to subjugate the Deccan sultanates: Ahmadnagar, Bijapur and Golconda.

The conquest of the Deccan proved to be a far more arduous task for the Mughals than the conquest of Hindustan; not even Akbar was entirely successful in his southern campaigns. For the Mughals, the Deccan wars were like fighting a triple-headed, twenty-four-armed octopus, of which they could never be sure which arm was of the ally and which of the adversary, which the subdued arm and which the battling one. Adding to the confusion were the Marathas, not yet a unified power, but the more dangerous for that reason, unpredictable roving bands of soldiers who kept darting in to tear at one party, then another, always there hovering in the background.

SHAH JAHAN ARRIVED in Malwa in December 1629 to oversee the operations against Khan Jahan Lodi. His presence was essential to give cohesion to the campaign, for, as Inayat Khan says, "discord and dissension existed among the chiefs and leaders of the army to such an extent, that they constantly sought to undermine each other's enterprise." Even with Shah Jahan around, it took the Mughals over a year of hard campaigning to achieve even their immediate objective of liquidating Khan Jahan. By end of 1630 Ahmadnagar, ravaged by famine and war, was forced to abandon the Khan and sue for peace. Khan Jahan attempted to escape into Punjab, but was intercepted and killed by the Mughals.

Still the Deccan war dragged on, with Bijapur, and to some extent

Golconda, getting entangled in it. At one point the Mughals did seem to be on the verge of final victory, having subdued Ahmadnagar and broken the resistance of Bijapur. Then suddenly the wind changed, as it would time and again in the Deccan wars. The Bijapuris, just as they were about to submit, realized that the Mughals had virtually run out of provisions, so they scuttled the peace negotiations, attacked the Mughals and chased them out of the kingdom.

Meanwhile Shah Jahan, troubled by a severe famine in the region, and broken by the death of Mumtaz Mahal, became disgusted with the Deccan, and left for Agra in December 1631, after a two-year stay in Burhanpur, leaving it to his generals to continue the campaign. The war went on along its tortuous course for another year and a half, till June 1633, when Mahabat Khan, who had taken over the Deccan command, stormed Daulatabad, the stronghold of Ahmadnagar, and captured Husain Shah, the boy king. And with that ended the nearly one-and-a-half-century long history of the Nizam Shahi dynasty. Husain Shah would spend the rest of his life in Gwalior, the prison for fallen royalty.

But there was now a fresh complication. Shahji Bhonsle, a prominent Maratha chieftain who had initially joined the Mughals against Ahmadnagar, now switched sides and set up a descendant of the Nizam Shahi dynasty as a figurehead king to oppose the Mughals. He had to be put down. And Bijapur still remained defiant. The Deccan wars would, it seemed, never cease. Mahabat Khan cracked under the pressure. Driven to distraction by chronic fistula and the frustrations of the interminable Deccan toil, the great general died in October 1634, a crushed and pathetic figure.

It then became imperative for Shah Jahan to return to the Deccan, to restore Mughal prestige. On the emperor's arrival in Daulatabad in February 1636, Golconda tamely capitulated and agreed to pay an annual tribute of 600,000 rupees. Shah Jahan then turned to Bijapur, and in a sharp, well-managed campaign lasting barely four months, he compelled Adil Shah, the Sultan of Bijapur, to sue for peace. By the terms of the treaty of May 1636, the sultan acknowledged Shah Jahan's overlordship and agreed to pay him an annual tribute of two million rupees; in return he was allowed to take over fifty parganas of the now extinct Ahmadnagar state. Bijapur also agreed to respect the territorial integrity of Golconda and cooperate with the Mughals in suppressing Shahji.

Shah Jahan confirmed the terms of the agreement in a letter authenticated by the vermilion imprint of his palm; later, the treaty was engraved on a gold plate and sent to Bijapur. In a while Shahji too submitted to the Mughals. He handed over all his strongholds and surrendered the Nizam Shahi pretender he was propping up, and then entered the service of Bijapur, which suited the emperor as well as the sultan since they could keep an eye on the ambitious Maratha.

THE PEACE ACCORD of 1636 endured for twenty years, and was beneficial to the Mughals as well as to the Deccan sultanates. Bijapur and Golconda took advantage of the security of their northern frontiers to expand southward into the Carnatic. The Mughal gain was that the settlement left them in possession of four Deccani provinces—Khandesh, Berar, Telingana and Daulatabad—yielding, according the Lahori, a revenue of fifty million rupees. Besides, the emperor was acknowledged by the sultans as their overlord.

With the Deccan affairs settled, Shah Jahan returned to Agra in July 1636, leaving eighteen-year-old Aurangzeb in charge of the region. Two decades would pass before he would turn to the Deccan again. In the intervening period he was primarily engaged with the north-west, though there were also a number of minor military campaigns elsewhere in the north during this time and earlier—the subjugation of the Mongoloid tribes along the north-eastern frontier of Assam; the annexation of Baglan and Garhwal; action in Chitor (to destroy new fortifications made in contravention of treaty) and Hugli (to punish defiant Portuguese), campaigns in Daman and Diu, Kangra, Little Tibet (Baltistan), Bundelkhand, Bihar, Malwa, and so on.

The most important of these minor campaigns, from the historical though not the military point of view, was the action against the Portuguese in Hugli, which was the first notable clash between Europeans and a major Indian power. The Portuguese had, since their arrival in India at the close of the fifteenth century, acquired a few tiny footholds along India's shores, primarily fortified trading posts which also served as Christian missionary centres. The main Portuguese naval base in India, in Goa, was well outside the Mughal empire, as were most of their trading posts, but they had a few settlements within the empire too, in outlying provinces like Gujarat and Bengal. The Portuguese of course ruled the Indian seas, but on land they posed no threat to any Indian state, let alone to the Mughal empire. Yet, because of their naval strength, they were at times tempted to defy local authority. This was what happened in Bengal.

Apart from Gujarat, Bengal was the major centre of Portuguese activity in the Mughal empire. In the mid-sixteenth century, around the time the Mughals were consolidating their power in Hindustan, the

Portuguese had set up a trade outpost at Hugli, up the river from modern Calcutta. As the settlement grew, a number of irritants developed between the Portuguese and the local Mughal authorities, such as the Portuguese levying tolls on ships that sailed past Hugli (thus choking the trade of the Mughal port of Satgaon further up the river) and conniving with—and sometimes participating in—the piracy and vicious slave trade carried on by pirates based in Chittagong. Jahangir ignored these incidents in a far corner of his empire, but Shah Jahan decided on action.

Shah Jahan had a personal grudge against the Portuguese in Bengal—they had aided the royal forces during his rebellion against Jahangir, had seized some of his boats and carried away a couple of his slave girls. Later, when he became the emperor, the Portuguese had omitted to send him the customary greetings and presents and make amends. So when Shah Jahan sent Kasim Khan as the governor of Bengal, he "impressed upon him the duty of overthrowing these mischievous people," says Lahori.

Matters came to a head when the Portuguese brashly raided a village close to Dacca, the Mughal provincial capital, and even molested a Mughal lady of noble lineage. That galvanized Kasim Khan into action, especially as a renegade Portuguese merchant named Alfonso had assured him that there was rich booty to be bagged in Hugli. In the summer of 1632 a small Mughal contingent—1400 horse, ninety elephants, 600 boats, and the usual rabble of infantry—appeared before Hugli, and settled down to besiege the town.

The siege was desultory and went on for three months, with negotiations and clashes alternating. In the end the Mughals stormed the town, killing thousands, though many of the townspeople managed to escape in boats in a dramatic river action. A few hundred Portuguese, mostly women and children, were captured, and were sent to Agra. Shah Jahan, according to Lahori, "ordered that the principles of the Muhammadan religion should be explained to them, and that they should be called upon to adopt it. A few appreciated the honour offered to them and embraced the faith . . . But the majority in perversity and willfulness rejected the proposal." The defiant ones were given to amirs for confinement, and many of them, says Lahori, "passed from prison to hell".

THE HUGLI ACTION was a minor provincial incident. The prestige of the empire was not at stake in it. But Kandahar was quite another matter. Shah Jahan had, soon after his accession, resumed diplomatic relations with Persia, which Jahangir had broken off in his pique over the loss of Kandahar. He sent his first ambassador to Persia in 1629, to condole the death of Shah Abbas, and followed it with other embassies to announce his various victories. The Shah (Shah Abbas II, successor of Shah Abbas) reciprocated these fraternal gestures. But the issue of Kandahar continued to smoulder behind the silken veil of cordiality woven by the ambassadors.

The loss of Kandahar was on Shah Jahan's conscience, for it was his rebellion that had aborted Jahangir's plan to recover the town. Luckily, in 1638 he was able to seize Kandahar in very much the same manner in which Akbar had taken it forty-three years earlier, without waging war, by luring Ali Mardan Khan, the Persian governor of Kandahar who had fallen out with the Shah, to surrender the fort—for a price, of course. Shah Jahan lavishly rewarded Ali Mardan with cash and presents and appointed him as the governor of Kashmir, to which Punjab was later added.

It was then the turn of the Persians to strike back. The Shah however made no immediate move, for he was beset with rebellions at home and was under pressure from the Turks on his western frontier. He would turn to Kandahar later, in his own time.

In the fall of Kandahar Shah Jahan saw another door of opportunity open: the conquest of Samarkand, Babur's magnificent obsession. Shah Jahan had no desire for Fergana, Babur's homeland. It was too far away, too obscure. Samarkand was nearer, a worthy and feasible objective, especially as the Uzbegs of Central Asia, riven by internal dissensions, were defenceless, and the Shah of Persia, who was himself in conflict with the Uzbegs, could be expected at least to remain neutral if the Mughals invaded Samarkand.

Still, it took Shah Jahan eight years after the fall of Kandahar to make a serious move in Central Asia. His opportunity came in 1646, when a major power struggle broke out among the Uzbegs. Boldly intervening, Shah Jahan sent prince Murad, twenty-two, and Ali Mardan Khan into the Uzbeg lands with an army of 50,000 horse and several thousand musketeers, artillerymen and rocketeers. The king of Balkh was helpless against such an overwhelming force—his regular army numbered no more than 3000, and his revenue was a meagre 2.5 million rupees a year, about the same as the stipend of a middle-rung Mughal amir—so he fled to Persia for refuge on the approach of the Mughal army. Murad occupied the city of Balkh without opposition, and after a brief halt there, stormed on to take Termez on the banks of the Amu Darya (Oxus) river. Some 250 kilometres due north of Termez lay the fabled but now decrepit city of Samarkand, less than two week's march away. But Murad refused to proceed beyond Termez. This was Babur's home turf, where he had often trudged through deep snow in the dead of winter to seek an elusive fortune. But Murad belonged to another time, another lifestyle. Though an intrepid soldier, he loved ease and luxury, and did not want to waste his youth in remote, frigid highlands, fighting obscure battles. Shah Jahan tried to spur Murad on by offering him the prestigious governorship of Samarkand, but Murad was not tempted. Instead, he abruptly relinquished his command without royal permission and returned to Lahore. Furious, Shah Jahan stripped him of his rank and forbade him from entering the court.

The Mughals were out of their element in Central Asia. They were continually tormented by the Uzbegs and wild Turkoman tribes, who forever hovered around them, fleeing when challenged, but returning to take advantage of any neglect or weakness in their prey. They kept the Mughal army ever on its toes, ever on the move. Mughal soldiers hated Central Asia, and longed to return to India. The "natural love of home, a preference for the ways and customs of Hindustan, a dislike of the people and manners of Balkh, and the rigours of the climate, all conduced to this desire," says Lahori. A Rajput contingent in fact abandoned its post around the time Murad left Balkh and trekked back to India—it was stopped at the Indus under the emperor's orders and forced to go back.

On Murad's return, Shah Jahan summoned Aurangzeb from Gujarat and rushed him to Balkh. Aurangzeb did not mind the hardships of Central Asia, but even he was not able to push ahead to Samarkand. Like a man caught in a quicksand, the harder the Mughals struggled, the deeper they sank in Central Asia. They won every engagement, but made no gains.

The only way out of the Central Asian quagmire was retreat. To do so honourably, Aurangzeb returned Balkh to its Uzbeg ruler on his nominal submission, and by the end of the summer of 1647 made a hasty retreat to Kabul before winter closed the mountain passes. Aurangzeb had lost only about 500 soldiers in the war, but he lost ten times as many men to the elements as the army crossed snow-bound high passes in the winter that set in early that year.

The Central Asian adventure, according to Inayat Khan, cost Shah Jahan twenty million rupees, several times more than the potential revenue of the region. "Not an inch of territory was annexed, no dynasty changed, and no enemy replaced by an ally on the throne of Balkh," comments Jadunath Sarkar.

THE DISASTER IN Central Asia presaged disaster in Kandahar. When

Shah Jahan wrote a transparently dissembling letter to the Shah about his Central Asian campaign—claiming that Murad had invaded Balkh without authorization—the Shah in reply bluntly asked Shah Jahan to restore Kandahar to him and Balkh to the Uzbegs. Then, in mid-December 1648, at the height of winter, when there was little chance of the Mughals sending reinforcements from the plains, the Shah attacked, personally leading an army against Kandahar.

The mere presence of the Shah at Kandahar was enough to unnerve the Mughal garrison there. Though they had a strength of 7000 men, enough provisions to withstand a long siege, and had lost only 400 men in the fight, they believed their position to be hopeless. Some of the Mughal captains then began to parley with the Persians, and when Daulat Khan, the Mughal governor, tried to enforce discipline, it led to a mutiny. Thus beset, Daulat Khan surrendered the fort to the Persians in mid-February 1649, after a resistance of just fifty-seven days, securing for the garrison a safe passage out of the fort.

Shah Jahan had received intelligence reports as early as September 1648 about the impending Persian attack, but he allowed himself to be persuaded by his indolent amirs to wait until after the winter to send reinforcements. They argued that the Shah was unlikely to attack in winter, and that even if he did, the Kandahar garrison would be able to withstand the siege for several months. This was wishful thinking. In mid-January 1649 Shah Jahan, who was then in Lahore, received a dispatch from Kandahar that the fort was under Persian siege. He immediately ordered Aurangzeb, then serving as the governor of Multan, to proceed to relieve the town. The emperor himself then moved to Kabul to supervise the operations. Aurangzeb, leading an army of 50,000, was delayed by winter hardships in the mountains, and could reach Kandahar only in mid-May, a full three months after its fall to the Persians.

On his arrival, Aurangzeb spiritedly set about besieging Kandahar, but there was little that he could achieve, as he, initially assigned only to relieve and reinforce the Kandahar garrison, had not brought with him the heavy cannons needed to breach the fort walls. The town, reputedly founded by Alexander the Great, nestled against a high ridge of bare rock, and had virtually impregnable walls of dried clay reinforced with straw and stones, in some places as thick as nine metres. A citadel high on the ridge guarded the town. It was impossible for Aurangzeb to wrest Kandahar from the Persians. So after a frustrating siege of 110 days, he retreated in early September, fearing the approach of a large Persian expeditionary force and the even more dreaded Afghan winter.

It would be three years before the Mughals would make another attempt on the town. In May 1652 Aurangzeb returned to Kandahar, again with an army of over 50,000 men, but with the addition of a large train of artillery. The besiegers were required to operate under the instructions of Shah Jahan, who moved to Kabul with a reserve force of over 40,000 men. Despite all these elaborate arrangements, it was humiliation again that awaited Aurangzeb at Kandahar. The Mughals, poor gunners, could not breach the fort walls, and it was impossible to storm the fort against heavy enemy fire. Shah Jahan therefore ordered Aurangzeb to retreat after a siege of just two months.

The emperor was bitter about the failure of the expedition and blamed it on Aurangzeb. "I greatly wonder how you could not capture the fort in spite of such vast preparations," he wrote. When the prince pleaded for another chance to prove himself, Shah Jahan scornfully replied, "If I had believed you to be capable of taking Kandahar, I should not have recalled your army."

The following year Shah Jahan sent yet another army against Kandahar, this time under the command of his eldest and favourite son, Dara Shukoh, an army even larger then the first two, consisting of 70,000 men, with a mighty train of cannons and several European gunners to man them. But Dara's campaign was as dismal a failure as the previous two campaigns. After investing Kandahar for five months, Dara too was obliged to retreat on the onset of winter.

The Mughals would make no further attempt on Kandahar. The Persians, says Waris in extenuation of the Mughal failure, were "expert in the capture and defence of forts . . . They were masters of firearms and artillery." The Shah put the matter differently. The Mughals, he said, knew only how to steal the city by bribery, not how to take it by force of arms. The taunt hurt the Mughals, because it was true—every time the Persians took Kandahar (including the first time when they captured it and gave it to Humayun), they took it by force, while all the Mughal occupations of Kandahar were by stratagem.

The three Kandahar campaigns cost Shah Jahan—including the value of equipment and supplies lost with the fort—an incredible 120 million rupees, "more than half the gross annual revenue of the entire empire", estimates Jadunath Sarkar. It was a colossal loss, but Shah Jahan could bear it. He was wealthy enough. In losing Kandahar, the Mughals also lost some commercial and strategic advantages, but they did not matter much either. What Shah Jahan could not bear was the loss of prestige. He would never quite recover from the humiliation he suffered in Kandahar. The confident enterprise that had marked his early career now disappeared; he became tentative, half-hearted; and he progressively retired from public life, delegating more and more power to Dara, the crown prince.

And what the emperor became, the empire became. With Kandahar was also gone the Mughal elan, their aura of invincibility. There would still be other victories, like Aurangzeb's push to the ends of the subcontinent, but they would be Pyrrhic victories, won by awful and unremitting toil, and ultimately futile. This is the true significance of the loss of the insignificant provincial town of Kandahar—what it did to the Mughal psyche.

THE ACTION NOW again shifted to the Deccan. After the failure of the second Kandahar campaign, Shah Jahan dispatched Aurangzeb to the Deccan, as governor. They would not see each other again.

This was Aurangzeb's second governorship of the Deccan, to which he was returning after an interval of about ten years. He found the Deccan in a sorry state. "The Deccan is in disorder," he wrote to Shah Jahan, "as it has not been governed well for the last ten years." Always self-righteous and ever ready to blame his difficulties on others, Aurangzeb is not entirely credible in his complaints about the Deccan. Though the Deccan was normally a deficit province (funds had to be brought in from other provinces to finance its government) and frequent changes of its governors (there were six between Aurangzeb's first and second governorship) had not helped matters any either, yet it seems improbable that twenty years of peace in the region had not brought some prosperity to it. At least one governor, Khan-i-Dauran, had managed to remit money from the Deccan to the imperial treasury, proudly claiming, "Other governors had to get money from Hindustan; I am sending money there!" Certainly there was good revenue potential in the province.

Shah Jahan therefore would not grant Aurangzeb the additional funds he requested, but advised him to promote cultivation and improve revenue collection. In response, Aurangzeb introduced Todar Mal's revenue system into the Deccan, advanced loans to poor peasants for farming, and tightened the administration by weeding out inefficient and venal officers. But these were long term solutions, while his needs were urgent. "How can I, in one season or two, bring back to cultivation a pargana which has been unproductive of revenue for twenty years?" Aurangzeb indignantly wrote to Shah Jahan.

A quick way out of his predicament was for Aurangzeb to conquer new territories, which would earn him the revenues he needed and also redeem his military reputation shattered by the Kandahar fiasco. In his quandary, Aurangzeb's ravening eyes fell on Golconda, which had submitted meekly to the Mughals in 1636, and could be expected to do so again. Golconda was easy prey, soft and flabby, ruled by a slothful monarch sunk in dissipation. Besides, Golconda was immensely rich, a mine of wealth, as its very name came to mean in English. The land was fertile and well cultivated, and there were flourishing textile and carpet industries, famed gold and diamond mines. Hyderabad, the capital of Golconda, was a renowned centre of the diamond trade to which merchants from all over the world flocked. In Machilipatnam (Masulipatam), the kingdom had a celebrated international port and emporium.

If the opulence of Golconda were not reason enough for invading it, Aurangzeb had the excuse that the tribute due from the kingdom by the treaty of 1636 was in arrears. Further, Golconda was charged with invading, without imperial sanction, the Carnatic, an extensive land stretching from the Krishna River to the Kaveri River, made up of a mosaic of small principalities, fragments of the shattered Vijayanagar empire.

GOLCONDA'S INVASION OF the Carnatic in the mid-seventeenth century was masterminded by Mir Jumla, one of the most colourful of the Persian migrants to rise to high office in India. He was "the son of an Oyl-man of Isfahan," says Thevenot, and had originally come to India as the personal attendant of a Persian merchant. In Golconda he set himself up as a trader, and, mixing business and politics with great finesse, soon amassed an immense fortune. Simultaneously he also rose in government service to become the prime minister of the sultanate, a position in which he entrenched himself, according to Bernier, through an advantageous liaison with the queen mother. Mir Jumla utilized his office to enrich himself further, by securing profitable trade monopolies, and by carrying on "extensive commerce with various parts of the world, as well as by the diamond mines which he farmed under feigned names," says Bernier. Further, by invading the Carnatic, he looted the long buried treasures of the ancient temples and royal families there.

Mir Jumla thus became one of the richest men in India, reputedly in possession of twenty *maunds* of diamonds, according to Thevenot. He ruled over an extensive jagir, some 500 kilometres long and eighty kilometres broad, which yielded an annual revenue of four million rupees. As befitted his power and wealth, Mir Jumla maintained, in addition to the divisions of the royal army under his command, a private army of 5000 cavalry, with matching infantry, artillery and elephant corps. He was thus virtually an independent ruler, the king of the Carnatic.

The peril inherent in the *imperium in imperio* situation was evident even to so indolent a monarch as Abdullah Qutb Shah, the sultan of Golconda, and he manoeuvred to clip the wings of his overweening minister. The issue came to a head suddenly and in an unexpected manner. Abdullah had patiently and for long suffered the haughty air and rude manners of Mir Jumla's son, Muhammad Amin, but one day when, in a drunken stupor, Muhammad curled up on the throne carpet and soiled it with his vomit, it was too much for the sultan to bear. He clapped Muhammad into jail and attached his property.

That drove Mir Jumla to Aurangzeb for protection, thus providing the prince with the handle he had been seeking to stir up trouble in Golconda. On Aurangzeb's recommendation, Shah Jahan appointed Mir Jumla and his son as imperial officers and forbade Abdullah from harassing them. As Abdullah balked at yielding to this gross interference in a matter between himself and his minister, Aurangzeb sent, early in 1656, an expeditionary force storming towards Hyderabad under the command of his son Muhammad Sultan, and himself followed with a large force, even though Abdullah had by then complied with the Mughal demands.

Aurangzeb's instructions to Muhammad Sultan were explicit and chillingly brutal. "Qutb-ul-mulk is a coward and will probably offer no resistance," he wrote. "Surround his palace with your artillery and also post a detachment to bar his flight to Golconda. But before doing so, send a carefully chosen messenger to him, saying, `I had so long been expecting that you would meet me and hospitably ask me to stay with you. But as you have not done so, I have myself come to you.' Immediately on delivering this message, attack him impetuously and, if you can manage it, lighten his neck of the burden of his head."

Abdullah saved his head by fleeing to the nearby fort of Golconda. Besieged there by Aurangzeb, the sultan tried to placate him with various presents and by making submissive offers, even sending his mother to plead for clemency. At the same time, he also sought Dara's intercession with Shah Jahan to restrain Aurangzeb.

Aurangzeb's objective was nothing short of the annexation of Golconda, and he tried to get Shah Jahan to sanction it by tempting him with the immense wealth of the kingdom. "What shall I write about the beauty of this country—its abundance of water and population, its good air, and its extensive cultivation . . . ?" he wrote to the emperor. "At every stage after crossing the frontier I met with many large tanks, springs of sweet water, running streams, inhabited villages with large patches of cultivated land attached to them. Not a piece of land without tillage. Such a money-yielding country!" And he pleaded:

327

"I hope your majesty will order annexation." Shah Jahan, mistrusting Aurangzeb's motives and under the influence of Dara, refused to sanction annexation; instead, he ordered Aurangzeb to accept Abdullah's offer of indemnity, lift the siege of Golconda and quit the kingdom—at once!

Aurangzeb complied. On 9th April 1656 he raised the siege and began to retreat. But he had by then managed to get most of what he wanted from Golconda. By the terms of peace, Abdullah ceded the district of Ramgir to the Mughals, committed himself to pay an indemnity of ten million rupees, and agreed to catch up with the payment of tribute. Further, he gave one of his daughters in marriage to Muhammad Sultan, and in a secret understanding with Aurangzeb, pledged (as he had no sons) to make the prince heir to the throne of Golconda. By such compromises Abdullah bought a little time for his dynasty from annihilation by the Mughals.

Around this time the last remnant of the Vijayanagar empire, Chandragiri, vanished from history. The principality, extending a mere 300 kilometres from Nellore to Pondicherry, was caught like a morsel between the thrusting jaws of Golconda and Bijapur. In imminent danger of being swallowed up, Sri Ranga Rayal, the raja of Chandragiri, sought the help of the Mughals to save himself—he offered to present Shah Jahan with twenty-five million rupees, 200 elephants, all his hoarded jewels, and in addition to pay an annual tribute; alternately, he suggested that his kingdom might be annexed by the Mughals and given to him to hold as a jagir; he even offered to become a Muslim, if only the emperor would protect him.

Inexplicably, Aurangzeb was not tempted, probably because the raja's extravagant offer was not credible, or because Chandragiri was not contiguous to the Mughal empire. The hapless Ranga Rayal, harassed by his faithless vassals, deserted by his courtiers, and with no army at his command, finally took refuge with the raja of Mysore, once his servant. His last historically significant act was to cede the site of Madras to the East India Company for them to set up a factory, where Robert Clive would, a century later, lay the foundations of the British empire in India.

FROM GOLCONDA AURANGZEB turned to Bijapur. The kingdom, at peace with the Mughals since the treaty of 1636, had in the intervening twenty years prospered greatly, extending its territory west into the Konkan, south into Mysore, and east into the Carnatic, thus straddling peninsular India from coast to coast. Throughout this period Bijapur was ruled by Muhammad Adil Shah, the seventh of the royal line of Bijapur, a pious and benevolent monarch, who provided stability to the kingdom and kept the Mughals at bay by carefully maintaining cordial relations with the emperor. When Muhammad died in November 1656, everything turned topsy-turvy in Bijapur—rebellions broke out in the newly conquered territories, top royal officers squabbled and fought among themselves, and the very legitimacy of the new sultan, Ali Adil Shah II, was questioned.

The time was thus ripe for the Mughal invasion of Bijapur. All that was lacking was an excuse, but that did not deter Aurangzeb. He pressed Shah Jahan for permission to invade Bijapur on the specious ground that Ali was not really the son of the deceased sultan. Aurangzeb's proposal was strongly supported at the court by Mir Jumla, and under his influence Shah Jahan sanctioned the invasion of Bijapur, cavalierly sweeping aside the treaty of 1636. He instructed Aurangzeb to annex the whole kingdom if possible, or at least the territories taken by Bijapur from Ahmadnagar, and collect an indemnity of fifteen million rupees. He was also given the option to extend the campaign to annex Golconda. Mir Jumla was sent to the Deccan to assist Aurangzeb. "Come quickly," Aurangzeb wrote to Mir Jumla, "so that we may both start together."

Meanwhile, anticipating the emperor's permission for the invasion, Aurangzeb opened the Bijapur campaign in his usual insidious manner, by offering 2,000 rupees for every Bijapuri captain who defected with 100 soldiers. Then, on 28th January 1657, the day Mir Jumla joined Aurangzeb, the Mughals began their advance on Bijapur. Their progress was slow, averaging only about nine kilometres a day, so it took Aurangzeb forty-three days to cover the 386 kilometres from Aurangabad to the Bijapuri town of Bidar, the old capital of the Badami sultans. The fort fell after a three-week siege, and the Mughal army moved on to its next target, Kalyani (once the Chalukya capital), which fell by the end of July.

There was nothing dashing or heroic in these victories. It was a slow, plodding though tenacious campaign, which was the hallmark of Aurangzeb's style. Shah Jahan was naturally impatient, for the monsoon had already broken over the peninsula, and during the rains military operations had to be suspended and the army quartered in cantonments. He therefore—possibly also under the influence of Dara, whose intercession was sought by Bijapuri agents—ordered Aurangzeb to conclude the campaign quickly. Aurangzeb then negotiated a treaty with Bijapur, by which the kingdom agreed to pay an indemnity of fifteen million rupees (from which Shah Jahan remitted five million) and also to surrender a number of forts.

Meanwhile another player had entered the field: Maratha captain Shahji Bhonsle's son Shivaji, who rampaged through the territories at the rear of the Mughal army while Aurangzeb was busy with the Bijapur campaign. But Shivaji was only a minor nuisance to the Mughals at this time, and he was easily chased off into the mountains by a punitive force sent by Aurangzeb. Later, when Bijapur submitted to Aurangzeb, so did Shivaji.

On the whole, Aurangzeb was able to achieve the Mughal goals in the Deccan, despite the restraints imposed on him by Shah Jahan. But presently everything was thrown into disorder in the Mughal empire, as Shah Jahan fell ill in Delhi and the imperial princes plunged into a brutal war of succession.

"Ya Takht, Ya Tabut!"

THE ORDER TO Aurangzeb to pull back from Bijapur was the last major act of Shah Jahan as emperor. Thereafter his sons would determine the course of events.

In March 1657 Shah Jahan had celebrated the thirtieth lunar anniversary of his accession. He was then at Mukhlispur, his summer retreat on the Yamuna at the foot of the Sirmur Hills, some 160 kilometres north of Delhi, where he had gone to avoid an epidemic that was raging in Delhi. He returned to Delhi towards the end of April 1657, but fell ill on 16th September. "The emperor was attacked with serious illness in the form of strangury, constipation and other sympathetic affections," says Muhammad Salih Kambu. "Physicians tried all the remedies of their art, but in vain, for the disorder increased." His legs swelled up, fever rose. He was in great pain. For a week he took no food, and as he grew weak, his life was despaired for.

Manucci and Bernier both attribute Shah Jahan's illness to the use of an astringent aphrodisiac. "Shah Jahan brought this illness on himself," says Manucci, "for being already an old man . . . he wanted still to enjoy himself like a youth, and with this intent took different stimulating drugs." Twenty years earlier, in March 1637, Shah Jahan had been laid up with a similar illness, probably from a similar cause, and had suffered "excruciating agony" for three weeks, says Inayat Khan. That time he recovered. But he was now a much older man, and his chances of survival seemed dim—sixty-five years old, he had already lived longer than any Mughal emperor before him.

For about a week Shah Jahan's condition was deemed critical, and he neither attended the durbar nor showed himself to the public at the jharokha. No one but Dara and a handful of trusted amirs had access to him. As the emperor disappeared from sight, the rumour that he was dead—poisoned by Dara, some said—raged through Delhi like wild fire, spreading panic. Merchants closed their shops, fearing riots. "This confusion lasted in the city for three days and three nights," says Manucci. Then, as the rumour spread to the provinces, the brittle web of royal authority that bound the empire together began to crumble. Frontiers were violated. Farmers resisted revenue collection; zemindars fought with each other and with imperial officers; and brigands, ever lurking in the shadows, emerged rampaging. Says Khafi Khan, "Turbulent men from every corner and quarter, and men eager for a fray, in every province and country, raised their heads in expectation of strife."

To still the rumours, Shah Jahan dragged himself to the window of his bedroom on 24th September, to show his face to the public gathered in the maidan below the fort walls. But many refused to believe their eyes. "There were present a very great number of men from the army and the common people, all of whom, heard and saw," writes Manucci. "But the greater part of them said that it was not Shah Jahan, but a made-up figure prepared by Prince Dara for that purpose."

Shah Jahan remained bedridden for another month, but gradually, on a diet of "mint and manna" soup, he began to recover his strength. By mid-October he was able to move about. He then shifted to Agra, travelling down the Yamuna in the royal barge, as physicians had recommended a change of air. By mid-November, nursed diligently by Dara and Jahanara, Shah Jahan fully recovered his health.

But he would never recover power. Though he would live for another nine years, it was really the end of him.

AS THE WILD RUMOURS about the emperor's condition reached the imperial princes in the provinces, they tensed with apprehension. They had their agents at the court, but with Shah Jahan in seclusion and the agents themselves watched, no authentic information reached the princes. If Shah Jahan was dead, or if he was incapacitated and had relinquished power to Dara, their fate was sealed. They had no alternative but to prepare for war—it was not merely an issue of succession, but of their very lives. As Bernier puts it, "Not only was the crown to be gained by victory alone, but in case of defeat life was certain to be forfeited."

Before Shah Jahan left Delhi for Agra, he had formally nominated Dara as his successor, and had commanded the amirs to obey him as their sovereign. This was a grave error. Shah Jahan should have known that only one of his sons could survive to occupy the throne, and that to hand over power to Dara without first disarming the other princes— each a powerful satrap, with his own army—would make a war of succession inevitable. But what was he to do? He wanted to secure the throne for Dara, but how could he arrange the liquidation of his other sons?

Shah Jahan had four sons. Dara, forty-two, was the eldest, followed by Shuja, forty-one, Aurangzeb, thirty-nine, and Murad, thirty-three. At the time that Shah Jahan fell ill, Dara was with the emperor in Delhi, Aurangzeb was in the Deccan, Shuja in Bengal, and Murad in Gujarat. Of the four, Dara's position was the strongest; he had the emperor's backing and had at his disposal the immense resources of the imperial treasury. Yet Dara would lose to Aurangzeb. Shah Jahan himself believed that Aurangzeb had the best chance of winning the throne. "At times I fear that my eldest son has become the enemy of good men," he is said to have remarked. "Murad Bakhsh has set his heart on drinking; Muhammad Shuja has no good trait except contentment. But the resolution and intelligence of Aurangzeb prove that he [alone] can shoulder this difficult task [of ruling India]."

There was a touch of anguish in this comment, for Dara was Shah Jahan's favourite. "In the eyes of his father the Emperor, Prince Dara Shukoh was superior to his brothers both in merit and age," says Kambu. "When his other sons departed to their respective governments, the Emperor, from excessive love and partiality, would not allow Dara Shukoh to go away from him. He also evinced the greatest partiality and affection for the Prince, providing for his honour and dignity."

Dara had long been groomed to succeed Shah Jahan, and was always kept at the court to familiarize him with imperial administration. Conferred the grand title Shah-i-buland-iqubal, Lord of the Lofty Fortune, he had the exclusive privilege of sitting in the durbar hall, in a gold chair just below the imperial throne. His rank as commander of 40,000, with an annual pay of fifteen million rupees, was unprecedented and well above that of the other princes. Even Dara's sons held ranks nearly as high as those of the emperor's younger sons, with Sulaiman Shukoh, Dara's eldest son, holding the rank of 15,000. In September 1657, during Shah Jahan's illness, Dara's rank was raised to 50,000, and in December raised again to 60,000, with a pay of twenty million rupees.

Dara was a popular prince. In contrast to dour Aurangzeb, he was genial, and Shah Jahan loved his company. Dara, complains Aurangzeb, won Shah Jahan's favour by "flattery, smoothness of tongue, and much laughing". Says Manucci: "Dara [was] a man of dignified manners, of a comely countenance, joyous and polite in conversation, ready and gracious of speech, of most extraordinary liberality, kindly and compassionate." Confirms Bernier: Dara "was courteous in conversation, quick at repartee, polite, and extremely liberal." He was a cultured, benevolent and warm-hearted prince, who often interceded to soften the harshness of Mughal rule.

Dara's fatal flaw was pride. "He entertained too exalted an opinion of himself," says Bernier, "believed he could accomplish everything by the powers of his own mind, and imagined that there existed no man

333

from whose counsel he could derive benefit. He spoke disdainfully of those who ventured to advise him, and thus deterred his sincerest friends from disclosing the secret machinations of his brothers. He was irascible, apt to menace, abusive and insulting even to the greatest Omrahs; but his anger was seldom more than momentary."

Dara had a mocking tongue. "If Dara had a failing, it was not to conciliate the great nobles and win them over to be his friends," writes Manucci. He "scorned the nobles, both in word and deed, making no account of them . . . He ordered his buffoons several times to imitate the gait and gestures of . . . Mir Jumla, making mock of him." Not surprisingly, Dara was not the favourite of the amirs. This hurt his fortune. The amirs, worldly creatures though they were, false and opportunistic, and generally lacking the aesthetic and intellectual refinements that Dara cherished, were nevertheless the intermediaries of power, without whom Dara could neither win nor exercise power. It was folly to alienate them.

The amirs probably found Dara mystifying. His preoccupation with religion and philosophy, instead of with power and glory, his artistic conceits, and his preference for the company of mystics and (as one Mughal writer puts it) "lunatics", were traits which the amirs could neither understand nor appreciate. What they could appreciate was valour, but Dara—unlike Aurangzeb, a veteran of many battles—was not field tested. He had only one major campaign to his credit, the third siege of Kandahar, and though he did no worse in it than Aurangzeb in his earlier campaigns, he lacked the aura of heroic leadership, the special blood bond with men forged in the thick of battle. Though personally fearless, he had little experience in leading men under pressure in the face of danger. Nor did Dara have the ruthlessness so essential to lead and command. He was too civilized. These would prove to be major handicaps in the war of succession.

An equally severe disability was Dara's heterodoxy. Aurangzeb's partisans in fact accused him of being an apostate. Mirza Muhammad Kasim, Aurangzeb's official chronicler, charges that Dara went beyond mere heresy to a definite partiality for Hinduism. "He was constantly in the society of brahmins, yogis and sanyasis, and he used to regard these worthless teachers of delusions as learned and true masters of wisdom," says Kasim. "He considered their books which they call Bed (Veda) as being the Word of God, and revealed from heaven." Dara got the Vedas translated into Persian, continues Kasim, and "he spent all his time in this unholy work, and devoted all his attention to the contents of these wretched books . . . Through these perverted opinions he had given up the prayers, fasting and other obligations imposed by the law . . . It became manifest that if Dara Shukoh obtained the throne and established his power, the foundations of faith would be in danger and the precepts of Islam would be changed for the rant of infidelity and Judaism."

This was a genuine anxiety. But Dara was not an apostate. "Born a Mahometan, he continued to join in the exercises of that religion," states Bernier. Dara was a devotee of Mian Mir, a celebrated Muslim saint, and he even compiled a biography of Muslim saints, which he would not have done had he ceased to be a Muslim. He was however eclectic, and inclined to pantheism. He wrote:

We have not seen an atom separate from the Sun,
Every drop of water is the sea in itself.
With what name should one call the Truth?
Every name that exists is one of God's names.

Dara studied the Talmud, the New Testament, the Upanishads and the works of Sufis, and he endeavoured to find a common ground between different religions. He especially sought to reconcile Hinduism with Islam, and wrote a book—*Majmua-ul-Baharain* (Mingling of Two Oceans)—to propound his thesis. With the help of Hindu pundits from Varanasi, Dara himself translated the Upanishads from Sanskrit into Persian, and maintained that the Upanishads were "without doubt or suspicion, the first of all heavenly books in point of time, the source of the fountain of reality and ocean of monotheism, in conformity with the Holy Koran and even a commentary thereon."

Such a view was not unusual for a liberal Muslim—Jahangir, for instance, had considered Vedanta as "the science of Sufism"—but from the point of view of the orthodox Muslim, it was an unpardonable heresy. As Khafi Khan saw it, Dara "had declared infidelity and Islam to be twin brothers, and had written treatises on this subject." To make matters worse, Dara damned the mullahs with such remarks as that "Paradise is there where no mullah exists." The mullahs, we should assume, did not reciprocate Dara's scorn with love.

In his religious attitudes Dara seems to have modelled himself consciously on his great-grandfather, Akbar, but there was this basic difference between them, that while Akbar was primarily a king who happened to be keenly interested in religion, Dara was primarily a mystic who happened to be a prince. The renunciatory impulse, latent in most Mughal emperors, was dominant in Dara. "Kingship is easy, acquaint thyself with poverty," wrote Dara; "why should a drop become a pearl when it can transform itself into an ocean?" And again:

"O friend, renounce worldly kingship and take up wisdom, knowledge and truth," he wrote, presumably addressing himself. But the Mughal blood would not let him renounce either.

Dara was the most cultured of the sons of Shah Jahan; he was in fact the finest scholar the Mughal dynasty had ever produced, and was the author of six books. He was also a poet and, like Babur, a skilled calligraphist. "I have acquired the kingdom of calligraphy and the connoisseurs of art have shown deference to it," he writes. Like Shah Jahan, he was fond of music and dance.

We do not know what dreams Dara had for the empire, but they certainly would not have been the same as the dreams of Aurangzeb. India was at a crossroads in the mid-seventeenth century; it had the potential of moving forward with Dara, or of turning back to medievalism with Aurangzeb. But India's destiny was with Aurangzeb.

AURANGZEB AND DARA despised and hated each other, Aurangzeb venomously, Dara with an aesthete's delicate revulsion. Aurangzeb, says Bernier, was "devoid of that urbanity and engaging presence, so much admired in Dara, but he possessed a sounder judgment, and was skillful in selecting . . . confidants." He was a consummate schemer, cold-blooded and ruthless, a self-righteous hypocrite who cunningly melded high principles with low practices. His will to win was indomitable, almost insane. While Dara cultivated culture, Aurangzeb sharpened his sword.

His sword, Aurangzeb claimed, was the fiery sword of Islam against Dara's diabolic heresy. While Dara contemptuously called Aurangzeb a *nemazi*, bigot, Aurangzeb damned Dara as a *mulhid*, infidel. As Aurangzeb would later say, "The fear of seeing the Muhammadan religion oppressed in Hindustan if my brother Dara ascended the throne; that of beholding the ruin of the kingdom, which I looked on as inevitable if my father's reign had continued, by reason of his bad government: these are the only causes why I have always opposed myself strongly and without self-seeking to the attempts of everyone to supplant me."

It was not personal ambition, Aurangzeb claimed, but the desire to protect Islam and the empire that made him imprison his aged father and slay his brothers. But behind that sanctimonious posturing were the more elemental passions of love and hate. Shah Jahan seems to have developed an almost pathological aversion for Aurangzeb, which often degenerated into petty and unbecoming squabbles. During Aurangzeb's second governorship in the Deccan, Shah Jahan accused the prince of tardiness, inefficiency, misgovernment, and of misappropriation of some of the treasure he had got from Golconda; he further reproached him for diverting the best weavers of Burhanpur from the imperial factory to his private factory, and even for keeping for himself the best mangoes from Shah Jahan's favourite Deccani tree, before forwarding the crop to the imperial table. Aurangzeb in turn complained of discrimination, mistrust and niggardly funding. "If your majesty wishes me to be honoured with a great viceroyalty, give me the means worthy of it," he wrote sharply to his father. Shah Jahan was irked by Aurangzeb's constant nagging and often spoke caustically about the prince in open court.

According to Manucci, when Aurangzeb was born an astrologer had warned that the child boded ill for Shah Jahan and his line. Maybe this prejudiced Shah Jahan. In any case, how could Shah Jahan, aesthete and voluptuary, love a frigid puritan like Aurangzeb! His affinity was for Dara. "Aurangzeb knew that his father put no faith in him, and did not love him," says Manucci. Aurangzeb would never forgive Shah Jahan for not loving him—or forgive Dara, for appropriating all their father's love.

Aurangzeb and Dara were the main contenders for the throne, and there was something portentous about their contest, involving issues far larger than those of their own lives and ambitions—the fate of the empire, the future of India. The motivations of the other princes were simpler: they merely wanted to occupy the throne, or at least save their lives. Not surprisingly, they were the first to make their moves in the crisis.

Shuja was the first to show his hand. He does not seem ever to have been very attached to Shah Jahan; as a child, he was brought up by Nur Jahan; as an adult, he was invariably away from the court. As the governor of Bengal, which he had ruled for seventeen years, he had earned a reputation for military skill and administrative efficiency. Bernier speaks of Shuja as an intelligent, discreet young man, firm of purpose and "dexterous in the management of intrigue". But he was a voluptuary, continues Bernier, "too much a slave to his pleasure, and once surrounded by his women, who were exceedingly numerous, he would pass whole days and nights in dancing, singing and drinking wine." Says Manucci, Shuja "followed the habits of his father, being a lover of songs, dances, and women . . . He had such a high idea of himself that he supposed his valour could conquer everybody."

Murad, the youngest of the brothers, born in the hill fort of Rohtas during Shah Jahan's rebellion against Jahangir, was a great soldier, but had no other merit. "He was a man of little wisdom, who could not plan anything beyond his amusements, drinking, singing, and dancing," says Manucci. "He was very bold and valorous, for ever practicing himself in the use of arms, and perfect in the use of bow and arrow." According to Bernier Murad was "inferior to his three brothers in judgment and address. His constant thought was how he might enjoy himself, and the pleasure of the table and of the field engaged his undivided attention. He was, however, generous and polite. He used to boast that he had no secrets: he despised cabinet intrigues, and wished it to be known that he trusted only to his sword and to the strength of his arm. He was indeed full of courage; and if that courage had been under the guidance of a little more discretion" he could have won the war of succession.

THE WAR OF SUCCESSION between the brothers was joined in the imperial harem too, where Jahanara and Raushanara, sisters and rivals, matched their wits against each other, with Jahanara supporting Dara and Raushanara intriguing for Aurangzeb. Jahanara, beautiful and talented, was everybody's beloved sister; even Aurangzeb loved her dearly, despite her favour for Dara. But she and Dara had a special bond. "I love my brother Dara Shukoh extremely both in form and spirit," she is reported to have said. "We are, in fact, like one soul in two bodies and one spirit in two physical forms." They were both inclined to Sufism, had a common love for philosophy and literature, and she, like Dara, was a writer, having to her credit *Munis-ul-arwah*, a biography of Sheikh Muinuddin Chishti.

Raushanara had no intellectual or artistic pretensions. "She was not very good-looking," says Manucci, "but very clever, capable of dissimulation, bright, mirthful, fond of jokes and amusement, much more so than her sister Begum Sahib (Jahanara)." Elsewhere Manucci says that Raushanara had "libidinous propensities". She was an implausible accomplice for the stern and ascetic Aurangzeb. Many years later, according to Manucci, Aurangzeb had her poisoned because of a love scandal, and she died "swollen out like a hog-head, and leaving behind her the name of great lasciviousness". The story seems farfetched. Whatever the truth of it, for the time being Aurangzeb and Raushanara were cohorts, united in their hatred for Dara.

SUCH THEN WAS the principal cast of this the most traumatic drama in Mughal history. In Agra, Shah Jahan, old and weary, was content to leave the management of the crisis to Dara. "Whatever he (Dara) submitted was accepted [by the emperor]," says Mughal chronicler Ishwardas Nagar. Shah Jahan played an advisory and moderating role, but decisions were left to the prince. Dara reciprocated this trust with devotion and deference. "He did nothing without communicating it to his father," says Manucci. Though Dara was provided with a golden chair near the throne in the durbar hall, he never sat in the presence of Shah Jahan. Dara alone among Shah Jahan's sons did not seem to have wished for his father's death. For the other princes, each having declared himself emperor one after the other, the emperor living on was an awful embarrassment.

Aurangzeb's courtier historians naturally blamed Dara for the civil war. When Shah Jahan fell ill, says Kazim, "irregularities of all sorts occurred in the administration, and great disturbances arose in the wide territories of Hindustan. The unworthy and frivolous Dara Shukoh considered himself heir-apparent, and notwithstanding his want of ability for the kingly office, he endeavoured with the scissors of greediness to cut the robes of the Imperial dignity into a shape suited for his unworthy person." Dara, says Kambu, "took upon himself to interfere in the direction of affairs of State, and induced His Majesty to do many unwise things which tended to create disturbances."

Such charges do not hold up against facts. Dara did not usurp power: power was delegated to him; he did not cause civil war: it was forced on him. And if he made any mistakes, it was mainly due to Shah Jahan's moderating advice in dealing with the rebel princes. Dara himself acted with prudence and resolution, and his political and military strategies were essentially sound. It was chance and ill luck that destroyed him.

Dara's immediate objective was to maintain law and order in the empire and to prevent his brothers from setting off a crisis before he was ready to deal with it. This was the reason why, when Shah Jahan suddenly fell seriously ill, the news was kept a secret, just as Humayun's death was once kept a secret, though under somewhat different circumstances. Later, when a civil war became inevitable, Dara sought to set his brothers against each other, or at least to prevent them from combining against him. These were sound and essential measures.

Dara's first move was to recall from the Deccan the imperial army and its battle-tested commanders engaged in the war against Bijapur. A firman was accordingly sent out to the commanders to return, and many of them immediately complied, several of them setting out for Agra without even taking leave of Aurangzeb. Dara however made a minor slip here; instead of recalling Mir Jumla forthwith, he was asked, probably on the advice of Shah Jahan, to secure the surrender of the fort of Parenda from Bijapur before returning. It proved to be a costly error. The delay enabled Aurangzeb to detain Mir Jumla and take over his army and treasure.

Dara's second move was to persuade Shah Jahan to shift Murad from the rich province of Gujarat to Berar. This had a double objective. If Murad obeyed, it would set him against Aurangzeb, to whom Berar then belonged; if he disobeyed, then his rebellion would be out in the open and he could be accordingly dealt with. As it happened, Murad did not obey, but declared himself emperor.

Even before the impetuous Murad acted, Shuja in Bengal, claiming that Dara had poisoned his father, proclaimed himself emperor, and had the khutbah read and coins struck in his name. He then started for Agra with his army, to avenge, as he claimed, his father's murder. "*Ya takht, ya tabut!*" he exclaimed as he set out—The throne or the tomb!

Murad in Gujarat followed suit, first in a secret enthronement, then, two weeks later, in a public ceremony. He was short of funds, and had sent an army into Surat to capture the imperial treasury in the fort there and to plunder the city, but even before the contingent could return, the auspicious moment for his accession was upon him—his astrologers had told him that four hours and twenty-four minutes past sunrise on 20th November 1657 was too rare a moment to be missed. So, with only a few amirs in attendance, Murad formally ascended the throne at that precious moment. His public accession followed on 5th December, when his name was read in the khutbah and coins struck in his name. He even dispatched an ambassador to Persia to announce his accession. Then, taking his cue from Aurangzeb, he began to strut about as the defender of the faith against Dara.

AURANGZEB HIMSELF HOWEVER did not make any overtly defiant moves, though he opened conspiratorial exchanges with Murad and Shuja, and intrigued with amirs at the imperial court. Cunning and cautious, he bided his time, waiting for the scene to clarify before he moved. Yet all eyes were on him. His would be the crucial role in the civil war. "Dara Shukoh," says Khafi Khan, "looked with an eye of apprehension upon the talents of Prince Aurangzeb, and was made uneasy by the vigour and wisdom which he displayed."

Aurangzeb's position was the strongest among the rebel princes— he had, as Kambu says, a "splendid army under his command", the Deccan veterans, and he was flush with funds, the tribute he had squeezed out of Golconda. Aurangzeb himself would, in a letter to Murad, boast of his "numerous army and powerful artillery as the means of securing . . . victory". Yet his actions at this time were timid and vacillating, more cautious than caution warranted. Aurangzeb seemed unsure of himself and racked with anxiety.

Events were moving fast. The flood-tide was upon him. Aurangzeb had to ride it, or drown. In his quandary, the prince sought the advice of Mir Jumla, then besieging Parenda, writing to him almost every day. "I have no friend or confidant but you," he wrote, requesting Mir Jumla to settle the matter of Parenda one way or other quickly and return, "in order that the most important business of all may be undertaken before it is too late."

Aurangzeb felt, as he wrote to Mir Jumla, that he should launch his campaign for the throne "only when the occurrence of Shah Jahan's death is verified". Yet he feared that if he waited too long, "worldlings and seekers of rank" would gravitate towards Dara. Even his own officers and army were in a state of confusion, Aurangzeb noted. "They are in greater trouble than can be described," he wrote to Mir Jumla. "Many (of my) officers want to return to the Emperor." And again: "What shall I write about my own troubled state or describe how the days pass over me? I have no remedy save patience."

By mid-November, Aurangzeb retreated from Kalyani to Aurangabad, to await developments. Meanwhile, he tried to settle matters with the Deccan sultanates. Though harsh and belligerent initially in his effort to get the promised payments and the surrender of forts from Golconda and Bijapur, Aurangzeb became progressively softer and more conciliatory as he became preoccupied with the developments in Hindustan. In the end, all he wanted was peace, peace at any cost, so that he might not be molested from the south when he turned to the north. He even apologized to Bijapur for invading the kingdom, blaming it on "Mir Jumla's wicked advice". "Let there be peace and happiness," he wrote to Adil Shah of Bijapur. To Qutb Shah of Golconda he wrote, "Now is the time for you to show your friendship and exert yourself that nothing unfriendly is done," and he repeated about the same words to Adil Shah: "Now is the time to show your loyalty and friendliness." He promised to reward the Deccan sultans for their support "after I have become Emperor".

At last Aurangzeb made up his mind. He would cross the Rubicon— the Narmada, in this case. He began to collect his forces, and had the ferries of the Narmada guarded to restrain officers from going to Agra and to prevent the news of his moves from leaking out; he intensified his intrigues with Murad and Shuja as well as with the amirs at the court. As Dara would complain to Shah Jahan, "Aurangzeb is winning over the nobles and pillars of the State. He is doing his work by means

341

of secret epistles." Notes Manucci, "There were many traitors at the court friendly to Aurangzeb."

Then suddenly Aurangzeb was confronted with an unexpected problem. In the last week of December 1657 Mir Jumla received a peremptory order from Shah Jahan to return to Agra. That threw Aurangzeb into gloom, as he was heavily dependent on the counsel and help of Mir Jumla, whom he affectionately called Babaji. What would Mir Jumla do? He was an Aurangzeb loyalist—Dara in fact had removed him from Viziership soon after the crisis broke—but it appeared that his loyalty did not extend to sacrificing his self-interest; his family was in Agra, and he feared that if he sided with Aurangzeb they would be in jeopardy. So he decided to obey the imperial command and return to Agra, "quite regardless of the duty and respect he owed to the Prince," says Kambu.

Aurangzeb could not afford to let Mir Jumla go. He tried to coax him to stay, and wrote him an ingratiating letter, reminding the amir of his assurance of readiness to sacrifice life and property for Aurangzeb. "Come to me," Aurangzeb cajoled, "so that with your advice I may engage in preparations for the work of gaining the crown."

Mir Jumla was not tempted. He said that he could not disobey the emperor's direct command. Aurangzeb then had no alternative but to have Mir Jumla arrested, his property and military equipment seized. Dara suspected the arrest to be a mere pretence, to enable Aurangzeb to acquire Mir Jumla's resources without compromising the amir in the eyes of the emperor. "It was all a trick and conspiracy," Dara is reported to have told Shah Jahan. And Manucci says that the arrest drama was just "comedy". These were legitimate suspicions, given Aurangzeb's sly and deceitful character. Still, the weight of evidence indicates that it was not a collusive arrest. Nor was it, however, a hostile act. Aurangzeb still highly valued Mir Jumla. Later, after he gained the throne, he would release Mir Jumla from confinement and appoint him as the Khan-i-khanan, the premier noble of the empire, and would virtually apologize to him, writing, "That I imprisoned you was not due to any disloyalty on your part. Only you showed remissness in exertion and insisted on going back."

AS AURANGZEB TARRIED, Murad was waiting impatiently for him to move, so that their two armies could march together against Dara. "We are losing time and letting our business suffer, by waiting for certain news of Shah Jahan. Our enemy is growing stronger," Murad wrote to Aurangzeb. When he received letters in Shah Jahan's own hand to assure him that he was alive and well, Murad claimed that they were forgeries by Dara, a plausible suspicion, as Shah Jahan and Dara wrote in the same style of hand. Nor was Murad convinced when his own agents wrote to say that the emperor had recovered, for he feared that the letters were written under duress. "Let us start together for Agra," Murad implored Aurangzeb. "It only remains for you to give the order."

Murad and Aurangzeb were in continual contact with each other at this time, exchanging letters through relays of runners stationed every sixteen kilometres. They also established contact with Shuja, to coordinate their moves against Dara. Confidential agents shuttled between the princes carrying oral messages too risky to put in writing, and Aurangzeb devised a cipher to encode their letters. Aurangzeb and Murad, and possibly also Shuja, then entered into an agreement among themselves to divide the empire after eliminating Dara.

Finally, when all arrangements were ready, Aurangzeb set out for Agra. War, he knew, was a risk, its result unpredictable, but it was a risk he had to take. The alternative was certain destruction. Still Aurangzeb, unlike Shuja and Murad, did not proclaim himself emperor, but with characteristic deceit tried to occupy a moral high-ground, claiming that he was proceeding to Agra only to visit his ailing father and to release him from the clutches of Dara. Aurangzeb maintained that he was not a rebel, but a dutiful son anxious about his father's welfare.

"For the Sake of the True Faith"

TO AURANGZEB, DARA was not just an adversary in the power struggle, but the very embodiment of evil, and the fight against him not a mere succession feud, but a holy war. Aurangzeb's personal ambition thus meshed smoothly with what he considered to be his historic obligation to defend the faith.

Dara was at a disadvantage in such posturings, for heterodoxy had no legitimacy in the medieval world. But then, Dara saw no issue of good and evil involved in the crisis, not even an issue of succession, for their father was alive and in control. For him, the matter was quite simple: his brothers had rebelled against their father. They had to be put down.

As the crown prince it was Dara's responsibility to suppress the rebels, and he believed that he had the necessary means to do so. His plan was to hold Murad and Aurangzeb in check in the south, meanwhile to deal with Shuja in the east, and then to wheel his army around to the south, to crush Murad and Aurangzeb. The sequence of events, the delay in Aurangzeb's advance, favoured Dara, giving him an interval of about three months between the time he had to meet the two challenges. Dara's strategy was simplicity itself. It almost worked.

WHEN THE NEWS OF Shuja's advance from Bengal reached Agra, Dara obtained Shah Jahan's permission to send an expeditionary force against him. The army that was marshalled for it was not, by Mughal standards, large, only some 20,000 cavalry and 2000 musketeers, but it was the pick of Dara's army, and was commanded by his eldest son, Sulaiman Shukoh, a charismatic prince, who was assisted by two great generals, Raja Jai Singh of Amber and Dilir Khan Ruhela.

Sulaiman set out from Agra in early December 1657. At this time, Shuja was the only rebel prince in the field. Neither Aurangzeb nor Murad had committed any overt act of rebellion yet. They were bound to enter the fray, Dara knew, but he felt that he would have time to deal with them after tackling Shuja. To make sure that he had time, Dara sent two armies to the south, one under Kasim Khan to take over

Gujarat from Murad, and another under Raja Jaswant Singh of Marwar to take over Malwa from Shayista Khan, a suspected Aurangzeb loyalist. The two armies were to act in concert under the overall command of Jaswant, to block Aurangzeb's path and to prevent Murad from combining with him.

By the end of January 1658 Shuja had reached Varanasi, about 550 kilometres east of Agra, with Sulaiman rapidly closing in on him. On 24th February, in an early morning surprise attack on the slumbering Shuja, Sulaiman scattered the Bengal army and drove Shuja eastward, chasing him as far as Munger, some 350 kilometres further east. This ten-week long chase was tactically unnecessary and in fact proved fatal to Dara's cause, as it made it impossible for Sulaiman to return in time to be with his father in the crucial battle with Aurangzeb.

Ironically, it was, in a sense, Shah Jahan who sealed Dara's fate. Shah Jahan had instructed Sulaiman's generals to be clement towards Shuja, so at Varanasi they let him escape, though they had him in their grasp. Says Manucci, "Raja Jai Singh so controlled matters that he (Shuja) was allowed to retreat and save himself." The mischief of this leniency was compounded by Sulaiman's decision, against Jai Singh's advice, to pursue Shuja.

In mid-May, when Sulaiman was preparing to engage Shuja at Munger, he received an urgent message from Dara, ordering him to make peace with Shuja and rush back to Agra, as Aurangzeb had smashed through Jaswant's army in Malwa. Sulaiman then ceded Bengal, Orissa and eastern Bihar to Shuja, and immediately set out for Agra. But it was already too late.

Events had moved too fast. Aurangzeb, who was initially slow in his movements, was now advancing rapidly—while it had taken him about ten weeks to cover the 400 odd kilometres from Aurangabad to Ujjain, it took him only a little over half that time to cover the somewhat greater distance from Ujjain to the river Chambal just south of Agra. Sulaiman would not be able to return in time to save his father, or to save himself.

Sulaiman was still some 400 kilometres from Agra when the decisive battle between Dara and Aurangzeb took place at Samogarh near Agra on 8th June. The grim news of Dara's defeat and flight to Delhi reached him on 12th June at Kora, 330 kilometres east of Agra. He then paused to consider his options. Jai Singh, whose counsel he sought, was ambivalent: he advised Sulaiman either to advance (to Delhi) or to retreat (to Allahabad), but himself refused to accompany the prince; instead, he along with Dilir Khan went off with their contingents to Agra to join Aurangzeb, from whom they had, according to Manucci, received inviting letters.

Abandoned by his generals, Sulaiman retreated to Allahabad with a rump army of 6000. But he had a plan. At Allahabad, he crossed the Ganga and swung north, and skirting the enemy in Agra by a wide arc, passed through Lucknow and Moradabad and headed for Haridwar, intending to recross the Ganga there to join Dara in Punjab. But Aurangzeb, thorough and relentless, had foreseen the move and closed the ferries. Unable to join Dara, Sulaiman then struck north to the mountains, and, deserted by all but a handful of followers, sought refuge with the raja of Garhwal.

The raja was hospitable. He even gave Sulaiman a daughter in marriage. For about a year and a half, the prince lived in Garhwal, roughing it out in the hill country, but safe. Then, in January 1561, the long arm of Aurangzeb (who had by then ascended the throne) reached into the mountains to snatch Sulaiman away, forcing the raja to surrender the prince.

In Delhi, Sulaiman was brought in chains before Aurangzeb. Bernier, who was at the court when Sulaiman was brought in, reports: "Many of the courtiers shed tears at the sight of this interesting young man, who was tall and extremely handsome. The principal ladies of the court had permission to be present, concealed behind a lattice-work, and were greatly moved." Aurangzeb was unmoved. "The tyrant gloated over the sight," says Manucci, a Dara partisan, "this being the last thorn that could prick him." But characteristically Aurangzeb feigned kindness. "Be comforted," he said to Sulaiman. "No harm shall befall you. You shall be treated with tenderness." Sulaiman's only request was that he might please be put to death right way rather than be administered pousta, a narcotic concoction made out of crushed poppy heads soaked overnight in water, which, given daily over a period of time, turned men into zombies and slowly drained out life. Sulaiman did not want to die such a degrading death. Aurangzeb assured him that pousta would not be given to him, and dispatched him to Gwalior fort for confinement—where he, on Aurangzeb's orders, was forced to drink pousta every morning! Sulaiman lingered on for a year, feeble and witless, more vegetable than man. He died in May 1622, aged thirty. He was Shah Jahan's favourite grandson.

THERE WAS NO EXIGENT reason, personal or political, for Aurangzeb to inflict on Sulaiman such a wretched fate. But that was Aurangzeb's way, to double bolt every door. Caution was his second nature, deception his policy.

By the time Sulaiman was caught, Aurangzeb had been emperor

for nearly two years; Shah Jahan and Murad were his prisoners; Dara and Shuja were dead. This story has now to be told.

Aurangzeb had set out from Aurangabad on 15th February 1658 on his quest for the throne. He had not yet declared himself king, but the ambiguity and hesitation that had initially marked his response to the crisis were not there any more. His course was set. By his actions he made it clear that, contrary to what he was still saying in public, he was indeed seeking the crown—it was essential for him to make that clear, in order to retain the adherence of his officers, who would stay with him only if there was a prospect of sharing the spoils of power. Aurangzeb therefore now began to function like a monarch, bestowing titles and honours. He even appointed his own viceroy in the Deccan, his son Muazzam.

On 28th February, Aurangzeb reached Burhanpur. He would stay there for a month, gathering intelligence, completing his preparations and coordinating his moves with Murad. On 30th March, he advanced from Burhanpur with an army of some 30,000 veterans, including some Maratha contingents and Mir Jumla's train of artillery manned by European gunners. On 13th April he crossed the Narmada, the boundary between the Deccan and Hindustan. He was now in the ring.

Ten days later, he was joined by Murad at the Dipalpur lake, and together they pushed on towards Ujjain to give battle to the army sent by Dara to block their advance. The commanders of Dara's army, Jaswant Singh and Kasim Khan, were at a disadvantage in opposing Aurangzeb and Murad, for they were mere mansabdars, and by convention only princes could fight princes. Their inhibitions in this were compounded by the soft-hard ambivalence of Shah Jahan's guidelines to them. "To these leaders the king gave secret orders that on no account were they to give battle unless compelled," says Manucci. Shah Jahan wanted them to persuade the princes to go back to their provinces, and to use force only as the last resort. He certainly wanted Dara to win, but he did not want his other sons to lose, not lose their lives at any rate.

Shah Jahan's pacific directives put the imperial commanders in a passive frame of mind, and that presumably was why Jaswant did not thrust forward aggressively to prevent Aurangzeb and Murad from converging. He had arrived in Ujjain at the end of February, in time—and in position—to halt Murad's eastward advance to join Aurangzeb. He failed to do that. Instead, he very nearly allowed himself to be browbeaten by Aurangzeb, who curtly ordered him to get out of the way.

Jaswant pleaded his inability to yield to that demand, for he was under a firm order from Shah Jahan to prevent the advance of the princes. He therefore moved his army to Dharmat, a village about twenty-two kilometres south-west of Ujjain, on the western bank of the Gambhira, a tributary of the Chambal River, to block Aurangzeb's path. At the same time he tried, as the emperor had asked him to try, to persuade Aurangzeb to withdraw. "I do not want to fight," he wrote to Aurangzeb, "and I have no power to show audacity to your highness. If you pardon me and give up your project of a fight, I shall go and wait on you."

This plea for accommodation was more a courtesy than a practical suggestion. It was too late to affect a reconciliation. Aurangzeb could not retreat any more than Jaswant could step aside. There was no alternative to battle. Inevitably, Jaswant's posture was defensive; he did not want to defeat Aurangzeb, but only to block his advance. So he chose a narrow ground flanked by ditches and swamps to deploy his army; he even poured water on the battlefield, to make the ground slushy and hamper the enemy onset. It was as if he were preparing to stand a siege rather than to give battle.

The opposing forces were fairly evenly matched, numbering about 35,000 men each, though Aurangzeb had a marginal superiority, because of his greater fire power. The battle was joined on 25th April, a couple of hours after sunrise. It could have gone either way. At one point, a fierce Rajput charge rammed through Aurangzeb's artillery line and tore into his van, very nearly routing his army. If Kasim Khan had then advanced to support the Rajput surge, the momentum could probably have carried the imperialists to victory. But Kasim Khan stood idly by, probably with treachery in his heart. His passivity enabled Aurangzeb to reinforce his van, surround the Rajputs and cut them down. That settled the outcome of the battle.

Still Jaswant fought on, and the battle continued to rage for some eight hours, well into the afternoon. In the end the imperial army fled, the Rajput as well as the Muslim contingents, leaving behind some 6000 dead, most of them Rajputs.

For the next three days Aurangzeb camped in Ujjain, conferring honours, distributing booty, receiving defectors, mending the war damage and tending the wounded. Then he resumed his onward march.

WHEN NEWS OF THE debacle at Dharmat reached Agra, Dara sent off an urgent message to Sulaiman to return, and himself prepared for the now inevitable direct confrontation with Aurangzeb. Shah Jahan however continued to dream of an amicable settlement. "Shah Jahan constantly advised Dara not to engage in war, and always recommended peace," says Kambu. He suggested that Aurangzeb and Murad might be allowed to visit him at the Agra fort, for him to arrange peace. This was an impractical suggestion. To allow the victorious rebel princes free entry into Agra would have been virtual capitulation. Dara could not agree to that. Shah Jahan then sought "to extinguish the war by going in person to the camp, and making peace by his own exertions and speeches," reports Kambu. "So he ordered his advance tents to be pitched between the two armies."

Would that have defused the crisis? Unlikely. Aurangzeb was determined to exterminate Dara. As he was advancing on Agra, Aurangzeb had received a letter from Jahanara, which in effect expressed Shah Jahan's sentiments. "The emperor has recovered and is himself administering the state," she wrote. "Your armed advance is therefore an act of war against your father. Even if it is directed against Dara, it is no less sinful, since the eldest brother, both by Canon Law and common usage, stands in the position of the father." To this Aurangzeb replied indignantly, charging Dara with usurping power and attempting to destroy his younger brothers. "Against such overt hostility I am bound to take up arms in self-preservation," he wrote. For the sake of form, he continued to profess loyalty to Shah Jahan. "My wish . . . is only to go to Shah Jahan's presence and reveal everything to him personally," he wrote, but went on to threaten: "I shall not brook any obstacle to this loving design." He demanded that Dara should be sent to Punjab to avoid conflict.

This was a preposterous demand. Shah Jahan could not possibly be expected to banish Dara from the court on Aurangzeb's demand. On the other hand, Shah Jahan was not realistic in expecting Aurangzeb to withdraw in peace and negotiate away what he had won by his sword at Dharmat. Clearly, the issue had to be settled on the battlefield. Dara therefore persuaded Shah Jahan to abandon the conciliatory course he had taken. Dara would hazard the battle. He was confident of victory.

His confidence was not altogether misplaced. Even without Sulaiman around, he had enough resources and military might to stop Aurangzeb in his tracks. He had with him a well equipped army of about 50,000 men, with numerous guns and elephants. True, it was not a battle tested army, and many of his captains were, as Sarkar puts it, "carpet knights of the court". "The greater number of the soldiers that Dara had newly enlisted were not very warlike," says Manucci, who commanded an artillery division in Dara's army. "They were butchers, barbers, blacksmiths, carpenters, tailors, and such-like. It is true that on their horses and with their arms they looked well at a review; but they had·no heart and knew nothing of war." A further weakness of Dara was that there were many secret adherents of Aurangzeb in Dara's camp—according to Bernier, Aurangzeb boasted that in Dara's army "there were thirty thousand Mongols devoted to his service." Still, even with all those disabilities, Dara's was a formidable army.

On 28th May, at an auspicious hour, Dara set out from Agra with his army to oppose Aurangzeb. Shah Jahan bid him a fond farewell at the Diwan-i-am, the durbar hall, showering him with gifts. His parting advice to Dara was for caution. "I . . . entreat you, my beloved son, to avoid a battle until the arrival of Sultan Sulaiman Shukoh, your son," he said. "You will thus increase your chance of victory. I beg of you to curb your ardour." As Dara beseeched for permission to depart, Shah Jahan held him in a long and tender embrace before letting him go. Then he turned away, and lifting his arms in supplication, fervently prayed to Allah for Dara's safety and victory. He would never see his beloved son again.

From the steps of the Diwan-i-am, Dara climbed into a chariot—as was prescribed by Indian custom, while going on a southern campaign— and amidst a flourish of drums set out to battle his mortal enemy, his brother. "*Ghareeb mu'af, maghrur marg!*" Dara cried as he marched out— To the humble, pardon; to the haughty, death! His generals responded: "*Inshallah*"—By god's favour!

AFTER PROCEEDING A short distance in the chariot, Dara mounted a towering, magnificently caparisoned elephant to lead his grand army towards the Chambal River, which Aurangzeb had to cross to reach Agra. "We began the march in such great order that it seemed as if sea and land were united," writes Manucci. "Prince Dara amidst his squadron appeared like a crystal tower, resplendent as sun shining over all the land . . . A marvellous thing was it to behold the march, which moved over the heights and through the vales like the waves of a stormy sea."

In four days the army reached Daulpur on the northern bank of the Chambal, where Dara planned to hold Aurangzeb till Sulaiman Shukoh returned from Bihar, and then launch the decisive attack. It was a good plan. He had all the known Chambal fords guarded to prevent Aurangzeb from sneaking across, and himself took up a well-entrenched position at Daulpur. It would have been impossible for Aurangzeb to smash through those defences.

Aurangzeb did not even try to do that. Instead, he skirted Daulpur by swerving east from Gwalior and, aided by a local Bundela chief, located a little-known and unguarded ford about sixty-five kilometres downstream, and reached it by forced marches on 1st June. The trek to the ford was through extremely rough terrain, and Aurangzeb lost many soldiers and camp followers along the way. But it got him across the river unopposed. In one stroke he thus wrecked Dara's elaborate defence preparations, and put himself in a position to storm into Agra without any army to oppose him. In response, Dara hurriedly pulled out his army from the bulwarks and trenches at Daulpur, and took up a fresh blocking position on a wide, sandy plain at Samogarh, thirteen kilometres east of Agra.

Crossing the Chambal and heading north-west, Aurangzeb arrived at Samogarh on 7th June, with an army that after Dharmat had swelled to about 50,000. As soon as Aurangzeb was sighted, Dara drew up his forces and advanced, as if to give battle right away. That would have been the right decision, for Aurangzeb's army was exhausted from a long march and his guns were not in position. Inexplicably, after advancing a short distance, with Aurangzeb just a couple of kilometres away, Dara halted. He did that, says Manucci, because "traitors intervened on astrological grounds by saying that neither the day nor the hour was favourable . . . All this they did solely that Aurangzeb might have time to take rest, to refresh his people, and secure the arrival of his guns."

None of the Mughal chroniclers mention treachery. Dara was in any case predisposed to take a defensive posture, and he did not have the military experience to improvise strategy in the flux of the battlefield—having planned a defensive campaign, he was not able deftly to shift gears to attack. Moreover, says Manucci, "Dara received a letter from his father Shah Jahan, directing his retreat to Agra, there to entrench himself until the arrival of Sulaiman Shukoh." Dara could not possibly accept this advice—to retreat in the face of the enemy would have been unmanly—but the letter apparently reinforced his decision to fight only when attacked.

So he waited. And so did Aurangzeb. On seeing Dara approach, he too had marshalled his army and advanced, but halted at a cannon-shot distance from Dara, not wanting to rush into battle, says Khafi Khan. All day long the two armies in steel armor stood in battle array on the blazing sands under a broiling summer sun. Many soldiers fell where they stood from exhaustion; horses and elephants wilted. "The day was so hot that many strong men died from the heat of their armor and want of water," writes Khafi Khan.

At the evening prayer, the armies, wearied by the waiting and the heat, plodded back to their camps. The next day, 8th June, well before dawn, both Aurangzeb and Dara began to marshal their forces. By eight Aurangzeb was on the move, and by nine he was within the sight of Dara, who greeted him with fierce salvos of artillery. Aurangzeb replied briefly, then held his fire, as the armies were still beyond the range of the guns. Dara kept up the cannonade.

THEN THE FIRING ceased, and suddenly Dara's left wing exploded into action. With a wild war whoop, some 10,000 braves under Sipihr Shukoh, Dara's teenage son, and Rustam Khan Dakhini, a legendary warrior, galloped out of the curtain of cannon smoke and swooped down on Aurangzeb's artillery in front of them. The contingent staggered as the cannon and musket shots of the enemy slammed into them, and finding it impossible to overwhelm the guns, swung to the right and tore into Aurangzeb's van, mauling it badly. "Great confusion rose in this part of the army," says Khafi Khan. Then Rustam Khan swung left and fell on Aurangzeb's right. "Aurangzeb's forces wavered, and seemed about to give way," reports Khafi Khan, but somehow the onslaught was stemmed, Rustam killed and Sipihr hurled back.

While the action thus raged furiously on Aurangzeb's right, the Rajputs in the imperial van under the command of Chhatra Sal Hada tore into Murad on Aurangzeb's left, scattered his forces and very nearly killed the prince. Several arrows hit Murad, and his howdah "was stuck as thick with arrows as a porcupine with quills," says Khafi Khan. "Confusion arose in the ranks of Murad Bakhsh, so that many were overpowered with fear and fell back." As Aurangzeb from the centre hastened to aid Murad, the Rajputs, still on the rip tide of adrenaline, swung on him. "Raja Rup Singh Rathor," says Khafi Khan, "sprang from his horse, and, with the greatest daring, having washed his hands of life, cut his way through the ranks of his enemies sword in hand, cast himself under the elephant on which the prince (Aurangzeb) was riding, and began to cut the girths which secured the howdah." For a moment Aurangzeb was in mortal danger, then his guards cut down Rup Singh.

Meanwhile Dara with some 20,000 cavalry advanced from his position at the centre of his army. "Dara, who was ignorant of the rules of war and lacked experience in command, foolishly hastened with the Centre and the Advanced Reserve in person, after the charge of Rustam Khan, and placed his own Van and Artillery behind himself," mocks Muhammad Kazim, the official chronicler of Aurangzeb. This is the victor's version. The fact seems to be that Dara had smelt victory and was adding his weight for the final push—he advanced, notes Manucci, beating all his drums.

Victory did indeed seem his that morning. Advancing from his position, Dara angled to his left, presumably to support Rustam Khan, but was met with formidable fire from the enemy. He therefore commanded his own artillery to move up, but it could not, because, says Manucci, the moment Dara left his artillery behind him, "the barbers, butchers, and the rest turned right-about face, abandoning the artillerymen and the guns. Many made for the baggage-train to plunder it." Thwarted thus in his effort to support Rustam Khan, Dara turned right to take on Aurangzeb already under attack by the Rajputs. "Dara's design was to continue his advance until he had closed with Aurangzeb, and could attack him in person," says Manucci.

Dara was moving in for the kill. But as he proceeded, he made a short halt, "owing to the difficulties of the ground, and to the fatigue that overcame him," according to Manucci. More likely, Dara paused to get his bearings. The battle scene had changed dramatically in the hour or so since he launched forth triumphantly from his ranks. Rustam Khan was dead, his braves routed, and the Rajput onslaught, which had swept off Murad and threatened Aurangzeb, had been contained. "He became distracted and irresolute, and knew not what to do," says Khafi Khan. It was critical for Dara that the Rajputs should hold; if they were routed, the battle would be lost. It was presumably to reassess his battle plan that Dara paused. But in pausing, he lost momentum, and gave time for Aurangzeb to dress his ranks. It "hindered his winning the day," says Manucci. "Aurangzeb's lucky star worked in his favour."

But the day was not yet lost. Dara, though now nearly surrounded and set on by Aurangzeb's van and right wing, and under heavy fire, "failed not at all in that which is expected of a valiant general," says Manucci. He was however an easy target on his lofty elephant, so when a rocket struck his howdah, one of his generals ("the traitor Khalilullah Khan", who had been bought off by Aurangzeb, state Manucci and Ishwardas) called out to him to dismount from the elephant. Dara then got down hastily, "without even waiting to put on his slippers, and he then without arms mounted a horse," says Khafi Khan.

This was the decisive moment. It was not uncommon in India for a commander to get down from his elephant in the thick of a battle and mount a horse, or even to get down from his horse to fight on foot, to show his do-or-die will. Akbar had done it—in his campaign against Uzbeg rebels, "as the battle grew hot," says Nizamuddin, "the emperor (Akbar) alighted from his elephant and mounted a horse." But Dara's circumstances were different. There was panic in the air. And the haste in which Dara dismounted intensified the panic. "This was as if he had quitted victory," observes Manucci. Dara's empty howdah—Aurangzeb and Murad were on their elephants for all to see, but not Dara—was taken by his army to mean that he had fallen. A sudden victory flourish, opportunistically sounded by Aurangzeb's band, confirmed the alarm of Dara's army. At this moment, records Aqil Khan Razi, a searing hot wind rose from Aurangzeb's position and struck Dara's army in the face. The imperial army then fled "like dark clouds blown by a high wind", says Manucci.

The fates had determined that Dara should snatch defeat from the jaws of victory. In a moment, as it happens every so often in battles, all was lost. One of Dara's attendants then caught hold of the bridle of his horse and turned him away from the fight.

The battle had lasted barely three hours; it began at around nine in the morning, and by noon all was over. Dara lost some 10,000 men.

Fleeing from the battlefield, Dara headed for Agra. Pausing along the way for a short rest, he reached the city by about nine in the night. By then Agra knew of his fate, and lamentations for the dead were already echoing through the night. "The whole city was in an uproar," reports Manucci. In the imperial harem, and in Dara's palace, women wailed. Shah Jahan tried to console Dara by removing the sting of shame from the defeat. "What has brought you down to such a state is only the decree of Fate," he wrote to Dara. "It is better for you now to come to the fort and see me. After hearing what I have to say, you may go wherever Fate leads you. What is predestined for you will happen in every place that you may be in." But Dara was too ashamed to meet his father. He replied: "I have not the face to appear before Your Majesty in my wretched plight. Then, again, if I stay here longer, the troops of death will encircle and slay me . . . I beg you to pronounce the benediction of farewell on this distracted and half-dead man in the long journey that he has before him."

Dara quickly gathered his family—his wife Nadira Banu, his children and grandchildren—and in the dead of night fled towards Delhi with just a handful of followers. Shah Jahan sent for him mule loads of gold, and ordered the governor of Delhi to open the treasury there for his use. In the following couple of days, about 5000 of his troops joined Dara on the way to Delhi. He could not yet be written off.

FOR AURANGZEB, HIS victory at Samogarh was the divine confirmation of the rightness of his cause against his infidel brother. When the fighting ceased, Aurangzeb got down from his elephant, spread his prayer carpet on the battlefield, and knelt to offer a prayer of thanksgiving. He then proceeded to Dara's tent and occupied it. Soon, Murad too arrived there. Severely wounded, he was the man of the moment, the hero. "Prince Murad Bakhsh had received many arrow wounds in his face and body," reports Khafi Khan. "Aurangzeb first applied to them the salve of praise and compliment, and then had them dressed by skillful surgeons . . . Then he wiped away the tears and blood from his brother's cheek with the sleeve of condolence." According to Manucci, Aurangzeb graciously credited the day's victory to Murad's valour, and announced that it was indeed the first day of Murad's reign.

There was revelry that night in the victor's camp, but the next day Aurangzeb was on the move again, rushing squadrons to blockade Agra, perhaps hoping to trap Dara. Two days later, Aurangzeb himself arrived at the city, and camped at the Nur-manzil (Abode of Light) garden in the suburbs, where the imperial amirs, ever loyal to their bread but seldom true to their salt, abandoned Shah Jahan and flocked to Aurangzeb. A large number of Dara's soldiers also joined him.

Aurangzeb's immediate problem was how to deal with Shah Jahan. Soon after the battle of Samogarh, Aurangzeb had written to Shah Jahan, says Khafi Khan, "excusing himself by referring all to the will of God." Shah Jahan now responded by sending to Aurangzeb the celebrated sword Alamgir (Conqueror of the Universe)—which name Aurangzeb would later, on his enthronement, adopt as his title—and other opulent presents, and inviting him to the fort for a parley. But the wary prince, fearing a trap, refused to go. Instead, needing the treasures of Agra to continue the fight against his brothers, he bid Shah Jahan to surrender the fort. But there was still fight left in the aged emperor. Incensed by his son's brazen demand, he shut the gates of the fort, and prepared to defend it with some 1500 slaves he had with him. He was not yet ready to leave himself at the mercy of his son.

Aurangzeb had till then worn the mask of a distraught son fighting to release his father from the evil clutch of Dara, but he now dropped this mask and strapped on another, claiming that his obligation as a true believer overrode his filial obligations, and that it was necessary to save the empire from his inept father.

It thus came to be that the issue between father and son had to be settled with cannons and muskets. Aurangzeb mounted his guns on the terrace of the Jama Masjid and Dara's riverside mansion and lobbed a few shells into the fort, more as a terror tactic than as a serious bombardment. In response, the guns at the fort opened up defiantly, and kept up the cannonade long after Aurangzeb's guns fell silent, inflicting little damage, but shaming Aurangzeb into changing his tactic. Clearly Shah Jahan could not be intimidated into submission. On the other hand, the fort was too strong to be stormed, and a siege would take too long. In that quandary, Aurangzeb had a better (or worse) idea—he cut off the water supply to the fort from the Yamuna, prompting Shah Jahan to fire yet another shot at Aurangzeb, a missive. He wrote:

> *My son, my hero!*
> *Why should I complain of unkind fortune,*
> *Seeing that not a leaf falls without God's will?*
> *Yesterday I had an army of nine hundred thousand,*
> *Today I am in need of a pitcher of water! . . .*
> *O, prosperous son, be not proud*
> *of the good luck of this treacherous world!*

On the back of Shah Jahan's letter Aurangzeb wrote his curt reply: "*Karda-i-khwesh ayed pesh*"—as we sow, so we reap! Later, as a salve to Shah Jahan's hurt feelings, he wrote: "If Your Majesty surrenders the gates of the fort to my men . . . I shall go and wait on you, consent to whatever you wish, and do nothing displeasing or harmful to you." Shah Jahan was not deceived. He would not surrender the fort. For three days he held out, then with several thousand inmates of the citadel in torment without water in the summer heat, he surrendered.

Aurangzeb sent his son Muhammad Sultan to take over the fort, with orders to seize the treasures and arsenals, to confine the dethroned emperor to his private apartments, and to keep a close watch over him. According to Khafi Khan, Aurangzeb ordered that "all means of intercourse with the outside world" should be cut off from Shah Jahan. When Muhammad presented himself to Shah Jahan, proffering his father's gifts and apologies, Shah Jahan broke down and wept. Aurangzeb himself would not ever go to see his father, not even to attend his funeral eight years later.

A couple of days after the surrender of the fort, Jahanara called on Aurangzeb, to propose a division of the empire between the four brothers. Aurangzeb would not hear of any mercy being shown to Dara. "Dara is an infidel and a friend of the Hindus," he said. "He must be extirpated for the sake of the true faith and the peace of the realm."

On 20th June, Aurangzeb held a grand durbar, to assume de facto control of the empire and to appoint imperial officers. He had not yet formally mounted the throne, but there was no doubt in anybody's mind who the emperor now was.

Murad was nowhere in the picture. He had been relegated to the background after his brief moment in the limelight at Samogarh. Aurangzeb had no further use for Murad. He could be done away with.

MURAD RESENTED THE neglect. The victory at Samogarh was his, he believed, but the rewards had all gone to Aurangzeb. As legend has it, Aurangzeb had strung Murad along till then by feigning that his own interest in the succession struggle was to ensure that the heretical Dara did not become emperor, and that he himself would retire to a religious life once Murad was securely placed on the throne. Aurangzeb had in fact written a letter to Murad stating this.

The letter, says Khafi Khan, was written "as a matter of prudence and expediency", and in it Aurangzeb told Murad, "I have not the slightest liking for or wish to take any part in the government of this deceitful and unstable world . . . But whatever course you have resolved upon in opposition to the good-for-nothing . . . disgraceful brother, you may consider me your sincere friend and ally." According to Ishwardas, Aurangzeb wrote: "My desire is that I should retire to a secret corner and spend the days and nights in the worship of the Almighty whose blessing constitutes the only true happiness. But, then I thought that at first I should place the dear brother firmly on the throne of the capital, Akbarabad, and after witnessing his auspicious and successful coronation, and gathering happiness and pleasure from it, return to fulfil my heart's desire . . ."

Aurangzeb, it is said, used to refer to Murad as Padishah-ji (Your Highness), while asking Murad to call him Hazrat-ji (Your Holiness). Such deceit was quite in character with the master dissembler that Aurangzeb was; also, in a formal sense, it would have been correct for Aurangzeb to address Murad as king, for Murad had declared himself king and Aurangzeb had not. But Aurangzeb certainly had not renounced political ambitions. There was in fact a proposal by Aurangzeb to partition the empire, by which Murad was to get Afghanistan, Kashmir, Punjab and Sind, nearly one-third of the empire, and Aurangzeb would take the remaining two-thirds, intending to offer half of his share to Shuja, in an equal division of the empire between the three anti-Dara princes. It is not however clear what the actual arrangement was between the two brothers, or what Aurangzeb said, what he concealed, and what Murad understood.

Whatever the deal, Aurangzeb had in his hour of need fawned over Murad, and Murad, impetuous and gullible, had fallen for the cajolery.

But now, as Aurangzeb's power and prestige grew by the hour, Murad's stature shrank by the same measure. Murad felt let down, and began to sulk. And his courtiers, whose fortune depended on his fortune, played on his resentment and aggravated the tension between the brothers. Some even suggested a preemptive strike to seize Aurangzeb. But such complicated machinations were beyond Murad. He however stopped visiting Aurangzeb as a precaution.

When, after a two-week stay in Agra, the brothers set out for Delhi in pursuit of Dara, Murad kept a few kilometres behind Aurangzeb, sullen and menacing. Aurangzeb moved very slowly. Twelve days out of Agra, we find him at Mathura, a mere fifty kilometres away. He did not want to close in on Dara without first eliminating the threat from behind. So he set about in his usual crafty manner to lay a trap for Murad, by showing him various favours and sending him beguiling messages to lull his suspicions. At Mathura the trap was sprung. One day, when Murad was returning from a hunt and was passing by Aurangzeb's camp, he was induced by one of his attendants—presumably bribed by Aurangzeb—to stop by. Aurangzeb received Murad with great cordiality, and the brothers feasted together, during which Murad was liberally plied with wine. "Drink in my presence," Aurangzeb told him, "as I long to see you supremely happy after so many adversities." Murad was then invited to rest a while in an adjoining tent, and a lovely slave-girl was sent in to massage him to sleep.

"Oppressed by wine, Murad Bakhsh went on sleeping," says Manucci. "But Aurangzeb was wide awake." As Murad slumbered, the slave girl left. Only his personal guard remained in the tent, armed and alert. But he too was induced to step out—bbeckoned by Aurangzeb himself, as if wanting to consult him on something, according to Manucci—and was garrotted by Aurangzeb's men lurking outside. Murad's weapons were then quietly removed from his side, where he had placed them when he lay down. Aurangzeb's officers then entered the tent and bound Murad's feet—in golden fetters, as a tribute to his princely status. This jolted Murad awake, but he found resistance futile, and submitted quietly, merely cursing Aurangzeb for breaking his word pledged on the Koran—to which Aurangzeb replied that what was being done was for his own good, and for the good of the state!

Before dawn broke, Murad was dispatched to Delhi in a covered howdah (of the type used by harem women) on an elephant, to be confined in Salimgarh, the island fortress on the Yamuna in Delhi. To confuse possible rescuers, three other elephants with identical closed howdahs were sent in different directions. But the precaution proved unnecessary. Nobody made an effort to rescue Murad. Instead, his officers and troops promptly went over to Aurangzeb.

From Salimgarh, Murad was later shifted to Gwalior fort, where Sulaiman Shukoh and Aurangzeb's rebel son Muhammad Sultan would join him in confinement. But Murad alive, even in confinement, was a threat to Aurangzeb, especially as the dashing though reckless prince had become a folk hero, and ballads about him were being sung in the bazaars. There was even an attempt one night to rescue Murad, which failed only because his concubine, Saraswati Bai, broke out in loud lamentations when he went to bid her farewell—"For whom are you leaving me?" she howled—which alerted the guards and aborted the plot.

Murad spent nearly three years in prison. Then Aurangzeb contrived a means to liquidate him, under the cover of judicial propriety, which was his preferred mode of political murder. A son of Ali Naqi, an amir whom Murad had a few years back slain in a rage in Gujarat, was persuaded to file a complaint against the prince in the courts, and to insist on enforcing the Islamic law of blood for blood. And Aurangzeb directed the Kazi at Gwalior that "after a lawful judgment had been given, the retaliation for blood should be exacted from the prince." Murad refused to degrade himself by pleading his case. Sentenced to death, he was executed in December 1661, and his corpse buried in the Traitors Cemetery in Gwalior Fort.

Dara's Last Stand

AFTER THE ARREST of Murad, Aurangzeb marched on to Delhi, from where Dara had long since fled to Lahore. It had been six and a half months since Aurangzeb set out from the Deccan to win the throne. The throne was now vacant and his to occupy. But Aurangzeb was in no hurry. He was concerned with the substance of power, not its form, and the substance of power was not yet quite secure in his hands. Dara and Shuja, defeated but not destroyed, were still lurking in the background. They had to be eliminated before Aurangzeb could be safe. There was also the embarrassment of the dethroned emperor still being around. The throne however could not be left vacant for long. The empire needed an emperor. So, on 31st July 1658 Aurangzeb ascended the throne in Delhi, somewhat reluctantly and in a token manner—not in the imperial palace, but at the Shalimar Garden in the suburbs of Delhi. He did not even bother to mint coins or have the khutbah read in his name, nor were there any grand festivities. There would be time enough for all this later.

Aurangzeb remained in Delhi for about three weeks, busy with preparations to continue his campaign against Dara, and looking into the pressing matters of administration. Then, a week after his accession, he proceeded to Lahore, where Dara was recruiting a fresh army.

Defeated at Samogarh, Dara had the option of fleeing to the east or to the west. Both had their attractions. In the east was the victorious army of Sulaiman Shukoh, with which he could join up to make a strong stand against Aurangzeb. The disadvantage of the eastern option was that if Shuja and Aurangzeb acted in concert, Dara would be trapped between them. By moving west, on the other hand, Dara could, by forming an alliance with Shuja, trap Aurangzeb in the middle. Moreover, in the west lay the vast treasures of Delhi and Lahore, with which a new army could be recruited and equipped; also in Lahore were the armaments that Shah Jahan had collected for the Kandahar campaigns. As for Sulaiman, he could skirt around Aurangzeb and join Dara in Delhi or Punjab. And if all failed, and Dara was not able to make a stand in Punjab, he would still have elbow room to manoeuvre, go to Kabul, Sind, Rajasthan or Gujarat or even to the Deccan and continue the fight, or escape to Persia. If he moved to the east, and his enterprise failed, he would be bottled up and destroyed.

These were, we must assume, the considerations that prompted Dara to flee westward. It was a sound move. But its success depended on Dara's ability to inspire confidence through heroic leadership and bold action. Aurangzeb now had an army that was much larger than any that Dara could deploy, and the only way Dara could win was by an Akbarian ferocity of attack. But Dara, gentle, humane and philosophical, lacked ferocity. Nor did he have the low cunning of Aurangzeb, to sow dissension among the enemy and win over deserters.

Dara's initial plan was to wait in Delhi for Sulaiman. But as the hope of Sulaiman joining him there faded, he had no alternative but to move on to Punjab, to gain time and to widen the distance between himself and his relentless adversary. On 22nd June, the day before Aurangzeb set out from Agra, Dara left Delhi for Lahore, destroying the boats as he crossed the Satluj into Punjab, to prevent easy pursuit. He had hoped that Aurangzeb, his forces exhausted by the long march from the Deccan and the two great battles he had fought, would not pursue him right away, but this was wishful thinking. Aurangzeb arrived in Punjab within weeks after Dara, forcing him to flee again. Though Dara had in Lahore an army that numbered a respectable 20,000, he did not dare to pit those raw recruits against Aurangzeb's much larger force of veterans. He needed respite to organize himself.

But there would be no respite. As Dara fled south towards Multan, Aurangzeb swung after him and began to close in by forced marches. There was at this time much disquiet in Dara's camp, and many, perceiving his cause to be hopeless, deserted him. Aurangzeb fished expertly in those troubled waters, planting forged letters to make Dara doubt the loyalty of even his trusted lieutenant, Daud Khan, and dismiss him from service. By the time Dara reached Multan, his army had shrunk to 14,000, and half of them deserted him as he fled again on the approach of Aurangzeb.

AS DARA RETREATED from Multan, Aurangzeb himself turned away from Dara and, leaving it to his generals to continue the chase, hastened back to Delhi to deal with a fresh emergency there, caused by Shuja's suspicious movement from Rajmahal to Patna. Covering two stages a day, Aurangzeb rushed to Delhi in double-quick time, and arrived there on 30th November.

Aurangzeb had been in correspondence with Shuja ever since the crisis broke, and after Samogarh had offered him the eastern third of the empire in return for cooperation against Dara. But Shuja was not Murad; he could recognize a ploy when he saw one. An empire is not partitioned in brotherly goodwill, he knew: whatever he got, would have to be won in the battlefield. So when Shuja learned that Aurangzeb had gone to Punjab in pursuit of Dara, he set out from Rajmahal, his capital on the southward bend of the Ganga, and arrived at Patna, some 400 kilometres to the west, in October 1658. He obviously meant to make a dash for Agra.

Shuja had a chance to seize Agra, as Aurangzeb's hot chase after Dara had left the city vulnerable, with no strong force between it and Bengal. He missed the chance by moving too slowly. It was only by the end of October that he advanced from Patna. By then Aurangzeb, alert to the danger, was already half way back to Delhi from Punjab, and by the time Shuja reached Varanasi, Aurangzeb was in Delhi, from where he ordered Muhammad Sultan in Agra to advance against Shuja. He himself followed soon after. So when Shuja reached Allahabad in early January 1659, he found Muhammad Sultan already at Kora, a short distance away, to contest the passage to Agra.

On 12th January, Aurangzeb too arrived at Kora, and was joined by Mir Jumla from the Deccan, who had been released from Daulatabad and summoned by Aurangzeb to assist him. Aurangzeb's army now numbered some 90,000 cavalry, mammoth enough to swallow up Shuja, who lay thirteen kilometres east of Kora, at the village of Khajwa, with just 23,000 horsemen. On 13th January Aurangzeb moved up intimidatingly to about a kilometre and a half from Shuja's position. "A dense cloud of dust hid the earth and sky," as his army advanced, writes Kazim.

Despite the overwhelming numerical preponderance of his army, Aurangzeb very nearly lost the battle to Shuja. He was in trouble even before the battle began. Around 4 a.m. on 14th January, a mere three or four hours before the battle was to be joined, Raja Jaswant Singh, who commanded Aurangzeb's right wing, incensed by some slight he had suffered, suddenly broke loose and deserted the army with a contingent of 14,000 Rajputs, "destroying and plundering as they went, and cutting down all who opposed them," writes Khafi Khan. For a while nobody knew what was happening and feared the worst. "A panic was spreading through the whole army," continues Khafi Khan. "Many men were so disheartened that they joined the plunderers, thinking that the best way of escaping disaster. One party fled to the open country; another approached the enemy's army, and set about ravaging . . . Without exaggeration, half the army had gone away to plunder or escape, and many had joined the enemy."

Fortunately for Aurangzeb, Jaswant Singh did not go over to Shuja, but returned to Rajasthan. Still, his flight put Aurangzeb in great peril. If Shuja had attacked in the midst of the confusion, he could possibly have defeated Aurangzeb. Jaswant Singh had in fact sent a message to Shuja about his intended betrayal and invited him to attack when he heard the clamour. But Aurangzeb's craftiness once again came to his rescue, this time by proxy. Shuja suspected that the message he received from Jaswant Singh was a ruse of Aurangzeb to lure him into an ambush. So when he heard the hubbub in the enemy camp he did nothing.

Aurangzeb's cool courage saved the situation. "For all this confusion in the army," notes Khafi Khan, "nothing shook the resolution of Aurangzeb." The news of Jaswant's flight was conveyed to Aurangzeb when he was at his pre-dawn prayer. Unperturbed, he finished his prayer, then rose to prepare calmly for the battle, dismissing Jaswant's flight as irrelevant. The sheer psychic pull of Aurangzeb's calm soon stilled the tumult among his men. As the day broke, and the reason for the commotion came to be known, and the flight of the Rajputs was recognized as inconsequential in that vast army, many of the scattered troops returned to the camp. Aurangzeb then rode out on his elephant to inspect his army and found that he yet had about 60,000 soldiers, nearly three times the strength of Shuja's army.

Still, Aurangzeb was sorely tried that day. Shuja was a more daring and innovative general than Aurangzeb, and he used the velocity of his small army to pierce the mass of Aurangzeb's horde. The battle began at 8 a.m. with an artillery duel, as usual. Then Shuja unleashed his right wing against Aurangzeb's left, leading with three furious, heavy-chain-wielding elephants, which swept all before them. Shuja then swung his left wing into action. Under this combined onslaught, Aurangzeb's left wing collapsed, his centre wavered, and his right wing "fell into confusion". But Aurangzeb himself stood firm. When he was attacked by one of Shuja's mammoths, he ordered the legs of his elephant to be chained together to prevent it from fleeing. There would be no retreat for him, no flight. This show of resolution rallied his men. The moment of danger passed. Aurangzeb then gathered the entire weight and firepower of his immense army and sent it rolling like a giant tidal wave to engulf the enemy. Shuja could save himself only by dismounting from his elephant and fleeing on a horse.

As Shuja fled, Aurangzeb sent an army of 30,000 under the command of Prince Muhammad Sultan and Mir Jumla to hunt him down. Shuja, with his army reduced to 10,000, made several stands on his way to Bengal, but was forced to retreat each time. Mir Jumla was ever at his heels, giving him no respite, though for a brief while Mir Jumla himself was in trouble, because of the disaffection of Muhammad Sultan who, chaffing under the command of Mir Jumla and enticed by the prospect of marrying Shuja's ravishing daughter, Gulrukh Begum, deserted to Shuja. (Muhammad Sultan would later re-defect, but his unforgiving father would keep him in prison for the rest of his life.) Mir Jumla however continued the relentless pursuit, till Shuja was driven out of Bengal in mid-May 1660, sixteen months after the battle of Khajwa.

Shuja with his family and about forty soldiers fled to seek refuge with the barbaric Magh pirate king of Arakan to the east of Bengal. How his life ended is uncertain. A plausible story, offered by the European traders in the area and mentioned by Manucci, is that in January 1561 Shuja, the would-be emperor, unable to reconcile himself to being a destitute refugee, plotted to overthrow his host, but was driven away into the jungles, where he was cut down by the Maghs. When the news of the likely death of Shuja reached Aurangzeb, he ordered funeral obsequies, to set at rest the spectre of Shuja's return. "In Arracan all traces of Shuja disappeared," writes Khafi Khan.

AT THE TIME Aurangzeb was confronting Shuja at Khajwa, Dara was in Gujarat. He had fled from Multan towards Tatta in southern Sind in mid-September 1658, his army reduced to 3000 on the way, a mere one fifth of the pursuing force. Along the way he thought of turning off to Kandahar for refuge in Persia, but his women, terrified of passing through the wild Baluchi country, dissuaded Dara. He therefore set his course to Gujarat, and in mid-November crossed over to the left bank of the Indus at Tatta. At that point the pursuing army, summoned back by Aurangzeb, turned around to rejoin the emperor then on his way to Delhi. They could ignore Dara for the time being. Shuja had to be tackled first.

Crossing the Indus, Dara headed south-east, and toiling through the forbidding, waterless Rann of Kachchh (Kutch), but hospitably received along the way by local chiefs eager for a Mughal connection, he reached Ahmadnagar, the capital of Gujarat, in January 1659. There he found favour with Shah Nawaz Khan, the governor, who, although he was Aurangzeb's father-in-law, opened the provincial treasury for Dara and helped him to recruit an army of 22,000. Cannons were procured from Surat.

Dara could now dream of the throne again. Garbled versions of Aurangzeb's tussle with Shuja had reached Gujarat—there was a rumour that Aurangzeb had been routed—and that buoyed up Dara's spirits.

Babur and his sons: miniature from Rajasthan, sixteenth century by Dip Chand. Victoria & Albert Museum, London/Bridgeman Art Library

Above left: The building of Fatehpur Sikri palace complex: *Akbar-nama*, sixteenth century. Victoria & Albert Museum, London/Bridgeman Art Library

Above right: A polo game: Mughal painting, seventeenth century. Victoria & Albert Museum, London/Bridgeman Art Library

Opposite page (clockwise)
Mughal garden entertainment: *Babur-nama*, sixteenth century. British Library, London/The Art Archive

Royal marriage festivity: *Akbar-nama*, sixteenth century. Victoria & Albert Museum, London/The Art Archive

Akbar hunting tigers: *Akbar-nama*, sixteenth century. Victoria & Albert Museum, London/Bridgeman Art Library

The siege of Chitor by Akbar: *Akbar-nama*, sixteenth century. Victoria & Albert Museum, London/Bridgeman Art Library

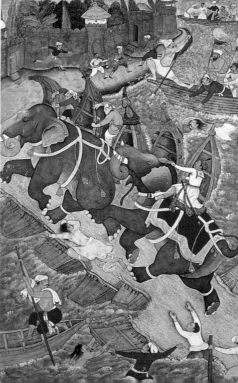

Above left: Jahangir riding, with hawk: Mughal painting, seventeenth century. The Bodleian Library, Oxford (MS Douce Or a1 folio 54r)/The Art Archive

Above right: Dancing girl: Mughal painting, seventeenth–eighteenth century. Phoenix Art Museum, Arizona/Bridgeman Art Library

Jahangir holding a portrait of Akbar: Mughal painting, seventeenth century. Musée Guimet, Paris/Bridgeman Art Library

Opposite page (clockwise)
Akbar at a fight between two Hindu ascetic sects: *Akbar-nama*, sixteenth century. Victoria & Albert Museum, London/Bridgeman Art Library

Imperial household celebrating the birth of Akbar's second son, Murad: *Akbar-nama*, sixteenth century. Victoria & Albert Museum, London/Bridgeman Art Library

Akbar controlling elephants rampaging across a bridge of boats on the Yamuna: *Akbar-nama*, sixteenth century. British Museum, London/Bridgeman Art Library

Dancing girls entertain Akbar: *Akbar-nama*, sixteenth century. Victoria & Albert Museum, London/Bridgeman Art Library

Clockwise

Sa'd-ullah Khan, Shah Jahan's prime minister, holding durbar: Mughal painting, seventeenth century. The Bodleian Library, Oxford (MS Douce Or a1 folio 21r)/The Art Archive

Shah Jahan: Mughal painting, seventeenth century. Victoria & Albert Museum, London/The Art Archive

Shah Jahan receives Persian general Ali Mardan Khan: Mughal painting, seventeenth century. The Bodleian Library, Oxford (MS Ousley Add 173 folio 13)/The Art Archive

The Taj Mahal, Agra by Thomas and William Daniell: aquatint, 1801. Private collection/Bridgeman Art Library

Murad Bakhsh on horseback: Mughal painting, seventeenth century. British Library, London/Bridgeman Art Library

Aurangzeb and courtiers: Mughal painting, eighteenth century. Chester Beatty Library, Dublin/Bridgeman Art Library

But neither Dara nor Shuja was moving with time and tide. If Shuja had advanced when Dara was still in Delhi, or if Dara had returned to Hindustan when Aurangzeb was marching against Shuja, Aurangzeb would have been in trouble. As it was, it was only on 24th February, more than a month after Shuja was overwhelmed at Khajwa, that Dara started from Gujarat towards Agra. Still he was hopeful. Raja Jaswant Singh of Marwar, who had deserted Aurangzeb, had offered to marshal the Rajputs for Dara. If Jaswant joined him with 15-or-20,000 Rajputs, Dara would have a fighting chance against Aurangzeb. With this hope he set out for Marwar, after securing from the "promise-breaking raja a covenant . . . confirmed with the most solemn Hindu pledges," says Kambu.

The fickle Jaswant broke his word. He had advanced some distance to join Dara when he got a letter from Raja Jai Singh, assuring him of Aurangzeb's pardon and the restoration of honours if he returned to loyalty, but threatening certain destruction if he did not. This made Jaswant change sides again. "Necessity turns lions into foxes," comments Khafi Khan. Dara even sent his son Sipihr Shukoh to plead with the raja, but to no avail.

Meanwhile Aurangzeb, having returned from the battle with Shuja, was rapidly closing in on Dara. So there was no time for Dara to withdraw safely into Gujarat. He had run enough, anyway. The time had come for him to make a last stand. So, advancing towards Ajmer, he took a carefully chosen position at Deorai, seven kilometres south of the town, his flanks protected by two hills of the Aravalli Range, and his front by embankments and trenches. His guns, behind the embankments and on a hillock overlooking the plain, dominated the battlefield.

On 21st March, Aurangzeb arrived at Deorai and encamped three kilometres east of Dara's position. The battle was joined the next day, and commenced as usual with an artillery duel. The tactical advantage clearly was with Dara. Aurangzeb had to clamber up a slope to give battle, and his huge army, squeezed tight into the narrow valley, was unable to use its strength, while Dara could mow it down with his well placed guns. The disadvantage of Dara's position was that it had little offensive potential—while it was difficult for Aurangzeb to overrun Dara, it was equally difficult for Dara to rout Aurangzeb. But given Dara's predicament, to stave off defeat would have been victory enough. From that point of view, Dara's strategy was masterly, his position virtually impregnable. What Dara lacked was not generalship, but luck.

Unlike the three-hour battle of Samogarh, at Deorai the battle raged on for an unprecedented three days. But at the end of the third day, by nightfall, in a confused mêlée in the dark, Aurangzeb managed to overrun one of Dara's entrenchments. And that, like breaching the wall of a fortress, immediately rendered Dara's fort-like position indefensible.

Dara did not tarry. Even while the battle was raging, he fled in the dark of the night, accompanied by his fifteen-year-old son Sipihr Shukoh and a small band of followers. In his hasty flight Dara even missed the rendezvous with his women who, along with his treasure, had been waiting since noon on the banks of Ana Sagar, a lake on the outskirts of Ajmer, mounted on elephants and ready for any contingency. When no word came from Dara they took off on their own, but not before the treasure with them was plundered by the very Rajput guards to whom Dara had entrusted its safekeeping. "Struggling and fighting with each other, every man seized what he could lay hands on," writes Khafi Khan. "The baggage was taken from the backs of the elephants and placed on camels, and the women were stripped of their jewels and taken off the camels to be mounted on the elephants; then the plunderers, with camels and horses laden with money and articles of great value, made off for the desert."

Luckily, the women, led by the faithful eunuch Khwaja Maqul, fled in the same direction as Dara, and joined up with him the following evening. The fugitives were pillaged along the way by rampaging soldiers as well as by villagers. Kulis, a tribe of professional robbers, followed Dara's convoy like hyenas, falling on stragglers. Dara headed for Gujarat, a "forlorn fugitive, in sore distress, without baggage, and despoiled by plunderers", as Khafi Khan describes him. His army had scattered in different directions in the confusion of the night flight, but some 2000 of them joined him along the way, in an extraordinary show of loyalty to a lost cause.

Aurangzeb would not let Dara escape. Immediately after the battle, he sent Raja Jai Singh and Bahadur Khan after Dara, and they were joined in the hunt by Jaswant Singh, Dara's one time would-be succourer. The local chiefs along Dara's path were alerted and urged to arrest the fugitive. Wherever he went, Dara was in peril. Somehow, though pursued by an imperial army of 20,000, he managed to reach Gujarat. There he found Ahmadnagar closed to him by Aurangzeb's adherents, who had taken over the city.

Dara's situation was pathetic. He was utterly destitute, dressed in a thin linen tunic and cheap shoes. He was not even able to provide privacy for his women, a matter of great dishonour for a Mughal aristocrat. Bernier, the French physician accompanying Dara, records that the panels shielding the harem tents were tied to the carriage in which he was resting! "The shrieks of the females drew tears from every eye," writes Bernier. "We were all overwhelmed with confusion and dismay, gazing in speechless horror at each other, at a loss what plan to recommend, and ignorant of the fate which perhaps awaited us from hour to hour. We observed Dara stepping out, more dead than alive, speaking now to one, then to another; stopping and consulting even the commonest soldier. He saw consternation depicted on every countenance, and felt assured that he should be left without a single follower."

There was no time even for rest. The pursuers were close behind. So Dara once again trudged through the Rann of Kachchh and escaped into Sind, pursued by Jai Singh. It was a wonder that he managed to escape. According to Manucci, this was possible because Jai Singh did not want to capture Dara, but only drive him out of the empire. "However much the men of Aurangzeb might follow and press upon Dara, Rajah Jai Singh still arranged the day's march that there was ever room for the unfortunate and dishonoured prince to escape," says Manucci. Finally, when Dara crossed the Indus at Sehwan and left the Mughal empire, Jai Sigh gave up the chase and proceeded to Delhi.

Dara could no longer fight for the throne. His only thought now was to save himself and his family from destruction. For that, the only way out for him was to flee to Persia. From Sehwan he therefore headed for the Bolan Pass to go to Kandahar. Dara also had the option, if fortune favoured him, of advancing from Kandahar to Kabul, and from there to try his fortune in India again.

NONE OF THAT would be. A malevolent fate still held Dara pinioned in its talons. On the way to the Bolan Pass, his favourite wife, Nadira Banu, his good companion in weal and woe and the mother of his three sons, passed away—she died of "dysentery and vexation", according to Khafi Khan, which is plausible, but it is equally plausible that, as Manucci says, she committed suicide by taking poison, for she hated to leave India and in any case had had enough of life. Nadira's death finally broke Dara's will to fight, even to live. "Mountain after mountain of trouble thus pressed upon the heart of Dara," writes Khafi Khan; "grief was added to grief, sorrow to sorrow, so that his mind no longer retained its equilibrium." It was time for him to give up the struggle.

Nadira's last wish was to be buried in India. Dara therefore sent her body to Lahore with an escort of the few soldiers still remaining with him, to be buried in the tomb of Mian Mir, his spiritual preceptor. He was now entirely without a military escort. Only a few eunuchs and servants remained with him.

Before he could resume his journey, Dara needed a little time to compose himself, to tap the very last reserves of will and energy to keep going. At Dadar, a mere fourteen kilometres east of the Bolan Pass and safety, Dara sought a moment's respite with an Afghan tribal chieftain named Malik Jiwan. Dara had good reason to expect hospitality from Malik, for Malik owed his very life to Dara, who had once interceded to save him after Shah Jahan had ordered him to be trampled to death by an elephant for an offence against the state. "This evil zemindar, Malik Jiwan, came out like a destroying angel to meet him," writes Khafi Khan. The fates had carefully chosen Malik for the final, grim act, for to be betrayed by a man with such a debt as Malik owed to Dara, was the fitting denouement of Dara's tragic life.

Dara's women pleaded with him not to go to the Pathan, but "Dara, as if hurried away by his evil genius", would not listen, says Bernier. When Dara arrived at Dadar, Malik waited on him three kilometres outside his fort and conducted him to his house with all honour and courtesy. For three days Dara rested there.

On 19th June, Dara began the short trek towards the Bolan Pass. There was no haste now. Safety was close at hand. But so was Malik. Tribal honour would not permit Malik to molest Dara as long as he was his guest, but once Dara left the fort, he was fair game for the predator. Dara was a limp prey. When Malik swooped down on the fugitives, there was no resistance, except from Sipihr Shukoh, who was too young to die.

Dara, his son and two daughters were then taken back to Jiwan's fort. On getting word from Malik of Dara's capture, Jai singh and Bahadur Khan, who were then proceeding north along the Indus after abandoning the pursuit of Dara, crossed the Indus to the right bank, and on 3rd July took charge of the captives.

Three months later, on 2nd September, Bahadur Khan arrived in Delhi with the captives. A week later, on 8th September, on Aurangzeb's specific orders, Dara and Sipihr were paraded through Delhi in an open howdah mounted on a filthy, small and mangy female elephant. Broken and weary, "like a crushed twig", Dara sat limply, dressed in rags, a dingy turban on his head, his feet chained. Sipihr sat beside him, and right behind them sat Aurangzeb's slave Nazar Beg, with a drawn sword, threatening instant death to the princes in case of a rescue effort. Squadrons of cavalry and mounted archers at the ready, led by Bahadur Khan, escorted the prisoner.

Entering Shahjahanabad through the Lahore gate, the sombre parade passed through the length of the city, through Chandni Chowk and the bazaar, and then went on to Khizirabad, a suburb of Delhi, where Dara was lodged. It was, says Manucci, "a melancholy spectacle, creating compassion in all those who saw him. For in such a brief space was this prince, so mighty, so rich, so famous, so powerful, reduced to the last stages of misery." Adds Bernier, "The crowd assembled upon this disgraceful occasion was immense; and everywhere I observed the people weeping, and lamenting the fate of Dara in the most touching language . . . From every quarter I heard piercing and distressing shrieks, for the Indian people have a very tender heart; men, women, and children wailing as if some mighty calamity had happened to themselves."

The next day there was a riot in the city. When Malik Jiwan—now dignified as Bakhtiyar Khan, a mansabdar of 1000—with his escort of Afghans was strutting through the city on his way to attend the imperial durbar, he was set on by the mob. "The idlers, the partisans of Dara Shukoh, the workmen and people of all sorts, inciting each other, gathered into a mob, and assailing Jiwan and his companions with abuse and imprecations, pelted them with dirt and filth, and clods and stones, so that several persons were knocked down and killed, and many were wounded," writes Khafi Khan. "Jiwan was protected by shields held over his head, and he at length made his way through the crowd to the palace. They say that the disturbance on this day was so great that it bordered on rebellion . . . Ashes and pots full of urine and ordure were thrown down from the roofs of the houses upon the heads of the Afghans . . . "

This show of people's devotion to Dara finally sealed his fate. There were, in any case, overwhelming political reasons for executing him. Aurangzeb's conniving counsellors, ever ready with the advice he wanted to hear, told him that if Dara did not die, people would be ever looking for his release, and this would be a source of disquiet in the empire. But Aurangzeb, hypocrite that he was, needed the sanction of law to execute Dara. On the evening of the day Dara was paraded through Delhi, his fate was debated in the Diwan-i-khas. Only one amir, Danishmand Khan, pleaded for mercy, but most, among them Dara's uncle Shayista Khan, recommended death. And behind the scenes, malevolent Raushanara—"his sister but his mortal enemy," as Manucci describes her—clamoured for blood.

So death it was. "The pillars of the Canonical Law and Faith apprehended many kinds of disturbance from his life," writes official chronicler Kazim. "So the Emperor, both out of the necessity to protect the Faith and Holy Law, and also for reasons of State, considered it unlawful to allow Dara to remain alive any longer as a destroyer of public peace."

On learning of the death decree, Dara made a direct appeal to Aurangzeb to save his life. "My Lord Brother and Emperor!" he wrote. "The desire for kingship is not at all left in my mind. Be (it) blessed to you and your sons. The plan of slaying me which you are cherishing in your heart is unjust. If you only grant me a house fit for (my) residence and one young handmaid out of my own handmaids to wait on me, I shall employ myself in praying for your (good) in the retired life of a pardoned man."

Aurangzeb did not want Dara's prayers. He wanted his life. On the margin of Dara's petition he wrote in his own hand: "You first acted as an usurper, and you were a mischief maker." On 9th September, a party of slaves entered Dara's prison house at about seven in the night to carry out the execution. Sipihr Shukoh, who was with Dara, wailed and clung to his father, but was torn away and taken to another room, where he continued to cry out. Dara appealed to the slaves to take a message to Aurangzeb, but they replied, "We cannot be anybody's messenger. We have only to carry out our orders." Dara then, in a futile gesture, attacked the slaves with a tiny dagger he had hidden in his pillow, but was overpowered and stabbed to death. They then hacked off his head and took it to Aurangzeb for verification.

"On that night Roushan Ara Begum gave a great feast," writes Manucci. He further tells a ghoulish tale of Aurangzeb jabbing his brother's severed head three times with his sword and then, "with great glee", sending the head to Shah Jahan in Agra, to be placed on the old man's table in a covered dish when he sat down to dinner—"to avenge himself for the love lavished on Dara and the little account made of himself." This seems too sadistic an act even for Aurangzeb. His probable response on being presented Dara's severed head, as recorded by Masum, was: "As I did not look at this infidel's face during his lifetime, I have no wish to do so now."

On Aurangzeb's orders, the headless corpse of the prince was paraded through the bazaar on an elephant—"so once alive and once dead he was exposed to the eyes of all men, and many wept over his fate," writes Khafi Khan—before being buried, unwashed and unadorned, in a vault in the tomb of Humayun, Dara's blighted ancestor.

LATER, WHEN HIS court chroniclers asked Aurangzeb how they should record the events of the civil war, he smiled knowingly and said: "Are you so ignorant as not to know the causes of such obvious and well-known events? Cannot you see that the Mughal Empire was in complete anarchy through the bad government of King Shah Jahan, my father, and his desire to make over the state to Prince Dara, an enemy of the Muhammadan faith? It was just punishment for the son to lose his life, he being an idolater, while the king was dispossessed of the kingdom and placed in confinement for being incapable to rule. As for the prince Shah Shuja, he was deprived of the kingdom because by his ambition he laid claim to the throne which did not belong to him . . . In regard to Prince Murad Bakhsh, a man of good qualities and an excellent soldier, I am innocent of his death. It was due to the demands of justice. Nor was he fit to reign, for he was a heretic, as I have ascertained since his death. If God made me emperor, it was from no other cause than that I had been ever a faithful defender of the Koran. Against my design and my will, which was to live as a poor fakir, I was exalted above other men, because that just Lord, who raises the meek and abases the haughty, had so determined."

Would Dara—or Shuja or Murad—have spared the lives of his brothers if he had become the emperor? It is difficult to say. To the Mughal emperor, his brothers were his deadliest enemies, and there were compelling political reasons for eliminating them. In fact, Manucci reports that when Aurangzeb asked Dara what he would have done if he had won, Dara recklessly replied that he would have had Aurangzeb quartered and gibbeted at the four gates of Delhi.

Manucci's story is improbable, but it reveals a characteristic Mughal attitude. The distinctiveness of Dara's reign would have been in the destiny of India, not in the fate of his brothers. In a sense then, Aurangzeb was right after all—the issue in the war of succession was not who should rule the empire, but what should be the future of India. Dara's promise was of a humane, progressive future. When he was executed, what was involved was not just the death of a prince, but the death of a future.

At the beginning of the war of succession, Father Buzeo, a European padre in Agra, had confidently predicted that Dara, despite all his advantages, would be destroyed. The reason? "The people of Hindustan," said the padre to Manucci, "are very malicious . . . [and] such a race required to be ruled by a more malignant king, not by a good-natured man like Dara."

Chapter Nine

OVER THE TOP

God's Elected Custodian

RETURNING TO DELHI after his victory over Dara at Deorai, Aurangzeb camped at Khizirabad on the outskirts of the city for some days, waiting for an auspicious day to move into the citadel. Early morning on the chosen day, 22nd May 1659, before the sun was up, the royal procession set out from Khizirabad, led by a band of drums, pipes and trumpets. A train of caparisoned elephants bearing the royal standards followed the band, then a cavalcade of thoroughbred horses, the camel corps, the musketeers, and columns of infantry. Finally, escorted by the grandees of the empire on richly accoutred horses, came Aurangzeb, seated on a golden throne atop a lofty, bejewelled elephant, showering gold and silver coins on the crowds along the route, as the procession solemnly wended its way through city and bazaar to the citadel.

The procession marked the commencement of Aurangzeb's formal coronation celebrations, which were the grandest in Mughal history, and were dazzling enough to divert people's attention from the stigma of his infamous usurpation. His earlier enthronement, in July 1658, was a token affair, held solely for administrative reasons. But now, with his father safely in confinement and his brothers eliminated—Murad imprisoned, Dara and Shuja chased away, and soon all three to be even more safely dead—Aurangzeb was secure enough to celebrate his accession with the pomp and grandeur that was expected of the Mughal.

Royal astrologers had specified three hours and fifteen minutes past sunrise on 15th June 1659 as the most auspicious time for Aurangzeb to ascend the throne. At the precise moment, on a signal from astrologers, the royal band sounded a flourish, and Aurangzeb, forty, resplendent in a ceremonial dress, emerged from behind the screen of the throne balcony of the Diwan-i-am and mounted the Peacock Throne.

The Diwan-i-am was opulently decorated for the ceremony with tassels of pearls and gem-studded gold ornaments, its floor covered with priceless carpets, its ceiling and pillars draped in velvet, flowered brocades and cloth of gold and silver. An immense tent was pitched in the courtyard of the durbar hall, raised on massive poles covered with silver plates. Incense and aloeswood smouldered in gold and silver burners. The amirs, dressed in their ceremonial best, stood in the hall in groups neatly segregated by rank, and they made their obeisance and invoked divine blessings on Aurangzeb as he ascended the throne. Musicians sang and nautch girls danced, while royal attendants distributed paan to the amirs and sprinkled scented water on them. The khutbah was then recited in Aurangzeb's name, and new coins issued, bearing the legend,

> This coin has been stamped on earth
> like a shining full moon,
> By King Aurangzeb, the conqueror
> of the world.

Aurangzeb spent nearly three hours at the durbar, bestowing robes of honour and conferring honours on nobles. Then he moved into the harem, to present gifts to palace inmates. Later, at a select gathering in the Diwan-i-khas, the hall of private audience, he gave presents to his sons, to the top amirs of the empire, and to distinguished scholars, poets and musicians.

The celebrations continued well into the night. By evening, the broad banks of the Yamuna flowing past the citadel were illuminated with lamps, and the river itself shimmered and glowed, as boats, bedecked with lamps and carrying musicians, plied about. Fireworks burst over the night sky. The festivities lasted fourteen weeks, from 22nd May to 29th August.

Thus began in grand and joyous celebration a singularly joyless reign.

IF ANY OF THE amirs crowding around Aurangzeb on his accession was troubled by the memory of the plight of Shah Jahan, to whom most of them owed their positions, perhaps the very robes they were wearing, there was no sign of it. Writes Bernier, "I can indeed scarcely repress my indignation when I reflect that there was not a single movement, nor even a voice heard, in behalf of the aged and injured Monarch; although the Omrahs, who bowed the knee to his oppressors, were indebted to him for their rank and riches, having been, according to the custom of the Court, raised by Chah-Jehan from a state of lowest indigence, and many of them even redeemed from absolute slavery." Comments Tavernier, "If perchance there were any who felt touched by his (Shah Jahan's) misfortunes, fear made them silent, and made them basely abandon a king who had governed them like a father."

Shah Jahan remained a prisoner in his marble palace in the Agra fort. But it was not a harsh life for him. "Although Aureng-Zebe kept his father closely confined in the fortress of Agra and neglected no precaution to prevent his escape, yet the deposed monarch was otherwise treated with indulgence and respect," says Bernier. "He was permitted to occupy his former apartments, and to enjoy the society of Begum-Sahib (Jahanara) and the whole of his female establishment, including the singing and dancing women, cooks, and others. In these respects no request was ever denied him; and as the old man became wondrously devout, certain Mullahs were allowed to enter his apartment and read the Koran." In the beginning, Prince Muhammad Sultan was in charge of Shah Jahan. On his departure, Mutamad, a mean-minded eunuch—who, according to Manucci, "looked like a baboon"—took over, and he seemed to have treated Shah Jahan with some pettiness, grudging even to supply him with proper slippers or to have his violins repaired.

Every precaution was taken to ensure that Shah Jahan did not interfere in the affairs of government in any way. People could visit him only with Aurangzeb's permission, and only in the presence of Muhammad Sultan. Everything that he said and did was reported to Aurangzeb. When Shah Jahan was found sending letters out of the fort, Aurangzeb asked him to stop doing so, and when Shah Jahan refused to comply—"Am I his son that I should obey his orders?" he asked—Aurangzeb punished the eunuchs carrying the letters and deprived Shah Jahan of writing materials. The loss of power could not have troubled Shah Jahan much, for he had been long weary of the burden of government, and had, even before the civil war, delegated his powers to Dara. It was wounded pride that grieved him, but he stoically bore his misfortune, though initially he seems to have tried to incite Murad and Shuja—as well as Muhammad Sultan—against Aurangzeb, and, according to Tavernier, himself once made an attempt to escape.

Aurangzeb had taken over the royal treasure in Agra soon after seizing the fort, and now he began to pester Shah Jahan to hand over his personal jewels, including his diamond thumb ring and pearl rosary, claiming that they were state property and had to be used for the good of the community. "Know that the royal property and treasures exist for the good of the people," he sanctimoniously wrote to his father. "A kingdom is not a hereditary private property. The king is merely God's elected custodian and trustee of His money for the good of the subjects." Abashed, Shah Jahan gave up the ring, but he refused to part with the rosary—it was made of 100 perfectly matched pearls worth 400,000 rupees—saying that he needed it to say his prayers and that he would rather pound it into dust than give it away.

Aurangzeb never once visited his deposed father; in fact, he never entered Agra as long as Shah Jahan was alive. But in the beginning they often wrote to each other, trading charges in bitter, acrimonious letters. "Many letters passed between the Emperor Shah Jahan and Aurangzeb, full of complaints and reproaches on one side, and of irritating excuses on the other," says Khafi Khan. Of these, we have only Aurangzeb's letters. He always took the high moral ground, asserting that he fought against his brothers only to defend Islam. "During your illness, Dara usurped all power, girt up his loins to promote Hinduism and destroy Islam, and acted as king, totally setting you aside . . . If, God forbid, the aim of that infidel had succeeded . . . it would have been hard [for us] to answer for it on the Last Day," wrote Aurangzeb. He blamed the civil war on Shah Jahan's partiality towards Dara and neglect of his other sons. "You did not love me," he charged.

Aurangzeb claimed divine sanction for his actions. "If God had not approved of my enterprise, how could I have gained victories which are only His gifts?" he asked rhetorically. He claimed that he took up "the perilous load of the crown, out of sheer necessity and not from free choice", and he told Shah Jahan that he (Aurangzeb) had done him a favour by relieving him of the burden of government, and that Shah Jahan should be grateful to him for that. "You have no cause of complaint in that I have relieved you of such a heavy load and taken it on my own shoulders and made my (hitherto) free mind the slave of a thousand afflictions and fatigue," he wrote, and went on to offer sage counsel to his father: "Submit to the will of God, and your sorrows and tribulations will turn into peace and contentment!" Finally, he taunted Shah Jahan: "How do you still regard the memory of Khusrav and Parviz, whom you did to death before your accession and who had threatened no injury to you?"

In the end Shah Jahan stopped complaining. Time formed a callous over his hurt; it no longer pained. The soothing presence of Jahanara, always there beside him, tending him with loving care, gave him the fortitude to endure his fate. In the last years of his life Shah Jahan became very pious, and spent most of his time studying the Koran and listening to religious discourses. He had entirely given up on the affairs of the world and prepared himself for the life hereafter.

He had to wait eight years for the final summons. On 17th January 1666, as a reaction to a massage with medicated oil, Shah Jahan had a recurrence of the complaints he had had nine years earlier, high and persistent fever and strangury. Soon his condition turned critical. As he lay ill in the octagonal tower of the Agra palace, he could, if he lifted his eyes, see the Taj Mahal down the river, the symbol of his long departed glory and happiness, which would be his own final resting place.

There was a passing improvement in his condition after nine days, then he began to sink. The end came on the fifteenth day of his illness, on 1st February 1666, a Monday. As death approached, Shah Jahan, seventy-four, remained perfectly composed and conscious. He had already signed, at Jahanara's persuasion, a letter pardoning Aurangzeb. Now he made his last will, gave directions for his funeral, presented keepsakes to those attending on him, and bade farewell. As Jahanara began to weep, Shah Jahan consoled her, and entrusted to her care his two surviving wives, Akbarabadi Mahal and Fatehpuri Mahal, and his daughter Purhunar Begum, his first child. Then the Koran was read to him, and he murmured his last prayer. Around 3 a.m. he breathed his last. Lamented Jahanara:

> I cry from grief like a reed, with only wind
>   to grasp;
> I burn from sorrow like a candle, but only
>   smoke rises from my head.

Aurangzeb had been informed of Shah Jahan's illness, but he chose to send only his son, Prince Muazzam, and even the prince did not reach Agra in time for the funeral. Jahanara had, according to Kambu, planned "a grand and honourable funeral" for Shah Jahan, but as Aurangzeb had not ordered a state funeral, she had to manage as best as she could.

Soon after Shah Jahan passed away, his chaplain, Sayyid Muhammad Qanauji, and Kazi Qurban of Agra were summoned to the fort, and they shifted his body to an adjoining hall, bathed and shrouded it, and placed it in a sandalwood coffin. At dawn the body was taken out of the fort by breaking open, as was customary, a wall of the palace, and was carried by boat down the Yamuna to the Taj Mahal, where he was buried, at noon, next to Mumtaz Mahal in the crypt of the mausoleum. No descendant of Shah Jahan, no grand amir, bore his bier. It was a humble funeral for the grandest of the Mughal emperors.

SHAH JAHAN'S FORLORN death did not assuage Aurangzeb's bitterness towards him. Courtier historians do speak of Aurangzeb's sorrow on hearing of his father's death—he "grieved much over his death," says Khafi Khan; "tears of grief poured forth uncontrollably on the auspicious cheeks," says Kazim—but these are mere pro forma statements, not factual descriptions. Aurangzeb had not seen his father for fourteen years, since the day he took leave of him in Kabul in 1652 to go to the Deccan, and had not cared to visit him in his illness or to attend his funeral. It was only late in February, a month after Shah Jahan's death, that Aurangzeb went to Agra, and even then his main object seems to have been to make up with Jahanara rather than to visit his father's grave.

Jahanara, though a partisan of Dara, was Aurangzeb's favourite sister, and he yearned to win her love and respect. He redesignated her as the first lady of the realm, the status she had enjoyed under Shah Jahan, but now with the high title Padshah Begum, Princess Royal, instead of Begum Sahib, Noble Princess, her title till then. At his next coronation celebrations, held in Agra, Aurangzeb presented Jahanara with gold worth 1.4 million rupees, and raised her annual allowance from 1 million to 1.7 million rupees.

Aurangzeb seems to have intended to shift his capital to Agra at this time, for he brought back to Agra the imperial treasures—they were brought in 1,400 carts—which he had earlier taken away to Delhi. But in October he returned to Delhi, and induced Jahanara also to move in there. He assigned for her residence the grand mansion of Ali Mardan Khan, and often visited her, spending hours in conversation with her, rare moments of affection and tenderness in this dour emperor.

With Jahanara's return to favour, Raushanara, who had ruled the roost in the imperial harem till then, receded into the background, to die in obscurity five years later, in September 1671, aged forty-seven. Ten years later, in September 1681, Jahanara, sixty-seven, passed away. The news of her death reached Aurangzeb when he was on his way from Ajmer to the Deccan, and he immediately ordered a halt of three days to mourn her. She was buried in the compound of the sepulchre of Sheikh Nizamuddin Auliya in Delhi, a Sufi sage of the fourteenth century, in a humble grave, a 5 metre by 3.5 metre patch of ground enclosed with screens of marble lattice work, open to the skies and covered with grass, marked only by a plain marble slab according to her wish as inscribed on the headstone: "Let no rich canopy surmount my resting place. This grass is the best covering for the grave of a lowly heart."

AT THE TIME OF Jahanara's death, Aurangzeb himself was on a final journey of sorts, leaving Hindustan for the Deccan, there to toil forlornly for the rest of his life, twenty-six long years, and to die there, never once returning to North India.

The Vindhya Range, separating Hindustan from the Deccan, was, in a sense, the fulcrum on which Aurangzeb's forty-nine years long reign turned, first tipping him into the north as he set out to battle for the throne, and then, after twenty-three years, tipping him back into the south for the remainder of his life. It was therefore fitting that his birthplace should be in those mountains, at Dahod, midway between Ahmadabad and Ujjain. He was born there on the night of 3rd November 1618, a Saturday, when his parents, Shah Jahan and Mumtaz Mahal, along with Jahangir, were on the way to Agra from Gujarat. Aurangzeb was sentimental about his birthplace, and cherished its memory all his life. "Noble son," he would write late in his life to Prince Azam, "the village of Dahod, in the province of Gujarat, is the birthplace of this sinner. Deem it proper to treat its inhabitants with kindness."

Shah Jahan was the rising star in the Mughal firmament at the time of Aurangzeb's birth, but fell from favour soon after, and was, in consequence of his unsuccessful rebellion, obliged to send Aurangzeb and Dara to Jahangir as hostages, to join Shuja, who was already being brought up by Nur Jahan. The princes could return to their father only after Jahangir's death. On Shah Jahan's accession, Aurangzeb, ten, was sanctioned a daily allowance of 500 rupees. By then his education was well advanced, having commenced at the age of four, as usual. Aurangzeb was a diligent but not a happy pupil; he worked hard because he was earnest, not because he valued what he was taught.

Much of what he was taught as a child was an awful waste of time, Aurangzeb believed, and he secretly loathed his tutors. When one of them, identified as "Melecsale" (Malik Salih?) by Manucci, turned up at the court soon after Aurangzeb's accession, hoping for favours from his former pupil, Aurangzeb ignored him for three months, then "weary at last of seeing him constantly in his presence", called him aside, and with only four or five amirs present, tore into him with uncharacteristic heat and candour. "What can I do but weep when I remember that in my tender age I fell into your hands," Manucci reports Aurangzeb as telling the mullah. Quotes Bernier: "Forgetting how many important subjects ought to be embraced in the education of a Prince, you acted as if it were chiefly necessary that he should possess great skill in grammar, and such knowledge as belongs to a doctor of law; and thus did you waste the precious hours of my youth in the dry, unprofitable, and never-ending task of learning words!"

Aurangzeb resented being taught in Arabic. "May not our devotions be offered up as acceptably, and solid information communicated as easily, in our mother tongue?" he asked. "I have a perfect remembrance of your having, during several years, harassed my brain with idle and foolish propositions, the solution of which yield no satisfaction to the mind—propositions that seldom enter into the business of life; wild and extravagant reveries conceived with great labour, and forgotten as soon as conceived; whose only effect is to fatigue and ruin the intellect, and to render a man head-strong and insufferable."

"Oh yes, you caused me to devote the most valuable years of my life to your favourite hypotheses, or systems," continued Aurangzeb; "and when I left you, I could boast of no greater attainment in sciences than the use of many obscure and uncouth terms, calculated to discourage, confound, and appall a youth of the most masculine understanding: terms invented to cover the vanity and ignorance of pretenders to philosophy; of men who, like yourself, would impose the belief that they transcend others of their species in wisdom, and that their dark and ambiguous jargon conceals many profound mysteries known only to themselves."

Dara would have cherished such learning, but not Aurangzeb. According to Manucci, Aurangzeb asked the mullah: "Was it not your duty to teach me the customs of the Mughal princes, to inform me that one day I should be forced to take the field, sword in hand, against my brothers, if not to gain a crown, at least to defend my life? Thus you should have told me how to gain friends, to take or besiege fortresses, and fight pitched battles . . . If you did not know the military art, you might at least have taught me the methods of governing the people when my father should send me to rule in some province. Thus you might have laid down rules for the equal administration of justice, the way of capturing a people's love . . . All this you ought to have taught me, but not a word did you breathe to me of such things. Thus I owe you nothing, for you misled me . . . Never again appear in my presence, for you made me waste a great deal of time, and by your fault I have also wasted this day."

AT SIXTEEN, AURANGZEB was given his first official posting, as a commander of 10,000 horse, and was granted the privilege of using the red tent. Soon after, in 1635, he was given the command of the Bundela campaign, his first field assignment. The following year he was appointed as governor of the Deccan, a post which he held for eight years, till May 1644, when he was abruptly dismissed from service during his visit to Agra to see Jahanara after her fire accident. We do not know why he was dismissed. Lahori mysteriously remarks that Aurangzeb had "done some acts which the Emperor disapproved of"; according to Khafi Khan, Aurangzeb, "to anticipate his father's punishment of his bad deeds, himself took off his sword" and resigned his office.

From an account written in Aurangzeb's old age, it seems that the dismissal had something to do with Aurangzeb's paranoid envy and fear of Dara—it appears that, while visiting Dara's new riverside mansion along with his father and brothers, and being shown an underground room, Aurangzeb refused to enter it, apprehending that Dara might kill them all there. He therefore sat in the doorway as a sentinel, and would not budge even when his father called him in. When pressed, he walked away in a huff. Ten years after the incident, Aurangzeb would recall it in a letter to Jahanara, and claim that he had at that time "known my life to be aimed at".

Some seven months after his dismissal, in February 1645, he was restored to favour, probably on Jahanara's intervention, and was appointed governor of Gujarat, where his strong government won him the approbation of the emperor, who raised his salary to six million rupees a year. From Gujarat he was called away at the end of 1646 to take charge of the Central Asian campaign. On his return, in March 1648, he was named governor of Multan. From there he was summoned to head the Kandahar campaigns, and after that, in July 1652, sent again to the Deccan as governor.

By then the trust between father and son had broken down completely. When Shah Jahan accused the prince of embezzling the jewels collected from the Sultan of Golconda, Aurangzeb indignantly asked, "Why should I grudge to give up a few jewels to His Majesty, when my life itself is at his service?" but nevertheless went on to complain that Shah Jahan did not, as promised, share the Golconda indemnity with him. Aurangzeb became so alienated from Shah Jahan at this time that he stopped writing to him altogether, confining himself to sending messages to the imperial Vizier. He was, as he wrote to Mir Jumla in July 1656, bitter and angry with his father.

"Fear the Sighs of the Oppressed"

AURANGZEB WAS A deeply worried man during his second term as the governor of the Deccan, apprehensive about what the future held for him. Ever since he had reached what medieval chroniclers call the age of discretion, he was conscious that his brothers were his deadly enemies, with whom sooner or later he would have to fight mortal duels, from which only one could emerge alive to sit on the throne. Now, with Shah Jahan increasingly delegating royal power to Dara, the day of reckoning seemed imminent. Aurangzeb's squabbles with Shah Jahan were the early gusts of this gathering storm.

To a superficial observer Aurangzeb would have seemed the most disadvantaged of the sons of Shah Jahan, lacking the martial prowess of Murad and Shuja, the suavity of Dara. But he would make up for all his deficiencies by sheer craftiness. He would trust nobody in his fight for survival, neither his father nor any of his brothers, not even his own sons. Ever. "The art of reigning is so delicate, that a King's jealousy should be awakened by his very shadow," he believed, and would act on this precept all his life, imprisoning his father, liquidating his brothers, and at one time or other imprisoning or driving into exile four of his five sons, the only exception being his hot-blooded third son, Prince Azam, towards whom he was inexplicably indulgent. "There can be no doubt that if any king ever had recourse to foresight to prevent disorder, it was Aurangzeb," says Manucci.

AURANGZEB WAS A sickly child, but he would, in an apparent triumph of mind over body, live far longer than any of his ancestors or siblings, to die at the ripe old age of eighty-nine. "There is great sickness and infirmity in his physical frame," Shah Jahan once said of Aurangzeb. Yet Aurangzeb was indefatigable in his labours, and would be seriously ill only once in his long reign. This was in May 1662, his fifth regnal year, when a combination of overwork, Ramadan fasting and the brutal Delhi summer exhausted him, and he "fell ill of a sudden fever, which was so severe that it caused delirium", and his life was despaired for, reports Manucci. The emperor's health crisis sent shivers of panic through Delhi, as it had five years earlier on Shah Jahan's illness, for fear of yet another civil war, as potential successors and their promoters manoeuvred for advantage.

After five days, Aurangzeb's fever began to abate, and he had himself carried to the durbar hall, to show his face to the courtiers and reassure them that he was alive and recovering. Full recovery took another month, but even then the illness left him with a speech disability—he had, says Manucci, suffered a partial paralysis of the tongue during his illness, and "remained a little defective in speech, and up to this day he speaks deliberately."

There was no further health crisis in his reign, and he retained all his faculties till the end, except for a slight shortness of hearing. "Strictly speaking, kings wanted nothing but sight and speech," Aurangzeb is once said to have remarked in his old age, adding that, although he was then eighty-six years old, god in his mercy had preserved for him both, "without counting the thirty sound teeth that I still possess." His memory was phenomenal even in old age. Says Ishwardas, "As nature had gifted the Emperor with two powerful qualities, viz, a sharp memory and the power of retention, he could recognize a person seen long back and could remember words once heard by him."

There are no descriptions of Aurangzeb as a prince, but there are some excellent portrait paintings, in which we see a handsome young man with an open face and a modest, sincere expression, small-made and fine-boned, his features delicate, except for an assertive, high-bridged, aquiline nose. There is no hint of deceit in this face. And it is the same face that we see in his portraits as an old man, a trifle weary now, his eyes soft and reflective, his face ascetically lean, the slight bend of his head reinforcing his expression of humility. The halo around his head seems both natural and fitting.

We have from Careri, an Italian traveller who saw Aurangzeb in 1695, a vivid portrait of Aurangzeb as an old man. "He was of a low Stature, with large Nose, Slender, and stooping with Age," says Careri. "The whiteness of his round Bear'd, was more visible on his Olive colour'd Skin. When he was seated they gave him a Scimiter, and Buckler, which he lay'd down on his left side within the Throne. Then he made a sign with his Hand for those that had business to draw near; who being come up, two Secretaries standing, took their Petitions, which they delivered to the King, telling him the Contents. I admir'd to see him Indorse them with his own Hand, without Spectacles, and by his cheerful, smiling Countenance seemed to be pleas'd with the employment." Bakhtawar Khan also speaks of Aurangzeb's "pleasing countenance and mild look". Said Aurangzeb about himself: "This weak old man, this shrunken helpless creature, is afflicted with a hundred maladies besides anxiety, but he has made patience his habit."

Aurangzeb's dress was simple, his demeanour gentle. "His clothes are plain, and he wears few ornaments, nothing but a small plume or aigrette in the middle of his turban and a large precious stone in front; on his stomach another," notes Manucci. "He wears no strings of pearls . . . His coats are always made of very moderately-priced material, for each qaba does not exceed ten rupees in cost." Careri too describes him in similar terms: "The King came, leaning on a Staff forked at the top, several Omrahs and abundance of Courtiers going before him. He had on a white Vest . . . The Cira or Turban of the same white stuff, was ty'd with a Gold Web, on which an Emerald of a vast bigness, appear'd amidst four little ones. He had a Silk Sash, which cover'd the Catari or Indian Dagger, hanging on the left. His Shoes were after the Moorish Fashion, and his legs naked without Hose. Two Servants put away the Flyes, with long, white Horse-tails; another at the same time keeping off the Sun, with a green Umbrella."

THESE PICTURES AND descriptions of Aurangzeb reveal a truth about him that is often missed—lost under layer upon layer of his all too well-known misdeeds—that he was the mildest, the least violent, the most law abiding of the Great Mughals. "Aurangzeb's humanity and kindness was such that the severest punishment was reduction of dignity, and this even was soon restored through the intercession and kind offices of men high in office," says Khafi Khan. Once, when he was in Burhanpur, and there was a fire near the citadel, thirty sacks of gunpowder were found in the cellar under his sleeping apartment. There was no foul play involved—the sacks had been left there many years earlier and forgotten—but it was a serious lapse of security. Yet Aurangzeb only censured and demoted the officials responsible, pointing out, in his characteristic self-righteous manner, that if such a thing had happened in the reign of Jahangir, that king would have had the culprits blown up along with the gunpowder.

The lowlier the offender, the more merciful was Aurangzeb. Once, when a eunuch stumbled against Aurangzeb and knocked him down, and himself collapsed in fright, Aurangzeb spoke to him kindly: "Wherefore fearest thou a created being, one like thyself? . . . Rise and be not afraid." Another time, when Aurangzeb was in Lahore, and an old man, who ran a water mill on a channel that flowed out from the royal palace, suffered inconvenience when fussy officials stopped up the channel, the emperor called the old man to him and compensated him, saying, "You are my neighbour, and my arrival has caused you hardship. Pardon me."

Aurangzeb, says Manucci, "assumes always great humility of attitude," and even when an officer disobeys him, he betrays no anger. "All he says is (and that in the softest voice) that he is only a miserable sinner, that there is no reason for astonishment if his orders are disregarded, since every day those of God Himself are neglected and repudiated. He does not forget, however, to repeat his orders, and adopt every exact means of getting them executed."

Even as a prince, Aurangzeb was mild in dealing with imperial officers, so mild that Shah Jahan had to upbraid him: "I have heard that in dealing with every one of my officers you show the greatest humility on your part. If you do so with a view to the future, [know that] all things depend on predestination, and that nothing but contempt will be gained by this meekness of spirit." Shah Jahan suspected that Aurangzeb was dissimulating humility merely to gain the support of amirs in the succession struggle.

Shah Jahan was wrong. Guile certainly was an element in Aurangzeb's humility, but the humility itself was not a pretence. Though he would not permit any weakness in himself and would strive hard to make others conform to his own dour ideals, he had throughout his life shown a more humane concern for the welfare of the people, and a greater tolerance for human frailty, than any other Mughal. This is evident in his numerous letters. "We must put up with every class of people; what is to be done with them? They are also people," he wrote in one letter. And in another: "Do you know who is a brave man? A brave man is he who puts up with his enemies..." In his last letter to his son Kam Bakhsh, he wrote: "Though my relatives and servants show wheat and sell barley, you should give them employment through kindness, mildness, and carelessness [towards their deception]."

"I wish you to recollect that the greatest conquerors are not always the greatest Kings," Aurangzeb wrote in a letter to Shah Jahan. "The nations of the earth have often been subjugated by mere uncivilized barbarians, and the most extensive conquests have in a few short years crumbled to pieces. He is the truly great King who makes it the chief business of his life to govern his subjects with equity." Acting on this maxim, Aurangzeb would endlessly badger his sons to uphold the law and avoid oppression. To Prince Azam he wrote: "For a long time I have heard that in your jagir districts oppression is practised openly . . . Fear the sighs of the oppressed." And to his vizier Asad

Khan he wrote: "Oppression will cause darkness on the day of judgment."

"Don't be so salty that [your subjects] would spit you out of their mouths, nor be so sweet that they may gulp you down," was Aurangzeb's dictum, as he once told Prince Muazzam. The moderation in speech and action that he practiced, he demanded of his officers too. "In his sacred Court no improper conversation, no word of backbiting or falsehood, is allowed," writes Bakhtawar Khan. "His courtiers . . . are cautioned that if they have to say anything which might injure the character of an absent man, they should express themselves in decorous language and at full detail . . . [Yet if a supplicant at the court] talks too much, or acts in an improper manner, he is never displeased, and he never knits his brows. His courtiers have often desired to prohibit people from showing so much boldness, but he remarks that by hearing their words and seeing their gestures, he acquired a habit of forbearance and tolerance . . . Under the dictates of anger and passion he never issues orders of death."

Clearly then, Aurangzeb was considered a saint by his contemporaries not merely because of his ostentatious religiosity, but because he was, contrary to his later reputation, benevolent and charitable.

Later historians saw Aurangzeb in an altogether different light, as the passage of time faded the memory of his innumerable small acts of everyday kindness, but magnified his few notable misdeeds, such as his religious intolerance, his ruthlessness as a conqueror, his use of stratagems to get the better of others, and, more than anything else, his harsh treatment of his father, brothers and sons. But his predecessors too were guilty of similar acts—Jahangir and Shah Jahan had rebelled against their fathers; Jahangir had imprisoned and blinded and had even thought of executing one of his sons; Shah Jahan was guilty of liquidating his brothers and nephews, and had also swerved from Akbar's liberal religious policy; as aggressors, none of them, not even Akbar, was much different from Aurangzeb. As for the use of stratagems, Sher Shah and Shivaji were equally culpable.

The only really exceptional act of Aurangzeb was the imposition of jizya, but this in itself was not enough to give him his dismal reputation. What damned Aurangzeb in the eyes of historians was his cold-bloodedness, which made him seem evil, and not just wilful, so that even his virtues appeared mean—he seemed kindly without being compassionate, his mildness dictated by expediency. It was his personality that damned Aurangzeb, not his deeds.

"Aurangzeb was not used to displaying passion openly," says

Manucci, and again: "This prince was very different from the others, being in character very secretive and serious, carrying on his affairs in a hidden way, but most energetically. He was of a melancholy temperament, always busy at something or another." Aurangzeb himself, in a letter to Prince Azam, enunciated his philosophy thus: "Manliness does not consist in audacity and recklessness . . . The perfection of manliness and humanity lies in self-control."

Aurangzeb's concern for self-control was so extreme that it almost bordered on sickness. And it had, as its corollary, a mind that was so insidious and convoluted that every thought and action of his seemed dishonest and crooked. It was not that Aurangzeb did not value honesty—"An honest man is like unalloyed gold," he once remarked, and at another time, "I, with a wounded heart, insensible, and needy, always seek for honest human beings"—but he was worldly-wise enough to know that, for rulers, honesty was not the best policy. Once, while considering an amir for a governorship, Aurangzeb hesitated, because, in his own words, the amir was "very honest and simple-minded, [and] he cannot at all understand fraud and stratagem." According to Manucci, Aurangzeb advised his officers that they might take false oaths to serve the interests of the state, and that, if they did so, it was enough to feed ten mendicants to remove the sin thus incurred.

"One cannot rule without practising deception," maintained Aurangzeb, and characteristically went on to find a theological justification for crookedness: "In the opinion of the common herd, cunning and deception are greatly scorned," he wrote in one of his epistles. "As God himself in His Holy Word has ascribed cunning to His own holy self, saying, 'God is the best of plotters,' it is contrary to the Koran to consider stratagem as blameable." Says Manucci: "The policy of the present Mogul is so fine and so delicate as to surpass that of all his predecessors." As Aurangzeb put it, "When you have an enemy to destroy, spare nothing rather than fail, neither deception, subterfuges, nor false oaths, for anything is permissible in open war . . . In one word, make use of every pretext in the world that you judge capable of bringing you success in your projects."

Success, Aurangzeb apparently believed, was the only earthly (or heavenly) judge of right and wrong. Yet he also tried to maintain in all his actions an appearance of righteousness and a semblance of legality, being anxious to preserve his reputation for orthodoxy and saintliness. For him, unlike for his predecessors, his whim was not the law. The shariah, the law of Islam, was inviolable, and he would always abide by the letter of the law, if not its spirit.

Aurangzeb would twist facts and concoct lies without compunction to suit his purpose and gain his goals, but would never overtly violate the law. Thus, unlike Shah Jahan, who peremptorily ordered the murder of his brother and nephews to protect his throne, Aurangzeb in a similar situation took care to execute his brothers strictly through the legal process, though the process itself was manipulated to suit his purpose. Similarly, towards the end of his life, during the siege of Satara, when a few Hindu and Muslim soldiers fighting for the Marathas were captured by the Mughals, and a Kazi gave the opinion that the Hindu prisoners had to be released if they accepted Islam and the Muslim prisoners could only be imprisoned, not executed, Aurangzeb asked the Kazi to examine the case again "so that control over the kingdom may not be lost", and he had the prisoners executed only after the Kazi reversed his verdict. The pretence of legality does not redeem Aurangzeb. Maybe it could even be said that he compounded his crime with hypocrisy. Still, obsession with righteousness (as he saw it) was a basic characteristic of Aurangzeb.

Paradoxically, this strict adherence to law was what distressed his subjects most, for the law he abided by was the law of Islamic theocracy, which was oppressive towards his predominantly Hindu subjects, and was troubling even to most Muslims, who had let human frailty loosen the corset of orthodoxy. Aurangzeb saw it differently. For him, the laws of Islam were sacred and immutable, the only possible laws, and to enforce them was his sacred and inexorable obligation.

NO MOGUL EMPEROR had worked harder at ruling than Aurangzeb— or got less pleasure out of his work. For his predecessors, being the emperor was usually (though not always) a joyous adventure. But not for Aurangzeb. For him it was ever a sombre, sacred duty. This rigorous but narrow, joyless and morbid sense of duty turned Aurangzeb into an adamant drudge, ever going round in the rut of routine. "So long as a single breath remains to this mortal life, there is no release from labour," he used to say.

"An emperor," Aurangzeb told his son Muazzam, "should never allow himself to be fond of ease and inclined to retirement." Once, late in his reign, when a well-intentioned amir suggested that he should lighten his burden of work, Aurangzeb bridled with scorn. "There can surely be but one opinion among you learned men as to the obligation imposed upon a sovereign, in seasons of difficulty and danger, to hazard his life, and, if necessary, to die sword in hand in defence of the people committed to his care," he said. "And yet this good and considerate man would fain persuade me that the public weal ought to cause me no solicitude; that, in devising means to promote it, I should never pass a sleepless night, nor spare a single day from the pursuit of some low and sensual gratification. According to him, I am to be swayed by considerations of my own bodily health, and chiefly to study what may best minister to my personal ease and enjoyment."

"No doubt he would have me abandon the government of this vast kingdom to some vizier," continued Aurangzeb. "He seems not to consider that, being born the son of a King, and placed on a throne, I was sent into the world by Providence to live and labour, not for myself, but for others; that it is my duty not to think of my own happiness except so far as it is inseparably connected with the happiness of my people. It is the repose and prosperity of my subjects that it behoves me to consult; nor are these to be sacrificed to anything besides the demands of justice, the maintenance of the royal authority, and the security of the State." Was there nothing at all for the monarch to gain from his office? "The only benefit which we kings derive from our position in the world is the gaining of fame," said Aurangzeb.

But fair name would elude Aurangzeb in history, despite his exalted view of kingship. He was not a heroic figure. There was nothing electrifying about him. Yet the sheer relentlessness of his toil and the unwinking intensity of his orthodoxy are overwhelming. Aurangzeb might not have been an admirable or exciting person, but there was something awesome about him, in his own perverse way.

ORTHODOX ISLAM WAS the iron grid to which Aurangzeb welded his life. For a man in whom little was as it seemed, his piety was undeniable. He spent a lot of his time in prayer, punctiliously observed all the prescribed fasts and more, and did nothing whatsoever in violation of the puritanically orthodox Sunni practices. British ambassador Norris, who saw Aurangzeb in the Deccan, has in his report an arresting description of the aged emperor engrossed in reading the Koran even while visiting the frontline: though Aurangzeb was surrounded by "greate numbers of Horse & vast numbers of people crowding to see Him . . . he himselfe tho' carryd openly saw nobody, having his eyes always affixed upon a Booke he carryd in his hands & reading all ye way he went without ever divertinge to any other object."

Aurangzeb, says Mustaid Khan, memorized the Koran completely, "with great exertion and angelic persistence", and made it his religious duty to labour at copying it. His dress and food, even the tableware he used, were as prescribed by orthodox custom. Says Bakhtawar Khan, "He never puts on clothes prohibited by religion, nor does he ever use vessels of silver or gold." Adds Manucci: "For a long time he pretended to be a fakir. Not content with pretending to be a fakir, Aurangzeb went further, and acted the mullah, catechizing this one and the other."

By and by people came to regard Aurangzeb as a saintly king, even as a miracle worker. Aurangzeb encouraged such fancies. When Satnamis, a fanatic Hindu sect supposedly having magical powers, rose in rebellion, and Mughal soldiers were afraid to fight against them, Aurangzeb, says Khafi Khan, "wrote some prayers and devices with his own hands, which he ordered to be sewn on the banners and standards, and carried against the rebels"—and sure enough, his spells exorcised the Satnami sorcery! Khafi Khan further reports that once when the Bhima River flooded Mughal encampments, "the King wrote out prayers with his own hand, and ordered them to be thrown into the water, for the purpose of causing it to subside." Aurangzeb, says Manucci in all seriousness, was "a past master in witchcraft".

To go with his reputation of saintliness, Aurangzeb adopted an ostentatiously ascetic lifestyle, and made much of meeting his personal expenses from what he earned by making caps (which he presented to nobles, who in turn made offerings to him) and by selling the calligraphic copies of the Koran he made, for he "deemed it sinful to eat the bread of idleness", says Jadunath Sarkar. Somewhere along the way he also bought a farm between Agra and Delhi to provide him with a private income. The farm cost him 500 rupees, and he spent another 500 rupees to plant and manage it, and received an annual income of 2000 rupees from it, "but ye Mogull is soe good a husband he layed up annually for 20 years 1000 Rupees or soe that this greate Emperour's meat drink & cloathinge cost but 1000 Rupees a yeare," says Norris. Says Careri: "His expense was but small, for a Vest of his did not cost above 8 Roupies, and the Sash and Circa or Cap, less." Whatever Aurangzeb needed for his own use he always paid for, never accepted as a present, says Norris.

In his youth Aurangzeb used to be fond of music, but as emperor he deliberately tore himself from that indulgence—"on account of his great restraint and self-denial," says Bakhtawar Khan. When an amir once asked his opinion about music, Aurangzeb said, "It is *mubah* (allowed), neither good nor bad," but went on to add, "I cannot listen to music without flutes, especially *pakhawaj* (drums), but that is unanimously prohibited; so I have left off hearing singing too." Says Mustaid Khan, "All the agents of pleasure and entertainment, such as sweet-voiced singers or charming players on musical instruments, were gathered in large number round his throne, and in the first few years of his reign he occasionally listened to their music and had a perfect expert's knowledge of this art; yet out of extreme abstinence he [later on] totally gave up listening to music."

Similarly, Aurangzeb spurned poets. "It is the erring who follow the poets," the Koran warns, so, according to Bakhtawar Khan, "to please Almighty God, he (Aurangzeb) never turned his eye towards a flatterer, nor gave his ear to a poet." Aurangzeb's favourite reading was theological works. And his favourite art, the one in which he had some talent, was calligraphy, a skill he needed to copy the Koran. "He writes a very elegant Naskh hand, and has attained perfection in this art," says Bakhtawar Khan. Aurangzeb also patronized painters, despite Koranic injunctions against figurative art, and even had several portraits of himself painted. But he had no feeling for architecture and most of his buildings, except the Pearl Mosque in Delhi, are quite pedestrian. Collecting fine china was his sole aesthetic passion.

The only indulgence of Aurangzeb that does not conform to the spartan rigour he had chosen as his lifestyle was his love for the pleasures of the table. "Exalted son," Aurangzeb once wrote to Prince Azam, "I remember the savour of your kichadi and biryani during the winter . . . I wanted to have from you Sulaiman, who cooks biryani; but you did not allow him to serve me as my cook. If you happen to find a pupil of his, skillful in the art of cookery, you will send him to me . . . The desire (for eating) has not entirely left me . . ." Like his ancestors, Aurangzeb had a passion for fruits, especially for mangoes, and there are numerous references to mangoes in his letters. "Exalted son," he wrote Prince Azam, "the delicious mangoes (sent by you) sweetened the palate of the old father."

For all his severity there was in Aurangzeb also a pleasantly surprising sense of humour, sardonic and self-deprecating, which enabled him, despite his puritanical rigour, to be tolerant of human foibles. Once, when a critically ill amir told him, "I had wished to die in battle and thus be of service to Your Majesty," Aurangzeb caustically replied, "You have been devoting yourself to my service all through your life, and yet your desire for it is not satisfied!" Similarly, when a man from Bengal approached him saying that he had come all the way to be his disciple, the emperor, reports Mustaid Khan, "smiled and took out of his pocket . . . about 100 rupees and bits of gold and silver to be presented to the man, and said, 'Tell him the favour he expects from me is this!'"

There was a cutting edge to Aurangzeb's humour, a touch of acid, and he often used irony to chasten pretentious amirs. When it was reported to him that a noble, Amir Khan Bahadur, was in the habit of having *naubat* (band music) played at his residence every day without that distinction being conferred on him by the emperor, Aurangzeb wrote on the report: "[Amir Khan] is not such a fool as to act so very audaciously. It is evident that there is some festival in his house every day. As even low persons do not require permission from the Emperor to play the *naubat* on festive occasions, why should he?"

As he mocked others, he forbore being mocked himself. So when an official, who had been derided by a Delhi satirist, appealed to the emperor to punish the offender, Aurangzeb wrote on the petition: "Formerly . . . he (the satirist) had not spared me; in return, I had increased his reward that he might not do it again; yet in spite of this [favour] he had not on his part been less [satirical]. It is not possible to cut out his tongue and sever his neck. We ought to repress our feelings and live in harmony [with others]."

AURANGZEB LACKED THE physical strength and exuberant vitality of the Mughals, but he did not lack the Mughal courage. He was in fact utterly fearless, and would never turn away from an adversary, man or beast, nor ever retreat from a battlefield. The most dramatic display of this nerveless intrepidity was his confrontation with a charging elephant on the banks of the Yamuna in Agra when he was fourteen years old. The incident occurred when he and his brothers on horseback were following an elephant fight. Suddenly one of the elephants turned and bore down fiercely on Aurangzeb. The prince met it head on. Without a moment's hesitation, "he galloped at it and rose in his stirrups and hurled his spear," reports Inayat Khan. And when the elephant knocked down his horse with its trunk, Aurangzeb "sprang nimbly up, and stood sword in hand, ready to strike", while all around him men ran helter-skelter, before Shuja and Raja Jai Singh galloped up to divert the elephant and save the prince.

Thus began the legend of Aurangzeb's courage and luck, later reinforced by many other similar incidents, such as he calmly spreading his prayer carpet on the battlefield and kneeling down to say the evening prayers in the midst of a raging battle against the Uzbegs in Central Asia. Aurangzeb was probably in no personal danger in doing that, as he was no doubt shielded by his troops; still, as a gesture, it was arresting, and Abdul Aziz, the Uzbeg chief, hearing of it exclaimed: "To fight with such a man is to court one's own destruction."

In his old age Aurangzeb would speak of hunting as "the business of idle persons", but in his youth he was Mughal enough to delight in it, and had built a monument to commemorate his hunting feat of felling two fighting antelopes with two shots. "During my viceroyalty, while I was living at Daulatabad and Aurangabad . . . I used in my folly to ride about, and make forced marches under the instigations of Satan and of my own passions," he would recall in a letter to his grandson Bidar Bakht. "I used to go far on horseback to hunt the nilgai and other kinds of game. Other idle deeds did I do. I used to visit the lake of Qatluq in the valley of the watershed . . . make pilgrimages . . . or climb up the hill fort of Daulatabad and to the caves of Ellora (which are wondrous examples of the Creator's art), sometimes with my family, at others alone."

It is hard to visualize Aurangzeb romping in the hills with his women, or of having any kind of fun, but there were apparently secret vulnerabilities in him, which he tried to burn out with the searing scowl of his will. But he was not always successful in suppressing his passions, and had once become helplessly infatuated with a Hindu dancing girl, Hira Bai. She very nearly turned him into a hedonist.

This was probably in 1653, when Aurangzeb was passing through Burhanpur on his way to assume the governorship of the Deccan for the second time. He was then in his mid-thirties and already the father of six children, having married his first wife, Dilras Banu Begum, in 1637, when he was nineteen. Dilras was the daughter of Shah Nawaz Khan, a distant relation of the Shah of Persia, and was, says Aurangzeb, a woman of "extreme imperiousness, but to the end of her life I continued to love her and never once did I wound her feelings." Later he acquired three more wives, and in all he sired ten children, five boys and five girls. He was a considerate husband and took good care of his wives, but he had no passionate attachment to any of them.

The Hira Bai affair was different, a fragrant but brief and tragic romance. She was originally a concubine of Mir Khalil, the husband of a maternal aunt of Aurangzeb. Aurangzeb chanced to see her while he, along with his aunt, was visiting a deer park on the banks of Tapi (Tapti) at Zainabad, a suburb of Burhanpur, where Mir Khalil was stationed. Hira Bai, a winsome, naughty lass in the retinue of the begum, was frolicking around the park, singing softly, seemingly indifferent to the presence of the prince, when Aurangzeb saw her. "Immediately on seeing her, the prince, unable to control himself, sat down there, and then fell down at full length on the ground in a swoon!" says Hamiduddin Khan Nimacha.

Masir-ul-umara, a Mughal chronicle of the eighteenth century, tells the story thus: Hira Bai, "whose musical skill ravished the senses, and who was unique in blandishments . . . on seeing a fruit-laden mango-tree, in mirth and amorous play advanced, leaped up and plucked a fruit, without paying due respect to the prince's presence. This move of her robbed the prince of his senses and self-control. With shameful importunity he procured her from his aunt's house, and became infatuated and given up to her, in spite of all his severe continence and temperance and pure training in theology . . . One day she offered him a cup of wine and requested him to drink it. All his profession of reluctance and entreaty were disregarded. When the poor prince was at last about to drink it, the sly enchantress snatched away the cup and said, 'My purpose was to test your love and not to embitter your mouth with this wicked and unlucky liquor!'"

Hira Bai, renamed Zainabadi, tragically died within a year, leaving Aurangzeb desolate. "By chance the rose of her life withered in its very springtime, and left the prince seared with the brand of eternal separation," notes *Masir-ul-umara*. Aurangzeb then "made a vow never to drink wine again nor to listen to music," says Manucci. "In after-days he was accustomed to say that God had been very gracious to him by putting an end to that dancing-girl's life, by reason of whom he had committed so many iniquities, and run the risk of never reigning through being occupied in vicious practices."

Born to Trouble Others

THE ZAINABADI AFFAIR, in the few months it lasted, was quite a scandal, and its echoes were heard in the imperial court in far away Lahore, where Dara is said to have remarked to Shah Jahan, "See the piety and abstinence of this hypocritical knave! He has gone to the dogs for the sake of a wench!" This probably was how Aurangzeb himself felt about the affair, in the moments when he could shake his head clear of his awful obsession. Terrible must have been the pangs of guilt he suffered about his dalliance with Zainabadi, by which he risked not only damnation in the life hereafter, but also the certain ruination of his earthly fortune. Never again would he stake salvation or dominion for transient pleasures.

Aurangzeb's guiding principle as emperor was to abide strictly by the shariah—he would walk the straight and narrow path of religious orthodoxy, and he would do his utmost to get fellow Muslims to walk the same straight and narrow path. As for Hindus, he would follow the shariah in dealing with them too, imposing on them such disabilities as the law required him to impose, but no more than that.

There would be no random, impulsive persecution of Hindus. He made this clear soon after his accession, in the firman he issued in 1659, the second year of his reign, to his officer in Varanasi, Abdul Hasan. "It has been decided according to our Canon Law that long standing temples should not be demolished, but no new temple allowed to be built . . ." wrote Aurangzeb. "Information has reached our . . . court that certain persons have harassed the Hindu residents in Benares (Varanasi) and its environs and certain Brahmans who have the right of holding charge of the ancient temples there, and that they further desire to remove these Brahmans from their ancient office. Therefore, our royal command is that you should direct that in future no person shall in unlawful ways interfere with or disturb the Brahmans and other Hindu residents in those places."

In issuing the ordinance, Aurangzeb was not favouring Hindus, but only enforcing Islamic law. He would destroy new temples, and would not allow old temples to be repaired, but he would not permit old temples to be demolished.

These were the principles that Aurangzeb followed even as a prince. The first recorded instance of temple demolition by him was in 1635, when he, seventeen, demolished, on Shah Jahan's orders, the great temple that Bir Singh had built at Orchha, and erected a mosque on its site. Ten years later, as the governor of Gujarat, he had, he says, "in Ahmadabad and other parganas of Gujarat . . . temples . . . destroyed by my order." Similar demolitions were presumably carried out during his governorship elsewhere. In the Deccan during his second governorship he boasted of demolishing a hill-top temple near Aurangabad "by God's grace" and forbidding "the temple dancers (*muralis*) to ply their shameful profession". Also during this time, he had a brahmin revenue officer, Chhabila Ram, beheaded for uttering "improper words with reference to the Prophet", and justified the execution saying, "It is proper for all Muslims to do their utmost to assert the rules of the Prophet's religion."

Despite this resolve, Aurangzeb was prudent enough not to make any major moves against Hindus in the first decade of his reign, till his authority was firmly established, though he continued to demolish temples here and there. Thus in November 1665 he issued an order to the imperial officers in Gujarat that the "formerly demolished and recently restored temples should be pulled down", and this was followed a couple of years later by an order to officers in Orissa that "every idol-house built during the last 10 or 12 years, whether with brick or clay, should be demolished without delay. Also, do not allow the . . . despicable infidels to repair their old temples. Reports of the destruction of temples should be sent to the Court under the seal of the Kazis and attested by pious Sheikhs."

The Orissa order implies that 'new' meant temples built since Aurangzeb's accession, but there was considerable ambiguity about this. Sometimes 'new' seems to have been taken to mean temples built after the Mughal conquest of a territory, or even temples built or rebuilt after the first Muslim conquest, as in the case of Aurangzeb's destruction of the temple of Somnath rebuilt in the twelfth century, after Mahmud Ghazni had destroyed an earlier structure.

Whatever the interpretation, there were no large-scale temple demolitions in the first decade of Aurangzeb's reign, no major discriminatory regulations against Hindus. The situation changed decidedly around 1668, when he came to realize that he had not done enough to promote Islam in the ten years of his reign. The continued proliferation and prosperity of Hindus even after 500 years of Muslim rule in India was, in his view, an intolerable affront to the true faith, and he considered it his imperative obligation to do everything possible under law to harass Hindus.

In 1669 he "issued orders to all governors of provinces to destroy with a willing hand the schools and temples of the infidels, and they were strictly enjoined to put an entire stop to the teaching and practising of idolatrous forms of worship," reports Mustaid Khan. It was at this time that the temple of Somnath, the Vishwanath temple at Varanasi, the great Keshav Rai temple in Mathura, and many other prominent temples were demolished. In 1670 "all temples" around Ujjain were destroyed; ten years later, numerous temples were destroyed in Rajasthan, beginning with Jodhpur, from where, according to Mustaid Khan, "several cart-loads of idols" were taken to Delhi to be "cast in the quadrangle of the Court and under the steps of the Jama Masjid for being trodden upon." Around this time, over 300 temples were destroyed in and around Chitor, Udaipur and Jaipur. In 1687 Aurangzeb ordered temples in Golconda to be destroyed, in 1698 the temples in Bijapur.

There was no let up. The more Aurangzeb did to promote Islamic theocracy, the more there seemed yet to be done. But he did not despair or give up; instead, he redoubled his efforts, believing that it was not his policy that was wrong but his exertion that was wanting. In the last decade of his reign, when he was mired down in the Deccan in a hopeless war against the Marathas, his thoughts again turned to the temples he had once destroyed, and he wrote to the royal officers in Gujarat: "The temple of Somnath was demolished early in my reign . . . It is not known what the state of things there is at present. If the idolaters have again taken to the worship of images at the place, then destroy the temple in such a way that no trace of the building may be left, and also expel them (the worshippers) from the place." The akbarat (daily newsletter) of 11th January 1705, just two years before Aurangzeb's death, records that "The Emperor . . . ordered . . . to demolish the temple of Pandharpur, and to take the butchers of the camp there and slaughter cows in the temple . . . It was done." So it went on, till death stilled his hand.

AURANGZEB'S PREDECESSORS, except Akbar, had also demolished temples, but there was a difference between them and him—while they in most cases demolished temples at random and on the impulse of the moment, Aurangzeb made it a deliberate and systematic policy of the state, an integral part of his larger policy to tighten the rigour of Islamic theocracy. It should however be noted that Aurangzeb proceeded cautiously with his anti-Hindu policies, turning the screw slowly though relentlessly, over a period of several decades, and that even in its most stringent phase, his reign was nowhere near as intolerant as the contemporary Muslim states in the Middle East and Central Asia.

The demolition of temples by Aurangzeb was accompanied by other related measures, such as the order he issued in 1668 to restrict Hindu festivals like diwali and holi. "It is ordered that in bazaars there should be no illumination at diwali, nobody's faggot should be taken by force or theft and flung into the holi bonfire, and no obscene language used," reports Ali Muhammad Khan. For good measure, Aurangzeb with sectarian fervour also prohibited the muharram procession of Shiahs, after a clash between rival processionists in Burhanpur in 1669. And he abolished sati—"The king issued an order that in all lands under Mogul control never again should the officials allow a woman to be burnt," reports Manucci. How effective these orders were is not known; they were probably little more than symbolic measures.

In 1671 Aurangzeb ordered that revenue officers in the crown lands should be only Muslims, hoping thereby to induce conversions with the lure of office. The policy did not work. Some Hindus did exchange faith for office, but not enough of them, and it was impossible to run revenue administration without Hindu clerks and accountants. Eventually Aurangzeb had to modify the rule to permit half of the officers to be Hindus. Similarly, the discriminatory customs duty he imposed on Hindus (they had to pay twice as much duty as Muslims) was frustrated by Muslim traders conniving with Hindu traders to cheat the government.

There was nothing that Aurangzeb could do to neutralize human greed, so he tried to exploit it to serve his goals. New converts were, for instance, favoured for succession to disputed property; they were given (if they were men of status) robes of honour and taken out in procession on elephants, "with flags flying and music playing", or were offered stipends and jobs, or, in the case of felons, given remission of prison sentences. At the same time, various penal disabilities were imposed on Hindus. Khafi Khan reports Aurangzeb ordered that "no Hindu should ride in a palanquin or on an Arab horse without permission", and of course they were not permitted to ride elephants.

These restrictions did not apply to Rajputs, nor presumably to the other Hindu martial communities whose services Aurangzeb needed. For all his fanaticism, Aurangzeb was pragmatic enough to let political expediency determine the scope of his theocratic regulations. Thus when an amir complained to him about the continuing prominence of Shiah Persians in the Mughal empire, he sensibly replied: "What connection have worldly affairs with religion? and what right have matters of religion to enter into bigotry? For you is your religion and for me is mine . . . [If your suggestion is accepted] it would be my duty to extirpate all the (Hindu) rajas and their followers. Wise men disapprove of the removal from office of able officers."

Manucci claims that Aurangzeb at one time "directed that the higher officers of the court who were Hindus should no longer hold their charges, but into their places Muhammadans should be put." If such a directive was indeed issued, it was done only as a formality, for Aurangzeb continued to employ Hindus in high offices. Though the percentage of Hindu officers in his service declined slightly in the first half of his reign, it rose again later, so that in the second half of his reign their percentage was higher than ever before under the Mughals— in the rank of commanders of 5000 and above, it was 32.9 per cent under Aurangzeb as against fourteen per cent under Akbar; among all officers of the rank of 500 and above, it was 31.6 per cent under Aurangzeb as against 22.5 per cent under Akbar. A brahmin, Raghunath, served for a while as Aurangzeb's acting revenue minister, one of the highest offices in the empire.

THE MOST DRAMATIC expression of Aurangzeb's anti-Hindu policy was the reintroduction of jizya, which Akbar had abolished in 1564. Now, 115 years later, on 12th April 1679, Aurangzeb reimposed it.

The promulgation of jizya immediately set off a howl of protest, and not from Hindus alone. According to Manucci, "All (meaning 'several', no doubt) the high-placed and important men at the court opposed themselves to this measure," arguing that the tax was against the practice of the Mughal empire, and that in any case the people did not have the strength to bear the burden. Aurangzeb was unmoved. "Think not I am like my grandfather, Jahangir, who spent his time listening to . . . music, or in looking on at plays and other games," he scolded. "No! No! It will never be like that with me. All my thoughts are turned towards the welfare and the development of my kingdom, and towards the propagation of the religion of the great Muhammad."

The omens at the imposition of jizya were sinister. According to Manucci, soon after Aurangzeb issued the decree, an earthquake struck Delhi, and the amirs, taking that as an ill portent, once again entreated Aurangzeb to reconsider his decision. Said Aurangzeb: "It is true that the earth lately trembled, but it is the result of the joy it felt at the course I am adopting. All nature shows marks of this feeling. The skies are darkened, they are covered with clouds, and weep tears of gladness . . ."

Among those who raised their voice against jizya was Jahanara.

"Just think, sire," she is said to have pleaded, "that the lands of Hindustan are like a vast ocean; your majesty and all the other members of our royal family are like ships navigating its waters and ploughing through its waves." It would not be wise, she argued, for Aurangzeb to stir up a storm in "the sea on which he sails . . . Abandon, then, sire, this purpose, lest there be a rebellion in this kingdom. Let your majesty reflect that violent winds usually rise and disturb the seas, swell high their waves, and transform the whole into a terrifying tempest. By its violence everything is swept to the shore, and the poor and persecuted people are ruined." The appeal had no effect on Aurangzeb. He replied that such taxes had been used by the Prophet to propagate Islam and that his own ideal was to follow that noble tradition. "Having finished these words," writes Manucci, "he bade her good-bye and turned his back upon her, a movement that cut the princess to the very quick."

Jahanara's warning about rebellion very nearly came true. "Upon the publication of this order, the Hindus all round Delhi assembled in vast numbers under the jharokha of the Emperor on the river front of the palace, to represent their inability to pay, and to pray for the recall of the edict," writes Khafi Khan. "But the Emperor would not listen to their complaints. One day, when he went to public prayer in the great mosque on the Sabbath, a vast multitude of Hindus thronged the road from the palace to the mosque, with the object of seeking relief. Money changers and drapers, all kinds of shopkeepers from the camp bazaar, mechanics, and workmen of all kinds, left off work and business, and pressed into the way. Notwithstanding the orders given to force a way through, it was impossible for the Emperor to reach the mosque. Every moment the crowd increased, and the Emperor's equipage was brought to a stand-still. At length an order was given to bring out the elephants and direct them against the mob. Many fell trodden to death under the feet of the elephants and horses. For some days the Hindus continued to assemble in great numbers and complain, but at length they submitted to pay the jizya." For a while brahmins in Delhi went on a fast to protest against jizya, but broke the fast when other Hindu castes agreed to pay jizya for them, says Muhammad Kazim.

There were disturbances in the provinces too. In Burhanpur, "the infidel inhabitants of the city and country round made great opposition to the payment of jizya," writes Khafi Khan. "There was not a district where the people, with the help of faujdars and mukaddams, did not make disturbances and resistance." Significantly, it was the common people and their local leaders who protested. There was hardly any opposition from the great Hindu chiefs serving the emperor. They had their careers to look to.

The only Hindu raja to protest was Shivaji, but he was Aurangzeb's foe, and had nothing to lose by antagonizing him. Shivaji's letter to the emperor on jizya, believed to have been drafted by his Persian secretary, Nila Prabhu, is a classic, sizzling with barbed wit. Aurangzeb, a master of sarcasm himself, could not but have admired it, even if the letter vexed him. "This firm and constant well-wisher Shivaji, after rendering thanks for the grace of God and the favours of the Emperor . . . begs to inform your Majesty that . . . he is ever ready to perform, to the fullest extent possible and proper, everything that duty as a servant and gratitude demand of him," wrote Shivaji, his tongue firmly in cheek.

He went on: "So, with a view of rendering good service and earning the imperial favour, I submit the following words in a spirit of devotion to the public welfare: It has recently come to my ears that, on the ground of the war with me having exhausted your wealth and emptied the imperial treasury, your Majesty has ordered that money under the name jizya should be collected from the Hindus and the imperial needs supplied with it." This, Shivaji reminded Aurangzeb, was contrary to the tradition established by Akbar, who abolished the poll tax, and so was blessed with success in every endeavour, as were Jahangir and Shah Jahan.

"But in your Majesty's reign," Shivaji mocked, "many of the forts and provinces have gone out of your possession, and the rest will soon do so, too, because there will be no slackness on my part in ruining and devastating them. Your peasants are down-trodden; the yield of every village has declined, in the place of one lakh [of rupees] only one thousand and in the place of a thousand only ten are collected, and that too with difficulty. When poverty and beggary have made their home in the palaces of the Emperor and the princes, the condition of the grandees and officers can be easily imagined. It is a reign in which the army is in ferment, the merchants complain; the Muslims cry, the Hindus are grilled; most men lack bread at night, and in the day-time inflame their own cheeks by slapping them [in anguish]. How can the royal spirit permit you to add the hardship of the jizya to this grievous state of things? The infamy will quickly spread from west to east and become recorded in books of history that the Emperor of Hindustan, coveting the beggars' bowls, takes jizya from Brahmans and Jains, yogis, *sanyasis*, *bairagis*, paupers, mendicants, ruined wretches, and the famine-stricken—that his valour is shown by attacks on the wallets of beggars—that he dashed down the name and honour of the Timurids!"

403

Shivaji then proceeded to give Aurangzeb a lesson on the Koran. Reminding Aurangzeb that the Koran refers to God as *"rabb-ul-alamin*, the lord of all men, and not *rabb-ul-musalmin*, the lord of the Muhammadans only," he told the emperor that Islam and Hinduism, despite all their differences, were merely the different pigments "used by the true Divine Painter."

The imposition of jizya, Shivaji argued, was unjustified. "In strict justice the jizya is not at all lawful. From the political point of view it can be allowed only if a beautiful woman wearing gold ornaments can pass from one country to another without fear or molestation. [But] in these days even the cities are being plundered, what shall I say of the open country? Apart from its injustice, this imposition of the jizya is an innovation in India and inexpedient. If you imagine piety to consist in oppressing the people and terrorizing the Hindus, you ought first to levy jizya from Rana Raj Singh, who is the head of the Hindus. Then it will not be very difficult to collect it from me, as I am at your service. But to oppress ants and flies is far from displaying valour and spirit. I wonder at the strange fidelity of your officers that they neglect to tell you of the true state of things, but cover a blazing fire with straw."

Shivaji closed the letter with the ironic greeting, "May the sun of your royalty continue to shine above the horizon of greatness!"

We have no record of Aurangzeb's reaction to Shivaji's solicitous letter, but nothing could divert him from his set policy. When some provincial officers pleaded for the remission of jizya in their districts on compassionate grounds, Aurangzeb's order was, "You are free to grant remissions of revenue of all other kinds; but if you remit any man's jizya—which I have succeeded with great difficulty in laying on the infidels—it will be an impious change and will cause the whole system of collecting the poll-tax to fall into disorder." When he was told that the tax was driving Hindu traders away from Mughal territory in the Deccan, he was indifferent. The only instance in which he is known to have relaxed the impost was in Hyderabad for one year after its annexation, when the governor there reported that the people of the city, already reduced to poverty by war, would flee if the tax was sought to be collected.

Aurangzeb appointed a whole new set of revenue officers to collect jizya, and in 1687, eight years after the tax was promulgated, he appointed an inspector-general to ensure its strict administration. The amount of revenue that the emperor received from jizya is not known, but it could not have been an insignificant amount. It is even possible that, apart from theocratic compulsions, revenue considerations motivated Aurangzeb to impose the tax—a review of the state finances in his thirteenth regnal year had revealed that in the previous twelve years expenses had exceeded income, and presumably this drain had continued in subsequent years too. Manucci says that Aurangzeb imposed jizya for two reasons: "First, because by this time his treasuries had begun to shrink owing to expenditure on his campaigns; secondly, to force Hindus to become Muhammadans." Of the two, the primary motive was probably religious. Thomas Roll, president of the English factory at Surat, writing in 1679, states that jizya was being collected to force conversions. Says Manucci: "Many Hindus, who were unable to pay, turned Muhammadan . . . Aurangzeb rejoices."

AURANGZEB COULD REJOICE because, contrary to fears, his anti-Hindu drive did not lead to any major rebellion, though there was considerable popular unrest. There was some localized opposition to temple demolition in the Rajput belt; in a few places mosques were demolished and the Muslim call for prayer stopped. Somewhere a jizya collector was "expelled after plucking his beard out", and in Delhi a Sikh once threw a brick at Aurangzeb when he was returning to the fort from the Jama Masjid. These were petty incidents, and created hardly a ripple in the vast empire.

The opposition to Aurangzeb's theocratic policies was more intense in south India than in the north. Temple demolitions, for instance, had caused no major turmoil in the north, but there was strong resentment against it in the south. F. Martin, the French diplomat in Pondicherry, noted in his diary in November 1689 that "the Muslims, having set about to destroy a temple in the Karnatak, as ordered by the Mughal, the Hindus rose to oppose it." The following month he noted that Lachmi Nayak, a local chieftain, who had at one time joined the Mughals, turned rebel on seeing the anti-Hindu policy of Aurangzeb and "wrote to all the Hindu princes to unite against the enemy of their race and religion."

In the north, there were three major uprisings against Aurangzeb around the time he began his drastic anti-Hindu thrust, but their outbreak at this time was coincidental, and had little to with his religious policy.

The first uprising was of the Jats. In 1669 the Jats in the Mathura district, a turbulent people barely held in restraint by coercion, erupted in one of their periodical revolts. Emboldened by a chance victory over the local Mughal officer, they set about looting and ravaging the district, and the prospect of plunder brought the local toughs swarming to Gokla, the Jat zemindar who headed the revolt. Soon Gokla had an army of some 20,000 men under his command, a menace serious enough for Aurangzeb to march personally into the district to quell the uprising. Gokla was captured and his limbs hacked off one by one in public, his family forced into Islam. This curbed the Jats, but only for the time being; they would rise again ten years later, when Aurangzeb was in the Deccan, and they would remain unsubdued for a long time.

No less troublesome was the uprising of Satnamis, a unitarian Hindu community of farmers and petty traders of strange appearance, who shaved off all the hair on their heads, even their eyebrows. Their name meant 'men of good name', but they were, says Ishwardas Nagar, "extremely filthy, unclean and dirty. They made no distinction between Hindus and Musalmans. They eat dirty pigs and other prohibited meats. If a dog eats from the same dish with them, they feel no distaste or aversion. They did not regard debauchery and adultery as sin." But they were a cohesive and spirited people, and, says Khafi Khan, "if any one attempts to wrong or oppress them by force, or by exercise of authority, they will not endure it."

The Satnami revolt was sparked off by a petty incident at Narnaul near Delhi in the summer of 1672, a fight between a peasant and a foot soldier. One thing led to another, and soon it flared into a major conflagration. The trouble would probably have died out by itself but for the appearance of a sorceress on the scene, a demented old crone who inflamed passions and convinced the Satnamis that her spell would protect them against enemy weapons. If any of them fell in battle, seventy would spring from the earth to take his place, she prophesied. The spell indeed seemed to work. Initially, nothing could stop the Satnami surge. Numbering barely 5000, but each mighty with a faith that could move mountains, they scattered the local Mughal officers and boldly took over the administration of the district. They then advanced on Delhi, coming as close as fifty kilometres to the city.

The Mughal contingents sent against them were terrified of the magical powers that the Satnamis were believed to possess. "It was said that swords, arrows, and musket-balls had no effect upon these men, and that every arrow and ball which they discharged against the royal army brought down two or three men," says Khafi Khan. "Thus they were credited with magic and witchcraft . . . They were said to have magic wooden horses like live ones, on which their women rode as an advanced guard." Magic, Aurangzeb realized, had to be countered with magic. So he had some spells of his own sewn on the banners of his army, and in the ensuing clash, his spells proved to be stronger than those of the Satnami sorceress, and the rebels were routed with great slaughter. (The Mughal army, incidentally, was led by a Hindu chieftain, Raja Bishnu Singh Kachhwah.)

The third major uprising was that of the Sikhs. This was of a different class altogether from the other two, though here too the issue was more political than religious. The Sikhs had by the mid-seventeenth century transformed themselves from a syncretic religious sect into a political community. Their guru was as much a monarch as a spiritual head, and was therefore a potential threat to the Mughal authority. Political as well as religious considerations therefore induced Aurangzeb to bear down on the Sikhs. This drove Tegh Bahadur, the Sikh guru, into rebellion, but he was arrested, tortured and beheaded.

To avenge Tegh Bahadur's death, his son and successor, Govind Rai, the last Sikh guru, transformed the Sikhs into the Khalsa, a military fraternity. His aim was openly political: he wanted to turn the Khalsa into an empire, and proclaimed that he would lead his men to "destroy the Mughals". Aurangzeb took up the challenge. The imperial forces then drove the guru out of Anandpur (his headquarters) to the hills, and finally out of Punjab altogether. The guru would return to Punjab only on the death of Aurangzeb.

AURANGZEB, SAYS MANUCCI, "had been born to trouble others and be troubled by them". That was the nature of his relationship with his father and brothers, with the Rajputs and the Marathas, with Hindus generally. And it was so even in his dealings with his Muslim brethren, on whom he tried to impose his own narrow, morose and joyless world-view. His reign was nearly as hard on Muslims as it was on Hindus. "The innovators, atheists, heretics who had deviated from the straight path of Islam, infidels, hypocrites and the spiritually indifferent who had spread over India, were chastised and forced to give up their wicked ways, obey the theologians and observe the fasts and prayers regularly," says Aquil Khan.

The vexation of his subjects did not bother Aurangzeb. He was, as he saw it, doing his duty as a Muslim and a king, and he believed that what he was doing was for the good of the people. "The king of happy disposition," writes Khafi Khan, "strove earnestly from day to day to put in force the rules of Law, and to maintain the Divine commands and prohibitions." Said Aurangzeb: "If I allow a single regulation to be violated, all of them will be disregarded."

Aurangzeb's very first act as emperor, after his grand enthronement in 1659, was to prohibit the stamping of the kalima, the Muslim confession of faith, on his coins, for fear of it being defiled by infidels.

Soon after, he abolished the carnival of Nauruz, the pre-Islamic Persian new year celebration which the Mughals had adopted, and transferred the customary formalities of the day to the anniversary of his accession. Later, in 1670, he severely curtailed his birthday festivities, viewing them as ostentatious and unlawful, and after another seven years abolished the celebration of the anniversary of his coronation, marking it merely by distributing paan and scents among the courtiers, whom he forbade from making any offerings to him.

Around 1670 he introduced a whole series of modifications in court regulations, to comply with Islamic prescriptions. Even the durbar hall was redecorated. "The uncanonical railings of gold and silver" were replaced with "railings of lapis lazuli set in gold", and the gold and silver censers for burning aloeswood removed, says Mustaid Khan. Gifts for distribution were thereafter required to be brought on shields instead of the usual silver trays; clerks were ordered to use porcelain and stone ink-pots in the place of silver ink-pots; dress of pure silk was forbidden in the court; and "embroidered cloth . . . instead of stuff with gold and silver flowers worked on it" was specified for robes of honour to be presented by the emperor.

In the eleventh year of his reign Aurangzeb forbade the writing of the chronicle of his reign as an impious conceit. Around this time he also gave up the Hindu royal practices that the Mughals had adopted, such as the emperor presenting himself to his subjects at sunrise; weighing himself on his solar and lunar birthdays against gold, silver and other commodities and giving away the value of the weight in charity; and the custom of applying the *tika* on the forehead of rajas at their investitures. Further, courtiers were forbidden to greet each other with Hindu salutations, but were to confine themselves to saying *salaam alekum*. Aurangzeb also decreed, to conform to Koranic law, that tombs should not be roofed over or lime-washed. He barred women from visiting shrines, as Firuz Tughluq had done 300 years earlier, to prevent lasciviousness in holy places. And he condemned shikar as an indulgence of the *bekar* (the idle).

The oddest of Aurangzeb's puritanical decrees was his 1668 banishment of music. "As the emperor had no liking for pleasure," says Mustaid Khan, "and his devotion to duty left him no time for festivity, he ordered that the chief musician . . . (and others) might come to the Court, but must not make music. Gradually (music) was entirely forbidden." Musicians who gave up their profession were given allowances by the emperor, says Bakhtawar Khan. According to Khafi Khan, "public proclamations were made prohibiting singing and dancing", and Manucci says that officials were empowered to enter and break musical instruments if anywhere they heard the sound of music. What this meant, presumably, was that, apart from banishing music from the court, public performances of music and dance were also banned. Aurangzeb could not have banned music as such from the empire, for that would have had no canonical justification.

Whatever the scope of the ban, the loss of royal patronage distressed artistes, and they protested by staging a charade. "About one thousand of them assembled on a Friday when Aurangzeb was going to the mosque," reports Manucci. "They came out with over twenty highly-ornamented biers, as is the custom of the country, crying aloud with great grief and many signs of feeling, as if they were escorting to the grave some distinguished defunct. From afar Aurangzeb saw this multitude and heard their great weeping and lamentation, and, wondering, sent to know the cause of so much sorrow. The musicians redoubled their outcry and tears . . . Lamenting, they replied with sobs that the king's orders had killed Music, therefore they were bearing her to the grave. Report was made to the king, who quite calmly remarked that they should pray for the soul of Music, and see that she is thoroughly well buried."

AROUND THE TIME that music was banished, Aurangzeb issued a number of orders to regulate public and private morals. "Prohibitions were promulgated against intoxicating drinks, against taverns and brothels, and against . . . *jatras* or fairs," says Khafi Khan.

The Mughal nobles, Muslim as well as Hindu, were addicted to liquor, which Aurangzeb found abominable. "It was so common to drink spirits when Aurangzeb ascended the throne, that one day he said in a passion that in all Hindustan no more than two men could be found who did not drink, namely himself and Abdul Wahab, the Kazi," says Manucci. "But with respect to Abdul Wahab he was in error, for I myself sent him every day a bottle of wine, which he drank in secret."

Aurangzeb imposed severe penalties on prohibition offenders—a hand and a foot of those who sold liquor were cut off, and the houses of those who made liquor at home were vandalized and plundered by the police—but none of that had any great effect on tipplers. "The nobles, who found it hard to live without spirits, distilled in their houses, there being few who did not drink secretly," says Manucci. Faced with such persistence, Aurangzeb was eventually obliged to yield to human nature and lighten the rigour of his prohibition law.

At the time of introducing prohibition, Aurangzeb also banned the cultivation of cannabis (there is no mention in the chronicles of banning opium) and the preparation of *bhang*, a common marijuana concoction. "Not a day passed that on rising in the morning we did not hear the breaking by blows and strokes of the pots and pans in which these beverages are prepared," says Manucci. Gambling too was forbidden. And of course prostitution. "In the reign of Shah Jahan female dancers and public women enjoyed great liberty . . . and were found in great numbers in the cities," writes Manucci. "For a time, in the beginning of his reign, Aurangzeb said nothing, but afterwards he ordered that they must either marry or clear out of the realm . . . some of them married and others went away, or, at least, concealed themselves."

In the same spirit, to curb wantonness, Aurangzeb ordered that women "must not wear tight trousers like those of men, but wide ones," says Manucci, and he issued an order to the governor of Kashmir to make the people there wear drawers, instead of just the heavy cloak under which they, men as well as women, usually wore nothing. He disapproved of dandyism, and once humiliated an amir in the open court by ordering a few inches of his cloak—which fell below his ankles, and was therefore considered improper—to be snipped off. Hedonistic refinements offended Aurangzeb, and he ordered that "the factory of *do dami* (superfine cloth) established at Chanderi should be abolished," says Mustaid Khan. He also forbade the planting of rose-beds in imperial gardens.

According to Manucci, Aurangzeb even sought to regulate the length of beards, decreeing that "no Muhammadan should wear a beard longer than four finger-breadths." An official, says Manucci, was appointed to enforce this regulation, and he importantly went about with attendants and soldiers "to measure beards in the middle of the street, and, if necessary, dock them . . . It was . . . amusing to see the official in charge of beards rushing hither and thither, laying hold of wretched men by the beard, in order to measure and cut off the excess, and clipping their moustaches to uncover the lips. This last was done so that, when pronouncing the name Allah, there might be no impediment to the sound ascending straight to heaven."

Enforcement of these Islamic edicts was overseen by the Muhtasib, the censor of morals. This officer was a part of the regular Muslim administrative apparatus, but Aurangzeb raised his stature by appointing a distinguished scholar to the office and giving him a high rank (commander of 1000) and a large staff. It was the censor's duty to enforce among Muslims canonical regulations about what was permitted and what was forbidden, to ensure that the prescribed prayers were said and fasts observed, and to prevent heresy and blasphemy.

There was however considerable confusion about the details of the religious discipline required of Muslims, because of the many conflicting interpretations of Islamic law and tradition. Aurangzeb therefore set up a council of theologians to compile a book of judicial decisions, and they produced the *Fatawa-al-Alamgiriyya*, one of the most authoritative works on Islamic jurisprudence. In discharge of his theocratic obligations, Aurangzeb also took care to repair old mosques and monasteries—there were some 600 mosques in Delhi at this time, and it cost Aurangzeb 100,000 rupees a year to maintain them—and he encouraged traditional learning by granting allowances to pupils.

AURANGZEB'S THEOCRATIC regulations are what gave his reign its distinctive colouration, but his reforms in other fields are also noteworthy. Mughal administration had collapsed during the civil war, and local chiefs had taken to collecting cesses and tolls as they pleased "on every highway, frontier and ferry", says Khafi Khan. This seriously impeded trade and made the price of essential commodities rise to famine levels. Aurangzeb sought to restore the efficiency of administration by issuing, soon after his accession, orders abolishing a large number (eighty, according to Khafi Khan) of vexatious petty cesses, and forbidding local officials from collecting illegal imposts.

He also showed similar concern to safeguard the interests of peasants, and gave detailed instructions to revenue officers about what had to be done to promote agriculture, to protect cultivators from exploitation by middlemen, as well as about the steps to be taken to alleviate the sufferings of peasants during natural calamities. Similarly, Aurangzeb abandoned the practice of the emperor confiscating the property of amirs on their death. "His Majesty . . . forbade the practice of escheating to the State the property of the dead nobles who had left behind them no debt due to the government, but he let their heirs succeed to their legacy," says Mustaid Khan.

Unfortunately, few of these regulations had any practical effect. His orders on illegal cesses, like similar orders by his predecessors, were generally ignored by local chiefs, who would comply with the orders only if the emperor dispatched mace-bearers to enforce his fiat, and that too only as long as the enforcers were around. "So the regulation for the abolition of most of the imposts had no effect," concedes Khafi Khan. As for escheat, Aurangzeb himself often violated his guideline, because of financial pressures.

In all his regulations, commendable or otherwise, Aurangzeb was strictly following Islamic law and conventions. He was in fact so heedful of observing laws and norms, that it almost amounted to a

411

weakness, and his authority lacked the coercive terror so essential to maintain law and order and administrative efficiency in the medieval state. Says Khafi Khan: "From reverence for the injunction of the Law he did not make use of punishment, and without punishment the administration of a country cannot be maintained."

It was, in a sense, the rule of law under Aurangzeb. This however was hardly a positive quality in him, but a lack of vision, an inability to see beyond the instant horizon.

"The More One Drinks . . ."

AURANGZEB HAD NO vision, only ambition; no reach, only grab. He was the least imaginative, the least creative of the Great Mughals. And the least dynamic. He laboured tirelessly, but was driven by will and routine rather than by genius. No other Mughal emperor, with the possible exception of Akbar, had spent as much time in the battlefield or won as many battles as Aurangzeb. He pushed the Mughal frontiers almost to the very ends of the subcontinent, making it the most extensive empire in Indian history. Yet he was a failure, and he died a defeated man, a tragic, almost pathetic figure. In every respect the reign of Aurangzeb marks the beginning of the end of Mughal glory.

Aurangzeb's military operations fall into two nearly equal halves: he spent the first twenty-three years of his reign in north India, and the next twenty-six years in the south. Though there were major campaigns in the south during Aurangzeb's northern phase—his entire tussle with Shivaji falls into that period—the emperor himself remained in the north; similarly, during his southern phase, the wars he had earlier launched in the north, especially the Rajput wars, would continue, but Aurangzeb himself would never cross the Narmada again.

A MAJOR AND SOMEWHAT exaggerated concern of Aurangzeb in the first half of his reign was the contingency of a Persian invasion of India, a menace the Mughals had had to live with ever since Shah Abbas II drove them out of Kandahar in 1649. During the war of succession, Murad as well as Dara had approached the Shah for support, and though the Shah did not get directly involved in the conflict, he did assemble a 30,000 strong force in Kandahar to be ready for any eventuality, and he did try to instigate the Shiah kingdoms of the Deccan to take advantage of the civil war to throw off the Mughal yoke. But when Aurangzeb emerged as the clear winner in the civil war, Shah Abbas sent him a grand embassy, to convey his felicitations.

The visit of the Persian ambassador, Budaq Beg, in the summer of 1661 created quite a flutter in Delhi. Persians were the cultural aristocrats of the eastern Muslim world, and the Mughals, quite provincial for all their wealth and power, craved for Persian approbation. The ambassador was therefore accorded a most magnificent reception. He was received at the Mughal frontier by a senior imperial officer, and from a distance of one day's journey to Delhi, he was escorted by a Mughal grandee with a contingent of a thousand select horsemen; in the city itself, for a distance of five kilometres, soldiers lined the streets, and "the principal streets were decorated with rich stuffs, both in the shops and at the windows, and the ambassador was brought through them, escorted by a number of officers, with music, drums, pipes and trumpets. On entering the fort . . . he was saluted by all the artillery . . . The whole court was adorned with a thousand marvellous things," writes Manucci, an eyewitness.

Aurangzeb was however apprehensive about what to expect of the ambassador. To protect his dignity against possible Persian insolence, he had sought through his officers an assurance from the ambassador that he would comply with the Mughal custom of saluting the emperor by bowing humbly and salaaming, instead of in the proud Persian manner of standing upright and placing his hands on the chest. Yet the ambassador, as he approached the throne, saluted the emperor in the Persian fashion, upon which four stalwart Mughal officers, specially assigned to meet the contingency, politely but firmly took hold of the ambassador and made him perform the Mughal salute, "without force or violence, as if they were teaching him," notes Manucci.

The ambassador showed no resentment at this. He then presented to the emperor the gifts he had brought from the Persian monarch—and a letter. The Shah's letter, though courteous as usual, was patronizing in its tone, and it annoyingly referred to his recent triumph in Kandahar and the earlier Persian role in restoring Humayun to power. The letter vexed Aurangzeb, but he kept his own counsel, and after a couple of months gave the Persian envoy leave to return, conferring on him and his entourage fabulous gifts. Two years later, in 1663, he sent to Persia his own ambassador, Tarbiyat Khan, who bore gifts worth over 700,000 rupees for the Shah, nearly double of what Aurangzeb had received from Abbas, presumably to demonstrate the superior grandeur of the Mughal emperor.

Aurangzeb in his letter to Abbas, sent through Tarbiyat Khan, sought to score a verbal victory over the Shah by speaking grandly about his own victories. The Shah was not impressed. He treated Tarbiyat Khan with scorn, muttered threats of invading India, and when the ambassador returned to Delhi, sent through him a blunt, rude letter to Aurangzeb. "I learn that most of the zemindars of India are in rebellion because their ruler is weak, incompetent and without resources," Abbas wrote. He taunted Aurangzeb for his failure to suppress Shivaji, and went on: "You style yourself as the Conqueror of the Universe while you have only conquered your father; and having gained composure of mind by the murder of your brothers . . . you have abandoned the royal practices of doing justice and charity . . . You have failed in every undertaking that required manliness."

The Shah signed off by virtually threatening to invade India. "Thanks to the favour of God and the Imams, it is my nature to cherish those who are cursed, and my ancestors have been the refuge of the kings of the world," he wrote. "Now that you . . . are in distress, it is my royal aim to go personally to India with my multitudinous army, meet you, . . . give you every help and extinguish the fire of disorder with the lustre of my sword . . . so that people might be delivered from the oppression of lawless men, and sing my praises. May God keep you safe amidst your misfortunes."

The letter was a gauntlet thrown down, but Aurangzeb dared not pick it up; instead, he profaned Persians as corpse-eating demons and (what must have been to Aurangzeb the ultimate insult) as *batil mazhaban*, heretics. He also vented his fury on poor Tarbiyat Khan—he was accused of failing in his mission, denied admission to the court, degraded in rank, and packed off to Orissa. The Shah's letter intensified Aurangzeb's anxiety about a possible Persian invasion, especially as there were rumours at this time about military preparations in Persia. He could breath easy only when the pugnacious Shah died in August 1667. Even then, before he shifted to the Deccan in 1681, Aurangzeb took the precaution of securing an agreement from the ruler of Balkh to be vigilant against any Persian move towards India.

THE IMMEDIATE REASON for Aurangzeb to shift his field of operations to the south was the rebellion of his son Akbar, but there was in any case the unfinished task of subjugating the Marathas and the Deccan sultanates. Like his predecessors, Aurangzeb too had a ravenous land hunger. He was an "insatiable beast of prey," says Manucci, and points out that "the more one drinks, the more one wants to drink." In the face of Persian belligerence, Aurangzeb could not dream of a Central Asian adventure. There was not even any thought of recovering Kandahar. Aurangzeb had to sate his land hunger in India itself.

There was hardly any land left in north India for Aurangzeb to bite into. Akbar had conquered most of Hindustan, and what little was left was mopped up by Jahangir and Shah Jahan. Aurangzeb could only expand into the south. He was involved with only one major campaign in the north, against the Rajputs, and that was to suppress a rebellion, not to conquer new territory. His other campaigns in the north were in remote, mountainous regions, where gains in territory and revenue hardly matched the effort and the cost of operations.

The Mughal campaign in Assam was typical of the hardships the army suffered in mountain wars. A lush tropical valley in the crook of the mountains, Assam was the land of the Ahoms, a fierce Mongoloid tribe who had by the mid-seventeenth century become Hinduized. The Mughal thrust into Assam had begun during the reign of Akbar, when Koch Bihar (Cooch Behar), nestling against the Himalayas just below Bhutan, was brought under Mughal suzerainty. From there, turning east at the mountains, the Mughals annexed Kamrup in the reign of Jahangir, thus extending the imperial domain up to the Bar River. This brought the Mughals into conflict with the Ahoms, who ruled the land across the river. The desultory war that ensued dragged on for twenty-six years, well into the reign of Shah Jahan. Then for two decades there was peace, but during the Mughal war of succession both Koch Bihar and Assam broke free.

There was no immediate Mughal response to the rebellion, but after Aurangzeb established himself securely on the throne, he ordered Mir Jumla, his governor in Bengal, to chastise the rebels. In a swift action Mir Jumla reoccupied Koch Bihar, and then swept into Assam, where he cut his way through the river-fissured jungles, scattered the Ahoms, and took Garhgaon, the Ahom capital. But there the Mughals got bogged down, as the monsoon broke over Assam and turned the land into a steamy swamp, marooning them in isolated outposts, where they were subjected to unremitting nightly attacks by the Ahoms, who had come into their own with the rains. The Mughal camps were cut off from each other and from the outside world. No supplies reached them, not even news. And with the rains came epidemics that felled hundreds every day. But Mir Jumla was equal to the crisis. He companionably shared every privation with his men, eating what they ate, living as they lived, and kept up their morale and conserved their strength.

The siege by rain lasted for six months, from May to November. Then at last the rains ceased, "pleasant breezes began to blow, and flowers to blossom". Communication between the camps was then restored. Fresh supplies arrived. Presently, the Mughals were on the move again, and the Ahoms in retreat. In the end, Mir Jumla's adamant will prevailed, and the Ahom king treated for peace. He agreed to pay a heavy indemnity, cede a part of his kingdom, give hostages, and send a princess for the imperial harem.

416

When the princess, the hostages and the first installment of the indemnity arrived, Mir Jumla began an orderly retreat from Assam. Unfortunately he died on the way, worn out by the campaign, but triumphant. The peace he secured lasted a few years, longer than any one could have expected. Then hostilities broke out again, and the Ahoms drove the Mughals out of Assam and even captured Gauhati, the capital of Kamrup. Though a fresh Mughal campaign tried to reassert imperial authority in Assam, it was not able to make any great headway and had eventually to retreat. Kamrup and Assam were lost.

Later, when Shayista Khan, Aurangzeb's maternal uncle, took over the governorship of Bengal, he restored Mughal authority in Koch Bihar, but did not attempt to retake Kamrup or Assam. Instead, he turned south to launch an extended campaign to pacify south-eastern Bengal, which had been in turmoil for a long time.

Deltaic Bengal was Mughal India's badlands, the swampy mouth of a thousand-headed hydra of a river, the home of the crocodile, the tiger and the desperado. The dregs of the foreign settlements in India drifted into this tract, which was dominated by the Portuguese and half-breed pirates operating out of Chittagong, a port in the domain of the Magh king of Arakan. "Men of hard heart . . . they boasted among themselves of having reached the acme of evil-doing," says Manucci. "The Arakan pirates, both Magh and Feringhee, used constantly to come by the water-route and plunder Bengal," reports Shihabuddin Ahmad Talish. "As they continually practised raids for a long time, Bengal daily became more and more desolate . . . Not a house was left inhabited on either side of the rivers lying on their track . . . The district of Bakla, which formerly abounded in houses and cultivated fields . . . was swept so clean with their broom of plunder and abduction that none was left to tenant any house or kindle a light in that region."

Shayista Khan ended this chaos. Rebuilding the shattered and demoralized Bengal flotilla, he launched a combined land and sea operation against Chittagong, routed the Arakanese on land and sea, and annexed Chittagong, thus virtually ending piracy in the region.

As in the north-east, so in the north-west too Aurangzeb was faced with a major law and order problem, because of the turbulence of the Turko-Iranian mountain tribes of eastern Afghanistan. These tribes, called Pathans in the north and Baluchis in the south, lived by war and rapine, because their land was too niggardly and they were in any case too proud and restless a people to live by humdrum productive labour. Fiercely free-spirited, they forever fought among themselves or ravaged their neighbours, fulfilling an age-old curse (or blessing) laid on them by a Pathan saint, that they would be always free, but never united.

Every Mughal emperor had despaired about them; even Akbar had suffered galling reverses at their hands.

In the late 1660s a couple of Afghan tribes crossed the Indus and occupied the Mughal plains, closed the Khyber Pass, cut off Kabul, and routed the Mughal expeditionary forces sent against them. This was a dangerous development, threatening Mughal rule in Kabul. As the situation got out of control, in 1674 Aurangzeb moved to Peshawar, and by concentrated effort over the next year and a half finally managed to pacify the region, by sowing dissension among the Afghan tribes ("breaking two stones by knocking them together," as he put it), giving generous subsidies to those who submitted, and battering down those who would not.

AMONG THE MAJOR Mughal casualties in Afghanistan was Raja Jaswant Singh Rathor of Marwar, who died at his command post near the Khyber Pass in December 1678, due to the severity of the winter. The raja left no heir, as his only son Jagat Singh too had died in Afghanistan. The decision about succession in Marwar therefore fell to Aurangzeb, the overlord of the principality.

The vacant throne, with no clear successor, predictably brought Rajput fractiousness to the fore. "Because of the death of the Maharaja, all the Rajputs of Marwar, from house to house were seething with pride . . . and were showing restlessness and readiness to create trouble," says Ishwardas, a Nagar Brahmin chronicler of Aurangzeb and a player in the Rajput drama. The strongest claimant to the Marwar throne was Indra Singh, a grandson of Jaswant's elder brother, but he was not acceptable to most Rathors. A further complication was that two of Jaswant's queens were in an advanced state of pregnancy at the time of the raja's death, so Aurangzeb had to wait for the birth of the babies before deciding on the succession. If a male child was born, the crown would naturally go to him.

The succession choice thus waited on developments, but Marwar could not be left without a government in the interregnum. Law and order had to be maintained, revenue had to be collected. Aurangzeb therefore, soon after he received the news of Jaswant Singh's death, sent his officers to take over the administration of Marwar. Further, he escheated the personal property of Jaswant, as the raja, a poor manager, owed large sums of money to the imperial treasury. These measures were normal, essential, and perfectly legal.

Yet, certain aspects of the emperor's action raised doubts about what he really meant to do in Marwar. For one thing, the top officers he appointed in Marwar were all Muslims, and they set about demolishing temples and building mosques in their place. Aurangzeb himself moved to Ajmer at this time, ostensibly on a pilgrimage but really to watch over developments in Marwar. It was as if he were planning some big move.

Meanwhile news reached Aurangzeb that Jaswant's pregnant widows had both delivered sons in Lahore. The Rathors therefore urged Aurangzeb to nominate Ajit, one of the sons, as successor to Jaswant. To this Aurangzeb raised certain difficulties: the child obviously could not rule, nor could the dominion government be conferred on the queen or on any Rathor noble, even as a regent, for that was against Mughal tradition. Aurangzeb therefore saw no reason to retrace the steps he had taken.

On 12th April 1679 he returned to Delhi from Ajmer, and that very day imposed jizya throughout the empire. This decision, coming close on the heels of the destruction of temples in Marwar and the taking over of the government of the principality, gave the impression that all these deeds were in some way connected and had an ominous common purpose.

What did Aurangzeb want? As a political move, aggressive action against Marwar did not make sense. Marwar was a vassal state, part of the empire, and its revenues belonged to the emperor, so there was no significant advantage in imposing direct Mughal rule over it. Marwar was a poor state, a good part of it desert, its very name a corruption of *marumar*, meaning the land of death. The region had some commercial importance, as the most convenient route between Delhi and the entrepots of Gujarat passed through it, but in this too there was no special advantage for Aurangzeb to gain by ruling Marwar directly.

We do not know whether Aurangzeb had a master plan for Marwar, or whether he was merely responding pragmatically to an evolving situation. He, unlike his predecessors, had no great regard for the Rajputs; even as a prince he had been unfriendly towards Rajputs, and Shah Jahan had once pulled him up on that. The traditional Mughal policy, as enunciated by Jahangir, was to avoid the destruction of the old ruling families of India as far as possible, but Aurangzeb saw the Hindu royal families as an impediment to the realization of his grand dream of Islamizing India. He seems to have felt that as long as there were powerful Rajput kingdoms around, patronizing and promoting Hinduism, and serving as symbols of the continuing high stature of Hindus, the battle against infidelity would never be won in India. Moreover, there was a risk of the Rajput states becoming the rallying points of Hindu resistance to his policies. It was therefore to his advantage to discredit and weaken the Rajput rajas. In Marwar he had an opportunity to do so.

Aurangzeb had never liked Jaswant, and for good reason—the raja had fought against him at Dharmat, betrayed him at Khajwa, and later had offered to support fugitive Dara. Moreover, Jaswant was, as Aurangzeb described him in one of his letters, an "infidel who has destroyed mosques and built idol temples on their sites". He could only be happy to see the ruination of the raja's family.

IN THE FIRST WEEK of June 1679, a full five months after Jaswant's death, Aurangzeb invested Indra Singh Rathor as the ruler of Marwar, on a payment of 3.6 million rupees as the succession fee. By this choice Aurangzeb probably hoped to divide Rajput loyalties. That did not happen. Indra Singh had no support among the Rathors, so Mughal officers had to be retained in the state to prop him up on the throne. Meanwhile, by the end of June, Jaswant's widows arrived in Delhi with their sons, and the Rathor nobles once again pressed for the recognition of Ajit as king.

Aurangzeb then explained to them the difficulty in handing over power to Ajit, but agreed to do so when the child came of age, and ordered him to be brought up in the imperial harem. According to Bhimsen Burhanpuri, a Bundela officer in the Mughal service and a chronicler of Aurangzeb's reign, the throne was offered to Ajit on condition that he become a Muslim—not an improbable manoeuver, given the general thrust of Aurangzeb's policies and the fact that he had settled some other disputed successions in favour of claimants who agreed to become Muslims. He would later make a similar offer to Shahu, Shivaji's grandson. In any case, Aurangzeb's proposal to bring up Ajit in the imperial harem was looked on by the Rathors with deep suspicion. "The emperor, who seems to be in a furious and angry mood, has demanded the surrender of the children. God alone knows what he has in mind regarding the youngsters," they fretted. Safety lay in flight, they decided.

The primary issue that was involved here, from the Rajput point of view, was political, not religious, though the issue also had strong religious undertones. Rajput chieftains and grandees, it should be noted, had never shown any fervour to defend their faith as long as their power was not threatened; indeed, they often connived with the Mughals in temple destruction. What now turned them against the emperor was not so much his religious policy as the political implications of that policy.

The Rajputs had for over a century, from the time of Akbar, enjoyed a special status in the Mughal empire: they were vassals of the emperor yet virtually independent, an arrangement that satisfied Rajput pride as well as Mughal prestige. This balance was upset by Aurangzeb. In fact, even before his reign, the role of the Rajputs in the Mughal empire had been declining, because of the induction of other Indian martial communities like the Marathas into Mughal service. By the second half of Aurangzeb's reign there were more Marathas than Rajputs among Mughal officers, and the Rajputs had ceased to play any major role in Mughal campaigns. Furthermore, Aurangzeb, who was more a tactician than a warrior, had little respect for the valour of the Rajputs, and scorned their daredevilry as mere foolhardiness. The Rajputs for their part had little regard for Aurangzeb, and could hardly trust him.

In that environment of mutual distrust it was only natural that the Rathors should suspect Aurangzeb's motives in wanting to bring up Ajit in his harem. They however tried to avoid a confrontation on the issue by pleading that the baby was too young to be separated from his mother. Aurangzeb saw the excuse for what it was, quibbling and insubordination, and it got his blood up. He ordered his officers to seize the queens and their sons.

The Rathors had anticipated that move and were prepared for it. A small contingent of Rajputs had already set a flight plan in motion by obtaining the prior permission of the emperor to return to their homes in Marwar. "Meanwhile the Rajputs had obtained two boys of the same age of the Raja's children," says Khafi Khan. "They dressed some of the female attendants in the garments of the ranis, and . . . left these women and the boys under the guard in their camp. The ranis, disguised as men, went off at night in charge of two trusty servants and a party of devoted Rajputs, and made their way with all speed to their own country." When the imperial officers went to seize the queens and the princes, the Rajputs fought as if they were indeed fighting to defend their royal family, and many were killed.

The substitute Ajit was taken to Aurangzeb and was brought up in the imperial harem in the care of Aurangzeb's daughter Zebunnisa; he was named, significantly, Muhammadi Raja. "The two boys which the Rajputs carried off were for a long time rejected by Aurangzeb, who refused to acknowledge that they were the sons of Jaswant, until all doubt was removed by the Rana of Chitor, who married Ajit Singh to a girl of his family," says Khafi Khan. For long, Aurangzeb spoke of the prince in Marwar as Ajit-i-jali, the duplicate Ajit.

The man who masterminded the escape of the princes from Delhi was Durgadas Rathor, son of Jaswant's minister Askaran. Durgadas, like Raja Jai Singh of Amber, was an unusual Rajput, who combined heroic valour with shrewd diplomacy and outstanding organizational skills, so that the Rathor bard would sing, "*Eh mata put esa jin Jesa Durgadas,*" wishing every Rajput mother a son like Durgadas. With Ajit safely hidden in the Aravalli Range, Durgadas prepared to resist the Mughals.

AURANGZEB NOW ONCE again moved to Ajmer, and from there sent a strong force under his son, Prince Akbar, to coerce Marwar. As Akbar advanced, the Rathors blocked his way, but were routed, and the prince entered Jodhpur, the Marwar capital, without resistance. Jaswant's widow Rani Hadi is then said to have offered to destroy the temples of Marwar if Aurangzeb would recognize Ajit as the raja; in the alternative, she suggested that Marwar might be taken over as Mughal crown lands, instead of handing it over to Indra Singh—a plausible offer, given the bitter internecine feuds among the Rajputs. Nothing came of the proposal. For a time, Aurangzeb seems to have considered partitioning the state to satisfy the rival claimants, but later, finding Indra Singh incompetent to rule, dethroned him, and took over the direct administration of the principality.

Around the time that Aurangzeb tightened the screws on Marwar, he also put pressure on Mewar, accusing Rana Raj Singh, the Sisodia chief, of repairing the fortifications of Chitor against treaty terms. Further, he demanded the payment of jizya from Mewar, and asked the Rana to secure the 'alleged sons' of Jaswant from Marwar, Ajit's mother being a sister-in-law of Raj Singh. The Rana refused to be provoked into a hasty war; he offered to cede two or three districts of Mewar in commutation of jizya, declared that he was not supporting the sons of Jaswant, and, according to Khafi Khan, "begged forgiveness for his offences". This mollified Aurangzeb. He had, he believed, humbled the Rajputs and won the contest in Rajasthan.

He was wrong. The struggle had only just begun.

In Marwar, the Rathors, though vanquished in pitched battles, kept up an obstinate guerrilla war against the Mughals, and in Mewar, Raj Singh reneged on his agreement with Aurangzeb and fled into the mountains to resist the Mughals. The Rathors and the Sisodias thus made common cause against the Mughals, united in their alarm that Aurangzeb meant to exterminate them. What followed was a war of attrition, with no possibility of a final victory for either the Rajputs or the Mughals. There was no way that the Rajputs could defeat the

Mughals—they could only harass them; equally, there was no way that the Mughals could crush the Rajputs—they could only keep them at bay. When the Mughals occupied the plains of Rajasthan, the Rajputs took to the mountains and the desert and continued the fight. The Mughals won nearly all the battles, but could not win the war.

The war went on. The Rajputs occupied the crests of the Aravalli Range, from where they could range either east into Mewar or west into Marwar, streaking in to cut off Mughal supplies, menace their outposts, and on occasion even attack Akbar's camp. The Mughal army dared not pursue the Rajputs into the mountains. "Our army is motionless through fear," wrote Akbar to the emperor. Aurangzeb then shifted Akbar from Mewar to Marwar and ordered him to advance into the hills from the west, while Prince Azam was ordered to advance from the east, and Prince Muazzam from the north. Of these three drives, only Akbar could make any significant gain, but even that was not to Aurangzeb's satisfaction.

Akbar got as far as Desuri in south Rajasthan, but dallied there instead of advancing to Kumbhargarh, the last stronghold of the Rana of Mewar. He resented being constantly badgered by Aurangzeb despite his successes. On the other hand, the Rajputs were at this time making much of him, urging him to usurp the throne and save the empire from the morass into which Aurangzeb was dragging it. Akbar listened and was tempted. The Rajput rebellion thus developed into a fight for the Mughal throne, which in turn dragged Aurangzeb into a self-destructive war with the Marathas.

"Now That the Shadows Fall . . ."

PRINCE AKBAR EASILY fell to the Rajput enticement, for what they proposed was what he himself was dreaming about, to be the great unifier of India, like his namesake ancestor. He, not Aurangzeb, was the true inheritor of the Mughal legacy, the Rajputs told him: Aurangzeb was an awful aberration. "If you wish that the honour of Hindustan should not be totally lost, we clasp the skirt of your robe and hope for deliverance and happiness at your hands," Rana Jai Singh of Mewar (son and successor of Raj Singh) told Akbar. The romance of the heroic role that the Rajputs offered him was temptation enough for the prince, but there were other considerations too. He was twenty-three then, his father sixty-three. He knew that sooner or later he would have to stake his life in a deadly struggle for succession, so why not now, when he had mighty allies on his side?

Akbar had always been a spirited child, aggressive and wilful, very much the son of his mother, the imperious Dilras Banu Begum, who had died soon after giving birth to him. He, like his full brother Azam, was in no particular awe of his baleful father, and often clashed openly with him. Yet Aurangzeb indulged him. Akbar was his favourite son. Aurangzeb was therefore inclined to ignore the early warning of Akbar's rebellion which Prince Muazzam conveyed to him, terming it, according to Khafi Khan, "sheer calumny". Aurangzeb was uncharacteristically trusting. At least, that was the impression he gave. In any case, he took no precaution against Akbar.

The Rajputs contacted Akbar at Desuri through his frontline commander Tahavvur Khan and assured him of their support if he chose to rebel. Akbar welcomed the offer. Then, taking a lesson in deception from his father, he attempted to throw Aurangzeb off the scent of rebellion by claiming that he was negotiating the surrender of the Rajputs, and would himself be conducting them to the emperor to solicit pardon for them. But he was uncomfortable with the subterfuge, and presently stood forth boldly as a rebel. When Aurangzeb wrote to him that he had heard rumours about his rebellion and wanted to know the truth, Akbar wrote back impudently that he had indeed rebelled, following, he said, the excellent example of Aurangzeb himself.

"The whole realm was . . . tired at seeing his tyrannical acts, more especially the abrogation of the rights and privileges that his far-off ancestors had conceded to different persons in Hindustan," wrote Akbar to his father, and advised him, according to Manucci, to "mount his horse and prepare for battle, for he (Akbar) was coming straight to fight him personally."

Akbar then issued an edict deposing Aurangzeb. Four ulema in his pay legitimized the action by decreeing that Aurangzeb had forfeited his right to reign by his infractions—of all things—of Islamic law! Then, on 11th January 1681, Akbar proclaimed himself emperor, and the next day set out with his Rajput allies to confront Aurangzeb.

His timing was perfect. Aurangzeb was then at Ajmer, some 170 kilometres north-east of Akbar's position. He was virtually defenceless. "All his retinue, counting the eunuchs and writers, did not exceed seven or eight hundred horsemen," writes Khafi Khan. "A great panic fell upon the royal camp, and wild confusion followed." Ishwardas gives the strength of Aurangzeb's retinue as six or seven thousand, which is more probable, but whatever its actual size, it was insignificant compared to Akbar's army, which included some 30,000 Rajput veterans. Victory was in Akbar's grasp, if he hastened to grab it.

AKBAR DID NOT hasten. He saw no need to. Having declared himself emperor, he assumed that he already was the emperor, and so proceeded with regal deliberation, taking a full fortnight to get to Ajmer, which he could have reached in less than half that time. This delay wrecked his chances. With each passing day his strength dwindled, as Mughal soldiers deserted to the emperor, doubting Akbar's ability to oust his indomitable father, while Aurangzeb's strength daily grew, as his sons and generals rushed to him on his urgent summons. Aurangzeb was amazed, though pleased, by Akbar's tardiness. "I am now defenceless. The young hero has got a splendid opportunity. Why then is he delaying his attack?" he wondered.

Manucci says that it was Aurangzeb's machination that delayed Akbar, by getting astrologers to advise the prince to delay his advance. The appearance of a comet at this time also caused much confusion. The opposing forces finally came face to face near Deorai, where Aurangzeb had won a great battle against Dara twenty-two years earlier. There Aurangzeb's strength was greatly augmented by the arrival of Prince Muazzam with an army, though for a while there was apprehension whether Muazzam meant to support or attack the emperor.

Aurangzeb was thus no longer vulnerable to easy defeat. But a battle was always a risk. Aurangzeb preferred to win without fighting. To gain that objective, he employed his time-tested ploy of fake letters, sending, on the night before the scheduled battle, a letter to Akbar, thanking him for successfully enticing the Rajputs into an ambush. "My dear son, my courageous son, . . . well done," wrote Aurangzeb. "You deserve praise and congratulation on the wisdom and foresight displayed by you . . . to entrap the uncultured and barbarous Rajputs." At the same time, Aurangzeb had a letter sent to Tahavvur Khan, Akbar's right hand man, threatening that if he did not surrender his women would be publicly outraged and his sons sold into slavery "at the price of dogs".

It was a night of storm and rain, perfect for mischief, and both of Aurangzeb's letters unerringly hit their target. Late that night Tahavvur Khan sneaked away to Aurangzeb's camp, maybe to surrender, or maybe to take personal revenge on the emperor, but was cut down by the royal guards, as the purpose of his visit was not clear and he refused to remove his arms before entering the royal tent. Aurangzeb's letter to Akbar fell into the hands of the Rajputs as intended. When Durgadas, who headed the Rajput army, went to Akbar's tent around midnight to seek clarification, he was told that the prince was sleeping and could not be awakened. Durgadas then sent for Tahavvur Khan, and was dismayed to learn that the Khan, who was the prime mover of the alliance between the Rajputs and Akbar, had gone over to Aurangzeb—and that confirmed the Rajput fears about Mughal treachery.

The Rajputs feared that they were in imminent danger of being trapped and decimated. So around three that night, as Akbar slumbered, they galloped homeward, plundering Akbar's camp as they went. When the flight of the Rajputs was known, the Mughal soldiers with Akbar also decamped, most of them defecting to Aurangzeb. When "Akbar rose . . . to make ready for the great attempt . . . it was already too late to begin," wryly notes Manucci, who, as an artillery officer under Muazzam, was a witness to the drama. "For all the mighty force which Prince Akbar brought against his father, the sword was not drawn, and no battle fought, but his army was completely broken," reports Khafi Khan. Akbar found himself totally deserted, except for his personal retainers of about 350 horsemen. So he too fled, following the wake of the Rajputs.

So once again Aurangzeb's sorcery triumphed. The ulema who had legitimized Akbar's usurpation were caught, and were stretched on racks and whipped, to make them see the light afresh. Zebunnisa, Akbar's full sister and Aurangzeb's favourite daughter, who was found from letters in Akbar's tent to have been in collusion with him, was deprived of her allowance, her property confiscated, and she herself confined in the fort of Salimgarh. Akbar's name was thereafter ordered to be written as *abtar* (worst) and *baghi* (rebel) in all official papers.

But Akbar himself had escaped. That was dangerous. Aurangzeb therefore sent Prince Muazzam in hot pursuit of Akbar, ordering him, according to Manucci, "to pursue until he had seized him". Muazzam warned Aurangzeb that the chase might lead to a battle in which Akbar might be killed, to which Aurangzeb replied that "even if Akbar were killed, it would be well, for a rebellious son is unworthy to live."

Meanwhile, on the second night of his flight, Akbar caught up with the Rajputs, and they, realizing that they had been tricked by Aurangzeb, took the prince under their protection. Durgadas with a contingent of 500 horsemen then personally escorted Akbar to safety in the Deccan, after a tortuous, harrowing flight lasting nearly five months, twisting and turning to avoid pursuers and the imperial pickets. Akbar took up residence in the village of Pale near Goa in the domain of Shambhuji, the Maratha king, and there he kept up a pretence of being emperor, hoping that Maratha help would one day turn his dream into reality.

What was dream for Akbar was nightmare for Aurangzeb. The Marathas had for years defied the Mughals in the Deccan, and now, with Akbar in their midst, their provincial turbulence could well turn into a threat to the very throne of the emperor. Aurangzeb therefore quickly made peace with Mewar and moved into the Deccan. At the same time, he tried to entice Akbar into his web. "My beloved son, light of my eyes, part of my heart, Akbar!" he wrote. "I write to you, swearing upon the word of the Ruler over kings, and be God my witness, that I esteem you and love you more than my other sons. You were ever my solace and consolation, and lightened my afflictions when you were present." Aurangzeb professed to believe that the prince had rebelled only because the "demoniac Rajputs" had led him astray, and pleaded with him to return to the family fold, assuring him that he would not be punished. "This invitation is not given solely from a desire to see you present here, but to obviate your being, as you are now, ruined, solitary, lost and dishonoured," wrote Aurangzeb.

Akbar knew his father too well to fall into the trap. He replied defiantly: "Quit the government, and I will rule the kingdom as it ought to be done. Journey to Mecca . . . During all these years you have ruled in grandeur and done what you pleased. Now that the shadows fall, it is time to retire and begin to care for your soul." When Aurangzeb renewed his plea to Akbar to return, the prince, according to Manucci, assured his father that he would surely return, but with sword in hand.

427

Akbar remained in the Deccan for nearly six years, receiving a daily allowance of 300 rupees from Shambhuji. Durgadas remained with him till the prince, having lost all hope of Maratha help to gain the throne, embarked for Persia in February 1687. He was received with royal honours in Persia, but the Shah would not accede to his request for military help, on the ground that, as he put it, "To do so in the lifetime of his father would be against the holy shariah." Akbar would die in Persia in 1704, three years before his father's death.

AT THE TIME OF Akbar's rebellion, the Rana of Mewar was in imminent danger of being crushed by the Mughals. The rebellion temporarily eased the Mughal pressure on him and emboldened him to range out into the Mughal territories in Gujarat and Malwa in Maratha style pillaging raids. But these raids were mere bravado gestures; Mewar was really beaten, its plains entirely occupied by the Mughals, even its hill refuges threatened, and the morale of its army low for lack of provisions. The Rana was therefore anxious for peace.

And so was Aurangzeb, though for entirely different reasons, as his attention had shifted from Rajasthan to the Deccan. So in June 1681, when the Rana approached Prince Azam to treat for peace, he was honourably received. By the peace agreement that was then concluded, Mewar ceded three districts to the Mughals in lieu of jizya, and the emperor in return confirmed "the Rana's ancient privileges", records Manucci. Three months later Aurangzeb left Rajasthan for the Deccan.

Aurangzeb's departure for the Deccan saved Marwar from annihilation. The Rathors could thus survive, but they could not prevail. The Mughals continued to occupy the plains of Marwar, but every now and then Rathor bands emerged from the hills or the desert to harass them. Terrible was the suffering of the people of Marwar at this time, for, as the Rajput bard lamented, "sword and pestilence united to clear the land". Rajput fortunes improved only when Durgadas returned to Marwar in 1687, on Akbar's departure from India. He brought Ajit Singh, eight years old then, out of concealment, and using him as the symbol of Rathor honour, gave focus and direction to Rajput resistance.

The Rathors then won some spectacular engagements against the Mughals. But Aurangzeb restored the balance by sending Shujaet Khan, a leader equal to Durgadas in ability, as the governor of Marwar. In 1694 Shujaet Khan negotiated a settlement with the Rathors (with chronicler Ishwardas Nagar acting as the intermediary) by which Akbar's daughter, who had been left in the care of Durgadas, was sent to Aurangzeb before she attained puberty; four years later, in 1698, a son of Akbar in Rathor care was also delivered to Aurangzeb. Grateful, Aurangzeb then reinstated Durgadas and Ajit to imperial favour. Though Marwar was not restored to Ajit—instead, he was given three parganas in southern Rajasthan as his jagir—the Rathors, weary of war, accepted the peace. Ajit, who had recently married, was anxious to settle down.

Mughal-Rathor hostilities broke out again in 1702, but there was now friction between Ajit Singh and Durgadas—the baby whom Durgadas had brought away from Delhi was now twenty-three years old and a householder; he wanted to be his own man—so the revolt fizzled out after a couple of years. In 1706, a few months before Aurangzeb's death, Ajit Singh and Durgadas united again to raise the Rathor standard, and when the emperor died in March 1707, Ajit Singh boldly rode into Jodhpur, expelled the Mughal officer there, and took possession of his ancestral capital. Thus ended the thirty-year Rathor struggle, in triumph.

The Rajput wars were damaging to Aurangzeb, but not crippling. They did not hamper Mughal operations elsewhere. Still, the prolonged tussle in Rajasthan damaged imperial prestige, made the Mughal highway into the Deccan vulnerable, and, more than anything else, ruptured the immensely productive Mughal-Rajput political partnership, thus depriving the emperor of the soldiers he needed to win against the Marathas. "For this campaign, Aurangzeb put in pledge the whole of his kingdom," writes Manucci. Aurangzeb could not redeem the pledge.

Chapter Ten

THE MARATHA NEMESIS

Maratha Beginnings

AURANGZEB HAD BEEN twenty-three years on the throne and was sixty-three years of age when he set out from Ajmer for the Deccan in September 1681. He would spend most of the next twenty-six years in the battlefield, living in tents, resolutely enduring appalling hardships, waging incessant wars. His campaigns would take him deep into the south, up to the Krishna River, some 1400 kilometres from Delhi, while his generals would advance a further 700 kilometres, to cross the Kaveri River and come within spitting distance of the land's end. Only then would the eighty-seven-year-old emperor, bent with age but still indefatigable, turn north again, perhaps dreaming of returning home to Delhi. He would get as far as Ahmadnagar, and there finally rest his weary bones, on 3rd March 1707, aged eighty-nine.

When Aurangzeb ascended the throne in 1658 he could hardly have imagined that he would spend more than half his reign in the Deccan. True, the conquest of the Deccan, begun by Akbar and pursued earnestly by Shah Jahan, was unfinished, interrupted by the war of succession at the end of Shah Jahan's reign, but the back of Deccani resistance had already been broken, and it did seem that a firm push by the Mughal provincial governor was all that would be required to send the effete, tottering, debauched sultans of Golconda and Bijapur tumbling into their graves. As for the Marathas, they were as yet no more than a peripheral nuisance, apparently well within the capacity of the local Mughal officers to deal with. There did not seem to be any need for the emperor to get involved personally in the Deccan.

That was not how it turned out. When the rebel Prince Akbar took refuge with the Marathas in 1681, it brought Aurangzeb scurrying into the Deccan, for Akbar and the Marathas potentiated each other, the Marathas as the bow, Akbar as the arrow, directed against the person of the emperor himself. Fortunately for Aurangzeb, the Akbar-Maratha alliance did not meld, and after six years of gnashing frustration the prince sailed away to seek sanctuary in Persia. In the meantime, Aurangzeb gained another of his major objectives, the annexations of Bijapur and Golconda, effected in 1686 and 1687 in quick succession. Two years later, in 1689, he captured and executed the Maratha king

Shambhuji and thereby wiped out organized Maratha resistance. Aurangzeb had thus, in an eight-year campaign, gained all that he had set out to accomplish in the Deccan.

Yet he would spend another eighteen years, the rest of his life, in the Deccan, in interminable wars—battling not so much to conquer as simply to survive, as packs of snarling Marathas hounded him relentlessly. They would be his nemesis.

THE MARATHAS WERE the sons of the soil, their character and history moulded over the centuries by their rugged homeland. The Maratha country stretches north-south down the spine of the Western Ghats, and eastward across its mountain ribs, the Harischandra, Satmala and Ajanta hills. In the north the land has a bastion in the Vindhya and Satpura ranges, and in the west it is protected by the Arabian Sea; only to the east and the south, into the Deccan plateau and Karnataka, is the land open. A wild, tossing country, the Maratha homeland is sundered by mountains, fissured by innumerable rivulets and the serpentine headwaters of the Penganga, Godavari and Bhima rivers.

The land here varies greatly in topography, fertility and climate, from the verdant coastal strip on the west and the rain-drenched, seething tropical forest of the ghats, to the rocky, scraggly highlands eastward beyond the ghats. In the ghats the monsoon has a fury seldom seen elsewhere. "The rains in that country last nearly five months, so that people cannot put their heads out of their houses," says Khafi Khan. "The heavy masses of clouds change day into night, so that lamps are often needed, for without them one man cannot see another of a party."

The rocky highlands, which Khafi Khan describes as "a specimen of hell", is the true Maratha country. The land there is dry as bone, with the ghats cutting off the nurturing south-west monsoon. Scarcely any rice grew there in medieval times, and very little wheat, the staple crops being hardy millets like jawar, bajra, ragi and maize. There were no highways in the Maratha country, only stony footpaths; in the mountains the paths were so precipitous that even a led horse could keep its footing only with difficulty. "In a military point of view, there is probably no stronger country in the world," notes Grant Duff, the mid-nineteenth century historian of the Marathas. The land itself was the prime enemy of the enemies of the Marathas.

As the land, so the people. A rugged, wiry breed of great endurance, the Marathas were, like the Afghans, a restless, turbulent people. The racial mix of the Marathas was, we should assume, shuffled and reshuffled over the centuries, but the character of the people, moulded by the land, hardened by the climate, remained the same. "The inhabitants are proud, spirited and warlike, grateful for favours and revengeful for wrongs, self-sacrificing towards suppliants in distress and sanguinary to death to any who treated them insultingly"—so wrote the seventh-century Chinese traveller Hsuan Tsang about the people of the Maratha country. A thousand years later, Jahangir noted in his memoirs: the Marathas are "a very hardy race of people, who are great movers of opposition and strife."

THE EARLY HISTORY of the Marathas is obscure, but they were predominantly of the sudra (peasant) class, though later, after they gained a political role in the Deccan, they claimed to be kshatriyas (warriors) and dressed themselves up with pedigrees of appropriate grandeur, with the Bhonsles (Shivaji's clan) specifically claiming descent from the Sisodias of Mewar. The fact however is that the Marathas were not even a distinct caste, but essentially a status group, made up of individual families from different Maharashtrian castes, who set themselves apart from others of their community by the military-political role they assumed and by the distinguishing social conventions they adopted.

Whatever their origin, the Marathas were valued as soldiers from early medieval times, and had probably fought on the side of Pulakesin II in his war against Harsha in the seventh century. Somewhere along the way, maybe after the Muslim invasion of the Deccan in the thirteenth century, the Marathas assumed the role of mercenary soldiers, fighting for pay and plunder. As mercenaries they served whoever employed them, fought against whoever they were required to fight, in professional disregard of race, religion, caste, clan and family.

They specialized in guerrilla warfare, in raids, ambushes and night attacks, and in time acquired a reputation for devilish cunning. Comparing the Marathas with the Rajputs, Elphinstone, a nineteenth century historian of India, writes, "A Rajput warrior, as long as he does not dishonour his race, seems almost indifferent to the result of any contest he is engaged in. A Maratha thinks of nothing but the result, and cares little for the means, if he can attain his object." For the Rajput, war was an end in itself, for the Maratha it was only a means. Rajputs played the game, Marathas played to win.

The Marathas moved from an auxiliary military role to a mainline political role in the Deccan in the mid-fourteenth century, when the newly founded Bahmini Sultanate began associating the local people with their government. Muslims in India were essentially an urban people, who hated to serve in the countryside, especially in the hill country, so the sultanate had to enrol a number of Maratha chieftains as feudatories to garrison the hill forts. Towards the end of the century, when a decade-long famine in the Deccan virtually depopulated the outlying districts of the Bahmini kingdom and the governmental machinery there collapsed, the Marathas further consolidated their position by stepping into the power vacuum and seizing a number of forts.

Around this time the Bahmini sultanate itself disintegrated into splinter kingdoms, and this opened up vast new opportunities for mercenaries, as the points of conflict multiplied. Maratha peasants then began increasingly to take to soldiering as a far more lucrative occupation than farming. In the process, some Maratha families, particularly the Jadhavas and the Bhonsles—the maternal and paternal families of Shivaji—became rich and powerful on plunder and the spoils of war. Such were the beginnings of the Maratha political ascension.

The Bhonsles were originally the headmen of a couple of villages near Pune, where they had lived for many generations, but late in the sixteenth century they moved north to Verul (or Elur) near Daulatabad. Maloji Bhonsle, the grandfather of Shivaji, was the first noteworthy personage of the clan. His rise began when he came into possession of a considerable treasure—"probably by robbery," says Duff—which he claimed was buried treasure shown to him by his family deity, Bhavani. Maloji invested the treasure wisely, to equip a small private army of his own and to buy from the Sultan of Ahmadnagar a lordly title (Maloji Raja Bhonsle) and a high rank (commander of 5000 horse). He also secured for his son Shahji the hand of Jija Bai, daughter of Lukhji Jadhava, the most prominent Maratha of the time. Maloji thus set the Bhonsles on the path to wealth and power.

The prevailing political situation in the Deccan favoured the rise of the Marathas. When Ahmadnagar began to crumble under the onslaught of the Mughals, many Maratha chieftains, including Lukhji and Shahji, joined Malik Ambar to prop up the tottering sultanate, thus expanding their own political role. Shahji himself was however a minor figure at this time, commanding no more than 2000 horse and possessing little land beyond his ancestral villages; he is not even mentioned in the Mughal or Deccani chronicles of the time, though several other Maratha chieftains are.

Shahji's opportunity for leadership came when Malik Amber died in 1626 and plunged Ahmadnagar into further turmoil. He had by then become quite a prominent figure, prominent enough to receive the surprisingly high rank of 5000 horse from the Mughals when he, along with the Jadhavas, defected to them for a while in 1630. Shahji however remained with the Mughals only for a couple of years, then returned to Ahmadnagar, where he seized an extensive territory around Nashik and Junnar, set up his own puppet sultan—Murtaza, a ten-year-old-child of the Ahmadnagar royal family—and assumed the role of a de facto monarch.

This was in 1633. Shahji's move had the support of Bijapur, which needed to prop up Ahmadnagar as a bulwark against the Mughal push into the Deccan. For three years Shahji reigned from Junnar in royal style, but when Bijapur submitted to Shah Jahan in 1636, so did Shahji, handing over Murtaza to the Mughals. Shahji then entered the Bijapur service, and was assigned to Karnataka.

PENINSULAR INDIA SOUTH of the Krishna River, constituting the modern states of Karnataka and Tamil Nadu, had been at this time in a state of chaos for some seven decades, following the collapse of the Vijayanagar empire after the battle of Talikota in 1565. The Nayaks—the provincial chiefs of Vijayanagar who had become virtually independent—continually fought among themselves as well as against Sri Ranga Rayal of Chandragiri, the last of the Vijayanagar monarchs, who struggled futilely to assert his suzerainty. In those internecine clashes, as well as in the various succession disputes, the Nayaks and the Rayal often sought the intervention of the Deccan sultans, particularly of the Sultan of Bijapur. "The old kings of this country appear, by their jealousies and imprudent action, to invite the conquest of entire India by the Muslims," noted Antoine de Proenza, a Jesuit missionary in Tiruchirappalli.

The interveners predictably turned invaders. The local rulers, crippled by civil war, could offer hardly any resistance. Yet it took over seventy years for the victors of Talikota to mop up the fragments of the Vijayanagar empire. This was because the Deccan sultanates were themselves engaged in intramural wars at this time, and were furthermore transfixed by the Mughal spectre that had suddenly loomed over the Vindhyas. By 1577, a mere dozen years after the battle of Talikota, Akbar had stormed into the Deccan, subjugating Khandesh. Though for several decades after that the Mughals applied only haphazard pressure on the Deccan, the sultans dared not go adventuring southward when their own survival was under threat from the north.

In 1636, with the accord reached between Shah Jahan and Muhammad Adil Shah of Bijapur, one phase of the Mughal campaign in the Deccan ended. For the next twenty years there was peace with the Mughals, and it was during this time that Bijapur and Golconda annexed the domains of the Nayaks, partitioning the tract in the proportion of 2:1 between them. It was a leisurely conquest. Setting out in the autumn of every year, the Deccani forces pushed their frontiers southward in steady annual increments, always returning home before the onset of the monsoon.

These southern wars, though they happened to be between Muslim and Hindu rulers, were by no means Hindu-Muslim wars. They were wars for land and power. Religion was hardly a factor. There were many Muslim soldiers and several Muslim captains in the Hindu armies, and among the invaders were numerous Hindu soldiers and several Hindu captains.

The most prominent Hindu officer in the Bijapur army was Shahji, who served the sultanate for a quarter of a century, from 1638 till his death in 1664. Though he was only the third in the chain of command in the Bijapur army in Karnataka, and it was only towards the end of his life that he rose to be second in command, he was nevertheless a highly valued officer, who was addressed by Adil Shah as "our son Shahji Bhonsle, the pillar of our State." When Bangalore was taken by the Bijapuris in 1640, Shahji was put in charge of the administration of that important district. But his career received a serious setback in mid-1648, during the Bijapuri siege of Gingee, when he was abruptly arrested, taken to Bijapur, and kept in confinement for some ten months.

The reasons for Shahji's fall from favour are not clear. It could be that he was coquetting with the local rajas or with Golconda. He also seems to have been tardy in obeying royal commands, which raised doubts about his loyalty, especially because his teenaged son Shivaji was in rebellion against Bijapur at this time. Shivaji's conduct does not however seem to have been the sole or even the primary reason for Shahji's fall—among the conditions for Shahji's release there was only one that concerned Shivaji, that he should surrender the fort of Sinhgarh near Pune, while Shahji's other sons were required to surrender Bangalore and Kandarpi in Karnataka. When these forts were surrendered, Shahji was released from confinement, presented a robe of honour and restored to his previous position.

Shivaji, though he surrendered Sinhgarh as instructed by Shahji, soon broke entirely free of his father's control, and began harassing the outlying districts of Bijapur as well as the Mughal Deccan. That worried Shahji. He feared that his own safety and the careers of his other sons would be jeopardized by Shivaji. Adil Shah heard of these anxieties and reassured Shahji: "The faults of Shivaji will not be laid upon you, but his offences are being imputed to him only . . . there will be no change or deprivation in your rank and fiefs," he wrote in a letter to Shahji dated 26th May 1658.

Shahji thus continued in royal favour till his death six years later, aged seventy. But long before Shahji's death, the focus of the Maratha action had shifted from Karnataka to Maharashtra, and from Shahji to Shivaji.

Enter Shivaji

THERE ARE NO contemporary records of Shivaji's birth, the earliest account being of 150 years later, but it is generally believed that he was born on 6th April 1627, in the hill fort of Shivneri in the Western Ghats, about a hundred kilometres east of Bombay. The child was named Shiva after the local goddess Shiva Bai, to whom Jija Bai, his mother, had prayed for the boon of a son.

Jija Bai had several other sons born to her before Shivaji, but only Shambhuji, the eldest, had survived, so she was keen to have another son. It might be also that, by having a young son, she hoped to revive her husband's flagging affection for her. This hope was not fulfilled. In fact, political as well as personal factors further estranged the couple. Shahji and the Jadhavas (Jija Bai's clan) had become adversaries at this time, with Shahji opposing the Mughals and the Jadhavas serving them; besides, Shahji had taken a young second wife, Tuka Bai of the Mohite clan, and it was she who thereafter accompanied him on his campaigns. Later, when Shahji took up service in Karnataka, it was Tuka Bai who moved in with him.

Jija Bai and Shivaji were left behind in Maharashtra, in Pune, where they lived for about ten years, in the new mansion built for them by Dadaji Kondadeve, the guardian to whom Shahji had entrusted their affairs. Neglected by Shahji, the mother and son clung to each other, and they both grew intensely religious. Dadaji played the surrogate father. An astute and loyal officer, Dadaji greatly augmented the prosperity of the Pune fief by his prudent management, and he took great care to protect and guide the restive youngster in his charge. But Shivaji does not seem to have received any formal education, and he, like Akbar, was in all probability illiterate. "Marathas seldom can write or read; they consider all such learning the business of a *carcoon* (clerk), and if not degrading, at least undignified," notes Duff. "Sivajee could never write his name."

Shivaji learned from life, not from books. Wandering about in the mountains with his tribal companions, he acquired the survival and leadership skills that were far more valuable to him than book learning. He became an intimate of the jungle, expert in disguise, dexterous in tracking, a skilled archer and marksman, a superb horseman. There was nothing that he could not do better than his men.

SHIVAJI'S CAREER BEGAN conventionally enough for a Maratha, with petty marauding. "From about his sixteenth year, he began to associate with persons of lawless habits, and to talk of becoming an independent Polygar (chieftain)," writes Duff. That troubled Dadaji, who viewed his escapades as unbecoming to the son of a great chief, and feared that they would ruin the family. It troubled Shahji too, and he summoned Shivaji and Jija Bai to Bangalore, presumably to chasten Shivaji, but with little effect.

Shivaji was only around sixteen then, and could hardly be termed a rebel; his activities were an annoyance to his father, but not something with which the sultan had to be concerned. His career however assumed an altogether different aspect in the next few years. Around 1646 he began capturing the hill forts around Pune, mostly by stratagem, sometimes by storming. Success conferred respectability on him, and even Dadaji, who had initially disapproved his raids, is said to have in the end, just before his death in 1647, blessed Shivaji, enjoining him to "protect Bramins, kine, and cultivators; to preserve the temples of the Hindoos from violation", according to Duff.

Shivaji's early campaigns did not involve any direct confrontation with Bijapuri forces, for the hill forts were mostly held by Maratha chieftains, and they were his first victims. Adil Shah therefore overlooked Shivaji's raids for quite a while. Moreover, the sultan was at that time preoccupied with the invasion of Karnataka, a region that was far more important to him than the hill country where Shivaji operated. Besides, Shivaji had taken care to write to Adil Shah that he was capturing the forts on the sultan's behalf, to control the turbulent region effectively and thus to serve him better; he even offered to remit to the royal treasury a higher revenue than had been realized from that region till then. Such were Shivaji's professions.

His actions revealed quite another intent. He is said to have found around this time a treasure of buried gold in the ruins of a fort, just as his grandfather is once said to have found buried gold in a field, both attributing the boon to the favour of goddess Bhavani, the family deity. Shivaji, again like his grandfather, used the treasure wisely to build up his military power. He now constructed a fort for himself, assumed the posture of an independent chieftain, and adopted a new seal which proudly proclaimed: "This seal of Shiva, son of Shah, shines forth for the welfare of the people and is meant to command increasing respect

441

from the universe like the first phase of the moon." He named his fort Raigarh, Royal Fort.

When Adil Shah came to know of these developments, he forbade the construction of the fort and summoned Shahji, to whom the Pune fief still officially belonged, to account for his son's activities. Shahji claimed that Shivaji had not consulted him, and that he "was as much in rebellion against him as against the King's government". This very likely was the truth, for Shivaji had by then stopped making remittances to his father, saying that his poor lands in Maharashtra produced no surplus and advising his father "to depend on his more extensive and fertile possessions in the Carnatic". Nevertheless Shahji was arrested—though there were also other and perhaps more weighty reasons for his arrest—and was kept in confinement in Bijapur for some months. That forced Shivaji to lie low for a while.

For about seven years, from 1649 to 1656, Shivaji was relatively quiet. In 1656 he struck again. His first target was Javli in the Mahabaleshwar Range south of Pune. There was no provocation for the aggression other than that the Mores, who ruled Javli, stood in the way of Shivaji's southward expansion. Shivaji tried persuasion to get the Mores to ally with him, but failing in that, and the Mores being too strong to be attacked openly, he seized the fort by having the leading members of the family slain by a brahmin agent during a pretended marriage negotiation. It was a treacherous act, but in the eyes of Shivaji entirely justifiable, because it succeeded, and because it avoided unnecessary bloodshed. He would use similar stratagems time and again in his career.

The capture of Javli was a high point in Shivaji's career, and it greatly extended the range of his forays. The very year after he seized Javli, taking advantage of the diversion of the Mughal provincial army for the invasion of Bijapur, he for the first time raided the Mughal Deccan, penetrating as far as the environs of Ahmadnagar. That proved to be nearly calamitous, for a strong force sent by Prince Aurangzeb, who was then the Mughal governor of the Deccan, routed Shivaji with great slaughter.

Shivaji fled into the mountains, pursued by Mughal officers, who had been ordered by Aurangzeb to "extirpate that miscreant" by "wasting the villages, slaying the people without pity, and plundering them to the extreme". Shivaji was able to save himself only because the Mughal army, reluctant to enter the mountains, abandoned the chase when the monsoon set in. Shivaji learned a lesson from the experience, and thereafter would be most circumspect in dealing with the Mughals. And when Bijapur submitted to Aurangzeb, so did Shivaji, writing to the prince in feigned humility to beg forgiveness for his transgressions and promising to remain faithful ever after. He also sent a couple of emissaries to plead his case with the prince, requesting that he be confirmed in the possession of his ancestral estates, and offering in return to send a contingent of "500 expert soldiers" to help the prince win the throne. "I shall myself join the imperial officers in protecting the boundaries of the imperial dominions and prevent disturbances from any source taking place there," he promised loftily.

This was hardly a credible offer from one who, from the Mughal point of view, was the chief disturber of peace in the Deccan. But Aurangzeb, preoccupied with the succession struggle, and badly needing quiet on his southern front, responded conciliatingly. From Burhanpur, on his way to Agra, he wrote to Shivaji: "Although your offences are too many and too grave to merit pardon, yet as you are professing an intention to render loyalty and service to me and showing penitence and a sense of shame for your past misdeeds, I draw the pen of pardon through the pages of your crimes, but on condition of your remaining firm in obedience and service in future." Later, after his accession, Aurangzeb wrote again to Shivaji from Delhi, sending him a robe of honour and exhorting him to remain loyal.

All that was pretence, on the part of Shivaji as well as Aurangzeb. Neither trusted the other. According to Inayat Khan, ten out of the forty forts of the former kingdom of Ahmadnagar were in the possession of Shivaji, which gave his depredations a potential which the Mughals could not ignore. "The mountain rat" (as Aurangzeb called Shivaji) would continue to nibble at the Mughal behemoth. Aurangzeb was well aware of that hazard, so he, before he left the Deccan, had cautioned his officers to be vigilant against Shivaji, warning them that "the son of a dog is waiting for his opportunity". Further, Aurangzeb advised Adil Shah that if he intended to give any fief to Shivaji, to give it only "in the Karnatak, far from the imperial dominions, so that he may not disturb them".

Shivaji on his part realized that to make any gain at all against the Mughals, or even against Bijapur, he had to build up his strength considerably, and he laboured tirelessly to revamp his administration, augment his finances and build up his army. He took special care to expand his cavalry, which was essential for any serious military contest; he even acquired a number of naval vessels, so he could scour the sea as well as the land.

Shivaji then pushed into the Konkan, the Maratha country between the ghats and the sea, bringing the entire northern Konkan, stretching some 140 kilometres from Bhiwandi to Mahad, under his rule. And with that, the Maratha state might be said to have come into existence. The "mountain rat" had transformed himself into a tiger.

THIS TRANSFORMATION BROUGHT Adil Shah into action against Shivaji. The sultan had till then left it to his local officers to deal with Shivaji, but now, acknowledging the gravity of the threat that Shivaji posed, he sent Afzal Khan, one of his top generals, against Shivaji, confronting him for the first time with the organized might of the state. As the Khan at the head of a strong cavalry force stormed north into· Maratha country, Shivaji hastily retreated to the hill fort of Pratapgarh, with the Khan in hot pursuit. Shivaji's position at this point seemed hopeless, and many urged him to sue for peace. Shivaji would not hear of it. He claimed that goddess Bhavani had, in a vision, assured him of victory.

Shivaji was resourceful enough to make the promise of that opportune vision come true. He had a plan. As an opening gambit, he pretended to cower before the Bijapuri advance, saying that he dared not oppose a general of the stature of Afzal Khan. He offered to surrender, provided his pardon was assured. It seemed a credible proposal to Afzal Khan, given the known poor morale of the Marathas. The Khan then sent an envoy, a brahmin named Gopinath, to assure Shivaji that he (Afzal Khan), as a close friend of Shahji, had only Shivaji's good at heart, and would therefore endeavour to secure him the favour of Adil Shah.

The arrival of Gopinath was a lucky break for Shivaji. The envoy was corruptible, and Shivaji had little difficulty in turning him into an accomplice, by appealing to his religious sentiment and pandering to his cupidity. Visiting Gopinath secretly at night, Shivaji claimed that all that he had done was at the behest of goddess Bhavani, to protect Hinduism, and he pleaded with the envoy, as a brahmin, to help him. That appeal was particularly effective at this time, as Afzal Khan, in an iconoclastic frenzy unusual in the Deccan, had, during his march against Shivaji, desecrated a number of Hindu holy places, including Pandharpur, the most sacred pilgrimage centre in Maharashtra. Gopinath was therefore responsive to Shivaji's exhortation, especially as Shivaji reinforced the appeal to faith with the bait of lucre, offering him rich presents and the free grant of a village. Gopinath then swore on Bhavani to serve Shivaji in his sacred mission, and together they hatched a plot to entice Afzal Khan to a meeting and assassinate him.

Returning to Afzal Khan, Gopinath reported that Shivaji was quaking with anxiety and could easily be persuaded to give himself up if the

Khan would meet him and assure him of protection. Unsuspecting, and in any case overconfident, the Khan readily agreed to the suggestion.

Shivaji chose the crest of a hillock below his fort as the venue for the parley, and there erected a magnificently furnished pavilion to indulge the Khan's vanity. He also had the jungle cut down to clear a path to the venue, to ensure that the Khan would arrive only by the route that suited Shivaji. On the night before the meeting Shivaji secretly sent a contingent of Maratha infantry to hide in the jungle close to the meeting site, and another contingent, much larger, to conceal itself near Afzal Khan's camp.

The meeting was arranged for the afternoon of Thursday, 20th November 1659. Afzal Khan set out for the venue with a retinue of 1500 troops, but the soldiers were, on the plea of Gopinath, halted some distance from the venue—in order not to alarm Shivaji, said Gopinath. Afzal Khan then proceeded to the pavilion in a palanquin, without armour, dressed in a thin muslin garment, attended, as had been agreed, by a single armed bodyguard, a renowned swordsman named Sayyid Banda. The Khan himself was armed, as usual, with a sword, but his mood was relaxed. He suspected no foul play. He waited in the pavilion, says Manucci, "building, I fancy, many castles in the air."

Meanwhile Shivaji emerged from the fort, after prostrating himself before his mother and receiving her blessing. He too was dressed suitably—for his purpose. He wore a steel cap under his turban and chain armour under his cotton gown; a vicious crooked dagger called *beechwa* (scorpion) was concealed in his right sleeve, and on his left hand was fixed the notorious Maratha weapon *wagnuck* (tiger claws), steel claws attached to the hand with rings and kept concealed by closing the hand.

From the pavilion Afzal Khan could see Shivaji approaching with seeming timidity, apparently unarmed, as required of a surrendering rebel, accompanied by one armed bodyguard. "Shivaji began to advance, bowing again and again, as if he was petitioning for a good reception and was in a state of apprehension," says Manucci. When he approached the pavilion, Afzal Khan's guard moved a few paces away, and Shivaji's guard too stopped at the same distance. The Khan, "a tall man, very corpulent", as Manucci describes him, was supremely confident, and had no anxiety at all in confronting the diminutive Shivaji.

As Shivaji entered the pavilion, Afzal Khan rose and, advancing a few steps, clasped him in a bear-hug. This was Shivaji's opportunity. Instantly he opened his clawed hand and tore into the Khan's ample abdomen. Startled, the Khan released Shivaji and sprang back, crying treachery and drawing his sword. As Shivaji launched at him again, the Khan swung at him with the sword, but the blow fell harmlessly with a metallic clang against Shivaji's hidden armour, and Shivaji felled him by plunging the scorpion dagger into him. By then Sayyid Banda had rushed in, but Shivaji, who had wrested the sword from the Khan, cut him down with the help of his own guard. During the melee, the Khan's bearers put him in his palanquin and tried to bear him away, but were intercepted by the Marathas hiding along the path. They cut off Afzal Khan's head and carried it to the fort.

Shivaji too hurried back into the fort, and ordered a blast of horn to be sounded, to signal his hidden soldiers to fall upon Afzal Khan's retinue. Soon after, at the sound of five salvos from the fort's cannons, another signal, the Marathas near the main Bijapuri camp pounced on the unwary enemy and scattered them. A large number of horses, some elephants and camels, and a vast treasure fell to Shivaji. All the enemy who surrendered were spared, and many Maratha soldiers in the Bijapur army entered Shivaji's service. His own soldiers who were wounded in the skirmish were honoured by Shivaji with "bracelets, necklaces, chains of gold and silver, and clothes . . . [which] were presented with much ceremony," says Duff.

There is a different version of what happened at the meeting between Afzal Khan and Shivaji, which states that the Khan pinioned Shivaji in his iron embrace and tried to stab him with a dagger, and that Shivaji acted in self-defence. Afzal Khan was certainly capable of such perfidy, and had in fact once murdered the raja of Sera when he came out of his fort to surrender to him. Shivaji therefore had good reason to fear foul play from the Khan. But there is no evidence that the Khan actually planned treachery against Shivaji. What is certain is that Shivaji executed a carefully plotted assassination.

The Afzal Khan episode turned the thirty-two-year-old Shivaji into a living legend. He now boldly pushed deep into Bijapur, advancing as far as Kolhapur, even menacing the city of Bijapur. Adil Shah himself then took the field, and this made Shivaji back off, but only temporarily, for he resumed his forays soon after, though he took care never to oppose Adil Shah personally, indicating the vassal-rebel ambiguity of his relationship with the sultan.

Around 1661 Adil Shah, weary of skirmishing with Shivaji, sent Shahji to arrange a settlement with him. Father and son had not seen each other for nearly twenty years, and their relative positions had changed in the interval, the son being now the greater hero. But Shivaji was punctilious, even emotional, in receiving Shahji. He advanced several kilometres from his fort to receive his father, and on seeing him, dismounted and walked beside his palanquin to escort him. And on reaching the fort, he stood in respectful attendance on his father till he was repeatedly commanded by Shahji to sit down. Whatever bitterness there had once been between father and son was now gone. Shahji, though himself a loyal servant of Bijapur, was proud of this rebel son of his, and Shivaji now, unlike in his turbulent youth, was receptive to his father's advice. So it was with Shivaji's promise of loyalty to Adil Shah that Shahji returned to Bijapur after a few weeks. Shivaji kept his word and remained at peace with Bijapur from then on till Shahji's death in 1664.

It was a peace of mutual convenience. Shivaji was glad to make peace with Bijapur, for a great new menace now threatened him from the north, in the person of Shayista Khan, Aurangzeb's uncle and the premier noble of the Mughal empire. Bijapur too wanted peace with Shivaji, for it was in its interest to shore him up as a defence against the advancing Mughal tide. So Adil Shah, although he kept up a pretence of campaigning against Shivaji in concert with Shayista Khan, entered into a secret pact with Shivaji, by which he acquiesced in Shivaji's aggressions against the semi-independent hill feudatories in the outlying provinces of Bijapur, while Shivaji agreed not to molest the central provinces under the sultan's direct rule.

Shivaji was now the master of fairly extensive territory stretching a couple of hundred kilometres, and he had an army of some 7,000 horse and a large infantry. The pact with Bijapur confirmed his stature as a Deccani power. He was no longer a mere predator or rebel, but an ally of Bijapur.

SHIVAJI'S NEW STATURE brought him new perils. As a territorial power, he now stood in the way of the southward expansion of the Mughal empire. This, and Shivaji's practice of pillaging the Mughal Deccan, brought the Mughals bearing down on him, with Aurangzeb sending Shayista Khan to the Deccan as governor soon after his accession and ordering him to quell the Maratha menace.

Shayista Khan arrived in Aurangabad in January 1660, and from there moved into the Maratha country with a strong force. As he advanced, the Marathas retreated, though here and there they offered resistance or harassed the Mughal lands at the rear of the Khan's army. For three years Shayista Khan exerted unremitting pressure on the Marathas and kept them on the run. Shivaji had lost the initiative.

To retrieve the initiative and to save his reputation, indeed even to keep the Maratha dreams alive, it then became imperative for Shivaji to do something sensational. His solution to the problem was typical of him, daringly unconventional yet spectacularly effective—a commando strike personally led by him, to assassinate the imperial commander right in the middle of his camp!

Circumstances favoured Shivaji. The Mughal army was at this time billeted in Pune, the town where Shivaji had spent his youth and which he knew intimately, and Shayista Khan himself had taken up residence in Shivaji's old home, in a symbolic seizure of the rebel. Shivaji was at Sinhgarh, some twenty kilometres south of Pune. Knowing that Shivaji was lurking nearby, and wary of what he might be up to, Shayista Khan had taken elaborate precautions to protect his camp, especially as Pune was not a walled town. "A regulation had been made that no person, especially no Maratha, should enter the city or the lines of the army without a pass, whether armed or unarmed, excepting persons in the Imperial service," notes Khafi Khan. "No Maratha horseman was taken into service." Still the sly "mountain rat" found a way to burrow into the Mughal camp.

Shivaji planned the audacious raid with meticulous care, after obtaining detailed information through his spies about the Mughal dispositions in Pune. The day of the raid, 15th April 1663, was picked with care, to coincide with the anniversary of Aurangzeb's accession in the month of Ramadan. It being the Muslim month of fasting, Shivaji knew that the night vigil at Shayista Khan's camp would be slack, as Muslim soldiers would be exhausted after the day-long fast and drowsy after the feast at night. He decided to strike at midnight, because the band at the camp would be, as was customary during anniversary celebrations, playing music at midnight, which would help to mask the sound of the raid.

On the chosen day, a party of Maratha infantrymen in the Mughal service, who had been won over by Shivaji's spies, obtained the permission of the Kotwal (city prefect) to admit into Pune some 200 Marathas of what they claimed to be a marriage party. "A boy dressed up as bridegroom, and escorted by a party of Marathas, with drums and music, entered the town early in the evening," says Khafi Khan. Another contingent of Shivaji's men was brought in on the same day, as if they were prisoners taken at one of the Mughal outposts. Among the infiltrators was Shivaji himself.

At midnight Shivaji and a squad of his men sneaked to the residence of Shayista Khan. Knowing every nook and corner of the house, Shivaji led the men to the cook-house abutting the women's apartments, where, after quietly dispatching the servants sleeping or at work there, they opened a passage into the harem by knocking down a lightly bricked up window. Meanwhile, another group of raiders went to the band room and ordered the musicians, as if on the Khan's instruction, to beat the drums and play music louder. "Such a din was raised that one could not hear another speak," says Khafi Khan. Yet another Maratha squad entered the guard-house and slaughtered all those there, thus securing the camp.

At the time of the break-in, Shayista Khan's household was sound asleep. When a servant, wakened by the sound of pick-axes and the groans of the dying in the cook-house, alerted the Khan, he dismissed the report saying that it could only be the cooks preparing for the pre-dawn Ramadan meal. But almost immediately, says Khafi Khan, "some maid-servants . . . came, one after another, to say that a hole was being made through the wall. The Amir then jumped up in great alarm, and seized a bow, some arrows, and a spear. Just then some Marathas came up in front, and the Amir shot one with an arrow; but he got up to the Amir, and cut off his thumb. Two Marathas fell into a reservoir of water, and Amir-ul-umara brought down another with his spear. In the midst of the confusion two slave-girls took Shayista Khan . . . by the hand and dragged him from the scene of strife to a place of safety." A quick-witted woman had meanwhile put out the lamps, which enabled the Khan to escape, and turned the raid into a chaotic scrimmage, with the Marathas slashing blindly in the dark, killing several women and servants.

The Marathas fled before the camp awoke to their presence. There was no attempt to pursue them. Jaswant Singh, who with a cavalry force of 10,000 lay encamped close by, did not stir during the fracas, but was there the next morning to offer his condolences to Shayista Khan, who had lost a son in the fight. Said the Khan to the Raja in an urbane sneer: "When the enemy fell upon me, I imagined that you had already died fighting against them." The rumour in the Mughal camp was that the Raja had connived with Shivaji in the raid. This was not impossible, given the character of Jaswant Singh, but Shivaji was quite capable of pulling off the daring raid all by himself.

The Pune exploit, though it yielded no great gains to the Marathas in material terms, immeasurably enhanced the prestige of Shivaji, who now came to be regarded as something of a sorcerer, capable of the most impossible feats. Further, it infused in the Marathas a new spirit of daring. While previously they used to flee in the face of the Mughal cavalry, the very morning after the Pune raid, when a Mughal contingent attacked Sinhgarh, the Marathas not only drove them off, but boldly pursued them, the first time they had dared to do so.

Aurangzeb was mortified by the Pune incident, blamed Shayista

Khan for carelessness and punitively transferred him to Bengal. Prince Muazzam then took over as the governor of the Deccan, but this only made matters worse, as that slothful prince remained ensconced in Aurangabad, leaving it to Jaswant Singh to carry on the operations against the Marathas. Shivaji took full advantage of Mughal apathy. His spies—some of whom, like Bahirji Naik, were as famous as his generals—roamed the land, identifying places to plunder or where the Mughals were vulnerable. As Muazzam plaintively reported to Aurangzeb in 1664, the Marathas were "growing more and more daring, and every day attacking and plundering the imperial territories and caravans." The Marathas also began to menace coastal shipping, even the Mughal pilgrim ships going to Mecca, which was particularly galling to Aurangzeb.

Shivaji followed the Pune action with a raid on the wealthy Mughal port town of Surat at the mouth of the river Tapi in Gujarat. Surat, not being a military or administrative centre, was a virtually defenceless town, protected only by an eroded mud wall. There was a fort abutting the town, but it was not of much use, as the Mughal officer there, who was paid to maintain a force of 500, merely pocketed the allowance in the typical Mughal fashion, instead of garrisoning the fort. So when Shivaji suddenly appeared at Surat in mid-January 1664, all that the citizens could do was to flee—the rich merchants into the fort, carrying what they could; the common people to the countryside. Only the foreign merchants stood their ground and prepared to defend their life and property.

Pitching his camp in a garden just outside Surat, Shivaji summoned the chief merchants of the town to appear before him and pay ransom for not sacking the town. No one responded, for fear that they themselves might be seized for ransom. Shivaji then sent his men into Surat, and for four days, from the 16th to the 20th, they plundered the town at leisure, facing no opposition from anyone except from the foreign merchants, whom the Marathas left well alone. Then suddenly, as suddenly as he had come, Shivaji struck camp and departed on hearing of the approach of Mughal reinforcements from Burhanpur.

Back in Raigarh, Shivaji learned that while he was in Surat his father Shahji had died in a hunting accident in Karnataka. He then assumed the chieftainship of the Bhonsle clan, by taking the title raja and minting his own coins. Shivaji was now king, though not yet crowned.

AURANGZEB THEN RAISED the level of military pressure on Shivaji by sending two of his ablest commanders, Raja Jai Singh and Dilir Khan, into the Deccan. Shivaji tried to intimidate the imperial officers by warning them about the difficulties they would face in Maratha country. "Even the steed of unimaginable exertion is too weak to gallop over this hard country," he wrote. "My home . . . is not situated on a spacious plain, which may enable trenches to be run or assault to be made. It has lofty hill ranges . . . everywhere there are streams hard to cross; sixty forts of extreme strength have been built . . ." Shivaji went on to remind the amirs of the fates of Afzal Khan and Shayista Khan, and signed off with the couplet:

> *The wise should beware of this river of blood*
> *From which no man has borne away his boat.*

The letter would have amused Jai Singh but not daunted him, for the raja, sixty, was one of the most remarkable personages of the age, an intrepid general and an astute yet honourable diplomat, a man of complex intelligence and great foresight. Jai Singh, says Ishwardas, "possessed great skill and had no rival in diplomacy". The raja was well aware of the difficulties of his mission, the forbidding land and its canny people, and the complex, ever-shifting alliances among the Deccani powers, but none of that inhibited him. "Not for a moment, in day or night, do I seek rest or ease from being busy about the task on which I have been sent," he wrote to Aurangzeb.

Jai Singh crossed the Narmada in mid-January 1665, and advancing rapidly through the ghats arrived in Pune in mid-March to take over the Deccan command from Jaswant Singh. Then in a sharp three-month campaign, skillfully combining military and diplomatic pressure, he forced Shivaji to submit. Shivaji tried to save face by claiming that his patron goddess Bhavani had ordered him to surrender, warning him in a vision that he could not prevail against the raja. In defeat as much as in victory, in every act of commission or omission, Bhavani abided with Shivaji.

When Shivaji treated for peace, Jai Singh initially disdained to respond, because, as he wrote to Aurangzeb, "I knew that unless a strong hand was laid on him, his words and stories would not contain a particle of truth." Dilir Khan, Jai Singh's pugnacious second in command, was in fact against seeking a negotiated settlement. He challenged Shivaji to "first fight then [seek] peace", and went on to ask him why he was not showing up for battle despite his earlier boasts about his "strong forts, sky-kissing hills, abysmal ravines, and brave soldiers lying in ambush." Shivaji swallowed that bitter taunt. He had no alternative but to surrender.

After several exchanges between Jai Singh and Shivaji, in which Shivaji retreated step by step from his initial negotiating position, a meeting was finally arranged between the two. Jai Singh, despite his seemingly tough stand, was careful not to press Shivaji too hard and drive him into the arms of Bijapur, the chief adversary of the Mughals in the Deccan. His attitude, as he wrote to Aurangzeb, was that though he could defeat a Maratha-Bijapur combine, "if policy can accomplish a thing, why should we court delay [by resorting to force]?"

On 21st June 1665, as previously arranged, at around nine in the morning, Shivaji arrived at Jai Singh's camp outside the fort of Purandhar which the Mughals were besieging. He had come from Raigarh, some fifty kilometres to the east, travelling in a palanquin, accompanied by six brahmins. Jai Singh, guarded by Rajputs against treachery, received Shivaji in durbar. "When Shivaji entered, the Raja arose, embraced him, and seated him near himself," reports Khafi Khan. "Shivaji then, with a thousand signs of shame, clasped his hands and said, `I have come as a guilty slave to seek forgiveness, and it is for you either to pardon or to kill me at your pleasure.'"

Such remarks were mere civility. There was tough bargaining ahead, which went on till midnight. The next day the terms of peace were finally agreed on. Shivaji surrendered all the territory and forts he had seized in the Mughal Deccan, in all twenty-three forts, including Purandhar and Sinhgarh, retaining for himself only twelve, including Raigarh. He was allowed to keep the Konkan coastal strip which he had wrested from Bijapur, and was told that he could have the Konkan highlands too, if he could conquer them from Bijapur. In return, Shivaji was required to pay a tribute to the emperor and also personally to assist Jai Singh in the war which the raja was about to launch against Bijapur.

By the terms of the agreement, Shivaji's son Shambhuji, twelve then, was required to enter the Mughal service—he was given a mansab of 5000—and to attend the imperial court, which was a means of holding him as a hostage. But Shivaji himself, who had never served under anyone, politely sought to be excused from attending court. "Hitherto I had no wisdom or prudence, and have trodden the path of shortsightedness. I have not the face to wait on the emperor . . . exempt me from mansab and service," he requested, and went on to assure: "So long as I live, I shall not draw my neck back from obedience to orders of service. Whenever in your Deccan wars I am appointed to any duty, I shall without delay perform it." At the end of the parley, Shivaji—adroitly acting out the role of subservience—"begged hard for the full suit of the robe of honour" worn by Jai Singh. "I made him wear it," reported the raja to Aurangzeb. Jai Singh also presented Shivaji with an elephant and two horses.

The convention between Jai Singh and Shivaji was subject to the emperor's approval, but was put into operation right away on Jai Singh's guarantee. As it happened, Aurangzeb raised several objections to the terms of the agreement and was doubtful about Shivaji's good faith. Jai Singh clarified the points raised by the emperor and pressed for the ratification of the agreement, assuring that "if Shiva strays by a hair's breadth from the path of obedience he can be totally annihilated by us with the slightest exertion." Jai Singh's main objective in the Deccan was the conquest of Bijapur, and he wanted to secure Shivaji's cooperation in that endeavour. "Now that Adil Shah and Qutb Shah have united in mischief, it is necessary to win Shiva's heart by all means," wrote Jai Singh to Aurangzeb.

Shivaji himself wrote to Aurangzeb with assumed humility to assure him that "this offender and sinner . . . hereafter . . . will remain firmly engaged in performing the Emperor's work, as a reparation for his past life and an amendment of his uselessly spent days; he will never deviate from the position of rendering service, risking his life and carrying out the imperial mandates . . . He hopes that out of the storehouse of (your Majesty's) grace . . . life to this slave may be granted, and an imperial firman may be issued pardoning his offences, granting security to his house and family, and bestowing life on him."

Even the ever-sceptical Aurangzeb could not resist such wily cajolery, and in the end, on 15th September 1665, he issued a firman to Shivaji, stamped with the impression of his palm, confirming the terms offered by Jai Singh. "I, out of my characteristic noble habit of shutting my eyes to faults and granting the pardon of lives, do forgive your past deeds and sins and grant all your prayers," wrote Aurangzeb. He sent Shivaji a robe of honour along with the firman.

Shivaji then wrote yet another effusive letter, to thank the emperor: "Shiva, the meanest of life-devoting slaves—who wears the ring of servitude in his ear and the carpet of obedience on his shoulder—like an atom . . . [acknowledges] the good news of his eternal happiness, namely favours from the Emperor . . . This sinner and evil-doer did not deserve that his offences should be forgiven or his faults covered up. But the grace and favour of the Emperor have conferred on him a new life and unimaginable honour . . ."

Lord of the Umbrella

AFTER HIS FACILE triumph in Maharashtra, in November 1665, soon after the rains ceased, Jai Singh turned confidently southward. He intended to sweep into the Mughal lap the last couple of kingdoms in India still remaining outside the empire, as the crowning achievement of his career. Initially, it was a smooth run for Jai Singh, as he, accompanied by Shivaji, stormed into Bijapur, but gradually, as the Bijapuri resistance stiffened, his campaign began to falter, and Shivaji himself, though successful in reducing several enemy positions in the hill country, was repulsed with heavy losses when he attacked the fort of Panhala in Kolhapur district. Worse, Shivaji's commander, Netaji Palkar, deserted to Bijapur, to join Ekoji and other Marathas serving Adil Shah.

If the Mughals were disappointed with Shivaji's battlefield performance, which did not match his reputation, they did not show it; instead, Aurangzeb commended his services, sent him a robe of honour and a jewelled dagger, and invited him to the imperial court. On 5th April 1666 he wrote to Shivaji: "Come here without delay, in full confidence in my grace and perfect composure of mind. After you have obtained audience of me, you will be glorified with my royal favours and given permission to return home." Jai Singh too urged Shivaji to go and guaranteed his safety.

It was surprising that Jai Singh wanted Shivaji to leave the Deccan at this time. The Mughal campaign in Bijapur was not going well, and Jai Singh was in no position to dispense with whatever help he could get from Shivaji. Why then did he send Shivaji away? Paradoxically, the reason could well be that the campaign was not going well, and the Mughals had become vulnerable in the Deccan. With the defection of Netaji to Bijapur, Jai Singh was very likely worried about what Shivaji himself would be up to. After all, Shivaji had just lost two-thirds of his domain to the Mughals, so would he not try to wrest it back with the help of Bijapur if he had the chance? This was a hazard that Jai Singh had to reckon with. In this quandary it was very much in the interest of Jai Singh to get his doubtful ally out of his backyard.

Circumstantial evidence strongly suggests that Aurangzeb and Jai

Singh acted in concert to remove Shivaji from the Deccan—not to do him any harm, but to get him out of where he could harm the Mughals. Later, when Shivaji was in Agra and causing problems, Jai Singh would expressly request Aurangzeb not to send him back to the Deccan. "Every moment has its special requirement," wrote the wise raja. "Under the present circumstances, it is not at all politic to permit him to come to this region."

Surprisingly, Shivaji did not see through the Mughal ploy. Why did he agree to go, especially as the treaty of Purandhar specifically exempted him from attending the Mughal court? Apparently Shivaji was in some awe of Jai Singh. This was the first time that he was seeing the Mughal military apparatus from within, and he could not but have been astounded by the immense power and prestige the raja enjoyed, and the seemingly limitless resources at his command. It is possible that the hill chieftain craved a similar grand role for himself. Shivaji must also have been curious about what the imperial court could be like if a mere general's circumstances could be so fabulous.

Still, Shivaji was apprehensive about going to Agra. He consulted his astrologers, and decided on the trip only on their assurance of his safe return. Once he decided to go, he set about the preparations with scrupulous attention to detail. He visited every one of his forts, made arrangements for their management, then summoned all his principal officers to a conference at Raigarh to set up a chain of command, so that the government of his domain would run smoothly during his absence. Then, with a small retinue of some 300 men, Shivaji, along with his son Shambhuji, set out for Agra, where Aurangzeb had just then set up court, soon after the death of Shah Jahan.

SHIVAJI ARRIVED IN Agra on 21st May 1666, during the festivities of the anniversary of Aurangzeb's accession. He halted at the outskirts of the city for a day. The next day he was met, on Aurangzeb's orders, by Kumar Ram Singh, son of Jai Singh, and escorted to a mansion near his own residence. From there, after a brief rest, Ram Singh conducted Shivaji to the imperial durbar, but by the time Shivaji arrived, Aurangzeb had moved from the Diwan-i-am to the Diwan-i-khas, and it was there that Shivaji was presented to the emperor.

Shivaji was probably piqued that Aurangzeb had sent only Ram Singh, not someone more senior, to receive him, but his tardy appearance at the court only made matters worse. On being presented to the emperor, Shivaji made the customary tributary offerings, but Aurangzeb, according to Jaipur records, "neither talked with him nor addressed any word to him." Shivaji was then unceremoniously led to stand in the third row of amirs, among the commanders of 5000 rank. Though a ceremonial robe, jewels and an elephant had been got ready to be presented to Shivaji, and they would have been bestowed on him immediately if he had presented himself at the public durbar, now at the private durbar, which was essentially a business rather than ceremonial session, the presents were set aside to be given to him at the end of the durbar.

The rank of the commander of 5000, to which Shivaji was assigned, was at one time a very high rank in the Mughal hierarchy, the highest rank in fact to which a noble could normally rise under Akbar. But since then much higher ranks had come to be routinely assigned to top officers, so the rank of 5000 had become crowded and undistinguished, especially under Aurangzeb, who invariably assigned the rank to any prominent adversary who joined the Mughal service. Shambhuji (Shivaji's young son) and even Netaji Palkar (Shivaji's former lieutenant now in the Mughal service) had been given this rank. Shivaji deserved better. He had expected at least the rank of 7000, the same as that of Jaswant Singh.

Shivaji was not immediately aware of the rank assigned to him, but he was fidgety standing neglected in a throng of unknown and obscure amirs. His visit was clearly not being treated by the emperor as the high point of the day's durbar. This upset him. He had imagined, or perhaps Jai singh had led him to expect, an entirely different reception. "Shivaji was shocked to receive such a cold treatment," says Ishwardas. When Shivaji realized that he had been assigned to a rank two rungs below the rank of Jaswant Singh, assigned in fact to the same rank as that of his son and his former lieutenant, he "flew into a rage and his eyes became wet," says a Jaipur diarist. When Ram Singh asked him what the matter was, Shivaji made a scene, and turning his back on the throne walked away, to sit in the portico to the side of the Diwan-i-khas.

Such behaviour was unheard of in the Mughal court, where high decorum and silence were the rule. When Aurangzeb inquired what the hubbub was about, Ram Singh suavely replied, "The tiger is a wild beast of the forest. He feels oppressed by heat in a place like this and has been taken ill." Ram Singh then went up to Shivaji to reason with him, but by then Shivaji was hysterical with rage, threatening to kill himself rather than appear before the emperor again. When Aurangzeb sent a couple of amirs with a *khilat* (dress of honour) to console Shivaji, he told them, "I refuse to accept the *khilat* . . . I decline the Emperor's *mansab*; I will not be his servant. Kill me, imprison me, if you like, but

I will not wear the *khilat.*" According to some, he swooned.

On hearing of Shivaji's outburst, Aurangzeb forbade him from attending the court thereafter. But that, in the eyes of several amirs, was not punishment enough. Rajput amirs in particular urged a more severe punishment—they generally resented the induction of Marathas into the imperial service, considering them as upstart petty chieftains, crude and unfit for the Mughal court, and a threat to their own position in the imperial hierarchy. Marathas had begun entering the Mughal service during the reign of Jahangir; under Shah Jahan there were as many as five Marathas holding the rank of 5000, and by the second half of Aurangzeb's reign the number of Marathas serving as Mughal amirs would rise to ninety-six. Rajput anxiety over this development was reflected in their condemnation of Shivaji. Said Jaswant Singh, whose rank Shivaji had presumed to claim: "He is a mere *bhumia* (country chieftain), and he came and displayed such discourtesy and violence! It is your Majesty's concern if you overlook it. But he ought to be punished." Among those demanding punishment was Jahanara, who was inimical towards Shivaji for humiliating her uncle Shayista Khan and for sacking Surat, the customs revenue of which was her due.

Returning to his camp, Shivaji continued to fume about Aurangzeb's breach of faith. It was feared that he might flee from Agra and take to rebellion again. A guard was therefore placed around his camp and, though his movements were not initially restricted, he was kept under constant surveillance. At one time Aurangzeb seems to have considered getting Shivaji out of the way by posting him to Kabul. There was also a rumour of a secret decision to confine Shivaji in a fortress or even to execute him, which, according to Rajput sources, was thwarted by Ram Singh, who asked the emperor to take his life first before taking Shivaji's, as Shivaji was under the guarantee of safety given by his father. Aurangzeb then asked Ram Singh to stand as surety for Shivaji, which he did. Ram Singh in turn took a pledge of good conduct from Shivaji. "Shiva came over to the Kumar's tent and there worshipped Mahadev, and pouring water on the idol gave his solemn assurance," says the Rajput diarist.

SHIVAJI HAD NO intention of keeping his pledge. To his own people, and in his own eyes, he was a great hero, but among the grandees of the Mughal empire he did not amount to much, just a small cog in a big wheel. That was not the life for Shivaji. He had to get away.

"His subtle brain," says Khafi Khan, "was not long in contriving a scheme" to escape from Agra. At first he tried petitioning Aurangzeb through imperial officers—whose favour he had won with presents—that if the emperor was not inclined to favour him, he might be permitted to return home, as the air and water of Hindustan were unhealthy for him. Aurangzeb would not hear of it. Shivaji then requested that he might be allowed to join the war against Bijapur so that, as he put it, he might "fight and die and thereby render service to you". Aurangzeb was not amused. Shivaji even made, in a variation of the trick he played on Afzal Khan, a request for a private interview with the emperor, in which he promised to reveal a great secret to him. The request was rejected out of hand as preposterous. In seeming despair, Shivaji then sought permission to go to Varanasi and become a religious mendicant, to which Aurangzeb graciously replied, "Let him turn fakir and live in the Allahabad fort . . . My *subedar* there will keep a good watch over him!"

All these moves were, says Khafi Khan, just a charade, to divert attention from what Shivaji was really planning. Aurangzeb suspected as much, and he made Shivaji's confinement steadily more rigorous, ordering that "he must not visit anybody, not even go to Kumar's house". He was kept under constant watch by the guards of the Kotwal as well as those of Kumar Ram Singh.

Yet Shivaji managed to escape, making his moves with calm ingenuity. His first manoeuvre was to send most of his men away from Agra, so that they would not be at the emperor's mercy after his escape. Aurangzeb readily gave permission for the men to leave, as he thought that this would render Shivaji even more helpless.

His men safely away, Shivaji made the next move. "He feigned to be ill," says Khafi Khan, "and groaned and sighed aloud. Complaining of pains in the liver and spleen, he took to his bed . . . For some time he carried on this artifice." During his 'illness' and while he was 'recovering', Shivaji sent out, as was customary, "presents to his doctors and attendants, food to brahmins, and presents of grain and money to needy Muslims and Hindus." Every day vast quantities of sweetmeats were carried out in a couple of huge covered baskets, each slung from a pole borne by two men. Initially, the guards inspected the baskets with care, but as the practice became routine they grew negligent. That was Shivaji's chance.

His escape was set for 29th August. That evening Shivaji and Shambhuji concealed themselves in sweetmeat baskets, and were carried past unsuspecting guards and taken to a secluded spot. There the fugitives got out and quickly proceeded to a suburb of the city, where Shivaji mounted a horse that had been kept ready for him, and set off with Shambhuji behind him. Meanwhile, at Shivaji's residence, his half-brother Hiraji, who resembled Shivaji, took Shivaji's place in his couch, wearing Shivaji's distinctive gold ring. "He was directed to throw a piece of fine muslin over his head, but to display the ring he wore upon his hand, and when anyone came in, to feign to be asleep," says Khafi Khan.

Shivaji's flight was discovered only late in the afternoon of the next day, so he had a nearly twenty-four-hour head start over his pursuers. When a spy first reported the escape to the Kotwal, he made inquiries, but finding the guards in place at Shivaji's camp, dismissed the report as unfounded. By then a second spy came to report the escape, so the Kotwal sent his men into Shivaji's camp to check, but they reported back that they found Shivaji asleep in his couch. It was only when a third spy came in with the same story that a thorough check was made and the truth discovered. Fulad Khan, head of the guards, attributed Shivaji's escape entirely to witchcraft. "The Raja was in his room," he reported. "We visited it regularly. But he vanished all of a sudden from our sight. Whether he flew into the sky or disappeared into the earth is not known, nor what magical trick he has played."

Meanwhile Shivaji had headed north, in a direction opposite to that which he would have been expected to take. Reaching Mathura, he shaved off his beard and disguised himself as a fakir, smearing his body with ash. From Mathura, where he was probably joined by some of his men, Shivaji swung east to Allahabad, then to Varanasi, and only then did he turn south. Taking the rough and unfrequented route through Bundelkhand, Gondwana and Golconda, changing disguises frequently, and often travelling by night, he reached Raigarh in November, after a trek of over two months. Shambhuji was left behind in Varanasi in the charge of 'Kabkalas' (Kavi Kalash), a brahmin who, according to Khafi Khan, "was the hereditary family priest of his family, and who happened at that time to be at Varanasi". We shall meet Kavi Kalash again in this story.

It is said that Shivaji did not throw off his disguise till he reached Raigarh, and a charming story is told that, on returning home disguised as an ascetic, he fell at the feet of his mother, and that even she could not recognize him.

Aurangzeb suspected—perhaps with justification, as Manucci, Bernier and Ishwardas indicate—that Ram Singh had colluded with Shivaji in his escape; he was, says Ishwardas, "rebuked and was deprived of his mansab". But mainly Aurangzeb blamed himself for his negligence, and would rue Shivaji's escape till the end of his days. "The greatest pillar of government consists in keeping of information about everything that happens in the kingdom—while even a minute's negligence results in shame for long years," he wrote in his last testament. "See, the flight of the wretch Shiva was due to carelessness, but it has involved me in all these distracting campaigns to the end of my days."

The general expectation was that Shivaji would be on the prowl again after his return to Raigarh. "If it be true that Sivajee hath escaped, Aurangzebe will quickly hear of him to his sorrow," wrote the English factors at Karwar in a letter dated 29th September 1666. But his long and arduous journey had worn him out, and he was laid up for several weeks after his return. Strangely, even after he recovered, Shivaji made no aggressive moves, either against the Mughals or against Bijapur, but remained quiet for over three years, using the time mainly to systematize the administration of his domain.

Equally strangely, Aurangzeb too remained passive, and took no steps to seize Shivaji—not because of any change of heart, but because he was then preoccupied with his Afghan campaign, and his governor in the Deccan, Prince Muazzam (who had returned as governor for the third time) was inclined to sloth. It was even suspected that Muazzam and his adjutant Jaswant Singh were receiving bribes from Shivaji.

Shivaji in any case took care not to provoke Aurangzeb. He kept up a pretence of servility, and Aurangzeb reciprocated with a pretence of forgiveness, both biding their time. In April 1667, Shivaji wrote to Aurangzeb seeking pardon, and entreated with Jaswant Singh to intercede for him. "The Emperor has cast me off," wrote Shivaji. "Otherwise I intended to have begged the task of recovering Kandahar with my unaided resources. I fled [from Agra] in fear of my life." Aurangzeb played along. Though he would not accede to Shivaji's plea for conferring on him a mansabdari rank and a fief, he granted Shivaji the chieftain's rights (*deshmukhi*) in his old domain, and advised him that "he was at liberty to seize as much of the Bijapur territory as he could". On the intercession of Muazzam, the emperor also conferred on Shivaji the title of raja. "Raja Shivaji!" wrote Muazzam in March 1668, "His Gracious Majesty has elevated your head by granting you the title of Raja, which was the extreme point of your desire."

Shivaji's unnatural passivity at this time gave many the impression that his career was past its peak, and that he was in the process of fading into obscurity as a petty hill chieftain. The English factors in India thought so. They were wrong. Shivaji would presently burst into action again, and would bring nearly half of the Deccan under his sway in the remaining ten years of his life. He was quiet between 1667 and 1670 only because he was gathering his strength and maturing his plans.

IN JANUARY 1670 Shivaji took to the field again. The prevailing political and military situation in the Deccan favoured him. In Bijapur, Ali Adil Shah II, who had at one time shown great martial enterprise, was now sunk in debauchery. The Mughals too were flaccid. Jai Singh was dead; Prince Muazzam, who had taken his place, was inert. And Aurangzeb, engaged in subduing the Afghans, paid little attention to the Deccan. In fact, he reduced his Deccan forces at this time, perhaps as an economy measure, perhaps to deny Muazzam the means to rebel. (Shivaji inducted many of the disbanded Mughal soldiers into his army—for him, the army was not an item of expenditure, but a source of revenue, through plunder.)

Shivaji's immediate objective was to recover the forts he had ceded to the Mughals in 1665. The first to fall was the great hill fort of Sinhgarh. Purandhar, at the foot of which Shivaji had surrendered to Jai Singh, fell the next month. Then the other forts. In October 1670, for a second time he raided Surat, and for three days sacked the town at leisure, sparing, as before, only the establishments of European trading companies.

Shivaji withdrew from Surat, as he had done in 1664, on the approach of Mughal reinforcements from Burhanpur, but this time he left a letter for the local Mughal officer (who had as usual taken refuge in the fort) demanding an annual ransom of 1.2 million rupees from the city. As the officer did not respond, Shivaji repeated the demand twice again, the last time in 1672, when he wrote, "I demand for the third time, which I declare shall be the last, the *chauth* or quarter part of the king's revenue under your government. As your Emperor has forced me to keep an army for the defence of my people and country, that army must be paid by his subjects. If you do not send me the money speedily, then make ready a large house for me, for I shall go and sit down there and receive the revenue and custom duties, as there is none now to stop my passage." Shivaji was bluffing. He was far too engrossed with other campaigns to turn to Surat again.

The raid on Surat was followed by Maratha incursions into other Mughal territories. A large Maratha fleet also roamed the coastal waters, swooping down on ports, preying on local shipping, once even clashing with the Portuguese navy. In December 1670, Shivaji's forces raided the Mughal province of Khandesh, plundering towns and extracting from village headmen agreements to pay *chauth* to Shivaji, so that he might protect them—from himself! This was the first time that Shivaji imposed *chauth* in a territory directly ruled by the Mughals, and with it began the process of Maratha authority overlying Mughal authority, which would, in the course of time, cover most of the empire, virtually obliterating Mughal power without ever formally replacing it.

As the situation in the Deccan deteriorated, Aurangzeb recalled Jaswant Singh and sent Mahabat Khan (Luhrasp) with a force of 40,000 to serve under Prince Muazzam. That yielded no gains either. In 1672 the emperor recalled both Muazzam and Mahabat Khan, and appointed Bahadur Khan (later titled Khan Jahan) as the governor of the Deccan. This created fresh problems. Bahadur Khan's brief was to protect the Mughal frontiers; he therefore adopted a defensive posture against the Marathas, while his second in command, Dilir Khan, favoured an aggressive thrust. Between the two opposed strategies, the Mughal campaign against Shivaji floundered.

Meanwhile, in December 1672 Ali Adil Shah of Bijapur suffered a paralytic stroke and died, and was succeeded by Sikandar Adil Shah, a boy barely five years old. This plunged Bijapur into chaos. Bijapur's adversity was Shivaji's opportunity. But before he could invade Bijapur, Shivaji had to secure Mughal neutrality, so once again he proffered subservience to the emperor. Bahadur Khan, eager to divert Maratha raids from Mughal lands, went along with the sham. In March 1673 Shivaji took Panhala, then pounced on the rich commercial town of Hubli, where the British factors were among his victims. Fort after fort, including Satara, fell to him; he even appeared in the environs of Bijapur, pillaging with impunity, and his naval wing swept down the coast, sacking such towns as Karwar and Ankola.

The whole of the Deccan was now Shivaji's hunting ground. He could roam wherever he pleased, strike at will wherever he wished. No one had the power to check him. Shivaji had thus become, in a sense, the dominant power of the Deccan. His potency was not however in the size of his domain but in his penetrative power. His kingdom was still tiny in extent, a barely 300-kilometre-long narrow strip along the ghats, the hill country shunned by the Mughals as well as by the Deccani powers. Large portions of even the Maratha homeland lay outside his rule. Bijapur and Golconda were far greater territorial powers; even Shivaji's younger brother Ekoji held, in fiefhold from Bijapur, lands more extensive and more prosperous than Shivaji's realm.

What distressed Shivaji however was not so much the smallness of his domain, as the fact that his power lacked conventional political legitimacy. For all his military might, and despite the title of raja he sported, Shivaji was considered by many of his contemporaries as a mere warlord or rebel, by some even as no more than a fabulously successful bandit. This status, of being a rebel, warlord or bandit, was the usual transitional position of the founder of a new dynasty in medieval India, but Shivaji craved for the distinction of being a legitimate Hindu monarch, to place himself incontrovertibly above all other Maratha chieftains.

There was a problem in Shivaji claiming royal legitimacy. He was a Maratha, a community commonly designated as sudra, while Hindu convention specified that only kshatriyas could be consecrated as kings. This however was not an insurmountable difficulty. Hindu society, despite its formal rigidity, had sufficient practical flexibility to deal with the problem. The anomaly of non-kshatriyas having to be acknowledged as rajas was not uncommon in Indian history, and the usual solution to it was to invest the upstart monarch with a mythical kshatriya lineage. It was then no surprise that Shivaji's accommodative genealogical sleuths found for him the best of all kshatriya lineages— he was, they discovered, a Sisodia, a scion of the solar dynasty of Mewar tracing its origin to the epic hero Lord Rama, indeed to god Vishnu himself!

Shivaji's newly discovered semi-divine ancestry was approved and sanctified (after some becoming and perhaps profitable hesitation) by Gaga Bhat, a renowned authority on Hindu scriptures, who had come all the way from Varanasi to consecrate Shivaji. Gaga Bhat further held, hedging his endorsement, that irrespective of genealogy, Shivaji had in any case proved himself a kshatriya by his deeds.

While Gaga Bhat thus exalted Shivaji, Shivaji in turn exalted Gaga Bhat, turning him into a kind of divine messenger, claiming that the coming of the sage was intimated to him by goddess Bhavani in a vision. Shivaji travelled some distance from Raigarh to welcome Gaga Bhat ceremonially, and escorted him into the fort in a grand procession. That ostentatious display of reverence enhanced, in the eyes of the common people, the holiness of Gaga Bhat, and, by reflection, the sanctity of the consecration he would perform.

THE CORONATION OF Shivaji was celebrated with great splendour, for the occasion was not just the crowning of a new king, but the founding of a new kingdom and a new dynasty. Even more than that, it was, in Shivaji's eyes, the beginning of the Hindu political renaissance, and he took care to have his pundits trace and restore ancient, long-neglected Hindu coronation rituals. Significantly, a new era was proclaimed to mark Shivaji's accession.

Preparations for the coronation took several months, and everything was done with the fastidious attention to detail that was typical of

Shivaji. Brahmins from all over India with their families were invited to Raigarh for the ceremony, and Shivaji housed and fed some 50,000 of them for four months. Meanwhile, Shivaji performed the pilgrimages, austerities and purification ceremonies required of him as penances for neglecting his kshatriya duties (out of ignorance of ascribed caste status). He was then invested with the sacred thread, which brahmins and kshatriyas, but not sudras, were allowed to wear. The priests further—for a fee—absolved him, as they insisted was necessary, of the sin of causing the "death of Brahmins, cows, women and children", even though he could not knowingly have committed such offences. Shivaji also desired to be taught the Vedic mantras, but the priests firmly rejected this request, because, they claimed, in the prevailing eon, the Kali Yuga, Vedic mantras could be taught only to the true twice-born.

Grand Hindu coronations were rare in seventeenth-century India, so Shivaji's installation was an exceptional professional opportunity for brahmins, and they made the most of it, exacting high fees and receiving rich presents at every stage of the ceremony. Shivaji was separately weighed against seven metals (gold, silver, copper, zinc, tin, lead and iron); against cloves, nutmeg and other spices, as well as against salt, camphor and fine linen; and finally against butter, sugar, fruits and all sorts of eatables, including betel-leaves. After the weighing, all items were distributed to brahmins.

On 16th June 1674, the day of the coronation, Shivaji, having fasted the previous day, bathed in Ganga water, put on a pure white robe, and adorned himself with garlands of flowers and gold ornaments. He then worshipped his household deities, adored the feet of his family priest, and took his seat on a low, gold-plated stool for the *abhishekham*, the consecration by holy water. Soyra Bai, his chief consort, sat to his left with her sari knotted to his robe, and Shambhuji, his eldest son, sat close behind. The Ashta-pradhans, Shivaji's eight ministers, formed a close circle around the royal family, standing at the cardinal and intermediate points of the compass, with gold jugs in their hands, filled with water from the Ganga and other holy rivers. They poured the water over the royal family amidst the chanting of Vedic hymns, while "sixteen pure-robed Brahmin wives, each with five lamps laid on a gold tray, waved the lights around his (Shivaji's) head to scare away evil influences," writes Jadunath Sarkar in his graphic and exquisitely detailed description of the coronation.

Continues Sarkar: After the *abhishekham*, Shivaji changed into "a robe of royal scarlet, richly embroidered with gold, put on sparkling gems and gold ornaments, a necklace, a garland of flowers, and a turban adorned with strings and tassels of pearls, worshipped his sword, shield, bow and arrows, and again bowed to his elders and Brahmins. Then, at the auspicious moment selected by astrologers, he entered the throne-room." As Shivaji mounted the octagonal throne, the congregation was showered with tiny lotuses wrought in gold and silver, and once again the sixteen brahmin wives waved their lamps as the priests chanted sacred hymns. Then, as the band struck up and musicians sang, and the artillery "of every fort in the kingdom" fired salvos, Gaga Bhat, the chief priest, raised the royal parasol over Shivaji and hailed him as Chhatrapathi, Lord of the Umbrella, the usual appellation of great Hindu monarchs. Later, Shivaji mounted a richly caparisoned elephant and, surrounded by his ministers and generals, went on a ceremonial procession through Raigarh. All along his path women waved lighted lamps and showered him with fried rice, flowers and holy grass.

The coronation rites, spread over nine days and nine nights, concluded with the distribution of gifts to the assembled brahmins. Shivaji, says Sarkar, "performed the sixteen varieties of great alms-giving (*maha-dan*) prescribed in the sacred books of the Hindus." The celebrations cost Shivaji some five million rupees.

Soon after the coronation, the monsoon auspiciously burst over Raigarh, in a heavenly shower of benediction. Shivaji's aged mother Jija Bai, who had lived only to see her son crowned king, closed her eyes a few days after the coronation, her life fulfilled.

Kirti Rupen

SHIVAJI WAS FORTY-SEVEN years old at the time of his coronation. Physically, he was hardly an imposing figure. Short and slightly built, he weighed under sixty-four kilograms at the time of his coronation. Yet there was an unmistakable aura of power about him, a radiant intelligence, of which his contemporaries speak. Though "at sight Shivaji's body looks lean and short," notes a Rajput diarist, "even without finding out who he is, one does feel instinctively that he is a ruler of men. His spirit and manliness are apparent."

The portraits of Shivaji painted in later times, which fairly tally with contemporary descriptions, show him with a high-bridged aquiline nose, large, deep-set, lustrous eyes and a lively, cheerful expression. He was fair-complexioned—"his appearance is wonderfully fair," notes the Rajput diarist—and full bearded, and wore his hair long. Duff, on the basis of the tradition among Shivaji's descendants and among the descendants of his ministers and domestics, describes Shivaji as "a man of small stature, and of an active rather than strong make; his countenance was handsome and intelligent; he had very long arms in proportion to his size, which is reckoned a beauty among the Mahrattas." His most striking features were his eyes. "The Raja (Shivaji) is short and tawny, with quick eyes that shew a great deal of wit," notes Thevenot. Chaplin Escaliot, on the basis of the reports of Englishmen who had seen Shivaji around 1664, also speaks of his "quick and piercing eyes".

Shivaji was an excellent judge of people, and had a persuasive tongue. "Shivaji is very clever, he speaks the right word, after which nobody needs say anything more on the subject," says the Rajput diarist. His lifestyle, like that of his great antagonist, Aurangzeb, was austere. Unlike most rulers of his time, Shivaji found no pleasure in debauchery, and throughout his life retained the simplicity and rigour of his arduous life in the hills around Pune in his teens. Though he was a polygamist—he had at least four wives—as was the custom among medieval rulers, Hindu as well as Muslim, he does not seem to have kept any concubines. Germain, a French envoy from Pondicherry who visited Shivaji when he was encamped near Thanjavur late in his reign, records that "the camp of Shivaji is without pomp, without women and without baggage. It has only twó tents—but of simple coarse stuff and very small—one of them for himself and the other for his prime minister." Says Duff, "No soldier in the service of Sivajee was permitted to carry any female follower with him in the field, on pain of death."

There was a strong moral streak in Shivaji, and a high respect for women, whether of his own or of the enemy. He invariably addressed all women as mother. Even Khafi Khan, who habitually damns Shivaji as "the hell-dog", praises his fair treatment of captives and subject people. "Shivaji had always striven to maintain the honour of the people in his territories," says Khafi Khan. "He persevered in a course of rebellion, in plundering caravans, and troubling mankind, but he entirely abstained from other disgraceful acts, and was careful to maintain the honour of the women and children of Muhammadans when they fell into his hands. His injunctions upon this point were very strict, and any one who disobeyed them received punishment." It was a standing order to his army that, even during pillaging raids, cows, cultivators and women were not to be molested, and only the rich (Hindu or Muslim) were to be taken as prisoners, for ransom.

In all this, the major influence on Shivaji was his mother, and it was she who instilled in him an abiding and intense religious faith. As a child, he was avid in attending the discourses of Tukaram, a renowned sage living near Pune; later he took Ramadas, another Maharashtrian sage, as his spiritual guide. As Shivaji grew older, the rigour of his religious devotion intensified. "He loved to distraction religious readings and songs (*kirtan*) and sought the society of Hindu and Muslim saints wherever he went," says Careri, an Italian aristocrat in India in the late seventeenth century. Shivaji's sense of heroic purpose, we must assume, was derived from the Hindu epics, the *Ramayana* and the *Mahabharata*— he himself seems to have been conscious of this influence, for he tried to inculcate the same ardour in his soldiers by having the war chapters of the *Ramayana* routinely recited to them.

Despite his intense faith, Shivaji, unlike Aurangzeb, was not obsessed with religion, and he certainly was not a bigot; he was Hindu, and would make no compromise on that, but he equally respected the devotion of other people to other religions. More importantly, in that harsh age and in his brutal environment, religious sensibility infused a certain probity even in his depredations.

Shivaji had in his army several Muslim soldiers and captains, by whom he was well served and for whom he built a mosque opposite to his palace in Raigarh. His confidential secretary was a Muslim, Kazi Haidar; he even had a Muslim guru, Baba Yakut of Kelsi. He never, except once in unusual circumstances, ravaged a Muslim holy place or hermitage, and whenever a Koran fell into his hands in the course of plunder, he took care to hand it over deferentially to some Muslim. Notes Duff, "Sivajee never sequestrated any allowance fixed by the Mahomedan government for the support of tombs, mosques or places of commemoration in honour of saints." This reverential treatment of the people of other religions was extended even to Europeans; Bernier reports that during the sacking of Surat, Shivaji ordered that "the Frankish Padrys are good men, and shall not be molested."

In many respects Shivaji was an unusual ruler for his age, but he could also be utterly ruthless as a medieval ruler needed to be. His cunning was legendary. "He was distinguished in his tribe for courage and intelligence," writes Khafi Khan in resentful admiration, "and for craft and trickery he was reckoned a sharp son of the devil, the father of fraud." According to English merchants, "Shivaji is so famously infamous for his notorious thefts that Report hath made him an airy body, and added wings, or else it were impossible he could be at so many places as he is said to be at, all at one time . . . They ascribe him to perform more than a Herculean labour that he is become the talk of all conditions of people." The Mughals believed that Shivaji was a sorcerer, who could fly through the air across forty or fifty yards to pounce on his victim.

All this was of course myth. Shivaji's sorcery was only intelligence soaring on the wings of opportunity. What he did was not always pleasant, especially as the prey saw it, but it was invariably effective. Writes Duff in a sensible assessment: "Sivajee was patient and deliberate in his plans, ardent, resolute, and persevering in their execution . . . duplicity and meanness were so much intermixed with his schemes . . . he always preferred deceit to open force when both were in his power . . ."

To prefer deceit to open force was perhaps not very gallant, but it was more humane, as it minimized casualties. For Shivaji, the right action was that which was the most efficient, yielding the best result with the least effort. He was tough and ruthless, but not savage. He avoided unnecessary risks in battle, and saw no dishonour in flight to save himself and his booty, considering it a greater merit to live to fight another day, than to fall in the battlefield. Being cunning was however only one facet of Shivaji's character. He could be sensationally intrepid when required. And more than anything else, he was marvelouslly inventive. He found a way out of every problem he faced, and a way to improve on any given situation. "Nothing," says Duff, "is more remarkable in regard to Sivajee than the foresight with which some of his schemes were laid, and the fitness of his arrangements for the genius of his countrymen."

SHIVAJI'S GENIUS PERFECTLY matched the Maratha potential. The potential itself was not however Shivaji's creation, for it had already been well demonstrated in the phenomenally successful career of Shahji. Shivaji's career was in a way the culmination of Shahji's career. Shahji had, it should be remembered, risen to become, for a while, the uncrowned monarch of the remnant Ahmadnagar kingdom, and he would probably have founded the Maratha state himself had he not had the misfortune of tangling with Shah Jahan; on the other hand, Shivaji probably would not have been crowned with as great a success as he was, if Aurangzeb had come into the Deccan during Shivaji's lifetime.

Yet Shivaji's career was not just an amplification of his father's career. While Shahji preferred to operate within the existing political system—seeking, even in rebellion, the legitimacy of acting on behalf of a (puppet) Nizam Shahi sultan—Shivaji opted out of the system altogether. Shahji sought a role within the established power structure in the Deccan, Shivaji sought to supplant the structure. Unfortunately, except in the *swaraj*, the core area which he ruled directly, Shivaji replaced the old structure not with a new structure, but with anarchy.

Shivaji's political system consisted of three concentric circles. At the centre was the *swaraj*. There Shivaji was benevolently paternalistic, and would not allow the people to be harassed in any way. "When you . . . [oppress] the poor peasants, who are holding on to their cottages, and somehow eking out a livelihood, [they] will . . . begin to run away," Shivaji warned his officers. "Some of them will starve. Then they will think that you are worse than the Mughals who overran the countryside."

In the second circle, the region contiguous with the *swaraj*, over which Shivaji claimed suzerainty but did not administer himself, he spared the people from pillage, but they were required to pay *chauth* (one-fourth of the revenue as protection money) and *sardeshmukhi* (an extra one-tenth, as the chieftain's due). These taxes were not Shivaji's invention. *Chauth* was current before Shivaji's time in Maharashtra, and probably elsewhere too. The Rajputs seem to have collected a similar toll—in 1688 Shujaet Khan, the Mughal officer in Marwar, conceded to the Rajputs one-fourth of the imperial customs duties for sparing traders on roads. Similarly, *sardeshmukhi* was also an existing practice in

Bijapur. Shivaji's distinction was that he collected these taxes aggressively and over a wide territory.

Beyond the suzerain lands was the third circle, where Shivaji's only objective was plunder. There he was dreaded by all the people, for he pillaged all, irrespective of race and religion. Once, when he seized Sringarpoor, the leading Maratha citizens in the town actually preferred to migrate to the region controlled by Muslims, deeming it more secure. Most Maratha campaigns were not directed against political or military targets, but against defenceless people of the countryside and small towns. For the Deccan as a whole, the sweep of the Maratha tornado was terrifyingly calamitous.

Pillaging raids would remain a primary activity of Shivaji even after he made the transition from warlord to crowned monarch, and they would remain a part of the Maratha political culture well into the nineteenth century. "To *plunder the enemy* is to this day used by Mahrattas to express victory, of which it is in their estimation the only real proof," says Duff, writing nearly 200 years after Shivaji's time.

Shivaji did not waste his resources in fruitless heroics, and whenever he felt that the gain he could expect did not match the effort required, he backed off, as he did in the face of the resistance by European traders in Surat, for they had cannons and he had none. Nor did he attack the castle in Surat, "though he knew very well that the richest things they had were conveighed thither, and especially a great deal of ready Money," says Thevenot. Similarly, he never attacked Goa, the rich Portuguese enclave nestling on the Maratha coast, for, as the English merchants in India reported in June 1674, "it is none of his business to lay siege to any place that is fortified against him, for it will not turn him to account. He is, and ever was, for a running banquet, and to plunder and burn those towns that have neither defence nor guard." For the same reason, Shivaji also took care never to attack Mughal provincial capitals like Aurangabad and Burhanpur directly, saying, "If we attack these places, the honour of Aurangzeb will be wounded, and he will march hither himself, and then, God knows how the strife will end!" Shivaji won most of his battles because he had the prudence not to fight the battles he could not win.

The Maratha campaigning season was the seven-month period from the end of October to the end of May, which was the dry season in the Deccan. Dasehra, the Hindu festival symbolizing the triumph of good over evil, which was celebrated at the end of the monsoon in October, was the high point of the year for the Marathas. Soon after the festival, a general review of troops was held, and then they took off, to swoop down on defenceless towns and habitations, bellowing their war cry, *Har, Har, Mahadev*! to invoke the blessings of god Shiva, under whose flag, the Bhagwa Jenda,—a swallow-tailed, deep orange pennant—they fought. The places to raid were selected by Shivaji's intelligence chief, the legendary Bahirji Naik, whose spies roamed the land. At the end of the dry season, the Marathas returned to their homeland, in time for the peasant soldiers to till their land. This went on year after year.

THE ARMY, NOT surprisingly, was the most critical element in Shivaji's government, and he gave its organization and training the utmost attention. In the beginning, the backbone of his army was the infantry—suited for the mountain terrain where he operated—but as his campaigns extended into the plains, his cavalry force grew in size and importance. Shivaji also had a naval wing consisting, in 1665, of eighty-five 'frigates'. "With these vessels he attacked and plundered ships which were proceeding to Europe and to Mecca," says Khafi Khan. In the coastal waters his navy fought the Siddis, an Abyssinian military clan in India who usually commanded the naval forces of Indian rulers; sometimes the Maratha navy even clashed with European navies, and on at least one occasion worsted them.

Shivaji had a fair number of non-Marathas in his army, even quite a few Muslim soldiers and captains, especially in the cavalry, but his soldiers were predominantly recruited from the sudra castes of his homeland. Every soldier was personally selected by Shivaji, and was taken into service only on the security of a soldier already in service. Discipline was strict in the Maratha army, despite its predatory character. All plunder had to be remitted to the state, and was formally received by Shivaji sitting in durbar; the captains were then rewarded in proportion to their capture, and "were praised, distinguished, and promoted according to their success." Soldiers too were rewarded, but none was allowed to keep anything on his own, and those who hid booty were severely punished.

The procedure was strict and thorough. At the time of setting out on a campaign, an inventory of each soldier's effects was taken, against which what he brought back at the end of the campaign was checked, and what he had in excess was taken away or adjusted against his salary; but equally, losses, including dead horses, were made good.

The Maratha cavalry lived off the enemy country during the fair season, but during the rainy season was cantoned in pasture-lands under the protection of forts. Shivaji took great care in the maintenance and security of his forts, for in them was the security of his government. Retired captains of high reputation were put in charge of the forts and were assigned rent-free lands hereditarily so that they would take care of their charge "as the mother that fed them". Notes Duff: "Orders in respect to ingress and egress, rounds, watches and patrols, care of water, grain, stores and ammunition, were most minute; and the officer of each department was furnished with distinct rules for his guidance, from which no deviation was permitted."

To prevent sedition, Shivaji permitted no fortifications of any kind, even village walls, to be built within his kingdom, except those manned by his own troops. He also disfavoured the jagir system, which tended to weaken the central authority. In all this, Shivaji's primary concern was efficiency. This was evident even in his patronage of religion: though he took care to maintain temples, as expected of a Hindu monarch, and those temples without provision were granted endowments, he also made the priests in charge of them accountable for their expenditure, to make sure that the grants served the purpose for which they were intended.

A significant aspect of Shivaji's rule was his attempt to revive ancient Hindu political traditions and court conventions. He introduced Marathi in the place of Persian as the court language, revived old Sanskrit administrative nomenclature, and compiled a dictionary of official terms, the *Raja-vyavahara-kosa*, to facilitate the change over. His council of eight ministers, the Ashta-pradhans headed by the Peshwa, too was modelled on old Hindu institutions. Shivaji was influenced by the Mughal revenue system, but assessments were made on the actual yield, with three-fifths left to the cultivator and two-fifths taken by the government. In judicial administration, civil cases continued to be decided by the panchayat, the village council, as from time immemorial, while criminal law was based on the *shastras*, the Hindu law books.

ALL THIS TIME, while Shivaji was expanding and consolidating his power, Aurangzeb made no major move against him. He did not even react to Shivaji's coronation, presumably viewing it only as a means for Shivaji to secure his position among the Marathas, and not as an act against the emperor, for the idea of an independent Hindu kingdom was inconceivable in India in Mughal times. But the coronation brought about a subtle change in Shivaji's operations. There was now a new gravity in his actions, and though he continued his annual pillaging raids, he now began also to annex land, not just seize possessions; and, instead of entering into subordinate deals with other monarchs, as he had been obliged to do until then, he now entered into treaty agreements with them as an equal.

These changes were dramatically evident in Shivaji's southern campaign of 1677, but even before that a new daring was evident in his actions, as he sent his forces ranging deep into Bijapur and the Mughal Deccan. In 1675 a Maratha army swept north to the environs of Burhanpur and crossed the Narmada River for the first time, to pillage the region around Bharuch in Gujarat, while another army struck southward to besiege Ponda near Goa. But the following year was relatively quiet for Shivaji, as he lay ill for several months in Satara.

During his illness, he was visited by Raghunath Pant Hanumante, the disaffected minister of his step-brother Ekoji. An overbearing and ambitious brahmin, Raghunath had served Shahji faithfully for many years but could not get along with Ekoji, and had left him in a huff, vowing vendetta. Raghunath first went to the Sultan of Bijapur, Ekoji's nominal overlord, but finding no favour there, proceeded to Golconda, where he established a rapport with Madanna Pant, the brahmin minister of Qutb Shah. From Golconda he shuttled to Satara to arrange a compact between Shivaji and Qutb Shah, to conquer Ekoji's realm and divide it between them.

Shivaji was eager for the campaign. Over several years he had stripped to the bone his traditional hunting grounds in the Deccan and now needed a rich and virgin territory to plunder—which was precisely what Ekoji had, an extensive and lush fief in Karnataka (which he had got as his patrimony) and the principality of Thanjavur (which he had seized from its effete Nayak ruler). Besides, Ekoji had crowned himself in Thanjavur in 1676, and Shivaji presumably considered that as an affront to his authority as the head of the Bhonsles. Shivaji moreover believed that it was a matter of honour for him to procure his rightful share of his father's lands in Karnataka. Lastly, in the context of his growing power and ambition, Karnataka offered an opportunity for him to extend his power beyond the Maratha homeland.

But before Shivaji could venture into Karnataka, he had to secure the neutrality of the Mughals, who were at his rear and eastern flank. So once again, now for the fourth time, he professed submission to the emperor. The Mughals played along, for Bahadur Khan, the Mughal governor in the Deccan, had just then suffered a crushing defeat at the hands of Bijapur and was eager for revenge, and in any case the Mughal strategy at this time was to encourage the Deccani powers to fight among themselves and exhaust each other, for the emperor to pick them off later. Besides, Shivaji had taken the precaution of paying a large sum of money to Bahadur Khan, part of it privately as a bribe, and part of it publicly as a tribute to the emperor. He viewed the payment as a profitable investment—the money paid to the Mughals, said Shivaji, was like "the oil-cake given to his milch cow", to be recovered in greater measure in another form.

In January 1677 Shivaji set out for Golconda with an army of 30,000 cavalry and 40,000 infantry. This was a state visit, not a pillaging expedition, so he took care to make his entry into Hyderabad a grand pageant, solemn and mannerly—his soldiers wore shiny new armour and his captains were adorned with strings of pearls and gold bracelets, and he himself rode in royal fashion, showering handfuls of gold and silver on the bystanders as he passed through city streets elaborately decorated for the occasion on the orders of Qutb Shah.

The sultan received Shivaji as an honoured royal guest, and their negotiations were cordial. An agreement was soon reached by which Golconda agreed to supply Shivaji with funds and a train of artillery, and Shivaji agreed to share with Golconda his southern conquests, excluding only Shahji's jagir, which was left to Shivaji to dispose of as he pleased. The terms also included an undertaking for joint defence against the Mughals, by which Golconda agreed to make a contribution of 300,000 rupees to Shivaji and pay him an annual subsidy of 100,000 *huns* (South Indian gold coins).

After a month in Hyderabad, Shivaji headed south, visiting places of pilgrimage on the way and performing penances. Then he advanced on Thanjavur, Ekoji's capital, taking the forts of Gingee and Vellore on the way. Arriving on the banks of the Kaveri River, he camped at Tirumalvadi, some fifteen kilometres north of the town. There he was visited by Ekoji, and the brothers spent a week together in negotiations. But they could not agree on dividing their patrimony, and one night Ekoji, fearing coercion, fled secretly to Thanjavur. That upset Shivaji. "Was I going to imprison him?" he lamented. "My fame has spread over the sea-girt earth. I asked for my father's property only because one should keep his heritage. If he does not wish to part with it, he is under no compulsion to give it. Why did he flee for nothing? He is very young and acted like a child."

Shivaji's attitude towards Ekoji was of a protective elder brother. He would not menace his brother's person. But this did not prevent him from wresting Ekoji's fiefs, imposing *chauth* and *sardeshmukhi* where he could, and plundering as he pleased. In the end, however, Shivaji retained only the tableland of Mysore for himself and returned the rest of the territory to Ekoji, who in turn agreed to share with Shivaji the treasure of Shahji as well as the revenue of the Karnataka fief.

The Karnataka campaign marked the peak of Shivaji's career, and he returned triumphant to Raigarh just before the onset of the south-west monsoon in 1678, after an absence of eighteen months.

MEANWHILE THE MUGHALS were on the move again in the Deccan, with Dilir Khan advancing to besiege Bijapur city. In its moment of peril, Bijapur had only Shivaji, the erstwhile rebel, to turn to for succour. Masud Khan, the Bijapuri regent, wrote to Shivaji: "We are neighbours. We eat the same salt. You are as deeply concerned [in the welfare of] this State as I am. The enemy (the Mughals) are day and night trying to ruin it. We two ought to unite and expel the foreigner." In August 1679 he wrote again, entreating, "The condition of this royalty is not hidden from you. There is no army, money or ally for defending the fort and no provision at all. The enemy is strong and ever bent on war. You are a hereditary servant, elevated by this Court. And, therefore, you will feel for this house more than others can. We cannot defend the kingdom and its forts without your aid. Be true to your salt; turn towards us. Command what you consider proper, and it shall be done by us."

Responding to the call, Shivaji advanced into Bijapur, and approached as close as thirty-eight kilometres to the Mughal camp, then abruptly veered away to ravage the Mughal lands between the Bhima and Godavari rivers, presumably to divert the Mughals and thus ease the pressure on Bijapur. In any case, it was far more profitable, and far less risky, for Shivaji to plunder the undefended Mughal territory than to battle the Mughals in Bijapur. Unfortunately, when he was returning with the plunder he was intercepted by a Mughal army. Shivaji lost some 4000 men in the action and had to abandon the plunder, and he himself was able to evade capture only with great difficulty, fleeing through obscure paths and marching incessantly for three days and nights.

Around this time Shivaji suffered yet another humiliation, when his son Shambhuji, who had been confined in the Panhala fort for his outrage on a married brahmin woman, escaped and defected to the Mughals. Shambhuji would return contritely to Shivaji after a year, but clearly Shivaji's luck was beginning to run out.

A few months after Shambhuji's return, Shivaji performed the thread ceremony of his young son Rajaram at Raigarh. Soon after this he fell ill with fever and dysentery, and a painful swelling of the knee joints. His condition rapidly turned critical, and after a few days' illness, he passed away at noon on 2nd April 1680. As Sarkar describes the death scene, after "giving solemn charges and wise counsels to his nobles and officers, and consoling the weeping assemblage with assurances of the spirit's immortality in spite of the perishableness of the body, the maker of the Maratha nation performed the last rites of his religion and then fell into a trance, which imperceptibly passed into death." Shivaji was fifty-three.

The date of Shivaji's death was noted by Khafi Khan with the chronogram, *Kafir ba-jahannam raft*—The infidel went to hell! Aurangzeb, then in Ajmer engaged in his campaign against the Rajputs, was relieved and exclaimed: "My armies were employed against him for nineteen years, but nevertheless his State has always been increasing." At the time of his death Shivaji was in possession of an extensive domain stretching down the western peninsular coast from Daman southward to Ankola (excluding the European settlements) and extending eastward to include a good part of modern Maharashtra, Karnataka and Tamil Nadu.

Shivaji's was a remarkable career, and even his adversaries could not help admiring him. "Although an infidel and a rebel, [he] was a wise man," says Khafi Khan. Says Tavernier: "Shivaji is both wise and liberal." Sang sage Ramadas: "*Shivarajas athavaven . . . kirti-rupen!*"— Remember Shivaji raja, glory incarnate! F. Martin, the founder of Pondicherry, had this to say about Shivaji: "The deceased may well hold a high rank among the great men of India, although all the conquests which he made during his life were done more by skillfulness and cleverness than by open force."

Much of what Shivaji did, especially in his early years, was little different from banditry. That cannot be denied. But as his power grew, so did his vision, transforming his role from that of a warlord to that of a great king. Shivaji was the right man at the right time in the right place. More than that, he created his own opportunities: transcending his circumstances he gathered into himself the Maratha energies, and gave his people an enduring historical role. By his achievements as well as by the example he set, Shivaji spun the strands from which the fabric of post-Mughal Indian history would be woven.

Maratha Collapse

THE DEATH OF Shivaji was followed by a short but vicious power struggle in Maharashtra. Shambhuji, twenty-three, the elder of Shivaji's two surviving sons, was the rightful heir, but the Ashta-pradhans, Shivaji's council of ministers dominated by brahmins, were uneasy about him, because of his turbulent ways and his well-known anti-brahmin bias. Shambhuji, says Martin, "was the declared enemy of Brahmans". The ministers therefore sought to raise the younger prince, Rajaram, a boy of ten, to the throne.

The prime mover of the plot was Anaji Datto, the finance minister, who worked in tandem with Soyra Bai, Rajaram's ambitious mother. The king-makers kept Shivaji's death a secret—the funeral obsequies were performed privately by a relative of Shivaji—and they dispatched a force to detain Shambhuji in Panhala, where Shivaji had kept him under guard after his re-defection from the Mughal camp. Unfortunately for the conspirators, Shambhuji scented the plot, and in a rushing move took command of Panhala.

Despite that setback, the ministers went ahead and raised Rajaram to the throne. But denied quick success, they lost momentum, and presently, with rivalries and jealousies among the Ashta-pradhans coming into play, the cabal disintegrated. Hambir Rao Mohite, the commander-in-chief, was the first to defect to Shambhuji. He was followed by Moro Pant Pingle, the Peshwa. With that the coup collapsed, so that when Shambhuji arrived in Raigarh in mid-June to claim the throne, there was no opposition to him at all. A few weeks later, on 28th July 1680, a day chosen by astrologers, Shambhuji formally ascended the throne.

MARATHA CHRONICLES SPEAK of the ill omens that appeared on Shambhuji's accession, but initially everything went off well, and the first phase of Shambhuji's reign was characterized by political moderation and martial energy. Though Shambhuji executed several of the would be king-makers, put Anaji in irons and confined Soyra Bai, most of the other partisans of Rajaram were pardoned and restored to royal favour. Rajaram himself was confined, but more as a precaution than as a punishment. He was not ill treated. Within a few months of his accession, at the end of the rainy season, Shambhuji sent his army sweeping into Khandesh, plundering the suburbs of Burhanpur, continuing Shivaji's practice of annual pillaging raids.

In all this, Shambhuji's reign neatly dovetailed into Shivaji's reign. Then, not unexpectedly, Shambhuji swerved into a path of his own. Says Khafi Khan: "Sambha . . . in his vile and evil course of life was ten times worse than his father Sivaji." Says Manucci: "Sambaji was a man of unruly habits, who seized other men's wives." "He diverts himself far too much with women and drink," noted the Dutch factors in India in a letter dated 10th February 1684.

Throughout his reign Shambhuji was under the sinister influence of Kavi Kalash, his Rasputin. Kavi Kalash was the hereditary priest of the Bhonsles in Varanasi, and it was he who took charge of Shambhuji during Shivaji's flight from Agra and later brought him safe to Raigarh. Though a distinguished scholar and poet, he was also a necromancer and tantric, a practitioner of occult rites disdained by the orthodox Hindu. Local brahmins suspected that he had cast a tantric spell on the prince, and they loathed him, if for no other reason than for worming his way into Shambhuji's favour to their exclusion.

With Shambhuji, the spirit of Maratha polity changed. Shivaji was daring but never a daredevil; meticulous preparation, caution and a fine sense of the possible marked his actions. Shambhuji, in contrast, was hot-blooded and mercurial, and therefore vulnerable. While Shivaji took care (after a disastrous early attack on Ahmadnagar) to avoid menacing Mughal political centres, fearing heavy reprisals, Shambhuji had no such inhibition, and in 1681, the second year of his reign, made an attempt on Ahmadnagar. He was too eager to prove himself.

Further, Shivaji, despite his predatory career, was an honourable man, exemplary in his personal life, principled even in his brigandage. Shambhuji had none of those high qualities. And, surprisingly for a man of his wanton ways, he was, unlike Shivaji, a religious fanatic, matching the bigotry of Aurangzeb. Thus in November 1682 he wrote a long letter to Raja Ram Singh of Amber, son of Jai Singh, taunting him to launch a holy war against Aurangzeb. Wrote Shambhuji: "The present wicked Emperor believes that we Hindus have all become effeminate and that we have lost all regard for our religion . . . We are prepared to sacrifice everything, our treasure, our land, our forts, in waging war against this satanic Emperor . . . The moment has now arrived when the Emperor himself can be captured and made prisoner with the result that we can rebuild our temples and restore our religious practices . . . When we ponder on this situation, we feel extremely surprised to find that you keep yourself so quiet and so unmindful of your religion."

Such taunts were just bravado. Shambhuji was incapable of resolute and sustained action. His campaigns were haphazard and impulsive, and what victories he won, says Manucci, "were not the fruit of his own labour, but were due to his officers. He was much more inclined to spend his time with women, amusement, and wine, than to take the field and emulate the example of valour and untiring exertion bequeathed to him by his father."

When Durgadas and Aurangzeb's rebel son Akbar arrived in Maharashtra for refuge soon after Shambhuji's accession, the Marathas had a great opportunity to form an axis with the Rajputs against Aurangzeb, but nothing came of it, for the elaborate and cool planning that the enterprise required was beyond the raja's ability. Far from being able to help Akbar, Shambhuji himself was in serious trouble during most of his reign, with clan and family feuds splintering the Maratha kingdom. Anaji Datto, whom Shambhuji had imprisoned during the succession tussle but later released and restored to office, showed his gratitude by hatching a plot to poison Shambhuji. The plot was discovered, and its ringleaders, including Anaji, were trampled to death under the feet of elephants. Soyra Bai, who was incriminated, was administered poison, and her family, the Shirkays, despoiled and hounded out. Moro Pant, the Peshwa, was again thrown into prison, along with several other senior officers. Kavi Kalash's dominance now became absolute.

THE MARATHAS UNDER Shambhuji were thus in no position to resist the Mughals when Aurangzeb arrived in the Deccan in 1681. Bijapur and Golconda, old and effete, were even more vulnerable. The emperor therefore confidently expected, according to Manucci, to complete his Deccan campaign in a couple of years. His immediate objective was to neutralize Akbar, a task that would brook no delay. Yet there was a curious hesitancy about Aurangzeb at this time. "The king's mind . . . is continually wavering and he is extraordinarily peevish and uneasy because of Sultan Akbar," English merchants in Surat noted. It was well within Aurangzeb's capacity to storm into the Maratha country and seize Akbar, but never once did he make a decisive move towards that. It was as if he did not want to capture Akbar but only to stymie him. And for that limited purpose, the mere presence of the emperor in the Deccan was enough.

This explains Aurangzeb's initial tentativeness towards the Marathas. Moreover, Aurangzeb's main goal in the Deccan was the annexation of Bijapur and Golconda, not the suppression of the Marathas, whom he continued to underestimate as mere rebels. Aurangzeb therefore made no major thrust against the Marathas for nearly a year after his arrival in the Deccan, and even when a campaign was finally launched, it was not sustained. This inaction was however mistaken for timidity by the English merchants in Karwar and Surat, who reported: "He (Aurangzeb) is so inveterate against the Raja (Shambhuji) that he hath thrown off his *pagri* (turban) and sworn never to put it on again, till he hath either killed, taken, or routed him out of his country", and yet, despite having "with him a great army . . . he sits still and attempts nothing, being under great jealousies and fears, thinks himself hardly secure."

By October 1687 the two sultanates had fallen to Aurangzeb. Then came the turn of Shambhuji. On 11th February 1689, a little over a year after the fall of Golconda, the Mughals captured Shambhuji in an ambush at Sangameshwar, a beautiful river valley surrounded by high mountains, where, says Khafi Khan, "Kabkalas (Kavi Kalash), the filthy dog, had built a house, embellished with paintings, and surrounded with a garden full of fruit trees and flowers." There Shambhuji sported, entirely "unaware of the approach of the falcon of destiny". When Maratha scouts warned him of the approach of the Mughal contingent, he dismissed it as impossible, and even "ordered the tongues of the reporters to be cut out" for babbling, says Khafi Khan. Shambhuji was certain that the Mughals could never penetrate the deep jungle.

Presently however, a small Mughal contingent under Muqarrab Khan swooped down on the unsuspecting carousers, scattered the guards, and seized Shambhuji and Kavi Kalash. "Although Sambha, in the brief interval, had shaved off his beard, smeared his face with ashes, and changed his clothes, he was discovered by a necklace of pearls under his garments, and by the gold rings upon the legs of his horse," says Khafi Khan.

Shambhuji's capture was probably facilitated by "the treachery of his leading Brahmans", as Martin notes in his diary of March 1689. Treachery is also indicated by the fact that no attempt at all was made to rescue Shambhuji during the long trek of the captors through the hills, during which they were vulnerable. Martin in fact had foreseen Shambhuji's doom, and had noted in his diary as early as November 1683: "Shambhaji Rajah continues to exercise his cruelty with regard to the . . . officers of his father, particularly against the Brahmans. It can be foreseen that this prince will ruin himself by his wicked conduct; the Brahmans never forgive, and besides their character is to govern among the Hindu princes."

There was general relief on the capture of Shambhuji, according to Khafi Khan. "The rejoicings," he says, were "great among all classes, from chaste matrons to miserable men . . . In every town and village on the road [by which Shambhuji was taken to Aurangzeb's camp] or near it, wherever the news reached, there was great delight; and wherever they passed, the doors and roofs were full of men and women, who looked on rejoicing." Khafi Khan no doubt exaggerates; most of the people, we must assume, had gathered out of curiosity, not necessarily to rejoice. Shambhuji's Maratha antagonists were of course happy to see him go; similarly, the men of property and the peaceable common people in the Deccan, to whichever community they belonged, were also probably relieved that this great disturber of peace had at last been captured. "Shambhaji Rajah had rendered himself odious to his subjects by his violence, his cruelty and his debauchery," notes Martin.

The Mughals exulted over the capture. "Satan was chained," crows Mustaid Khan. Aurangzeb received the prisoners in durbar in his camp at Bahadurgarh. The two were taken in all trussed up, especially Kavi Kalash, as a precaution against his sorcery—"his head and neck and every limb was firmly secured so that he could use only his eyes and tongue," says Khafi Khan. When they were brought in, the emperor stepped down from his throne and knelt in a prayer of thanksgiving. Seeing this, Kavi Kalash commented mockingly: "O Raja, at the sight of thee the King Alamgir, for all his pomp and dignity, cannot keep his seat upon his throne, but has perforce descended from it to do thee honour."

What was to be done with Shambhuji? Some of Aurangzeb's counsellors advised him that his life should be spared, if he surrendered his forts and revealed where his treasures were hidden. But Shambhuji and Kavi Kalash foreclosed that option by their deliberately violent abuse of the emperor. They knew, says Khafi Khan, that even if their lives were spared, "they would be kept in confinement, deprived of all the pleasures of life, and every day of life would be a new death. So both Sambha and Kabkalas indulged in abusive language, and uttered the most offensive remarks in the hearing of the Emperor's servants." Told of this, Aurangzeb ordered their tongues to be cut out, then their eyes to be gouged.

Finally, on 21st March 1689, about six weeks after their capture, they were "put to death with a variety of tortures," says Khafi Khan. The skins of their heads were then stuffed with straw and sent to be exhibited "in all the cities and towns of the Dakhin, with the beat of drum and sound of trumpet." Aurangzeb, who viewed Shambhuji as "the infernal son of the infernal infidel", would not treat him as a vanquished prince, but only as a captured bandit. And Shambhuji on his part behaved like an outlaw.

This is essentially the story as told by Khafi Khan. Other chroniclers add frills to it. Manucci says that Shambhuji on his arrival at Aurangzeb's camp was paraded through the town like a clown, before being taken to the emperor, and that "when there he ordered his side to be cloven open with an ax and his heart extracted. The body was then flung on a dunghill and abandoned to the tender mercies of the dogs." Duff, basing his story on Maratha manuscripts, says that Aurangzeb offered to save Shambhuji's life if he became a Muslim, to which Shambhuji, who "expected and wished for nothing but death", replied, "Tell the Emperor that if he will give me his daughter I will become a Mussulman"—not an improbable response from Shambhuji.

Shambhuji's nine-year reign marked the transformation of the Maratha government from Shivaji's tightly disciplined fighting machine into a barely functioning anarchy. As the state slid towards bankruptcy, Shambhuji, contrary to Shivaji's policy, farmed the revenue. This led to speculators callously exploiting peasants who, unable to bear the hardship, often abandoned their fields, further impoverishing the state.

The pernicious effect of Shambhuji's reign was worst felt in the army. Discipline, so rigorously enforced by Shivaji, now virtually disappeared. "Stragglers were allowed to join, plunder was secreted, women followers . . . were not only permitted, but women were brought off from the enemy's country as an established article of plunder, and either retained as concubines, or sold as slaves," notes Duff. As troops could not be paid regularly, they were encouraged to take to the field on their own to make up for the deficiencies in their pay—they were, says Manucci, allowed "to plunder wherever they pleased". Maratha armies were often accompanied by auxiliary marauding bands, later to be infamous as Pindaris.

The term Maratha thus became a generic term for all bandits, irrespective of their community. Soldiers disbanded from the crumbling Bijapur and Golconda sultanates joined the Maratha warlords, and occasionally even formed gangs of their own and took to the field. No loyalty bound any of them, no law or morality restrained them, and in a short time they turned the Deccan into a hellish jungle, where the omnivorous, predatory, humanoid animal roamed and hunted as he pleased. So the very name Maratha came to evoke a nameless terror among the people. Maratha lawlessness, more than anything else, was responsible for the ruination of India in early modern times, and they so vandalized India's political fabric that it crumbled at the mere touch of the British.

ON 18TH FEBRUARY, a week after Shambhuji was captured, but nearly five weeks before his execution—again indicating premeditation—the brahmin oligarchs, whom Shambhuji had disdained to favour, brought Rajaram, now nineteen, out of confinement and crowned him king in Raigarh. "They planned their measures with wisdom, unanimity, and firmness," says Duff. Shambhuji's son Shahu was only·six then, and not even his mother, Yesu Bai, made a claim for him.

Rajaram had little chance of surviving on the throne. With Bijapur and Golconda fallen, the entire focus of Mughal attention was now on the Marathas. Rajaram was not safe in Raigarh, or anywhere else in Maharashtra. For his own safety, as well as for the survival of the state, it was essential to put a great distance between the raja and the Mughals. In this crisis, Prahlad Niraji, a high Maratha noble, took charge of Rajaram, carried him out of Raigarh, and with an escort of just 300 soldiers took him first to the southern fort of Panhala, where they rested during the monsoon, and finally to Gingee in the Tamil country, as far away from the Mughal reach as they could get.

The fugitives travelled disguised as religious mendicants. Even then, it was a most hazardous journey, menaced all along the way by Mughal patrols alerted by Aurangzeb. On a couple of occasions they were very nearly captured. Often they travelled on foot, with Niraji "frequently carrying him (Rajaram) on his own shoulders when the Raja was too weak to walk," notes Martin in his diary. On 11th November 1689, after a seven-month odyssey, they finally reached Gingee and took over the fort from the reluctant hands of Ambika Bai, Shivaji's daughter (whose deceased husband had been the governor of the region) and her minor son.

Prahlad Niraji saved the Maratha state. In October 1689 the Mughals stormed Raigarh and seized Shambhuji's family, including his wife Yesu Bai and her young son Shahu. Aurangzeb treated the captives with courtesy—Shahu was conferred the title raja and given the rank of 7000, two steps higher than what had once been given to Shivaji—but they would be detained by the Mughals for eighteen years, until Aurangzeb's death. If Prahlad had not taken Rajaram to Gingee, the Maratha state would not have had a legitimate nucleus around which to cohere, and probably would not have survived.

Not surprisingly, Rajaram treated Prahlad "as a father", notes Martin. Prahlad was not of course labouring solely out of love for

Rajaram; he had, as Martin writes, "his own designs". As Prathinidhi, Royal Deputy, a post specially created for him, Prahlad became the de facto ruler of the Marathas. Rajaram did not mind. He was an easygoing prince, addicted to opium and sensual pleasures. Notes Martin: Prahlad "threw the young prince into pleasures and amusements . . . he made him marry three or four women during the first two or three months after his arrival. The dancing girls, without whom the Hindus do not believe any feast to be complete, were brought by the minister to the Court in many troupes . . . and they served for other purposes [as well]."

When Rajaram mounted the throne in Gingee, "gold bangles, clothes, shawls, and letters announcing the event were secretly forwarded and . . . presented to all the principal Hindoos throughout Maharashtra," notes Duff. That bore the promise that the Maratha state would endure.

But before we take up the story of Maratha revival, we have to turn to the fates of Bijapur and Golconda.

Rafizi-kush

DURING THE FIRST twenty-three years of his reign, Aurangzeb had paid only partial attention to Deccan affairs. He remained in the north, first waiting for Shah Jahan to die, and then occupied with several military campaigns as well as with the formulation of his theocratic policies. During that period he confined himself primarily to a holding operation in the Deccan, keeping his frontiers intact while attempting to weaken the Deccan kingdoms by setting them against each other and by fomenting internal dissension. Occasionally the Mughals did make forays into Bijapur and Golconda, but made no significant gains, as the Mughal army in the Deccan was often weaker than the opposing Deccani forces. Aurangzeb, who saw the world in the image of his own paranoid self and would trust no one, especially his sons, was reluctant to assign strong armies to his proconsuls in the Deccan, for fear of rebellion.

The Deccan sultanates did what they could to avert or delay their annihilation. Ali Adil Shah II, the Sultan of Bijapur, tried to propitiate Aurangzeb on his accession with substantial gifts, and later cooperated (at least outwardly) with both Shayista Khan and Jai Singh in their operations against Shivaji. But Adil Shah was playing a double or triple role, as dictated by his own survival requirements. Towards the Mughals he was overtly submissive, but secretly subversive, knowing that conflict with them was in the end inevitable. Similarly, in his dealings with the Marathas, he sought to discourage them from making incursions into Bijapur, and at the same time secretly encouraged them to resist the advance of the Mughals.

The Mughals were no doubt aware of all this. "Adil Khan in his folly played false with me," wrote Jai Singh to Aurangzeb. "He outwardly sent an army into Shiva's territory; but he considered the utter destruction of Shiva to be harmful to his interests and wished Shiva to stand as a wall between the imperial troops and Bijapuris." Furthermore, Jai Singh noted, Adil Shah had persuaded Golconda to send money to Shivaji "while he was all the time breathing loyalty to the Emperor". These actions of Adil Shah gave the Mughals an excuse to invade Bijapur. Moreover, substantial amounts of war indemnity were still due from Bijapur to the emperor. So in 1666, when Jai Singh, after securing the submission of Shivaji, sought permission to invade Bijapur, Aurangzeb acceded to the request.

Jai Singh opened his campaign in November 1665, after softening up some of the Bijapur officers with bribes. As the Mughals approached, the sultan tried to avoid war by offering to meet the Mughal demands, but the raja spurned the offer. Jai Singh was determined to cap his career with the conquest of Bijapur. He was confident of a quick victory.

Bitter disappointment awaited the raja. Bijapur, though a small kingdom compared to the Mughal empire, had substantial resources and a strong enough army to thwart the Mughals. It had, in 1656, an annual revenue of 78.4 million rupees and in addition received 52.5 million rupees as tribute from vassal rajas and zemindars; it had an army of 80,000 cavalry, 250,000 infantry and 530 elephants. Though a part of this wealth and power had since then attenuated, Bijapur was still a major power, and was furthermore buttressed by a contingent of 12,000 cavalry and 40,000 infantry sent from Golconda to counter the Mughal invasion. The morale of the Bijapuri army, despite many of its officers being corrupted by the Mughals, was high, and they fought tenaciously. Though Jai Singh did make rapid progress initially and was at Bijapur city by the first week of January 1666, once he got there he realized that it would be impossible for him to capture the fort by force.

He had brought no siege guns with him, expecting to capture the city by bribery and stratagem. That did not work. Bijapuris had prepared themselves with ruthless thoroughness for the defence of the city. "The embankments of the tanks were cut," writes Khafi Khan, "poisonous matters and carrion were thrown in the wells, the trees and lofty buildings near the fortress were destroyed, spikes were fixed in the ground and the gardens and houses on both sides of the city were so destroyed that not a trace of culture was left near the city." Bijapuri flying columns hung around the invading forces, harassing them, raiding imperial territories in the rear, and threatening the Mughal lines of communication and supply. Jai Singh then pleaded with Aurangzeb to advance into the Deccan himself, to clinch the victory, but the emperor refused.

Despite all the handicaps, Jai Singh invested Bijapur for eight months, spending, in addition to the four million rupees Aurangzeb allotted to the campaign, ten million rupees of his own funds, hoping to recover the amount on the annexation of Bijapur. All of it came to nothing, and in the end he was compelled to lift the siege and pull out.

Fighting his way back, harassed continually by the enemy, he returned to Aurangabad by the end of the year.

The campaign was an unmitigated disaster. A great career thus ended in a sorry whimper. Censured by Aurangzeb and recalled to court, Jai Singh died on the way at Burhanpur in mid-July 1667.

FOR ABOUT SIX years, from Jai Singh's retreat until 1673, Bijapur was not molested either by the Mughals or the Marathas—Prince Muazzam, who replaced Jai Singh as governor in the Deccan, was sluggish, and Shivaji was in one of his rare quiet phases. It was however only a respite from war, not peace. Perhaps realizing the hopelessness of the future, Ali Adil Shah II, who had toiled for a decade and half for the preservation of his kingdom, now sank into a life of amnesic dissipation. Predictably, when he died in December 1672, felled by a paralytic stroke, the kingdom itself fell into its death spasm.

This was an opportunity that the Mughals and the Marathas could not pass up. Shivaji was the first to pounce. When Ali was succeeded by his four-year-old son, Sikandar, and the kingdom split into squabbling factions, Shivaji swept into Bijapur, seizing several forts and pillaging extensive tracts of the kingdom, even the neighbourhood of Bijapur. The Mughals were slow to react, as Bahadur Khan, who had in 1672 taken over the Deccan command under Prince Muazzam, had been advised by the emperor to concentrate on the defence of the imperial frontiers, not on expansion. He had been well advised, for when in 1676 he finally invaded Bijapur, he suffered an embarrassing defeat. Though Bahadur Khan later succeeded in bullying Bijapur into surrendering a couple of forts, Aurangzeb was displeased with him, and replaced him with the hyperactive Dilir Khan, who promptly plunged into the vortex of Deccani politics.

In 1678, Dilir Khan helped Sidi Masud, an Abyssinian amir, to become the Vizier of Bijapur, on the understanding that he would rule as a Mughal agent. The deal outraged Bijapuris. Even more galling to them was Masud's offer to send Shahr Banu, the royal princess, to Delhi to marry Prince Azam. The precocious princess, sixteen, wise beyond her years and beautiful, was the pride of the people of Bijapur, and they resented her being bartered away.

In the face of the public tumult, Masud backed out of his agreement with Dilir Khan and entered into a secret pact with Shivaji against the Mughals. But no secret in medieval India was ever a secret, so the pact precipitated the immediate Mughal invasion of Bijapur. Shahr Banu, in a melancholy bid to save her brother's crown, then voluntarily went off to the Mughals—the people of Bijapur lined the streets to bid her an emotional farewell—but Dilir Khan, though he received the princess with due honours and sent her on to Aurangabad, continued to advance towards Bijapur city.

Dilir Khan was no more successful than Jai Singh or Bahadur Khan in seizing Bijapur, so he skirted the city and set about ravaging the countryside, especially Shivaji's Karnataka lands, in retaliation for the Maratha pillage of Mughal lands. But in the end he too had to retreat from Bijapur in disgrace, after suffering a humiliating defeat in March 1680 at the hands of the tribal Berads in their belt between the Krishna and Bhima rivers. Aurangzeb was furious. "Your first duty was to guard the imperial dominions," he wrote to Dilir Khan. "What folly is this that you have practised? You have neither protected my dominions, nor gained your object. Withdraw quickly from the siege of Bijapur to the defence of the empire."

Soon after Dilir Khan's retreat, the scene in the Deccan changed dramatically. Shivaji died in April 1680, the rebel prince Akbar arrived in the Deccan, and, chasing him, Aurangzeb himself. Once Aurangzeb arrived, it was only a matter of time before the Mughal juggernaut rolled over virtually all of peninsular India.

There were several proximate causes and provocations for the Mughal annexation of Bijapur and Golconda, but their fate was in any case sealed by the inevitable tidal swell of Mughal imperial expansion into the Deccan. Aurangzeb however had a problem which had not troubled his predecessors: his Chief Kazi, Abdul Wahab, declared that it was unlawful for Aurangzeb, the champion of Islam, to attack fellow Muslim monarchs. Aurangzeb's answer was that the Deccan sultans, being Shiahs, were little different from infidels—a predictable response from a monarch who habitually called the Shiahs *rafizi*, heretics, abused them in his letters as *ghul-i-bayabani*, corpse-eating demons, and named his favourite dagger Rafizi-kush, heretic slayer.

Initially, for about four years after Aurangzeb's arrival in the Deccan, there was not much Mughal pressure on Bijapur, because of the emperor's preoccupation with Prince Akbar, but in the summer of 1685 the Mughals intensified their campaign against the sultanate, and advanced to besiege the city of Bijapur. The siege, under the overall command of Prince Azam, went on for some thirteen months, still Bijapur remained defiant. In July 1686 the emperor himself arrived at Bijapur to take charge of the campaign, and two months later, the Bijapur army, having withstood the siege for over fifteen months, their ranks reduced to just 2000 men, surrendered the city. On 22nd September 1686, Sikandar Adil Shah, the boy-king now eighteen, the last ruler of the two-century-old dynasty, came out of the city and surrendered to Aurangzeb.

Sikandar was received graciously by Aurangzeb in durbar, and was given a seat on the emperor's right, the place of honour. "I shall exalt you with many favours and gifts. Be composed in mind," Aurangzeb told him. A pension of 100,000 rupees was settled on him, and for fourteen years he vegetated in Mughal captivity, till his death in 1700.

Aurangzeb entered Bijapur seated on a portable throne, scattering gold and silver coins. He was, it turned out, performing the last rites of this once gracious and prosperous city. A devastating bubonic plague felled half the city's population soon after its fall, and Bijapur became a ghost city, its nobility impoverished, its artisans, scholars and poets scattered and without sustenance.

AFTER BIJAPUR CAME the turn of Golconda. The kingdom had been ruled for forty-six long but undistinguished years by Abdullah, the sixth king of the Qutb Shah dynasty. During most of his reign he was content to leave the government to his masterful mother Hayat Bakhsh Begum, and when she died, to his eldest son-in-law, Nizamuddin Ahmad, who governed for six years. "The King has lost all mental energy and has ceased to hold the reins of government," says Bernier. "He never appears in public to give audience and administer justice according to the custom of the country, nor does he venture outside the walls of the fortress of Golconda. Confusion and misrule are the natural and unavoidable consequences of this state of things. The grandees, totally disregarding the commands of a monarch for whom they no longer feel either affection or respect, exercise a disgusting tyranny."

Abdullah spent most of his time with dancing girls, "practising ingenious forms of sensuality". Under his indulgent rule, Golconda became notorious for its decadent lifestyle. Hyderabad, the capital city, abounded in prostitutes—reputedly some 20,000 of them—and taverns. According to Tavernier, 1200 large leather bottles of toddy were drunk daily in Hyderabad.

Abdullah had no sons, only three daughters, so when he died in 1672 the choice of his successor had to be made from among his sons-in-law. The eldest of them, Nizamuddin, was unacceptable to the amirs because of his arrogance; the second, Aurangzeb's rebel son Muhammad Sultan, was a prisoner in Gwalior; so the choice fell on Abul Hasan, the youngest son-in-law, whom the amirs expected to be pliable in their hands. Abul Hasan did not disappoint them. As prince, says Manucci,

Abul Hasan was "poor and despised, passing his life in taverns and shops, looking on at dancing and listening to music." As sultan, he affected some dignity, but still preferred pleasure to power, and engrossed himself with music and dance, wine and women. His pride was in being known as Tana Shah, Refined King.

Like his father-in-law, Abul Hasan was happy to leave the chores of government to others, in his case to his Vizier Madanna, a Vaishnavite brahmin from a poor family who had joined government service as a clerk and wormed his way to the highest office through talent, guile and intrigue. For twelve years, till his violent death in March 1686, Madanna in effect ruled Golconda, assisted by his brother Akkanna and his nephew Rustam Rao. "Madanna has sole control, and nothing is thought of but peeling and squeezing the people," reported the English factors in Madras in July 1676. "The government of the country is now in so bad hands that nothing but fraud and oppression [prevail], and [officials are] so void of shame that no credit can be given to either agreements, promises, *qauls* or *farmans*."

Abul Hasan was no doubt aware of what was going on, but he preferred to overlook it. He knew that the days of his dynasty were numbered, that the Mughal annexation of Golconda was inevitable, no matter what he did to avert it. The most he could do was to delay that fate, and with that object in mind he took care not to offend Aurangzeb in any manner. As an alternative line of defence, he also entered into a secret pact with Shivaji, paying him an annual subsidy of 500,000 rupees.

The abject subservience of the sultan, instead of pleasing the emperor, displeased him greatly, for Abul Hasan's humility was an impediment to the emperor's plan to annex the kingdom. He therefore sent Mirza Muhammad, a rough and impudent amir, as his special emissary to Golconda, somehow to provoke the sultan into doing something improper. Ostensibly, Muhammad was sent to ask for two famous diamonds said to be in Abul Hasan's possession, but Aurangzeb, according to Khafi Khan, told the ambassador confidentially: "I am not really sending you there to get these useless bits of stone, which I do not care for. My sole intention is that you should not humour him, but bandy words with him so fearlessly that he too may be harsh to you and thus give me a justification for extirpating him. As far as possible quarrel with him, and never treat him politely in private or public."

Aurangzeb professed not to care for the "bits of stone", but he kept on exacting whatever money and treasure he could from the Sultan. "Thus did the poor King of Golconda become a petty prince," says Manucci. "He attempted no further to turn himself into a valiant warrior, but passed his time continuously in feasting among musicians and dancers." Whatever the provocation, Abul Hasan refused to be provoked, preferring, as Sarkar puts it, "ease at the expense of honour." He knew and accepted his fate, and tried to make the best of it, meeting Mirza Muhammad's insolence with good humour and ready wit. Once, when the ambassador objected to the sultan calling himself king, Abul Hasan twitted: "If we are not to be called kings, how can Aurangzeb be styled the king of kings?"

But neither good humour nor humility would save the sultan from the humourless, pitiless emperor. In the end, however, it was an indiscretion of Abul Hasan that gave an opening to Aurangzeb. In a confidential letter to his representative in Aurangzeb's camp in Bijapur, the sultan wrote: "The emperor is a great man, and has acted magnanimously up to this time, but now, finding Sikandar a helpless orphan, he has laid siege to Bijapur and pressed him hard," and went on to state that he intended to send an army of 40,000 men for the defence of Bijapur. Unfortunately, the letter fell into the hands of Aurangzeb.

AURANGZEB RESPONDED TO the provocation of Abul Hasan's indiscreet letter by sending, in July 1685, an army into Golconda under the command of Prince Muazzam, expecting quick victory. But the Mughal advance was blocked for more than two months by a numerically superior Golconda army, and Muazzam could eventually clear his way only by bribing the commander-in-chief of Golconda. When the news of the commander's treachery reached Abul Hasan in Hyderabad, he fled precipitately from the city into the nearby Golconda fort, to escape capture by the rapidly advancing Mughal army. "Without consulting with any of his nobles, or even caring anything for his property or the honour of his own women and family, or of others, he fled with a few servants by night, with boxes full of such valuables as he could carry, to the fort of Golconda," says Khafi Khan.

As the sultan fled, so did the citizens, and the city was taken over by looters and rapists. "A noise and tumult arose like that of doomsday," says Khafi Khan. "Carpets of great value, which were too heavy to carry, were cut to pieces with swords and daggers, and every bit was struggled for." Property worth forty or fifty million rupees was looted, according to Khafi Khan. "Even the doors were taken off their hinges," says Bhimsen, an eyewitness to much of what happened during Aurangzeb's Deccan campaign. "The women of the soldiers and of the inhabitants of the city were subjected to dishonour, and great disorder and destruction prevailed," reports Khafi Khan. "Many thousands of high-born persons, being unable to take horses and carry off their property, in the greatest distress took the hands of their children and wives, many of whom could not even seize a veil or sheet to cover them, and fled to the fortress."

Beaten, Abul Hasan continued to cringe, sending peace appeals to Muazzam, "most humbly and earnestly begging forgiveness of the sins which he had and had not committed", as Khafi Khan puts it. Aurangzeb then dictated the terms of peace, by which Abul Hasan agreed to dismiss Madanna and Akkanna, cede the districts of Malkhed and Seram to the Mughals, pay twelve million rupees towards past dues of tribute, and thereafter pay an annual tribute of 200,000 *huns*.

The execution of a part of the accord was taken over by the Muslim mob in Golconda, who, at the instigation of what Khafi Khan calls "some women of great influence in the harem", murdered Madanna and Akkanna in the streets of Golconda as they came out of the palace one night, sacked their residences and raided the Hindu quarters in the fort, looting and killing. "Many Brahmins lost their lives and property that day," says Khafi Khan. "The heads of the two brothers were cut off, and were sent to Prince Shah Alam (Muazzam) by the hands of a discreet person" as a peace offering. Aurangzeb then ordered Muazzam to withdraw from Golconda.

However, within weeks of Muazzam's retreat, Aurangzeb himself advanced against Golconda, cavalierly sweeping aside the assurances he had given to the hapless Sultan. He furthermore "added meanness to his want of faith", says Duff, by instructing Sadat Khan, his ambassador in Golconda, to extract as much of Golconda's treasure as he could "by working on the hopes and fears of that weak prince". Abul Hasan even stripped off the jewels of his women, hoping to pacify Aurangzeb and stave off annexation. Still Aurangzeb kept advancing. So Abul Hasan once again took refuge in the Golconda fort, from where he wrote to Aurangzeb with protestations of obedience and seeking forgiveness. "But the Emperor's only reply was the sword," says Mustaid Khan.

Characteristically, Aurangzeb claimed that he was motivated by high moral purpose to invade Golconda, and listed the crimes of Abul Hasan that justified the invasion. "The evil deeds of this wicked man pass beyond the bounds of writing; but by mentioning one out of a hundred, and a little out of much, some conception of them may be formed," he wrote. "First, placing the reins of authority and government in the hands of vile, tyrannical infidels; oppressing and afflicting the Sayyids, Sheikhs, and other holy men; openly giving himself to excessive debauchery and depravity; indulging in drunkenness and wickedness night and day; making no distinction between infidelity and Islam, tyranny and justice, depravity and devotion; waging obstinate war in defence of infidels; want of obedience to Divine commands and prohibitions, especially to that command which forbids assistance to an enemy's country . . . Letters full of friendly advice and warning upon these points had been repeatedly written, and had been sent by the hands of discreet men. No attention had been paid to them; moreover, it had lately become known that a lakh of *pagodas* (*huns*) had been sent to the wicked Sambha . . ."

Faced with Aurangzeb's implacability, Abul Hasan finally decided to go down fighting. Golconda was a virtually impregnable fort, well provisioned and heavily armed. The Mughals on the other hand were handicapped by dissensions and rivalries among their commanders—Prince Muazzam was in treasonable contact with Abul Hasan and was taking bribes from him; imperial officers, envious of each other, often worked at cross purposes; the emperor's Shiah officers were slack in the campaign against the last Shiah ruler in India; Aurangzeb's orthodox Chief Kazi condemned the invasion as sinful. But nothing deterred Aurangzeb. He ordered the arrest of Prince Muazzam and his sons—they were kept in confinement for several years, their properties confiscated—and proceeded with the siege.

Abul Hasan was equally resolute. He poured such incessant fire on the besiegers that, according to Mustaid Khan, "the fort looked as if made of fire; the smoke turned the day into night." Outside the fort, a Golconda army of 40,000 continually harassed the Mughals. The siege, which began on 7th February 1687, dragged on for eight months. An attempt to escalade the fort secretly at night was discovered and frustrated by the defenders alerted by the barking of a pariah dog. (Abul Hasan honoured the dog with a gold chain, a jewelled collar and a gold-embroidered coat, and, says Khafi Khan, "directed that the dog should be kept chained near to himself.")

Golconda's position was of course hopeless. Abul Hasan could only delay defeat, not avert it. He knew that. So, even while stoutly defending the fort, he tried to reason with Aurangzeb. "If Golconda is left to me as a vassal paying tribute, it would be more profitable to the Emperor than if he annexes it and governs it by a viceroy, as the expense of the latter course would swallow up the entire revenue of the province," he wrote Aurangzeb. "It will take seven or eight years to restore cultivation and population to this war-wasted land, and during that period the Mughals will get nothing out of it. If, on the other hand, Aurangzeb makes peace and retires beyond my frontiers, I shall pay him one crore (ten million) of rupees as an indemnity, besides one crore in honour of every assault that he has led in person." The Sultan even offered to send grain from the fort for the provision-short imperial army. But Aurangzeb would not relent. "If Abul Hasan is really submissive to me, as he professes to be, let him come with his arms tied together and rope round his neck, and then I shall confer on him any favour that I may consider proper," he replied.

Aurangzeb would not relent even when conditions in the Mughal camp turned grim, as the enemy's flying columns cut off supplies and reduced the Mughals to a state of virtual famine. On top of that, the monsoon burst over Golconda, miring the Mughals in ankle-deep slush. As the Mughal army grew dispirited and weary, the Deccanis, showing unexpected spirit, made daring sorties out of the fort, on occasion capturing Mughal forward positions and spiking their guns. The defenders also effectively counter-mined to neutralize the mines run by the Mughals to the fort walls, and on a couple of occasions when the mines were fired, the stones rained on the Mughals themselves, killing many, but doing little damage to the fort. And when Aurangzeb, to show his firmness, himself advanced to the frontline to order an assault, a tempest broke over the battlefield, so that the assailants were forced to fall back drenched in rain.

The portents were not good for the Mughals. Conditions got even worse when a pestilence broke out in the famine-ravaged Mughal camp. "The city of Hyderabad was utterly depopulated; houses, river, and plain were all filled with corpses," says Mustaid Khan. "The same condition prevailed in the Mughal camp. At night piles of the dead used to accumulate, and next day the sweepers used to fling them, without funeral, on the bank of the river. This happened day after day. The survivors in the agony of hunger ate the carrion of men and beasts. For miles and miles around, the eye rested only on mounds of corpses. Happily, the ceaseless rain melted away the flesh and the skin, otherwise the rotting carcasses would have poisoned the air and dispatched even the men spared by the famine." Says Ishwardas, "Gradually things came to such a pass that not a single person could keep his balance of mind. Everybody lost hope of life. It was not a war but an example of The Divine Curse."

None of that weakened Aurangzeb's resolve. Rather, he now redoubled his efforts, setting up a stockade of wood and mud to encircle the fort, to prevent all ingress and egress and thus to starve the defenders into submission. But that did not work either, for the fort was well provisioned. Finally, bribery opened the gates of the fort. At around 3 a.m. one night early in October 1687, a traitor let a small

Mughal contingent sneak into the fort and open a gate for the Mughal army to storm in. As Khafi Khan puts it, "the fortune of Alamgir at length prevailed, and after a siege of eight months and ten days, the place fell into his hands; but by good fortune, not by force of sword or spear."

Abul Hasan surrendered with grace and dignity. When he realized that the Mughals had penetrated the fort, "he went into his harem to comfort his women, to ask pardon of them, and take leave of them," says Khafi Khan. "Then, though his heart was sad, he controlled himself, and went to his reception room, and took his seat upon the *masnad* (throne), and watched for the coming of his unbidden guests. When the time for taking his meal arrived, he ordered food to be served. As Ruhulla Khan (a Mughal commander) and others arrived, he saluted them all, and never for a moment lost his dignity. With perfect self-control he received them with courtesy, and spoke to them with warmth and elegance." He then called for his horse and accompanied the Mughal amirs to Prince Azam, who escorted him to Aurangzeb.

The emperor received the sultan courteously, and sent him to be confined in Daulatabad. An annual pension of 50,000 rupees was settled on him. Property worth sixty-eight million rupees, "besides jewels, inlaid articles and vessels of gold and silver", was seized from the fort. The kingdom, which had a potential annual revenue of thirty million rupees, was then annexed to the empire.

After the fall of Golconda, only the Marathas remained outside the Mughal grasp. Sixteen months later, the Mughals captured and executed Shambhuji. And with that Aurangzeb's triumph seemed complete. "There are many different princes in the Carnatic, but they could not agree to a joint defence," writes Manucci; "then he (Aurangzeb), like a dexterous falcon, pounced upon them." An immense sweep of land, from Kabul across the entire Indian subcontinent, except the southernmost tip beyond the Kaveri River ruled by petty chieftains, lay at the feet of one man. Aurangzeb, seventy-one, had become the master of the largest empire India had known.

But at the moment of his supreme triumph, Aurangzeb found to his horror that the very ground on which he stood was crumbling. The Maratha dragon which he thought he had slain, turned out to be a hydra: each head that he cut off grew as two, the serpent slithering and pullulating in eerie, maddening chaos. It was a nightmare from which Aurangzeb would not awaken.

Maratha Eruption

AFTER THE EXECUTION of Shambhuji in 1689, there seemed to be nothing more for Aurangzeb to do in the Deccan. All that he had set out for had been achieved. Would he then return to Delhi? Asad Khan, his Vizier, suggested that he should. "Praised be God! that through the grace of the great Omnipotent and the never-to-decay fortune [of your Majesty], two great kingdoms have been conquered," Asad petitioned. "It is now good policy that the imperial standards should return to Paradise-like Hindustan, so that the world may know that nothing more remains for the Emperor to do."

Aurangzeb knew better. "I wonder how an all-knowing hereditary servant like you could make such a request," he indignantly wrote across the petition. "If your wish is that men might know that no work now remains to be done, it would be contrary to truth. So long as a single breath of this mortal life remains, there is no release from labour and work." And so it would be. For nearly another two decades, till the end of his life, Aurangzeb would toil on unremittingly in the Deccan, fighting endless battles, besieging obscure hill forts, subjugating petty tribal chieftains. He did not know how to stop. His victories were all Pyrrhic now; the more battles he won, the weaker he grew.

This awful fate was not, however, evident in 1689. In fact, the next ten years were a relatively quiet and peaceful time for Aurangzeb, a good part of it spent in tranquil pastoral settings, in villages like Galgala on the Krishna south-west of Bijapur and Brahmapuri on the Bhima near Solapur. During this period Aurangzeb occupied himself with overseeing the consolidation of the newly conquered lands, but was not personally engaged in any campaigns. The only military task that remained, it seemed to him, was to mop up the remnants of the shattered Deccani states, a task that his generals were accomplishing with fair success. There were of course the Maratha bands lurking in the background, but Aurangzeb tended to underestimate their potential.

FOR ABOUT A year after the capture of Shambhuji the Marathas were quiet. Then they erupted again, rumbling out of the earth into which

Aurangzeb thought he had pounded them. Curiously, it was the destruction of the Maratha central authority that gave the Marathas their explosive potency. Says Manucci, "It is a remarkable thing to see these leaders, so many in number, yet without any prince to direct them, make war on the Mogul . . . by their foresight and valour they continue to be constantly victorious." As Duff puts it, the breakdown of the organized Maratha state "had a wonderful effect in extending predatory power". More than that, the virtual absence of a centralizing royal authority gave the Maratha campaigns the aspect of a people's war, almost a nationalist aspect.

This baffled Aurangzeb. He could not comprehend what he was up against. He thought that all that remained for him to do was to take a few hill forts. But taking a fort or a town or even crushing a particular army meant nothing in the fight against the Marathas. They had no one centre, no particular base. Not even any regular army. The numerous bands into which they divided to sweep the land, most of them led by desperadoes, often would not even stand and fight, for their objective was not power, but plunder; they were not interested in defeating the Mughals but only in pillaging and fleeing. As the Mughals kept spinning around, chasing the elusive Marathas everywhere, they lost all bearing and all control.

Aurangzeb initially viewed Rajaram as the person to be attacked, and Gingee, his seat, as the fort to be taken, and he sent a large force under Zulfiqar Khan to besiege it. It took Zulfiqar eight years to capture Gingee—not because of the fierceness of Maratha resistance, but because the general was in no hurry to take the fort.

The siege was a sham. It had become the established custom for Mughal field commanders to drag on campaigns as much as possible, for as long as they were in the field they wielded enormous power, while back at court they would be just flunkeys. The Mughal army was not so much besieging Gingee as camping beside it. Sometimes Zulfiqar set out on tangential campaigns, such as his foray down the east coast towards Thanjavur, to exact the submission of Shahji II, son and successor of Ekoji, but he delayed the capture of Gingee as much as possible. "Zulfiqar Khan has been frequently ordered to take Gingee," reported the English merchants in Madras in November 1696, "and it has been in his power to do so and destroy all the Marathas in the country. But instead of that it appears plain that he hath joined council with them." Confirms Bhimsen: "If he had wished it, he could have captured the fort on the very day that he reached Gingee. But it is the practice of generals to prolong operations." It was suspected that Zulfiqar was in secret correspondence with Rajaram, wanting to set up his own principality in the Deccan on the expected imminent death of Aurangzeb.

Zulfiqar was later joined at Gingee by his father Asad Khan, the imperial Vizier, and Prince Kam Bakhsh, but that only created fresh complications for the Mughals, setting off new tensions, spawning new traitorous plots, which in the end led to the arrest and confinement of the prince by the general for intriguing with the Marathas. The siege made little progress, and the Marathas dominated the countryside, virtually besieging the besiegers. It was only when Aurangzeb pressed hard on Zulfiqar to produce results that the general finally, in January 1698, stormed Gingee, but not before, it was suspected, warning Rajaram about the intended action, to enable the raja to escape. Rajaram fled north to Satara, which then became the seat of his government.

IF THE MUGHALS worked at cross purposes, so did the Marathas. "Among the Marathas not much union was seen," writes Bhimsen. "Every one called himself a sardar and went out to plunder [on his own account]." The Maratha factions often fought against each other, and several of the premier Maratha clans, including the Jadhavas (Shivaji's mother Jija Bai's family) and the Shirkeys (the family of Rajaram's mother) fought on the Mughal side against their compatriots.

There was no unity even among the Maratha royalists. Some semblance of centralized authority was maintained by Prahlad Niraji as long as he was alive, but when he died the year before the fall of Gingee, the latent tensions among the Maratha leaders came to the fore. The most destructive of these conflicts was the rivalry between Dhanaji Jadhav and Santaji Ghorpare, the legendary Maratha generals.

Santaji was a military genius, an unrivalled master of guerrilla warfare. He was the terror of the Mughals. "Everyone who encountered him was either killed or wounded and made prisoner; or if any one did escape, it was with his mere life, with the loss of his army and baggage," says Khafi Khan. "Nothing could be done, for wherever the accursed dog went and threatened an attack, there was no imperial amir bold enough to resist him, and every loss he inflicted on their forces made the boldest warriors quake . . . Aurangzeb was greatly distressed."

Meticulous planning which left no chance for failure, rapid movement, precise timing and coordination were the key to Santaji's success. He therefore demanded instant and unquestioning execution of his orders, and was a ruthless disciplinarian. "For a trifling offence he would cast a man under the feet of an elephant," says Khafi Khan.

Santaji was egomaniacal, arrogant, hot-tempered and dictatorial. Few liked him, though he was held in awe by all. In contrast, Dhanaji, a great-grandson of Shivaji's maternal uncle, was suave, cool, gracious, generous and unfailingly courteous. Dhanaji was a lesser general, but a greater man. And he was liked by all. Except, of course, by Santaji. The two generals were bitterly jealous of each other and jostled for the office of the commander-in-chief of the Maratha army. Niraji had managed to get them to work in tandem, but on his death the rivals became enemies and clashed openly, which led to the defeat and eventual assassination of Santaji.

The crisis of leadership among the Marathas deepened further when Rajaram, who had been suffering from "a spitting of blood and inflammation of the lungs", died in March 1700 at Sinhgarh. His two surviving wives then set up their infant sons as rival kings—Tara Bai Mohite raised her son as Shivaji II, while her rival, Rajas Bai, raised her son as Shambhuji II, splitting the Marathas into two warring groups. There was even a third party, supporting the claim of Shahu, son of Shambhuji, still in Mughal custody.

The Marathas, it seemed likely, would rip themselves apart limb from limb. What saved them was the genius of Tara Bai, Rajaram's widow, a woman of spirit, sagacity and finely tuned Maratha craftiness. She "was a clever, intelligent woman, and obtained a reputation during her husband's lifetime for her knowledge of civil and military matters," says Khafi Khan. On the death of Rajaram, she moved swiftly to assert herself. She secured the support of top Maratha officials, placed Rajas Bai in confinement, and, assisted by Parashuram Trimbak, who was appointed Prathinidhi, took charge of the Maratha destiny.

Tara Bai confounded not only her Maratha rivals, but Aurangzeb as well. According to Khafi Khan, when Aurangzeb received the news of Rajaram's death, he "ordered the drums of rejoicing to be beaten . . . the soldiers congratulated each other . . . saying that another prime mover in the strife was removed . . . and that it would not be difficult to overcome two young children and a helpless woman. They thought their enemy weak, contemptible and helpless; but Tara Bai . . . showed great powers of command and government, and from day to day the war spread and the power of the Mahrattas increased."

Initially Tara Bai sought to buy peace by offering to surrender several forts to Aurangzeb, in return for her son being recognized as Rajaram's successor and given the Mughal rank of 7000. This was a ploy to gain time, Aurangzeb suspected, and he rejected the offer. There could at best be a truce, but not peace. And presently, as expected, Tara Bai "took vigorous measures for ravaging the imperial territory," says Khafi Khan. "She won the hearts of her officers, and for all the struggles and schemes, the campaigns and sieges of Aurangzeb up to the end of his reign, the power of the Mahrattas increased day by day."

SOON AURANGZEB WAS in deeper trouble than he had ever been. "By hard fighting, by the expenditure of the vast treasures accumulated by Shah Jahan, and by the sacrifice of many thousands of men, he had penetrated into their wretched country, had subdued their lofty forts, and had driven them from house and home; still the daring of the Mahrattas increased, and they penetrated into the old territories of the Imperial throne, plundering and destroying wherever they went," writes Khafi Khan. "Their daring went beyond all bounds . . . They fall upon and plunder large caravans within ten or twelve *kos* (thirty or forty kilometres) of the imperial camp, and have even had the hardihood to attack royal treasure." In villages where no ready money was available, Maratha raiders now began to accept promissory notes from the headmen, confident of their power to redeem them later. From traders they collected protection money for each cart or laden bullock. Says Bhimsen: "From the Narmada southwards, throughout the entire Deccan, in every pargana and village, the Marathas have spread like ants and locusts."

Tara Bai did not initiate or control all this action; she merely rode the wave of Maratha insurgency and gave it a general direction. Clearly, what was emerging out of the chaos in the Deccan was not a unified Maratha kingdom but a loose military confederacy, which was linked to the central authority but not governed by it. Shivaji's system of paying salaries to officers had by now completely disappeared. "The servants of the Maratha state support themselves by plundering on all sides, and pay a small part of their booty to their king, getting no salary from them," says Bhimsen.

Despite such anarchic tendencies, the Maratha captains were at this time gradually making the transition from banditry to conquest. Instead of raiding and fleeing, the Marathas now "cast the anchor of permanence wherever they penetrated," says Khafi Khan. "As the imperial dominions have been given out in fief to the jagirdars, so too the Marathas have made a distribution of the whole empire among their generals," writes Bhimsen, "and thus one kingdom has to support two sets of jagirdars . . ." Maratha forts began to come up in every part of the Mughal Deccan, and village headmen in Mughal territories, with the backing of Marathas, began to dictate terms to imperial officers regarding the payment of revenues.

Simultaneously, there came about a change in Maratha military tactics. While previously they used to hit and run, now they boldly faced the imperial forces, and invariably it was the Mughals who ran. "The imperial officers had become so dastardly, and the troops so shameless, that the mere appearance of Dhunnajee's cavalry made them turn to flight," says Duff. Military initiative thus shifted from the Mughals to the Marathas. Often Mughal commanders entered into secret understandings with the Marathas, giving them protection money, says Manucci; "if they (the Marathas) think fit, they take it; if not, they burn and destroy in all directions." Sometimes Mughal officers enriched themselves by colluding with the Marathas in plunder.

Gradually, these changes in the Maratha ethos came to be reflected in their military organization, and they began to move about in regular military formations, like the imperial army. "These [Maratha] leaders and their troops move in these days with much confidence, because they have cowed the Mogul commanders and inspired them with fear," says Manucci. "At present time they possess artillery, musketry, bows and arrows, with elephants and camels for all their baggage and tents . . . In short, they are equipped and move about just like the armies of the Mogul . . . Only a few years ago they did not march about in this fashion. In those days their arms were only lances and long swords two inches wide. Armed thus, they prowled about on the frontiers, picking up here and there what they could; then they made off home again. But at the present time they move like conquerors, showing no fear of any Mogul troops." Such was the growing feeling of insecurity among the Mughals that many prudent amirs now began to send their families back to Hindustan, says Bhimsen.

AURANGZEB WAS CONSCIOUS of the gravity of the situation, and had, even before Rajaram's death, taken direct command of the operations against the Marathas. His plan was to split his forces into two divisions, one to engage the Marathas in the field, and the other, under his own command, to reduce their forts. Prince Bidar Bakht, seventeen, son of Prince Azam, with Zulfiqar Khan as his lieutenant, was put in charge of the expeditionary force. And in October 1699 the aged emperor, eighty-one now, himself issued out of Brahmapuri. "Aurangzeb," says Manucci, "is well aware that if he does not go in person at the head of his armies, it is impossible to become master of any fortress."

The subjugation of the Marathas, even with Aurangzeb himself in command, was a daunting task. Predicted Manucci: "It may . . . be asserted that if the monarch (Aurangzeb) maintains his design of becoming the master of all Shiva Ji's (Maratha) fortresses, he will need, before he succeeds, to live for as many years more as he had already lived."

At his age, battle could not have been a thrill for Aurangzeb. But he had to do his duty. And he set about it with some show of spirit. "The old king still shows his eagerness for war by the gestures he uses on the march," says Manucci. "While seated in his palanquin, he unsheathes his sword, makes cuts in the air, first one way, then the other, and smiling all the while, polishes it with a cloth, then returns it to its scabbard. He does the same with his bow, to show that he can still let fly an arrow. But most of the time he sits doubled up, his head drooping so much that his beard lies on his chest, and it looks to you as if it grew out of his throat. When his officers submit any petition, or make report to him on any occurrence, he gently raises his head and straightens his back. He gives them such an answer as to leave no opening for reply, and still looks after his army in the minutest particulars."

Emerging from Brahmapuri, Aurangzeb headed due west. His first target was the fort of Basantgarh, which surrendered in three days. Fort after fort then fell to him and his commanders, including the great forts of Satara, Rajgarh, Parli, Vishalgarh and Panhala. Most of the forts were, however, taken by bribing Maratha commanders. Sometimes, as in the capture of Vishalgarh, rival Mughal commanders bid against each other to bribe the Maratha garrison commander—to get the credit for capturing the fort! Aurangzeb, says Khafi Khan, "paid sums of money to the commandants, and so got the forts into his possession". Capturing forts by bribery gave the Mughals an illusion of success without actually defeating the enemy, but such sham victories made them lose sight of their real objective, of destroying Maratha power.

But Aurangzeb pressed on. Such was his "longing and passion for taking all the [Maratha] forts," says Bhimsen, "that he personally runs about panting for a heap of stones." He won everywhere, but his victories were hollow, for in many instances the forts he captured were retaken by the Marathas the moment he turned his back. Aurangzeb seemed punch drunk at this time, lurching and jabbing blindly, unable to stop.

Frustrated in his Maratha campaigns, Aurangzeb in 1703 thought of releasing Shahu in the hope of sowing dissension among the Marathas, or even of agreeing to grant the Marathas *sardeshmukhi* rights for the Deccan and making them responsible for the maintenance of peace there. But nothing came of these plans, as he could not trust the Marathas and they were too demanding.

Aurangzeb's last military campaign, in February-May 1705, was against Wagingera, in the Gulbarga district of modern Karnataka, the seat of the aboriginal Berad chief, Pidia Nayak—that was what the great Mughal emperor was up to at the zenith of his career, personally leading the imperial army against a petty tribal chief!

Terrible were the hardships that the Mughals had to face during the last, six-year long campaign of Aurangzeb, as he pursued the elusive final solution to the Maratha problem. He had already spent a good part of his long reign in camps so that, says Bhimsen, "a new generation was thus born [under canvas]; they passed from infancy to youth, from youth to old age, and passing beyond old age girt up their loins for the journey to the world of angels, and yet never once saw the look of a house, but only knew that in this world there is no other shelter than a tent." The Mughal nobles were heartily sick of their lifelong grind in the Deccan; one homesick noble even offered to pay Aurangzeb 100,000 rupees for permission to spend a year in Hindustan; the Rajputs complained that their breed was dying out because they had been away from their women for so long.

After the fall of Wagingera, with no more forts to take, Aurangzeb, eighty-seven, triumphant, though only in his own eyes, finally decided to return to Delhi. But the Marathas would not let the broken old man go with dignity. A horde of some 50,000 exultant Marathas dogged his feet as Aurangzeb dragged himself to Ahmadnagar, keeping just a few kilometres to the rear of the imperial army.

WHILE NIGHT THUS descended on the Deccan, the rest of the empire too was sliding into darkness. The Maratha success inspired many imitators who, realizing the vulnerability of the Mughals, now began ravaging various parts of the empire and biting off chunks of it here and there. In Gujarat a former brewer named Inu Mand, who had taken to highway robbery, combined with the Marathas to sack Baroda. In Rajasthan, a desultory war against Marwar rebels had been going on for over two decades, with no end in sight. Further north, the Jats, tough, brave and ever turbulent, were on the move, menacing even Agra and despoiling Akbar's tomb. Aurangzeb sent his grandson Bidar Bakht to suppress the marauders, and the prince was able to rout the Jats and drive their leaders into hiding, but the restoration of order was only transitory. There were troubles elsewhere too, in Malwa, Bihar and Gondwana. Pirates roamed the Indian seas, menacing Mughal shipping and the pilgrim traffic to Mecca.

The hyenas and carrion birds were closing in on the dying lion.

"Of the Future There Is No Hope . . ."

THE DECCAN WAS swirling in chaos as Aurangzeb trekked back homeward. For nearly forty years, ever since Jai Singh's 1666 campaign, the Deccan had been in a state of continuous turmoil, with rare short intervals of peace. The "war never ceases," says Manucci.

"Aurangzeb withdrew to Ahmadnagar, leaving behind him the fields of these provinces devoid of trees and bare of crops, their places being taken by the bones of men and beasts," continues Manucci. "Instead of verdure all is black and barren. The country is so entirely desolated and depopulated that neither fire nor light can be found in the course of a three or four days' journey." The loss in life, if Manucci's figures are at least proximate, was staggering: "There have died in his armies over a hundred thousand souls yearly, and of animals, pack-oxen, camels, elephants, et cetera, over three hundred thousand."

The people were crushed under the weight of two separate governments, Mughal and Maratha, that simultaneously lay on the land, one over the other. The peasants, unable to bear this double exaction, often abandoned their fields, collected arms and joined the marauders, rather than labour for others to plunder the fruits of their labour. "All administration has disappeared . . . the realm is desolated, nobody gets justice, they have been utterly ruined," notes Bhimsen. "The ryots have given up cultivation; the jagirdars do not get any money from the fiefs . . . Many mansabdars in the Deccan, starving and impoverished, have gone over to the Marathas."

Bandits freely roamed the land, Marathas as well as the disbanded soldiers of the extinct Deccani kingdoms, freebooters of many races and different religions. Even the Mughal jagirdars pillaged, sometimes their own jagirs, as that was the only way they could collect any revenue. "No man from sardar down to ryot ate his bread for a single day in peace; none from the Sultan down to the pauper slept for a single night in happiness," says Bhimsen.

HOW DID THE great empire come to such a sorry pass? In broad terms, the reasons are no different from those for the fall of any great empire; only the particulars distinguish the Mughals. Empires are created by conquest and sustained by oppression. Such aggrandizements are possible only when the aggressor has a clear advantage over the victim in military might, which the Mughals had in the beginning, in martial ferocity, and, for a short while, in military technology, in the use of cannons and muskets in field battles. Of these, the crucial factor was martial spirit, which reached its peak under Akbar, then declined, as the Mughal ruling class grew secure in its power and soft in its lifestyle. And it continued to decline even under Aurangzeb, despite his being personally austere and industrious. Though the empire, having achieved critical mass under Akbar, continued to expand, it did so by inertia rather than dynamism. Its vitality no longer matched its size; its spirit could not sustain its body. Territorial expansion under Aurangzeb in fact diminished rather than increased Mughal strength.

In the end the Mughal empire had become ungovernable. It was much too large. An efficient administrative system—like that of the complex and tightly cross-woven imperial fabric of the Mauryas two thousand years earlier—could have sustained the empire longer, but the Mughals, basically a predatory people, did not have the genius for administration. Even the very bureaucratic Aurangzeb was a mediocre administrator.

The emperor had of course a great advantage over his adversaries in the immense resources in men and materials at his command—but even that proved to be illusory, as the Mughals were unable to marshal their resources efficiently because of group rivalries, corruption and administrative incompetence. Says Duff of the state of the Mughal empire under Aurangzeb: "There was motion and bustle, without zeal or efficacy: the Empire was unwieldy, its system relaxed, and its officers were corrupt beyond all example. It was inwardly decayed, and ready to fall to pieces as much by its own irrecoverable weakness, as by the corroding power of the Mahrattas."

The empire was virtually bankrupt towards the close of Aurangzeb's reign, and the emperor, unable to meet his expenses from his revenue, had to draw on the accumulated treasures of his ancestors. Most of the provinces produced hardly any surplus revenue, and their remittances were irregular. "The actual revenue collection in the Deccan was sometimes one-tenth of the normal assessment," says Sarkar. Only the revenue from Bengal came with any regularity, and was always eagerly awaited; on one occasion, when this remittance was delayed, the arrears to artillerymen fell to fourteen months. Sometimes soldiers were in arrears of pay for as much as three years.

By the end of Aurangzeb's reign it was evident that the Mughal giant was crippled in body and spirit. The empire was collapsing under its own weight, its vital energy spent, having grown too ravenous, bloated too big, for its own good.

The early symptoms of decay were noticeable even in the reign of Shah Jahan, but the general expectation at the time of Aurangzeb's accession was that he would restore the vigour of the empire. That was the promise implicit in his ardent labours as a prince, and in his emphatic victory over his brothers in the war of succession. He was extremely hardworking, and was pitiless and crafty. He had no vices to sway his judgment or sap his energy. And, though not a brilliant general, he was tenacious in war. By all conventional calculations, he should have been a great success.

Why then did he fail? Because of his religious bigotry? Hardly. After all, by Aurangzeb's time Muslims had ruled India for over 500 years. There were other Muslim rulers in India before him who were far more balefully fanatical than he, and yet there had never been any serious religious uprising against any of them. Nor were there any against Aurangzeb—none of the rebellions during his reign are really attributable to his religious policy.

This is true of the Maratha wars as well. The Mughal-Maratha conflict was essentially a power struggle. Predictably, several prominent Maratha clans, some of them closely related to the Bhonsles, including a nephew of Shivaji, were arrayed on the side of the Mughals, just as several Muslim captains fought for the Marathas. True, the Maratha uprising had a strong communal element in it and was often energized by the religious fervour deliberately whipped up by its leaders, yet the primary goal of the Marathas was to exploit the prevailing political and military situation for their material gain, rather than to defend Hinduism. Maratha depredations were in fact totally nonsectarian, and Hindus were as much their victims as Muslims. The fact that the adversaries of Marathas were Muslim rulers was incidental; they were rebelling against the established political authority in the region, not against Muslim rule as such. Nor were they rebelling against exploitation and oppression; rather, they wanted to be the oppressors and exploiters themselves, and were generally worse in that role, even against fellow Hindus, than Muslim rulers.

In the case of the Rajput rebellion too, its cause was not so much Aurangzeb's religious policy as his failure to manage and channelize Rajput turbulence and give scope to their ambitions. The

Rajputs had no objection to fighting against Hindus or against fellow Rajputs, or even to the demolition of temples—they invariably stood docilely by when major temples were demolished, as when Shah Jahan demolished the great Rajput temples in Orchha before the very eyes of the captains of the heroic Rajput clans, the Sisodias, Rathors, Kachhwahs and Hadas. In any case, during the second half of Aurangzeb's reign, when he was in the Deccan and his troubles began to mount, he was not as rigorous in his anti-Hindu policy as before; he demolished very few temples in the Deccan, some of them only because of their military potential, for, as Bhimsen notes, "many of the forts were temples".

Aurangzeb's religious fanaticism has therefore to be seen only as a contributing factor, not as the crucial factor, in the decay of the Mughal empire. There was no single crucial factor. Everything contributed, even, ironically, Aurangzeb's unremitting attention to government. Aurangzeb failed in part because he tried to do too much. Instead of providing leadership and getting others to do the work, he, who had no faith in man, tried to do everything himself. Inevitably, he failed. Furthermore, he did not have the broad vision to match his vast empire; his was a petty mind and he ruled by rote, with the mentality of a clerk. He was cunning without being inventive; active without being dynamic. Though he remained alert till the end, knew what was happening to the empire and what it portended, he did not know what to do about the growing crisis, except to keep on doing what he had been doing all along.

PERHAPS AURANGZEB'S GREATEST failing was that he was, contrary to common perception, a weak ruler, hesitant to coerce obedience. "From reverence for the injunction for the Law he did not make use of punishment, and without punishment the administration of a country cannot be maintained. Dissension had arisen among his nobles through rivalry. So every plan and project that he formed came to little good; and every enterprise which he undertook was long in execution, and failed of its object," laments Khafi Khan. And again: "Throughout the imperial dominions in the reign of Aurangzeb, no fear and dread of punishment remained in the hearts of the jagirdars, faujdars and zemindars." Says Manucci: "If he would only abandon his mock sainthood, and behead a few of those in his empire, there would not be so much disorder, and he would be better obeyed." Lamented Aurangzeb, "I have become garrulous by talking and talking; but none of you have taken heed from my words." At times he seemed resigned:

"In my time all rules are without force." Once, exasperated with the endless complaints about corruption and inefficiency, he told a supplicant, "If you do not find your grievances redressed, pray to the Almighty to grant you some other ruler!"

"All administration has disappeared," writes Bhimsen. "Those who are at a distance [from the court] pay very little attention to his (Aurangzeb's) orders," says Manucci. "They make excuses, they raise difficulties; and under cover of these pretexts, and by giving large sums to the officials at court, they do just as they like." Bengal which yielded a net revenue of 1.7 million rupees during the reign of Shah Jahan now yielded no more than 500,000 rupees, according to Manucci. "He asked the grand vizier the cause of the falling off. The vizier replied hypocritically that the government of Shah Jahan was tyrannical and the people oppressed, whereas that of His Majesty was compassionate and holy, leaving people to live in peace and happiness. These words satisfied His Majesty."

Aurangzeb's theocratic bias also contributed to his administrative difficulties, as the prominence he gave to Kazis in government was resented by the military aristocracy. Says Khafi Khan: "Aurangzeb established the Kazis so firmly in the affairs of the state, and with reference to administration, that the leading and responsible officers of the empire began to regard them with envy and jealousy." Once, when Aurangzeb was fretting about a military problem, Mahabat Khan, a prominent general, sarcastically told the emperor that to gain victory he had only to ask the Chief Kazi to issue a fatwa and that there was no need to send an army.

Aurangzeb's lack of trust in men was another major problem. As he once told Prince Muazzam, he trusted no one, and was suspicious of even his own shadow. In the face of such paranoia, no one dared to show any initiative. "None of ym dare move a step without his Leave," noted British ambassador Norris. Aurangzeb repeatedly clipped the wings of his sons, often humiliated them in public, using such epithets as "ignorant and narrow-minded", "fearful and cowardly", "proud and foolish", "short-sighted, base-minded and foolish". He drove one of his sons into exile, and imprisoned three others, two of them for long years. All the princes were kept under constant surveillance. Understandably, not being trusted with responsibility, his sons and officers did not function responsibly.

So it was that the foundations of the empire crumbled during the last years of Aurangzeb, and India began to collapse in turmoil, first the Deccan, then Hindustan. This was Aurangzeb's legacy. But the lords of chaos were not the Mughals, but the Marathas. The Marathas vandalized and plundered the disintegrating empire, but did not care to supplant the Mughals and impose their own authority, for they had a vested interest in prolonging anarchy. "I have heard that every week they (Marathas) gave away sweets and money in charity, praying for the long life of the Emperor, who had proved [to them] the Feeder of the Universe!" says Bhimsen. "Many of the Moghul officers in charge of districts were in the pay of both parties, and likewise wished that the existing confusion might continue," adds Duff. Maratha and Mughal officers when they met often parted with a mocking prayer for the long life of Aurangzeb.

It took the Marathas a long time to realize that they had the historic opportunity to be the successors of the Mughal empire. "Their plundering hordes," says Duff, "did not comprehend that they were conquerors." The Marathas tore at the flesh of the dying lion, but did not have the vision to see that they could be the kings of the forest themselves.

THE LAST FEW years of Aurangzeb were pathetic. For six long years, from 1699 to 1705, the octogenarian emperor wearily trudged through mire from battlefield to battlefield, from fort to fort, resolute till the end, till at last his body gave up, and he submitted to the inevitable end of all human endeavour.

After the fall of Wagingera, in May 1705 Aurangzeb shifted his camp to Devapur, a village on the Krishna River, to give himself and his troops some much needed rest. There the cumulative strain of the tireless labour of the previous six years finally overcame him, and he fell ill. He had, says Khafi Khan, "severe pains in his limbs". Still he continued to labour, attending the durbar and issuing orders, so that his condition grew worse and he became critically ill. Several times he slid into unconsciousness, and, according to Manucci, "for twelve days he did not appear at the public audiences". As Aurangzeb began to sink, consternation gripped the imperial camp, for fear of civil war, and for fear of the Marathas.

Miraculously, Aurangzeb recovered. In October, after a six-month stay at Devapur, he began his homeward journey. On the way, he halted on the banks of the Bhima for forty days to observe the month of fasting, and reached Ahmadnagar on 31st January 1706. He pitched his camp at exactly the same spot where he had camped twenty-two years before, when he first arrived there to direct the campaign against the Deccan kingdoms. He had completed a cycle.

From Ahmadnagar he was expected to proceed to Aurangabad,

and from there to Delhi, but when the imperial officer at Aurangabad requested permission to repair the citadel there to receive him, the forlorn emperor wrote, "Ahmadnagar . . . [is] my journey's end."

It was a woebegone old man who returned to Ahmadnagar. Writes Manucci, "The old and wily king, Aurangzeb . . . we find him, then, with his army not far from the fortress of Ahmadnagar . . . feeble and old, full of disillusions, and near to the day of his death."

He was eighty-nine years old now. All his brothers and sisters were dead; some of his own children, even some of his grandchildren, were dead. When Goharara Begum, his last surviving sister, died in 1706, Aurangzeb lamented her death, repeating again and again, "She and I alone were left among Shah Jahan's children." He could himself then hear the footfalls of the dread reaper.

At Ahmadnagar, the emperor continued to work as best as he could. Till the end, even during his final illness, he kept up the appearance, maintaining the royal routine, even holding a kind of make-believe durbar, reviewing from his bed the assemblage in the courtyard of his tent. There would be no negligence, no lack of attention on his part. For his age, Aurangzeb, once a sickly child over whom Shah Jahan had fretted, was remarkably well-preserved. "Although he lived for ninety years, his five senses were not at all impaired, except his hearing, and that to only so slight an extent that it was not perceptible to others," says Khafi Khan. He was looked after with devotion by his daughter Zinatunnisa—an old maid of sixty-three herself—and by his wife Udipuri.

A major concern of Aurangzeb in the last weeks of his life was to prevent his sons from fighting for the throne over his deathbed. Kam Bakhsh, his youngest son born to Udipuri when Aurangzeb was forty-nine, was with him, and the aged emperor doted on him. But the prince was menaced by Azam, Aurangzeb's impetuous and ambitious third son, who was also in the camp, having arrived there from Gujarat. The emperor's favours to Kam Bakhsh, says Khafi Khan, made Azam "writhe like a poisonous serpent". Aurangzeb realized that he could not leave "two unchained lions . . . together", and so in the third week of February 1707 he separated the brothers, sending Kam Bakhsh to Bijapur and Azam to Malwa. He knew that he would not see them again, and broke down and wept when Kam Bakhsh took leave of him.

Whatever precautions Aurangzeb took, a war of succession immediately after his death was inevitable. "Thus do matters go on in the Mogul kingdom," writes Manucci. "Sons, grandsons and great-grandsons are making preparations for the terrible wars which must ensue upon the death of the old king. For there are many aspirants to dominion, it being among them a saying that in such a case a father should not trust a son, nor a son his father."

There were seventeen "princes of full age" who had a claim to the throne, notes Manucci: sons who were already old men, gray-bearded grandsons, and great-grandsons in their mid-twenties. "What an event to behold will be the tragedy following the death of this old man!" reflects Manucci. "One only of these princes can succeed, and thereby protect his family; the rest of them will be decapitated, or lose their lives in various ways. It will be a much worse tragedy than that which happened at the end of King Shah Jahan's reign."

On 28th February 1707, four days after he sent Azam away, Aurangzeb fell ill with high fever. Even then, for a few days he continued to visit the court room to say the five daily prayers with the nobles. "He was very weak," says Khafi Khan, "and death was clearly stamped upon his face." Aurangzeb knew that his end was near, and often recited,

> In a twinkle, in a minute, in a breath,
> The condition of the world changes.

Court astrologers, fearing the worst, advised Aurangzeb to give away in charity an elephant and a valuable diamond, to avert the evil influences of the stars. Aurangzeb, who still had his wits about him, disagreed with the suggestion, and noted on the petition that "the giving away of an elephant was the practice of the Hindus and of star-worshippers." Instead, he sent 4,000 rupees to the Chief Kazi for alms-giving. To the note sanctioning the grant, he added a funeral instruction: "Carry this creature of dust quickly to the first (burial) place, and consign him to the earth without any useless coffin."

A few days before his death, Aurangzeb wrote farewell letters to Azam and Kam Bakhsh, and possibly also his will. "I know not who I am and what I have been doing," he wrote to Azam. "The days that have been spent except in austerities have left only regret behind them. I have not at all done any (true) government of the realm or cherishing of the peasantry. Life, so valuable, has gone away for nothing . . . Of the future there is no hope . . . I brought nothing with me (into this world), and am carrying away with me the fruits of my sins. I know not what punishment will fall on me . . .

> Whatever the wind may be
> I am launching my boat on the water."

511

To Kam Bakhsh the emperor wrote: "My son, my liver! . . . Now that I am dying . . . anxiety about the army and camp-followers has been the cause of [my] depression of mind and fear of final torment . . . When I was full of strength, I could not at all protect them; and now I am unable to take care of myself! My limbs have ceased to move. The breath that subsides, there is no hope of its return. What else can I do in such a condition than to pray? . . . I am in trepidation. I bid farewell . . ." The bells were tolling. For Aurangzeb as well as for the Mughal empire.

In his last will, said to have been found under his pillow after his death, Aurangzeb recommended the partitioning of the empire among his sons. In another document, more a testament than a will, he laid down various precepts for the guidance of his successors, and advised: "Never trust your sons, nor treat them during your lifetime in an intimate manner . . . The main pillar of government is to be well informed in the news of the kingdom. The negligence for a single moment becomes the cause of disgrace for long years . . . "

The document also gave instructions for his funeral. "Four rupees and two annas, out of the price of the caps sewn by me, are with Aia Beg, the *mahaldar*," he wrote. "Take the amount and spend it on the shroud of this helpless creature. Three hundred and five rupees, from the wages of copying the Koran, are in my purse for personal expenses. Distribute them to the fakirs on the day of my death . . . do not spend it on my shroud and other necessaries . . . Bury this wanderer . . . with his head bare, because every ruined sinner who is conducted bareheaded before the Grand Emperor (God), is sure to be an object of mercy . . . Cover the top of the coffin on my bier with a coarse white cloth called gazi. Avoid the spreading of a canopy . . ."

THE END CAME on Friday, 3rd March 1707. That morning, when he was saying his prayers, he slipped into unconsciousness, and slowly, tranquilly slid to death. Even as he lost consciousness, says Mustaid Khan, "the force of habit prevailed, and the fingers of the dying King continued mechanically to tell the beads of the rosary they held." Khafi Khan places the time of Aurangzeb's death "at about one watch of the day", around 9 a.m. The day of his death, Friday, and the moment of his death, while at his prayers, were as Aurangzeb would have desired. If we are to believe Manucci, "At the time the king died, a whirlwind arose, so fierce that it blew down all the tents standing in the encampment. Many persons were killed, being choked by the dust, and also animals. The day became so dark that men ran into each other, being unable to see where they were going; villages were destroyed, and trees overthrown. The whirlwind lasted up to six o'clock in the evening."

The next morning, Prince Azam, who had tarried outside Ahmadnagar instead of proceeding to Malwa, arrived at the imperial camp, and conveyed Aurangzeb's body for burial at the tomb of saint Sheikh Zain-ul-Haqq in Khuldabad, four miles to the west of Daulatabad. It was Aurangzeb's wish that his tomb, like that of his beloved sister Jahanara, should be lowly and simple. His grave was therefore marked only by a slab of stone, nine feet by seven feet, with a trough cut into it, which was filled with earth and planted with green herbs. The tomb has no platform, nor any dome over it, but is open to the skies.

"*Az ma-st hamah fasad-i-baqi!* (After me, chaos!)" Aurangzeb had once said. He died with the woeful knowledge that his titanic endeavour had all been in vain. In a note to one of his amirs, he wrote of himself:

Alas, my life has been wasted in vain! . . .
I have [merely] consumed a quantity of
    water and fodder.

And to his Vizier, Asad Khan, he wrote: "Praised be God that in whatever place and abode I have been, I have by passing [through it] withdrawn my heart from all things connected with it, and made death easy for myself."

The loneliness and misery of his last years do not redeem Aurangzeb, but they soften the light on him. It is tempting to see him as a tragic figure, but he would himself have preferred to be judged sternly, without sentimentality or compassion.

AFTER AURANGZEB THERE would be yet other Mughal emperors, so called, on the throne of Delhi for a century and a half, till 1858, when the last emperor—the eleventh after Aurangzeb—Bahadur Shah, a feeble old man of eighty-two, was bundled off to prison in Rangoon by the British after the suppression of the Sepoy Mutiny. Bahadur Shah had grand titles but no empire; he was in reality only the king of Delhi, barely a king at that, subsisting on a pension from the British. The empire was gone long before his time, gone a hundred years, bludgeoned by Persian and Afghan invaders, dismembered by the Marathas and the British. Even before the empire was gone, hardly five years after the death of Aurangzeb in fact, the emperor had become a mere puppet in the hands of ruthless king-makers at the court.

Thus it was that when Aurangzeb stood at the pinnacle of the Mughal imperial glory, he was looking into the abyss.

It had been, for Aurangzeb and his forebears, a long, arduous climb to the summit. For his successors, it would be but one step into the abyss.

Epilogue

Death of the Future

IN A MERE century and a half, covering just four reigns from Akbar to Aurangzeb, Mughal rule changed the face of India, by which India would recognize itself and the world would recognize India. In every facet of life the Mughal achievement was matchless, and it transformed the lifestyle of the elite throughout India. What the Mughals were, was what the rich and the powerful everywhere in India aspired to be. In customs and manners, dress and cuisine, architecture and gardening, language and literature, art and music and dance, the standards of excellence for a long time thereafter would be Mughalai.

Yet in a fundamental sense India did not change at all. What changed was lifestyle, not life, and that too only of a minuscule elite. There was no transmutation of civilization. Behind the Mughal facade lay the immense body of Hindu culture, ancient and torpid but still breathing. The Hindu world did not change under Muslim influence, nor did the Muslim world change under Hindu influence, despite their 600-odd-year coexistence. There was some interaction between the two cultures, but no synthesis. Nor did either community respond creatively to the stimulus of resurgent Europe, which had reached out across the great oceans and linked up with India even before the Mughals arrived on the scene. There were no stirrings of new life in Mughal India. The Mughal efflorescence was a flowering of the old trees. And it turned out to be the last spring of the old cultures in India.

"IT LOOKS AS if everything in India were being made ready for some remarkable revolution"—this was how India at the turn of the seventeenth century seemed to Niccolao Manucci, an astute Italian observer who had lived in India through the entire long reign of Aurangzeb and beyond. India, it appeared to him, was barrelling towards chaos.

Outwardly, the Mughal empire still glittered mesmerizingly, but within the golden, jewelled chrysalis, the flesh was rotting, the spirit dead. The land was desolate, the empire crumbling, its economy shattered, its government inefficient and irredeemably corrupt, its mammoth army flaccid and impotent, its culture effete, its people broken and spiritless. Only the Marathas displayed any vitality. But there was no future with the Marathas either. They could have seized the imperial sceptre: it was theirs to take. They had the power. But they had no vision. The Marathas too were captains of the medieval, Hobbesian hell into which India was collapsing in the eighteenth century. India seemed to be a land where the future had died.

This was not how India's destiny had seemed a century earlier, at the end of Akbar's reign. Indeed, in many respects the Mughal age was progressive. The Mughals had integrated almost all of India into one empire, and provided it with a fair amount of political stability and administrative unity; under them the Indo-Gangetic Plain, the heartland of India, had for over a century enjoyed such peace as it had not known in a very long time. Culture luxuriated under Mughal patronage, and India now acquired, after the decline of Sanskrit as a living language, a new lingua franca, Urdu. Urbanization had advanced notably under the Mughals, and so had the monetization of the economy, which, along with improvements in the standardization of currency, weights and measures, facilitated the growth of trade. And, coincidentally, new and vital trade links with Europe had turned the Indian economy, though tentatively, in a new direction.

Yet, despite all this, in several areas crucial to the growth and transformation of society, Mughal India lagged way behind Europe, behind even China, Japan and Persia. There was hardly any vigour in the economy, scant spirit of enterprise among the people. In agriculture, industry and trade, Indian practices were archaic. There was no ferment of ideas, and curiosity about the new science and technology of Europe did not go beyond the dilettantism of a few amirs. Except in a few minor gadgets, India showed little interest in European inventions. Even in military technology, so close to the Mughal heart, adoption of improvements was slow and haphazard. While numerous Europeans from every stratum of society were arriving in India in Mughal times, only one Indian of note is known to have travelled to Europe—"Haji Habibullah, who had visited Europe, . . . had brought with him fine goods and fabrics for His Majesty's inspection," says Nizamuddin Ahmad, chronicler of Akbar. There were no Indian books on Europe or European learning. Such indifference was not mere insensitivity to new knowledge, but a denial of the very possibility of change and progress.

Most shocking of all was the debasement of the character of man in Mughal India. From the highest amir, indeed from the emperor himself, down to the man in the street there was a near total absence of civic morality and personal integrity. "No one ever says a word to be relied upon," writes Manucci. "It is continuously requisite to think the worst and believe the contrary of what is said . . . They deceive both the acute and the careless; thus, when they show themselves the greatest friends, you require to be doubly careful." Says Roe: "It is not the costome of the best or the worst in this countrey to be as good as their word, being certaine only in dissembling." Adds Pelsaert: "Everything in the kingdom is uncertain. Wealth, position, love, friendship, confidence, everything hangs on a thread."

Hypocrisy and sycophancy were the characteristic traits of the Indian ruling class. According to Manucci, Indians seldom spoke openly, but held "confabulations with nods and metaphors", which made it easy for them to break faith and still feel decent. The amir probably viewed sycophancy merely as good manners, a formal courtesy, and had therefore no feelings of personal degradation in being a sycophant, especially as the practice was universal. But sycophancy was not just good manners. Lack of earnestness in speech—using words to dress up and disguise thoughts and feelings, rather than to reveal them—led to lack of earnestness in thought and action, corrupted values, and perverted both individual character and social process.

The evil of this was compounded by the peculiarity of Indian society being at once servile and tyrannical—those who bowed and scraped before their masters tyrannized their underlings, and thus all the way down the social ladder. The entire Indian socio-political system was iniquitous, and shot through and through with corruption, inefficiency and oppression. There was no sense of justice or fair play. Everything was for sale.

In a way, the flaws of Indian society were the flaws of medieval society, which was nearly the same the world over. But the helix of medievalism in India had a few additional twists of its own, such as the ossified Hindu caste system and the fatalistic values underpinning it, the grinding poverty of the people, the debilitating climate of India, and, more than anything else, the near total absence of the spirit of individualism among Indians—and these, combining with the pernicious nature of Mughal rule, disabled India. There were some stirrings of the new during the reign of Akbar, the spirit of open inquiry breaking through the crust of medievalism, but the inertial forces of India, like a viscous, black tide, enveloped and quiesced the new energies.

Meanwhile Europe had broken free, to go adventuring across far horizons, to the ends of the earth and the confines of the mind. Columbus had discovered America when Babur was still a lad in what he considered to be "the very farthest limits of the civilized world", and by the time Babur arrived in Agra, Magellan's expedition had circumnavigated the world, and the Portuguese had already been in

India for over a quarter century. Copernicus, Michelangelo, Leonardo da Vinci and Machiavelli were Babur's contemporaries; Shakespeare, Kepler and Galileo were the contemporaries of Akbar and Jahangir; Newton of Aurangzeb. Europe was on the up spiral, India on the down spiral.

This was plain to see. But few could see the obvious, being blinded by the glitter of the Mughal emperor's mountainous hoard of gold and gems, his marble palaces, the peacock throne, the Taj. But behind the shimmering imperial facade, there was another scene, another life— people in mud hovels, their lives barely distinct from those of animals, wretched, half-naked, half-starved, and from whom every drop of sap had been wrung out by their predatory masters, Muslim as well as Hindu. Only chieftains and amirs fattened, and kings lived like kings.

Not surprisingly, at the height of Mughal splendour under Shah Jahan, over a quarter of the gross national product of the empire was appropriated by just 655 individuals, while the bulk of the approximately 120 million people of India lived on a dead level of poverty. No one gave a thought to their plight. Famine swept the land every few years, devouring hundreds of thousands of men, and in its wake came, always and inevitably, pestilence, devouring several hundreds of thousands more. In Mughal India, the contrast between legend and reality was grotesque.

"India of the seventeenth century must have been an inferno for the ordinary man," says Moreland, a fair and perceptive early modern economic analyst of Mughal India. But the common folk were not mere innocent victims either. They were weak, but not innocent. Held in check only by the brute coercive power of the state, they went on a rampage whenever authority slackened, pillaging and killing the unwary and the helpless. The idyllic, peaceable rustic of poetic imagination did not exist. In the towns, too, the common people were unruly, and it took very little to set them rioting. Victims were victimizers awaiting their turn. In the medieval jungle men were beasts.

THE JUNGLE ITSELF of course antedated the Mughals. It in fact antedated even the establishment of the first Muslim empire in India at the end of the twelfth century, for by then the Dark Ages in India, which roughly coincided with a similar epoch in Europe, were already some 500 years old. The culpability of the Mughals was in their failure to lead India out of the medieval morass through the broad path opened up by Akbar.

The decline of India's position relative to the rest of the civilized world, especially Europe, is reflected in the contrasting perceptions of travellers in ancient and medieval India. Some 2000 years before Mughal times, Megasthenes, the Greek envoy in the Mauryan court, said of Indian character: "Truth and virtue they hold alike in esteem." Seven hundred years after Megasthenes, Fa Hsien, a Chinese traveller, had about the same thing to say of Indians, as did Hsuan Tsang in the seventh century, who wrote, "They do not practice deceit, and they keep their sworn obligations . . . They will not take anything wrongfully, and they yield more than fairness requires."

These are no doubt sweeping generalizations, expressions of sentiment rather than statements of fact— and this is equally true of the blanket condemnations of Mughal India by European travellers. Yet undeniably they contain substantial elements of truth. Besides, the fact that the predominant attitude towards India in ancient times was of goodwill, and that such goodwill was almost totally absent in Mughal times, is in itself significant.

THE EIGHTEENTH CENTURY turned out to be, as Manucci had predicted, the age of revolutionary transformation in India—the first half of the century saw the collapse of the old world, while the second half marked the beginning of the new. The dissolution of Mughal India was largely due to its internal vicissitudes—the decrepitude of the Mughals and the waywardness of the Marathas—but the pivotal role in building a new India was played by an external power, the British. India by itself did not have the vitality either to sustain its old cultures or to transform and renew itself. Under the circumstances, the European domination of India seemed not only inevitable, but desirable—not as the domination of one people over another, but of modernism over medievalism. For the future to be born. If at all.

Incidental Data

Chapter 1

■ When Babur first arrived in Agra, the Lodi capital, Humayun, who had preceded him to the city, presented him with a huge and lustrous diamond, the value of which was put by Babur at "two and a half day's food for the whole world". With characteristic generosity he gave it back to Humayun. "I just gave it back to him," writes Babur. The diamond did not have a name then, but it is generally believed that it was the Kohinur, the most famous gem in history.

The diamond, along with a tray of jewels, had been given to Humayun by the Rajput royal family of Gwalior, in gratitude for protecting them from pillagers when they got trapped in Agra after the battle of Panipat, in which the raja, a tributary of Ibrahim Lodi, was slain.

The Kohinur, some claim fancifully, was the Samantik Mani that once adorned the bracelet of the *Mahabharata* hero, Arjuna. More credibly, but again without proof, it is maintained that the diamond originally came from the Kollur diamond mine along the river Krishna in the Deccan—this is not improbable, as the diamond mines in the Kurnool and Anantapur districts of Andhra Pradesh were at one time reputed to have been the richest diamond mines in the world. Later, the diamond is said to have been in the possession of the royal family of Malwa for several generations, from whom it was seized by Alauddin Khilji, the Sultan of Delhi, in the fourteenth century. Babur conjectured that the gem that Humayun presented to him was "the famous diamond which Alauddin must have brought" to Delhi. How it got to Gwalior from Delhi is not known.

Humayun took the diamond with him when he sought refuge in Persia, but nearly lost it there once. The prince, says Jauhar in his memoirs, used to carry "his valuable diamonds and rubies in a purse in his pocket", but once, after performing his ablutions, he absentmindedly left the purse behind. Luckily, Jauhar, who was then a personal attendant of Humayun, found the purse and returned it to the prince, who then presented the diamond, along with several other gems, to Shah Tahmasp.

From Persia, the diamond somehow found its way back to India—the conjecture is that Shah Tahmasp sent it as a present to the Nizam Shahi Sultan of Ahmadnagar, though it is also probable that it came through regular diamond trade channels. Later, it came into the possession of Mir Jumla (diamond-trader and Vizier of Golconda), and he, when he defected to the Mughals in 1656, presented it to Shah Jahan. Says Bernier: "On this occasion it was that Mir Jumla presented Shah Jahan with that celebrated diamond which had been generally deemed unparalleled in size and beauty."

The story so far is hypothetical, though plausible; it is not certain that the same diamond was involved in all of the above transactions, though it seems unlikely that more than one such unique diamond could have figured in the history of medieval India. The subsequent history of the Kohinur is, however, well documented.

In Shah Jahan's court the diamond was examined and evaluated by Tavernier, a French jewel merchant. It was originally reputed to have weighed 756 carats, but when Tavernier saw it, it weighed only a little over 268 carats, as it had been inexpertly ground down by a Venetian diamond cutter named Hortensio Gorgio. Gorgio was fined Rs 10,000 by Shah Jahan for spoiling the stone.

In 1739 Nadir Shah of Persia carried away the diamond when he sacked Delhi, and it was he who gave it its name: Kohinur, Mountain of Light. Eight years later, on the assassination of Nadir Shah, the diamond was seized by Ahmad Shah Abdali, a Persian general, who then set himself up as the ruler of Afghanistan. Shah Shuja, Ahmad Shah's descendant (who is said to have chipped off pieces from it), brought the diamond back to India when he arrived in Punjab as a fugitive, and Ranjit Singh, the Sikh ruler, took it from him around 1815, and set it on the bracelet he wore at official functions.

The British got hold of the diamond when they annexed Punjab in 1849. An amusing but improbable story is often told that John Lawrence, the Chief Commissioner of Punjab, had absentmindedly left it forgotten in his waistcoat pocket for six weeks. The diamond was sent to England by Dalhousie, the Governor General of India, to be presented to Queen Victoria. It thus became a part of the British crown jewels. In 1852 the diamond, which was considered lumpy and lacking in fire, was recut—the process took thirty-eight days and cost 8000 pounds—reducing it to 108.93 carats. Kohinur was never placed on the crown of a reigning British monarch, probably because it was reputed to bring ill luck to men, but it adorned the tiaras of several British queens.

In 1947, newly independent India demanded that Kohinur be returned to India, on the ground that it rightfully belonged to the temple of Lord Jagannath, to which Ranjit Singh had vowed to present it. The claim was repeated in 1953. In 1976, Zulfikar Ali Bhutto, the president of Pakistan, claimed it for his country. The Kohinur remains in the Jewel House in the basement of the Tower of London.

■ Bisexuality was common among Central Asian aristocrats in medieval times. Writes Babur about his uncle, Sultan Mahmud Mirza of Badakshan: "If anywhere in his territory there was a handsome boy, he used, by whatever means, to have him brought for a catamite; of his begs' sons and of his sons' begs' sons he made catamites, and laid command for this service on his very foster brothers and on their own brothers. So common in his day was that vile practice, that no person was without a catamite; to keep one was thought a merit, not to keep one, a defect."

■ In Herat almost every one was a poet. Writes Babur: "Ali-sher at a chess-party, in stretching his leg, touched Bana'i (both poets of Herat) on the hinder parts, and said jestingly, 'It is a sad nuisance of Herat that a man can't stretch his leg without touching a poet's backside'. 'Nor draw it up again,' retorted Bana'i."

■ Babur was a heavy but finicky drinker, and he took care not to mix opium eaters and wine drinkers. "Never does a *majun* party go well with a drinking party," he observes, and so set aside Saturday, Sunday, Tuesday and Wednesday for wine, the other days for *majun*. Babur disliked arrack, the common alcoholic drink of India; he was, he says, "disgusted by its bad flavour". Despite his fastidiousness, Babur did occasionally get so drunk that he could not recall on the following morning what he had done the previous night.

■ Timur is said to have remarked that there was no need to fear elephants, "for their trunks are empty sleeves, and they carry their tails in front; in Hindustan everything is reversed."

■ Babur was a resourceful and daring commander, but never foolhardy. He writes of the precautions he took during a campaign: "So cautious were we that at night our right and left, centre and van were just in the way they had dismounted, each according to its place in battle, each prepared for its own post, with men on foot all round the camp, at an arrow's distance from the tents. Every night the army was posted in this way and every night three or four of my household made the rounds with torches, each in his turn. I for my part made the round once each night." Laxity in guard duty was severely punished by Babur. "Those not at their posts had their noses slit and were led round through the army."

Despite his easy camaraderie, Babur was a tough disciplinarian, even as a boy-king. In 1497 in Samarkand, when Babur was just fourteen years old, his soldiers had plundered a caravan of traders without permission, but "such was the discipline of my army," writes Babur, "that on my issuing an order that no person should presume to detain any part of the effects or property that had been so seized, but the whole should be restored without reserve, before the first watch of the next day was over, there was not, to the value of a bit of thread, or a broken needle, that was not restored to the owner."

■ The Mughals were seen, as indeed they wished to be seen, as ogres by their victims. Babur would not have been displeased if he had heard that Guru Nanak, the founder of the Sikh religion, had described him as "Yama (the Hindu god of death) disguised as the great Mughal". Lamented the guru: "This age is like a drawn sword, the kings are butchers!"

■ Rana Sanga traced his descent from Sri Rama, but he had not modelled himself on the chivalrous mythical hero of the *Ramayana*—it was by wading through the blood of his brothers that the Rana ascended the throne of Mewar in 1509.

525

■ Rajput historians speak of Babur seeking a negotiated peace before the battle of Khanua, and also that the Mughal victory was facilitated by the treachery of the commander of the Rajput vanguard. Neither of these are improbable, though they are not corroborated by any other source. Babur's position was weak, and a deferred battle would have suited him. Subversion too was not unlikely—Rajput chieftains were ever at each others' throats, and Mewar itself, both before and after the reign of Rana Sanga, was riven with internecine squabbles, in which the intervention of outside rulers was sometimes sought. In fact, just a few months after Khanua, Babur was offered the great fort of Ranthambhor by Rana Sanga's second son, Vikramajit, in return for help against his elder brother who had become the ruler of Mewar after Rana Sanga's death.

■ Rana Sanga died in 1529, poisoned by his sardars, and with him died the Rajput imperial ambitions, though it took the Mughals nearly ninety years more to bring Mewar finally under their sway. The Mewar royal family itself endured long after the Mughals became extinct.

Chapter 2

■ Babur's plan to divide the empire, as given in a letter he wrote to Humayun on 27th November 1528: "As thou knowest, the rule has always been, when thou hadst six parts, Kamran had five; this having been constant, make no change . . . Live well with thy brothers. Elders must bear the burden. I have hope that thou, for thy part, will keep on good terms with him; he, who has grown up an active and excellent youth, should not fail, for his part, in loyal duty to thee." Askari was assigned Shambal and Hindal given Alwar as their fiefs.

■ Humayun was finicky about ritual washings, and was ever proper in speech and action. Superstitious, he was always careful to make his entrances with his right foot first, and required the same care in others—if anyone entered his presence with the wrong foot, he was liable to be sent out to enter again with the right foot, says Badauni.

■ Mirza Haidar on camp followers: If an amir had 100 retainers, he would, "for himself and them, have perhaps five hundred camp-followers, who on the day of battle do not attend on their masters . . . so that they wander at large . . . however much they may be beaten back on face and head . . ."

■ Was Hamida in love with Hindal? It seems probable, though there is only circumstantial evidence for it. "In those days Hamida-banu Begum was often in the mirza's mahal," says Gulbadan.

Hamida and Gulbadan were close friends, and their tents were always pitched next to each other. Gulbadan married Khizr Khwaja Khan, who later became the governor of Lahore; she died at the age of eighty, in the reign of

Akbar, and Hamida was with her when she breathed her last. Hamida herself died in the autumn of 1604, sixty-three years after her wedding. She was seventy-seven years old, forty-nine years a widow.

Chapter 3

■ Portraits show Sher Shah as a moon-faced, heavy-jowled, stout man, with powerful, bulging shoulders and a thin, curled moustache.

■ There were a number of Dravidian tribes in the hills of south Bihar in medieval times, like Cheroes and Savars. Dravidians were dominant from Gorakhpur to Bundelkhand, but were gradually displaced by Rajputs.

■ Sikandar Lodi's succession rules for jagirdars: "If any noble dies, whatever money or other effects he may leave should be divided among his heirs according to the laws of inheritance, but his office and his jagirs and his military retinue, let him confer on whichever of the sons he thinks most able, and these no one else has a right to share, nor is any remedy open to them." This was the principle on which Sher Shah based his refusal to share his father's jagir with his stepbrothers.

■ Sher Shah, says Abul Fazl, was "a stranger to friendship's realm".

■ Sher Shah on the ways of Afghans: "The custom of the Afghans is that, if any man has four kinsmen more than another, he thinks little of killing or dishonouring his neighbour."

■ Sher Shah's strategy in Rajasthan was to seize and hold the important forts, leaving the countryside to the rajas.

■ Sher Shah was particular about throwing up entrenchments wherever he camped, but found it impossible to do so in the desert sands of Rajasthan. But where Sher Shah was foxed, a child showed him the way—his seven-year-old grandson, Mahmud Khan, suggested that bags could be filled with sand to build the defences, says Abbas. This was probably the first time that sandbags were used in war in India. The ingenious boy was the son of Adil Khan; he was put to death by Islam Shah as a potential rival.

■ In dealing with corruption, Sher Shah, despite his orthodoxy, was strict even with religious officers, and dealt firmly with corrupt imams, resuming their fraudulently acquired lands, as Akbar would later do.

■ There were, according to Niamatullah, four tasks that Sher Shah on his deathbed regretted he was unable to accomplish: he had wanted to shift the Afghans of his native Roh to Punjab as a shield against Mughal incursions, and raze Lahore to the ground so that such a great city might not exist as an easy prey for the Mughals; he had also wanted to build a fleet of ships for pilgrims from India to go to Mecca, and raise a tomb for Ibrahim Lodi at Panipat. "I shall carry these regrets with me to my grave," he lamented.

■ Nothing much is known about Sher Shah's literary efforts, but he is said to have composed witty verses. Poetry was an obsession with Islam Shah. He was himself a poet, clever in extempore compositions, like the jesting ditty he wrote on Parasuram, the Raja of Gwalior, who was not, as Abdullah notes, "particularly good-looking":

> I do not know how to salute Parasuram,
> When I behold him, I am distracted,
>   and exclaim, Ram! Ram!

Chapter 4

■ Kamran died in 1557, and Askari in 1558: they lived long enough to hear about Humayun's re-conquest of Hindustan, and the accession of Akbar.

■ Akbar was the first Mughal emperor who was a natural-born Indian, but he had no Indian blood in him; he was in fact more Persian than Mughal in blood, as his mother, as well Humayun's mother, were Persians.

■ Akbar's favourite wet nurse was Jiji Anaga; he grew so attached to her that the other foster-mothers accused her of practising witchcraft to prevent the baby from accepting milk from anyone else. Jiji Anaga's husband was the amir who pulled Humayun out of the Ganga after the rout at Kanauj; he was later given the title Atga (Foster-father) Khan, and rose to become Vakil under Akbar, but only to be murdered soon after by Adham Khan, the envious son of another foster-mother, Maham Anaga.

■ Maham Anaga, according to Gulbadan, was related to Hamida; her husband was Nadim Khan.

■ When Hamida joined Humayun in Kabul, Akbar was brought before a group of women, and the child, then about three, is said to have recognized her at once and run to her, though he had not seen her since he was two. The story is plausible. Akbar had exceptional visual memory, and could vividly recall the incidents of his childhood—like the first steps he took as an infant, and how his uncle Askari then struck him with his turban and brought him down to perform the customary spell against the evil eye. "This striking and falling are visibly before me. Also, at the same time they took me for good luck to have my head shaved at the shrine of Baba Hasan Abdal. That journey and the taking of my hair are present before me as in a mirror," Akbar would recall later.

■ The size of the Mughal army that engaged Hemu at Panipat is uncertain.

Abul Fazl states that the Mughal army was only 10,000 strong, "but perhaps only 5000 were men of battle", but Yadgar mentions that they had 26,000 cavalry, though two paragraphs later in his account he says that "the Mughal army did not exceed 20,000 horse and foot". Hemu's army is put at 40,000 cavalry by Yadgar. Jahangir says that Hemu had a force of 30,000 against Biram Khan's four or five thousand.

■ Yadgar mentions that Akbar struck prostrate Hemu with his sword, but Abul Fazl and Badauni state that Akbar refused. Nizamuddin says that "Biram Khan . . . then put Himun to death with his own hand." British historians maintain that the story of Akbar's refusal is a cover-up by court historians. But that is just conjecture. It seems out of character for Akbar to hit an inert and helpless man. Nor can we assume that Akbar, a wilful child, would have automatically complied with Biram Khan's wish. Says Jahangir: "Not defiling his hand with his [Hemu's] blood, he [Akbar] told one of his servants to cut off his head."

Further, if Akbar had indeed fleshed Hemu, it would not have been concealed, but trumpeted, by Mughal chroniclers, at least by orthodox Badauni, as a meritorious deed, for in their eyes that would have made Akbar a ghazi, a slayer of infidels.

■ When the news of Hemu's defeat reached Delhi, his resourceful wife—yes, there was a woman behind his success—escaped to Mewat with his treasure. Pir Muhammad Khan pursued her, but she managed to elude him. Hemu's father was however captured in Alwar. Pir Muhammad offered to save his life if he changed his religion, but he refused. "For eighty years I have worshipped my god, according to this religion," said the old man. "Why should I, merely from fear of my life, without understanding it, come into your way of worship?" Angered, Pir Muhammad, as Abul Fazl puts it, "answered him with the tongue of his sword".

■ Throwing Adham Khan head first from the harem terrace was a punishment based on the principle of retaliation—as Adham Khan had entered head first into a prohibited area, he had to be thrown out head first. (Aurangzeb is said to have inflicted a similar punishment on his daughter's paramour.)

Chapter 5

■ It is usually recorded that Akbar slept for just three hours at night, but this should be taken not as a precise measure of time, but only as a conventional way of saying that he slept little. Jahangir says that Akbar slept for about four and half hours. Abul Fazl's detailed description of Akbar's daily schedule indicates that he slept for seven and half hours. As for the nature of Akbar's sleep, Abul Fazl says that it was "more like waking".

■ The name of the Amber princess Akbar married is not recorded. Her royal title was Maryam Zamani (Mary of the Age), and she was buried, like a Muslim, in a sepulchre near Akbar's tomb at Sikandra.

■ A potential rival to Akbar's throne was Abul Kasim, Kamran's son, a slightly older childhood friend of Akbar from his Kabul days. Abul by himself was probably harmless, but there was no saying who would use him for what purpose against Akbar. Akbar therefore prudently kept him in prison in Gwalior, and later, during the Uzbeg rebellion, had him executed, to deny him to rebels as a pretender to the throne.

■ Rani Durgavati was a princess of the ancient Chandel dynasty of Mahoba. She had, according to Mughal chroniclers, the "complete share of beauty and grace", and was moreover "distinguished for courage, counsel and munificence". She personally led the Gond army against the Mughals, riding a mighty elephant, and when the battle was lost, she plunged a dagger into her chest and "died in a virile fashion", preferring death to surrender, says Nizamuddin Ahmed.

■ Badauni on Rajputs in the Mughal army: "a Hindu wields the sword of Islam."
Akbar tried to encourage the formation of mixed regiments of Hindus and Muslims. They were not popular, but the lower pay of Rajput soldiers was an inducement for amirs to recruit Rajputs to fill their quota. During the reign of Jahangir, Mahabat Khan's contingent was predominantly Rajput.

■ Historians generally, following Vincent Smith, hold Mansur guilty of treason, but the evidence is against it. What is curious about the incriminating letters is that they were all letters to Mansur, so that their genuineness could not be immediately verified. Though Abul Fazl and Monserrate do refer to letters by Mansur, it is not stated where and when they were found or what they said.

■ Sending courtier historian Asad Beg to the Deccan, Akbar ordered, "You must . . . remain in each place so long as may be necessary, to collect whatever they may have of fine elephants and rare jewels throughout their dominions, to bring back with you. Their money you may keep. I want nothing but their choice and rare elephants and jewels . . . You must not relax your efforts as long as there is one fine elephant or rare jewel out of your grasp in the Dakhin."

■ So lucky was Akbar in everything that his good fortune became celebrated in the saying, "As fortunate as Akbar."

Chapter 6

■ Irked by the anti-Muslim vehemence of the Jesuits in the Ibadat Khana, a mullah once challenged them to a fire-walking ordeal, saying, "Let us make a peat fire, and in the presence of His Majesty we will pass through it, and whoever gets safely through it, will prove thereby the truth of his religion."

When the fire was made, the mullah pulled one of the Jesuits by the coat and exhorted, "Come on, in the name of God!" But the Jesuit shrank away. So writes Badauni.

Abul Fazl says that it was a Jesuit who proposed the ordeal, but the mullah angrily spurned it. Monserrate says that the proposal was made by Akbar to humiliate a wicked mullah who professed great sanctity, but that the Jesuits refused to collaborate.

■ When Aquaviva celebrated the Holy Mass (which involved taking a sip of wine and eating a small piece of bread as part of the Divine Mystery) Akbar, who attended, commented teasingly: "You ate and drank, but did not invite me!"

■ Sometimes the Jesuits answered taunts with wit. Jerome Xavier, when asked why more Christians than Muslims were possessed by devils, replied that the devil, having the Muslims already in his power, could afford to neglect them.

■ Akbar had, in his own eyes, one qualification to be a prophet—he was illiterate. "The prophets were all illiterate," Akbar used to point out, and thought that it would be good for believers to keep one of their sons illiterate.

■ A possible motive of Akbar in issuing the Infallibility Decree could have been his desire to appropriate the "caliphal authority from the Ottomans".

■ Abul Fazl was one of the most colourful amirs in Akbar's court. He was a man of prodigious intellect—and an equally prodigious appetite. "He had an extraordinary appetite," records Massir-ul-Umara. "It is said, that . . . he consumed daily twenty-two *seers* (nearly fourteen kilos) of food . . . When Abul Fazl was in the Deccan, his table luxury exceeded all belief. In an immense tent one thousand rich dishes were daily served up and distributed among the amirs; and near it another large tent was pitched for all-comers to dine, whether rich or poor, and kichery was cooked all day and was served out to anyone that applied for it."

Known throughout India as "the great munshi", Abul Fazl, like his father Sheikh Mubarak (the author of the 'Infallibility Decree') and brother Faizi (a well-known poet in Akbar's court), was a Sufi, so his religious views were in harmony with those of Akbar. That helped, but Abul Fazl's phenomenal success was largely due to his adroitness as a courtier and his flair for elegant flattery, which seduced even Akbar. An unabashed sophist, Abul Fazl could argue any side of a case with great persuasiveness, but he lacked strong convictions, perhaps even intellectual integrity. His main rival, Badauni—burning with envy but still essentially truthful—describes him as "officious, time-serving, openly faithless, continually studying the emperor's whims, a flatterer beyond all bounds." Once, when Badauni in private challenged Abul Fazl on his heresies, he (Abul Fazl) replied arrogantly, "I wish to wander for a few days in the vale of infidelity for sport."

Jahangir describes Abul Fazl as one who had "excelled . . . in wisdom and learning, had adorned himself outwardly with the jewel of sincerity, and sold it to my father at a heavy price." Akbar valued and admired Abul Fazl,.and it was to him that he entrusted the task of preparing the chronicle of his reign, advising him to "write with the pen of sincerity the account of the glorious events and of our dominion-increasing victories". Abul Fazl added considerable gloss to the glory of those "glorious events", but he does not seem to have falsified facts as such—he wrote, he claims, "with a pen perfumed with sincerity".

Abul Fazl was born on 14th January 1551; he died aged fifty-two. Of Arab extraction, his parents originally lived in Sind, but later moved into Rajasthan and settled down at Nagaur. Abul Fazl entered Akbar's service at the age of twenty-three—which he calls his "second birth"—and rose to be a commander of 4000. He was a brilliant foil for Akbar's intellectual jousts, and was as much a companion as a courtier, to whom Akbar once said, quoting,

Serene is the night and pleasant moonlight,
I wish to talk to thee on many a subject.

■ Once Akbar was gored by a deer during a hunt, and "one of the testicles was lacerated, and blood flowed." The injury, because of Akbar's neglect, "became serious, and the swelling increased . . . The application of the medicine was left to the writer of the book of fortune," says Abul Fazl.

■ Todar Mal was a Khattri from Lahore, but little is known about his background. It is possible but not certain that he had served under Sher Shah, for there is a Todar Khattri mentioned in Mughal chronicles as an outstanding manager of money, to whom Sher Shah had entrusted the construction of the fort of Rohtas in Punjab.

A brilliant administrator and a great general, Todar Mal is best remembered for organizing the Mughal revenue system, in which his contribution was great, and would probably have been even greater had he not been periodically called away to lead the army. His only fault, according to Abul Fazl, was that he was ill-tempered, obdurate and vindictive. "Though Todar Mal possesses a sharp intellect for the ins and outs of political and financial affairs, I do not like his pride," Akbar is said to have remarked, according to Shah Jahan quoted by Aurangzeb. "He served with honesty and the absence of avarice," says Abul Fazl. "There was no cupidity in his administration. Would that he had not been spiteful and revengeful so that a little opposition would cause dislike to spring up in the field of his heart and acquire strength and substance . . . If bigotry in religion had not coloured his nature he would not have had any bad qualities. But in spite of these defects, if we look to the nature of men in general, in fullness of courage, absence of avarice . . . in the performance of service, in diligence and skill, he was a man such as is seldom seen, or rather he was incomparable."

Todar Mal was touchy in matters of religion. Once, when a Mughal officer demolished some temples in Varanasi and converted them into a Muslim school, Todar Mal punished him by rack-renting him. "Just as he was of the unique of the age for practical wisdom and trustworthiness, so was he at the head of mortals for superstition and bigotry," says Abul Fazl. "His rule was that until he had performed in a special manner his idols-worship, and had adored them after a thousand fashions, he would not attend to business nor eat or drink. Suddenly, in the turmoil of moving camp, the idols of the simpleton were lost. In his heartfelt folly he abandoned sleep and food. His Majesty had compassion on him and administered consolations to him. He recovered somewhat and addressed himself to his duties."

Under Akbar we first notice Todar Mal in 1565, performing military duties, and he would later distinguish himself in several campaigns, but he is best remembered as a revenue administrator. He was first assigned to revenue work by Akbar in 1574, when he was sent to Gujarat to organize the revenues of that newly conquered province, and he did such a thorough job there—measuring the land and grading it according to soil, nature of irrigation and crops grown—that the province was soon yielding five million rupees of surplus revenue a year; Todar Mal was probably also associated with the graded organization of the bureaucracy, the conversion of fiefs into crown lands, and the regulation requiring the branding of horses, which were all initiated around the time Todar Mal was sent to Gujarat. Later he served as Akbar's Diwan for several years, and was associated with most of the revenue reforms of Akbar.

Getting on in years, in 1589, when Akbar was in Kabul, he, according to Abul Fazl, submitted a petition to Akbar that "old age and sickness had prevailed over him" and sought "permission to resign in order that he might go to the bank of the Ganga, and spend his last breaths in remembering God." At first Akbar agreed to relieve him, and Todar Mal set out on his pilgrimage, but "afterwards admonitions were sent to the effect that no worship of God was equal to the soothing of the oppressed, and that it would be better for him to give up his idea (of retirement) and to spend his last breath in serving man, and to make that the provision for his final journey." Akbar's order reached Todar Mal near Lahore, and he obediently turned back, but only to die on the way, in November 1589.

Todar Mal's son, Raja Kalyan served under Jahangir.

Chapter 7

■ The earliest reference to the Salim-Anarkali liaison (later celebrated in folklore) is to be found in the journal of William Finch, an English merchant in India from 1608 to 1611. While visiting Lahore, Finch says he saw in the suburbs of the town ("without the town, in the way to the gardens"), "a faire monument for Don Sha (Daniyal), his mother, one of the Acabar his wives, with whom it is said Sha Selim had to do (her name was Immacque Kelle, or Pomgranate kernell); upon notice of which the King (Akbar) caused her to be inclosed quicke within a wall in his moholl, where shee dyed, and the King (Jahangir), in token of his love, commands a sumptuous tombe to be built of stone in the midst of a foure-square garden richly walled, with a gate and divers roomes over it. The convexity of the tombe he hath willed to be wrought in workes of gold, with a large faire jounter with roomes over-head."

No other contemporary writer mentions the Anarkali incident, but the story is told by some late Mughal writers like Khafi Khan. A building in Lahore (used as a parish church in the second half of the nineteenth century, and later as a record office) is often pointed out as the tomb that Jahangir built for Anarkali on his accession. The inscription on the presumed tomb of Anarkali: "I would give thanks unto my God till the day of resurrection, if only I could behold the face of my beloved once more."

According to William Finch, Anarkali was the mother of Daniyal. That would make her at least thirteen years older than Salim, as Salim was born in 1569 and Daniyal in 1572. This age difference, instead of making the story improbable, in fact makes it probable, given the Oedipal tensions between Akbar and Salim.

■ Jahangir on Nur Jahan's marksmanship: "My huntsmen reported to me that there was in the neighbourhood a tiger which greatly distressed the inhabitants. I ordered his retreat to be closely surrounded with a number of elephants. Towards evening I and my attendants mounted and went out. As I had made a vow not to kill any animal with my own hands, I told Nur Jahan to fire my musket. The smell of the tiger made the elephant very restless and he would not stand still, and to take good aim from a howdah is a very difficult feat. Mirza Rustam, who after me has no equal as a marksman, had fired three or four shots from an elephant's back without effect. Nur Jahan, however, killed this tiger at the first shot."

■ Itimad-ud-daula was an aesthete who devoted his leisure to the "study of poetry and style", says Mutamid Khan. Itimad's wife, Asmat Begum, was the inventor of attar of roses, which became renowned as Attar-i-Jahangiri, the name given to the perfume by Salima Begum. Writes Jahangir: "It is of such strength in perfume that if one drop be rubbed on the palm of the hand it scents a whole assembly, and it appears as if many red rosebuds had bloomed at once. There is no other scent of equal excellence to it."

■ Among the presents offered by Roe to Jahangir was an English coach, which cost the East India Company 151 pounds and 11 shillings. Jahangir got the coach refurbished for Nur Jahan's use, and had a replica of it made locally for his own use—the Mughal emperor never sat on a saddle or howdah or carriage on which anyone else had sat.

Jahangir wanted Roe to procure for him some English dogs and an English horse; he thought that if six were sent by ship from England, at least one might survive.

■ When an eye ailment of Shahryar was cured, and the matter was reported to Jahangir, he said: "Yes, they will no doubt continue to be quite well, if they be not deprived of light by his brothers."

Chapter 8

■ According to legend, when Mumtaz was in labour with her last child, the baby cried in the womb, portending the death of the mother on childbirth. A woman who dies on childbirth is considered a *shaheed* (martyr), and her tomb an urs, a holy spot.

■ On Mumtaz's death, Shah Jahan, "gave up the practice of plucking out gray hair" from his beard, says Qazvini.

■ The Taj had minor construction flaws, and it began to leak soon after it was built, as Aurangzeb reported to Shah Jahan when he visited it in December 1652. Repairs were carried out, apparently with success. Minor cracks were noticed in 1810, 1874 and 1937.

■ Dara's Persian translation of the Upanishads, rendered in turn into Latin and published in Europe a century and half later, in 1801, was read by Schopenhauer, the German philosopher, who spoke of the book as "the solace of my life, the solace of my death".

■ Aurangzeb's agreement with Murad to partition the empire, as given in his letter to Murad: "Whereas the design of acquiring the throne has now been set on foot, and all (my) pious aim is to uproot the bramble of idolatry and infidelity from the realm of Islam and to overwhelm and crush the idolatrous chief with his followers and strongholds, so that the dust of disturbance may be allayed in Hindustan,—and whereas my brother, dear as my own heart, has joined me in this holy enterprise, has confirmed anew with strong (professions of) faith the terms of co-operation (between us previously) built on promises and oaths, and has agreed that after the extirpation of the enemy of Church and State and the settlement of public affairs he will stay firmly in the station of alliance and help, and in this very manner, at all times and places, and in all works, he will be my companion and partner, the friend of my friends, the foe of my foes, and will not ask for any land besides the portion of imperial dominions that will be left to him at his request,—therefore, I write that, so long as this brother does not display any (conduct) opposed to oneness of aim, oneness of heart, and truthfulness, my love and favour to him will daily increase; I shall consider our losses and gains as alike, and at all times and under all conditions I shall help him; I shall favour him even more than now, after my object has been gained and the godforsaken idolater has been overthrown. I shall keep my promise, and, as previously settled, I shall leave to him the Punjab, Afghanistan, Kashmir, and Sind (Bhakkar and Tatta),—the whole of that region to the Arabian Sea, and I shall make no objection to it. As soon as the idolater has been rooted out and the bramble of his tumult has been weeded out of the garden of the empire—in which work your help and comradeship is necessary—I shall without the least delay give you leave to go to this territory. As to the truth of this desire I take God and Prophet as witnesses!"

Chapter 9

■ Mumtaz's coffin is directly below the point of the central dome of the Taj, and Shah Jahan's coffin to one side of it, for the custom was that the first to die took the central position. (It was the same arrangement in Itimad-ud-daulah's tomb also.) The plinth of Shah Jahan's coffin is however slightly higher than that of Mumtaz.

■ Initially, the holy men of Mecca refused to accept gifts from Aurangzeb, because he had imprisoned his father and usurped the throne. But later their cupidity got the better of their principles and they accepted the gifts—not only that, the Sharif of Mecca began to appropriate for himself the money Aurangzeb sent for charity, so towards the end of his life Aurangzeb had to ask his Vizier to "devise some means by which . . . the hands of this unrighteous exactor may not touch it". To avoid the risk of the money being misappropriated, he then began sending it in small amounts through Arab traders, bypassing the Sharif.

■ According to Manucci, during Aurangzeb's 1662 illness, Raushanara dictatorially took charge of him and would not let anyone but her own confidants to see him, once even dragging his wife Nawab Bai by the hair from the royal chamber.

■ Though Aurangzeb disliked Hindu customs, he once wrote to Bidar, his grandson: "Though to weigh the body of a person against gold, silver, copper, corn, oil and other commodities [and giving away the value of the weight in charity] is not the practice of the country of our ancestors and of the Mohemmadans of this country, many needy and poor persons are benefited by this practice." He allowed his sons to be weighed on their recovery from illness, for the money to be given away in charity.

■ Aurangzeb's favourite fruit was, appropriately, corinda (Carissa carandas), an acidic fruit; he also enjoyed "a sort of chewing gum called khardali". He disliked the Indian habit of chewing paan, adopted by the Mughals. "I do not chew paan," he says with curt distaste.

■ Aurangzeb's daughter Zebunnisa Begum was a patron of literature and the arts, and was herself a linguist. "She appreciated the value of learning and skill; and all her heart was set on the collection, copying and reading of books and she turned her kind attention to improving the lot of scholars and gifted men. The result was that she collected a library the like of which no man has seen," says Mustaid Khan. She wrote a book of odes and quatrains under the pen-name Makhfi, the Concealed One.
    Imprisoned for her complicity in Prince Akbar's rebellion, she spent the last 21 years of her life in the fort of Salimgarh, and died in 1702. She was buried in the Garden of Thirty Thousand Trees outside the Kabul Gate in Delhi; her tomb was later demolished to lay a railway track.

■ Desperadoes of deltaic Bengal: There was even a monk among the bandits, "clothed in scarlet" and playing petty despot, says Manucci. Writes Bernier: "On this spot the notorious Fra-Joan, an Augustinian monk, reigned, as a petty Sovereign, during many years."

The most notorious of the European desperadoes was Sebastian Gonzalves Tibao, a Portuguese adventurer, who captured Sandwip and a couple of other islands at the mouth of the Ganga, and scoured the coastal seas and the many arms of the Ganga, pillaging and enslaving. He was eventually defeated by the Arakanese, and driven out of Sandwip. The bandits thereafter served as the mercenaries of the Arakanese king, raiding Bengal on behalf of the king and giving him half the plunder, for providing them a sanctuary in Chittagong. Shayista Khan once asked the bandits, after he had induced them to defect to the Mughals, what pay the Arakanese king had assigned to them, and they replied, "Our salary was the Mughal empire. We considered the whole of Bengal as our jagir!"

Chapter 10

■ Aurangzeb on Bengal: "A hell well-stocked with bread."

■ Shahji was named after a Muslim sage, Shah Sharif of Ahmadnagar, by whose blessing Maloji, childless for long, had a son born to him, after his supplications to Hindu deities Mahadev and Bhawani had proved fruitless.

■ During the Mughal siege of Purandhar, Manucci, who was then in the service Jai Singh, and used play cards with him at night, met Shivaji when he (Shivaji) came into the raja's tent one night. Shivaji wanted to know of which country Manucci was the raja, and Jai Singh said that he was a Feringhee raja. They met again several times later, talked about Christianity and the kings of Europe.

■ Shortly before he died, Shivaji wrote a long letter to his younger brother Ekoji, calling him to attend to kingly duties. "Many days have elapsed without my receiving any letter from you, and in consequence I am not in comfort," he wrote. "Ragoo Punt has now written, that you, having placed melancholy and gloom before yourself, do not take care of your person, or in any way attend to yourself as formerly; nor do you keep up any great days or religious festivals. Your troops are inactive, and you have no mind to employ yourself on state affairs. You have become a Byragee (recluse), and think of nothing but to sit in one place accounted holy, and let time wear away . . . I am surprised, when I reflect, that you have our father's example before you—how did he encounter and surmount all difficulties, perform great actions, escape all dangers by his spirit and resolution, and acquire a renown which he maintained to the last? . . . Is it then for you, in the very midst of opportunity, to renounce all worldly affairs, and turn Byragee—to give up your affairs to persons who will devour your estate—to ruin your property and injure your bodily health?"

"What kind of wisdom is this," Shivaji continued, "and what will it end in? . . . Throw off despondency, spend your days properly; attend to fasts, feasts, and customary usages, and attend to your personal comforts. Look to the employment of your people, the discipline of your army, and turn your attention to affairs of moment . . . and gain fame and renown. What a comfort and happiness it will be to me to hear the praise and fame of my younger brother . . . Above all do not be slothful . . . This is the time for performing great actions. Old age is the season for turning Byragee. Arouse! bestir yourself. Let me see what you can do. Why should I write more, you are wise."

■ On Shivaji's death an inventory of his possessions was taken on the orders of Shambhuji. It lists, apart from treasure, 100,000 pieces of gold embroidered cloth, 100,000 do-patta (scarves), 400,000 pieces of silk cloth, 32,000 quires of white paper, 6800 kg of pepper, 2200 kg of ambergris, 4500 kg of gulal (red powder used for Holi festival), 227 kg of dried grapes, 454 kg of almond, nearly 15,900 kg of dates, 11,350 kg of coconut kernel, 681 kg of cardamom, nearly 16,000 kg of betelnut, 22,700 kg of opium, 1.8 million kg of snuff, 3.9 million kg of paddy, 11.4 kg of gram, 5.7 million kg of ghee, 15.9 million kg of mustard oil, nearly 23,000 kg of honey, 31,000 horses of various types, 3,000 camels, 500 elephants, 100 cows, 1000 sheep, and 1000 male and 500 female slaves. Weapons were relatively few in number, as Maratha soldiers usually brought their own weapons: only 500 swords, 600 lances, 4000 spears and 1,000 daggers are listed, but there were 45.4 million kg of gunpowder and 22.7 million iron balls (shots), because ammunition was supplied by the state.

■ Khafi Khan on the contrast between Shivaji and Shambhuji: Shivaji used to sit at a tank he had dug near the fort of Raigarh, "and when the women of the traders and poor people came to draw water, he would give their children fruits, and talk to the women as to his mother and sisters. When the raj descended to Sambha, he also used to sit upon this bench; and when the wives and daughters of the ryots came to draw water, the vile dog would lay one hand upon their pitcher, and another upon their waist, and drag them to the seat. There he would handle them roughly and indecently, and detain them for a while."

■ Aurangzeb to his son and successor Muazzam: "The passages of my horoscope—composed by Fazil Khan Ala-ul-mulk, [and giving the incidents] from the day of my birth till after my death—have all been verified by actual experience. In that horoscope it is written that after me will come an Emperor, ignorant, narrow-minded, overpowered by injuries—whose words will be all imperfect and whose plans will be all immature. He will act towards some men with so much prodigality as almost to drown them, and towards others with so much rigour as to raise the fear of [utter] destruction. All these admirable qualities are praiseworthy characteristics found in your nature!"

■ Bangalore was sold by Ekoji to Deo-Raj, the Raja of Mysore, for 300,000 rupees in 1687.

Notes

Dates in the book generally conform to those in the *Cambridge History of India*, Vol. IV.

The sources of all quotations are given in the text. All quotations, except a few comments by modern historians, are from works of the Mughal period. In about half a dozen instances, the wording of the English translations of Persian sources has been slightly altered, or sentences from different translations integrated, for the sake of clarity. Where sources differ in minor detail, I have chosen the version that seemed plausible to me, or have combined bits from different sources to tell a consistent and credible story—for instance, in the description of Prince Murad's arrest by Aurangzeb.

Bibliography

Medieval Sources

Abbas Khan Sarwani (an Afghan noble in Akbar's service): *Tuzuk-i Sher Shahi* in H. M. Elliot & John Dowson (E&D): *The History of India as Told by Its Own Historians* (London, 1867-1877 / Delhi, 1990) (Vol iv, pp. 301-434)

Abdulla (a contemporary of Jahangir): *Tarikh-i Daudi* (E&D iv, pp. 434-513)

Abul Fazl (courtier of Akbar): *Akbar-nama*. 3 vols. (Tr: H. Beveridge) (Calcutta, 1907-1929 / Delhi, 1989)

Abul Fazl: *Ain-i-Akbari*, 3 vols. (Tr: H. Blochmann & H. S. Jarrett) (Calcutta, 1873-94 / Delhi, 1977)

Asad Beg (courtier of Akbar): *Wikaya-i Asad Beg*. (E&D vi, pp. 150-74)

Aurangzeb (Mogul emperor): *Ruka'at-i-Alamgiri or Letters of Aurangzeb* (Tr: Jamshid H. Bilimoria) (London, 1908 / New Delhi, 1972)

Babur (Mogul emperor): *Babur-nama* (Tr: Annette Beveridge) (London, 1922 / Delhi, 1979)

Badauni (courtier of Akbar): *Muntakhab-ut-Tawarikh*. 3 vols. (Tr: Ranking, Lowe & Haig) (Calcutta, 1884-1925 / Delhi, 1980)

Bakhtawar Khan (courtier of Aurangzeb): *Mirat-i-Alam*. (E&D vii, pp. 145-65)

Bernier, Francois (a French physician in mid-17th century India): *Travels in the Mughal Empire*. (Tr: Archibald Constable) (Westminster, 1891 / Delhi, 1968)

Bhara Mal (courtier of Shah Jahan and Aurangzeb): *Lubbu-t Tawarikh-i-Hind*. (E&D vii, pp. 168-73)

Careri, J. F. G. (an Italian in India at the close of the 17th century): His account in *Indian Travels of Thevenot and Careri* (Ed: Surendranath Sen) (New Delhi, 1949)

Coryat, Thomas (an Englishman in India in the second decade of the 17th century): His letters in William Foster: *Early Travels in India* (London, 1921 / Delhi, 1989. pp. 234-87)

De Laet, Joannes (a mid-17th century Dutch compiler of Mogul history from Humayun to Jahangir, based on contemporary European sources): *The Empire of the Great Mogol* (Tr: J. S. Hoyland) (Bombay, 1928 / Delhi, 1975)

Du Jarric, Fr. Pierre (an early 17th century French compiler of Mogul history, based on Jesuit sources): *Akbar and the Jesuits* (Tr: C. H. Payne) (Oxford, 1926)

Ferishta (contemporary of Jahangir): *Tarikh-i-Ferishta*, 4 vols (Tr: John Briggs) (London, 1829 / Delhi, 1989)

Finch, William (An Englishman in India in the first decade of the 17th century): His journal in Foster: pp. 122-87 (London, 1921 / Delhi, 1985)

Fitch, Ralph (an English trader in India in late 16th century): His journal in Foster: pp. 1-47

Foster, William: *Early Travels in India*, 1583-1619 (Oxford, 1921 / Delhi, 1985)

Fryer, John (an Englishman in India in late 17th century): *A New Account of East India and Persia* (1672-1681) (Hakluyt Society, London, MDCCCCXV)

Guerreiro, Fr. Feranao (an early 17th century Portuguese historian, who based his account on the reports of Jesuits): *Jahangir and the Jesuits* (Translated by C. H. Payne from the *Relations* of Fr. Guerreiro) (London, 1931)

Gulbadan Begum (sister of Emperor Humayun): *Humayun-nama* (Tr: Annette Beveridge) (1902 / Delhi, 1972)

Haidar, Mirza, Muhammad (cousin of Emperor Babur): *Tarikh-i-Rashidi* (Tr: N. Elias and E. Denison Ross) (London, 1895 / Delhi, 1986)

Hamid-ud-din Khan Nimcha (courtier of Aurangzeb): *Ahkam-i-Alamgiri* (translated by J. Sarkar as *Anecdotes of Aurangzeb*) (Calcutta 1928 / 1988)

Hanafi, Muhammad Sharif (a contemporary of Shah Jahan): *Majalisu-s Salatin*. (E&D vii, pp. 134-40)

Hawkins, William (East India Company's trade representative at Jahangir's court): His account in Foster pp. 60-121.

Inayatu-lla (a courtier of Akbar): *Takmila-i Akbar-nama* (E&D vi, pp. 103-15)

Inayat Khan (Shah Jahan's courtier): *Shahjahan-nama* (Tr: W. E. Begley & Z. A. Desai) (Oxford: Delhi, 1990]

Ishwardas Nagar (courtier of Aurangzeb): *Futuhat-i Alamgiri* (Tr: Tasneem Ahmad) (Delhi, 1978)

Jahangir (Mughal emperor): *Tuzuk-i-Jahangiri*, 2 vols. (Tr: Alexander Rogers) (London, 1909-14 / New Delhi, 1989)

Jauhar (a personal servant of Emperor Humayun): *Tazkirat-ul- Waqiat* (Tr: Charles Stewart) (London, 1832 / Delhi, 1972)

Khvand Amir (Khondamir) (courtier of Humayun): *Humayun-nama* (E&D v, pp. 116-26)

Khafi Khan (courtier of Aurangzeb): *Muntakhabu-l Lubab*. (E&D vii, pp. 207-533)

Lahori, Abdul Hamid (courtier of Shah Jahan): *Badshah-nama*. (E&D vii, pp. 3-72)

Linschoten, John Huighen Van (a Dutch trader in India in late 16th century): *The Voyage of John Huighen Van Linschoten to the East Indies* in *Purchas*, Vol. X pp. 222-318 (Hakluyt Society, 1884)

Manucci, Niccolao (Italitan adventurer in India in the second half of the 17th century): *Storia do Mogor*, 4 vols. (Tr: William Irvine) (London, 1907-8 / Delhi, 1989)

Maulana Ahmad and others (courtiers of Akbar): *Tarikh-i-Alfi* (E&D v, pp. 150-76)

Mildenhall, John (an English merchant at Akbar's court): (his account in Foster, pp. 48-59)

Monserrate, Fr. Anthony (a Jesuit at Akbar's court): *Journey to the Court of Akbar* (Tr: J. S. Hoyland) (London, 1922)

Muhammad Hadi (courtier of Jahangir): *Tatimma-i Wakiat-i Jahangiri* (E&D vi, pp. 392-99)

Muhammad Kazim (a courtier of Aurangzeb): *Alamgir-nama*. (E&D vii, pp. 174-80)

Muhammad Salih Kambu (courtier of Shah Jahan): *Amal-i Salih*. (E&D vii, pp. 123-33)

Mufazzal Khan (contemporary of Aurangzeb): *Tarikh-i Mufazzali*. (E&D vii, pp. 141-44)

Muhammad Amin (a contemporary of Jahangir): *Anfau-l Akhbar* (E&D vi, pp. 244-50)

Mundy, Peter (an English traveller in Shah Jahan's India: *Travels in Europe and Asia* (Ed: R. C. Temple) Vol. II (Hakluyt Society, 1914)

Manrique, Sebastien (an Augustinian friar in India in mid-17th century): *Travels*. 2 vols.(Tr: C. E. Luard) (Hakluyt Society, 1926-7)

Mustaid Khan, Muhammad Saqi (a late contemporary of Aurangzeb): *Maasir-i-Alamgiri* (Tr: J. Sarkar) (Calcutta, 1947)

Mushtaqui, Shaikh Raiq Ullah (a late contemporary of Shah Jahan): *Waqi'at-e-Mushtaqui* (Tr: I.H. Siddiqui) (Delhi, 1993)

Mutamid Khan (Jahangir's courtier): *Ikbal-nama-i Jahangiri*. (E&D vi, pp. 400-38)

Niamatu-lla (courtier of Jahangir): *Tarikh-i Khan-Jahan Lodi* (E&D v, pp. 67-115)

Nizamuddin Ahmad (courtier of Akbar): *Tabaqat-i-Akbari* (Tr: B. De) (Calcutta, 1936)

Norris, William (British ambassador in the court of Aurangzeb): *Journals* (in Harihar Das: *The Norris Embassy to Aurangzeb*) (Calcutta, 1959)

Nurul Hakk (courtier of Jahangir): *Zubdatu-t Tawarikh* (E&D vi, pp. 182-194)

Ovington, J (an Englishman in India in late 17th century): *A Voyage to Surat in the year 1689* (Ed: H. G. Rawlinson) (Oxford, 1929)

Pelsaert, Francis (a Dutch trader in India in the second decade of the 17th century): *Remonstrantie* (translated by W. H. Moreland as *Jahangir's India*) (Cambridge, 1925/ Delhi, 1972)

Qandahari, Muhammad Arif (courtier of Akbar): *Tarikh-i-Akbari* (Tr: Tasneem Ahmad) (Delhi, 1993)

Roe, Sir Thomas (British ambassador at Jahangir's court): *Observations Collected out of the Journal of Sir Thomas Roe in Purchas His Pilgrims* Vol iv, pp. 310-469. (Glasgow, MCMV]

Sirhindi, Faizi (a contemporary of Akbar): *Akbar-nama* (E&D vi, pp. 116-146)
Stevens, Thomas (an English Jesuit in India in the last quarter of the 16th century) His letter in *The Principal Voyages, Traffiques & Discoveries of the English Nation* by Richard Hakluyt, Vol. IV (London, MCMXXVII)

Tavernier, Jean-Baptiste (a French jewel merchant in India in mid-17th century): *Travels in India*, 2 vols. (Tr: V. Ball) (Calcutta, 1905)
Terry, Edward (an English clergyman at Jahangir's court): His account in Foster, pp. 288-332)
Thevenot, M. de (a Frenchman in India in mid-17th century): His account in *Indian Travels of Thevenot and Careri* (Ed: Surendranath Sen) (New Delhi, 1949)
Tirmzi, S.A.I.: *Edicts from the Harem* (Idarah-i Adabiyat-i-Delhi, 1979)

Varthema, Ludovico di: (an Italian traveller in India in the first decade of the 16th century): *The Itinerary of Ludovico di Varthema of Bologna from 1502-1508* (Tr: J. W. Jones) (London, 1928)

Waris, Muhammad (courtier of Shah Jahan): *Badshah-nama*. (E&D vii, pp. 121-122)
Withington, Nicholas (English traveller in India in the second decade of the 17th century): his account in Foster, pp. 188-233

Yadgar, Ahmad (a late contemporary of Humayun): *Tarikh-i Salatin-i Afaghana* (E&D v, pp. 1-66)

Zain Khan, Shaikh (courtier of Babur): *Tabaqat-i Baburi* (Tr: Sayed Hasan Askari) (Delhi, 1982)

Later Works

Abul Khadir Muhammad Farooque: *Roads and Communication in Mughal India* (Delhi, 1977)
Ali, Athar: *Mogul Nobility Under Aurangzeb* (Bombay, 1970)
Ali, Meer Hasan: *Observations on the Mussalmauns of India* (Oxford, 1832 / 1917)
Altekar, A. S.: *The Position of Women in Indian Civilization* (Delhi, 1938 / 1959)
Amini, Iradj: *Koh-i-noor* (New Delhi, 1994)

Ansari, Muhammad Azhar: *Social Life of the Mughal Emperors* (New Delhi, 1983)
Asher, Catherine B.: *Architecture of Mughal India* (Cambridge, 1992)

Basham, A. L.: *The Wonder That Was India*, Vol I (New York, 1954)
Beach, M. C.: *Mughal and Rajput Painting* (Cambridge, 1992)
Beagley, Raymonds (Ed): *Voyages & Travels*: 2 vols. (Westminster, 1903)
Begley, W.E. & Desai, Z. A.: *Taj Mahal.* (Harvard, 1989)
Bharatiya Vidya Bhavan: *History and Culture of the Indian People*: Vol vii: *The Mughal Empire.* (Bombay, 1984)
Binyon, Laurence: *Akbar* (Edinburgh, 1932)
Brown, Percy: *Indian Architecture* (1942 / Bombay, 1956)
Brown, Percy: *Indian Painting Under the Mughals* (Oxford, 1924)

Chandra, Satish: *Mughal Religious Policies, The Rajputs & The Deccan* (Delhi, 1993)
Cambridge Economic History of India, Vol i (Ed: Tapan Raychaudhuri and Irfan Habib) (Orient Longman, 1982 / 1991)
Cambridge History of India: Vol iv: *The Mughal Period.* (Ed: Wolseley Haig and Richard Burn) (Delhi, 1937 / 1987)
Chopra, P. N.: *Some Aspects of Social Life During the Mughal Age* (Jaipur, 1963)
Cole, Owen W. & Piara Singh Sambhi: *The Sikhs* (Delhi, 1989)
Cunningham, J.D.: *History of the Sikhs* (Delhi 1849/ 1990)

Dabisttan: The Religion of Sufis (London, 1979)
de Bary (Ed): *Sources of Indian Tradition.* (Columbia, 1958)
Duff, James Grant: *History of The Mahrattas.* 3 vols. (1863 / Delhi 1990)

Embree, Ainslie T (Ed.): *Sources of Indian Tradition* (Penguin, 1991)
Erskine, William: *A History of India Under the First Two Sovereigns of the House of Timur, Babur and Humayun.* 2 vols. (Oxford, 1854 / 1974)
Edwards S.M & Garrett H.L.O.: *Mughal Rule in India* (Delhi, 1974)

Findly, Ellison Banks: *Nurjahan* (Oxford, 1993)

Gascoigne, Bamber: *The Great Moghuls.* (London, 1971)
Godden, Rumer: *Gulbadan* (New York, 1980)
Gordon, Stewart: *The Marathas —1600-1818* (Cambridge, 1993)
Gupta, I. P.: *Agra* (Delhi, 1986)

Habib, Irfan (Ed): *Medieval India 1* (Oxford, Delhi, 1992)
Habib, Irfan: *Agrarian System of Mughal India* (Bombay, 1963)
Hasrat, Bikrama Jit: *Dara Shikuh.* (Visvabharati, 1953)
Hutchinson, Lester: *European Freebooters in India* (Bombay, 1964)

Ikram, S. M. (Ed): *The Cultural Heritage of Pakistan* (Oxford, Karachi, 1955)

544

Kaul, H.K (Ed): *Historic Delhi* (Delhi, 1985)
Kaul, H. K.: *Traveller's India* (Delhi, 1979)
Kulke, Hermann & Rothermund, Dietmar: *A History of India* (Delhi, 1991)

Lall, John & Dubey, D.N.: *Taj Mahal.* (Delhi, 1982)
Lane-Poole, Stanley: *Babur* (Delhi, 1964)
Lane-Poole, Stanley: *Aurangzeb* (Delhi, 1971)

Maclagan, Edward: *Jesuits and the Great Mogul* (London, 1922)
Moosvi, Shireen: *The Economy of The Mughal Empire* (Oxford, 1987)
Moreland, W. H.: *From Akbar to Aurangzeb* (London, 1923)
Moreland, W. H.: *India at the Death of Akbar* (Delhi, 1990 / 1920)
Moreland, W. H.: *The Agrarian System of Moslem India* (Delhi, 1990 / 1929)

Nizami, Khaliq Ahmad: *State and Culture in Medieval India* (New Delhi, 1985)
Nizami, Khaliq Ahmad: *Akbar and Religion* (New Delhi, 1989)

Prasad, Beni: *History of Jahangir.* (Allahabad, 1930)

Qanungo, K: *Sher Shah* (Calcutta, 1921)

Randhawa, M. S.: *A History of Agriculture in India* Vol ii (New Delhi, 1982)
Richards, John F: *The Mughal Empire* (Cambridge, 1993)
Rizvi, S.A.A.: *The Wonder That was India*, Vol II (London: 1987)
Ruby Maloni (Ed): *European Merchant Capital and the Indian Economy* (New Delhi, 1993)

Saksena, Banarsi Prasad: *History of Shah Jahan of Delhi.* (Allahabad, 1932 / 1969)
Sarkar, Jagadish N: *Studies in Economic Life in Mughal India* (Calcutta, 1975)
Sarkar, Jadunath: *History of Aurangzeb*, 5 vols (Calcutta, 1912-24 / Longman, 1973-74)
Sarkar, Jadunath: *Historical Essays* (Calcutta, 1912)
Sarkar, Jadunath: *House of Shivaji* (Calcutta, 1940 / 1978)
Sarkar, Jadunath: *Shivaji and His Times* (Calcutta, 1920)
Sarkar, Jadunath: *Mughal Administration* (Calcutta, 1924)
Sarkar, Jadunath: *Military History of India* (Orient Longman, 1960)
Sharar, A. H.: *Lucknow: The Last Phase of an Oriental Culture* (Colorado, 1975)
Singh, Dhananajaya: *The House of Marwar* (New Delhi, 1994)
Singh, Khushwant: *History of The Sikhs* (Oxford, 1963)
Smith, V. S.: *Akbar The Great Mogul* (Oxford, 1917 / Delhi, 1966)
Spear, Percival: *Delhi, a Historical Survey* (Oxford, 1937)
Spear, Percival: *India* (Michigan, 1961)
Spear, Percival: *A History of India* Vol 2 (Penguin, 1965)
Srivastava, M. P.: *Society and Culture in Medieval India* (Allahabad, 1975)
Srivastava, M. P.: *Socio-Economic Culture in Medieval India* (Allahabad, 1993)

545

Thapar, Romila: *History of India* Vol. I (Penguin, 1966)

Tod, James: *Annals of Mewar* (part of Tod's *Annals and Antiquities of `Rajasthan* published between 1829 and 1832) (Ed: C. H. Payne) (Delhi, no date)

Veluthat, Kesavan: *The Political Structure of Early Medieval South India* (Orient Longman, 1993)

Williams, Rushbrook: *An Empire Builder of the 16th Century* (1918 / Delhi, no date)

Yasin, Mohammad: *A Social History of Islamic India* (Lucknow, 1958)

Zinat Kausar: *Muslim Women in Medieval India* (Patna, 1992)

Index